BIOGRAPHICAL DICTIONARY OF AMERICAN NEWSPAPER COLUMNISTS

Biographical Dictionary of American Newspaper Columnists

SAM G. RILEY

GREENWOOD PRESS
Westport, Connecticut • London

Library of Congress Cataloging-in-Publication Data

Biographical dictionary of American newspaper columnists / Sam G.
  Riley.
      p.   cm.
    Includes bibliographical references and index.
    ISBN 0–313–29192–6 (alk. paper)
      1. Journalists—United States—Biography—Dictionaries.
    I. Riley, Sam G.
    PN4871.B57   1995
    070'.92'273—dc20   95–7185
    [B]

British Library Cataloguing in Publication Data is available.

Library of Congress Catalog Card Number: 95–7185
ISBN: 0–313–29192–6

First published in 1995

Greenwood Press, 88 Post Road West, Westport, CT 06881
An imprint of Greenwood Publishing Group, Inc.

Printed in the United States of America

The paper used in this book complies with the
Permanent Paper Standard issued by the National
Information Standards Organization (Z39.48–1984).

10 9 8 7 6 5 4 3 2 1

To my daughter, Heather Marie,
now Mrs. Neil Chadwick,
but always daddy's girl

Contents

Preface

The *Biographical Dictionary of American Newspaper Columnists* provides concise professional biographical sketches of six hundred columnists—from the time men and women having this job description appeared on U.S. papers in the Civil War era to the present. Each entry contains the following items, if they could be ascertained: a heading consisting of the columnist's full name and dates of birth and death, below which appear a statement of the individual's principal accomplishments, the place of birth, the name under which the columnist has normally written, the columnist's education, a career summary, further information about the nature of the individual's column, a list of the earliest editions of all known books authored or edited by the columnist, and references, where good general references could be found. Abundant citations are available on the more well known columnists, but many of these writers have not been written *about* in spite of all they themselves have written. In some cases, the columnist's autobiography is the best available source; inasmuch as autobiographies appear under the BOOKS rubric, they are not repeated under REFERENCES. In the cases of columnists who write under a pen name or professional name (Larry Zeiger writing as Larry King, Eppie Lederer as Ann Landers, Merle Kessler as Ian Shoales), the entry appears under the individual's actual name with references (See Landers, Ann) provided by pen name in the index. Listings of the columnists' books were compiled via the Virginia Tech Library's Online Computer Library Center (OCLC) data base terminal.

The selection of columnists was limited to those whose subject matter is of relatively general interest: political and humor columnists, plus those who variously describe their job as "personal columnist," "op-ed columnist," "general columnist," "life-style columnist," "items columnist" and the like. Not included are columnists whose work focuses on chess, bridge, finance, health, astrology, computers, or other such specialized topics. Exceptions are a handful of advice, society, and Hollywood or Broadway columnists who were pioneers in their field, or who became so well known and thoroughly identified with column writing that it would seem unfair to exclude them. Examples are Broadway's Earl Wilson and Ed Sullivan, Hollywood's Louella Parsons and Hedda Hopper, advice mavens Emily Post and Amy Vanderbilt, and society chronicler Maury Biddle Paul.

Included in these pages are local columnists who write exclusively for one newspaper, self-syndicated columnists who sell their work to a variety of papers, and columnists whose work is distributed more widely by established syndicates. Entries are arranged alphabetically by columnists' last names, and the phrase "American newspaper columnists" is interpreted somewhat loosely to mean persons whose columns appear or appeared in U.S. papers. A few columnists who are not U.S. citizens appear here, for example, former Soviet premier Mikhail Gorbachev and prominent Mexican writer Carlos Fuentes, who are distributed by the New York Times Syndicate, and former Soviet journalist Vladimir Voina, handled in America by Creators Syndicate.

In selecting the six hundred columnists to be profiled, the author attempted to include all the true giants of column writing, living or dead—men and women such as Franklin Pierce Adams, Raymond Clapper, Irvin S. Cobb, Eugene Field, Doris Fleeson, Frank Kent, Arthur Krock, Walter Lippmann, Anne O'Hair McCormick, Ernie Pyle, Carl Rowan, Mike Royko, Bert Leston Taylor, and Dorothy Thompson. This part of the selection process was easy. The most difficult part was determining what *local* columnists to include. No one individual is qualified to make these choices alone. Accordingly, the means of selection used here was to write to two respected journalism professors in each state, asking for "nominations" for the best local columnists in their city, state, or region. From the resulting list, the author wrote to the "nominees," asking them to complete a biographical information sheet. The same method was used earlier for the author's 1993 book *The Best of the Rest: Non-Syndicated Newspaper Columnists Select Their Best Work* (Greenwood Press), an anthology of the work of local columnists. All these columnists were also asked to recommend other columnists, living or dead, who, in their opinion, warranted inclusion in this book. These individuals were also contacted by the author. A few other local columnists were added after having won various writing awards or because the author especially admired their work.

The remainder of the columnists profiled here are syndicated or self-syndicated writers whose work, in the author's judgment, appeared of good quality or, in the case of new columnists, showed considerable promise, and for whom sufficient information could be found by library research, by direct contact, or by contact with the columnist's syndicate.

Finally, the author has chosen to include individuals who wrote newspaper columns but are not mainly remembered as columnists. Examples are novelist John O'Hara, humorists Joel Chandler Harris and James Thurber, writer Christopher Morley, social critic H. L. Mencken, satirist Ambrose Bierce, muckraker Ray Stannard Baker, poet Carl Sandburg, and scholar W.E.B. DuBois. The reader will also find several men and women who wrote columns but, in the main, are known as newspaper owners: William Randolph Hearst, John Knight, Dorothy Schiff, and Charles McClatchy. A few other column writers are principally remembered for their nonliterary pursuits: billionaire H. L. Hunt, business demigod Lee Iacocca, and entertainment impresario Billy Rose, for example.

Entries show the routes individuals have followed in becoming columnists. The most common career path is to begin as a reporter; move through a variety of reportorial, editing, or feature writing assignments; and finally emerge with one's own column. It is not at all uncommon, however, to find persons who got their column after having had various kinds of political experience (Eugene McCarthy, William Safire, Jim Wright, Eleanor Roosevelt) or academic experience (John Roche, Garry Wills). Also, media switching is more fluid than it once was, and innumerable columnists supplement their income and reputation by doubling as radio or television commentators. Some, such as Charles Kuralt, left newspaper journalism altogether in favor of broadcasting; others, such as Tex McCrary, Morrie Ryskind, and Cal Thomas, have come to column writing *after* careers in broadcasting. Still others, such as Ben Hecht and Mark Hellinger, have found that their column writing provided a ticket to Hollywood as motion picture writers, actors, or even producers.

A great many columnists have used their column as a stepping-stone to the literary world. The author hopes that the arrangement of this book will graphically demonstrate the considerable link between the spheres of the columnist and the book author. The column is a sort of intersection where journalism and literature sometimes meet, or at least brush by one another at close range. Without question, columnists have contributed mightily to both the fiction and nonfiction of America since the mid-1800s. Academics who appear to define the term *literary journalism* as being basically synonymous with the *New Journalism* of the 1960s would do well to expand their scope to include the work of many of our better columnists, especially those who write not of politics but of the human condition—work that can be rich in literary value.

Scholars and students who make use of this reference book will perhaps notice that some of the very earliest columnists were women, probably given columns by editors or publishers not from altruistic motivation, but from the desire to bolster the number of their women readers. Pioneer women columnists were Sara Parton, whose column work dates from 1855; Jane Croly, whose first column was launched in 1856; Mary Clemmer Ames and Emily Briggs, who began their work as columnists in 1866; and Sallie Joy White, who launched her column in 1875. Other pioneering columnists were men of literary inclination who had contributed to newspapers on a fairly regular basis and who further regularized their output in the form of a column. Examples are Benjamin Perley Poore, whose column "Waifs from Washington" began to appear in 1854, satirist Ambrose Bierce, who began writing a column in 1868; and writer Lafcadio Hearn and humorist/folklorist Joel Chandler Harris, who began columns in the 1870s. A final group of early columnists were the humorists, who for years had contributed humorous stories and sketches to newspapers and who eventually regularized their contributions (and their income) with columns that appeared on a set schedule. Perhaps the earliest of these was Henry Wheeler Shaw, creator of the literary character Josh Billings, who began a column in 1867. Others were the previously mentioned Joel Chandler Harris (1870), Edgar Nye (1881), Eugene Field (1883), and, in 1893, Finley Peter Dunne, creator of Mr. Dooley, and George Ade.

Readers will also find evidence of the growth in the number of minority columnists in the United States, long painfully slow but greatly accelerated during the 1990s. Pioneers in this category are Gertrude Mossell (1885), Lillian Lewis (1889), and Ida Wells-Barnett (1892).

A fairly extensive Selected Bibliography on columnists and column writing is provided as an aid to further reading and research.

Next, the author offers a pair of apologies. To the many talented columnists who, for various reasons, do not appear in this collection, I regret that I did not learn of your work or else could not find sufficient information about you to write a reasonably complete entry. The second apology is to the six hundred columnists who *were* profiled. In order to include as many as six hundred without exceeding the total page limit set by the publisher, I have had to omit mention of the many, many awards and honors you have received, with the exception of the Pulitzer or Nobel prize. I hope you will understand that in making this choice, I do not intend in any way to disparage the other awards and recognition your work has won.

Finally, sincere thanks are offered to Virginia Polytechnic Institute & State University for granting me the semester-long research leave that enabled me to complete this book.

Profiles of Newspaper Columnists

A

Adams, Franklin Pierce (15 Nov. 1881–23 March 1960). "F.P.A.," as he signed his writing, was one of the best-known columnists of the 1920s and 1930s. He is best remembered for his witty column "The Conning Tower."

Having graduated from the Armour Institute of Technology in 1889, Adams worked in insurance for three years, then in 1903 joined the *Chicago Journal,* where he first wrote a weather column, then a humor column, "A Little About Everything," which used contributions sent in by readers. In the same way, Adams himself had contributed to Bert Leston Taylor's earlier *Chicago Journal* column "A Line o' Type or Two." In 1904 Adams moved to the *New York Evening Mail,* writing a daily humor column, "Always in Good Humor." In 1911 he introduced a second column, a parody of Samuel Pepys's *Diary* that recounted Adams's own adventures in reading, the arts, and gaming.

Adams moved to the *New York Tribune* in 1914, continuing his Pepys parody on a weekly basis and renaming his column "The Conning Tower," using both prose and verse and again including contributions from readers, many of whom were up-and-coming young writers, such as Dorothy Parker, Robert Benchley, James Thurber, and John O'Hara.

Adams served in military intelligence during World War I and wrote an occasional column, "The Listening Post," for *Stars and Stripes* under editor Harold Ross. At war's end, Adams returned to the *Tribune.* "The Conning Tower" appeared in the *New York World* from 1922 to 1931, in the *New York Herald Tribune* from 1931 to 1937, and finally in the *New York Post* from 1938 to 1941.

From 1938 to 1948 Adams was a panelist on the radio quiz program "Information Please," and with the short-story writer O. Henry he wrote a musical comedy entitled *Lo.*

BOOKS: *In Cupid's Court* (Evanston, Ind., 1902); *Tobogganing on Parnassus* (Garden City, N.Y., 1911); *In Other Words* (Garden City, N.Y., 1912); *By and Large* (Garden City, N.Y., 1914); *Weights and Measures* (Garden City, N.Y., 1917); *Something Else Again* (Garden City, N.Y., 1920); *Overset* (Garden City, N.Y., 1922); *Women I'm Not Married To* (Garden City, N.Y., 1922); *So There!* (Garden City, N.Y., 1923); *So Much Velvet* (Garden City, N.Y., 1924); *Half a Loaf* (Garden City, N.Y., 1927); *The Column Book of F.P.A.* (New York, 1928); *Christopher Columbus and Other Patriotic Verse* (New York, 1931); *The Diary of Our Own Samuel Pepys,* 2 vols. (New York, 1935); *The Melancholy Lute* (New York, 1936); *Innocent Merriment* (New York, 1942); *Nods and Becks* (New York, 1944).

REFERENCES: Sally Ashley, *F.P.A.* (New York, 1986); Clifton Fadiman, "The Education of Franklin P. Adams," *New Yorker* 11 (9 November 1935): 81–82; "F.P.A. of the New York Tribune," *Everybody's* 34 (May 1916): 598–599; Rupert Hughes, "F.P.A.," *Everybody's* 42 (April 1920): 52–53; Thomas L. Masson, "Franklin P. Adams," in *Our American Humorists* (New York, 1922): 21–25; John Wheelwright, "Poet as Funny Man," *Poetry* 50 (July 1937): 210–215.

Ade, George (9 Feb. 1866–16 May 1944). Humorist George Ade was one of the most successful and famous of America's early newspaper columnists. With a deft ear for dialect and a rare gift for extracting humor from the ordinary, he provided a chronicle of Chicago street life in the late 1800s and early 1900s.

Ade was born in the small Indiana town of Kentland. He earned a B.S. from Purdue University in 1887 and was editor of the school's monthly literary magazine, the *Purdue*. Later in life, he received two honorary degrees: the L.H.D. from Purdue in 1925 and the LL.D. from Indiana University in 1926.

Ade began reading for the law in Lafayette, Indiana, but abandoned this plan after only seven weeks and instead took a reporting job with a new paper, the *Lafayette Morning News*. When that paper went out of business, he became a reporter for another Lafayette paper, the *Call*. He left this job to write advertising copy for a patent medicine company but was soon let go, after which he moved to Chicago in June 1890 to join his friend and Sigma Chi fraternity brother, the illustrator John McCutcheon, at the *Morning News*. There he moved quickly from cub to star reporter.

Ade's "big break" came in 1893 when he and McCutcheon collaborated on a series of editorial page columns describing the Columbian Exposition, then being held in Chicago. The success of these pieces prompted the birth of Ade's regular column for the *News* (by this time, renamed the *Record*), "Stories of the Streets and of the Town," which was run on the same page with Eugene Field's popular "Sharps and Flats" column. The first of Ade's "fables in slang" appeared in 1897. These columns were written in the style of the fable with Midwest dialect added and became widely syndicated throughout the nation. The *Record* published in book form eight collections of Ade's columns from 1894 to 1900, including those columns written and illustrated while Ade and McCutcheon traveled in Europe in 1895. Returning to the paper, Ade began to use fictitious characters in his columns. The first was the fast-talking youth Artie

Blanchard, a forerunner of present-day Chicago columnist Mike Royko's character Slats Grobnik.

In 1900 Ade left journalism and began writing plays, musicals, and screenplays. He was popular on the speaking circuit and did promotional work for the alma mater and for the Republican party. His career in full-time journalism was quite brief, roughly twelve years, his time as a playwright even more so. Yet his work had made him wealthy. He spent the final decades of his life at his four hundred-acre Indiana estate, Hazelden, golfing and entertaining.

BOOKS: *The Chicago Record's "Stories of the Streets and of the Town"* (Chicago, 1894); *Second Series of "Stories of the Streets and of the Town"* (Chicago, 1894); *Third Series of "Stories of the Streets and of the Town"* (Chicago, 1895); *Fourth Series of "Stories of the Streets and of the Town"* (Chicago, 1895); *What a Man Sees Who Goes Away from Home* (Chicago, 1896); *Circus Day* (Chicago and New York, 1896); as John Hazelden, *Stories from History* (Chicago and New York, 1896); *Artie, A Story of the Streets and Town* (Chicago, 1896); *Pink Marsh, A Story of the Streets and Town* (Chicago and New York, 1897); *Fifth Series of the Chicago Record's "Stories of the Streets and of the Town"* (Chicago, 1897); *Sixth Series of "Stories of the Streets and of the Town"* (Chicago, 1898); *Seventh Series of "Stories of the Streets and of the Town"* (Chicago, 1899); *Doc' Horne: A Story of the Streets and Town* (Chicago and New York, 1899); *Fables in Slang* (Chicago and New York, 1900); *Eighth Series of The Chicago Record's Stories of the Streets and of the Town* (Chicago, 1900); *More Fables* (Chicago and New York, 1900); *Grouch at the Game, or Why He Changed His Colors* (Chicago, 1901); *Forty Modern Fables* (New York, 1901); *The Girl Proposition: A Bunch of He and She Fables* (New York, 1902); *People You Know* (New York, 1903); *The Sultan of Sulu: An Original Satire in Two Acts* (New York, 1903); *In Babel: Stories of Chicago* (New York, 1903); *Breaking into Society* (New York and London, 1904); *True Bills* (New York and London, 1904); *In Pastures New* (New York, 1906); *The Slim Princess* (Indianapolis, 1907); *Verses and Jingles* (Indianapolis, 1911); *Knocking the Neighbors* (Garden City, N.Y., 1912); *Ade's Fables* (Garden City, N.Y., 1914); *Hand-Made Fables* (Garden City, N.Y., 1920); *Single Blessedness and Other Observations* (Garden City, N.Y., 1922); *The Mayor and the Manicure: A Play in One Act* (New York and London, 1923); *Nettie: A Play in One Act* (New York and London, 1923); *Speaking to Father: A Play in One Act* (New York, 1923); *The College Widow: A Pictorial Comedy in Four Acts* (New York and London, 1924); *Father and the Boys: A Comedy Drama* (New York and London, 1924); *The Country Chairman: A Comedy-Drama* (New York and London, 1924); *Just Out of College: A Light Comedy in Three Acts* (New York and London, 1924); *Bang! Bang! A Collection of Stories Intended to Recall Memories of the Nickel Library Days When Boys Were Supermen and Murder a Fine Art* (New York, 1928); *The Old-Time Saloon: Not Wet—Not Dry Just History* (New York, 1931); *One Afternoon with Mark Twain* (Chicago, 1939); *Stories of the Streets and of the Town* (Chicago, 1941); *The Permanent Ade,* ed. by Fred C. Kelly (Indianapolis, 1947); *Chicago Stories,* ed. by Franklin J. Meine (Chicago, 1963).

REFERENCES: Lee Coyle, *George Ade* (New York, 1964); James DeMuth, *Small Town Chicago: The Comic Perspectives of Finley Peter Dunne, George Ade, and Ring Lardner* (Port Washington, N.Y., 1980); Bergen Evans, "George Ade, Rustic Humorist," *American Mercury* 70 (March 1950): 321–327; William Dean Howells, "Certain of the Chicago School of Fiction," *North American Review* 176 (March 1903): 734–746; Fred C.

Kelly, *George Ade: Warmhearted Satirist* (Indianapolis and New York, 1947); Lowell Matson, "Ade: Who Needed None," *Literary Review* 5 (Autumn 1961): 99–114; Dorothy Ritter Russo, *A Bibliography of George Ade* (Indianapolis, 1947).

Alden, William Livingston (9 Oct. 1837–14 Jan. 1908). Although he did not refer to himself as a "columnist," William Alden began a miscellaneous feature on the *New York Times*'s editorial page titled "Minor Topics." It was also known as the "Sixth Column," as it appeared in the sixth column of the editorial page. This feature was renamed "Topics of the Times" in 1896 and handled as a miscellany column by Frederick Craig Mortimer until 1926, after which it was taken over by Simeon Strunsky, who kept it running until 1948.

Alden was born in Williamstown, Massachusetts. He studied at two Pennsylvania schools for which his father worked, Lafayette College in Easton and Jefferson College in Canonsburg. He finished in Jefferson College's class of 1858, then read for the law and was admitted to the New York bar in 1860. He practiced law for five years and began writing for various magazines, such as *Scribner's* and the *Atlantic,* then New York City newspapers, including the *World* and *Graphic* as well as the *Times.* From 1885 to 1890 he was U.S. consul-general in Rome; he then lived in Paris until 1893 and wrote for the Paris edition of the *New York Herald.* Thereafter he lived and wrote in London. He was author of numerous books and is credited with having popularized canoeing in the United States.

BOOKS: *Domestic Explosives and Other Sixth Column Fancies* (New York, 1877); *Shooting Stars as Observed from the "Sixth Column" of the Times* (New York, 1878); *The Canoe and the Flying Proa* (New York, 1878); *The Moral Pirates* (New York, 1880); *Christopher Columbus (1440–1506) the First American Citizen* (New York, 1881); *The Cruise of the "Ghost"* (New York, 1882); *The Cruise of the Canoe Club* (New York, 1883); *The Comic Liar* (New York, 1883); *The Coming Girl* (New York, 1884); *The Adventures of Jimmy Brown* (New York, 1885); *A New Robinson Crusoe* (New York, 1888); *Trying to Find Europe, by Jimmy Brown* (London, 1889); *The Loss of Swansea* (Boston, 1889); *Told by the Colonel* (New York, 1893); *Among the Freaks* (New York, 1896); *His Daughter* (London, 1897); *Drewitt's Dream* (New York, 1902); *Cat Tales* (London, 1905); *Jimmy Brown Trying to Find Europe* (New York, 1905).

Alexander, Holmes Moss (29 Jan. 1906–5 Dec. 1985). Holmes Alexander was a syndicated political columnist from 1947 until 1981. He was handled by the McNaught Syndicate.

Alexander was born in Parkersburg, West Virginia; received his B.A. from Princeton University in 1928; and attended Trinity College, Cambridge, 1928–1929.

He began his work life as an English teacher at the McDonogh School in McDonogh, Maryland (1929–1931), and spent the years 1931–1935 as a Democratic member of the Maryland House of Delegates. He was a free-lance writer and author of biographies until he began his column. He worked as a reporter and book reviewer for the *Baltimore Sun* and from 1942 to 1945 was an officer in the U.S. Army Air Forces. Among the magazines for which he wrote were *Harper's, American Mercury, Nation's Business, Collier's* and *Saturday Evening Post.*

BOOKS: *Twenty of Their Swords* (Philadelphia, 1930); *The American Talleyrand: The Career and Contemporaries of Martin Van Buren, Eighth President* (New York, 1935); *Aaron Burr, the Proud Pretender* (New York, 1937); *American Nabob* (New York, 1939); *Dust in the Afternoon* (New York, 1940); *Selina* (New York, 1942); *Tomorrow's Air Age: A Report on the Forseeable Future* (New York, 1953); *The Famous Five* (New York, 1958); *Shall Do No Murder* (Chicago, 1959); *How to Read the Federalist* (Boston, 1961); *West of Washington* (New York, 1962); *The Equivocal Men: Tales of the Establishment* (Boston, 1964); *Washington and Lee: A Study in the Will to Win* (Boston, 1966); *The Spirit of '76* (New Rochelle, N.Y., 1966); *Between the Stirrup and the Ground: A Book About Horses and People* (Washington, D.C., 1967); *Pen and Politics: The Autobiography of a Working Writer* (Morgantown, W.Va., 1970); *With Friends Possess'd: A Personal Story About Man-to-Man Friendship and Its Place in the History of the Human Heart* (Caldwell, Idaho, 1970); *To Covet Honor: A Biography of Alexander Hamilton* (Boston, 1977); *The Hidden Years of Stonewall Jackson* (Richwood, W.Va., 1981); *Never Lose a War: Memoirs and Observations of a National Columnist* (Greenwich, Conn., 1984).

Allbright, Charles Wilson (5 Feb. 1929–). Charles Allbright has written his humor column, "Arkansas Traveler," at the *Arkansas Democrat-Gazette* since 1991 and at the *Arkansas Gazette* from 1973 to 1991.

Allbright was born in Oxford, Mississippi. He was an English major at the University of Arkansas but did not complete the degree. In 1955 he worked for the *Arkansas Gazette* as a general assignment reporter, and from 1956 to 1965 he was that paper's "Our Town" columnist. From 1966 to 1973 Allbright was a speech writer for Winthrop Rockefeller. He has written three books.

BOOKS: *The Night of the Possum Concert and Other Comedies* (Little Rock, Ark., 1987); *Gravely the Mules Stopped Dancing* (Little Rock, Ark., 1988); *The Consecrated Cross-Eyed Bear* (Little Rock, Ark., 1990).

Allen, Robert Sharon (14 July 1900–23 Feb. 1981). Robert S. Allen is remembered as cofounder with Drew Pearson of the immensely successful column "Washington Merry-Go-Round," which Allen left in 1942, and for his own later column, "Inside Washington" (1949–1980).

Allen was born in Latonia, Kentucky. At thirteen, he was a copyboy at the Louisville *Courier-Journal.* He enrolled at the University of Kentucky at age sixteen but after a year joined the army, enrolling at the University of Wisconsin after returning from the war in France in 1919. Allen worked part-time for the *Capital Times* in Madison while a student and graduated in 1921. He was awarded a liberal arts fellowship at the University of Munich, which he put off for two years in order to work at the *Capital Times* and *Wisconsin State Journal.* One of his most risky assignments involved his joining the Ku Klux Klan, then writing an expose series about his experiences. In 1923 he went to Munich to study at the university; there he also wrote for United Press (UP) and the *Christian Science Monitor*. Allen arrived in Munich just prior to Hitler's beer hall putsch and claimed to have been the first American to despise Hitler.

He returned to the United States in 1924, worked on publicity for the La-Follette campaign for president, then wrote briefly for the UP in New York City. In 1925 he moved to Washington, D.C., and a job on the *Christian Science Monitor*'s bureau, of which he became head in 1930. At about the same time, Allen began writing personality profiles of government figures for the *American Mercury* magazine. He met Drew Pearson, coauthored two books with him, and then, with Pearson, started the gossipy, tipster-fed muckraking column "Washington Merry-Go-Round."

Allen left the column to Pearson in 1942 to join Army Intelligence. He served under Gen. George Patton and lost an arm during a mission. After the war, Allen decided to start his own solo column, "Inside Washington" (1949–1980). Ill health plagued him, and he committed suicide in 1981.

BOOKS: With Drew Pearson, *Washington Merry-Go-Round* (New York, 1931); with Pearson, *More Merry-Go-Round* (New York, 1932); *Why Hoover Faces Defeat* (New York, 1932); with Pearson, *The Nine Old Men* (Garden City, N.Y., 1936); with Pearson, *Nine Old Men at the Crossroads* (Garden City, N.Y., 1937); *Lucky Forward: The History of Patton's Third Army* (New York, 1947); ed., *Our Fair City* (New York, 1947); ed., *Our Sovereign State* (New York, 1949); with William V. Shannon, *The Truman Merry-Go-Round* (New York, 1950).

REFERENCES: Charles Fisher, *The Columnists* (New York, 1944): 210–248.

Alsop, Joseph Wright, V (11 Oct. 1910–28 Aug. 1989). Jovian political columnist Joseph Alsop is remembered for the column "Matter of Fact," initially cowritten with his younger brother, Stewart, and from 1958 to 1974 written solo for the *New York Herald Tribune*.

Alsop (pronounced All-sop) was born in Avon, Connecticut. His family, relatives of the Roosevelts, sent him to Groton prep school and to Harvard, where he graduated cum laude in 1932.

His first job was reporting for the *New York Herald Tribune,* a paper owned by family friends. Alsop liked to tell people that he had never so much as read a newspaper before taking this job. Still, his writing had style, and he made rapid progress as a reporter. He became something of a protégé of the critic Alexander Woollcott, who declared him the only truly educated young American he had ever met. Alsop attracted favorable attention by his reporting of the Lindbergh kidnapping trial of Bruno Hauptmann and thereafter was sent to cover the White House, at that time occupied by his distant cousin Franklin Roosevelt.

In 1937 Alsop and Robert E. Kintner, who later was president of NBC, collaborated on a column, "The Capitol Parade," which gained national syndication. When the United States entered World War II, Alsop left the paper and entered the navy as an officer after having been turned down by the army for medical reasons. Through the intervention of influential friends in Washington, he was allowed to resign his Navy commission and join the "Flying Tigers" in Burma. Alsop was captured but released by the Japanese and at one point worked as aide to General Claire Chennault, the Flying Tigers' commander.

After the war Alsop returned to the *Herald Tribune* and invited brother Stewart to join him in writing a new political column. Whereas Joseph tended to be bellicose and confrontational, Stewart was more reticent in approach, and after twelve years, in 1958, Stewart left the column to become political editor of the *Saturday Evening Post.* Joseph wrote the column alone until his retirement in 1974. The column was distributed by the Los Angeles Times Syndicate to well over one hundred papers, and Joseph Alsop maintained his formidable reputation. He was a supporter of Roosevelt and Kennedy, was known for his rather English writing style, and traveled extensively to cover the conflicts in Korea and Vietnam. He authored or coauthored several books, most of which were on political topics, though some were on his hobbies, art and archaeology.

BOOKS: With Turner Catledge, *The 168 Days* (Garden City, N.Y., 1938); with Robert Kintner, *The Men Around the President* (New York, 1939); *An American White Paper* (New York, 1940); with Stewart Alsop, *We Accuse! The Story of the Miscarriage of Justice in the Case of J. Robert Oppenheimer* (New York, 1954); with Stewart Alsop, *The Reporter's Trade* (New York, 1958); *From the Silent Earth: A Report of the Greek Bronze Age* (New York, 1964); *Drink, Eat and Be Thin* (New York, 1965); *FDR, 1882–1945: A Centenary* (New York, 1982); *The Rare Art Traditions* (New York, 1982); *I've Seen the Best of It: Memoirs* (New York, 1992).

REFERENCES: Leann Grabavoy Almquist, *Joseph Alsop and American Foreign Policy* (Lanham, Md., 1993); Barnard Law Collier, "The Joe Alsop Story," *The New York Times Biographical Edition* 27 (May 1971): 1693–1698.

Alsop, Stewart (17 May 1914–26 May 1974). Stewart Alsop (pronounced All-sop) cowrote the *New York Herald Tribune* political column "Matter of Fact" with his older brother, Joseph Alsop, from 1946 to 1958.

Alsop was born into a prominent family in Avon, Connecticut. Like his older brother, he attended Groton prep school. He earned the B.A. at Yale University in 1936. He became an editor for Doubleday, Doran in New York and also contributed to various magazines. Unable to join the U.S. military because of medical problems at the onset of World War II, he was accepted by the British army, then was transferred to the U.S. army as an OSS officer. He parachuted into occupied France in 1944 to work with the resistance.

After the war he accepted brother Joseph's invitation to cowrite a column for the *Herald Tribune.* Then in 1958 Stewart Alsop left column writing to become political editor of the *Saturday Evening Post,* for which he wrote many articles; he held this position for the next decade, after which he wrote a political column for *Newsweek.* Unlike his brother Joseph, he opposed U.S. involvement in Vietnam. He coauthored a book on reporting with his brother and later wrote a memoir about his battle with leukemia.

BOOKS: With Thomas Braden, *Sub Rosa: The O.S.S. and American Espionage* (New York, 1946); with Joseph Alsop, *We Accuse! The Story of the Miscarriage of American Justice in the Case of J. Robert Oppenheimer* (New York, 1954); with Joseph Alsop, *The Reporter's Trade* (New York, 1958); *Nixon and Rockefeller: A Double Portrait* (Garden City, N.Y., 1960); *The Center: People and Power in Political Washington* (New York, 1968); *Stay of Execution: A Sort of Memoir* (Philadelphia, 1973).

Ames, Mary Clemmer (6 May 1831–18 Aug. 1884). One of the pioneer women columnists of America, Mary Clemmer Ames was a Washington columnist for the New York *Independent* from 1866 until 1884.

She was born Mary Clemmer in Utica, New York, and moved with her family to Westfield, Massachusetts. While attending Westfield Academy, she published poetry in the *Springfield Republican.* When she was older, she again wrote on a free-lance basis for the *Republican,* as well as for the *Utica Morning Herald.* She was married to, then divorced from a minister and lived with him in New York, Minnesota, and West Virginia. She was imprisoned for a short period by Confederate forces at Harper's Ferry and later worked as a nurse in Washington.

Ames's political column, "A Woman's Letter from Washington," first appeared in the New York weekly *Independent* in March 1866. She was quite possibly the first American woman columnist to use her actual name on her column, rather than signing a pen name, as did Emily Briggs ("Olivia") and Sara Lippincott ("Grace Greenwood"). Ames wrote seriously about the political scene and eschewed the gossip and fashion tittle-tattle expected of women writers in those days. She was a critic of President Andrew Johnson, a supporter of Ulysses Grant until the corruption of his administration became apparent, and a warm admirer of Rutherford B. Hayes. She also wrote for the *Cincinnati Commercial* during Hayes's years in the White House. From 1869 to 1872 she also wrote for the *Brooklyn Daily Union,* which, like the *Independent,* was owned by Henry Bowen.

Ames spoke out in favor of suffrage for women and succeeded in a field dominated at that time by men, yet her concern with being a proper lady prompted her to cover Congress not from the press gallery, but from the ladies' gallery instead.

REFERENCES: Edmund Hudson, *An American Woman's Life and Work: A Memorial of Mary Clemmer* (Boston, 1886).

Amory, Cleveland (2 Sept. 1917–   ). Versatile writer/broadcaster Cleveland Amory wrote a syndicated newspaper column titled "Animail" that reflected his growing interest in animals and in the relationship between animals and people. He also was a *Saturday Review* columnist from 1952 to 1972.

Amory was born in Nahant, Massachusetts, and received the A.B. from Harvard University in 1939. He was a reporter for the *Nashua Telegraph* in Nashua, New Hampshire, and at the *Arizona Star* in Tucson. He then became managing editor of the *Prescott* [Arizona] *Evening Courier.*

From 1939 to 1941 Amory was associate editor of the *Saturday Evening Post,* and since that time, he has worked free-lance. He was a reviewer for *TV Guide* from 1960 to 1974; he once wrote of the "Donny and Marie Show," "What's needed here is a 16-year-old critic," a splendidly curmudgeonly comment on the youth culture. He has also been a contributing editor of *Parade,* starting in 1983.

Amory has hosted his own radio program, "Curmudgeon at Large," and has worked as a television commentator. He has authored a number of books, some taking a satiric look at "Society," others showing his interest in animals and wildlife. In 1967, Amory founded the Fund for Animals.

BOOKS: *The Proper Bostonians* (New York, 1947); *Home Town* (New York, 1950); *The Last Resorts* (New York, 1952); ed. with Earl Blackwell, *Celebrity Register* (New York, 1959); ed. with Frederic Bradlee, *Vanity Fair: Selections from America's Most Memorable Magazine* (New York, 1960); *Who Killed Society?* (New York, 1960); *The Proper Bostonians Revisited* (New York, 1972); *Man Kind? Our Incredible War on Wildlife* (New York, 1974); *Animail* (New York, 1976); *The Trouble with Nowadays: A Curmudgeon Strikes Back* (New York, 1979); *The Cat Who Came for Christmas* (New York, 1987); *The Cat and the Curmudgeon* (Boston, 1990); *The Best Cat Ever* (Boston, 1993).

Anders, Smiley (20 Nov. 1937–). Items columnist for the *Advocate* in Baton Rouge, Louisiana, since 1979, Smiley Anders is known for his gentle humor.

Anders was born in Natchez, Mississippi, and received both a B.A. and an M.A. from Louisiana State University (1959 and 1971). He began his career as oil and gas editor for the *Shreveport Times* (1960–1962), then was information director of the Louisiana Farm Bureau (1963–1967) and public relations director of the Baton Rouge Chamber of Commerce (1967–1973). He was first employed by the *Advocate* in 1973 as a business reporter. Then in 1979, managing editor Mike Walker offered him a position as full-time columnist. Anders has also worked as a book reviewer for the *Sunday Advocate Magazine* and as a freelance writer for automotive and real estate periodicals.

Anders's six-times-weekly column is tightly geared to its Louisiana audience and makes use of varied humor forms, including short verse.

Anderson, Jackson Northman (19 Oct. 1922–). Jack Anderson was an employee of muckraker Drew Pearson on the widely syndicated column "Washington Merry-Go-Round" (1947–1965), the column's cowriter from 1965 to 1969, and its proprietor after Pearson's death in 1969.

Anderson was born in Long Beach, California, and moved with his family to Salt Lake City, Utah, in 1924. He contributed to a weekly, the *Murray Eagle,* at age twelve; edited his school newspapers in junior high and high school; learned typing and shorthand; and in high school was a stringer for the *Deseret News,* for which he also became editor of the Boy Scout page. While attending the University of Utah (1940–1941) he was a reporter for the *Salt Lake Tribune.* Anderson, a Mormon, put in his missionary years in Alabama, Georgia, and

Florida in 1941–1944, then joined the Merchant Marine in 1944 for a short tour. In 1945 he left the Merchant Marine to become a *Deseret News* correspondent behind Japanese lines in China, where he also free-lanced for the Associated Press. He was drafted into the U.S. Army and worked for part of his two-year hitch as a *Stars and Stripes* reporter in Shanghai.

In 1947 Anderson arrived in Washington, D.C., and was hired as one of Drew Pearson's legmen. Eventually he became Pearson's most valued assistant and in 1954 supplemented his modest income by becoming Washington editor for *Parade* magazine, a Sunday newspaper supplement. He held this position until 1968 and after that date was *Parade*'s D.C. bureau chief.

When Pearson died in 1969, Anderson became the column's proprietor. In the next three years, he increased the number of papers that carried his column from roughly six hundred to around nine hundred. In 1972 he won the Pulitzer Prize for national reporting for his columns based on inside information regarding Nixon's support of Pakistan over India at a time when the administration's "official" policy was neutrality.

For many years Anderson's chief assistant was Joseph Spear. Another noteworthy legman on his staff in the 1970s was Brit Hume. Anderson shared the column byline with Dale Van Atta from 1985 to 1991, when Van Atta resigned to concentrate on book projects and was replaced by Michael Binstein, who had made a reputation for his investigation of the savings and loan scandal. The column, formerly sent out seven times a week, is now distributed by United Feature Syndicate four times weekly.

While still America's best known muckraker, Anderson himself has never again been so much in the public eye as he was during the Watergate era, when the Nixon administration had him tailed by both the FBI and the CIA and audited at great length by the IRS. He is unwavering in his general opinion of politicians and bureaucrats as censorship-prone, self-important rascals. Attempts at secrecy in official Washington are sometimes thwarted by tips from Anderson's network of government sources or from disaffected underlings who offer leads or documents, sometimes by phone, sometimes by mail. The column, now written more by a substantial staff of employee-reporters than by Anderson himself, uses a colorful, relatively simple style designed for wide appeal.

The busy Anderson has long been a regular on the profitable lecture circuit, has hosted both radio and television programs, and has been part owner of the *Annapolis Evening Capital* and publisher of *Investigative Reporter*. He has published a number of books, mainly coauthored, that elaborate on his experiences as a major investigative columnist.

BOOKS: With Ronald W. May, *McCarthy: The Man, the Senator, the "ism"* (Boston, 1952); with Fred Blumenthal, *The Kefauver Story* (New York, 1956); with Drew Pearson, *U.S.A.: Second-Class Power?* (New York, 1958); *Washington Exposé* (New York, 1967); with Drew Pearson, *The Case Against Congress* (New York, 1968); with Carl Kalvelage, *American Government . . . Like It Is* (New York, 1972); with George Clifford, *The An-*

derson Papers (New York, 1973); with James Boyd, *Confessions of a Muckraker* (New York, 1979); with Bill Pronzini, *The Cambodia File* (Garden City, N.Y., 1981).

REFERENCES: Neil A. Grauer, *Wits and Sages* (Baltimore, 1984): 15–34.

Ashby, Lynn (4 Sept. 1938–). Lynn Ashby writes a general column for the *Houston Post.*

Ashby was born in Dallas and earned the B.J. at the University of Texas at Austin in 1961. He served in the Marine Corps and has worked for the *Houston Post* since 1968. Ashby is known for his history-based columns and is well versed in the history of Texas. He has published two books.

BOOKS: *As Your Acknowledged Leader* (Austin, Tex., 1983); *As I Was Saying* (Austin, Tex., 1984).

Asman, David (1954–). David Asman writes the "Americas" column for the *Wall Street Journal* and formerly wrote a second column, "Manager's Journal." Both date from 1983.

Asman was born in Hollis, New York. He received a B.A. with high honors from Marlboro College and did graduate work at Northwestern University (1977–1978).

He edited *Prospect* in Princeton, New Jersey, from 1978 to 1980 and the *Manhattan Report on Economic Policy* in New York City from 1980 to 1982. He has been with the *Wall Street Journal* since 1983. He is also senior editor of the *Journal*'s editorial page.

BOOKS: Ed. with Adam Meyerson, *The Wall Street Journal on Management* (New York, 1985).

Atwater, Richard Tupper (29 Dec. 1892–21 Aug. 1948). Richard Atwater wrote a humor column for the *Chicago Evening Post* and the *Chicago Daily News,* writing as "Riq."

Atwater was born in Chicago as Frederick Mund Atwater. He had his given names legally changed in 1913. Atwater was a 1910 graduate of the University of Chicago and did graduate work there, doubling as an instructor of Greek at that university. He held jobs as an editor and book editor. He published a volume of humor verse from his column, translated the *Secret History of Procopius,* wrote the 1933 operetta *The King's Sneezes,* authored a children's book, and, with his wife, Florence, coauthored the successful humorous children's book *Mr. Popper's Penguins* (1938).

BOOKS: *Rickety Rimes of Riq* (Chicago, 1925); translator of Procopius of Caesarea, *Secret History of Procopius* (Ann Arbor, Mich., 1927); *Doris and the Trolls* (New York, 1931); *The King's Sneezes* (Chicago, 1933); with Florence Atwater, *Mr. Popper's Penguins* (Boston, 1938).

August, Robert Olin (6 Oct. 1921–   ). Robert August wrote the nationally syndicated column "The Wiser Side of 60" from 1982 to 1986; it was handled by Universal Press Syndicate. He also wrote a general column for the *Cleveland* [Ohio] *Press* from 1979 to 1981 and has, in addition, written sports columns.

August was born in Ashtabula, Ohio. He received the B.A. from the College of Wooster in Wooster, Ohio, in 1943, then served in the Navy until 1946. August went to work for the *Cleveland Press* in 1946 as a sportswriter, rising to the position of sports editor in 1958. He was a sports columnist for the paper from 1964 to 1979 and was the *Press'* associate editor from 1981 to 1982.

From 1982 to 1989, August was sports editor of the *Lake County News-Herald,* and he wrote a sports column for the Ingersoll newspapers starting in 1982.

Aurandt, Paul Harvey (4 Sept. 1918–   ). Paul Harvey Aurandt, who works under the professional name Paul Harvey, has written a syndicated newspaper column since 1954.

He was born in Tulsa, Oklahoma, and began working as a broadcaster at age fourteen. From 1941 to 1943 he was a KVOO radio announcer in Tulsa; station manager for a Salina, Kansas, station; special events director for KXOX radio in St. Louis, Missouri; and program director of WKZO radio in Kalamazoo, Michigan. During that same period, he was also the Michigan and Indiana director of news and information for the Office of War Information.

Harvey became a commentator for ABC in Chicago in 1944 and in 1954 began writing a column distributed by General Features Corporation, now the Los Angeles Times Syndicate. Both his radio commentary and his column tend to be carried more in small towns than in large cities, and Harvey's distinctive style—a mixture of conservative opinion, offbeat news, old-fashioned storytelling, and down-home humor—has made him familiar to millions. On radio, his pronunciation of the word *news* is like no one else's, and he is a master of the dramatic use of the pause on a medium where the prevailing conventional wisdom considers dead air time anathema.

Harvey gives his readers and listeners a feeling of getting the news behind the news. He was a supporter of the late Sen. Joseph McCarthy, Richard Nixon, and Ronald Reagan, and he appears to see the nation's public morality as sliding inexorably downhill.

He has also done television commentary for ABC and has several books to his credit.

BOOKS: *Remember These Things* (Chicago, 1952); *Autumn of Liberty* (Garden City, N.Y., 1954); *You Said It, Paul Harvey,* comp. by Lynne Harvey (River Forest, Ill., 1969); *Our Lives, Our Fortunes, Our Sacred Honor* (Waco, Tex., 1975); *The Rest of the Story,* ed. by Lynne Harvey (Garden City, N.Y., 1977); *Destiny: From Paul Harvey's The Rest of the Story,* ed. by Lynne Harvey (New York, 1983); *Paul Harvey's For What It's Worth,* ed. by Paul Harvey, Jr. (New York, 1991).

Austin, Curtis Russell (6 Feb. 1953–   ). Curtis Austin was a columnist for both the *Times Herald* and the *Morning News* in Dallas, Texas, until his resignation from the latter paper in August 1992. He now heads the editorial department of Guild, Inc., a Hyattsville, Maryland, public relations firm.

Austin was born in Washington, D.C. He received the B.A. in communications from the University of Hartford in 1975 and in 1978 completed course work for a master's degree in English literature at Howard University.

Austin began his career at the Washington (D.C.) *Afro-American* (1978–1979), then signed on as a general assignment reporter for the *Knickerbocker News* in Albany, New York (1979–1980). He was a feature-side news writer for *The News and Observer* in Raleigh, North Carolina (1980–1982); a general assignment reporter for the Chicago *Sun-Times* (1982–1984); a reporter in the Clearwater bureau of the *St. Petersburg Times* (1984–1986); and education reporter for the Charleston (West Virginia) *Gazette* (1986–1989). Austin became a staff writer and, in February 1990, columnist at the *Dallas Times Herald* in February 1986. His column ran until the *Times Herald* folded in December 1991. In January 1992 he switched to the *Morning News* in the same capacity. His general interest column in the *Times Herald* made Austin the first section front black columnist in the history of Texas journalism. From January until August 1992 his award-winning *Morning News* column was syndicated by the Knight-Ridder news wire. Differences with the management of the *Morning News* led to Curtis's resignation, after which he worked briefly as associate editor of *Defense News* in Springfield, Virginia (January–May 1993), then joined Guild, Inc. Austin has also had short stories published in *Facet,* a literary magazine.

REFERENCES: David Astor, "Columnist Focuses on the Family," *Editor and Publisher* 25 (July 1992): 34, 36; David Astor, "A Columnist Controversy in Dallas," *Editor and Publisher* 19 (September 1992): 38–39.

B

Bacharach, Bertram Mark (10 March 1898–   ). Bert Bacharach wrote "Stag Lines," a general column for men, that was syndicated to nearly ninety newspapers starting in 1951.

Bacharach was born in Philadelphia and became a graduate of Virginia Military Institute. He served in the Marine Corps during World War I prior to his graduation. He learned his specialty, men's clothing, as a buyer and manager for Saks Fifth Avenue in New York City. In 1929 he founded his own trade periodical for men's wear, *Buyer's Outlook,* and in 1933 he began writing a column for *Men's Wear* magazine and for the *Daily News Record.* In 1934 he became editor/publisher of the *Men's Apparel Reporter.*

During the 1930s, Bacharach was a consultant for Macy's and in the early 1940s, had his own ABC radio show, "Letters to Your Serviceman." When television came to New York, Bacharach adapted his radio show to the new medium. He became men's fashion editor of two magazines in the late 1940s, *Pic* in 1947 and *Collier's* in 1948. In 1957, he started a new radio program on Mutual Broadcasting System, "Men's Corner." He contributed to various magazines and newspapers on a free-lance basis and published two books. Through the 1950s, Bacharach was known as *the* authority on men's clothing, but in more recent years, his fame has been eclipsed by that of his musician/songwriter son of the same name.

BOOKS: *Bert Bacharach's Book for Men* (New York, 1953); *Right Dress: Success Through Better Grooming* (New York, 1955).

Baer, Arthur (9 Jan. 1886–18 May 1969). "Bugs" Baer wrote a humor column titled "One Word Led to Another" for the Hearst papers starting in

1914 and, later, another on Sundays, "The Family Album." His columns were syndicated by King Features.

Baer was born in Philadelphia. He began his work life at age fourteen designing lace. Next he was a staff artist for the *Philadelphia Ledger* and from there moved to Washington as a *Washington Times* sports columnist/artist. The comical insects he added to his drawings were responsible for his nickname. Prior to joining the Hearst papers, he wrote on sports for the *New York World*. He wrote, he said, for the common man. He published one book, a collection of his Sunday columns.

BOOKS: *The Family Album* (New York, 1925).

Baker, Ray Stannard (17 April 1870–12 July 1946). Ray Stannard Baker is chiefly remembered as a Progressive Era muckraker for such magazines as *McClure's* and the *American*, but he also worked as a columnist for the *Chicago Record* in the 1890s.

Baker was born in Lansing, Michigan. He was an 1889 graduate of Michigan Agricultural College, now the University of Michigan. After two years working as a clerk for his father, Baker moved to Chicago and a job with the *Record*. During his six years with the paper he was a reporter, subeditor, and columnist. His newspaper years taught him much about the economic and social problems of turn-of-the-century city life. He left the *Record* in 1887 to write for McClure's Syndicate, and from 1899 to 1905 he was associate editor of *McClure's Magazine*. There he worked with fellow muckrakers Ida Tarbell and Lincoln Steffens. From 1906 to 1915 he wrote for *American* magazine. He devoted twenty-one years to writing an eight-volume biography of Woodrow Wilson. He was a prolific nonfiction author and free-lance magazine writer.

BOOKS: *The Boy's Book of Inventions* (New York, 1899); *Our New Prosperity* (New York, 1900); *Seen in Germany* (New York, 1901); *Boys' Second Book of Inventions* (New York, 1903); as David Grayson, *Adventures in Contentment* (Garden City, N.Y., 1906); *Following the Color Line* (New York, 1908); *New Ideals in Healing* (London, 1909); *The Spiritual Unrest* (New York, 1910); as David Grayson, *A Day of Pleasant Bread* (Garden City, N.Y., 1910); as David Grayson, *Adventures in Friendship* (Garden City, N.Y., 1910); as David Grayson, *The Friendly Road* (Garden City, N.Y., 1913); as David Grayson, *Hemphill; a Novel* (Garden City, N.Y., 1915); *Great Possessions* (New York, 1917); *What Wilson Did at Paris* (New York, 1919); *The New Industrial Unrest* (Garden City, N.Y., 1920); *Woodrow Wilson and World Settlement* (Garden City, N.Y., 1922); *The Versailles Treaty and After* (New York, 1924); as David Grayson, *Adventures in Understanding* (Garden City, N.Y., 1925); *Adventures of David Grayson* (New York, 1925); *American Pioneer in Science; the Life and Service of William James Beale* (Amherst, Mass., 1925); *Woodrow Wilson: Life and Letters,* 8 vols. (Garden City, N.Y., 1927–1939); as David Grayson, *Adventures in Solitude* (Garden City, N.Y., 1931); as David Grayson, *The Countryman's Year* (Garden City, N.Y., 1936); *Native American: The Book of My Youth* (New York, 1941); *Under My Elm* (Garden City, N.Y., 1942); *American Chronicle* (New York, 1945); *David Grayson Omnibus* (Garden City, N.Y., 1946); *More Adventures with David Grayson* (Garden City, N.Y., 1946).

REFERENCES: Robert C. Bannister, *Ray Stannard Baker* (New Haven, Conn., 1966); David Mark Chalmers, *The Social and Political Ideas of the Muckrakers* (New York, 1964); William Parmenter, *Muckraking and Ray Stannard Baker,* M.A. Thesis, University of Maryland, 1975; C. C. Reiger, *The Era of the Muckrakers* (Chapel Hill, N.C., 1932).

Baker, Russell Wayne (14 Aug. 1925–   ). A wry, intelligent humorist with a literary touch, Russell Baker has been writing his "Observer" column for the *New York Times* since 1962.

Baker was born in Morrisonville, Virginia, the son of a stonemason. When his father died, Baker, age five, moved with his mother to Belleville, New Jersey, and again, when he was eleven, to Baltimore. He attended Johns Hopkins University, editing the campus paper and serving in the Navy Reserve. After receiving his A.B. in 1947, he was hired by the *Baltimore Sun* to work the crime beat. He also worked in rewrite and in 1953 was made chief of bureau in London, England, undoubtedly picking up some of the style that marks the better journalistic writing in that country. In 1954 he returned to the United States to be the *Sun*'s White House correspondent. Later in the same year he was hired by the *New York Times* as a Senate reporter. In neither position had he found his true niche, and in 1962, James Reston offered him a general column on the *Times*'s editorial page. His spoofs and highly individual commentary have appeared in the *Times* ever since, making the "Good Gray Lady" much less gray than she would be without him. Content is sometimes political, sometimes social, sometimes hard to classify. Column length is usually around 750 words. Baker's "Observer" is sent out by the New York Times News Service to nearly five hundred papers. It is perhaps misleading to call Baker a "humor columnist," since he does not use humor for its own sake, but as a means to what is frequently a more serious end.

Baker has twice won the Pulitzer Prize, in 1979 for his thrice weekly "Observer" commentary, and in 1983 for biography after the 1982 appearance of his book *Growing Up,* the first of two autobiographical volumes he has written. His career has been helped along by not only his books, but by his longer articles in the *New York Times Magazine,* the first of which appeared in 1955, and in *Holiday, Sports Illustrated, McCall's,* and other magazines.

BOOKS: *Washington: City on the Potomac* (New York, 1958); *An American in Washington* (New York, 1961); *No Cause for Panic* (Philadelphia, 1964); *Baker's Dozen* (New York, 1964); *All Things Considered* (Philadelphia, 1965); *Our Next President: The Incredible Story of What Happened in the 1968 Elections* (New York, 1968); *Poor Russell's Almanac* (Garden City, N.Y., 1972); *Better Times* (New York, 1975); *The Upside Down Man* (New York, 1977); *So This Is Depravity* (New York, 1980); *Growing Up* (New York, 1982); *The Rescue of Miss Yaskell and Other Pipe Dreams* (New York, 1983); ed., *The Norton Book of Light Verse* (New York, 1986); *Inventing the Truth: The Art and Craft of Memoir* (New York, 1987); *The Good Times* (New York, 1989); *There's a Country in My Cellar* (New York, 1990); ed., *Russell Baker's Book of American Humor* (New York, 1993).

REFERENCES: Neil A. Grauer, *Wits and Sages* (Baltimore & London, 1984): 37–53; Woodford A. Heflin, "Russell Wayne Baker," in *American Humor*, ed. by John C. Gerber (Scottsdale, Ariz., 1977): 153–169; John Skow, "The Good Humor Man," *Time* (4 June 1979): 48–52, 55–56.

Balfour, Robert Llewellyn (16 May 1918–). Robert Balfour writes a general weekly column for various papers in Florida and Georgia.

Balfour was born in Wyocena, Wisconsin. He attended Kalamazoo College in Michigan in 1935–1937 and received his bachelor's in journalism from the University of Missouri in 1940.

After graduation, Balfour was news editor for the Albia papers in Albia, Iowa (1940–1941), then business editor of the *Flint Journal* in Flint, Michigan (1941–1942). He served in the U.S. Navy during 1943–1946, and again in 1950–1951, and was aboard the USS *Missouri* in 1945 when the peace accord was signed in Tokyo Bay. Balfour was campaign manager for Harold Stassen in his 1952 bid for the presidency and later traveled fifty-one thousand miles as a member of the Eisenhower campaign staff. From 1953 to 1978 he was vice president and sales manager of the Calgon and Purex subsidiaries of Johns-Manville and sales manager of Club Car Golf Car Company in Augusta, Georgia, until he retired in 1978. While with Club Car, he published one book and wrote for various magazines. Balfour believes that he and Harold Stassen were the only two Americans to have served on the staffs of both a five-star admiral (Halsey) and a five-star general (Eisenhower).

Balfour began his column in 1989, writing weekly for the *Clayton County News* and *Henry County Herald* in the southern suburbs of Atlanta. After moving to Florida in 1993, he began writing another column for the *Ocala Star-Banner* and other Florida papers.

BOOKS: *A Nobody Gives Hell to Everybody* (New York, 1970).

Balmaseda, Elizabeth R. (17 Jan. 1959–). Liz Balmaseda, winner of the 1993 Pulitzer Prize for commentary, has been a *Miami Herald* columnist since 1991.

Balmaseda was born in Puerto Padre, Oriente, Cuba, seventeen days after the 1959 revolution. She grew up in Miami, edited the campus newspaper for and received the associate of arts degree from Miami-Dade Community College, and received the B.S. in communications from Florida International University in 1981.

She was a student intern with the *Miami Herald* in 1980 and was hired by that paper in 1981 to write for its Spanish-language publication, *El Herald*. Later, she worked on the city desk and as a general assignment reporter. Balmaseda left in 1985 to become Central America bureau chief for *Newsweek*, based in El Salvador, after which she was employed by NBC News as a field producer working out of Honduras. In November 1987 she returned to the *Herald* as a feature writer, and in 1990 she began writing for *Tropic*, the paper's

Sunday magazine. She became a columnist in 1991; her column appears on Wednesdays and Saturdays and explores the political, social, and cultural aspects of the highly diverse city of Miami.

REFERENCES: David Astor, "Post-Pulitzer 'Blitz' and Bliss for Writer," *Editor and Publisher* (2 October 1993): 30–31.

Bandow, Douglas (15 April 1957–). Doug Bandow writes "The Capital Eye," which is syndicated by Copley News Service.

Bandow was born in Washington, D.C. His B.S. (1976) was from Florida State University, his J.D. (1979) from Stanford University. After law school, he worked for the Reagan for President campaign, and from 1980 to 1982 he was an assistant to President Reagan. Bandow was editor of *Inquiry* from 1982 to 1984 and became a fellow of the Cato Institute in 1984. He is also a contributing editor of *Reason* and has published several books on politics.

BOOKS: Ed., *U.S. Aid to the Developing World* (Washington, D.C., 1985); ed., *Beyond Good Intentions: A Biblical View of Politics* (Westchester, Ill., 1988); *Human Resources and Military Manpower* (Washington, D.C., 1989); *The Politics of Plunder: Misgovernment in Washington* (New Brunswick, N.J., 1990); *The Politics of Envy: Statism as Theology* (New Brunswick, N.J., 1994); ed., *Perpetuating Poverty* (Washington, D.C., 1994).

Barberich, Kathy (30 July 1948–). Kathy Barberich has been a columnist for the *Fresno Bee* since 1982.

Barberich was born in Fresno, California, and received her bachelor's degree in communications at Fresno State University in 1971. She began working for the *Bee* her freshman year at Fresno State, writing wedding and engagement stories for the Women's Activities Department. She eventually became a feature writer, then began her family and took six years off, returning to the paper in 1981. Her column, "The Family Tree," is sometimes personal, sometimes humorous, sometimes both. Its general thrust, as its title implies, is an examination of family life. In addition to her duties as columnist, Barberich is youth editor; as such, she is responsible for a weekly teen section and a Saturday children's page.

Barry, Dave (3 July 1947–). Dave Barry is arguably the funniest newspaper humor columnist of the 1980s and 1990s. His widely syndicated column is based at the *Miami Herald*.

Barry was born in Armonk, New York. In 1969, he received the B.A. from Pennsylvania's Haverford College, where he wrote for his school paper, as he had in high school. Barry began his career as a reporter for a small suburban paper outside Philadelphia, the *Daily Local News* of West Chester (1971–1975). During 1975–1976 he was with the Associated Press in Philadelphia, and from 1975 to 1983 he taught business writing for the consulting firm of R. S. Burger Associates.

Barry began free-lancing his humor copy in 1980. A long feature article on natural childbirth he wrote during this period is surely one of the classics of newspaper humor writing. His ability to capture that which is essentially silly in modern life began to attract attention, and in 1983 he was hired as a full-time humor columnist by the *Miami Herald.* He is wildly creative in approach and strives, he has said, to make his column read as though he had hurriedly dashed it off while carpet-chewing drunk. Strange as that might sound, he works at it seven days a week. He won the Pulitzer Prize for commentary in 1988, a year after he had poked fun at the Pulitzers, saying that he would never win one by writing about ''goat boogers.'' Occasionally, papers balk at some of the topics Barry chooses; in 1991 the *Portland Oregonian* pulled a column he had written about the antigas product Beano. Still, he is syndicated to several hundred papers via the Knight-Ridder/Tribune News Information Service wire and, since November 1989, Tribune Media Services. Thus far, Barry has published a dozen books, most of them collections of his columns.

BOOKS: *The Taming of the Screw* (Emmaus, Pa., 1983); *Babies and Other Hazards of Sex: How to Make a Tiny Person in Only 9 Months, With Tools You Probably Have Around the House* (Emmaus, Pa., 1984); *Bad Habits: A 100% Fact Free Book* (Garden City, N.Y., 1985); *Stay Fit and Healthy Until You're Dead* (Emmaus, Pa., 1985); *Claw Your Way to the Top* (Emmaus, Pa., 1986); *Dave Barry's Guide to Marriage* (Emmaus, Pa., 1987); *Dave Barry's Greatest Hits* (New York, 1988); *Homes and Other Black Holes* (New York, 1988); *Dave Barry Slept Here* (New York, 1989); *Dave Barry Does Japan* (New York, 1992); *Dave Barry Is Not Making This Up* (New York, 1994).

REFERENCES: Tricia Drevets, ''A Talk with a Pulitzer-Winning Humorist,'' *Editor and Publisher* (16 July 1988): 40–42.

Barry, Joseph Amber (13 June 1917–   ). Joseph Barry was Paris columnist for the *New York Post* from 1958 to 1965 and for the *Village Voice* for some years thereafter.

Barry was born in Scranton, Pennsylvania. He received two A.B. degrees from the University of Michigan in 1939 and 1940 and did graduate study in 1946 at the Sorbonne in Paris, where he came to know Gertrude Stein. From 1941 to 1946 he served as an officer in the U.S. Army.

Barry began his work life as a librarian at the New York Public Library (1940–1941). He worked with the Paris edition of *Newsweek* from 1946 to 1949 and was Paris bureau chief of the *New York Times*'s Sunday edition from 1949 to 1952. From 1952 to 1957 he was editorial director of *House Beautiful* in New York City, and in 1958, he launched his column. He has contributed to such magazines as *Smithsonian, Holiday,* and *Horizon* and has authored or edited eight books.

BOOKS: *Left Bank, Right Bank* (New York, 1951); ed., *Architecture as Space* (New York, 1957); *The House Beautiful Treasury of Contemporary American Homes* (New York, 1958); *France* (New York, 1965); *The People of Paris* (Garden City, N.Y., 1966); *Passions and Politics: A Biography of Versailles* (Garden City, N.Y., 1972); *Infamous*

Woman: The Life of George Sand (Garden City, N.Y., 1976); ed., *In Her Own Words: George Sand Translated and Edited by Joseph Barry* (Garden City, N.Y., 1979).

Bartels, Lynn (1957–   ). Lynn Bartels was until July 1993 a general columnist for *The Albuquerque* [New Mexico] *Tribune.* She is now a crime reporter for the *Rocky Mountain News* in Denver, Colorado.

She was born in Vermillion, South Dakota. She edited her high school newspaper and received a bachelor's degree in journalism from Northern Arizona University. From 1980 to 1983 she worked as a reporter on a paper in Gallup, New Mexico, then in 1984 moved to the Albuquerque paper as city hall reporter and columnist. Her column was witty and was frequently self-effacing and personal.

Bartlett, Charles Leffingwell (14 Aug. 1921–   ). Charles Bartlett's *Chicago Daily News* column "News Focus" was syndicated by the Field Syndicate from 1971 to 1981. The column had appeared in the *Daily News* since 1975, and prior to that time, Bartlett had been a columnist for the *Chicago Sun-Times* from 1963 to 1975.

Bartlett was born in Chicago. He received the A.B. from Yale University in 1943. He was in the navy from 1943 to 1946, then from 1946 to 1963 was a reporter for the *Chattanooga Times* in Tennessee. From 1958 to 1963 he was an editor for the News Focus Service. He won the Pulitzer Prize for reporting in 1955 and coauthored one book.

BOOKS: With Edward Weintal, *Facing the Brink: An Intimate Study of Crisis Diplomacy* (New York, 1967).

Battelle, Phyllis Marie (4 Jan. 1922–   ). Phyllis Battelle wrote "Assignment America," a three-times-a-week column syndicated by King Features Syndicate, starting in 1955.

Battelle was born in Dayton, Ohio, and earned her B.A. at Ohio Wesleyan University in 1944. She began her career as a feature writer/police reporter/teenage columnist for the *Dayton Herald* (1944–1947). From 1947 to 1954 she was women's editor and fashion editor for the International News Service, then began writing her column in 1955. The sometimes cynical Battelle married commentator Art Van Horn in 1957. She coauthored one book and wrote for various magazines.

BOOKS: With Joseph and Julia Quinlan, *Karen Ann: The Quinlans Tell Their Story* (New York, 1977).

Baye, Betty Winston (12 April 1946–   ). Louisville *Courier-Journal* editorial writer and columnist Betty Baye is syndicated by Gannett News Service. Her column is general, personal, and often political and is focused on the African-American experience.

Born in Brooklyn, Baye received the B.A. in 1979 from Hunter College of the City University of New York, and the M.S. in 1980 from Columbia University's graduate school of journalism.

Baye's career began as a reporter for the *Daily Argus* of Mount Vernon, New York (1980–1984). From 1984 until 1986 she was a reporter for the *Courier-Journal* in Louisville, where she has also served as assistant city editor (1986–1988) and assistant editor (1988–1990). During 1990–1991 she was a Nieman Fellow at Harvard University, after which she returned to the *Courier-Journal* in her present capacity. She has contributed to *Essence* magazine and has been a vice president of the National Association of Black Journalists.

BOOKS: *The Africans* (Wayne, Pa., 1983).

REFERENCES: Craig Polite and Audrey Edwards, *Children of the Dream: The Psychology of Black Success* (New York, 1992); Leslie C. Shields and Cydney Shields, *Work, Sister, Work* (New York, 1994).

Beagle, Benjamin Stuart, Jr. (24 April 1927–). Semiretired senior writer and columnist for the *Roanoke Times and World News* Ben Beagle still writes two personal humor columns a week plus an occasional essay for this paper.

Beagle was born in Staunton, Virginia, and spent most of his youth in two other Virginia towns, Waynesboro and Radford. He received the B.A. in English from Roanoke College in 1952.

Beagle's career began with three months at the Radford *News-Journal* in 1952, followed by a public relations position with Roanoke College in 1952–1953. In 1953 he went with the Staunton *News-Leader,* then joined the *Roanoke Times and World News* in 1954. His column first appeared in 1957. In his column Beagle frequently refers to himself as El Viejo (the Old One), or as "the aging, semihysterical reporter," and to his wife as "the greatest station wagon driver of them all."

BOOKS: *World I Never Made* (Roanoke, Va., 1986); *El Viejo Writes Again* (Roanoke, Va., 1990).

Beale, Betty (?–). Betty Beale (Mrs. George K. Graeber) was a Washington, D.C., columnist of long experience.

Beale, about whom little has been written, was born in Washington, D.C., and received the A.B. degree, magna cum laude, from Smith College. She wrote a column for the *Washington Post* from 1937 to 1940, then worked as a reporter and columnist for the Washington *Evening Star* from 1945 to 1981. Her work was handled by the Hall Syndicate and by the North American Syndicate. From 1953 she used the title "Betty Beale's Washington" for her weekly column. Her writing combined hard news and glamour. One of her best remembered scoops involved mistreatment of laboratory animals, and she was also known for her interviews with hard-to-get subjects, such as U.S. presidents and foreign heads of state. Her column often dealt with presidential politics.

Beasley, Delilah Leontium (9 Sept. 1871–18 Aug. 1934). Delilah Beasley, apparently the first African-American woman to write on a regular basis for a white U.S. newspaper, did a Sunday items column that appeared in the *Oakland* [California] *Tribune* from 1923 to 1934.

Beasley was born in Cincinnati, Ohio, and attended the public schools of that city. At age twelve she began contributing short items of church news for a black newspaper, the *Cleveland Gazette,* and at fifteen she began to contribute occasionally to the *Cincinnati Enquirer.* Meanwhile, she worked as a housemaid and as a masseuse in Chicago, Buffalo, and other locations. In 1910 she relocated from the Midwest to Berkeley, California, to work as a private nurse. She became interested in the history of the black pioneers who had helped settle California and after nine years of research and writing, privately published a book on that topic.

Beasley began contributing to the *Oakland Tribune* in June 1915; she also wrote for a black audience in the *Oakland Sunshine.* Her column, "Activities Among Negroes," first appeared in the *Tribune* in September 1923. Beasley's motivation was to give the white readers of the *Tribune* a positive picture of the black community. She kept clear of reporting incidents of racial discrimination and instead documented the achievements of successful black men and women, in Oakland and elsewhere. She was a gentle activist who followed the path chosen by Booker T. Washington rather than that taken by those who would be more militant. She also campaigned, apparently with some success, to eliminate the use of such ethnic slurs as "darkey" and "pickaninny."

Beasley, who never married, was national historian of the National Association of Colored Women and was active in the League of Women Voters.

BOOKS: *Negro Trail Blazers of California* (Los Angeles, Calif., 1919).

REFERENCES: Roger Streitmatter, "Delilah Beasley: A Black Woman Journalist Who Lifted As She Climbed," *American Journalism* 11 (Winter 1994): 61–75.

Beck, Joan Wagner (5 Sept. 1923–   ). Joan Beck began an editorial page column for the *Chicago Tribune* in 1974. Prior to that time, she had written syndicated columns for young people and for children.

She was born Joan Wagner in Clinton, Iowa. Her B.J., cum laude (1945), and her M.S. in journalism (1947) were from Northwestern University.

She was a radio scriptwriter for Voice of America in 1945–1946 and a copy writer for Marshall Field and Co. from 1947 to 1950. In 1950 she joined the *Chicago Tribune* as a feature writer. She began writing her syndicated column about young people in 1956 and in 1961 switched to writing another column concerning younger children. This second column was continued until 1972, when she became editor of the *Tribune*'s features section. Beck became a member of the paper's editorial board in 1975 after having begun her editorial page column in the previous year. She has also published several books regarding parenting.

BOOKS: *How to Raise a Brighter Child: The Case for Early Learning* (Cleveland, Ohio, 1967); with Virginia Apgar, *Is My Baby All Right? A Guide to Birth Defects* (New York, 1972); *Effective Parenting* (New York, 1976); *Best Beginnings: Giving Your Child a Head Start in Life* (New York, 1983).

Beckley, Zoë (?–   ). Zoë Beckley, known for her interview stories, began writing a daily column for the McNaught Syndicate in 1917.

Beckley was born in New York City. Her formal education was limited to the public schools. She learned typing from an aunt and shorthand at night school and did secretarial work for factories, a detective, a butcher, a broker, and an author. Columnist Helen Rowland suggested that she look into a career in journalism; her first job was reporting for the *New York Press.* She also wrote a double-page feature for the *Press* entitled "Little Stories of Manhattan." Her next job was at the *New York Mail,* for which she did war-related stories during World War I. In 1917 she convinced her editor, Edward Rumely, to send her on a tour of the United States to do interviews. Not long thereafter, she was hired by the *New York Evening World;* she also wrote for the Newspaper Enterprise Association (NEA) and the North American Newspaper Alliance.

One of Beckley's more unusual assignments for NEA in 1920 was to go to the Netherlands and get an interview with the German kaiser, who was visiting there. The kaiser did not deign to be interviewed by mere journalists, but Beckley did manage to get several candid photos of him. She also sailed on the S.S. *Mauretania* to interview Lady Astor.

Upon the sale of the *New York Mail,* Beckley went to work for the *New York Telegram* for a brief period, then took a job as columnist for Famous Features Syndicate. During this period she interviewed Queen Marie of Rumania and convinced the queen to write an exclusive series of articles for Famous Features. She also interviewed her least talkative subject, President Calvin Coolidge. Beckley did most of her writing at her home in Connecticut.

Beebe, Lucius Morris (9 Dec. 1902–4 Feb. 1966). Lucius Beebe, bon vivant, wrote a column for the *New York Herald Tribune* from 1921 to 1951. His primary interests were the habits of the upper class and travel by rail.

Beebe was born to a wealthy family at Wakefield, near Boston, Massachusetts. Because of his penchant for practical jokes, he was expelled from several private schools in New England, and from Yale, as well, finally graduating from Harvard in 1927. He studied poetry at Harvard for an additional year, then worked briefly for the Boston *Transcript.*

In 1929 he was hired as a reporter by the *New York Herald Tribune.* Soon his editors saw that he did not have the makings of a reporter and thought his peculiar talents would be better put to use if he were given a column. From El Morocco, the Stork Club, and other such haunts of the rich Beebe produced a chronicle of the extravagances and vagaries of America's financial and social elite. His widely syndicated column ran for thirty years. In 1952 Beebe gave up his column and moved to Virginia City, Nevada, to become copublisher of the *Territorial Enterprise,* the paper that had employed Mark Twain. In 1960 he was employed as a writer by the *San Francisco Chronicle* and also wrote for *Gourmet* and other upscale magazines. He was a prolific author and made a mark as a photographer and promoter of railroad trains.

BOOKS: *Fallen Stars* (Boston, 1921); *Corydon, and Other Poems* (Boston, 1924); *Aspects of the Poetry of Edwin Arlington Robinson* (Cambridge, Mass., 1928); *A Biography of the Writings of Edwin Arlington Robinson* (Cambridge, Mass., 1931); *Boston and the Boston Legend* (New York, 1935); *High Iron: A Book of Trains* (New York, 1938); *Highliners, a Railroad Album* (New York, 1940); *Trains in Transition* (New York, 1941); *Highball, a Pageant of Trains* (New York, 1945); *The Stork Club Bar Book* (New York, 1946); *Mixed Train Daily* (New York, 1947); *Snoot If You Must* (New York, 1948); with Charles Clegg, *Dreadful California* (Indianapolis, 1948); with Charles Clegg, *Virginia and Truckee* (Oakland, Calif., 1949); *Legends of the Comstock Lode* (Oakland, Calif., 1950); with Charles Clegg, *Cable Car Carnival* (Oakland, Calif., 1951); *Hear the Train Blow* (New York, 1952); *Comstock Commotion* (Stanford, Calif., 1954); with Charles Clegg, *The American West* (New York, 1955); with Charles Clegg, *Narrow Gauge in the Rockies* (Berkeley, Calif., 1958); *Mansions on Rails: The Folklore of the Private Railway Car* (Berkeley, Calif., 1959); with Charles Clegg, *San Francisco's Golden Era* (Berkeley, Calif., 1960); *Mr. Pullman's Elegant Palace Car* (Garden City, N.Y., 1961); with Charles Clegg, *When Beauty Rode the Rails* (Garden City, N.Y., 1962); *The Overland Limited* (Berkeley, Calif., 1963); with Charles Clegg, *Great Railroad Photographs U.S.A* (Berkeley, Calif., 1964); *Two Trains to Remember* (Virginia City, Nev., 1965); with Charles Clegg, *The Trains We Rode,* 2 vols. (Berkeley, Calif., 1965–1966); *The Big Spenders* (Garden City, N.Y., 1966); *The Provocative Pen of Lucius Beebe* (San Francisco, 1966); *The Lucius Beebe Reader* (ed. by Charles Clegg and Duncan Emrich, 1967); with Charles Clegg, *Steamcars to the Comstock* (Berkeley, Calif., 1970); *The Age of Steam* (Berkeley, Calif., 1972); *U.S. West: The Saga of Wells Fargo* (New York, 1974); *The Savoy of London* (London, n.d.).

Beeghly, Nancy Ward (30 May 1945–   ). Nancy Beeghly has written a general/human interest column for the *Vindicator* in Youngstown, Ohio, since 1989.

Beeghly was born in Cleveland, Ohio, and received a B.S. in English and education from Mount Union College. Beeghly raised three children and was an English teacher, community volunteer, naturalist, and bibliophile before being hired as columnist by the *Vindicator*'s publisher. She regards the bringing together of readers with the people featured in her columns as "sacred moments" and says, "I punch the 'send' button on my computer and wince as I send a little of myself to my editors for scrutiny."

Bell, Edward Price (1 March 1869–23 Sept. 1943). Standout Chicago journalist Edward Price Bell wrote a weekly column, "The Marching World," in the *Chicago Daily News* from 1927 to 1931.

Bell was born on a farm near Terre Haute, Indiana. He was a graduate of Wabash College. Prior to his college years, he had worked as a reporter for several Indiana papers and had briefly published a newspaper of his own, the *Rosedale Bee*.

After graduation, Bell took a reporting job with the *Chicago Record*. In 1900 he was dispatched to London as head of the paper's new foreign service. Next he held the same office for the *Chicago Daily News*, then in 1922 returned to Chicago and a job as a reporter for the *Daily News*. He traveled extensively and wrote about world politics. He also worked as a commentator for the paper's Chicago radio station, WMAQ, during the 1920s.

Bell ended his column in 1931 when he resigned from the *Daily News* and moved to Pass Christian, Mississippi. For his efforts to arrange meetings between world leaders and to press for disarmament, in 1930 Bell was nominated for the Nobel Peace Prize, a rare distinction for a journalist. He wrote for *Literary Digest* in the 1930s, again traveling the world to gather his material. His last employment was in 1941 as a writer for the weekly *Saturday Spectator* in Terre Haute. He published two books.

BOOKS: *World Chancelleries* (Chicago, 1926); *Europe's Economic Sunrise* (Chicago, 1927).

REFERENCES: James D. Startt, *Journalism's Unofficial Ambassador: A Biography of Edward Price Bell, 1869–1943* (Athens, Ohio, 1979); Benedict K. Zobrist, *Edward Price Bell and the Development of the Foreign News Service of the Chicago Daily News*, Ph.D. Dissertation, Northwestern University, 1953.

Bell, Lillian Smith (?–   ). One of the relatively few individuals to teach at a university and write a regular newspaper column, Lillian Bell is on the American Studies faculty at the University of Notre Dame and is an editorial page columnist with the *Elkhart Truth* in Elkhart, Indiana.

Bell was born in South Bend, Indiana, and received her B.S. from the Medill School of Journalism at Northwestern University in 1945, her M.A. from Case-Western University in 1955, and her Ph.D. from Northwestern in 1973.

Bell's first newspaper work was as a reporter and assistant editor for the Baltimore *Afro-American* (1945–1947). From 1947 until 1955 she edited the *Cleveland Herald* in Cleveland, Ohio. Her work in education began at Hampton Institute in Hampton, Virginia, where she was assistant director of public relations (1956–1958); she then taught English at Froebel High School in Gary, Indiana (1958–1964), followed by St. Joseph's Calumet College (1967–1975), Northwestern's Medill School of Journalism (1970–1971), Atlanta's Clark College (1975—as a visiting professor), and Northern Illinois University (1975–1988).

Bell's first column was with *Info*, a Gary, Indiana, weekly (1972–1982). From 1977 to 1987 she wrote a weekly column for the Gary *Post-Tribune;* during those years she also covered the Urban League and the National Association for the Advancement of Colored People (NAACP) for the same paper. She has been on the Notre Dame faculty since 1988, was an op-ed columnist for the South

Bend *Tribune* during 1988 and 1989, and began her Sunday editorial page column for the *Elkhart Truth* in 1990.

Berger, Meyer (1 Sept. 1898–8 Feb. 1959). *The New York Times*'s ace reporter Meyer "Mike" Berger launched the long-lived *Times* column "About New York" in 1939, had to discontinue it as a result of wartime paper shortages, then revived it in 1953 and kept it going until his death in 1959.

Berger was born on the Lower East Side of New York City, the son of Czech immigrants. He was a paper boy at age eight, a newspaper night messenger at eleven for the *New York World*, and later that paper's head office boy. Family financial troubles forced him to drop out of high school. He served in the army in France during World War I, then found work as a Brooklyn police reporter for the *World*. He next became the head of rewrite for the Standard News Association in Brooklyn, then in 1928, the top rewrite man and reporter for the *New York Times*. He became known for his coverage of the legal entanglements of such gangsters as Al Capone and Dutch Schultz.

Berger left the *Times* for one year, 1937, to write for *The New Yorker* but found that he preferred newspaper work. Back at the *Times,* he launched "About New York" in 1939, later went to London as a war correspondent for two months, and in 1950 won the Pulitzer Prize for local reporting for his coverage of an insane multiple murderer, Howard Unruh. He sent the $1,000 prize money to Unruh's mother.

During 1950 and 1951, Berger researched and wrote the history of the *Times,* which turned one hundred in 1951. Then in 1953 he resumed writing his column, continuing to discuss his city until his death in 1959. (The column was again revived in 1979 and written by several other *Times* staffers.) Berger was a master of color writing, human interest, and humor. He published eight books and was warmly regarded by all who knew him. He holds what must surely be a unique distinction as the only Jewish U.S. columnist to have been blessed by the pope. The blessing took place at a private audience with Pope Pius XII after Berger had cowritten a touching book about Roman Catholic missionaries, the Maryknoll Fathers of New York state.

BOOKS: *The Eight Million: Journal of a New York Correspondent* (New York, 1942); with James Keller, *The Men of Maryknoll* (New York, 1943); *Growth of an Ideal, 1850–1950* (Philadelphia, 1950); *The Story of the New York Times, 1851–1951* (New York, 1951); *New York: City on Many Waters* (New York, 1956); *The Library* (New York, 1956); *Meyer Berger's New York* (New York, 1960).

REFERENCES: John C. Devlin, "The Most Unforgettable Character I've Met," *Reader's Digest* 75 (October 1959): 77–81; "Mike Berger, Reporter," *Newsweek* 53 (16 February 1959): 16.

Bernstein, Theodore Menline (17 Nov. 1904–27 June 1979). One-company man Theodore Bernstein of the *New York Times* wore many hats, one of which was that of writer of the syndicated column "Bernstein on Words."

Bernstein was born in New York City and earned his B.A. from Columbia University in 1924. He joined the *Times* as a copy editor (1925–1930), was a suburban editor (1930–1932), and was foreign editor (1939–1948). Thereafter, he was assistant night managing editor (1948–1951), news editor (1951–1952), assistant managing editor (1952–1969), and editorial head of the company's book division (1969–1971). He also edited the *Times*'s splendid house organ, *Winners and Sinners,* which explored the dos and don'ts of journalistic writing (1951–1978). He was founding editor of the international edition, published in Paris (1960), and executive editor of the *New York Times Encyclopedic Almanac* (1969–1971).

Bernstein's column, started in 1972 and handled by the Times Special Features Syndicate, displayed not only his erudition, but his sparkling wit. Many a journalism professor has drawn inspiration from his comments on usage, some of which employed the fictitious public school teacher Miss Thistlebottom, whose rules, sadly, had no exceptions. Bernstein's reputation as an authority on usage was increased by the several books he published on the subject. He also contributed to *Saturday Review,* was a consultant for *Random House Dictionary* and *American Heritage Dictionary,* and taught journalism at Columbia University (1925–1950).

BOOKS: With Robert E. Garst, *Headlines and Deadlines: A Manual for Copy Editors* (New York, 1933); *Watch Your Language* (New York, 1958); *More Language That Needs Watching* (New York, 1962); *The Careful Writer* (New York, 1965); *Miss Thistlebottom's Hobgoblins* (New York, 1971); *Theodore Bernstein's Reverse Dictionary* (New York, 1975); *Dos, Don'ts and Maybes of English Usage* (New York, 1977).

Bierce, Ambrose Gwinnett (24 June 1842–Jan. 1914?). Remembered as the most bitter, caustic, and misanthropic of all America's humorists, Ambrose Bierce was a newspaper columnist from 1868 to 1872 in the *San Francisco News Letter and California Advertiser,* from 1881 to 1886 in the *Wasp,* and from 1887 to 1897 in the *San Francisco Examiner* and other Hearst papers. He also wrote a column, "The Prattler," in *Argonaut* magazine and a monthly column for *Cosmopolitan* that he continued until 1909.

Bierce was born on a farm in Horse Cave Creek, Ohio. His family moved to another farm, near Warsaw, Indiana, in 1846. From age fifteen to seventeen, he worked as a printer's devil on a small paper, the *Northern Indianan,* and in 1859 he left home for a year's study at Kentucky Military Institute, where he learned drafting and surveying. He enlisted in the Union Army as soon as war broke out and fought in such major battles as Shiloh, Chickamauga, and Missionary Ridge, rising from private to sergeant-major to first lieutenant. He left the army after being seriously wounded in January 1865, worked as a U.S. Treasury agent in Alabama, and went from Nebraska to California on a surveying and map-making expedition in 1866–1867. While working as a watchman and later a clerk for the Treasury office in San Francisco, Bierce was tutored in writing by James Watkins, managing editor of the *San Francisco News Letter and California Advertiser.* After publishing some of his work in various California periodicals, Bierce was hired by the *News Letter* and in December 1868 replaced Watkins as managing editor. He also began writing a weekly column, "The Town Crier" (5 December 1868–9 March 1872), in which his barbed wit was directed at local politicians, lawyers, police, clergy, and others. He became famed as "the wickedest man in San Francisco."

When Bierce married, the bride's father gave the couple a honeymoon trip to London, where they remained from 1872 to 1875. Bierce wrote for such witty English periodicals as *Figaro* and *Fun* and also published his first three books while living there.

Back in San Francisco, he worked briefly for the U.S. Mint, wrote a humor column titled "The Prattler" for *Argonaut,* and joined the Bohemian Club. He took two years to work as manager of a Black Hills mining company in South Dakota, then returned to San Francisco, where from 1881 to 1886 he edited the *Wasp,* and wrote his column, renamed "Prattle," for this weekly paper. "Prattle" was moved to William Randolph Hearst's *San Francisco Examiner* in March 1887; it later appeared in the *New York Journal,* as well. Bierce kept up the column until 1897 and also wrote editorials and other articles for the Hearst papers. He moved to Washington, D.C., in 1899 and from 1905 to 1909 wrote a column for Hearst's magazine *Cosmopolitan.*

Bierce's final literary project was a twelve-volume collection of his own works, published between 1909 and 1912. With this project complete, Bierce set out for Mexico, arriving in Juarez in November 1913. He traveled with Pancho Villa's army during Mexico's civil war and was last heard from in late December 1914, just prior to the Battle of Ojinaga, where it is thought that Bierce died.

BOOKS: As Dod Grile, *The Fiend's Delight* (London, 1873); as Dod Grile, *Nuggets and Dust Panned Out in California* (London, 1873); as Dod Grile, *Cobwebs from an Empty Skull* (London and New York, 1874); with Thomas A. Harcourt, as William Herman, *The Dance of Death* (San Francisco, 1877); *Tales of Soldiers and Civilians* (San Francisco, 1892); with Gustav Adolph Danziger, *The Monk and the Hangman's Daughter* (Chicago, 1892); *Black Beetles in Amber* (San Francisco and New York, 1892); *Can Such Things Be?* (New York, 1893); *Fantastic Fables* (New York and London, 1899); *Shapes of Clay* (San Francisco, 1903); *The Cynic's Word Book* (New York, 1903); *A Son of the Gods and a Horseman in the Sky* (San Francisco, 1907); *The Shadow on the Dial and Other Essays,* ed. by S. O. Howes (San Francisco, 1909); *Write It Right* (New York and Washington, D.C., 1909); *The Collected Works of Ambrose Bierce,* 12 vols. (New York and Washington, 1909–1912); *Battlefields and Ghosts,* ed. by Hartley E. Jackson and James D. Hart (Palo Alto, Calif., 1931); *Selections from Prattle by Ambrose Bierce,* ed. by Carroll D. Hall (San Francisco, 1936); *Enlarged Devil's Dictionary,* ed. by Ernest J. Hopkins (Garden City, N.Y., 1967); *The Ambrose Bierce Satanic Reader,* ed. by Ernest J. Hopkins (Garden City, N.Y., 1968).

REFERENCES: Adolphe de Castro, *Portrait of Ambrose Bierce* (New York, 1929); Paul Fatout, *Ambrose Bierce: The Devil's Lexicographer* (Norman, Okla., 1951); Fatout, *Ambrose Bierce and the Black Hills* (Norman, Okla., 1956); M. E. Grenander, *Ambrose*

Bierce (New York, 1971); Carey McWilliams, *Ambrose Bierce: A Biography* (New York, 1929); Richard O'Connor, *Ambrose Bierce: A Biography* (Boston, 1967); Robert A. Wiggins, *Ambrose Bierce* (Minneapolis, Minn., 1964); Stuart C. Woodruff, *The Short Stories of Ambrose Bierce: A Study in Polarity* (Pittsburgh, Pa., 1964).

Binstein, Michael (27 June, 1956–   ). Known especially for his investigative stories on America's savings and loan industry, Michael Binstein currently shares the "Washington Merry-Go-Round" byline with Jack Anderson. The column is handled by United Feature Syndicate.

Binstein was born in Chicago and graduated in 1980 from American University. He founded and ran the *Washington Observer*, a D.C.-based paper aimed at the college market. He worked as a contributing editor for the business/political magazine *Regardie's* and has been an ABC News and PBS "Frontline" consultant.

Binstein joined Jack Anderson's staff in 1982 and was named his cocolumnist in January 1992. Binstein's investigative scoops include the 1987 revelations about former House speaker Jim Wright's involvement in the savings and loan crisis, which led to Wright's resignation, and the 1992 account of questionable practices in the financial conduct of the United Way.

Bishoff, Don (30 Dec. 1936–   ). Don Bishoff has twice been a daily columnist for the *Register-Guard* in Eugene, Oregon: 1976–1977 and from 1983 to the present.

Bishoff was born in Martinsburg, West Virginia; attended high school in Richmond, Virginia; and received his B.S. from the Medill School of Journalism at Northwestern University in 1958. The following year he received the M.S. in journalism from Northwestern and in 1966 was a Professional Journalism Fellow (now known as a Knight Fellow) at Stanford University.

In 1959 he was a reporter with the City News Bureau of Chicago. Later in the same year he became a reporter for the *Richmond Times-Dispatch* in Virginia, moving to the *Register-Guard* in 1960. There he has worked as reporter (1960–1968), assistant city editor (1968–1976), daily columnist (1976–1977), associate editor and editorial writer (1977–1983), and again as daily columnist from 1983. He also wrote a weekly column for the *Register-Guard* from 1961 to 1976 and was drama reviewer from 1967 to 1984. He has cohosted "Town Meeting," a two-hour Sunday morning interview and listener call-in program on Eugene's radio station DAVE-FM, since 1992.

Bishop, James Alonzo (21 Nov. 1907–26 July 1987). A gifted storyteller and author of roughly twenty books, Jim Bishop wrote a thrice-weekly column for King Features Syndicate from 1957 until his death.

Bishop was born in Jersey City, New Jersey. He was mainly self-educated, though he learned shorthand and typing in 1923 at Drake Secretarial College in Jersey City. He worked as a *New York Daily News* copyboy in 1928 and as a cub reporter for that paper in the following year. He switched to the *New York Daily Mirror* as a reporter in 1930 as a low-paid assistant to columnist Mark Hellinger, then did rewrite and feature writing for the *Mirror* until 1943. In that year he went to *Collier's* magazine, as associate editor (1943–1944) and then as war editor (1944–1945). He was executive editor of *Liberty* magazine from 1945 to 1947, then from 1947 to 1949 directed the literature department of Music Corporation of America. He was founding editor of Gold Medal Books (1949–1951), then editor of *Catholic Digest* (1954) and founding editor of that magazine's book club (1954–1955).

Bishop began his syndicated column in 1957 and had his own weekly WABC-TV show, "Byline—Jim Bishop," during 1961–1962. His column appeared in more than two hundred papers, and he authored numerous books that combined history with journalism. He produced an autobiography, *A Bishop's Confession,* and contributed to many magazines, including *Good Housekeeping, Look,* and *McCall's.*

BOOKS: *The Glass Crutch: The Biographical Novel of William Wynne Wister* (Garden City, N.Y., 1945); *The Mark Hellinger Story* (New York, 1952); *The Girl in Poison Cottage* (New York, 1953); *The Making of a Priest* (N.p., 1954); *The Day Lincoln Was Shot* (New York, 1955); *Fighting Father Duffy* (New York, 1956); *The Golden Ham: A Candid Biography of Jackie Gleason* (New York, 1956); *The Day Christ Died* (New York, 1959); *Go with God* (New York, 1958); *Some of My Very Best* (New York, 1960); *The Day Christ Was Born* (New York, 1960); *The Murder Trial of Judge Peel* (New York, 1960); *Honeymoon Diary* (New York, 1963); *A Day in the Life of President Kennedy* (New York, 1964); *A Day in the Life of President Johnson* (New York, 1967); *The Day Kennedy Was Shot* (New York, 1968); *The Days of Martin Luther King* (New York, 1971); *FDR's Last Year* (New York, 1974); *Mother Tongue* (Portland, Me., 1975); *A Bishop's Confession* (Boston, 1981).

Bledsoe, Jerry (15 July 1941–   ). Now an author/publisher, Jerry Bledsoe was a columnist for the *Greensboro* [North Carolina] *Daily News* from 1966 to 1971 and from 1972 to 1977, then a *Charlotte* [North Carolina] *Observer* columnist from 1977 until he resigned to concentrate on writing books.

Bledsoe was born in Danville, Virginia. He served in the army from 1960 to 1963, then in 1966 began a productive stay at the Greensboro paper, which was interrupted for a few months in 1971 by work as a *Louisville* [Kentucky] *Times* feature writer. In addition to his newspaper column writing, he was also a contributing editor for *Esquire* from 1972 to 1975. Bledsoe has a dozen books to his credit as author.

BOOKS: *The World's Number One, Flat-Out, All-Time Great Stock Car Racing Book* (Garden City, N.Y., 1974); *You Can't Live on Radishes* (Greensboro, N.C., 1976); *Just Folks: Visitin' with Carolina People* (Charlotte, N.C., 1980); *Where's Mark Twain When We Really Need Him? He's Living with a Nice Couple in Independence, Missouri, and His Sense of Humor Is Shot* (Greensboro, N.C., 1982); *From Whalebone to Hot House: A Journey Along North Carolina's Longest Highway, U.S. 64* (Charlotte, N.C., 1986); *Bitter Blood: A True Story of Southern Family Pride, Madness, and Multiple Murder*

(New York, 1988); *Country Cured: Reflections from the Heart* (Atlanta, Ga., 1989); *The Bare-Bottomed Skier: And Other Unlikely Tales* (Ashboro, N.C., 1990); *Blood Games: A True Account of Family Murder* (New York, 1991); *Blue Horizons: Faces and Places from a Bicycle Journey Along the Blue Ridge Parkway* (Ashboro, N.C., 1993); *Before He Wakes: A True Story of Money, Marriage, Sex, and Murder* (New York, 1994).

Bloom, John (?–   ). Former investigative reporter John Bloom has created the fictitious character Joe Bob Briggs, a wisecracking, beer-guzzling Texas-style redneck. Briggs began by writing satirical movie reviews, then branched out into general humor. Creators Syndicate now distributes two columns by Bloom: "Joe Bob Goes to the Drive-In" and the more general "Joe Bob's America."

Bloom has been secretive about his actual past, and some standard reference works treat Joe Bob Briggs as a real person, complete with date of birth and parents. Actually, Bloom appears to have been born in Dallas and is a graduate of Vanderbilt University. His fictitious character emerged in the early 1980s at the *Dallas Times Herald*, where Bloom was a city columnist. His readers perked up and responded with more than normal enthusiasm when in March 1984, he introduced Briggs, whose favorite movie was and remains *The Texas Chainsaw Massacre* and whose zany movie reviews were written in intentionally bad taste.

The column was picked up by the Los Angeles Times Syndicate (LATS) and achieved considerable notice. Both the *Times Herald* and LATS dropped the column in the spring of 1985 as a result of a Briggs parody of "We Are the World," a song and music video through which various popular musicians raised money for famine relief in Africa. Briggs satirized this effort as "We Are the Weird." Bloom then resigned from the *Times Herald* and sued the paper and syndicate over the cancellation and over rights to his fictitious character. He was successful in retaining rights and was next handled by Universal Press Syndicate. He took Briggs on the comedy club circuit and in 1986 to television on the Movie Channel's "Drive-In Theater" and on "Moonlight Madness." Briggs recommends movies heavy in "blood, breasts and beasts." Bloom has also made Joe Bob Briggs a book author five times over, in addition to writing an earlier coauthored book under his own name.

BOOKS: With Jim Atkinson, *Evidence of Love* (Austin, Tex., 1984); *Joe Bob Goes to the Drive-In* (New York, 1986); *A Guide to Western Civilization, or, My Story* (New York, 1988); *The Cosmic Wisdom of Joe Bob Briggs* (New York, 1990); *Joe Bob Goes Back to the Drive-In* (New York, 1990); *Iron Joe Bob* (New York, 1992).

REFERENCES: David Astor, "Expert on Blood, Breasts and Beasts," *Editor and Publisher* (15 December 1984): 30–31; Astor, "Joe Bob Briggs in a One-Person Show," *Editor and Publisher* (19 October 1985): 38–39; Astor, "Who Has Joe Bob Briggs Rights?" *Editor and Publisher* (22 February 1986): 52–53.

Bode, Carl (14 March, 1911–   ). Writer/English professor Carl Bode became a columnist for the *Baltimore Evening Sun* in 1967 and for the *Chronicle of*

Higher Education in 1979. He is known for his work on the *Sun*'s H. L. Mencken.

Bode was born in Milwaukee, Wisconsin. His degrees include the Ph.B. in 1933 from the University of Chicago and the M.A. (1938) and Ph.D. (1941) from Northwestern University. From 1933 to 1937 he taught at Milwaukee Vocational School. He served in the army during 1944–1945, then in 1946 began his career as an English professor, first at the University of Chicago, then from 1947 to 1982 at the University of Maryland.

He was founder and first president of the American Studies Association (1952) and founder and first president of the Mencken Society (1976–1979). Bode also was president of the Thoreau Society (1960–1961) and the Popular Culture Association (1978–1979). He has been a prolific author/editor of books on American letters and culture. A collection of Bode's columns appears in *Highly Irregular* (1974).

BOOKS: Ed., *The Portable Thoreau* (New York, 1947); *The Sacred Seasons* (Denver, Colo., 1953); *The American Lyceum: Town Meeting of the Mind* (New York, 1956); ed. with Walter Harding, *The Correspondence of Henry David Thoreau* (New York, 1958); *The Man Behind You* (New York, 1959); *The Anatomy of American Popular Culture, 1840–1861* (Berkeley, Calif., 1959); ed., *The Young Rebel in American Literature* (New York, 1959); ed., *The Great Experiment in American Literature* (New York, 1961); ed., *Collected Poems of Henry Thoreau* (Baltimore, 1964); *The Half-World of American Culture: A Miscellany* (Carbondale, Ill., 1965); ed., *American Life in the 1840s* (Garden City, N.Y., 1967); ed., *The Selected Journals of Henry David Thoreau* (New York, 1967); *Mencken* (Carbondale, Ill., 1969); ed., *Ralph Waldo Emerson: A Profile* (New York, 1969); ed., *Midcentury America: Life in the 1850s* (Carbondale, 1972); ed., *The Young Mencken* (New York, 1973); *Highly Irregular* (Carbondale, Ill., 1974); ed., *The New Mencken Letters* (New York, 1977); *Maryland: A Bicentennial History* (New York, 1978); ed. with Malcolm Cowley, *The Portable Emerson* (New York, 1981); ed., *P. T. Barnum, Struggles and Triumphs* (New York, 1982); ed., *Horatio Alger, Ragged Dick and Struggling Upward* (New York, 1985); ed., *The Editor, the Bludenose, and the Prostitute: H. L. Mencken's History of the "Hatrack" Censorship Case* (Boulder, Colo., 1988); ed., *American Perspectives: The United States in the Modern Age* (Washington, D.C., 1990).

Bombeck, Erma Louise (21 Feb. 1927–   ). America's best known and most widely syndicated woman humor columnist, Erma Bombeck has written "At Wit's End" since 1965.

Born Erma Harris in Dayton, Ohio, she wrote her first humor column for her high school newspaper, was a copy girl at the *Dayton Journal-Herald,* and worked nights as a technical manual proofreader. She entered the University of Dayton in 1945; one of her part-time jobs was writing a column for a department store periodical. After receiving her B.A. in English in 1949, she was a reporter for the *Journal-Herald,* where she soon became a feature writer and author of a column titled "Operation Dustrag." She left the paper in 1953 to raise children, returning to journalism in 1964 to write her column "At Wit's End" for a small suburban weekly in Dayton, the *Kettering-Oakwood Times.* Before the year 1965 was out, she was writing the column for the *Journal-Herald,* and a mere several weeks from that change, her work was being syndicated to about sixty-five papers by the Newsday Syndicate. In 1967 her column was picked up by the Field Newspaper Syndicate, which placed it in roughly nine hundred papers, making it one of the most widely distributed and successful columns. She was hailed as "the female Art Buchwald," and, as *Life* magazine put it in 1971, "the Socrates of the ironing board," inasmuch as her usual subject matter was the often lonely, sometimes frustrating world of the American homemaker. "At Wit's End" has also been distributed by Publishers-Hall Syndicate (renamed North American Syndicate) (1970–1985), the Los Angeles Times Syndicate (1985–1988), and, since 1988, the Universal Press Syndicate.

Bombeck's thrice-weekly column was originally sold as a women's page column, but today it appears on feature or comics pages and has more male readers than when it first appeared. Her work brings understanding and a sense of affirmation to wives—and their husbands—as they cope with the demands of family and domestic life. Also, as the women's movement has taken women out of the home and into the workplace, Bombeck has followed the times in the topics she addresses.

Bombeck has written more than a dozen books; contributed to numerous magazines; written a magazine column, "Up the Wall," for *Good Housekeeping* (1969–1975); written for and appeared on "Good Morning, America" (1975–1986); and made a comic record album titled "The Family That Plays Together . . . Gets on Each Other's Nerves." Of all her projects, the one clunker was an ABC television sitcom titled "Maggie" that barely made a splash before being axed. Bombeck and her husband, a retired school principal, relocated from Dayton to Paradise Valley, Arizona, where she does her writing in a home office. Profits from her most serious book, *I Want to Grow Hair, I Want to Grow Up, I Want to Go to Boise,* about children fighting cancer, were donated to the American Cancer Society.

BOOKS: *At Wit's End* (New York, 1967); *Just Wait Till You Have Children of Your Own* (New York, 1971); *I Lost Everything in the Post-Natal Depression* (New York, 1973); *The Grass Is Always Greener over the Septic Tank* (New York, 1976); *If Life Is a Bowl of Cherries, What Am I Doing in the Pits?* (New York, 1978); *Aunt Erma's Cope Book* (New York, 1979); *Motherhood: The Second Oldest Profession* (New York, 1983); *Erma Bombeck Giant Economy Size* (New York, 1983); *Laugh Along with Erma Bombeck* (New York, 1984); *Four of a Kind* (New York, 1985); *Family: The Ties That Bind . . . and Gag!* (New York, 1987); *I Want to Grow Hair, I Want to Grow Up, I Want to Go to Boise: Children Surviving Cancer* (New York, 1989); *When You Look Like Your Passport Photo, It's Time to Go Home* (New York, 1991); *A Marriage Made in Heaven, or Too Tired for an Affair* (New York, 1993).

REFERENCES: Neil A. Grauer, *Wits and Sages* (Baltimore & London, 1984): 55–71; John Skow, "Erma Bombeck: Syndicated Soul of Suburbia," *Reader's Digest* (November 1984): 39–40.

Boxmeyer, Don (11 February 1941–). Celebrant of individuality and enemy of blandness Don Boxmeyer is a general columnist for the *St. Paul* [Minnesota] *Pioneer Press,* where he has worked since 1965.

Boxmeyer is a native of St. Paul and a journalism graduate of the University of Minnesota. He has worked for the *Pioneer Press* as a city hall reporter, capitol correspondent, and science/environmental reporter. He began writing his column in 1981. Boxmeyer has an especially fine way with humorous dialog.

Braden, Thomas Wardell (22 Feb. 1918–). Tom Braden has been a columnist with the Los Angeles Times Syndicate since 1968, although he is probably better known as the author of the book *Eight Is Enough.*

Braden was born in Greene, Iowa. He was editor and publisher of the *Blade-Tribune* in Oceanside, California, from 1954 to 1968, taught English at Dartmouth, and served in the CIA. He was able to buy the paper thanks to a $100,000 loan from Nelson Rockefeller and sold it for a profit.

His book *Eight Is Enough,* drawn from his own years as a father of eight children, was the basis of a popular ABC television show of the same name. Braden had earlier collaborated with fellow columnist Stewart Alsop on a book about espionage. Braden's column is cowritten with Frank Mankiewicz, Robert Kennedy's onetime press secretary. The occasionally whimsical, but mainly investigative column was regarded as less sensational than the Drew Pearson–Jack Anderson column. The pair also did commentary five days a week on WTOP-TV in Washington.

BOOKS: With Stewart Alsop, *Sub Rosa: The O.S.S. and American Espionage* (New York, 1946); *Eight Is Enough* (Greenwich, Conn., 1975).

REFERENCES: ''Washington's Third Pair,'' *Time* (15 August 1969): 68.

Brady, James Winston (15 Nov. 1928–). James Brady wrote a syndicated column for the *New York Post* from 1980 to 1983, but he is principally known for his magazine work, which included both writing and editing, and for his biographical feature that has appeared on Sundays in *Parade* since 1986.

Brady was born in Brooklyn, New York, and in 1950 received the A.B. from Manhattan College. He also attended New York University during 1953–1954.

He began his work life in 1956 as a correspondent for Fairchild Publications in New York City and Washington, D.C., then was Fairchild's bureau chief in London from 1958 to 1959 and in Paris from 1960 to 1964. He was publisher (1964–1971), senior vice president (1967–1971), and editorial director (1968–1971) of *Women's Wear Daily,* before becoming editor and publisher of *Harper's Bazaar* from 1971 to 1972. During 1973 and 1974 he wrote a column for *New York* magazine and was editor of *National Star* in 1974–1975. Brady was named editor at large of *Advertising Age* in 1983 and worked as a vice president of Capital Cities Broadcasting (1969–1971) and of the Hearst Corporation (1971–1972). He was a talk show host in 1973–1974 and a WCBS-TV news commentator (1981–1987). In addition to his column in the *New York Post,* he also wrote columns for *Advertising Age* and King Features.

BOOKS: *Superchic* (Boston, 1974); *Paris One* (New York, 1977); *Nielsen's Children* (New York, 1978); *The Press Lord* (New York, 1982); *Holy Wars* (London, 1984); *Designs* (New York, 1987); *The Coldest War: A Memoir of Korea* (New York, 1990); *Fashion Show, or, The Adventures of Bingo Marsh* (Boston, 1992).

Brasch, Walter M. (2 March 1945–). Walter Brasch writes "Wanderings," a weekly humor/satire column that appears in more than thirty newspapers. He is also a journalism professor at Bloomsburg University of Pennsylvania.

Brasch was born in San Diego, California. He received the A.B. in sociology from San Diego State College in 1966, the M.A. in journalism from Ball State University in 1969, and the Ph.D. in mass communications/journalism from Ohio University in 1974. He has taught journalism at Temple University (1974–1975) and at Bloomsburg since 1980.

Brasch has worked as a sportswriter for two years for the *Daily Report* in Ontario, California; for a year as sports editor of the Porterville (California) *Evening Recorder;* for one year as reporter and city editor of the Anderson (Indiana) *Daily Bulletin;* for two years as public affairs/investigative reporter for the Waterloo (Iowa) *Daily Courier;* and for two years as a correspondent for the Cleveland *Plain Dealer.* He has also worked as a free-lance writer and media consultant. His column, which he launched in 1992, is syndicated by Spectrum Features.

BOOKS: With Ila Wales Brasch, *A Comprehensive Annotated Bibliography of American Black English* (Baton Rouge, La., 1974); *Black English and the Mass Media* (Amherst, Mass., 1981); *Columbia County Place Names* (Orangeville, Pa., 1983); *Cartoon Monickers: An Insight into the Animation Industry* (Bowling Green, Ohio, 1984); *A Zim Self-Portrait* (New York, 1986); with Dana R. Ulloth, *The Press and the State: Sociohistorical and Contemporary Interpretations* (Washington, D.C., 1987); *Forerunners of Revolution: Muckrakers and the American Social Conscience* (Lanham, Md., 1991); *With Just Cause: Unionization of the American Journalist* (Lanham, Md., 1991).

Breslin, James (17 Oct. 1930–). Longtime New York City columnist Jimmy Breslin, now with *Newsday,* is the voice of the city's Irish Americans: brash, gruff, combative, street-wise, and well worth reading.

Breslin was born in Jamaica, New York. He attended Long Island University from 1948 to 1950, though he claims not to have graduated from high school. He was a *Long Island Press* copyboy in 1948 and in 1950 left college to write sports. He was a copyreader for half a year at the *Boston Globe,* then a feature writer for the Newspaper Enterprise Association. Breslin next wrote for the *New York Journal-American,* leaving the paper in 1960 for three years of free-lancing. A story he wrote on the New York Mets and their owner, Mrs. Charles Payson, led to a job in 1963 as a sports columnist for the *New York Herald Tribune,* owned by Mrs. Payson's brother, John Hay Whitney. Soon he abandoned sports in favor of a general column on the front page of the local section. Breslin had found his niche: the quirky, dramatic, highly personal presentation of New York as displayed via its more interesting denizens. He left the *Herald Tribune* to write his column for the *New York Post* for roughly a year (1968–1969) and was one of the writers for the city magazine, *New York,* for which he wrote until 1971. Breslin was near Robert Kennedy in the Ambassador Hotel in Los Angeles when he was shot to death and soon thereafter left the *Post* to concentrate on more profitable work writing books.

Breslin resumed his column in 1978, this time writing it for a decade in the *New York Daily News.* He moved to *Newsday* in 1988 and has remained there. He has ventured into television: as a commentator on WABC-TV in the late 1960s and on WNBC-TV in 1973. In 1987 he hosted "Jimmy Breslin's People" for ABC-TV and has even done a limited amount of acting. He has written for *Sports Illustrated, Time, Saturday Evening Post,* and other magazines and has published more than a dozen books. As with most columnists of the more outspoken, combative persuasion, Breslin has had his ups and downs. In 1986 he won the Pulitzer Prize for commentary, but in 1990 he was suspended without pay for two weeks for comments he made about fellow *Newsday* journalist Ji-Yeon Yuh, a Korean American. He was also the object of much criticism years earlier for his handling of the letters serial killer David Berkowitz sent him during the "Son of Sam" murders in New York. Some of his critics, the *New Yorker* among them, said that the space he gave Berkowitz encouraged him to kill again, but in the end, Berkowitz was caught partially as a result of handwriting samples from the letters he had sent to Breslin.

BOOKS: *Sunny Jim, the Life of America's Most Beloved Horseman, James Fitzsimmons* (Garden City, N.Y., 1962); *Can't Anybody Here Play This Game?* (New York, 1963); *The World of Jimmy Breslin* (New York, 1967); *The Gang That Couldn't Shoot Straight* (New York, 1969); *World Without End, Amen* (Harmondsworth, Middlesex, England, 1973); *How the Good Guys Finally Won* (New York, 1975); with Dick Schaap, *Son of Sam* (London, 1978); with Dick Schaap, *.44* (New York, 1978); *Forsaking All Others* (New York, 1982); *The World According to Breslin* (New York, 1984); *Table Money* (New York, 1986); *He Got Hungry and Forgot His Manners: A Fable* (New York, 1988); *Damon Runyon* (New York, 1991).

REFERENCES: Neil A. Grauer, *Wits and Sages* (Baltimore & London, 1984): 73–94; David Nyhan, "Jimmy Breslin, the Bard of Queens," *Washington Journalism Review* (October 1986): 25–28, 30.

Briggs, Emily Pomona Edson (14 Sept. 1830–3 July 1910). One of America's pioneer columnists, Emily Briggs wrote a daily column of social news under the pen name "Olivia" for the *Philadelphia Press* from 1866 to 1882.

Briggs was born Emily Edson in Burton, Ohio. She attended the public schools in Chicago and taught school briefly in Painesville, Ohio. In or around 1854 she married John R. Briggs, a former Wisconsin legislator, who was a friend of Abraham Lincoln. The couple moved to Keokuk, Iowa, where John bought part ownership of the *Daily Whig.* His connection with Lincoln led to his appointment as assistant clerk of the U.S. House of Representatives under clerk John Forney, owner of the *Washington Chronicle* and the *Philadelphia Press.* Forney hired Emily Briggs to write a column in the *Press* and assigned her the pseudonym "Olivia." The column appeared for more than twenty years. Her main concerns were the glitter of Washington society and news that affected women. She was apparently the first woman to get White House news regularly, one of the first newswomen permitted into the congressional press gallery, and one of the first of her gender to use the telegraph to relay news stories. In 1872 she and her husband bought a Capitol Hill mansion, the Maples, and her later years were spent as a prominent Washington hostess.

BOOKS: *The Olivia Letters: Being Some History of Washington City for Forty Years as Told by the Letters of a Newspaper Correspondent* (New York, 1906).

REFERENCES: Maurine H. Beasley, *The First Women Washington Correspondents,* George Washington University Studies No. 4 (1976); Marion Marzolf, *Up from the Footnotes: A History of Women Journalists* (New York, 1977).

Brisbane, Arthur (12 Dec. 1864–25 Dec. 1936). Arthur Brisbane was one of the most financially successful and famous newspapermen of his time and one of the most widely syndicated columnists of the early to mid-1900s.

Brisbane was born in Buffalo, New York, to a wealthy family that educated him in France and Germany. His career began in 1882 when Charles Dana hired him as a *New York Sun* reporter. He was later the *Sun*'s London correspondent, then editor of the new *Evening Sun.* In 1890 Joseph Pulitzer hired Brisbane as managing editor of the New York *Sunday World;* under Brisbane, circulation soared, and in 1897 William Randolph Hearst hired him to do the same for the *New York Evening Journal;* he did so with great success. He was the editor of the *Journal* from 1897 until 1921. Hearst also put Brisbane in charge of his Chicago paper, the *American,* in 1900; Brisbane edited this paper until 1936. Journalism had brought Brisbane considerable wealth, and he bought the *Washington* [D.C.], *Times* (1917–1919) and the *Wisconsin News* in Milwaukee (1918–1919). In addition he edited Hearst's sensationalistic tabloid *New York Mirror* from 1934 to 1936 and wrote for *Cosmopolitan, Pictorial Review,* and other magazines.

As a newspaper writer, Brisbane was mainly known for his editorials in the *New York Journal* and for his two syndicated columns: "Today," which was run in all of Hearst's dailies, and "This Week," a recast version of "Today" that appeared in a reported twelve hundred weekly papers. For all that, his writing is remembered as sensationalized, oversimplified, and given to the use of platitudes. He was one of the first columnists to dictate his column into a dictaphone for later transcription.

BOOKS: *Editorials from the Hearst Newspapers* (New York, 1906); *Brisbane on Prohibition* (New York, 1908); *Mary Baker Eddy* (Boston, 1908); *Three Brothers: An Editorial*

(New York, 1916); *The Book of Today* (New York, 1923); *Today and the Future Day: An Analysis of Two New Books, with Other Articles* (New York, 1925); *What Mrs. Eddy Said to Arthur Brisbane: The Celebrated Interview of the Eminent Journalist with the Discoverer and Founder of Christian Science* (New York, 1930); *How to Be a Better Reporter* (Eugene, Ore., 1933).

REFERENCES: Oliver Carlson, *Brisbane: A Candid Biography* (New York, 1937).

Britt, Donna (?–   ). Donna Britt has written a twice-weekly column for the *Washington Post*'s Style section since March 1992. Her column has been syndicated by the Washington Post Writers Group since 1993.

Britt was born in Gary, Indiana. She received the B.A. in mass media arts from Hampton University in Virginia and a master's degree in journalism from the University of Michigan (1979). Her career began in 1979 at the *Detroit Free Press,* where she was a city desk reporter. She also wrote about life-styles and fashions for the *Free Press,* then was Los Angeles bureau chief for *USA Today.* She joined the *Post* in 1989.

Britt's entertainingly written column usually deals with subjects of special interest to the African-American community.

Broder, David Salzer (11 Sept. 1929–   ). One of America's most respected and best-connected political columnists, David Broder has written a column for the *Washington Post* since 1975.

Broder was born in Chicago Heights, Illinois. He entered college at age fifteen and earned the B.A. in 1947 and M.A. in political science in 1951 at the University of Chicago. He was rejected for admission to the journalism graduate program of Columbia University and instead enlisted in the army, spending a year working for a base newspaper in Salzburg, Austria.

After his two years of military service, Broder found a reporting job in 1953 on the *Bloomington* [Illinois] *Pantagraph.* He left that paper in 1955 for five years as a reporter for the *Congressional Quarterly* in Washington, D.C., and from 1960 to 1965 was a *Washington Star* reporter and columnist. He spent eighteen months with the Washington bureau of the *New York Times* in 1965 and 1966 but was dissatisfied with conflicts between the bureau and the home office. In 1966 he joined the *Washington Post* as senior political reporter and columnist. At first the column appeared weekly, but after a short while it was increased to twice weekly. Broder won the Pulitzer Prize for commentary in 1973 for his coverage of the Nixon White House, and in 1975 he became the *Post*'s associate editor.

The Broder column, which is mainly reportorial as opposed to ruminative, was initially sent out free to Los Angeles Times–Washington Post News Service subscribers. When Broder's children reached college age (the tuition-paying wonder years), he asked to be able to realize some extra income from republication of his writing, and at that time, editor Benjamin Bradlee created the Washington Post Writers Group. Broder's columns benefit from his extensive personal contacts on the political scene. His writing is known for its serious, no-nonsense style. Broder continues to combine reporting with column writing and has authored or coauthored six books concerning politics.

BOOKS: With Stephen Hess, *The Republican Establishment: The Present and Future of the G.O.P.* (New York, 1967); *The Party's Over: The Failure of Politics in America* (New York, 1971); *American Politics in the Carter Era* (Manhattan, Kan., 1977); *Changing of the Guard: Power and Leadership in America* (New York, 1980); *Behind the Front Page, a Candid Look at How the News Is Made* (New York, 1987); with Bob Woodward, *The Man Who Would Be President: Dan Quayle* (New York, 1992).

REFERENCES: Neil A. Grauer, *Wits and Sages* (Baltimore, Md., 1984): 97–118.

Brothers, Joyce Diane Bauer (20 Oct. 1929–). Psychologist Dr. Joyce Brothers is familiar to television viewers and has been a syndicated newspaper columnist since 1961.

Born Joyce Diane Bauer in New York City, she earned the B.S. with honors from Cornell University in 1947 and the M.A. (1950) and Ph.D. (1953) from Columbia University. She was a teaching fellow (1948–1950) and instructor (1950–1952) at Hunter College in New York City and a UNESCO researcher in 1949. During 1952–1953 she was an American Association of University Women research fellow.

Brothers first came to public attention as the first woman winner of the grand prize on the television quiz show "The $64,000 Question." She hosted her own television programs in the late 1950s and the 1960s: "Dr. Joyce Brothers," NBC (1958–1963); "Consult Dr. Joyce Brothers," ABC (1961–1966); "Tell Me, Dr. Brothers," Triangle Films (1964–1970); and "Ask Dr. Brothers" (1965–1975). She also did radio programs for NBC and ABC from 1966 to 1969.

She has published books about how to cope with life since 1957 and began her career as a syndicated columnist in 1961 for North American Newspaper Alliance, a relationship that lasted until 1972. She was handled by the Bell-McClure Syndicate from 1963 to 1971 and has been with King Features Syndicate since 1972. Her column has appeared in as many as 350 newspapers. She has also written a column for *Good Housekeeping* magazine since 1963 and has appeared as a guest on many television talk and panel shows. Some members of Dr. Brothers's profession dismiss her as a popularizer; other observers point out that she has brought the findings of psychology to people who cannot afford $100 an hour to find out these things in private.

BOOKS: With Edward P. F. Eagan, *10 Days to a Successful Memory* (Englewood Cliffs, N.J., 1957); *Woman* (Garden City, N.Y., 1961); *How to Persuade Others to Do What You Want* (New York, 1968); *It's More than Skin Deep* (New York, 1969); *Sex, Dating, and the Teenager* (New York, 1969); *How to Face Up to Disappointments and Turn Them to Work in Your Favor* (New York, 1969); *Getting the Most from Family Relationships* (New York, 1969); *The Brothers System for Liberated Love and Marriage* (New York, 1972); *Better than Ever* (New York, 1975); *How to Get Whatever You Want Out of Life* (New York, 1978); *What Every Woman Should Know About Men* (New York, 1981); *What Every Woman Ought to Know About Love and Marriage* (New York, 1984); *Widowed* (New York, 1990); *Positive Plus: The Practical Plan for Liking Yourself Better* (New York, 1994).

Broun, Heywood Campbell (7 Dec. 1888–18 Dec. 1939). Heywood Broun (pronounced Broon) was one of the best known columnists of the 1920s and 1930s, working for New York City papers from 1911 to 1939.

He was born in Brooklyn, New York, and was a 1906 graduate of the private Horace Mann School, where he was editor of the school paper. He went to Harvard but dropped out in 1910 without a degree and became a baseball and Broadway reporter for the *New York Morning Telegram.* Fired when he asked for a raise, Broun found work as a copyreader for the *New York Tribune* in 1911 and later became a reporter and sportswriter for that paper, writing about such heroic figures as Babe Ruth and Ty Cobb. In 1915 he became the *Tribune*'s drama critic and was unsuccessfully sued for libel by the actor Geoffrey Steyne. Broun covered World War I as a *Tribune* war correspondent. Next he became the paper's literary editor, writing a book review column, ''Books and Things,'' three times a week. He was a regular at the Algonquin Round Table and a figure well-known to New Yorkers.

Broun went over to the *New York World* in 1921, and his general column ''It Seems to Me'' began its long run in September of that year. The outspoken columnist became stridently critical of authority wherever he found it, irritating the *World* management. He was suspended in 1927 over his criticism of Harvard University and the American judiciary in the Sacco-Vanzetti case. After writing a column for a short period in the *Nation,* he was reinstated at the *World* in January 1928 but was fired for criticizing the paper itself four months later.

He was promptly hired by the *New York Telegram,* where he used his column to crusade for the underdog. When the economy soured, he used his column as an employment service, matching roughly one thousand people with job opportunities. He ran unsuccessfully for Congress as a Socialist in 1930 and afterward continued speaking out in his column for women's rights, freedom of expression, and other causes and against religious and racial prejudice. In 1931 his paper merged and became the *World-Telegram,* in which ''It Seems to Me'' was continued. With the column as a forum, he helped unionize reporters in 1933 and was founding president of the American Newspaper Guild.

In 1938 he started the *Connecticut Nutmeg,* a weekly tabloid paper that later was renamed *Broun's Nutmeg.* In the following year, Broun was let go for the last time and moved his column to the *New York Post,* though because of a cold that became pneumonia, the portly, rumpled crusader was able to write but one column for the *Post* before his death. Broun wrote more than a dozen books, the most successful of which was *Anthony Comstock: Roundsman of the Lord,* which he cowrote with Margaret Leech.

BOOKS: *The A.E.F.: With General Pershing and the American Forces* (New York and London, 1918); *Our Army at the Front* (New York, 1918); *Seeing Things at Night* (New York, 1921); *Pieces of Hate: And Other Enthusiasms* (New York, 1922); *The Boy Grew Older* (New York and London, 1922); *The Sun Field* (New York and London, 1923); *Sitting on the World* (New York and London, 1924); *A Shepherd* (New York, 1926); *Gandle Follows His Nose* (New York, 1926); with Margaret Leech, *Anthony Comstock: Roundsman of the Lord* (New York, 1927); *Christians Only: A Study in Prejudice* (New York, 1931); *It Seems to Me: 1925–1935* (New York, 1935); *Collected Edition of Heywood Broun,* comp. by Heywood Hale Broun (New York, 1941); *A Tale of Toyland,* ed. by Charles Fleming (Richmond, Va., 1957).

REFERENCES: Heywood Hale Broun, *Whose Little Boy Are You? A Memoir of the Broun Family* (New York, 1983); Dale Kramer, *Heywood Broun: A Biographical Portrait* (New York, 1949); John L. Lewis et al., *Heywood Broun as He Seemed to Us* (New York, 1940); Frank O'Connor, *Heywood Broun* (New York, 1975); M. B. Schnapper, *Heywood Broun* (Washington, D.C., 1940).

Brower, William Alston (8 October 1916–). William Brower, associate editor of the *Blade* in Toledo, Ohio, writes a wide-ranging general column for that paper. The column often deals with national issues, with special emphasis on racial matters. Brower believes that he may well be the oldest African-American journalist in years of service currently working for a U.S. daily.

Brower was born in McCall, South Carolina, and grew up in High Point, North Carolina. He received the B.A. in journalism from Wilberforce University in 1939.

In 1942 he began reporting for the *Washington Tribune,* a black D.C. weekly. After three months he moved to the *Afro-American* newspaper chain in Baltimore, Maryland, and a year later, in January 1943, became editor of that chain's Richmond, Virginia, edition. In July 1945 he became editor of the chain's Philadelphia edition. Later in 1945 Brower became the first black newsman for the *Blade.* He worked for the *Blade* in rewrite in 1947, as news editor (1968), and as assistant managing editor in 1971. He has been associate editor since 1976. During 1979 and 1980 he was on leave to teach journalism at Temple University in Philadelphia.

Brunvand, Jan Harold (23 March 1933–). Folklorist Jan Harold Brunvand has written the unusual United Feature Syndicate column "Urban Legends" since 1987.

Brunvand was born in Cadillac, Michigan. He earned the B.A. from Michigan State University in 1955, spent 1956–1957 at the University of Oslo, then received the Ph.D. from Indiana University in 1961. He served in the army during 1962–1963, then taught a combination of English and folklore at three universities: the University of Idaho (1961–1965), Southern Illinois University at Edwardsville (1965–1966), and the University of Utah since 1971.

Brunvand has written free-lance for various newspapers and folklore journals. He has served *Midwest Folklore* as assistant editor (1959–1960) and book review editor (1961–1964) and the *Journal of American Folklore* as associate editor (1963–1967 and 1973–1976), book review editor (1967–1973), and editor (1976–1980). His interest, in his column and his several books, is the curious folklore of white middle-class America, especially the urban contingent of that group.

BOOKS: *A Dictionary of Proverbs and Proverbial Phrases from Books Published by Indiana Authors Before 1890* (Bloomington, Ind., 1961); *The Study of American Folklore: An Introduction* (New York, 1968); *A Guide for Collectors of Folklore in Utah* (Salt Lake City, 1971); *Folklore: A Study and Research Guide* (New York, 1976); ed., *Readings in American Folklore* (New York, 1979); *The Vanishing Hitchhiker: American Legends and Their Meanings* (New York, 1981); *The Choking Doberman and Other "New" Urban Legends* (New York, 1984); *The Mexican Pet: More "New" Urban Legends and Some Old Favorites* (New York, 1986); *Curses, Broiled Again! the Hottest Urban Legends Going* (New York, 1989); *The Taming of the Shrew: A Comparative Study of Oral and Literary Versions* (New York, 1991); *The Baby Train and Other Lusty Urban Legends* (New York, 1993).

Brush, Stephanie (2 Oct. 1954–   ). Humor columnist Stephanie Brush has been distributed by Creators Syndicate since 1993. Prior to that time, she was handled by Tribune Media Services (1990–1993) and was with the Washington Post Writers Group (1988–1990).

Brush was born in Cleveland, Ohio. She majored in theater at Northwestern University, then attended the University of Oregon and studied French at the University of Paris. She was associate editor of *Viva* from 1976 to 1978 and wrote on staff for *SELF* from 1979 to 1982. She has contributed to such magazines as *Vogue, Mademoiselle, Conde Nast Traveler,* and *Cosmopolitan* and has authored two humor books.

BOOKS: *Men: An Owner's Manual* (New York, 1984); *Life: A Warning* (New York, 1987).

Buchanan, Patrick Joseph (2 Nov. 1938–   ). With brief interruptions, arch-conservative Patrick Buchanan has been a syndicated newspaper columnist since 1975. He is currently handled by Tribune Media Services.

Buchanan was born in Washington, D.C. He earned the A.B. cum laude from Georgetown University in 1961 and the M.S. in journalism from Columbia University in 1962.

From 1962 to 1964 he worked as an editorial writer for the *St. Louis Globe Democrat.* He was assistant editorial editor of that paper from 1964 to 1966, then worked as an assistant to President Richard Nixon from 1966 to 1973 and from 1973 to 1974 as a consultant to Nixon and President Gerald Ford. For part of 1974 he wrote for "News Watch," a short-lived column in *TV Guide* magazine.

In 1975 Buchanan began his own column, which was syndicated by New York Times Features until 1985, when Buchanan became President Ronald Reagan's assistant and director of communications. He resumed writing his column, "Dividing Line," in 1988, interrupting it once again in 1992 in order to make his own (unsuccessful) bid for the Republican presidential nomination. He again resumed his column in February 1993. Buchanan delights in ruffling liberal feathers and in 1991 was given the Jesse Helms Defamer of the Year award by the Gay & Lesbian Alliance Against Defamation.

BOOKS: *The New Majority: President Nixon at Mid-Passage* (Philadelphia, 1973); *Conservative Votes, Liberal Victories: Why the Right Has Failed* (New York, 1975); *Right from the Beginning* (Boston, 1988).

Buchwald, Arthur (20 Oct. 1925–   ). America's premier political humor columnist Art Buchwald has been at it since 1949. His column is now syndicated by the Los Angeles Times Syndicate to around 550 papers, at least 50 of which are outside the United States.

Buchwald was born in Mount Vernon, New York. His mother died when he was five, and his father, unable to cope financially, had to put the Buchwald children into foster homes for a number of years. Part of this period of his life was spent in the Hebrew Orphan Asylum in New York. After dropping out of high school at seventeen, Buchwald lied about his age and joined the Marine Corps, serving in the Pacific between 1942 and 1945. He was enrolled at the University of Southern California from late 1945 until the spring of 1948. Here he wrote a column for the campus paper, the *Daily Trojan,* and was managing editor of the school's humor magazine, *Wampus.* When he received a veteran's bonus check, he used it to book passage on a ship headed for Europe. In Paris, he found a job writing about nightclubs and restaurants for *Variety* and, several months thereafter, began a nightclub column, "Paris After Dark," for the Paris edition of the *New York Herald.* In 1951 he began a more general *Herald* column, "Mostly About People." In this column he gave his readers celebrity interviews and adroitly dealt with what might be called "tourist clichés": the six-minute Louvre; the Mona Lisa crouch, the reverential stance tourists usually assume when examining this DaVinci masterpiece; and the "Oriental ritual" of Chapping, mainly engaged in by tourist women who appease the gods with large amounts of Mun-nee. He himself was a Paris celebrity by the time the *Herald* began selling his work, in yet another column titled "Art Buchwald in Paris," to U.S. papers.

In 1961 he returned to the United States to work out of Washington, D.C., as a political humorist. His *Tribune* column was renamed "Capitol Punishment." The Herald Tribune Syndicate had no difficulty placing the column all over the nation, yet Buchwald had his own difficulties in adjusting to his success and suffered a period of depression that required two and a half years of counseling. His popularity continued to mount, however, and he later switched to the *Washington Post* and the Los Angeles Times Syndicate, dropping the column title. His column now simply appears under the standing head "Art Buchwald."

As a humorist, Buchwald does nothing terribly literary. He merely scans the news for items that contain comic possibilities, then turns reality inside out via exaggeration, anticlimax, and comic dialog. He has poked good-natured fun at every administration from Eisenhower to Clinton, seldom lacking excellent material. His only difficulty, he has said, is that so much that now happens on the political scene appears to anyone of whimsical inclination already to *be* satire. When earnest-sounding politicians do things that are inherently clownish, he says, his best approach is to compress and dramatize them to bring out the humor. He describes his columns as political cartoons set to words—usually 600 to 650 of them. Part of what makes his work funny is a matter of juxtaposition: it appears next to serious, often gloomy news stories, or next to the somber comments of the more serious pundits.

Buchwald has largely avoided television work but has made an enormous amount of money on the lecture circuit, where he is as funny in person as he is on paper. He has collected his columns into a long list of humor books, has done a couple of children's books, and has written a play, *Sheep on the Runway,* that played with some success on Broadway in 1970. In 1990, Buchwald won a lawsuit in Superior Court in Los Angeles. The court ruled that the comedian Eddie Murphy's 1988 Paramount movie *Coming to America* was based on an idea originally put forward by Buchwald.

Fairly few people have the ability instantly to recognize the absurd and to write about it in a humorous way. A modest number can write good humor copy from time to time. Buchwald is perhaps most remarkable in that he has written successfully in this difficult genre for going on half a century.

BOOKS: *Paris After Dark* (Paris, 1950); *Art Buchwald's Paris* (Boston, 1953); *The Brave Coward* (New York, 1955); *More Caviar* (New York, 1957); *A Gift from the Boys* (New York, 1958); *Don't Forget to Write* (London, 1960); *How Much Is That in Dollars?* (Greenwich, Conn., 1961); *Is It Safe to Drink the Water?* (Greenwich, Conn., 1962); *I Chose Capitol Punishment* (Cleveland, Ohio, 1963); *Son of the Great Society* (New York, 1966); *Have I Ever Lied to You?* (New York, 1968); *The Establishment Is Alive and Well in Washington* (New York, 1969); *Counting Sheep: The Log and the Complete Play, "Sheep on the Runway"* (New York, 1970); *Oh, to Be a Swinger* (London, 1970); *Getting High in Government Circles* (New York, 1973); *I Never Danced at the White House* (New York, 1973); *"I Am Not a Crook"* (New York, 1974); *The Bollo Caper: A Fable for Children of All Ages* (Garden City, N.Y., 1974); *Irving's Delight: At Last! A Cat Story for the Whole Family!* (New York, 1975); *Washington Is Leaking* (Greenwich, Conn., 1976); *Down the Seine and up the Potomac with Art Buchwald* (New York, 1977); *The Buchwald Stops Here* (New York, 1978); with Ann Buchwald, *Seems Like Yesterday* (New York, 1980); *Laid Back in Washington* (New York, 1981); *While Reagan Slept* (New York, 1983); *You Can Fool All of the People All of the Time* (Boston, 1985); *I Don't Think I Remember* (New York, 1987); *Whose Rose Garden Is It Anyway?* (New York, 1989); *Lighten Up, George* (New York, 1991); *Leaving Home: A Memoir* (New York, 1994).

REFERENCES: David Astor, "He's Still Satirizing After All These Years," *Editor and Publisher* (6 September 1986): 44–46; Neil A. Grauer, *Wits and Sages* (Baltimore and

London, 1984): 121–139; Roger Piantadosi, "Art Buchwald," *Washington Journalism Review* (September 1982): 27–28, 32–34.

Buckley, William Frank, Jr. (24 Nov. 1925–   ). Dazzlingly unusual conservative William F. Buckley, Jr., has written his syndicated newspaper column, "On the Right," since 1962. He also founded the influential opinion journal *National Review* in 1955 and since 1966 has hosted the weekly television program "Firing Line."

Buckley was born into wealth and privilege, the son of an oil millionaire. The family fortune has been estimated at $100 million. His birthplace was New York City, though he spent most of his early youth in Paris and London. Privately tutored, he learned French and Spanish, and later was sent to St. John's Beaumont in England and the Millbrook School in New York, from which he graduated in 1943. Intelligent and self-assured, he developed such a superior manner that his own siblings dubbed him "the young Mahster." He studied at the University of Mexico in 1943–1944 and later in 1944 was drafted into the U.S. Army Infantry, rising from private to second lieutenant by his separation date in 1946. He then entered Yale University, where he was a star debater and editor of the nation's oldest student newspaper, the *Yale Daily News,* in which his editorials often instructed the Yale faculty in how to do their jobs. He graduated in 1950 with honors in economics, political science, and history and a year later published his much talked about first book, *God and Man at Yale: The Superstitions of "Academic Freedom,"* in which he blasted his alma mater's faculty for being antireligion and for pushing collectivism (as opposed to individualism). With the publication of this book, he became the enfant terrible of intellectual conservatism.

Buckley taught Spanish at Yale from 1947 to 1951, then served in Mexico with the CIA during 1951–1952. He left intelligence work to serve briefly as associate editor of *American Mercury* magazine in 1952 and from 1952 to 1955 was a free-lance writer. In 1955 he founded his own magazine, *National Review,* for which he was editor in chief through the issue of 5 November 1990. Buckley and his magazine have been influential in coordinating the various branches of American conservatism and in helping defang some of its extremists, such as the John Birch Society.

His television show "Firing Line" first appeared on commercial television in 1966, then in 1971 became affiliated with PBS. It is here that America has come to know Buckley the character as he converses one-on-one with a different guest each week. His mannerisms are beyond quirky. His tongue licks out like that of a serpent, his normally heavy-lidded eyes roll heavenward, his Cheshire Cat grin appears suddenly and disappears just as suddenly. He punctuates his thoughts with "ah" as only the wealthy, ah, ah, ah . . . can, with a supercilious English undertone and inflection that suggest a superior understanding. A favorite Buckley device is slipping into the conversation a word likely culled from the *Oxford English Dictionary*—one that hasn't been uttered aloud for perhaps two hundred years. Buckley is, in short, good theater: a man of another time, a Tory holdover imbued with noblesse oblige and an unshakable confidence in his own vision of what is right.

Of all his projects, he has said his magazine is his favorite, his column the least enjoyable. The thrice-weekly column, which is sent out to roughly 350 papers by the Universal Press Syndicate, usually runs to about 850 words and is researched by three assistants who have office space at the *National Review.* Buckley has stated that he does not enjoy the act of writing. Probably he does it to be able to say something of substance to a general audience, having established his persona on "Firing Line" and having already reached the more elite conservatives with his magazine.

Buckley has also written for other magazines and has been a busy author, especially for someone who doesn't like to write: he has written books on politics and sailing, which is one of his several hobbies, as well as spy novels.

BOOKS: *God and Man at Yale* (Chicago, 1951); with L. Brent Bozell, *McCarthy and His Enemies: The Record and Its Meaning* (Chicago, 1954); *Up from Liberalism* (New York, 1959); *Rumbles Left and Right: A Book About Troublesome People and Ideas* (New York, 1962); *The Unmaking of a Mayor* (New York, 1966); *The Jeweler's Eye: A Book of Irresistible Political Reflections* (New York, 1968); *The Governor Listeth* (New York, 1970); *Quotations from Chairman Bill,* comp. by David Franke (New Rochelle, N.Y., 1970); ed., *Odyssey of a Friend: Whittaker Chambers' Letters to William F. Buckley, Jr., 1954–1961* (New York, 1970); *Cruising Speed* (New York, 1971); *Inveighing We Will Go* (New York, 1972); *Four Reforms: A Guide for the Seventies* (New York, 1973); *United Nations Journal: A Delegate's Odyssey* (New York, 1974); *Execution Eve and Other Contemporary Ballads* (New York, 1975); *Airborne: A Sentimental Journey* (New York, 1976); *Saving the Queen* (Garden City, N.Y., 1976); *A Hymnal: The Controversial Arts* (New York, 1978); *Stained Glass* (Garden City, N.Y., 1978); *Who's on First* (Garden City, N.Y., 1980); *Atlantic High: A Celebration* (Garden City, N.Y., 1982); *Marco Polo, If You Can* (London, 1982); *Overdrive: A Personal Documentary* (Garden City, N.Y., 1983); *The Best of Bill Buckley,* comp. by Rick Broodhiser and David Brooks (New York, 1984); *The Story of Henri Tod* (Franklin Center, Pa., 1984); *Right Reason* (Garden City, N.Y., 1985); *The Temptation of Wilfred Malachey* (New York, 1985); *See You Later Alligator* (Thorndike, Me., 1985); *High Jinx* (Garden City, N.Y., 1986); *Racing Through Paradise: A Pacific Passage* (New York, 1987); ed., with Charles R. Kesler, *The Tablet Keepers: American Conservative Thought in the 20th Century* (New York, 1987); *Mongoose, R.I.P.* (New York, 1987); *On the Firing Line* (New York, 1989); *Gratitude: Reflections on What We Owe to Our Country* (New York, 1990); *Tucker's Last Stand* (New York, 1990); *Windfall: The End of the Affair* (New York, 1992); *In Search of Anti-Semitism* (New York, 1992); *The Culture of Liberty: The Calisthenics of a Libertarian Journalist* (New York, 1993); *A Very Private Plot: A Blackford Oakes Novel* (New York, 1994).

REFERENCES: Neil A. Grauer, *Wits and Sages* (Baltimore and London, 1984): 141–160; John B. Judis, *William F. Buckley, Jr.* (New York, 1988); Charles Lam Markmann, *The Buckleys: A Family Examined* (New York, 1973); Dan Wakefield, "William F. Buckley, Jr.: Portrait of a Complainer," *Esquire* 55 (January 1961): 49–52; Garry Wills, "Buckley, Buckley, Bow Wow Wow," *Esquire* 69 (January 1968): 72–76, 155, 158–159.

Burney, Joan R. (30 Oct. 1928–   ). Hartington, Nebraska, columnist Joan Burney has self-syndicated a variety of columns to newspapers and magazines in her part of the United States since 1980.

Burney was born in Walthill, Nebraska. She earned the B.A., cum laude, in communications and music from Mount Marty College in Yankton, South Dakota, in 1973 and the M.S. in psychological counseling from Wayne State College in 1986.

Burney writes weekly columns under the titles "At Random" and "Joan Burney" in the *Sioux City Journal, Norfolk Daily News, Missouri Valley Observer, Cedar County News,* and Maverick Media newspapers. She does biweekly columns under the titles "Offer It Up" in the *Catholic Voice* and "Joan Burney" in the *Omaha World Herald* and a monthly motivational column, "Comes the Dawn," in the *Nebraska Farmer* and the *Colorado Farmer Rancher.* Finally, her bimonthly column "Over the Feeder's Fence" appears in the *Nebraska Cattleman.*

Burney has also contributed articles and feature stories to the *Magazine of the Midlands,* the *Midlands Business Journal,* the *Catholic Digest,* and *Common Lot.* In addition, she has authored two books of her columns and has coauthored two books of religious advice. Since 1972, she has been a motivational/inspirational speaker, averaging between fifty and seventy-five talks and workshops yearly.

BOOKS: With Phyllis Chandler, *Sharing the Faith with Your Child (From Birth to Age Six): A Handbook for Catholic Parents* (Liguori, Mo., 1984); *The Keepers,* Vol. 1 (Sutton, Neb., 1987); *The Keepers: Comes the Dawn,* Vol. 2 (Lincoln, Neb., 1989); with Phyllis Chandler, *Sharing the Faith with Your Child (From Age Seven to Fourteen): A Handbook for Catholic Parents* (Liguori, Mo., 1992).

Byrne, Dennis (8 Jan. 1942–   ). Dennis Byrne has been a *Chicago Sun-Times* columnist since 1986.

Byrne was born in Chicago. He earned the B.A. in journalism from Marquette University in 1963, held a Russell Sage Fellowship in social science writing from 1964 to 1965 at the University of Wisconsin at Madison, and received the M.S. in urban affairs in 1967 from the University of Wisconsin at Milwaukee. He was a student intern at the *DePere* [Wisconsin] *Journal-Democrat* in 1962.

Byrne was with the *Chicago Daily News* in 1965–1966 and 1970–1978 as a general assignment reporter, urban affairs writer, and assistant financial editor. He went with the *Sun-Times* in 1978. From 1984 to 1986 he was director of public relations for the Specialty Chemicals Group of Allied-Signal Inc. in Des Plaines, Illinois. He returned to the *Sun-Times* in 1986 and has been a transportation writer, science writer, and editorial board member in addition to writing his general op-ed column.

C _____

Caen, Herb Eugene (3 April 1916–). San Francisco institution Herb Caen has written a daily column in his city since 1938.

Caen was born in Sacramento, California, and attended Sacramento Junior College in 1934. From 1932 to 1936 he was a *Sacramento Union* reporter, after which he moved to San Francisco and in July 1938 began a column for the *Chronicle.* In 1950 he switched to the *San Francisco Examiner,* writing his column for that paper until 1958, when he returned to the *Chronicle,* taking an estimated twenty thousand readers with him. From 1942 to 1945 he served in the U.S. Army Air Forces, rising from private to captain. His gossipy, name-filled column of brief items on his city is syndicated by Chronicle Features to papers in other cities, as well. His style, he says, was influenced by that of the late Walter Winchell. He prides himself on typing his work, which now appears thrice weekly, on an antiquated standard Royal typewriter and he may well be America's longest running columnist. His column title has been ''It's News to Me,'' but it is also popularly known as the ''three dot column'' because the individual items in it are separated by ellipses. In 1993 the National Society of Newspaper Columnists gave Caen its first lifetime achievement award. By force of personality, he has transformed what purports to be a ''gossip column'' into something decidedly more, and it is said that the only San Francisco institution better known than the witty, pun-loving Caen is the Golden Gate Bridge.

BOOKS: *The San Francisco Book* (Boston, 1948); *Baghdad-by-the-Bay* (Garden City, N.Y., 1949); *Baghdad, 1951* (Garden City, N.Y., 1950); *Don't Call It Frisco* (Garden City, N.Y., 1953); *Herb Caen's Guide to San Francisco* (Garden City, N.Y., 1957); *New Guide to San Francisco and the Bay Area* (Garden City, N.Y., 1959); *Only in San Francisco* (Garden City, N.Y., 1960); *San Francisco: The Guide to the City and the Bay Area Today* (Garden City, N.Y., 1965); with Dong Kingman, *San Francisco, City on*

Golden Hills (Garden City, N.Y., 1967); *One Man's San Francisco* (Garden City, N.Y., 1976); *Benny Goodman: An Album* (New York, 1976); *The Cable Car and the Dragon* (Garden City, N.Y., 1976); *Nostalgia: Or, What Happened to Etaoinshrdlu* (Lafayette, Calif., 1983); *The Best of Herb Caen, 1960–1975* (San Francisco, 1991).

REFERENCES: John Alan King, *Literature in a Hurry: Herb Caen's Newspaper Column and Its Role in San Francisco,* M.A. Thesis, Indiana University, 1986; Jacques Leslie, "San Francisco's Powerful and Prolific Herb Caen," *Washington Journalism Review* (April 1986): 31–36.

Cain, James Mallahan (1 July 1892–27 Oct. 1977). Known principally for his crime novels that were made into movies, James Cain was a columnist and editorial writer for the *New York World* from 1924 to 1931.

Cain was born in Annapolis, Maryland. He received the A.B. in 1910 and the A.M. in 1917 at Washington College. Between the two degrees, he had aspirations for a singing career but concluded that he lacked the necessary talent.

After his master's program, Cain took a job as a reporter for the *Baltimore Sun.* After less than a year, he enlisted in the army and sailed for France. He was named editor of the *Lorraine Cross,* a military weekly newspaper published for the American Expeditionary Forces. Returning home in 1919, he resumed his reporting job at the *Sun.* His biggest assignment was covering unrest in the West Virginia coal fields. To gain a better understanding of his topic, he took a job as a miner in 1922, and even joined the United Mine Workers of America.

Cain briefly taught journalism at St. John's College in Annapolis during parts of 1923 and 1924, then spent seven years on the *New York World,* where he did his only column writing. He also contributed to *American Mercury* and, in the mid-1930s, to *Ladies' Home Journal.* In the 1940s, he was a contributor to *Liberty* magazine, as well.

Cain's best known novel, *The Postman Always Rings Twice,* was made into a movie by MGM in 1946. Prior to its issue, earlier Cain successes had been *The Root of His Evil,* filmed by Universal in 1943 as *Interlude; Double Indemnity* (Paramount, 1944); and *Mildred Pierce* (Warner Brothers, 1945). His success as a novelist allowed him to leave journalism and concentrate on his books. Cain's favorite theme was the murder plot hatched against the husband by the wife and her lover. He was known for his lean prose and realistic dialog.

BOOKS: *Our Government* (New York, 1930); *The Postman Always Rings Twice* (New York, 1934); *Serenade* (New York, 1937); *Mildred Pierce* (New York, 1941); *Love's Lovely Counterfeit* (New York, 1942); *Double Indemnity* (New York, 1943); *Three of a Kind* (New York, 1943); *Cain Omnibus* (Garden City, N.Y., 1943); *The Embezzler* (New York, 1944); ed., *For Men Only* (Cleveland, 1944); *Past All Dishonor* (New York, 1946); *The Butterfly* (New York, 1947); *Sinful Woman* (New York, 1947); *Career in C Major* (New York, 1947); *The Moth* (New York, 1948); *Three of Hearts* (London, 1949); *Jealous Woman* (New York, 1950); *Galatea* (New York, 1953); *Root of His Evil* (New York, 1951); *Mignon* (New York, 1962); *The Magician's Wife* (New York, 1965); *Cain × 3: Three Novels* (New York, 1969); *Rainbow's End* (New York, 1975); *The Institute* (New York, 1976); *Hard Cain* (Boston, 1980); *The Baby in the Icebox and Other Short Fiction,* ed. by Roy Hoopes (Franklin Center, Pa., 1981); *50 Years of Journalism,* ed. by Roy Hoopes (Bowling Green, Ohio, 1985).

Caldwell, Earl (?–   ). One of America's most experienced columnists, Earl Caldwell has made national headlines twice: in 1970 in a legal case involving reporters' shield laws, and in 1994 when he and his employer, the *New York Daily News,* parted company.

Caldwell was born in Clearfield, Pennsylvania, and is a graduate of the University of Buffalo. His first newspaper job was with the *Clearfield Progress,* his second with the *Lancaster* [Pennsylvania] *Intelligencer-Journal,* where he both covered sports and was a general assignment reporter. In later years he wrote for the *New York Herald Tribune* and the *New York Post.* He joined the *New York Times* in 1967, working first as a metropolitan reporter in New York, then at the paper's San Francisco office starting in 1969. It was here that Caldwell began covering the militant Black Panther party, which led to his being subpoenaed before a federal court in November 1970. He refused to testify, reasoning that if he did so, he would lose access to his sources. In a complex decision, the U.S. Supreme Court refused to create a national shield law that would allow news people to withhold testimony with impunity, yet the aftermath of this decision saw numerous individual states create reporters' shield laws of their own.

Caldwell again hit the headlines in April 1994 when he either quit or was fired from the *New York Daily News.* A Caldwell column about allegations that a white policeman had raped six black New York cab drivers was spiked by the paper's editorial page editor, Arthur Browne, who contends that Caldwell quit over the incident. Caldwell maintains that Browne fired him by phone. The disappearance of Caldwell's thrice-weekly column has spawned a spin-off controversy between Wilbert Tatum, editor and publisher of New York's black weekly *Amsterdam News,* and the *Daily News*'s remaining black columnists, Playthell Benjamin and Stanley Crouch.

During his many years as a reporter and as a columnist, Caldwell has interviewed innumerable public figures, among them Fidel Castro, Justice Thurgood Marshall, Jesse Jackson, migrant worker advocate Cesar Chavez, South African Nelson Mandela, and jazz legend Miles Davis. Some of this material is to appear in book form in a collection of Caldwell's writings to be published by a new African-American firm, Lion House Publishing.

REFERENCES: George Garneau, "Dispute About Column Turns Radical," *Editor and Publisher* (30 April 1994): 9–10; Garneau, "N.Y. Daily News Reporters Charge Double Standard," *Editor and Publisher* (14 May 1994): 17, 29; M. L. Stein, *Blacks in Communications* (New York, 1972): 51–53.

Caldwell, William Anthony (5 Dec. 1906–11 April 1986). After a long career writing the "Simeon Stylites" column for the *Hackensack* [New Jersey] *Record,* William Caldwell in 1972 entered into semiretirement on Martha's Vineyard,

Massachusetts, where he continued writing a Sunday column for the *Record* and also did an editorial page column for the *Vineyard Gazette.*

Caldwell was born in Butler, Pennsylvania, and grew up in Titusville, where his father was managing editor of the *Herald.* He did not attend college but later was the recipient of several honorary degrees as well as a Pulitzer Prize for commentary in 1971. He joined the *Record* as a sportswriter in 1926, when the paper was called the *Bergen Evening Record.* He evolved into a news reporter, then an editorial writer and columnist. Caldwell published two books.

BOOKS: *In the Record: The Simeon Stylites Columns of William A. Caldwell* (New Brunswick, N.J., 1971); *How to Save Urban America* (New York, 1973).

Campbell, Susan (31 July 1959–   ). Susan Campbell has been a columnist since 1982 and is presently at the *Hartford* [Connecticut] *Courant.*

She was born in Ft. Campbell, Kentucky, and received the B.S. in journalism from the University of Maryland in 1981.

Campbell's first job was as a general assignment/police reporter for the *Joplin* [Missouri] *Globe* (1981–1982). From 1982 to 1986 she was a reporter, feature writer, and columnist for the *Wichita* [Kansas] *Eagle-Beacon.* In 1986 she moved to the *Courant* in Hartford, where she writes her general/humor column "Snapshots" and also writes features.

Canham, Erwin Dain (13 Feb. 1904–3 Jan. 1982). Principally remembered as the longtime editor in chief of the *Christian Science Monitor* and as a radio and television commentator, Erwin Canham was also a *Monitor* columnist. His column "Down the Middle of the Road" was launched in 1940; later it ran under the title "Let's Think."

Canham was born in Auburn, Maine. He received the B.S. from Bates College, took a job as a general assignment reporter with the *Monitor,* then was the recipient of a Rhodes Scholarship and spent the next three years studying modern history at Oxford University, where he was awarded both a B.A. and an M.A. in 1929. He rejoined the *Monitor* and became its managing editor in 1942, editor in 1945, and finally editor-in-chief (1964–1974). He also wrote on a regular basis for the British periodical *Round Table* and in 1945 began work on ABC radio as a *Monitor*-sponsored commentator.

Canham's best friend, fellow columnist Roscoe Drummond, gave the quiet, dignified Canham the most inappropriate nickname possible: Spike. Canham was known for his reasoned view of national and international affairs and garnered many honors. He received thirteen honorary degrees and was decorated by several foreign governments. He was chosen as head of the American Society of Newspaper Editors in 1948 and as president of the U.S. Chamber of Commerce in 1959. After his retirement from the *Monitor,* he was resident commissioner of the Northern Mariana Islands in the 1970s.

BOOKS: *Awakening: The World at Mid-Century* (New York, 1951); *New Frontiers for Freedom* (New York, 1954); *Commitment to Freedom: The Story of the Christian Science Monitor* (Boston, 1958); *A Christian Scientist's Life* (Englewood Cliffs, N.J., 1962); *The Ethics of United States Foreign Relations* (Columbia, Mo., 1966).

REFERENCES: William Dicke, "Erwin Canham, Longtime Editor of Christian Science Monitor, Dies," *New York Times* (4 January 1982), B10.

Cannon, Louis S. (3 June 1933–   ). Lou Cannon writes a weekly column of news commentary for The Washington Post Writers Group. He earlier wrote a monthly column titled "Letter from Washington" for the *California Journal* in Sacramento.

Cannon was born in New York City. He attended the University of Nevada (1950–1952) and San Francisco State University (1952), served in the army in 1953–1954, then worked as a truck driver from 1954 to 1956.

He held reporting jobs at various papers from 1956 to 1959, then was managing editor of the *Contra Costa Times* in Walnut Creek, California, from 1959 to 1961. He went with the *San Jose Mercury-News* in 1961, as a copy editor until 1965, then as the paper's state capitol bureau head from 1965 to 1969. Cannon became Washington correspondent for Ridder Publications in 1969. He has written five books, three of which are about Ronald Reagan.

BOOKS: *Ronnie and Jessie: A Political Odyssey* (Garden City, N.Y., 1969); *The Mc-Closkey Challenge* (New York, 1972); *Reporting: An Inside View* (Sacramento, Calif., 1977); *Reagan* (New York, 1982); *President Reagan: The Role of a Lifetime* (New York, 1991).

Carlinsky, Dan (9 March 1944–   ). Dan Carlinsky is author of the column "It's on the Tip of My Tongue," handled by Newspaper Enterprise Association.

Carlinsky was born in Holyoke, Massachusetts. He received the B.A. in 1965 and the M.S. in 1966 from Columbia University. He has worked as a free-lance author/journalist. In addition to a long list of books geared to entertainment, he has written for such magazines as *Playboy, TV Guide,* and *Travel and Leisure.*

BOOKS: With Edwin Goodgold, *Trivia* (New York, 1966); with Goodgold, *More Trivial Trivia* (New York, 1966); with Goodgold, *Rock 'n' Roll Trivia* (New York, 1970); comp., *A Century of College Humor* (New York, 1971); with David Heim, *Bicycle Tours in and Around New York* (New York, 1975); with Goodgold, *The Compleat Beatles Quiz Book* (New York, 1975); with Goodgold, *The World's Greatest Monster Quiz* (New York, 1975); *The Complete Bible Quiz Book* (New York, 1976); *Typewriter Art* (Los Angeles, 1976); *The Great 1960s Quiz* (New York, 1978); *The Jewish Quiz Book* (Garden City, N.Y., 1979); *Do You Know Your Husband?* (Los Angeles, 1979); *Do You Know Your Wife?* (Los Angeles, 1979); *The Great Bogart Trivia Book* (New York, 1980); *Are You Compatible?* (Los Angeles, 1981); *Do You Know Your Mother?* (Los Angeles, 1981); *Do You Know Your Father?* (Los Angeles, 1981); *Celebrity Yearbook* (Los Angeles, 1982); *College Humor* (New York, 1982); *Do You Know Your Boss?* (Los Angeles, 1983); with Goodgold, *The Status Game* (New York, 1986); *Stop Snoring Now!* (New

York, 1987); with Goodgold, *The Armchair Conductor: How to Lead a Symphony Orchestra in the Privacy of Your Own Home* (New York, 1991).

Carter, Boake (28 Sept. 1898–16 Nov. 1944). Boake Carter (born Harold Thomas Henry Carter) emigrated from England to the United States and became a syndicated columnist out of the *Philadelphia Public Ledger* and a radio commentator.

Carter was born in Baku, Azerbaijan, to an English-Irish couple. He attended Tunbridge Wells and Christ College, Cambridge University, where he was a reporter for the *Cantabrian.* He also studied at the Slade School of Art in London.

After brief experience at the London *Daily Mail,* Carter came to the United States and wrote for various southwestern papers, including the *Tulsa World* and the *Excelsior* in Mexico City. Then he settled in Philadelphia and was hired by the *Daily News* as rewrite man and copy editor. He became assistant city editor of this paper and in 1933 became an American citizen. His start in radio came in 1930 with station WCAU in Philadelphia; soon thereafter he changed his name to Boake in order to sound more distinctive for air purposes. He became well known for his emotional live coverage of the Lindbergh kidnapping trial and soon became a high-paid CBS commentator. He spoke with an English accent, signing off each broadcast with "Cheerio." His popularity waned when he became a severe critic of Roosevelt's New Deal policies. After parting company with CBS, he worked for Mutual Broadcasting System and began a syndicated daily newspaper column titled "But. . . ." Late in his life he was attacked as anti-Semitic even though he had become convinced that the Anglo-Saxon and Celtic peoples were actually the lost tribes of Israel.

BOOKS: *Black Shirt, Black Skin* (London, 1935); *Johnny Q. Public Speaks: The Nation Appraises the New Deal* (New York, 1936); *Made in U.S.A.* (New York, 1936); with Thomas H. Healy, *Why Meddle in Europe?* (New York, 1936); with Thomas H. Healy, *Why Meddle in the Orient?* (New York, 1936); *I Talk as I Like* (New York, 1937); *This Is Life* (New York, 1937).

REFERENCES: David Culbert, *News for Everyman* (Westport, Conn., 1976); Irving E. Fang, *Those Radio Commentators!* (Ames, Iowa, 1977).

Carter, William Hodding, III (1935–   ). Hodding Carter, once editor of his family's Greenville (Mississippi) *Delta Democrat-Times,* has been a columnist for the *Wall Street Journal* and is now writing a column for the Newspaper Enterprise Association (NEA).

Carter was born in New Orleans. He was in 1957 a summa cum laude graduate of Princeton University and served in the Marine Corps for the following two years.

Carter's career began at the *Delta Democrat-Times* in 1959. He was named editor in 1965, having progressed from reporter to editorial writer to managing editor to associate publisher. He became active politically, working for Lyndon

Johnson in 1964 and with the Jimmy Carter campaign in 1976. In 1977 he became an assistant secretary of state for public affairs and was the administration's chief spokesman during the Iranian crisis. He resigned from the State Department in 1980 and since that time has divided his efforts between broadcasting and column writing. He became anchor of "Inside Story," a PBS weekly press critique, in 1981 and was chief correspondent for another PBS show, "Capitol Journal," which offers commentary on Congress. Carter has written a *Wall Street Journal* column and in 1991 began a new column for NEA. He has written three books.

BOOKS: *The South Strikes Back* (Garden City, N.Y., 1959); *The Reagan Years* (New York, 1988); *Westward Whoa: In the Wake of Lewis and Clark* (New York, 1994).

Casey, Maura (circa 1957–   ). Maura Casey is a social/political columnist for the *Day* in New London, Connecticut.

Casey was born in Buffalo, New York. She received the B.A., magna cum laude, in political science from State University College at Buffalo in 1979 and the M.A. in journalism and public affairs from the American University in 1983.

From 1983 to 1988 she was editorial page editor of the *Lawrence* [Massachusetts] *Eagle-Tribune*. She has been associate editorial page editor and columnist for the *Day* since 1988.

Chamberlain, John Rensselaer (28 Oct. 1903–   ). John Chamberlain wrote a daily general column for King Features Syndicate. He had earlier written a book column for the *New York Times.*

Chamberlain was born in New Haven, Connecticut, and in 1925 received the Ph.D. from Yale University. He began his career as a copywriter for the Thomas F. Logan advertising agency in New York City but entered journalism the following year as a *New York Times* reporter stationed in the paper's Washington bureau. From 1928 to 1933 he was assistant editor of the *Times Book Review* and wrote a daily book column from 1933 to 1936. He was also associate editor of the *Saturday Review of Literature* in 1933. From 1936 to 1941 he was editor of *Fortune,* the business magazine, and was also book editor of *Scribner's Magazine* from 1936 to 1938.

Chamberlain was book editor of *Harper's* from 1939 to 1947, book columnist for a second time at the *New York Times* (1942–1944), and editor of *Life* from 1945 to 1950. From 1950 to 1952 he edited the *Freeman,* and he was associate editor of *Barron's* from 1953 to 1955. He taught journalism at Columbia University at various times in the 1930s and 1940s, lectured at the New School for Social Research in 1935, and was journalism dean at Troy State University in Alabama from 1972. He wrote, cowrote, and edited several books.

BOOKS: *Farewell to Reform, Being a History of the Rise, Life and Decay of the Progressive Mind in America* (New York, 1932); *John Dos Passos: A Biographical and Critical Essay* (New York, 1939); *The American Stakes* (New York, 1940); ed. with Benfield Pressey and Reginald E. Watters, *Living, Reading and Thinking: 56 Essays in*

Exposition (New York, 1948); with Charles A. Willoughby, *MacArthur, 1941–51* (New York, 1954); ed., *The National Review Reader* (New York, 1957); *The Roots of Capitalism* (Princeton, N.J., 1959).

Charen, Mona (?–). Conservative political columnist Mona Charen has been distributed by Creators Syndicate since 1987. Her column now appears in more than one hundred papers.

Charen grew up in a liberal New Jersey family. Her own conservatism was influenced by her discovery at age thirteen of the *National Review* and its founder, William F. Buckley, Jr. During her senior year at Barnard, she served an internship at the *National Review,* then went to George Washington University for a law degree.

Her first job was as a speech writer for Nancy Reagan. Next she was a staffer for Pat Buchanan in the White House communications office, and in 1986 she worked as a writer in Senator Jack Kemp's reelection campaign, after which she began a semimonthly column for the *Republican Study Committee Bulletin,* which goes to that party's members of Congress. It was at this point that she began to contact syndicates and was picked up by Creators.

REFERENCES: Maria Braden, *She Said What? Interviews with Women Newspaper Columnists* (Lexington, Ky., 1993): 137–147.

Cheshire, Maxine (5 April 1930–). Experienced reporter Maxine Cheshire began writing the "VIP" column for the *Washington Post* and the Los Angeles Times Syndicate in 1965.

Born Maxine Hall in Harlan, Kentucky, she studied at the University of Kentucky (1949–1950) and Union College (1951–1952). She was a reporter for two Kentucky papers, the *Barboursville Mountain Advocate* and the *Harlan Daily Enterprise;* then worked as a police reporter for the *Knoxville* [Tennessee] *News-Sentinel* (1951–1954). In 1954 Cheshire joined the *Washington Post* as a society reporter, holding this position until 1965. From 1965 to 1981 she wrote "VIP" ("Very Interesting People"), filled with inside information on politicians and others. Cheshire went beyond the usual tittle-tattle of the gossip column and often scooped her fellow reporters on more serious matters, such as influence peddling and unreported gifts to government officials. She wrote one book, her autobiography.

BOOKS: With John Greenya, *Maxine Cheshire, Reporter* (Boston, 1978).

Childs, Marquis William (17 March 1903–). Winner of the first Pulitzer Prize for commentary (in 1966), Marquis Childs was a columnist for United Feature Syndicate from 1944 to 1954 and for the *St. Louis Post-Dispatch* until 1981.

Childs was born in Clinton, Iowa. He received the A.B. from the University of Wisconsin in 1923, then was a United Press reporter in Chicago for a brief period and returned to school for the A.M., which he received from the University of Iowa in 1925.

He then went back to work for United Press, writing out of Detroit, New York, and St. Louis during 1925 and 1926. He became a *St. Louis Post-Dispatch* feature writer (1926–1930), after which he took a leave of absence to study and write in Sweden. Of his books on that country, *Sweden: The Middle Way* (1936) was the most acclaimed. He returned to the *Post-Dispatch* in 1934 as a member of the paper's Washington bureau, going to Europe to report on the Spanish Civil War. From Washington he covered the Roosevelt administration and World War II from the domestic perspective.

Childs left the *Post-Dispatch* to write a column for United Feature Syndicate (1944–1954). The column appeared in roughly 150 newspapers and furthered his reputation as an intelligent, moderate, thoughtful observer of American politics, economic problems, and social issues. In 1954 he again returned to the *Post-Dispatch* as a special correspondent and columnist. He was the paper's chief Washington correspondent from 1962 to 1968. He continued his column for the paper until May 1981, though in all other respects he retired in 1974. He wrote for *New Republic, Reader's Digest, Yale Review,* and other magazines and was an active book author.

BOOKS: *Sweden: Where Capitalism Is Controlled* (New York, 1934); *Sweden, the Middle Way* (New Haven, Conn., 1936); *Washington Calling* (New York, 1937); *This Is Democracy: Collective Bargaining in Scandinavia* (New Haven, Conn., 1938); with William V. Stone, *Toward a Dynamic America* (New York, 1941); *This Is Your War* (Boston, 1942); *I Write from Washington* (New York, 1942); *The Cabin* (New York, 1944); with Douglas Cater, *Ethics in a Business Society* (Westport, Conn., 1954); *The Ragged Edge: The Diary of a Crisis* (Garden City, N.Y., 1955); *Eisenhower: Captive Hero* (New York, 1958); ed. with James Reston, *Walter Lippmann and His Times* (New York, 1959); *The Peacemakers* (New York, 1961); *Taint of Innocence* (New York, 1967); *Witness to Power* (New York, 1975); *Sweden: The Middle Way on Trial* (New Haven, Conn., 1980); *Yesterday, Today and Tomorrow: The Farmer Takes a Hand* (Washington, D.C., 1980); *Mighty Mississippi: Biography of a River* (New Haven, Conn., 1982).

Clapper, Raymond Lewis (30 May 1892–1 Feb. 1944). One of the most respected journalists of the 1930s and 1940s, Raymond Clapper was a political columnist from 1934 to 1944, first for the *Washington Post* and later for Scripps-Howard Newspapers and United Feature Syndicate.

Clapper was born on Memorial Day on a farm at La Cygne, Kansas. His family moved to Kansas City, where his first contact with newspapers was delivering them. While in high school, he worked nights as a printer's devil and journeyman printer; his journalistic hero was William Allen White, editor of the *Emporia Gazette.* Clapper attended Kansas University and was managing editor of the campus paper, the *Daily Kansan,* plus campus correspondent for the *Kansas City Star.* He was hired full-time by the *Star* in 1916 but shortly left to work for the United Press (UP), first in Chicago, then in Milwaukee, St. Paul, and New York. In 1917 he attained his goal—a UP job in Washington, D.C. In 1920 he scooped the rest of the capital press corps in revealing that the Republicans planned to nominate Warren Harding for president, and in 1925 he covered the celebrated Scopes trial in Tennessee.

Clapper took a new job with the *Washington Post* in 1933 as head of its national bureau. In September 1934, at the suggestion of *Post* assistant general manager Mark Etheridge, Clapper launched his daily column, "Between You and Me," a pioneer effort at behind the scenes political analysis and interpretation. Before the year was out he went back to Scripps-Howard and wrote the same style column, this time titled "Watching the World Go By." This column first appeared in the chain's twenty-four papers, then was picked up by United Feature and syndicated to roughly 180 papers, giving Clapper an impressive readership.

As a political columnist, Clapper was so concerned with remaining impartial he even refused to register to vote. His was one of the earliest voices warning of the dangers of Nazi Germany, the coming of war, and the need for the United States to intervene. He was proved right in all this, though he was incorrect in predicting that the East Coast of America would be bombed by the Nazis.

After the attack on Pearl Harbor, Clapper became a war correspondent for Scripps-Howard, covering both the European and Pacific theaters. He died tragically in 1944 when the plane in which he was riding to cover the U.S. invasion of the Marshall Islands collided with another aircraft.

Clapper was respected as a straightforward, essentially modest "think columnist" and was sometimes referred to as "the average man's columnist." Journalism educator John Drewry once pointed out, "A Clapper column never floats a trial balloon." In 1939 Clapper was president of the Gridiron Club, and in 1940 he was picked by his fellow members of the D.C. press corps as the nation's most significant, fair, reliable columnist.

Clapper also did a twice-weekly radio news broadcast for Mutual Broadcasting Company, sponsored by the White Owl Cigar Company, and wrote for such periodicals as *Reader's Digest, Forum, Life,* and *Yale Review.* He wrote two books, one about corruption in the nation's capital, the other a collection of Clapper's writing done in the latter part of his career, edited by his widow.

BOOKS: *Racketeering in Washington* (Boston, 1933); *Watching the World,* ed. by Olive Ewing Clapper (London and New York, 1944).

REFERENCES: Olive Ewing Clapper, *One Lucky Woman* (Garden City, N.Y., 1961); Charles Fisher, *The Columnists* (New York, 1944); 151–165; Otto Fuerbinger, "Average Man's Columnist," in *More Post Biographies,* ed. by John E. Drewry (Athens, Ga., 1947): 75–87.

Clark, Stephen Cutlar, Jr. (11 Feb. 1941–   ). Steve Clark writes a general-interest column for the *Richmond Times-Dispatch* and from 1976 to 1992 was a columnist for the *Richmond News Leader.*

Clark was born in High Point, North Carolina, and in 1963 received the A.B. from Davidson College.

Clark worked as a reporter on the *Knoxville* [Tennessee] *News-Sentinel* in 1964 and was a sportswriter for the *Winston-Salem Journal* in 1965 and at the *Atlanta Journal* from 1965 to 1968. He was a reporter/columnist for the *Dayton Daily News* from 1968 to 1980, then returned to sportswriting: at the *Atlanta Constitution* (1970–1972) and the *Richmond News Leader* (1972–1976). In 1976 he began to work as a full-time columnist. His column is of general content and is often humorous.

BOOKS: *Alden Aaroe: Voice of the Morning* (Richmond, Va., 1994).

Cobb, Irvin Shrewsbury (23 June 1876–10 March 1944). Outstanding turn-of-the-century humorist Irvin S. Cobb wrote his first column for the *Louisville* [Kentucky] *Evening News,* but his fame rests more on his subsequent column in the *New York World* (1905–1911).

Cobb was born in Paducah, Kentucky, and attended public school there. In 1893 he became a cub reporter/illustrator for the *Paducah Daily News,* and by age nineteen he was that paper's managing editor—briefly. He was not ready for the job and was demoted to reporter; he began also to contribute humor verse and other amusing copy.

Cobb's work started to be noticed, and from 1898 to 1901 he was a reporter for the *Louisville Evening Post,* where he also wrote his first humor column, "Kentucky Sour Mash." His big story during this period was the murder of Kentucky's governor, William Goebel, whom Cobb later described as "a Mussolini of politics." He returned to Paducah and from 1901 to 1904 was the *News-Democrat*'s managing editor, this time with more success. Cobb then spent a year and a half as a reporter for the *New York Sun,* for which he also wrote humor pieces. Then in 1905 he joined the *New York World,* working as reporter, rewrite man, and correspondent for out-of-town assignments. Although originally hired by the *World* for his skill as a reporter of straight news, Cobb's lasting fame is derived far more for his humor column in that paper: "New York Through Funny Glasses." During this period, 1905–1911, he also wrote other humor articles for the *World* and did a humor page for the Sunday magazine section titled, at different times, "The Hotel Clerk Says" and "Live Talks with Dead Ones." Most of his copy was syndicated to other papers, making his name well known around the nation. His biggest straight-news story during this part of his career was the sensational murder of architect Stanford White by millionaire Harry Thaw. Before leaving the *World,* Cobb began writing short stories for *Saturday Evening Post,* for which he went on to become a staff writer from 1911 to 1922. His last decade as a staff writer was from 1922 to 1932 with Hearst's *Cosmopolitan.* Cobb wrote for still other magazines, among them *Reader's Digest, Current Opinion,* and *Good Housekeeping,* and was a remarkably prolific author of humorous books.

BOOKS: *Cobb's Anatomy* (New York, 1912); *Back Home* (New York, 1912); *Cobb's Bill-of-Fare* (New York, 1913); *The Escape of Mr. Timm* (New York, 1914); *Europe Revised* (New York, 1914); *"Speaking of Operations—"* (Garden City, N.Y., 1916); *Paths of Glory* (New York, 1915); *Fibble* (New York, 1916); *Local Color* (New York, 1916); *Old Judge Priest* (New York, 1916); *Those Times and These* (New York, 1917); *"Speaking of Prussians—"* (New York, 1917); *Lost Tribes of the Irish and the South* (New York, 1917); *The Thunders of Silence* (New York, 1918); *The Glory of the Coming* (New York, 1918); *Life of the Party* (New York, 1919); *Eating in Two or Three Languages* (New York, 1919); *"Oh Well, You Know How Women Are!"* (New York, 1919); *The Abandoned Farmers* (New York, 1929); *From Place to Place* (New York, 1920); *A Plea for Old Cap Collier* (New York, 1921); *One Third Off* (New York, 1921); *J. Poindexter, Colored* (New York, 1922); *Sundry Accounts* (New York, 1922); *Stickfuls: Composition of a Newspaper Minion* (New York, 1923); *A Laugh a Day Keeps the Doctor Away* (New York, 1923); *Snake Doctor, and Other Stories* (New York, 1923); *Irvin Cobb at His Best* (Garden City, N.Y., 1923); *Goin' on Fourteen* (New York, 1924); *Indiana: Cobb's America Guyed Books* (New York, 1924); *Kansas: Cobb's America Guyed Books* (New York, 1924); *Kentucky: Cobb's America Guyed Books* (New York, 1924); *Maine: Cobb's America Guyed Books* (New York, 1924); *New York: Cobb's America Guyed Books* (New York, 1924); *North Carolina: Cobb's America Guyed Books* (New York, 1924); *Alias Ben Alibi* (New York, 1925); *"Here Comes the Bride"—and So Forth* (New York, 1925); *Many Laughs for Many Days* (New York, 1925); *On an Island That Cost $24.00* (New York, 1926); *Prose and Cons* (New York, 1926); *Some United States* (New York, 1926); *Chivalry Peak* (New York, 1927); *Ladies and Gentlemen* (New York, 1927); *All Aboard: Saga of the Romantic River* (New York, 1927); *Red Likker* (New York, 1929); *This Man's World* (New York, 1929); *To Be Taken Before Sailing* (New York, 1930); *Both Sides of the Street* (New York, 1930); *Incredible Truth* (New York, 1931); *Down Yonder with Judge Priest and Irvin S. Cobb* (New York, 1932); *Murder Day by Day* (Indianapolis, 1933); *One Way to Stop a Panic* (New York, 1933); *Faith, Hope and Charity* (Indianapolis and New York, 1934); *Judge Priest Turns Detective* (Indianapolis and New York, 1937); *Azam, the Story of an Arabian Colt and His Friends* (New York, 1937); *Favorite Humorous Stories of Irvin Cobb* (New York, 1940); *Glory, Glory Hallelujah* (Indianapolis, 1941); *Exit Laughing* (Indianapolis and New York, 1941); *Roll Call* (Indianapolis and New York, 1942); *Cobb's Cavalcade* (New York, 1945).

REFERENCES: Elisabeth Cobb Chapman, *My Wayward Parent: A Book About Irvin S. Cobb* (Indianapolis and New York, 1945); R. H. Davis, *Irvin S. Cobb, Storyteller* (New York, 1924); Anita Lawson, *Irvin S. Cobb* (Bowling Green, Ohio, 1984); Fred Gus Neuman, *Irvin S. Cobb: His Life and Achievements* (Paducah, Ky., 1934).

Cockburn, Alexander (6 June 1941–). A native of Ireland, Alexander Cockburn (pronounced CO-burn) has been an American journalist since 1973. He writes a liberal biweekly column for the *Nation,* "Beat the Devil," and now also does a newspaper column distributed by Creators Syndicate.

Cockburn was born in Ardgay, Scotland; was educated in Ireland, England, and Scotland; and was a 1963 honors graduate of Oxford University.

Known for both his liberal viewpoint and for his gifts as a stylist, Cockburn comments on politics, economics, international policy, labor, and the environment. He has published six books; has contributed to such diverse magazines as *Harper's, Playboy,* and *House and Garden;* and has made frequent television appearances. He presently lives in Northern California.

BOOKS: Ed. with Robin Blackburn, *Student Power* (Baltimore, Md., 1969); *Idle Passion: Chess and the Dance of Death* (New York, 1974); with James Ridgeway, *Smoke: Another Jimmy Carter Adventure* (New York, 1978); ed. with James Ridgeway, *Political Ecology* (New York, 1979); *Corruptions of Empire* (London and New York, 1987); *Fate of the Forest: Developers, Destroyers and Defenders of the Amazon* (London and New York, 1989).

Coffey, Thomas Francis (14 Feb. 1923–). Tom Coffey is a longtime columnist for the Savannah (Georgia), *Morning News* and *Evening Press.* His column currently appears twice weekly in the *Morning News.*

Coffey was born in Walthourville, Georgia, is a graduate of Savannah High School, and attended both the 1964 American Press Institute at Columbia University and the 1970 Urban Management Course at the Massachusetts Institute of Technology.

He began his career at the Savannah papers in 1940 as a reporter for the *Press.* He was that paper's sports editor from 1950 to 1956 and held the same position at the *News* from 1957 to 1960. He was city editor, then managing editor of the *Press* (1964–1967) and managing editor of the *News* (1967–1970). Coffey was associate editor of the *News-Press* from 1974 to 1987 and editor from 1987 until his retirement in 1989. His title is now contributing columnist; his column, run untitled, is general and personal. Earlier column titles were "Coffey Time" (in the *Press*), "Coffey Break" (in the *News*), and "Another Week," which he used while serving as city editor.

BOOKS: *Working For God* (Savannah, Ga., 1991); *Only in Savannah* (Savannah, Ga., 1994).

Cohen, Richard (6 Feb. 1941–). Richard Cohen writes a general, and generally liberal, column for the *Washington Post.*

Cohen was born in New York City. He received the B.A. from New York University in 1967, the M.A. from Columbia University in 1968. He has been with the *Post* since 1968 and since 1976 has been part of the Washington Post Writers Group. His column appears twice weekly.

BOOKS: With Jules Witcover, *A Heartbeat Away: The Investigation and Resignation of Vice President Spiro T. Agnew* (New York, 1974).

Condon, Thomas J. (7 Feb. 1946–). Tom Condon does a general column with an urban slant for the *Hartford Courant.*

Condon was born in New London, Connecticut, and received his B.A. from the University of Notre Dame in 1968. He later earned the J.D. from the University of Connecticut School of Law. He is a longtime employee of the *Cour-*

ant, having worked there since 1971 as general assignment reporter, chief investigative reporter, special projects editor, and, since 1985, New Haven bureau chief and columnist. He is also a Vietnam War veteran.

BOOKS: *Fire Me and I'll Sue* (Maywood, N.J., 1986); with Anne Condon, *Legal Lunacy: Unbelievable but True Laws—Past and Present* (Los Angeles, 1992).

Conniff, Frank (24 April 1914–May 1971). Frank Conniff (pronounced con-NIFF) wrote three columns for the Hearst newspapers: "East Side, West Side," "Capital Corner," and "Conniff's Corner."

Conniff was born in Danbury, Connecticut. He studied at the University of Virginia. His first job was at the *Danbury News-Times* as a sportswriter. He joined the Hearst papers in New York a year later, working as reporter, feature writer, and rewrite man. Conniff spent World War II as a war correspondent in Africa, Italy, and Germany, then returned to New York. He wrote his first column, "East Side, West Side," until the outbreak of hostilities in Korea, which he covered as a combat correspondent.

Conniff returned in 1951 and worked as personal assistant to William Randolph Hearst, Jr., who in that year inherited the job of running his father's media empire. In 1955, Conniff, Kingsbury Smith, and William Hearst shared a Pulitzer Prize for international reporting, and in 1958 Conniff became director of the Hearst Headline Service, which handled news features. During this time he wrote his Washington column, "Capital Corner," and later, a New York City column that he titled "Conniff's Corner."

Conniff's last post was as editor of the *World Journal Tribune* (1966–1967). He ran unsuccessfully for the House of Representatives in 1964, losing to Ogden R. Reid, whose father had been publisher of the *New York Herald Tribune.* Conniff coauthored one book.

BOOKS: With William Randolph Hearst, Jr., and Bob Considine, *How Russia Is Winning the Peace—Uncensored* (New York, 1958).

Considine, Robert Bernard (4 Nov. 1906–25 Sept. 1975). Remembered more as a sportswriter and as a Hearst color reporter and war correspondent in both World War II and Korea, Bob Considine early in his career wrote an unusual Washington column titled "The Drifter," which appeared in the *Washington Post.*

Considine was born in Washington, D.C. He studied journalism and creative writing at George Washington University's night school and in 1923 was employed as a messenger by the Census Bureau. He moved on to other government jobs at the Bureau of Public Health, Treasury Department, and Department of State before 1930, the year he became employed at the *Washington Post.*

By any reasonable standard, Considine's journalistic career was unusual in that he began as a columnist. His first column was "Speaking of Tennis"; his second, a city column titled "The Drifter," for which he wandered various sections of Washington, writing about their origins, physical features, and the like. After dropping his "Drifter" column, he became the *Post*'s baseball writer in 1933 and during that same year moved to the *Washington Herald* as sports editor, in which position he wrote a new daily column that was picked up by more than one hundred other papers. The column's title was "On the Line with Considine." He kept the column going for years after moving again in 1936 to the *New York American* and later to the *New York Daily Mirror*.

As a favorite Hearst writer, he also wrote for the International News Service and by 1942 was writing solely for that agency. During the 1940s and 1950s he was one of America's best-known journalists, did radio and television commentary, wrote a few movie scripts, and authored or edited more than twenty books, including an autobiography, *It's All News to Me* (1961).

BOOKS: *MacArthur the Magnificent* (Philadelphia, 1942); *General Wainwright's Story* (Toronto and New York, 1946); *The Babe Ruth Story* (New York, 1948); *Innocents at Home* (New York, 1950); *The Maryknoll Story* (New York, 1950); *The Panama Canal* (Eau Claire, Wis., 1951); ed., *Short Short Stories* (New York, 1953); *Thirty Seconds over Tokyo* (New York, 1953); *Man Against Fire: Fire Insurance—Protection from Disaster* (Garden City, N.Y., 1955); *Christmas Stocking* (New York, 1958); *That Many May Live: Memorial Center's 75 Year Fight Against Cancer* (New York, 1959); with Jack Dempsey, *Dempsey, by the Man Himself* (New York, 1960); *It's the Irish* (New York, 1961); with Joseph O'Keefe, *The Men Who Robbed Brink's* (New York, 1961); *Ripley, the Modern Marco Polo* (Garden City, N.Y., 1961); ed., *True War Stories: A Crest Anthology* (Greenwich, Conn., 1961); *The Unreconstructed Amateur: A Pictorial Biography of Amos Alonzo Stagg* (San Francisco, 1962); *General Douglas MacArthur* (Greenwich, Conn., 1964); *It's All News to Me* (New York, 1967); *Toots* (New York, 1969); with Fred G. Jarvis, *The First Hundred Years: A Portrait of the NYAC* (New York, 1969); *The Remarkable Life of Dr. Armand Hammer* (New York, 1975); *They Rose Above It* (Greenwich, Conn., 1977).

Cook, Sam (25 Oct. 1948–   ). Sam Cook is a columnist and an outdoor writer for the *Duluth News-Tribune* in Minnesota.

Cook was born in Sabetha, Kansas, and received a B.S. in journalism from the University of Kansas, Lawrence, in 1970. He writes two columns for the *News-Tribune,* for which he has worked since 1980. One is a general interest column that often deals in a humorous way with family life. The other is an outdoor column that ranges, as Cook puts it, "from fishing to hunting to dog-sledding or blueberry picking."

BOOKS: *Up North* (Duluth, Minn., 1986); *Quiet Magic* (Duluth, Minn., 1988); *Camp-Sights* (Duluth, Minn., 1991).

Corry, John (?–   ). In the early 1970s, John Corry began a column titled "About New York" for the *New York Times*. Corry had been a *Times* employee since the 1950s, with the exception of a three-year period in which he worked for *Harper's* under editor Willie Morris.

Corry grew up in Brooklyn. He graduated from Michigan's Hope College and served in the army.

Corry joined the *Times* in 1956 as a sports department copyboy. He worked next as a copyreader and finally, in 1966, as a reporter. During his years writing for the *New York Times,* Corry was perhaps the first reporter to cover the sex research of Drs. Masters and Johnson. He also scooped his competition in reporting Jackie Kennedy's attempts to block publication of William Manchester's book *The Death of a President.* For the latter story, he was treated to a far less than favorable account in *Esquire* written in acid by Gay Talese. Corry is also remembered for having defended Polish novelist Jerzy Kosinski from charges in the *Village Voice* that Kosinski had used a ghostwriter and had worked for the CIA. Corry's final job with the *Times* was as a television critic, and broadcasters remember him without fondness for the barbed comments he made about their shallowness and concentration on appearances rather than substance.

Corry has authored two books: one about Irish Americans, the other, a memoir of his years at the *Times.*

BOOKS: *Golden Clan: The Murrays, the McDonalds, and the Irish American Aristocracy* (Boston, 1977); *My Times: Adventures in the News Trade* (New York, 1993).

REFERENCES: Gay Talese, ''The Corry Papers,'' *Esquire* (June 1967): 92–94.

Craven, Charles (29 April 1929–   ). Charles Craven was a colorful local columnist for the *News and Observer* in Raleigh, North Carolina.

Craven attended East Carolina Teachers College (now East Carolina University) for two years, then served in the U.S. Army during World War II. He received his bachelor's degree in journalism from the University of North Carolina at Chapel Hill in 1948, then was a reporter for a few months with the *Wilmington* [North Carolina] *Star.* In 1949 he joined the *News and Observer* and worked there for the remainder of his career. At the behest of publisher Jonathan Daniels, managing editor Sam Ragan gave Craven his own column, which he used to chronicle everything from debutantes to the Ku Klux Klan. Craven especially liked to write about the misadventures of those down-and-out denizens of Raleigh's Martin Street whom publisher Daniels called ''wastrels, wobblies and winos.'' These scenes of 1950s Raleigh from the underside were often set in a fictitious café called Rusty's, modeled on a small eatery just around the corner from the newspaper's offices. Craven's columns became so popular that the café's owner eventually changed his establishment's name to Rusty's— life imitating art. Craven wrote six columns a week and also did court and police reporting. He retired on 1 January 1981 and in a real sense was Raleigh's own Damon Runyon.

BOOKS: *Charles Craven's Kind of People: Selected Columns from the News and Observer* (Chapel Hill, N.C., 1956).

REFERENCES: ''Craven Retires After 31 Years at N&O,'' *News and Observer* (1 January 1981): 39, 50.

Crawford, Kenneth Gale (27 May 1902–13 Jan. 1983). Kenneth Crawford is most remembered as a magazine columnist for his "Washington" column in *Newsweek,* but much earlier he was a political columnist for the *Buffalo Times* in Buffalo, New York.

Crawford was born in Sparta, Wisconsin. He received the B.A. from Beloit College in 1924.

He began his career as a United Press correspondent, working in St. Louis, Cleveland, Lansing, Indianapolis, and Washington, D.C., from 1924 to 1929. From 1929 to 1932 he wrote the column "Politics" for the *Buffalo Times,* after which he became Washington bureau chief for the *New York Post.* In 1940 he moved to the just-founded New York paper *P.M.* as their Washington bureau chief and capital correspondent.

In 1943 Crawford left newspapering for a magazine job as a war correspondent for *Newsweek.* He was the first U.S. reporter to land with the troops on D Day (6 June 1944). Later in 1944 he returned to Washington and occupied a succession of positions with *Newsweek,* the last of which was as writer of the "Washington" column (1960–1970). He also wrote the "TRB" column in *New Republic* from 1940 to 1943 and was the American Newspaper Guild's second president (1939–1940). After his retirement in 1970, he was a free-lance writer. Crawford was a liberal, an internationalist, and a supporter of U.S. involvement in Vietnam.

BOOKS: *The Pressure Boys: The Inside Story of Lobbying in America* (New York, 1939); *Report on North Africa* (New York, 1943).

REFERENCES: Katy Louchheim, *The Making of the New Deal: The Insiders* (Cambridge, Mass., 1983).

Croly, Jane Cunningham (19 Dec. 1829–23 Dec. 1901). An important pioneer feminist and early full-time woman journalist, Jane Croly was a columnist intermittently from 1856 to 1898.

She was born Jane Cunningham in Market Harborough, Leicestershire, England, and moved with her family to the United States in 1841. The family lived in Poughkeepsie and later Wappingers Falls, New York. She was taught at home in her early years, then went to school in Southbridge, Massachusetts, where she edited the school paper. While working as a housekeeper for her older brother, she cowrote a news sheet for a church audience.

After her father's death, she became the first woman journalist to have her own desk at a New York newspaper when she went to work for the *New York Tribune* in 1855. It was at this time that she took a pen name, Jennie June, which she borrowed from a poem, "January and June," by Benjamin F. Taylor. The poem had been given to her at age twelve by her minister.

It is likely that she was hired by the *Tribune*'s Charles Dana not only out of liberal motives, which that paper did often display, but in a conscious attempt to increase that paper's appeal to women readers.

On Valentine's Day of the following year, she married a fellow journalist, David Croly. Jennie June began writing a column, "Parlor and Side-Walk Gossip," for the *Sunday Times and Noah's Weekly Messenger*. She worked out a means of what she termed "duplicate correspondence" in order to increase her income by having her work appear in multiple outlets: the *Richmond* [Virginia] *Enquirer, New Orleans Delta, New Orleans Daily Picayune,* and *Louisville* [Kentucky] *Journal.* She also provided these papers with new material of special interest to women readers.

David Croly was named editor of the Rockford (Illinois) *Register* in 1860. After a year, however, the couple returned to New York City, where he became editor of the *New York World* and she was that paper's fashion editor. The work of Jennie June was again published simultaneously in a number of papers, now including the *Chicago Times, Richmond Whig,* and *New Orleans Democrat.* She remained with the *World* until 1872 and was also fashion editor of the *New York Times* from 1864 to 1872; afterward she became woman's editor and columnist for the *New York Daily Graphic* and remained with this paper until 1878. In her columns she cut a wide swath, giving women advice on many topics: shopping (in a separate column, "Returning to Town,"), sewing, polite behavior, cooking, and, mainly, fashion. Her work prefigured the more specialized advice columns of later years. In her own later years she became more active as a feminist, arguing for careers for women outside the home, but at the same time honestly discussing from her own experience the strains that could accompany this dual life-style. She wrote serious copy about working conditions for women, public education, public sanitation, and ecological concerns for the *Graphic* before leaving the paper in 1878 to concentrate on her column, which she continued to self-syndicate to various papers, which now also included the *Baltimore American.*

A watershed experience in her life had occurred in 1868, when New York's all-male Press Club put on a dinner at Delmonico's for the English author Charles Dickens but refused tickets to Croly and other women journalists. Their response was to found Sorosis, one of the first American women's clubs, later that year. Croly was its president not only in 1868, but in 1870 and from 1886 to 1888. In 1889 she also helped found and was first president of the Woman's Press Club of New York City. She was also active with the General Federation of Women's Clubs, founded in 1889.

Croly also had a busy magazine career. In 1860 she became assistant editor of the *Mirror of Fashion* and in 1865, editor of *Demorest's Illustrated Monthly and Mme. Demorest's Mirror of Fashions* (later rechristened *Demorest's Illustrated Monthly*). Croly bought part interest in the sagging *Godey's Lady's Book* in 1887 but gave up on it two years later to edit *Home-Maker* instead and to found the *Women's Circle,* a periodical of the General Federation of Women's Clubs.

BOOKS: *Jennie Juneiana: Talks on Women's Topics* (Boston, 1864); *Jennie June's American Cookery Book* (New York, 1866); *For Better or Worse: A Book for Some Men and*

All Women (Boston, 1875); *Knitting and Crochet: A Guide to the Use of the Needle and the Hook* (New York, 1885); ed., *Needle Work: A Manual of Stitches and Studies in Embroidery and Drawn Work* (New York, 1885); *Ladies Fancy Work* (New York, 1886); *Sorosis: Its Origins and History* (New York, 1886); ed., *Letters and Monograms for Marking on Silk, Linen and Other Fabrics* (New York, 1886); *Thrown on Her Own Resources; or, What Girls Can Do* (New York, 1891); *The History of the Woman's Club Movement in America* (New York, 1898).

REFERENCES: Barbara Belford, *Brilliant Bylines: A Biographical Anthology of Notable Newspaperwomen in America* (New York, 1986): 38–45; Madelon Golden Schlipp and Sharon M. Murphy, *Great Women of the Press* (Carbondale and Edwardsville, Ill., 1983): 85–94.

Crosby, John Campbell (18 May 1912–). John Crosby was both a general columnist and a television columnist for the *New York Herald-Tribune* in the 1960s. He later wrote a column in England for the *Observer.*

Crosby was born in Milwaukee, Wisconsin. He attended Phillips Exeter Academy and in 1936 was enrolled at Yale University.

His first experience in journalism was as a reporter for the *Milwaukee Sentinel* in 1934. In 1936 he became a police reporter for the *New York Herald-Tribune,* leaving in 1941 to serve in the U.S. Army until 1946. He returned to the *Herald-Tribune* in 1960 and wrote his columns until 1963, when he moved to Paris and worked at the *Paris Herald.* In 1965 he moved to London and began a weekly column for the *Observer,* which he wrote until 1975. Crosby also wrote for a variety of magazines, such as *Playboy, Look, Life,* and *Ladies' Home Journal.*

BOOKS: *Out of the Blue: A Book About Radio and Television* (New York, 1952); *With Love and Loathing* (New York, 1963); *Sapho in Absence* (London, 1970); *Never Let Her Go* (New York, 1970); *Contract on the President* (New York, 1973); *The Literary Obsession: A Novel* (London, 1973); *The White Telephone* (London, 1974); *An Affair of Strangers: A Novel* (New York, 1975); *Nightfall: A Novel* (New York, 1976); *The Company of Friends: A Novel* (New York, 1977); *Dear Judgment: A Novel* (New York, 1978); *Party of the Year* (New York, 1979); *Penelope Now: A Novel* (New York, 1981); *Men in Arms* (New York, 1983); *Take No Prisoners* (New York, 1985).

Cullen, Edward J. (25 Aug. 1946–). Long an employee of the Baton Rouge *Advocate,* Ed Cullen writes a personal/humor column titled "Attic Salt."

Cullen is a 1972 journalism graduate of Louisiana State University and has worked for the *Advocate* since his student days—as an obit clerk. He has been a police beat reporter, has covered city hall and the school board in Baton Rouge, and has also been a full-time feature writer. His column runs on the front page of the People section on Sundays.

Cuneo, Ernest L. (1905–2 March 1988). Mainly remembered as owner of the North American Newspaper Alliance (NANA) from the mid-1950s until 1963, Ernest Cuneo wrote a syndicated column for the NANA until 1980.

Cuneo was born in East Rutherford, New Jersey. He was admitted to the New

York Bar in 1932 and moved to Washington, D.C., where he worked for Congressman Fiorello LaGuardia. Cuneo subsequently established his own law practice in Washington and was associate counsel for the Democratic National Committee.

Cuneo worked with the Office for Strategic Services during World War II doing liaison work with the White House, FBI, and British intelligence. He became president of the NANA in 1949 and bought the agency shortly thereafter. After selling the NANA in 1963, he served the agency as columnist and military analyst and continued to practice law until 1981.

BOOKS: *Life with Fiorello: A Memoir* (New York, 1955); *Science and History* (New York, 1963).

Cutler, Bernard Joseph (26 May 1924–). B. J. Cutler writes a foreign affairs column for Scripps-Howard News Service.

Cutler was born in New York City. He received the B.S. in mechanical engineering in 1945 at Pennsylvania State University.

From 1945 to 1951 he worked as a reporter for the *Pittsburgh Press,* and from 1951 to 1956 as a *New York Herald Tribune* reporter. He was, successively, the *Herald Tribune*'s Moscow correspondent (1956–1958), head of the Paris bureau (1958–1960), European edition managing editor (1960), and European edition editor (1961–1966).

From 1966 to 1969 Cutler was European correspondent for Scripps-Howard Newspapers, stationed in Paris. He was a Scripps-Howard editorial writer in Washington from 1969 to 1972 and was promoted to head editorial writer in 1972.

D

Dalton, Thomas Sarsfield (18 Oct. 1946–). Tom Dalton writes a humor column for the *Daily Evening Item* of Lynn, Massachusetts.

Dalton was born in Boston. He received the B.A. from Colgate University in 1968 and the M.A. from Illinois State University in 1971.

In 1974–1975 Dalton worked as editor of the *Belmont* [Massachusetts] *Citizen.* Since 1976 he has been with the *Daily Evening Item*—as sports reporter, assistant sports editor, sports editor, life-style editor, news reporter, and columnist. His column usually deals with the often whimsical minutiae of family life.

Daly, Thomas Augustine (28 May 1871–4 Oct. 1948). Columnist/humorist/reporter/poet/speaker T. A. Daly is included here for his columns that appeared in three Philadelphia newspapers in the early 1900s.

Daly was born in Philadelphia. He attended Villanova College and Fordham University but did not earn a degree. In 1891 he became a cub reporter with the *Philadelphia Record.* He later wrote editorials for the *Record* and was named its associate editor in 1918. His columns were carried by the *Record* (1918–1924) and two other Philadelphia papers, the *Evening Bulletin* (1929–?) and the *Evening Ledger* (1915–1918). He also became general manager of the *Catholic Standard and Times,* a church weekly, in 1898. He published several volumes of his humor verse, which tended toward the sentimental and frequently employed dialect.

BOOKS: *Canzoni* (Philadelphia, 1906); *Carmina* (Carmina, N.Y., 1909); *Madrigali* (Philadelphia, 1912); *Little Pollys Pomes* (New York, 1913); *Songs of Wedlock* (New York, 1916); *McAroni Ballads and Other Verses* (New York, 1919); *The Friendly Sons of St. Patrick* (Philadelphia, 1920); *Herself and the Houseful: Being the Middling-Mirthful*

Story of a Middle-Class American Family of More Than Middle Size (New York, 1924); with Christopher Morley, *The House of Dooner: The Last of the Friendly Inns* (Philadelphia, 1928); *McAroni Medleys* (New York, 1932); *Selected Poems of T. A. Daly* (New York, 1936); *Late Lark Singing* (New York, 1946).

REFERENCES: Franklin P. Adams, "Interesting People: T. A. Daly," *American Magazine* 70 (October 1910): 750–751; Dorothy Emerson, "Poetry Corner: T. A. Daly," *Scholastic* 30 (20 February 1937): 9; Ted Robinson, "A Timeless Troubadour," *Saturday Review of Literature* 29 (23 November 1946): 42.

Danzig, Fred Paul (17 Sept. 1925–   ). Fred Danzig wrote two columns for United Press International (UPI) from 1951 until 1962.

Danzig was born in Springfield, Massachusetts. He received the B.A. from New York University in 1949 after having served in the U.S Army in Europe during 1943–1946. His first contact with journalism came in the position of copyboy with the Associated Press in New York City. He was hired as a reporter by the *Evening Telegram* in Herkimer, New York (1949–1950), then took a similar job with the Port Chester (New York) *Daily Item* (1950–1951). He signed on as a reporter and columnist with UPI in 1951 and until 1962 wrote two columns: "Time Out" and "Television in Review." In 1962 he became executive editor of *Advertising Age.*

BOOKS: With Fred Danzig, *How to Be Heard: Making the Media Work for You* (New York, 1974).

Davis, Merlene (?–   ). Merlene Davis writes a column for the *Lexington* [Kentucky] *Herald-Leader.* Her columns on the funny side of family life have led some to call her the "black Erma Bombeck," though she is more a general columnist than a humorist.

Davis majored in journalism at the University of Kentucky and attended a summer program for minority journalists held at the University of California, Berkeley. Thereafter, she went to work as a reporter for the *Memphis Press Scimitar* until offered a job by John Carroll, editor of the *Lexington Herald-Leader.* After two years she was assigned to the Lifestyle section and shocked Lexington's black community with a story about internal discrimination among African Americans according to lightness or darkness of skin coloration. She prides herself in being just as willing to criticize shortcomings in the black community as she is to point out prejudice among whites. Davis has often written columns with the idea of showing her white readers that their concerns are basically the same as hers. When Davis suggested to her paper's white editors that they might not dare to hire a black columnist, they offered the job to her.

In 1991, when the queen of England visited the United States and was somewhat taken aback by having been given a big hug by a black woman, virtually every U.S. paper carried the picture, yet Davis was one of the very few journalists to conduct a sympathetic interview with the hugger, sixty-seven-year-old Alice F. Frazier.

REFERENCES: Maria Braden, *She Said What? Interviews with Women Newspaper Columnists* (Lexington, Ky., 1993): 164–173.

Davis, Paxton (7 May 1925–27 May 1994). Paxton Davis, former newspaper reporter and journalism professor, wrote a weekly op-ed column for the *Roanoke Times and World News* from 1976 until early 1994.

Davis was born in Winston-Salem, North Carolina. He attended Virginia Military Institute (1942–1943), then served in World War II in the China-Burma theater of operations. After the war, he enrolled at Johns Hopkins University, where he received the B.A. in 1949.

Davis began his newspaper career as a reporter on the *Winston-Salem Journal* (1949–1951), then reported for the *Richmond Times-Dispatch* (1951–1952) and the *Twin City Sentinel* in Winston-Salem (1952–1953). Later in 1953, he began teaching journalism at Washington and Lee University in Lexington, Virginia; he remained there until 1974. He was department head from 1968 to 1974, and beginning in 1961, he spent his summers with the *Roanoke Times and World News* as book page editor. In his column for the Roanoke paper, Davis is known for having pulled no punches as regards political leaders and others who aroused his ire.

BOOKS: *Two Soldiers* (New York, 1956); *The Battle of New Market: A Story of V.M.I.* (Boston, 1963); *One of the Dark Places: A Novel* (New York, 1965); *The Seasons of Heroes: A Novel* (New York, 1967); *A Flag at the Pole: Three Soliloquies* (New York, 1976); *Ned* (New York, 1978); *Three Days* (New York, 1980); *Being a Boy* (Winston-Salem, N.C., 1988); *Frederick Womble Speas: A Memoir* (Winston-Salem, N.C., 1989); *A Boy's War* (Winston-Salem, N.C., 1990); *A Boy No More* (Winston-Salem, N.C., 1992).

Dawkins, Wayne J. (19 Sept. 1955–). Wayne Dawkins has been a general op-ed page columnist for the *Courier-Post* in Camden–Cherry Hill, New Jersey, since November 1991.

Dawkins was born in New York City and holds the B.A. from Long Island University, Brooklyn campus (1977), and the M.S. from the Columbia University School of Journalism (1980).

From 1980 until 1984 Waters worked as a reporter for the *Daily Argus* in Mount Vernon, New York. He joined the *Courier-Post* in 1984 as a reporter, then became an editorial writer and assistant metro editor.

BOOKS: *Black Journalists: The NABJ Story* (Sicklerville, N.J., 1993).

Delaplane, Stanton Hill (12 Oct. 1907–18 April 1988). Stanton Delaplane's column dealt with travel, but he is included here because it was at the same time a humor column.

Delaplane was born in Chicago and went to high school in that city and in Santa Barbara and Monterey, California.

His start in journalism was a job as editor of *Aperitif* magazine (1933–1936).

In 1936 he took a reporting job with the *San Francisco Chronicle* and remained with that paper for the rest of his career. He won a Pulitzer Prize in 1942 for a series of stories on counties in California and Oregon that wanted to secede and form a separate state. He reported and did rewrite until 1953 and served in 1944 and 1945 as a war correspondent in the Pacific. In 1953 he began his humorous travel column, which was syndicated.

BOOKS: *Postcards from Delaplane* (Garden City, N.Y., 1953); *The Little World of Stanton Delaplane* (New York, 1959); with Robert de Roos, *Delaplane in Mexico: A Short Happy Guide* (New York, 1960); *And How She Grew* (New York, 1961); *Pacific Pathways* (New York, 1963); with Stuart Nixon, *Stan Delaplane's Mexico* (San Francisco, 1976).

DeMott, John Edward (15 Aug. 1923–). Recently retired Memphis State University journalism professor John DeMott is possibly unique in being the only white American to write a column for a black newspaper. His general column has appeared since 1987 in the *Tri-State Defender,* which is published in Memphis, Tennessee, and also serves northern Mississippi and eastern Arkansas.

DeMott was born in Topeka, Kansas. He received the A.A. degree from the Junior College of Kansas City (Missouri) in social science in 1944, the B.S. in education from the University of Kansas in 1946, the M.A. in history and English literature from the University of Missouri/Kansas City in 1960, and the Ph.D. in journalism and mass communication from Northwestern University in 1971.

DeMott's journalistic career began as a reporter and later editor for the *Kansas City Star and Times* (1946–1962). He taught journalism at the University of Kansas from 1962 to 1967 and was on the journalism faculties of Northwestern University (1967–1971), Northern Illinois University (1971–1976), Temple University (1976–1980), and Memphis State University (1980–1993). He also taught at the American University in Cairo, Egypt, in 1982–1983 and was journalism department chair at Memphis State from 1984 to 1987.

DeMott has also contributed columns on an occasional basis for other papers, including the Memphis *Commercial Appeal,* Memphis *Press Scimitar, Philadelphia Inquirer, Philadelphia Tribune, Kansas City Star, Kansas City Times,* and DeKalb [Illinois] *Daily Chronicle.*

BOOKS: With Alfred P. Klausler, *The Journalist's Prayerbook* (Minneapolis, 1975).

Deupree, Michael Harold (23 March 1946–). Mike Deupree is a thrice-weekly columnist for the *Cedar Rapids Gazette* in Cedar Rapids, Iowa.

Deupree, a native of Council Bluffs, Iowa, enrolled at Iowa State University in 1964 to study aerospace engineering, then in 1966 switched to a journalism major. A year thereafter, he transferred to the University of Iowa and in 1968 was awarded a B.A. in journalism.

His first job was as a general assignment reporter and sports editor for the

Blackfoot News in Blackfoot, Iowa. He also wrote editorials and did a weekly general-interest column for the *News*. In 1973 he became city hall reporter for the *Cedar Rapids Gazette,* where five years later he was named state editor, a position he held for three years. He also contributed film reviews, editorials, and occasional columns to the *Gazette* before becoming a full-time editorial writer in 1982. His regular column, which at first was done weekly, began in 1986; it has appeared three times weekly since February 1987. Deupree's column has been distributed by the New York Times News Service.

Dickinson, Brian (?–   ). Brian Dickinson writes a thrice-weekly column for the *Providence* [Rhode Island] *Journal-Bulletin* and the Scripps-Howard News Service.

Dickinson is a 1959 graduate of Harvard University. He reported for the *New York Times* for two years after graduation, served in the army for the next two years, then returned to the *Times* as a Washington bureau reporter. In 1964 he became a reporter for the *Journal-Bulletin.* He was an editorial writer and editorial page editor prior to starting his column in 1985. Scripps Howard began handling it in 1988. The column's subject matter is frequently foreign affairs, but Dickinson also uses his column's roughly eight hundred words to address the arts, the economy, environmental issues, and anything else he finds interesting.

Di Sandro, Deborah Jean (20 June 1959–   ). Deb Di Sandro self-syndicates her humor column, "Slightly Off," out of Cary, Illinois.

She was born in Chicago and received the B.A. in communications from Chicago's Columbia College in 1983.

Di Sandro started her column at the *Sussex Sun,* a weekly in Sussex, Wisconsin. She had worked there as a reporter since 1989. Her column was picked up by the *Freeman,* a daily, in Waukesha, Wisconsin, in 1992; by a monthly periodical, the *Country Gazette,* in 1993; and by the *Arlington Heights* [Illinois] *Daily Herald* in late 1993. Her column specializes in family-oriented humor.

Doogan, Gerald Michael (7 June 1948–   ). Mike Doogan's general-interest metro column has appeared since 1990 in the *Anchorage Daily News.*

Doogan was born in Fairbanks, Alaska, and received a B.A. in 1970 at the University of San Francisco.

His newspaper career began at the *Anchorage Daily Times* in 1972, and until 1977 he worked at that paper as sportswriter, political reporter, copy editor, Sunday editor, and assistant city editor. He left journalism for a few years to work as a legislative aide, campaign manager, and consultant and also worked as a radio reporter. Then in 1985 he became assistant city editor of the *Anchorage Daily News* and in 1990 became that paper's metro columnist. He is also a columnist for the monthly *Alaska Magazine.*

BOOKS: *Dawson City* (Anchorage, Alaska, 1988); *How to Speak Alaskan* (Seattle, Wash., 1993).

Driscoll, Charles Benedict (19 Oct. 1885–16 January 1951). Charles Driscoll was the heir to O. O. McIntyre's column "New York Day by Day" after the latter's death in 1938. He had earlier written the column "The World and All" for twelve years.

Driscoll was born on a farm outside Wichita, Kansas, and was a 1912 A.B. graduate of Friends University in Wichita. He also studied at the University of Kansas, the University of Minnesota, and the New School for Social Research. He worked for the *Wichita Eagle* for two years, then was hired by the *Omaha* [Nebraska] *News* and later by the *St. Paul* [Minnesota] *News.* At the St. Paul paper he originated and edited an education page. Three years later he went with the United Press in New York City, then in 1919 returned to Kansas as editor of the *Eagle.* In 1924 Driscoll became associate editor of the *Cleveland Press* and from 1925 to 1938 he was executive editor of the McNaught Syndicate. He wrote his column "The World and All" from 1927 to 1938, at which time he took over the enormously popular McIntyre column.

Driscoll was said to have owned the world's largest private library on pirates and pirate treasure. Pirates were the subject of several of his own books. He was also O. O. McIntyre's biographer.

BOOKS: *Complete Story of Omaha's Disastrous Tornado* (Omaha, Neb., 1913); *Doubloons: The Story of Buried Treasure* (New York, 1930); *Treasure Aboard* (New York, 1931); *The Book of Feminine Names: Women's Names and Their Meanings* (Dayton, Ohio, 1932); *Driscoll's Book of Pirates* (Philadelphia, 1934); *The Life of O. O. McIntyre* (New York, 1938); *Pirates Ahoy!* (New York, 1941); *Kansas Irish* (New York, 1943); *Country Lake* (New York, 1946).

REFERENCES: Charles Fisher, *The Columnists* (New York, 1944): 273–276.

Drummond, James Roscoe (13 Jan. 1902–30 Sept. 1983). Roscoe Drummond was known for his widely syndicated political column, "State of the Nation," and for his long career at the *Christian Science Monitor.*

Drummond was born in Theresa, New York. He was a 1924 B.S. graduate of Syracuse University, where he was editor of the campus paper, the *Daily Orange,* and worked part-time for the Syracuse *Journal.* He was employed as a reporter by the *Monitor* immediately after graduation and went on to hold a variety of positions at that paper: assistant city editor, assistant to the executive editor, head editorial writer, European editorial manager in London (1930–1933), and news editor. He was executive editor from 1934 to 1940 and head of the Washington, D.C., bureau (1940–1953).

Soon after becoming D.C. bureau chief, Drummond began his front-page column "State of the Nation," which he continued to write, with some interruptions, until 1981, when he was injured in an automobile accident.

In 1949 Drummond became European director of information for the Marshall

Plan, replacing Alfred Friendly of the *Washington Post.* From his post in Paris he wrote a Saturday column titled "State of Europe" for the *Monitor.* His year-long replacement in Washington was Joseph C. Harsch.

In 1954 he left the *Monitor* to become D.C. bureau chief for the *New York Herald-Tribune.* A little more than a year later, he gave up the bureau job to write a new column, "Washington," which became nationally syndicated. He eventually was picked up by the Los Angeles Times Syndicate and returned to the column title "State of the Nation." His writing won him many honors, plus the nickname "Bulldog Drummond." He also contributed to *Reader's Digest, Saturday Evening Post,* and other U.S. and English magazines, and coauthored one book.

BOOKS: With Gaston Coblentz, *Duel at the Brink: John Foster Dulles' Command of American Power* (Garden City, N.Y., 1960).

DuBois, William Edward Burghardt (23 Feb. 1868–27 Aug. 1963). The leading African-American intellectual of the twentieth century, the incredibly prolific W.E.B. DuBois wrote columns for a number of newspapers in addition to his many books and periodical articles.

DuBois was born in Great Barrington, Massachusetts. He earned the A.B. in 1888 at Fisk University and a second A.B., cum laude, in 1890 at Harvard. He remained at Harvard for the M.A. in 1891, studied abroad for two years at the University of Berlin, then returned to Harvard for the Ph.D. in 1895. DuBois was the first black American to earn this degree at Harvard.

He taught language courses from 1895 to 1897 at Wilberforce University and both economics and history at Atlanta University from 1897 to 1910. DuBois founded several periodicals, the first of which was the *Moon Illustrated Weekly* (1905). In 1906 he started a monthly, *Horizon,* which continued until 1910, and after becoming director of publications for the National Association for the Advancement of Colored People (NAACP) in 1910, he founded that organization's official journal, the *Crisis,* which he edited for about twenty-five years. He also founded a magazine for black children, *Brownies' Book* (1920–1921).

In 1934 DuBois resigned his NAACP post and returned to Atlanta University as chair of sociology. In 1940 he founded *Phylon,* a scholarly journal devoted to research on racial issues. He resumed a connection with the NAACP in 1944 and became increasingly outspoken regarding his conviction that improvement of the lot of American blacks lay in socialism. His column appeared in such papers as the *New York Amsterdam News* and the *Pittsburgh Courier* between 1936 and 1948. He also wrote a column for the *San Francisco Chronicle.* In addition, DuBois was active in the black literary movement known as the Harlem Renaissance.

BOOKS: *The Suppression of the African Slave-Trade to the United States of America, 1638–1870* (New York and London, 1896); ed., *Mortality Among Negroes in Cities* (Atlanta, 1896); ed., *Some Efforts of American Negroes for Their Own Social Betterment* (Atlanta, 1898); *The Philadelphia Negro: A Social Study* (Philadelphia, 1899); ed., *The*

Negro in Business (Atlanta, 1899); ed., *The College-Bred Negro* (Atlanta, 1900); ed., *The Negro Common School* (Atlanta, 1901); ed., *The Negro Artisan* (Atlanta, 1902); *The Souls of Black Folk: Essays and Sketches* (Chicago, 1903); ed., *The Negro Church* (Atlanta, 1903); ed., *Some Notes on Negroes in New York City* (Atlanta, 1903); ed., *Some Notes on Negro Crime* (Atlanta, 1904); ed., *A Select Bibliography of the Negro American* (Atlanta, 1905); ed., *The Health and Physique of the Negro American* (Atlanta, 1906); with Booker T. Washington, *The Negro in the South* (Philadelphia, 1907); ed., *Economic Co-Operation Among Negro Americans* (Atlanta, 1907); ed., *The Negro American Family* (Atlanta, 1908); *John Brown* (Philadelphia, 1909); ed. with Augustus Dill, *The College-Bred Negro American* (Atlanta, 1910); *The Quest of the Silver Fleece: A Novel* (Chicago, 1911); ed. with Augustus Dill, *The Common School and the Negro American* (Atlanta, 1911); ed. with Augustus Dill, *The Negro American Artisan* (Atlanta, 1912); ed. with Augustus Dill, *Morals and Manners Among Negro Americans* (Atlanta, 1914); *The Negro* (New York, 1915); *Darkwater: Voices from Within the Veil* (New York, 1920); *The Gift of Black Folk: The Negroes in the Making of America* (Boston, 1924); *Dark Princess: A Romance* (New York, 1928); *Africa: Its Geography, People and Products* (Girard, Kan., 1930); *Black Reconstruction* (New York, 1935); *Black Folk Then and Now: An Essay in the History and Sociology of the Negro Race* (New York, 1939); *Dusk of Dawn: An Essay Toward an Autobiography of a Race Concept* (New York, 1940); *Color and Democracy: Colonies and Peace* (New York, 1945); *The World and Africa: An Inquiry into the Part Which Africa Has Played in World History* (New York, 1947); ed., *An Appeal to the World* (New York, 1947); *In Battle for Peace: The Story of My 83rd Birthday* (New York, 1952); *The Ordeal of Mansart* (New York, 1957); *Mansart Builds a School* (New York, 1959); *Worlds of Color* (New York, 1961); *Selected Poems* (Accra, Ghana, 1963); *The Autobiography of W.E.B. DuBois,* ed. by Herbert Aptheker (New York, 1968); *An ABC of Color* (New York, 1969); *W.E.B. DuBois Speaks: Speeches and Addresses,* ed. by Philip S. Foner (New York, 1970); *W.E.B. DuBois: The Crisis Writings,* ed. by Daniel Walden (Greenwich, Conn., 1972); *The Education of Black People: Ten Critiques, 1906–1960,* ed. by Herbert Aptheker (Amherst, Mass., 1973); *The Complete Published Works of W.E.B. DuBois,* ed. by Herbert Aptheker (Millwood, N.Y., 1973–1986).

REFERENCES: Francis L. Broderick, *W.E.B. DuBois: Negro Leader in a Time of Crisis* (Stanford, Calif., 1959); Shirley Graham DuBois, *His Day Is Marching On: A Memoir of W.E.B. DuBois* (Philadelphia, 1971); Leslie Alexander Lacy, *Cheer the Lonesome Traveler* (New York, 1970); Elliott M. Rudwick, *W.E.B. DuBois: Propagandist of the Negro Protest* (New York, 1968).

Dunne, Finley Peter (10 July 1867–24 April 1936). Finley Peter Dunne, a competent political reporter and editor, mainly for papers in his native Chicago, is remembered for his satirical columns written in Irish dialect and featuring his literary mouthpiece "Mr. Dooley."

Dunne graduated from high school in 1884—last in a class of fifty. He began writing humor copy during high school but had to create his own handwritten newspaper, the *Missionary,* to get it published. He went to work as a gopher and part-time crime reporter for the *Chicago Telegram* in 1884, and later in that year switched to the *Chicago Daily News,* where he wrote news, sports, features, and editorials. He moved again in 1888 to the *Chicago Times,* reporting on politics and writing editorials. He was promoted to city editor but in 1889 was let go. He was unemployed for only part of one day, going with the *Chicago Tribune* as a reporter. He was named editor of the *Tribune*'s Sunday edition in 1890 but later that year switched papers yet again to cover politics for the *Chicago Herald.* In 1892 he was made editorial page editor of the *Herald*'s affiliate paper, the *Chicago Evening Post.*

Dunne came to know many of Chicago's outstanding journalists of that era, including Booth Tarkington, Carl Sandburg, Ben Hecht, Sherwood Anderson, and George Ade, and was one of the founders of the Whitechapel Club, a sort of offbeat literary/political "fraternity." Dunne found a supporter and literary tutor in the novelist Mary Ives Abbott, who encouraged him to make use of his talent for satire. His first Irish dialect sketches appeared in the *Post* in December 1892, featuring "Col. McNeery," a character based on a real Chicago tavern owner named James McGarry. When McGarry complained about being made into a figure of fun, Dunne created his more enduring literary character, Martin Dooley of Archey Street, bachelor, saloonkeeper, and self-appointed adviser to another of Dunne's characters, Mr. Hennessy, an uneducated laborer in a Chicago steel mill. Dunne used Mr. Dooley, himself uneducated but full of opinions, to "explain" the times, complain about corruption, and in an indirect way explore the life of the Irish urban immigrant in the turn-of-the-century American "melting pot." Dooley made his first appearance on 7 October 1893 and was immediately popular.

Dunne again changed papers in 1897, becoming managing editor of the *Chicago Journal* and continuing his Dooley column. Papers in other cities began running the Dooley column, and Dunne spoke out against U.S. involvement in what became the Spanish-American War. In 1898 he began the practice of collecting his columns into books. Then in 1900 Dunne moved to New York City to take advantage of the national play his first two books had given him. His newspaper column was widely syndicated by the McClure's Syndicate, and he began writing regularly for *Harper's Weekly* and for *Collier's,* also contributing to *Literary Digest, Century, Cosmopolitan,* and other magazines. From 1902 to 1904 he was editor of the *New York Morning Telegraph,* resigning after the death of its owner and Dunne's chum William Whitney.

Dunne's circle of friends now included Theodore Roosevelt and Samuel Clemens, and Mr. Dooley was commenting on national issues. Dunne joined in the founding of the *American Magazine* in 1906, contributing commentary in a department titled "In the Interpreter's House," as well as his Dooley pieces. He also kept up a weekly Dooley column for the McClure's Syndicate and, starting in 1911, did a monthly column for *Metropolitan Magazine,* a labor periodical. By 1915 he had severed all these ties and had begun writing a commentary page for *Collier's,* in which he advocated a strong U.S. military response to Germany in World War I. Dunne wrote no dialect columns during the war but in the 1920s revived Mr. Dooley for *Liberty* magazine. Then in

1927, Dunne's immensely wealthy friend Payne Whitney died, leaving Dunne a half million dollars, after which the writer retired.

BOOKS: *Mr. Dooley in Peace and in War* (Boston, 1898); *Mr. Dooley in the Hearts of His Countrymen* (Boston, 1899); *Mr. Dooley's Philosophy* (New York, 1900); *Mr. Dooley's Opinions* (New York, 1901); *Observations by Mr. Dooley* (New York, 1902); *Dissertations by Mr. Dooley* (London and New York, 1906); *Mr. Dooley Says* (New York, 1910); *Mr. Dooley on Making a Will and Other Necessary Evils* (New York, 1919); *Mr. Dooley at His Best,* ed. by Elmer Ellis (New York, 1949); *Mr. Dooley: Now and Forever,* ed. by Louis Filler (Stanford, Calif., 1954); *The World of Mr. Dooley,* ed. by Louis Filler (New York, 1962); *Mr. Dooley on the Choice of Law,* ed. by Edward J. Bander (Charlottesville, Va., 1963); *Mr. Dooley Remembers: The Informal Memoirs of Finley Peter Dunne,* ed. by Philip Dunne (Boston, 1963); *Mr. Dooley and the Chicago Irish,* ed. by Charles Fanning (New York, 1976).

REFERENCES: James DeMuth, *Small Town Chicago: The Comic Perspective of Finley Peter Dunne, George Ade, and Ring Lardner* (Port Washington, N.Y., 1980); Grace Eckley, *Finley Peter Dunne* (Boston, 1981); Elmer Ellis, *Mr. Dooley's America: A Life of Finley Peter Dunne* (New York, 1941); Charles Fanning, *Finley Peter Dunne and Mr. Dooley: The Chicago Years* (Lexington, Ky., 1978); Barbara C. Schaaf, *Mr. Dooley's Chicago* (Garden City, N.Y., 1977); Norris W. Yates, *The American Humorist: Conscience of the Twentieth Century* (Ames, Iowa, 1964): 81–99.

E

Eban, Abba Solomon (2 Feb. 1915–). An interesting new column about the Middle East for American readers is being written by Abba Eban, the Israeli diplomat who once, in a moment of frustration, called the United Nations "an umbrella that folds up when it rains."

He was born Abba Solomon in Cape Town, South Africa. He went with his mother to England in 1915, adopting the surname of his stepfather and during his school days, calling himself Aubrey rather than Abba. He was a 1931 graduate of Queen's College, Cambridge, where he studied modern languages and literature. Thanks to his years of study and travel, he speaks English, Hebrew, French, German, Arabic, and Persian. He remained at Cambridge for an M.A., with high honors, in 1938, after which he tutored briefly at Cambridge, then served as an officer in the British Army from 1936 to 1946.

He returned to Israel in 1946 and began his career in government, which included assignments as head of the Israeli mission to the United Nations (1948–1953), Israeli ambassador to the United States (1950–1959), minister of education and culture (1960–1963), deputy prime minister (1963–1966), and minister of foreign affairs (1966–1974). He is known in the United States as a supremely gifted public speaker.

Eban's column is distributed by Cartoonews International. His columns are accompanied by illustrations by Ranan Lurie, a former Israeli paratrooper who is reportedly the most widely syndicated cartoonist in the world and who also illustrates the recently launched column of the former Soviet leader Mikhail Gorbachev. Eban has authored nine books; most are about his homeland.

BOOKS: *Voice of Israel* (New York, 1957); *The Tide of Nationalism* (New York, 1959); *My People: The Story of the Jews* (New York, 1968); *My Country: The Story of Modern Israel* (New York, 1972); *Abba Eban: An Autobiography* (New York, 1977); *Promised*

Land (Nashville, Tenn., 1978); *The New Diplomacy: International Affairs in the Modern Age* (New York, 1983); *Heritage: Civilization and the Jews* (New York, 1984); *Personal Witness: Israel Through My Eyes* (New York, 1992).

Ebron, Betty Liu (25 July 1956–   ). Betty Liu Ebron of the *New York Daily News* writes a general column that tends to focus on diversity issues.

Ebron grew up in New York City, graduating from Stuyvesant High School in 1974. She earned the B.B.A. from Baruch College in 1979 and the M.A. from Columbia University's School of Journalism in 1980.

Her career in journalism began at the *Hudson Dispatch,* where she was a police reporter during 1980–1981. She was a *Newark Star Ledger* reporter from 1981–1985, then worked for *New York Business* during 1985–1986. Ebron joined the *Daily News* in 1986, working through 1991 as a business reporter and gossip columnist. Her present column began in 1991.

Eckel, Sara (?–   ). A newcomer to syndication via the Newspaper Enterprise Association (NEA) is Sara Eckel, who began a weekly women's issues column in autumn 1994.

Eckel is a graduate of Fordham University, where she took concentrations in literature, creative writing, and women's studies. Prior to beginning her own column, she wrote for *New York Newsday* and *Eating Well* magazine and worked as an editor of some of the columnists handled by NEA and United Feature Syndicate.

Eckel's column delves into such issues as why wife-beaters tend to get lighter sentences than persons who assault strangers, women's safety, and how women's rights activists can at times exploit the very women they intend to help.

Eliot, George Fielding (22 June 1894–21 April 1971). Fielding Eliot wrote a syndicated column for General Features Syndicate on military/political affairs from 1950 to 1967.

Eliot was born in Brooklyn, New York. He moved with his father to Melbourne, Australia, when he was eight. He graduated from Melbourne University and fought during World War I with the Australian infantry, from August 1914 until November 1918. After his release from the service, he immigrated to the United States, settling in Kansas City and working as an accountant. He wrote pulp magazine war stories to make extra money and in 1928 gave up accounting for writing. He wrote for *The Infantry Journal* and other military periodicals and collaborated with R. Ernest Dupuy on a well-received book about U.S. military preparedness, *If War Comes* (1937).

In 1939 Eliot became a military writer for the *New York Herald Tribune,* and during World War II he was a CBS military analyst and commentator. He wrote a column for the *New York Post* before launching his syndicated column in 1950. Eliot also contributed to such periodicals as *New Republic, Current History, American Mercury, Harper's,* and *Fortune* and authored sixteen books.

BOOKS: *The Eagles of Death* (New York, 1930); *The Purple Legion: A G-Man Thriller* (New York, 1936); with R. Ernest Dupuy, *If War Comes* (New York, 1937); *The Military Consequences of Munich* (New York, 1938); *The Ramparts We Watch: A Study of the Problems of American National Defense* (New York, 1938); *Defending America* (New York, 1939); *Bombs Bursting in Air: The Influence of Air Power on International Relations* (New York, 1939); *Hour of Triumph* (New York, 1944); *The Strength We Need: A Military Program for America* (New York, 1946); *Hate, Hope and High Explosives: A Report on the Middle East* (Indianapolis, 1948); *If Russia Strikes—* (Indianapolis, 1949); *Caleb Pettengill, U.S.N.* (New York, 1956); *Victory Without War* (Annapolis, Md., 1958); *Sylvanus Thayer of West Point* (New York, 1959); *Reserve Forces and the Kennedy Strategy* (Harrisburg, Pa., 1962); *Daring Sea Warrior Franklin Buchanan* (New York, 1962).

Ellerbee, Linda (15 Aug. 1944–   ). Familiar television figure Linda Ellerbee began writing a weekly column for King Features in 1988. Her column appears in roughly one hundred papers.

Ellerbee was born in Bryan, Texas. She dropped out of Vanderbilt University before graduating and became a disk jockey and newscaster for WVON radio in Chicago (1964–1967). She was program director for KSJO radio in San Francisco (1967–1968) and worked for KJNO radio in Juneau, Alaska, from 1969 to 1972, when she joined the Dallas bureau of the Associated Press (AP). Six months later she was fired because of an unusual incident. She had used her terminal to write a personal letter that criticized her employer, Dallas and its newspapers, and U.S. involvement in Vietnam. She somehow sent the letter out to Texas stations, provoking an uproar that resulted in her being sacked by the AP but hired by KHOU-TV in Houston as a reporter (1972–1973).

From there Ellerbee moved to New York City and station WCBS-TV, where she was a reporter from 1973 to 1976. She moved to NBC as a Nightly News reporter out of Washington, D.C., from 1976 to 1978 and coanchor of the newsmagazine show "NBC News Weekend" from 1978 to 1982. In 1982–1983 she coanchored "NBC News Overnight" and in 1984, "Summer Sunday U.S.A."

In 1986 she switched to ABC to anchor "Our World," a historical series for which her writing won her an Emmy. In 1987 she left the network and formed her own company, Lucky Duck Productions, which makes nonfiction programs. She has authored two books about any broadcaster's favorite topic.

BOOKS: *"And So It Goes": Adventures in Television* (New York, 1986); *Move On: Adventures in the Real World* (New York, 1991).

Emory, Alan Steuer (7 May 1922–   ). Alan Emory wrote the editorial page political column "From Washington," which he began in 1951 for the *Watertown* [New York] *Daily Times*. Starting in 1954, he wrote a syndicated column for United Feature–North American Newspaper Alliance. His column appeared in roughly two hundred papers until it was discontinued in 1980.

He was born Alan Epstein in New York City and had his name legally changed to Emory in 1951. He earned the A.B. from Harvard University in 1943 and the M.S. from Columbia University in 1947.

He began his career as a city reporter for the *Watertown Daily Times* (1947–1948). He was the *Daily Times*'s state editor (1948–1949), legislative correspondent (1949–1951), and Washington correspondent (1949–1951) prior to launching his editorial page column in 1951. He was Washington correspondent for several New York papers: the *Oswego Palladium Times* (1951–1980), the *Schenectady Gazette* (1954–?), the *Middletown Record* (1956–1962), and the *Binghamton Sun Bulletin* (1962–1964). In 1959–1960 he was a correspondent for *Radio Press International.* Beginning in 1980, he worked as Washington columnist for *Empire State Report.* His syndicated column with United Feature–North American Newspaper Alliance ran from 1954 to 1980.

Emory made appearances on the NBC television program "Meet the Press" and contributed to *Nation, Business Week, Reporter,* and other periodicals.

Engram, Sara M. (6 May 1949–   ). Sara Engram writes an op-ed column on Sundays for *The Evening Sun* in Baltimore, Maryland. From 1988 to 1992, she wrote "Mortal Matters," a weekly column about death and dying; it was syndicated by Universal Press Syndicate.

Engram was born in Enterprise, Alabama. She received the B.A. in religion from Salem College in Winston-Salem, North Carolina, in 1971; the M.Ed. from Wake Forest University in 1975; and the M.Div. from Yale Divinity School in 1979. Her first job experiences (1973–1977) were in education, as an elementary school counselor in Enterprise, Alabama, and later as a career/financial adviser at the college level.

She began her career in journalism reporting on the Delaware legislature for the *Philadelphia Inquirer,* then was editorial page editor at the *Baltimore News American.* She went to the *Evening Sun* in 1981 as deputy editorial page editor and was promoted to editorial page director in January 1992. She writes editorials for both the *Sun* and the *Evening Sun.* Her present column deals with social and political issues. She has authored one book, on the subject of death and dying.

BOOKS: *Mortal Matters: When a Loved One Dies* (Kansas City, Mo., 1990).

Erbe, Bonnie (?–   ). Bonnie Erbe writes two columns for the Scripps-Howard news wire. One is a point-counterpoint column she coauthors with Betsy Hart; its focus is domestic issues. It is sent to roughly four hundred papers. The other is Erbe's solo op-ed column, which she says is built on the premise that all politics are personal. She is also host of "To the Contrary," a weekly news analysis program that airs on approximately 240 PBS stations. Finally, she is a lawyer and a legal affairs correspondent for the Mutual/NBC radio networks.

Erbe was born in New York City. She received the B.A. in English from Barnard College in 1974, the master's in journalism from Columbia University in 1975, and a law degree with honors from Georgetown University in 1987. She is a member of the D.C. and New York bars.

Most of Erbe's media experience is in broadcasting. She worked for the CBS-TV affiliate in Washington, D.C., for a year in the 1970s, then for the CBS affiliate in Tampa, Florida, for three years. She then worked in NBC-TV's Atlanta bureau as a general assignment correspondent and from 1983 to 1989 covered national politics for the United Press International (UPI) Radio Network. She joined Mutual/NBC in July 1989. Her solo column was launched in April 1994.

Evans, Medford Stanton (20 July 1934–   ). M. Stanton Evans was syndicated by the Los Angeles Times Syndicate beginning in 1974 and also wrote a *National Review* column that started two years later.

Evans was born in Kingsville, Texas. He received the B.A., Phi Beta Kappa, from Yale University in 1955 and did graduate study at New York University later that same year.

Also in 1955, Evans became assistant editor of *Freeman* in Irvington-on-Hudson, New York. In 1956 he was on the staff of *National Review,* and from 1956 to 1959 he was managing editor of *Human Events.* He was head editorial writer for the *Indianapolis News* in 1959 and 1960, then served as that paper's editor from 1960 to 1974. In addition to his column, Evans was on CBS's "Spectrum" series starting in 1971. The conservative columnist authored a number of books addressing political issues, and he was associate editor of *National Review* from 1960 to 1973 as well as a contributing editor of *Human Events* from 1968.

BOOKS: *Revolt on Campus* (Lanham, Md., 1961); *The Liberal Establishment* (New York, 1965); *The Politics of Surrender* (New York, 1966); *The Usurpers* (Boston, 1968); *The Lawbreakers: America's Number One Domestic Problem* (New Rochelle, N.Y., 1968); *The Future of Conservatism: From Taft to Reagan and Beyond* (New York, 1968); *The Assassination of Joe McCarthy* (Boston, 1970); *Clear and Present Dangers: A Conservative View of America's Government* (New York, 1975); *Champions of Freedom,* ed. by Ronald L. Trowbridge (Hillsdale, Mich., 1980).

Evans, Rowland, Jr. (28 April 1921–   ). Rowland Evans writes the political column "Inside Report" with Robert Novak. The column has appeared since 1963.

Evans was born in White Marsh, Pennsylvania. He studied at Yale University (1940–1941) and at George Washington University (1950) and was on active duty with the Marine Corps from 1942 to 1945.

Evans was an Associated Press reporter from 1945 to 1955, then worked in the editorial section of the *New York Herald Tribune* from 1955 to 1963. He has been a roving editor for *Reader's Digest* and has contributed to such magazines as *Esquire, Harper's, New Republic,* and the *Reporter.* He and Novak have been praised for the quality of reporting that goes into their column, and into the three books the two have coauthored. The two columnists have also appeared on various television programs and have cohosted CNN's "Evans and Novak" show.

BOOKS: With Robert D. Novak, *Lyndon B. Johnson: The Exercise of Power: a Political Biography* (New York, 1966); with Robert D. Novak, *Nixon in the White House: The Frustration of Power* (New York, 1971); with Robert D. Novak, *The Reagan Revolution* (New York, 1981).

F

Farrell, Francis Thomas (9 Oct. 1912–17 Feb. 1983). Frank Farrell was a columnist for the *New York World-Telegram, World-Telegram Sun,* and *World Journal Tribune* from 1947 until 1967.

Farrell was born in New York City. He received the B.S. from New York University in 1936 and studied law there during 1936–1937. In his youth he was a reporter for the *Brooklyn Standard Union* (1928–1930) and the *Brooklyn Times-Union* (1930–1936). During 1936–1937 he was assistant editor of the *New York World-Telegram*'s *Weekend Magazine,* after which he was a staff writer (1937–1939) and features editor (1939–1942) for that paper.

Farrell served in the Pacific theater as a Marine Corps officer from 1942 to 1945. He rescued Allied war prisoners, helped uncover a Nazi spy network that had operated in Japan, and took part in prosecuting Japanese war criminals after VJ Day.

Returning to civilian life, he wrote his column (1947–1967) until the *World Journal Tribune* folded, then became president of the firm PR Associates in New York.

Feder, Don (25 November 1946–). A conservative columnist in liberal Boston, Massachusetts, Don Feder, who is syndicated out of the *Boston Herald,* likes to examine traditional morality in present-day America.

Feder grew up in the Adirondack Mountains of New York. He free-lanced for various newspapers from his high school days until 1983, when he became a full-time columnist. Feder graduated cum laude in political science from Boston University in 1969, then in 1972 completed his law degree at the same institution. From 1972 to 1976 he practiced law in Johnstown, New York. Then in 1976 he became executive director of the conservative group Citizens for Limited Taxation.

In 1980 he relocated to Seattle as executive director of the Second Amendment Foundation, an organization dedicated to Americans' right to bear arms. During 1980–1981 he also wrote a column for the Bellevue (Washington) *Journal-American*. With his partner Mark Isaacs, Feder edited and published a newsletter, "On Principle," during the years 1981–1983, and in 1983 Feder became editorial director of WEEI Radio, an all-news station in Boston. The articles he free-lanced to the *Boston Herald* during the early part of 1983 led to a full-time job as a *Herald* columnist later in that same year. He is charged with writing two columns and five editorials a week.

Feder's column was picked up by Heritage Features Syndicate in 1986; in 1991 Heritage was taken over by Creators Syndicate, which presently distributes Feder's column. He has also written for *Reader's Digest, National Review,* and other magazines and has authored one book.

BOOKS: *A Jewish Conservative Looks at Pagan America* (Lafayette, La., 1993).

Field, Eugene (2 Sept. 1850–4 Nov. 1895). Eugene Field enjoys dual fame: as one of America's most admired early city columnists for his "Sharps and Flats," which appeared in the *Chicago Morning News* from 1883 to 1895, and as one of the best loved children's poets for his "Wynken, Blynken, and Nod," "Little Boy Blue," and other similar efforts.

Field was born in St. Louis, Missouri. He attended three colleges, Williams College, Knox College, and the University of Missouri, but never completed a degree.

In 1873 Field began working for a succession of newspapers: the *St. Louis Evening Journal* as a reporter (1873–1875); the *St. Joseph Gazette,* where he was city editor for one year; the *St. Louis Times-Journal* as an editorial writer and writer of the column "Funny Fancies" for four years; the *Kansas City Times* for one year as managing editor; and in 1880 the *Denver Times* as managing editor and columnist ("Odds and Ends"). In 1883 he moved to Chicago to write a column for Melville Stone's *Chicago Morning News*. His original column title was "Current Gossip," but after a few days he changed it to the more interesting "Sharps and Flats," which he borrowed from a play he had attended. It was this six-days-a-week column roughly two thousand words long that earned him a lasting reputation among columnists. He is sometimes referred to today as the first American columnist, although he was not, yet his column was indeed one of the truly outstanding early city columns and served as a model for many writers who followed him. Sometimes the column was serious; often it was funny. He included both prose and verse and showed a marked interest in sports, especially baseball and boxing. He often printed the work of other writers, and, forever fond of pranks and practical jokes, occasionally attributed some of his own work to other people. He continued his column until his death. He wrote and published just under twenty books, and many of his children's poems were first published in magazines such as *Ladies' Home Journal* and *Youth's Companion.* Field was also a dedicated bibliophile, whose private library contained about thirty-five hundred books.

BOOKS: *The Tribune Primer* (Denver, 1881); *Culture's Garland: Being Memoranda of the Gradual Rise of Literature, Art, Music and Society in Chicago, and Other Western Ganglia* (Boston, 1887); *A Little Book of Profitable Tales* (Chicago, 1889); *A Little Book of Western Verse* (Chicago, 1889); with Roswell M. Field, *Echoes from the Sabine Farm* (New Rochelle, N.Y., 1891); *With Trumpet and Drum* (New York, 1892); *Second Book of Verse* (Chicago, 1892); *The Holy-Cross and Other Tales* (Cambridge and Chicago, 1893); *Love-Songs of Childhood* (New York, 1894); *The Love Affairs of a Bibliomaniac* (New York, 1896); *The House: An Episode in the Lives of Reuben Baker, Astronomer, and of His Wife Alice* (New York, 1896); *Songs and Other Verse* (New York, 1896); *Second Book of Tales* (New York, 1896); *Sharps and Flats,* 2 vols., comp. by Slason Thompson (New York, 1900); *A Little Book of Tribune Verse,* ed. by Joseph G. Brown (Denver, 1901); *Nonsense for Old and Young* (Boston, 1901); *The Stars: A Slumber Story* (New York, 1901); *Hoosier Lyrics,* ed. by Charles W. Brown (Chicago, 1905).

REFERENCES: Ida Comstock Below, *Eugene Field in His Home* (New York, 1898); Robert Conrow, *Field Days: The Life, Times, and Reputation of Eugene Field* (New York, 1974); Charles H. Dennis, *Eugene Field's Creative Years* (Garden City, N.Y., 1924); Slason Thompson, *Eugene Field: A Study in Heredity and Contradictions,* 2 vols. (New York, 1901); Slason Thompson, *Life of Eugene Field, The Poet of Childhood* (New York, 1927).

Fields, Suzanne (7 March 1936–   ). Suzanne Fields writes a syndicated general interest column from the *Washington Times* in Washington, D.C. She is syndicated by the Los Angeles Times Syndicate.

Fields was born in Washington, D.C. She received the B.A. with honors (1957) and the M.A. (1965) from George Washington University and the Ph.D. (1971) from Catholic University.

Fields taught English literature at Catholic University from 1965 to 1970 and was editor of *Innovations* magazine from 1971 to 1981. She has authored one book.

BOOKS: *Like Father Like Daughter: How Father Shapes the Woman His Daughter Becomes* (Boston, 1983).

Fitzgerald, James E. (5 Aug. 1926–   ). Veteran columnist Jim Fitzgerald has written a general humor column for the *Detroit Free Press* since 1976.

Born in Port Harbor, Michigan, Fitzgerald received a B.A. from Michigan State University in 1951.

After serving in World War II, Fitzgerald worked from 1951 until 1976 as ad salesman, reporter, and for fifteen years editor for the Lapeer (Michigan) *County Press.* For most of those years he wrote a column, as well. In 1976 he became a columnist for the *Free Press* in Detroit; his column is modestly syndicated. Some of the papers that carry the column run it under the column title "If It Fitz."

BOOKS: *If It Fitz: The Best of Jim Fitzgerald* (Detroit, 1985).

Fleeson, Doris (20 May 1901–1 Aug. 1970). Tough but liberal columnist Doris Fleeson did her first column for the *New York Daily News* (1933–1943), then was syndicated by the Bell Syndicate (1945–1954) and United Feature Syndicate (1954–1969).

Fleeson was born in Sterling, Kansas. She earned the B.A. from the University of Kansas in 1923, then became a reporter for the *Pittsburg* [Kansas] *Sun*. She moved to Evanston, Illinois, as society editor of the *News-Index,* then to Long Island, New York, as city editor of the *Great Neck News.* Finally, in 1927, she realized her goal of getting on a metropolitan daily when she became a general assignment reporter for the *New York Daily News.* Several years later she was sent to Albany to cover state politics. She married fellow reporter John O'Donnell in 1930, and after the couple were transferred to the paper's Washington bureau, they cowrote the column "Capitol Stuff" from 1933 until their divorce in 1942.

Fleeson left the *Daily News* in May 1943 and during 1943–1944 was a war correspondent for *Woman's Home Companion.* She covered the war in France and Italy, and when she returned to the United States, started writing a political column for the *Boston Globe* and the *Washington Evening Star.* The five-times-a-week column was picked up in 1945 by the Bell Syndicate and in 1954 by United Feature Syndicate. At its peak around 1960, Fleeson's column was in roughly one hundred papers. She was a great admirer of Eleanor Roosevelt and Adlai Stevenson but was a sharp critic of those less statesmanlike politicians who in her opinion had succumbed to what she termed "Potomac fever." Her fellow columnist Mary McGrory once called her "a tiger in white gloves," and President John F. Kennedy remarked that he preferred being "Krocked" to being "Fleesonized."

Fleeson was instrumental in founding the American Newspaper Guild in 1933 and served as president of the Women's National Press Club in 1937.

REFERENCES: Barbara Belford, *Brilliant Bylines* (New York, 1986): 259–269; "Core of the Corps," *Time* 58 (9 July 1951): 55; "Hundreds of Washington Bylines Daily . . . and Here Are Some Big Ones," *Newsweek* 54 (18 December 1961): 68–69; Ishbel Ross, *Ladies of the Press* (New York, 1974): 350–352.

Floyd, E. Randall (12 Aug. 1947–). E. Randall Floyd teaches history at Augusta College in Augusta, Georgia, and self-syndicates the column "Mysteries" to about sixty-five papers.

Floyd was born in Hazelhurst, Georgia, and received the B.A. in modern foreign languages in 1977 and the M.A. in history in 1984 from Valdosta State University.

He entered newspaper work as a reporter for *Stars and Stripes* during the war in Vietnam. He was a reporter and copy editor for the *Florida Times-Union* in Jacksonville (1970–1972), a reporter in Europe for United Press International (1972–1974), and state editor of the *Valdosta Daily Times* (1974–1977). He edited and published his own regional magazine, *High Country Living,* in Boone, North Carolina, from 1977 until 1984, when he joined the journalism faculty at Georgia Southern University in Statesboro. He joined the history department at Augusta College in 1988. "Mysteries" was formerly published as "American Mysteries." In its revised format, the column is international in scope and focuses on historical and scientific oddities and curiosities.

BOOKS: *Great Southern Mysteries* (Little Rock, Ark., 1989); *More Great Southern Mysteries* (Little Rock, Ark., 1990); *Great American Mysteries* (Little Rock, Ark., 1991); *Ghost Lights and Other Encounters with the Unknown* (Little Rock, Ark., 1993).

Frazier, George (10 June 1911–13 June 1974). A grand eccentric among columnists was George Frazier, a daily columnist from 1961 to 1965 for the *Boston Herald* and a four-times-weekly columnist for the *Boston Globe* from 1970 to 1974. He also wrote a column for *Esquire* magazine from 1967 to 1974.

Frazier was born in Boston. He received the A.B. in 1933 from Harvard University. Though born of humble lineage, Frazier molded himself into a sort of do-it-yourself Boston Brahmin. The dapper, well-starched, Brooks Brothers–clad Frazier affected a snobbish air that did not endear him to all. He was, for example, once selected by Boston feminists as the city's worst "male chauvinist pig." Awarded a muzzle as part of this honor, he had it bronzed and hung over his mantel.

He began as a free-lancer, then from 1941 to 1946 was *Life*'s entertainment editor. He wrote about books, jazz, theater, film, and sports for various magazines and served as media critic for "CBS Morning News" and as a commentator for Boston's WNAC-TV.

Among Frazier's favorite targets were politicians, feminists, hunters, sportscaster Howard Cosell, and anyone who dressed in poor taste. He was fired from the *Boston Globe* in 1971 for making sport of how some of that paper's reporters were dressed for a television show but was rehired after hiring a plane to trail a banner reading, "Bring back George Frazier." Among his other eccentric acts was once reporting a Yankee–Red Sox baseball game in Latin.

BOOKS: *The One with the Mustache Is Costello* (New York, 1947).

REFERENCES: Charles Fountain, *Another Man's Poison: The Life and Writings of Columnist George Frazier* (Chester, Conn., 1984).

Freeman, Gregory Bruce (18 Aug. 1956–   ). Gregory Freeman writes a political and social commentary column titled "Urban View" for the *St. Louis Post-Dispatch.*

Freeman was born in St. Louis, Missouri, and in 1978 received the B.A. from Washington University.

His first journalistic experience was as reporter and later associate editor for the *St. Louis American* (1977–1978). He then moved to Pontiac, Michigan, where he was a reporter for the *Oakland Press* (1978–1979), then for the Belleville (Illinois) *News-Democrat* (1979–1980). He joined the *St. Louis Post-Dispatch* in 1980 as a reporter and also served as assistant night city editor and assistant city editor before launching his column in 1989. Freeman also does weekly commentaries for KWMU radio and KXOK-FM in St. Louis. He has been president of the Press Club of Metropolitan St. Louis, his city's chapter of the Society of Professional Journalists, and the Greater St. Louis Association of Black Journalists.

Freidin, Seymour Kenneth (27 April 1917–). Seymour Freidin was a columnist with the *New York Post* syndicate from 1949 to 1961 and is also remembered for his long years as a foreign correspondent.

Freidin was born in New York City and studied at Columbia University and the University of Vienna. He was a *New York Herald Tribune* reporter and foreign correspondent from 1936 to 1949. In 1949 he began his column but continued for some years to do foreign correspondence out of Europe for the *Herald Tribune* and for *Collier's* magazine. He was a prolific contributor to U.S. magazines and authored four books.

BOOKS: *Fatal Decisions* (New York, 1956); *The Forgotten People* (New York, 1962); with George Bailey, *The Experts* (New York, 1968); *A Sense of the Senate* (New York, 1972).

Friddell, Guy (14 April 1921–). The dean of Virginia columnists, Guy Friddell has been with Norfolk's *Virginian-Pilot* since 1963.

Friddell is a Georgia native who began public school in Atlanta, where he edited and published a periodical titled *Community Life,* circulation sixty, while in fifth grade. He later moved with his family to Richmond, Virginia, where he graduated from Thomas Jefferson High School. He received his bachelor's degree at the University of Richmond (Virginia) and a master's from the Columbia University School of Journalism.

Friddell's long career has included work as a city hall reporter for the *Lynchburg* (Virginia) *News* (now the *News and Advance*), county reporter for the Nyack, New York., *Journal-News,* and for the twelve years preceding his present job, political writer for the Richmond, Virginia, *News-Leader.*

His column currently appears in the *Virginian-Pilot* and in Norfolk's other paper, the *Ledger-Star.* Friddell also holds the title of special writer for Landmark News Service. His longtime specialty is politics, yet his columns range widely in subject matter. He has written nine books, most of which are about his adopted state, Virginia.

BOOKS: *Jackstraws* (Richmond, Va., 1961); *I Hate You, I Love You* (Garden City, N.Y., 1965); *What Is It About Virginia?* (Richmond, Va., 1966); *We Began at Jamestown* (Richmond, Va., 1968); *The Virginia Way* (Offenbach, W. Germany, 1973); with Wolfgang Roth, *Washington, D.C., the Open City* (Richmond, Va., 1974); *Colgate Darden: Conversations with Guy Friddell* (Charlottesville, Va., 1978); *Miracle at Yorktown* (Richmond, Va., 1981); *Hello, Hampton Roads* (Richmond, Va., 1987).

Fritchey, Clayton (circa 1905–). Clayton Fritchey was a syndicated political columnist during the 1960s. During a part of this period, he also was a special assistant to the U.S. ambassador to the United Nations.

Fritchey was born in Bellefontaine, Ohio. His career in journalism began in 1924; he was a *Baltimore American* reporter. In 1944 he became editor of the *New Orleans Item,* holding this position until 1950. From 1950 to 1952 he was director of the public relations bureau of the Department of Defense and was an assistant to the secretary of defense. A liberal Democrat, Fritchey was an assistant to President Harry Truman in 1952 and was deputy chairman of the Democratic National Committee from 1953 to 1957. During these years he also edited *Democratic Digest,* the organ of the Democratic National Committee, and in 1956 he was press secretary to Adali Stevenson in the latter's second bid for the presidency.

Fritchey bought the *Northern Virginia Sun* in Arlington in 1957; he published the paper until 1961. From 1961 to 1965 he was a special assistant to the ambassador to the United Nations and also began writing his column.

Frye, William Ruggles (15 Dec. 1918–). Longtime *Christian Science Monitor* staffer William R. Frye wrote a weekly column titled "World in Focus" starting in 1957.

Fyre was born in Detroit, Michigan. He earned the B.A., cum laude, from Harvard University in 1940, then went to work for the *Monitor* as a reporter. From 1941 to 1946 he served in the army and for part of that period was on the staff of *Stars and Stripes.*

From 1946 to 1950 Frye was assistant foreign editor of the *Monitor,* and from 1950 to 1963 he was head of the paper's United Nations bureau. In 1963 he formed his own firm, the Frye Syndicate, writing about the UN and U.S. diplomacy. Another of his self-syndicated features was "Diplomatic Pouch," a commentary on news events. A third column, "Footloose with Frye," a travel series, still appears. He also authored three books in the 1950s and 1960s.

BOOKS: *Disarmament: Atoms into Plowshares?* (New York, 1955); *A United Nations Peace Force* (London, 1957); *In Whitest Africa: The Dynamics of Apartheid* (Englewood Cliffs, N.J., 1968).

Fuentes, Carlos (11 Nov. 1928–). The prominent Mexican writer, former ambassador, and educator Carlos Fuentes began writing a monthly column for the New York Times Syndicate in 1993.

Fuentes, the son of a Mexican diplomat, was born in Panama City, Panama. He studied law, earning the LL.B. in 1948 from the National University of Mexico, after which he did graduate study in international law at the Institute des Hautes Etudes in Geneva, Switzerland. He worked in Geneva as a writer for the International Labor Organization and as secretary of the Mexican delegation until 1952, then returned to Mexico City to become assistant chief of the press section of the Ministry of Foreign Affairs. In 1955–1959 he was an official of the National University of Mexico.

In 1955 Fuentes and Emmanuel Carballo founded the *Revista Mexicana de Literatura,* a bimonthly literary periodical of which Fuentes was editor until 1958. From 1959 to 1961 he was editor of *El Espectador,* and in 1960 he edited *Politica and Siempre.* It was during these years that he began his career as a serious author of short stories and novels.

Fuentes was Mexico's ambassador to France from 1975 to 1977, after which he has held numerous prestigious teaching posts: at the University of Pennsylvania, Harvard, Cambridge, the University of Paris, and several other schools.

He has been a highly prolific writer and has won innumerable literary awards. Several of his books have been translated into English.

BOOKS: *Where the Air Is Clear* (New York, 1960); *The Good Conscience* (New York, 1961); *Aura* (New York, 1962); *The Argument of Latin America: Words for North Americans* (Ann Arbor, Mich., 1963); *The Death of Artemio Cruz* (New York, 1964); *Aura* (New York, 1965); *A Change of Skin* (New York, 1968); *Holy Place* (New York, 1972); *Terra Nostra* (New York, 1976); *Hydra Head* (New York, 1978); *Burnt Water* (New York, 1980); *Distant Relations* (New York, 1982); *On Human Rights: A Speech* (Dallas, Tex., 1984); *The Old Gringo* (New York, 1985); *Myself with Others: Selected Essays* (New York, 1988); *Christopher Unborn* (New York, 1989); *Constancia and Other Stories* (New York, 1990); *The Campaign* (New York, 1991); *The Hurried Mirror* (New York, 1992); *Witnesses of Time* (New York, 1992); *The Orange Tree* (New York, 1994).

Furgurson, Ernest Baker, Jr. (29 Aug. 1929–   ). Ernest Furgurson was a national affairs columnist for the *Baltimore Sun* from 1964 and began being syndicated by the Los Angeles Times Syndicate in 1970.

Furgurson was born in Danville, Virginia. He studied at Averett College from 1948 to 1950, then received both the A.B. (1952) and the M.S. (1953) from Columbia University. He served in the Marine Corps from 1953 to 1955. He then did a year's postgraduate work at Georgetown University in 1961.

While at Averett College, Furgurson worked as a reporter for the Danville *Commercial Appeal* (1948–1951) and as sports editor of radio station WDVA (1949–1950). He reported for the *Roanoke* [Virginia] *World-News* during part of 1952 and from 1955 to 1956 was a reporter for the *Richmond* [Virginia] *News Leader.* He was a *Baltimore Sun* reporter in 1956–1961, the *Sun*'s Moscow bureau chief (1961–1964), and the paper's Saigon correspondent in 1964. Starting in 1975 he was the *Sun*'s Washington bureau head. Furgurson has written three books.

BOOKS: *Westmoreland: The Inevitable General* (Boston, 1968); *Hard Right: The Rise of Jesse Helms* (New York, 1986); *Chancellorsville: The Souls of the Brave* (New York, 1992).

G

Gabriele, Tony (26 Aug. 1947–   ). Tony Gabriele's thrice-weekly humor column "Get Serious!" appears in the Newport News (Virginia) *Daily Press.*

Gabriele was born in New York City, grew up there and in New Jersey, and received the B.A. from Rutgers University in 1968.

Gabriele worked for part of 1968 as a reporter for the *Daily Register* of Red Bank, New Jersey, then served a two-year hitch in the U.S. Army. In 1971 he became a reporter and weekly columnist for another New Jersey paper, the *News Tribune,* in Woodbridge. He left that paper in 1987 to assume his present duties with the Newport News *Daily Press.* One of his columns per week has been distributed nationally by KRTN Wire Service since 1990.

Garchik, Leah (2 May 1945–   ). Leah Garchik has been a columnist with the *San Francisco Chronicle* since 1984.

Garchik was born in Brooklyn, New York, and earned the B.A., with honors, in creative writing from Brooklyn College in 1966. Her first job was as a secretary to a Yale professor who was editing the prose works of the poet John Milton.

Garchik has been with the *Chronicle* since 1972, initially as a part-time steno clerk and editorial assistant (1972–1979), then as a full-time writer/editor (1979–1983). She has written book reviews and feature articles, some of which have been profiles of modern American authors. From 1983 to 1984 she was editor of *This World* magazine, then began her column with the *Chronicle* in 1984. Run under the title "Personals," her frequently satirical column tends to cover the well-to-do or famous. It is, she says, a humor/items column; it is distributed via the New York Times wire. She also reviews movies for the *Chronicle;* her favorites are baseball films. She is a panelist on the KPFA quiz show "Minds over Matter" and is a bell-ringer in a German polka band.

Gardner, Hy (2 Dec. 1908–17 June 1989). Hy Gardner was a Broadway columnist for the *New York Herald Tribune* from 1951 to 1966. Starting in 1967, he and his wife, Marilyn Gardner, cowrote the gossip column "Glad You Asked That," syndicated by the Field Newspaper Syndicate. He also wrote a column in *Parade*.

Gardner was born in New York City. He attended Columbia University but did not complete a degree. He served as an army officer from 1942 to 1945.

Gardner first worked in advertising before launching his column for the *Herald Tribune*. He edited *Trib TV* in addition to writing the column. He was host of various radio and television programs, including the "Hy Gardner TV Show" and "Hy Gardner Calling." He was also a panelist on the CBS-TV program "To Tell the Truth." Gardner had a brief fling with Hollywood, acting in *The Girl Hunters* and producing *Hi-Yank*. Gardner wrote or cowrote five books.

BOOKS: *Champagne Before Breakfast* (New York, 1954); *So What Else Is New!* (Englewood Cliffs, N.J., 1959); *Tales out of Night School* (New York, 1959); *Hy Gardner's Offbeat Guide to New York* (New York, 1964); with Marilyn Gardner, *Glad You Asked That* (New York, 1976).

Gary, Weller Kays (28 Oct. 1920–). Kays Gary, now retired from day to day journalism, still writes his column on an occasional basis for the *Charlotte* (North Carolina) *Observer*.

Gary was born in Springfield, Kentucky. He received the A.B. in journalism in 1942 at the University of North Carolina, Chapel Hill.

Gary's career began with an editing job at the *Thomasville Tribune* in 1942. In November 1945 he moved to another North Carolina paper, the *Shelby Daily Star*, where he worked as sports editor and feature writer until November 1951 and doubled as a stringer for the *Charlotte Observer*. He chose to work solely with the *Observer* in 1951, remaining there as human interest columnist and reporter until his retirement in 1986. He has covered every beat, he says, except the women's pages.

Gary has published one book: a collection of his columns.

BOOKS: *Kays Gary, Columnist* (Charlotte, N.C., 1981).

Geist, William E. (circa 1945–). Droll humorist Bill Geist conducted the *New York Times* column "About New York" from 1980 to 1987. The column was originated by Meyer Berger in 1939, ran through 1940, then was written by Berger again from 1953 to 1959.

Geist is a graduate of the University of Illinois and also is a journalism graduate of the University of Missouri. He was an army photographer in Vietnam, after which he was employed at the *Chicago Tribune* until joining the *New*

York Times in 1980. He has been a reporter/commentator for CBS since 1987, contributing to the evening news and to ''Sunday Morning with Charles Kuralt.'' He has authored five humor books.

BOOKS: *Millicent Fenwick, Marching to Her Own Drum* (New York, 1982); *Toward a Safe and Sane Halloween and Other Tales of Suburbia* (New York, 1985); *Merchandising Dr. Ruth* (New York, 1985); *City Slickers* (New York, 1987); *Little League Confidential: One Coach's Completely Unauthorized Tale of Survival* (New York, 1992).

Gelb, Leslie Howard (4 March 1937–   ). Leslie H. Gelb began writing the *New York Times*'s foreign affairs column in January 1991.

Gelb was born in New Rochelle, New York. He earned the A.B., magna cum laude, from Tufts University in 1959 and the M.A. (1961) and Ph.D. (1964) from Harvard University. In 1964–1965 he taught political science at Wesleyan University, then spent 1966–1967 as an assistant to Sen. Jacob Javits.

Gelb joined the U.S. Department of Defense in 1967, working in international security affairs and as director of the department's Vietnam Task Force. He was acting deputy assistant secretary of defense for policy planning and arms control in 1968–1969. From 1969 to 1973 he was a fellow at the Brookings Institution. He was diplomatic correspondent of the *New York Times* from 1973 to 1976, then returned to the State Department as director of the Bureau of Politico-Military Affairs and chief arms control negotiator for the SALT III agreement, 1977–1979. After spending 1979–1981 at the Carnegie Endowment for International Peace, Gelb returned to the *Times* as national security correspondent. He later became deputy editorial page editor and op-ed page editor of the *Times* before launching his twice-weekly column in 1991. He has authored or coauthored three books.

BOOKS: With Richard Betts, *The Irony of Vietnam: The System Worked* (Washington, D.C., 1979); *Our Own Worst Enemy: The Unmaking of American Foreign Policy* (New York, 1984); *Anglo-American Relations, 1945–1949: Toward a Theory of Alliances* (New York, 1988).

Geller, Uri (20 Dec. 1946–   ). One of the most unusual columnists of them all, Uri Geller, paranormal performer, began writing a syndicated column in 1975.

Geller was born in Tel Aviv, Israel; moved with his mother to the island of Cyprus, where he studied at Terra Santa College; then returned to Israel and served in the Israeli Paratroopers (1965–1968). He was wounded in the Six-Day War in 1967.

After his release from military duty, Geller worked as a photographer's model until becoming a performer/entertainer in 1970. His act was, in essence, a magic show, involving mental telepathy, the starting of broken watches, and the bending of metal objects without applying direct pressure. Geller came to the United States in 1972 and put his unusual talents to the test at the Stanford Research Institute, with inconclusive results. His performances in America began in 1973, after which he took up residence in New York City. While some believe he has genuine paranormal powers, others, such as the professional magician James Zwinge ("The Amazing Randi"), consider him a fraud. Geller has published four books.

BOOKS: *My Story* (New York, 1975); *Pampini* (New York, 1980); with Guy Lyon Playfair, *The Geller Effect* (New York, 1986); *Uri Geller's Fortune Secrets* (London, 1986).

REFERENCES: Martin Ebon, ed., *Amazing Uri Geller* (New York, 1976); Andrija Puharich, *Uri* (New York, 1974).

Germond, Jack W. (30 Jan. 1928–   ). Experienced reporter Jack Germond is three times a columnist: in the *Washington Star* (1977), in the *Baltimore Evening Sun* from 1981, and, with Jules Witcover, in "Politics Today," syndicated by Tribune Media Services since 1977.

Germond was born in Newton, Massachusetts. He served in the army from 1946 to 1947 and in 1951 received both the B.A. and B.S. degrees from the University of Missouri. From 1951 to 1953 he wrote sports, then city news, then political news for the *Evening News* in Monroe, Michigan. He was hired in 1953 as a reporter for the *Rochester* [New York] *Times-Union* and worked there and for other Gannett papers until 1973. He served as head of Gannett's Washington bureau from 1969 to 1973, then joined the *Washington Star* as its political editor (1974–1981). He was the *Star*'s assistant managing editor and wrote a column in 1977.

The Germond-Witcover column is mainly concerned with the national political scene. Both men also do television commentary and have coauthored four books on national politics.

BOOKS: All with Jules Witcover, *Blue Smoke and Mirrors: How Reagan Won and Why Carter Lost the Election of 1980* (New York, 1981); *Wake Us When It's Over: Presidential Politics of 1984* (New York, 1985); *Whose Broad Stripes and Bright Stars? The Trivial Pursuit of the Presidency* (New York, 1989); *Mad as Hell: Revolt at the Ballot Box, 1992* (New York, 1993).

Geyelin, Philip Laussat (27 Feb. 1923–   ). Philip Geyelin has written columns for the *Wall Street Journal* and *Washington Post* and has served as editorial page editor of the latter paper.

He was born in Devon, Pennsylvania. He received the B.A. at Yale in 1944, then served in the Marine Corps until 1946. Geyelin was employed by the Associated Press in its Washington bureau (1946–1947), after which he spent 1947–1967 with the *Wall Street Journal*. He joined the editorial page staff of the *Washington Post* in 1967 and became editor of its editorial page in 1968. Geyelin won the Pulitzer Prize for editorial writing in 1969. He has authored or coauthored two books.

BOOKS: *Lyndon B. Johnson and the World* (New York, 1966); with Douglass Cater, *American Media: Adequate or Not?* (Washington, D.C., 1970).

Geyer, Georgie Ann (2 April 1935–). Accomplished foreign correspondent Georgie Anne Geyer has been a syndicated columnist since 1975: with the Los Angeles Times Syndicate from 1975 to 1980 and since 1980 with Universal Press Syndicate.

Geyer was born in Chicago and received the B.S. from Northwestern University in 1956. During her junior year, she studied for three months at the University of Mexico, and after graduation, studied on a Fulbright Scholarship at the University of Vienna during 1976–1977.

She began her career as a reporter for Chicago's *Southtown Economist* in 1958. In 1959 she was hired by the *Chicago Daily News* and from 1964 to 1975 was a foreign correspondent for that paper, at first working in Latin America, then in other parts of the world. Geyer speaks German, Russian, Portuguese, and Spanish. Her thrice-weekly column is now handled by Universal Press Syndicate. During her long career, she has interviewed an impressive array of world leaders, among them the Ayatollah Khomeini, PLO leader Yassar Arafat, King Hussein of Jordan, Khaddafy, Prince Sihanouk of Cambodia, and Juan Peron. In 1966 she located and interviewed escaped Nazi Walter Rauff in Chile, in 1973 she was detained as an Israeli spy, and in 1976 she was incarcerated in Angola. Her goal, she has said, is to explain one part of the world to the others via interpretative journalism. In doing so, she reports not only on events, but on attitudes and ideas.

Geyer has contributed to many magazines, including *New Republic, Atlantic, Saturday Review, Progressive, National Observer,* and *Look,* and has authored a number of books.

BOOKS: *The New Latins: Fateful Change in South and Central America* (Garden City, N.Y., 1970); *The New 100 Years War* (Garden City, N.Y., 1972); *The Young Russians* (Homewood, Ill., 1975); *Buying the Night Flight: The Autobiography of a Woman Foreign Correspondent* (New York, 1983); *Guerrilla Prince: The Untold Story of Fidel Castro* (Boston, 1991); *Waiting for Winter to End: An Extraordinary Journey Through Soviet Central Asia* (Washington, D.C., 1994).

Giago, Tim Allen (12 July 1934–). One of the biggest names in Native American journalism today is Tim Giago, publisher of the *Lakota Times/Indian Country Today* and writer of the nationally syndicated column "Notes from Indian Country."

Giago, whose Lakota tribal name is Nanwica Kciji, was born on the Pine Ridge Indian Reservation. He attended and graduated from the Holy Rosary Mission School, studied at San Jose State College in California, and earned the B.S. in 1961 from the University of Nevada. Giago also spent 1991 as a Nieman Fellow at Harvard University.

From 1967 to 1973 he worked for J. C. Penney and owned a doughnut shop. He began his career in journalism with the *Farmington Daily News* (1974–1979), then was with the *Rapid City* [South Dakota] *Journal* from 1979 to 1980. He has been in his present position since 1980. His column, as its title implies, is mainly concerned with issues of importance to Native Americans. Giago has written or edited three books.

BOOKS: *The Aboriginal Sin* (San Francisco, Calif., 1978); *Notes from Indian Country* (N.p., 1984); ed., *The American Indian and the Media* (Minneapolis, 1991).

Gilbreth, Frank Bunker, Jr. (17 March 1911–   ). Under the pen name "Ashley Cooper," Frank Gilbreth wrote a humorous items column for over forty years in the *Charleston* [South Carolina] *News and Courier.*

Gilbreth was born in Plainfield, New Jersey, the eldest son of the family made famous by the book and film *Cheaper by the Dozen.* His parents were efficiency engineers who pioneered the management device they called time-and-motion study. Gilbreth Jr. spent one year as a student at St. John's College in Maryland, then completed his B.A. in 1933 at the University of Michigan, where he was managing editor of the *Michigan Daily.*

After college, he worked as a reporter for the *New York Herald* for about a year, then moved to Charleston as a police reporter on the *News and Courier.* In 1936 he became night editor for the Associated Press (AP) in Raleigh, North Carolina, working there until 1942, when he entered the navy. There he was an aerial photographer and aide to Rear Admiral Frank D. Wagner in the Pacific. In 1945 he returned to the AP in Raleigh. In 1947 he again moved to Charleston as a *News and Courier* editorial writer. With his sister, Ernestine Carey, he wrote a best-selling family memoir, *Cheaper by the Dozen* (1948), and two years later, a second, *Belles on Their Toes* (1950). Both books were made into movies by Twentieth Century Fox.

Gilbreth moved up to associate editor of the *News and Courier* in 1951, and in 1957 became assistant publisher. In 1958 he became vice president of Packet Motor Lines and in 1962 became an executive with Aiken (South Carolina) Communications and Aiken Cablevision.

His column, "Doing the Charleston," first appeared in the late 1940s and ran until 20 February 1993. His penname was borrowed from Anthony Ashley Cooper, Lord Ashley and the first earl of Shaftesbury, an English aristocrat who figured in Charleston's founding. This unusual persona was well suited to his city, which considers itself an aristocrat among U.S. municipalities. His column often defended historic preservation in Charleston from the onslaughts of developers. It also represented the humorous side of Charleston society. Charlestonians, he wrote, similar to the Chinese, eat rice and worship their ancestors. By his own count, Gilbreth wrote a total of around thirteen thousand columns in the guise of "Lord Ashley."

BOOKS: With Ernestine Gilbreth Carey, *Cheaper by the Dozen* (New York, 1948); *Belles on Their Toes* (New York, 1950); *I'm a Lucky Guy* (New York, 1951); with John Held, Jr., *Held's Angels* (New York, 1952); *Inside Nantucket* (New York, 1954); *Of Whales and Women* (New York, 1956); *How to Be a Father* (New York, 1958); *Loblolly* (New York, 1959); *He's My Boy* (New York, 1962); *Time Out for Happiness* (New York, 1970); *Ashley Cooper's Doing the Charleston* (Charleston, S.C., 1993).

Gilles, T. J. (?–   ). T. J. Gilles was until 1994 columnist and agriculture editor for the *Great Falls Tribune* in Great Falls, Montana.

Gilles was born in Laurel, Montana, and studied journalism at the University of Montana (1967–1970).

From 1971 to 1980 he was a reporter for livestock industry newspapers and magazines in Montana, and from 1973 to 1980 he was also a farmer-rancher in the area of Laurel, Montana. He was editor of *Roustabout* magazine in Shelby, Montana, and a sportscaster for KSEN Radio (1981–1982), then became managing editor of the Denver (Colorado) *Record Stockman* (1982–1984). He joined the Great Falls paper as agriculture editor in 1984.

Gilliam, Dorothy Butler (24 Nov. 1936–   ). Dorothy Gilliam has been with the *Washington Post* for more than twenty years; since 1979 she has written a column about life in the nation's capital.

She was born Dorothy Butler in Memphis, Tennessee. She studied at Ursuline College from 1953 to 1955, then transferred to Lincoln University in Jefferson City, Missouri, where she received the B.A., cum laude, in 1957. She went on to earn the M.S. in journalism from Columbia University in 1961, after which she worked for three years as a reporter specializing in welfare issues for the *Washington Post.* From 1964 to 1971 she was a reporter for WTTG-TV in Washington, D.C., on the program "Panorama," for which she won an Emmy.

Gilliam returned to the *Post* in 1972 and became an assistant editor of the Style section. She began writing her twice-weekly column in 1979. She has written one book.

BOOKS: *Paul Robeson, All-American* (Washington, D.C., 1976).

Gilmer, Elizabeth Meriwether (18 Nov. 1861–16 Dec. 1951). Elizabeth Gilmer began writing a personal advice column as "Dorothy Dix" in the late 1890s for the *New Orleans Picayune* and took her column national via three syndicates from 1901 to 1949.

She was born Elizabeth Meriwether on a large farm in Montgomery County, Tennessee. The family moved to another Tennessee community, Clarksville, where Elizabeth attended the Female Academy of Clarksville. Her only other formal education was a six-month term at Hollins Institute in Virginia. She married early, had a nervous breakdown, and recuperated on the Gulf Coast of Mississippi, where her next-door neighbor was Mrs. E. J. Nicholson, owner of the *New Orleans Picayune.* At Mrs. Nicholson's direction, Gilmer was "tutored" in journalism by *Picayune* managing editor Nathaniel Burbank. At first she covered women's organizations, church meetings, and the like. Later she began writing about people's personal problems for the Sunday paper, using the pen name "Dorothy Dix." Dix was derived from "Mr. Dicks," an old family servant of whom she was fond, and Dorothy was picked for its alliterative value.

When she was given a regular *Picayune* column as Dorothy Dix, she called it ''Sunday Salad.''

Some of her columns began to be used by other papers in or around 1900, including the *New York Journal.* In that year, the *Journal* also asked Gilmer to locate and interview Carry Nation, the intemperate temperance advocate. She did so and in 1901 was hired by the *Journal,* where she wrote her column, short stories, and black dialect sketches. She also achieved a reputation as a crack reporter of major crimes and trials and, under the paper's free-spending owner, William Randolph Hearst, was reportedly the highest paid woman reporter in the United States. In addition, she wrote often for Hearst's magazines, mainly *Good Housekeeping* and *Cosmopolitan,* sometimes as Dorothy Dix, sometimes under her actual name.

She left the *Journal* in 1916 after signing with the Wheeler Syndicate, and moved to New Orleans, where she worked out of her home for the remainder of her writing career. She switched to the Ledger Syndicate in 1923 and shortly thereafter had considerable success with a book titled *Dorothy Dix—Her Book: Every-Day Help for Every-Day People* (1926). From 1942 to 1949 her column was handled by the Bell Syndicate. Her mail from men and women who wanted advice about their problems sometimes came in at more than two thousand letters a week, and through her innovative handling of this new kind of column, in which she concentrated more on practical advice than flowery language, she died a millionaire. Her eight books, as well as her famous column, were written as Dorothy Dix.

BOOKS: *Fables of the Elite* (New York, 1902); *Mirandy* (New York, 1914); *Hearts a la Mode* (New York, 1915); *My Joy-Ride Round the World* (London, 1922); *Mirandy Exhorts* (Philadelphia, 1925); *Dorothy Dix—Her Book: Every-Day Help for Every-Day People* (New York and London, 1926); *Mexico* (Gulfport, Miss., 1934); *How to Win and Hold a Husband* (New York, 1939).

REFERENCES: Ella Bentley Arthur, ed., *My Husband Keeps Telling Me to Go to Hell* (Garden City, N.Y., 1954); Barbara Belford, *Brilliant Bylines* (New York, 1986): 70–78; Harnett T. Kane and Ella Bentley Arthur, *Dear Dorothy Dix: The Story of a Compassionate Woman* (Garden City, N.Y., 1952); Madelon Golden Schlipp and Sharon Murphy, *Great Women of the Press* (Carbondale, Ill., 1983): 112–120.

Glaser, Vera Romans (?–   ). Vera Glaser was a Knight-Ridder columnist from 1969 to 1981 and a Maturity News Service columnist from 1988.

Glaser was born in St. Louis, Missouri. She attended Washington University (in St. Louis), George Washington University, and American University from 1937 to 1940.

In 1943–1944 she was a writer for *National Aeronautics* magazine. She was a reporter for the *Washington Times Herald* from 1944 to 1946, then worked in public relations for the Great Lakes–St. Lawrence Association. Glaser did both writing and promotion work for Congressional Quarterly News Features from 1951 to 1954 and was with radio station WGMS in Washington, D.C., during 1954–1955. She worked in 1955–1956 in the Washington bureau of the *New York Herald Tribune,* and from 1956 to 1959 was press aide to Sen. Charles E. Porter. After serving as director of PR for the women's division of the Republican National Committee from 1959 to 1962, she spent 1962–1963 as press aide to Sen. Kenneth Keating.

Glaser was D.C. correspondent for the North American Newspaper Alliance from 1963 to 1969 and its D.C. bureau chief from 1965. After writing her column for more than a decade, she became associate editor of *Washingtonian* (1981–1988) and has remained a contributing editor to that magazine.

Golden, Harry Lewis (6 May 1902–2 Oct. 1981). Readers of Harry Golden's column and of his own paper, the *Carolina Israelite,* will forever remember his satirical "solutions" to racial segregation in the South: the Vertical Negro Plan, the White Baby Plan, and the Out of Order Plan. Golden's support of integration was truly of a unique sort.

Golden was born Harry Goldhurst to immigrant parents in New York City. He studied literature at City College in New York in the 1920s but dropped out before earning a degree. He held a number of jobs and wrote pamphlets for the Socialists. After four years in prison for a mail fraud violation regarding stocks to be purchased on margin, Golden worked as a reporter for the *New York Post* and *New York Mirror,* taught school briefly, then in 1939 moved south for a fresh start as a salesman. He sold ads for the *Charlotte Observer,* for which he also reported, then worked at the *Hendersonville* [North Carolina] *Times-News.*

In 1941 Golden moved back to Charlotte and started a liberal monthly paper, the *Carolina Israelite,* initial circulation about eight hundred. Most of its copy was written by Golden himself. He published a number of books, the most acclaimed of which was *Only in America* (1958), and wrote for such influential magazines as *Nation* and *Commentary.* These efforts, plus his column, which was handled by Bell-McClure Syndicate, gave him widespread recognition in the late 1950s and 1960s.

Golden also suggested a tongue-in-cheek plan to eliminate anti-Semitism: that all America's Jews convert en masse to Christianity. Christians, he reasoned, would be so horrified that they would form an Anti-Defamation League of their own and would try to talk the Jews out of it. Golden's antidiscrimination humor did not defeat prejudice, of course, but it certainly made a lot of people sheepish about it. His paper began to lose money in the 1960s, and in 1968 he put it to rest. He continued to be a prolific author of books.

BOOKS: *Only in America* (New York, 1958); *You're Entitle'* (Cleveland, 1962); *Forgotten Pioneer* (Cleveland, 1963); *Mr. Kennedy and the Negroes* (Cleveland, 1964); *So What Else Is New?* (New York, 1964); *A Little Girl is Dead* (Cleveland, 1965); *Ess Ess, Mein Kindt* (New York, 1966); *The Lynching of Leo Frank* (London, 1966); *The Best of Harry Golden* (Cleveland, 1967); *The Right Time: An Autobiography* (New York, 1969); *So Long As You're Healthy* (New York, 1970); *The Israelis: Portrait of a People* (New York, 1971); *The Golden Book of Jewish Humor* (New York, 1972); *The Greatest Jewish*

City in the World (Garden City, N.Y., 1972); with Richard Goldhurst, *Travels Through Jewish America* (Garden City, N.Y., 1973); *Our Southern Landsman* (New York, 1974); *Long Live Columbus* (New York, 1975).

Gonzales, Patrisia (3 June 1959–   ). With her husband, Roberto Rodriguez, Patrisia Gonzales writes the weekly column "Latino Spectrum" for Chronicle Features.

Gonzales, of Mexican and Kikapu ancestry, was born in Fort Worth, Texas. She holds a journalism degree from the University of Texas at Austin, and she has been a Ford Fellow at the Center for International Journalism at the University of Southern California.

Her career as a reporter has included employment at the *Corpus Christi* [Texas] *Caller* (1981–1982), *Tucson* [Arizona] *Citizen* (1982–1984), and *Philadelphia Inquirer* (1984–1992). While with the *Inquirer,* she worked with migrant Puerto Rican blueberry pickers to gather material for an investigative piece regarding their working conditions.

"Latino Spectrum" has a dual purpose: to provide copy especially meaningful to Latino readers, and to interpret that large ethnic community to non-Latino readers. The column was launched in March 1994.

REFERENCES: "Writing Team Covers a Latino Spectrum," *Editor and Publisher* (19 February 1994): 47.

Goodman, Ellen Holtz (11 April 1941–   ). A distinctive voice among syndicated columnists, Ellen Goodman began as a columnist with the *Boston Globe* and is distributed by the Washington Post Writers Group.

Born Ellen Holtz in Newton, Massachusetts, she is a 1963 cum laude graduate of Radcliffe College, where she majored in modern European history. Her first job out of college was as a researcher/fact checker in the television department of *Newsweek.* She married and in 1963 moved with her husband to Detroit, where she found work as a reporter/feature writer on the *Free Press.* In 1967 the Goodmans returned to Boston, where she was initially a feature writer for the women's section and later began a column titled "At Large." In 1971 her column was moved from the features section to the op-ed page. Goodman was a Nieman Fellow at Harvard University during 1973–1974, researching the social changes that had stemmed from the women's movement. The results of her work not only appeared in her column, but in her first book, *Turning Points* (1979).

Goodman became a full-time columnist on her return to the *Globe* in 1974. By 1976 her column appeared in roughly twenty-five other papers, and during that year she became part of the Washington Post Writers Group. Her twice-weekly column is now syndicated to about four hundred papers. Her specialty is to meld material normally found in personal/general columns into that which is usually addressed by the more strictly political columns—a mixture of social and political commentary. She writes with considerable wit and clarity of reasoning and seems concerned, in the main, with change and its effect on people's lives.

Certainly Goodman is a serious feminist, but at the same time, she does not hesitate to aim an occasional barb at women themselves, as in a column declaring 1987 the "Year of the Bimbo" or a 1985 column on the absurdity of Styrofoam hip pads sewn into skirts. Still, she celebrated the closing of Hugh Hefner's Playboy Clubs with a fantasy: a club where former bunnies "are served drinks by middle-aged businessmen in funny little costumes. For eternity." Goodman takes on big issues but is hardly a dry pundit as she does so. She has said she regards partisan politics as a game played mainly by men—"like any other sport."

She was a "Spectrum" commentator for CBS radio in 1978 and a "Today Show" commentator in 1979. She has written for *Ms., TV Guide,* and other magazines; won the Pulitzer Prize for commentary in 1980; and has written five books.

BOOKS: *Turning Points* (Garden City, N.Y., 1979); *Close to Home* (New York, 1979); *At Large* (New York, 1981); *Keeping in Touch* (New York, 1985); *Making Sense* (New York, 1989).

REFERENCES: David Astor, "Fusing the Political with the Personal," *Editor and Publisher* (16 June 1984): 48–49; Barbara Belford, *Brilliant Bylines* (New York, 1986): 330–349; Neil A. Grauer, *Wits and Sages* (Baltimore and London, 1984): 163–177.

Gorbachev, Mikhail Sergeyevich (2 March 1931–). Former chairman of the Presidium of the Supreme Soviet of the USSR Mikhail Gorbachev writes a column that originally was published in *La Stampa* (Turin, Italy) and that began to be distributed to U.S. papers via the New York Times Syndicate in February 1992.

Gorbachev was born in Privolnoye, Stavropol, in the Soviet Union. He received a law degree from Moscow State University in 1955 and an agricultural degree from Stavropol Agricultural Institute in 1967. His rise to power began in 1956 when he joined the Komsomol, or Young Communist League. He became a member of the Politburo in 1980, and general secretary and a member of the Presidium in 1985. He was chairman of the Presidium from 1988 to 1991, during which time he introduced the world-altering policies of glasnost (openness) and perestroika (restructuring) that broke the hold of the Communist party and moved the former USSR toward a free market economy.

Gorbachev's column found an immediate welcome in roughly one hundred U.S. papers, including the *New York Times, Los Angeles Times, San Francisco Chronicle,* and *Denver Post.* It offers historical analysis of the former USSR, the writer's views on the other world leaders of his acquaintance, and a look at progress and problems in his changing, troubled homeland. Since March 1992 the Gorbachev package has included the political cartoon illustrations of Ranan Lurie.

BOOKS: *A Time for Peace* (New York, 1985); *Perestroika: New Thinking for Our Country and the World* (New York, 1987).

REFERENCES: David Astor, "Mikhail Gorbachev Starts Writing Column," *Editor and Publisher* (29 February 1992): 30.

Gottlieb, Martin (24 Feb. 1946–   ). Martin Gottlieb has been a political columnist for Ohio's *Dayton Daily News* since 1984.

He was born in Melrose Park, Illinois, and received the B.S. in journalism from Northern Illinois University in 1968. He has also done graduate work in political science at the University of Chicago and the University of California at Santa Barbara.

Gottlieb first worked as a reporter/copy editor for the Portland (Indiana) *Commercial Review* (1968–1969), then as a reporter for the Kokomo (Indiana) *Tribune* (1970–1971). After several years of graduate work, he was from 1977 to 1983 a free-lance writer, covering the nation's capital for small dailies and trade publications. Gottlieb moved to San Francisco and began writing book reviews and commentary for various California papers. Then in 1984 he was hired as columnist and editorial writer by the *Dayton Daily News*. His column, which has been distributed by the New York Times wire, is more often than not political, but also includes some life-style material and some use of humor.

REFERENCES: David Astor, "Ohio Is Base for National Political Writer," *Editor and Publisher* (28 April 1990): 60–61.

Gould, John Thomas (22 Oct. 1908–   ). Newspaper owner/farmer/regional humorist John Gould wrote the weekly column "Dispatch from the Farm" for the *Christian Science Monitor* starting in 1942.

Gould was born in Boston and grew up in Freeport, Maine. He earned the A.B. in 1931 from Bowdoin College, then worked for the *Brunswick Record* from 1931 to 1939. He contributed features to the *Boston Sunday Post* from 1924 to 1954 and the *Baltimore Sun* from in 1975. From 1945 to 1951 he owned and published the *Lisbon Enterprise* in Lisbon Falls, Maine. Since 1930 Gould has operated his family farm and has also owned a florist and greenhouse business. His columns offer wry Down East humor applied to small-town and rural subject matter, written to appeal to city dwellers. He has authored seventeen books.

BOOKS: *New England Town Meeting: Safeguard of Democracy* (Brattleboro, Vt., 1940); *Pre-Natal Care for Fathers* (Brattleboro, Vt., 1941); *Farmer Takes a Wife* (New York, 1945); *The House That Jacob Built* (New York, 1947); *And One to Grow On* (New York, 1949); with F. Wenderoth Saunders, *The Fastest Hound Dog in the State of Maine* (New York, 1953); *Monstrous Depravity* (New York, 1963); *The Parables of Peter Partout* (New York, 1964); *You Should Start Sooner* (New York, 1965); *Last One In* (New York, 1966); *Europe on Saturday Night* (New York, 1968); *The Jonesport Raffle* (New York, 1969); *Twelve Grindstones* (New York, 1970); *The Shag Bag* (New York, 1972); with

Lillian Ross, *Maine Lingo: Boiled Owls, Billdads and Wazzats* (Camden, Me., 1975); *Glass Eyes by the Bottle* (New York, 1975).

Grafton, Samuel (7 Sept. 1907–). Sam Grafton, a publishing company executive in his later years, wrote the syndicated political column "I'd Rather Be Right" from 1939 to 1949.

Grafton was born in Brooklyn, New York, but was raised mainly in Philadelphia. He earned the A.B. from the University of Pennsylvania in 1929, writing for humor magazines during his college years as well as for *North American Review* and *New Republic.* In 1929 he won a $500 prize from the *American Mercury* in a contest for the best article on the faults of U.S. colleges and universities. Grafton intended to go on to law school but was convinced otherwise by J. David Stern, publisher of the *Philadelphia Record,* for which Grafton went to work as an editorial writer (1929–1934). From 1934 to 1949 he was associate editor of the *New York Post,* and in 1939 he began writing his column, whose title came from the old, no doubt fictitious political chestnut "I'd rather be right than president."

Grafton was editor of *Lithopinion* from 1966 to 1969 and was founder and president of Grafton Publishers, Inc., in 1969. He edited several reports concerning crime, youth, and substance abuse and wrote four books. His column was known for its stylish writing and for Grafton's dead certainty that that he was right, whatever the topic. He was a liberal, a supporter of the New Deal, and, during World War II, a frequent critic of the U.S. Armed Forces' leadership.

BOOKS: *All Out! How Democracy Will Defend America* (New York, 1940); *An American Diary* (Garden City, N.Y., 1943); *What Kind of Peace Shall We Make with Germany?* (New York, 1945); *A Most Contagious Game* (Garden City, N.Y., 1955).

REFERENCES: Charles Fisher, *The Columnists* (New York, 1944): 249–260.

Graham, Sheilah (15 Sept. 1904–17 Nov. 1988). Sheilah Graham, like Hedda Hopper and Louella Parsons, was one of the most successful Hollywood gossip columnists.

Born Lily Shiel in the East End of London, she was placed in the East London Home for Orphans at age six. She left the orphanage at fourteen to work as a housemaid and later as a toothbrush demonstrator in a department store. Her physical beauty lifted her from these dreary jobs and took her to the London stage after three months of study at the Royal Academy of Dramatic Arts. She changed her name to Sheilah Graham, lost her Cockney accent, and rose quickly from chorus girl to headliner, also contributing articles to the *Daily Mail* and other papers.

Graham entered the United States in 1933 with plans for a career in journalism. She did some free-lancing for the *New York Mirror* and the *Evening Journal,* then in 1935 was hired as a syndicated Hollywood columnist ("Hollywood Today") by the North American Newspaper Alliance (NANA). At a party in

1937, she met the writer F. Scott Fitzgerald. The two had a three-year affair that ended with Fitzgerald's death.

Graham was a war correspondent in London for NANA (1940–1945), then returned to Hollywood, where from 1945 to 1970 she wrote two NANA gossip columns, "Hollywood Everywhere" and "Speaking for Myself," and during 1952–1953 did a daily column for *Daily Variety*. From 1970 to 1976 she wrote a non–Hollywood celebrity column, "Speaking Frankly," for the Bell-McClure Syndicate. During the same period she also wrote a movie column for the *Hollywood Citizen-News* in Los Angeles.

Graham also did radio and television work in the 1950s and wrote ten books.

BOOKS: *The Rest of the Story* (New York, 1964); *College of One* (New York, 1967); *Confessions of a Hollywood Columnist* (New York, 1969); *The Garden of Allah* (New York, 1970); *A State of Heat* (New York, 1972); *For Richer, For Poorer: The Truth Behind Some of the World's Most Fabulous Marriages* (London, 1974); *How To Marry Super Rich* (New York, 1974); *The Real F. Scott Fitzgerald Thirty-Five Years Later* (New York, 1976); *The Late Lily Shiel* (New York, 1978); *Hollywood Revisited* (New York, 1985).

Greeley, Andrew Moran (5 Feb. 1928–   ). One of America's most prolific writers, a sociologist, and a Roman Catholic priest, Andrew Greeley writes the weekly syndicated column "People and Values" and has been a *Chicago Sun Times* guest columnist since 1985.

Greeley was born in Oak Park, Illinois. He first studied to become a priest, then pursued sociology degrees. He received the A.B. (1950), S.T.B. (1952), and S.T.L. (1954) from St. Mary of the Lake Seminary and the A.M. (1961) and Ph.D. (1962) from the University of Chicago.

From 1954 to 1964, Greeley was a priest at a Chicago church. He was with the National Opinion Research Center at the University of Chicago from 1961 to 1970, then in 1971 became director of that university's Center for the Study of American Pluralism. He also lectured in the sociology of religion at the University of Chicago from 1962 to 1972. Since 1978 he has been a professor of sociology at the University of Arizona in Tucson.

In his columns and in his remarkable outpouring of books, Greeley has had something to say about virtually every question faced by the church in recent times. He is liberal as to church doctrine and a supporter of what is called diversity by those who like it and political correctness by those who do not. He has appeared in the broadcast media and has been a frequent contributor to the more thoughtful periodicals.

BOOKS: *The Church and the Suburbs* (New York, 1959); *Strangers in the House: Catholic Youth in America* (New York, 1961); *Religion and Career* (New York, 1963); *Letters to a Young Man* (New York, 1964); *Letters to Nancy* (New York, 1964); with Peter H. Rossi, *The Education of Catholic Americans* (Chicago, 1966); *The Hesitant Pilgrim: American Catholicism After the Council* (New York, 1966); *The Catholic Experience: An Interpretation of the History of American Catholicism* (Garden City, N.Y., 1967);

Changing Catholic College (Chicago, 1967); *And Young Men Shall See Visions* (Garden City, N.Y., 1968); *Crucible of Change: The Social Dynamics of Pastoral Practice* (New York, 1968); *Uncertain Trumpet: The Priest in Modern America* (New York, 1968); *Youth Asks, Does God Talk?* (Camden, N.J., 1968); *From Backwater to Mainstream: A Profile of Catholic Higher Education* (New York, 1969); *A Future to Hope In* (Garden City, N.Y., 1969); *Life for a Wanderer: A New Look at Christian Spirituality* (Garden City, N.Y., 1969); *Religion in the Year 2000* (New York, 1969); *A Fresh Look at Vocations* (Chicago, 1969); *The Friendship Game* (Garden City, N.Y., 1970); *New Horizons for the Priesthood* (New York, 1970); with William E. Brown, *Can Catholic Schools Survive?* (New York, 1970); with Joe L. Spaeth, *Recent Alumni and Higher Education* (New York, 1970); *America's White Ethnic Groups* (New York, 1971); *Come Blow Your Mind with Me* (Garden City, N.Y., 1971); *The Jesus Myth* (Garden City, N.Y., 1971); *The Touch of the Spirit* (New York, 1971); *What a Modern Catholic Believes About God* (Chicago, 1971); *The Deminational Society: A Sociological Approach to Religion in America* (New York, 1972); *Priests in the United States: Reflections on a Survey* (Garden City, N.Y., 1972); *The Sinai Myth* (Garden City, N.Y., 1972); *That Most Distressful Nation: The Taming of the American Irish* (Chicago, 1972); *The Unsecular Man: The Persistence of Religion* (New York, 1972); *What a Modern Catholic Believes About the Church* (Chicago, 1972); *The Catholic Priest in the United States: Sociological Investigations* (Washington, D.C., 1972); *The New Agenda* (Garden City, N.Y., 1973); *Sexual Intimacy* (Chicago, 1973); ed. with Gregory Baum, *The Persistence of Religion* (New York, 1973); *Building Coalitions: American Politics in the 1970s* (New York, 1974); *The Devil You Say! Man and His Personal Devils and Angels* (Garden City, N.Y., 1974); *Ecstacy: A Way of Knowing* (Englewood Cliffs, N.J., 1974); *Ethnicity in the United States: A Preliminary Reconnaissance* (New York, 1974); with Gregory Baum, *The Church as Institution* (New York, 1974); *MEDIA: Ethnic Media in the United States* (Hanover, N.H., 1974); *Love and Play* (Chicago, 1975); *May the Wind Be at Your Back: The Prayer of St. Patrick* (New York, 1975); *The Sociology of the Paranormal: A Reconnaissance* (Beverly Hills, Calif., 1975); with William C. McCready and Kathleen McCourt, *Catholic Schools in a Declining Church* (New York, 1976); *The Communal Catholic* (New York, 1976); *Death and Beyond* (Chicago, 1976); *Ethnicity, Denomination, and Inequality* (Beverly Hills, Calif., 1976); *The Great Mysteries* (New York, 1976); *Nora Maeve and Sebi* (New York, 1976); with William C. McCready, *The Ultimate Value of the American Population* (Beverly Hills, Calif., 1976); *The American Catholic: A Social Portrait* (New York, 1977); *The Mary Myth: On the Femininity of God* (New York, 1977); *Neighborhood* (New York, 1977); *No Bigger Than Necessary: An Alternative to Socialism, Capitalism, and Anarchism* (New York, 1977); *An Ugly Little Secret: Anti-Catholicism in North America* (Kansas City, Mo., 1977); *Everything You Wanted to Know About the Catholic Church but Were Too Pious to Ask* (Chicago, 1978); ed. with Gregory Baum, *Communication in the Church Concilium* (New York, 1978); with J. N. Kotre, *The Best of Times, the Worst of Times* (Chicago, 1978); *Crisis in the Church: A Study of Religion in America* (Chicago, 1979); *The Making of the Popes: The Politics of Intrigue in the Vatican* (Kansas City, Mo., 1979); *Women I've Met* (Kansas City, Mo., 1979); *The Magic Cup: An Irish Legend* (New York, 1979); ed., *The Family in Crisis or in Transition* (New York, 1979); *Death in April* (New York, 1980); *The Irish Americans* (New York, 1980); with William C. McCready, *Ethnic Drinking Subcultures* (New York, 1980); *The Cardinal Sin* (New York, 1981); *Thy Brother's Wife* (New York, 1982); *Ascent into Hell* (New York, 1983); *Angry Catholic Women* (Chicago, 1984); *How to*

Save the Catholic Church (New York, 1984); *Lord of the Dance* (New York, 1984); *Ethnicity in the United States* (New York, 1985); *The Great Mysteries* (New York, 1985); *Happy Are the Meek* (New York, 1985); *Virgin and Martyr* (New York, 1985); *Angels of September* (New York, 1986); *Confessions of a Parish Priest* (New York, 1986); *The God Game* (New York, 1986); *An Andrew Greeley Reader* (Chicago, 1987); *Angels of September* (New York, 1987); *The Final Planet* (New York, 1987); *Happy Are the Clean of Heart* (New York, 1987); *Happy Are Those Who First for Justice* (New York, 1987); *The Passover Trilogy: Three Complete Novels* (New York, 1987); *Patience of a Saint* (New York, 1987); *Angel Fire* (New York, 1988); *Conversations with Andrew Greeley* (Boston, 1988); *The Incarnate Imagination* (Bowling Green, Ohio, 1988); *The Irish Americans: The Rise to Money and Power* (New York, 1988); *All About Women: Stories by Andrew M. Greeley* (New York, 1989); *Complaints Against God* (Chicago, 1989); *Love Song* (New York, 1989); *Myths of Religion* (New York, 1989); *Religious Change in America* (Cambridge, Mass., 1989); *Saint Valentine's Night* (New York, 1989); *When Life Hurts* (Garden City, N.Y., 1989); *The Bible and Us: A Priest and a Rabbi Read Scripture Together* (New York, 1990); *The Cardinal Virtues* (New York, 1990); *A Book of Irish American Blessings* (Chicago, 1991); *An Occasion of Sin* (New York, 1991); *Faithful Attraction* (New York, 1992); *Happy Are the Merciful* (Thorndike, Me., 1992); *Love Affair: A Prayer Journal* (New York, 1992); *The Sense of Love* (Ashland, Ohio, 1992); *Fall from Grace* (New York, 1993); *The Sociology of Andrew M. Greeley* (Atlanta, Ga., 1993).

Greenberg, Paul (21 Jan. 1937–). A syndicated columnist since 1970, Paul Greenberg made his considerable national reputation on a small-town paper, the *Pine Bluff* [Arkansas] *Commercial.*

Greenberg was born in Shreveport, Louisiana. He received the B.A. in journalism in 1958 and the M.A. in history in 1959 from the University of Missouri, then did graduate study at Columbia University from 1960 to 1962.

His original intention was to be a professor, but after failing his oral examinations, he instead, in 1962, became editorial page editor for the *Commercial.* He held this position until 1966, when he spent a year as an editorial writer for the *Chicago Daily News,* then returned to his old job on the *Commercial* in 1967. He launched a weekly column in 1970 and in 1971 began self-syndicating it. The column was picked up by the *Philadelphia Inquirer, Newsday,* and a few more papers. He was handled for a time by Universal Press Syndicate, then returned to self-syndication and eventually was distributed by the Los Angeles Times Syndicate. His column, now thrice weekly, appears in roughly fifty papers. In 1992 he became editorial page editor for the *Arkansas Democrat Gazette,* also in Pine Bluff.

Greenberg won the Pulitzer Prize in 1969 for his editorial writing on the race issue and has done commentary for National Public Radio's "Sunday Weekend Edition." While a social liberal, he provides a generally conservative voice from small-town America, which is read and appreciated by big-city readers for its wit, style, and good sense.

BOOKS: *Resonant Lives: Fifty Figures of Consequence* (Washington, D.C., 1991); *Entirely Personal* (Jackson, Miss., 1992).

REFERENCES: George T. Wilson, "Pulitzer-Winning Pundit from Pine Bluff," *Editor and Publisher* (7 April 1990): 34–35.

Greene, Robert Bernard, Jr. (10 March 1947–   ). Chicago's Bob Greene has written a column since 1971 and has been nationally syndicated since 1976. He has also been a columnist for *Esquire.*

Greene was born in Columbus, Ohio. He earned the B.J. from Northwestern University in 1969, and from that year until 1971 worked as a reporter for the *Chicago Sun-Times.*

Greene's first column, other than the one he wrote for the *Daily Northwestern* in 1968 and 1969 while in college, was for the *Sun-Times* (1971–1978). He was distributed by the Field Newspaper Syndicate from 1976 to 1978, then moved his column to the *Chicago Tribune* and remained there. He has been syndicated by Tribune Media Services since 1978. The column is of the general variety, heavy on human interest written from the point of view of the baby-boomer generation. The reach of Greene's column was pointed up in 1991 when his account of a library fire in Ohio resulted in contributions of $25,000 and donation of twenty thousand books. More recently, Greene was charged with "journalistic terrorism" by an Illinois Supreme Court justice over a column on the "Baby Richard" custody case.

Greene began his *Esquire* magazine column in 1980 and in 1981 became a correspondent for ABC-TV's "Nightline." His work has also appeared in numerous other magazines and major papers, and he has exercised his talent as a storyteller by authoring more than a dozen books, including one cowritten with his sister and fellow columnist, D. G. Fulford of the *Los Angeles Daily News.*

BOOKS: *We Didn't Have None of Them Fat Funky Angels on the Wall of Heartbreak Hotel, and Other Reports from America* (Chicago, 1971); *Running* (Chicago, 1973); *Billion Dollar Baby* (New York, 1974); *Johnny Deadline Reporter: The Best of Bob Greene* (New York, 1976); *American Beat* (New York, 1983); *Good Morning, Merry Sunshine: A Father's Journal of His Child's First Year* (New York, 1984); *Cheeseburgers, the Best of Bob Greene* (New York, 1985); *Diary of a Newborn Father* (Minneapolis, 1986); *Be True to Your School: A Diary of 1964* (New York, 1987); *Homecoming: When the Soldiers Returned from Vietnam* (New York, 1989); *He Was a Midwestern Boy on His Own* (New York, 1991); *Hang Time: Three Days with Michael Jordan* (New York, 1992); with D. G. Fulford, *To Our Children's Children: Preserving Family Histories for Generations to Come* (New York, 1993); *All Summer Long* (New York, 1993).

REFERENCES: Mark Fitzgerald, "Journalistic Terrorism?" *Editor and Publisher* (23 July 1994): 12–13.

Greenfield, Jeff (10 June 1943–   ). Jeff Greenfield, mainly known for his television work as a political and media analyst and for his books, has written a weekly syndicated newspaper column, as well.

Greenfield was born in New York City. He received the B.A., with honors, from the University of Wisconsin in 1964 and the LL.B, also with honors, from Yale University in 1967.

In 1967–1968, he was an aide to the late Sen. Robert Kennedy, and from 1968 to 1970, on the staff of New York's Mayor John Lindsay. From 1970 to 1976 he was a consultant with Garth Associates in New York City.

Greenfield began working with Charles Kuralt on the CBS "Sunday Morning" show in 1979 and in 1983 became an ABC analyst. He has authored or coauthored nine books.

BOOKS: With Jerry Bruno, *The Advance Man* (New York, 1971); with Jack Newfield, *A Populist Manifesto: The Making of a New Majority* (New York, 1972); *No Peace, No Place: Excavations Along the Generational Fault* (Garden City, N.Y., 1973); *The World's Greatest Team: A Portrait of the Boston Celtics* (New York, 1976); *Tiny Giant* (Milwaukee, Wis., 1976); *Television: The First Fifty Years* (New York, 1977); *Jeff Greenfield's Book of Books* (New York, 1979); *Playing to Win: An Insider's Guide to Politics* (New York, 1980); *The Real Campaign: How the Media Missed the Story of the 1980 Campaign* (New York, 1982).

Grimes, David (8 July 1952–   ). Humor columnist David Grimes has worked for the *Sarasota* [Florida] *Herald-Tribune* since 1976 and is syndicated by the New York Times News Service.

Grimes was born in Sharon, Pennsylvania. He was a member of the class of 1974 at the University of Maryland, where he was an English major.

Grimes's column appears three times a week.

Grimsley, James Edward (25 May 1927–   ). Ed Grimsley writes a column that is syndicated by the Creators Syndicate and has, since June 1992, been chairman of the editorial board of the *Richmond* (Virginia) *Times-Dispatch.*

Grimsley was born in Buchanan County, Virginia. He received the bachelor's degree in government in 1951 at the College of William and Mary.

From March 1951 to September 1952, Grimsley was a reporter with United Press International. He served as public relations director of the College of William and Mary from September 1952 to October 1953, at which time he joined the *Richmond Times-Dispatch* as a reporter. He has remained with this paper, working as reporter and columnist until 1970. From 1970–1992 he was editor of the editorial page.

Grimsley's column, "Crosscurrents," offers humorous/satirical commentary on general topics of current interest. He has published one book, a collection of his columns.

BOOKS: *Coming Through Awry* (Richmond, Va., 1967).

Grizzard, Lewis M., Jr. (20 Oct. 1946–20 March 1994). Lewis Grizzard, infuriatingly funny proponent of all things southern, was a humor columnist for the *Atlanta Journal* from 1979 until his death in 1994.

Grizzard (pronounced Gri-ZARD) was born in Columbus, Georgia, but grew up in the Georgia town of Moreland. He received the A.B.J. from the University of Georgia in 1967. He began writing sports for the *Atlanta Journal* while still a college student and by age twenty-three was the paper's executive sports editor. He advanced to associate city editor but didn't like the executive role, remarking later that he might as well have been selling insurance. He took a new job as sports editor of the *Chicago Sun-Times* but missed the South and in 1977 took a $12,000 pay cut to return to Atlanta, this time as a *Journal* sports columnist. A little more than a year thereafter he began the general humor column that soon made him Georgia's most recognized newspaperman. His column persona was the modern, sophisticated "good ol' boy" who clung to the old ways in the face of encroaching modernity.

Grizzard's work was a careful mixture of the hilarious and the poignant. He, the good ol' boy in Guccis, boosted grits, beer in longneck bottles, John Wayne movies, dogs, barbecue, and good ol' girls. He set himself up as a male chauvinist pig, taking potshots at gays, feminists, television evangelists, McDonald's, northerners, and anything the least bit politically correct. Readers liked his outrageous style, and eventually his column went into national syndication with King Features Syndicate, appearing in as many as 450 papers.

The Grizzard column was often highly personal. His readers learned in detail about his three failed marriages, his series of heart surgeries, the death of his favorite dog, Catfish. Toward the end of his career, he scaled back from four to three columns a week and established Grizzard Enterprises, a small firm whose several employees arranged his speaking and book-signing schedule and handled his finances. His columns were collected into twenty outlandishly titled books, most of which were hot sellers. He worked as a stage comedian, made comedy record albums, and occasionally appeared on such television shows as "Designing Women" and the "Tonight Show" with Johnny Carson. Before his death of complications during heart surgery, Grizzard had become a one-man humor industry.

BOOKS: *Kathy Sue Loudermilk, I Love You* (Atlanta, Ga., 1979); *Won't You Come Home, Billy Bob Bailey?* (Atlanta, 1980); *Don't Sit Under the Grits Tree with Anyone Else but Me* (Atlanta, 1981); with Loran Smith, *Glory! Glory! Georgia's 1980 Championship Season: The Inside Story* (Atlanta, 1981); *They Tore out My Heart and Stomped That Sucker Flat* (Atlanta, 1982); *If Love Were Oil, I'd Be About a Quart Low: Lewis Grizzard on Women* (Atlanta, 1983); *Elvis Is Dead and I Don't Feel So Good Myself* (Atlanta, 1984); *Shoot Low, Boys—They're Ridin' Shetland Ponies: In Search of True Grit* (Atlanta, 1985); *My Daddy Was a Pistol and I'm a Son of a Gun* (New York, 1986); *When My Love Returns from the Ladies Room, Will I Be Too Old to Care?* (New York, 1987); *Don't Bend over in the Garden, Granny, You Know Them Taters Got Eyes* (New York, 1988); *Lewis Grizzard on Fear of Flying: Avoid Pouting Pilots and Mechanics Named Bubba* (Atlanta, 1989); *Lewis Grizzard's Advice to the Newly Wed . . . and the Newly Divorced* (Atlanta, 1989); *Chili Dawgs Always Bark at Night* (New York, 1989); *Gettin' It On: A Down-Home Treasury* (New York, 1989); *Does a Wild Bear Chip in the Woods? Lewis Grizzard on Golf* (Atlanta, 1990); *If I Ever Get Back to Georgia, I'm Gonna Nail My Feet to the Ground* (New York, 1990); *A Heapin' Helping of True Grizzard: Down*

Home Again with Lewis Grizzard (New York, 1991); *Don't Forget to Call Your Mamma—I Wish I Could Call Mine* (Atlanta, 1991); *I Haven't Understood Anything Since 1962, and Other Nekkid Truths* (New York, 1992); *I Took a Lickin' and Kept on Tickin': And Now I Believe in Miracles* (New York, 1993).

REFERENCES: Peter Applebome, "Is It True What He Says About Dixie?" *The New York Times Magazine* (8 April 1990): 26, 34, 36, 38; Robert Coram, "Grizzard Inc.," *The Quill* (November 1986): 34–38; Kathy Grizzard Schmook, *How to Tame a Wild Bore and Other Facts of Life with Lewis* (Atlanta, 1988).

Groening, Matt (15 Feb. 1954–   ). Cartoonist/businessman Matt Groening (pronounced "GRAY-ning") began writing a syndicated humor column in 1986. He is much better known as the creator of "The Simpsons," an animated television show.

Groening was born in Portland, Oregon. He received the B.A. from Evergreen State College in Olympia, Washington, in 1977 and was editor of the campus newspaper.

Groening's early jobs included stints as a chauffeur, ghostwriter, record store clerk, dishwasher, and cemetery groundskeeper in the Los Angeles area. The sum total of these experiences contributed to his first comic strip, "Life in Hell," which featured three put-upon rabbits: Binky, Bongo, and Sheba. This alternative strip first appeared in 1979 in the *Los Angeles Reader,* where Groening also wrote a rock music column titled "Sound Mix" (1979–1984). In the mid-1980s Groening formed a partnership with Deborah Caplan, doing business as the Life in Hell Cartoon Company and Acme Features Syndicate. Their far more popular cartoon feature, "The Simpsons," first appeared in the mid-1980s as lead-in material written by Groening on the Emmy-winning "Tracey Ullman Show," then became a hit stand-alone show around 1990. Groening has also published a number of books of his cartoons.

BOOKS: *Love Is Hell* (N.p., 1984); *Work Is Hell* (New York, 1986); *School Is Hell* (New York, 1987); *Childhood Is Hell* (New York, 1988); *Akbar and Jeff's Guide to Life* (New York, 1989); *Greetings from Hell* (New York, 1989); *The Big Book of Hell* (New York, 1990); *Greetings from the Simpsons* (New York, 1990); *The Simpsons' Xmas Book* (New York, 1990); *With Love from Hell* (New York, 1991); *How to Go to Hell* (New York, 1991); *Matt Groening's The Simpsons Fun in the Sun Book* (New York, 1992); *Making Faces with the Simpsons* (New York, 1992); *Bart Simpson's Guide to Life* (New York, 1993).

Gross, Milt (4 March 1895–28 Nov. 1953). Cartoonist/illustrator/humor writer Milt Gross did a weekly illustrated column for the *New York Sunday World* from 1923 until the paper folded in 1931. He was also known for his several comic strips.

Gross was born in New York City of Jewish immigrant parents and grew up in the Bronx. His formal education ended after a year and a half of high school, and at age twelve he became a copyboy for the art department of the *New York*

American. In 1913, at age eighteen, he became a staff artist for the American Press Association, then in 1915 joined the *New York Evening Journal,* where he began drawing the comic strip "Henry Peck, a Happy Married Man." He served in the army during part of World War I, was a cartoon producer for Bray Studios, and in 1922 joined the *New York World.* In 1923 he launched his column, "Gross Exaggerations," written in zany Bronx Yiddish dialect. His most popular strip was introduced in 1926: "The Feitlebaum Family." From this daily feature, he spun off a Sunday strip, "Nize Baby," which was replaced in 1929 by a new strip, "Count Screwloose from Tooloose."

One of Gross's admirers was Charlie Chaplin, who had him hired in 1927 to help with the writing of Chaplin's movie *The Circus.* Gross also did screenwriting for Republic Studios in the 1930s. After the *New York World* closed in 1931, "Count Screwloose" continued to be syndicated by King Features.

Scholars of American humor credit Gross with popularizing Yiddish slang, thereby paving the way for the many Jewish comedians who would follow. Gross also published eight books of humor.

BOOKS: *Nize Baby* (New York, 1926); *Hiawatta, witt No Odder Poems* (New York, 1926); *De Night in de Front from Chreesmas* (New York, 1927); *Dunt Esk!* (New York, 1927); *Famous Fimmales, witt Odder Ewents from Heestory* (Garden City, N.Y., 1928); *He Done Her Wrong* (Garden City, N.Y., 1930); *Dear Dollink* (New York, 1945); *I Shoulda Ate the Eclair* (Chicago and New York, 1946).

Guest, Edgar Albert (20 Aug. 1881–5 Aug. 1959). America's "Norman Rockwell of poetry," Edgar A. Guest wrote a weekly column and later a syndicated daily column for the *Detroit Free Press.*

It is ironic that Guest, famed for his old-fashioned American values and sentiments, was born in Birmingham, England. His family immigrated to the United States in late 1891 and made their home in Detroit. Guest became a U.S. citizen in 1902. As a result of family financial problems, Guest never completed high school. He was a "soda jerk," then in 1895, an office boy in the *Detroit Free Press*'s accounting department. He became a cub reporter, then exchange editor, then police reporter for the paper. Noticing his talent for writing light verse, his editors gave him a weekly column, "Chaff." The column title was later changed to "Blue Monday Chat." His work proved so popular that he eventually gave up reporting in favor of writing a daily column, "Edgar A. Guest's Breakfast Table Chat," that combined prose sketches and the homespun verse that reportedly made him America's best-paid poet of any kind.

Guest's own favorite poets were Whitman and Browning, but his work was far more simple and less literary. He celebrated the virtues of home, motherhood, patriotism, neighborliness, and friendship. In 1925, Michigan's legislature selected him as its state's first poet laureate, but the governor vetoed the post, probably to the delight of most English teachers. Guest's homey lines, such as "It takes a heap o' livin' to make a house a home," held little allure for intellectuals and prompted Dorothy Parker to write: "I'd rather flunk my Wasserman test / than read a poem by Edgar Guest.'' His brand of pop culture poetry, however, was syndicated to roughly three hundred papers. His work was collected into numerous books, which also sold well. In the 1930s, Guest hosted two radio programs, ''It Can Be Done'' and ''Welcome Valley,'' and in 1951 he made the transition to television in ''A Guest in Your Home.''

BOOKS: *Home Rhymes: From "Breakfast Table Chat"* (Detroit, 1909); *Just Glad Things* (Detroit, 1911); *Breakfast Table Chat* (N.p., 1914); *If Only I Were Santa Claus* (Detroit?, 1914); *Every Day a Christmas* (N.p., 1915); *A Heap o' Livin'* (Chicago, 1916); *Just Folks* (Chicago, 1917); *Over Here* (Chicago, 1918); *The Path to Home* (Chicago, 1919); *A Dozen New Poems* (Chicago, 1920); *When Day Is Done* (Chicago, 1921); *All That Matters* (Chicago, 1922); *Poems of Patriotism* (Chicago, 1922); *The Passing Throng* (Chicago, 1923); *My Job as a Father, and What My Father Did for Me* (Chicago, 1923); *Rhymes of Childhood* (Chicago, 1924); *Home* (Chicago, 1925); *Friends* (Chicago, 1925); *Mother* (Chicago, 1925); *What My Religion Means to Me* (Chicago, 1925); *The Light of Faith* (Chicago, 1926); *Harbor Lights of Home* (Chicago, 1928); *The Herald Newsboy's Greeting* (Grand Rapids, Mich., 1928); *Father* (Chicago, 1930); *Poems for the Home Folks* (Chicago, 1930); *The Friendly Way* (Chicago, 1931); *Life's Highway* (Chicago, 1933); *Between You and Me* (Chicago, 1933); *Collected Verse of Edgar A. Guest* (Chicago, 1934); *Edgar A. Guest Broadcasting* (Chicago, 1935); *All in a Lifetime* (Chicago, 1938); *Just Folks* (Chicago, 1940); *Selected Poems* (Chicago, 1940); *Poems of Patriotism* (Chicago, 1942); *Today and Tomorrow* (Chicago, 1942); *Letters* (Detroit, 1946); *Living the Years* (Chicago, 1949); *Favorite Verse* (New York, 1950); *The Favorite Verses of Edgar A. Guest* (Detroit, 1954).

Guisewite, Mickey (?–   ). Mickey Guisewite (pronounced GUISE-wyte), sister of cartoonist Cathy Guisewite who draws the comic strip ''Cathy,'' writes a humor column syndicated by King Features.

Before launching her column, Mickey Guisewite worked as an advertising agency vice president and associate creative director. She is the author of a 1993 book of humorous essays, excerpts from which have appeared in *Cosmopolitan, Family Circle,* and other periodicals.

The material for the column comes from the foibles of daily life. Her aim, she says, is to give her readers a short ''humor break between disasters.''

BOOKS: *Dancing Through Life in a Pair of Broken Heels* (New York, 1993).

Gusewelle, Charles W. (22 July 1933–   ). C. W. Gusewelle has been associate editor and personal columnist for the *Kansas City Star* since 1979. His articles and short fiction have appeared in a variety of excellent periodicals.

Gusewelle was born in Kansas City, Kansas, and received the B.A. in English from Westminster College in Fulton, Missouri, in 1955.

He is unusual among today's journalists in that he joined the *Kansas City Star* after his graduation in 1955 and has been with that paper ever since. After a decade as a general assignment reporter, he became an editorial writer in 1966 and foreign editor in 1979. He has traveled extensively on assignment in Africa, the Middle East, Europe, the former Soviet Union, and Latin America.

Aside from his newspaper work, he has been a contributor to *Paris Review, Antioch Review, Virginia Quarterly Review, Texas Quarterly, transatlantic review,* and *Harper's.* In 1977 he won *Paris Review*'s Aga Khan Prize for fiction with his short story "Horst Wessel." He has also written nonfiction for *American Heritage* and *Blair & Ketcham's Country Journal* and has published four books of essays.

Gusewelle has served as lecturer and visiting professor at a number of universities: Westminster College (autumn 1982), Baylor University (autumn 1987, autumn 1988, and autumn 1990), Baker University (winter 1988), and the universities of Lagos and Ibadan, Nigeria (May 1989). He does roughly fifty speaking engagements a year and in 1979 was one of three subjects of a National Endowment for the Humanities–sponsored film on midwestern writers. In 1991 he was the American leader of a joint U.S.-Russian expedition from the source to the mouth of the Lena River in Siberia, on which he wrote, produced, and narrated a television documentary, "A Great Current Running." His column is distributed nationally by the New York Times News Service.

BOOKS: *A Paris Notebook* (Kansas City, 1985); *An Africa Notebook* (Kansas City, 1986); *Quick as Shadows Passing* (Loose Creek, Mo., 1988); *Far from Any Coast* (Columbia, Mo., 1989).

H

Haggart, Robert R. (17 Aug. 1933–). Robert Haggart's column appears five times a week in the Syracuse (New York) *Post-Standard.*

Haggart was born in Lawrence, Kansas, to a sea captain father and an opera singer mother. After one year at Kansas University, he joined the army as an alternative to going to jail for a prank—letting two hundred pigs out of a pen in the town of Tonganoxie. On the troop ship from Seattle to Korea, he had his first writing job—doing the ship's newsletter. His first job after leaving the army in 1955 was selling subscriptions for the San Jose (California) *Mercury News.* After working briefly for the *Elmira Advertiser* in Elmira, New York, he attended Syracuse University and worked nights as a copyboy for the *Post-Standard.*

After graduation from Syracuse with a B.A. in liberal arts, Haggart took a job with the Syracuse *Herald-Journal,* where he became chief political writer and Albany correspondent. In 1972 he began working the copy desk and later became assistant city editor. For most of 1974 he was chief photographer for both the *Post-Standard* and the *Herald-Journal,* which had a joint operating agreement. He returned to the *Post-Standard* in 1975 as metropolitan editor and became its assistant managing editor in 1977. After a triple heart bypass operation in 1982, he became a columnist. His general interest column appears on the local news page.

In 1976 and 1977 Haggart was an adjunct professor at the Newhouse School of Public Communications at Syracuse University, and in 1994 he began hosting a local television show, ''Haggart Live!''

Hale, Leon (30 May 1921–). Leon Hale began writing a column for the *Houston Post* in 1956 and took his column to the *Houston Chronicle* in the 1980s.

Hale was born in Stephenville, Texas, and received the B.A. in 1946 from Texas Technological College, which is now Texas Tech. He was in the Army Air Forces from 1942 to 1945.

From 1946 to 1948 Hale worked as an editor for the Extension Service of Texas A & M University, after which he was farm editor of the *Houston Post* (1948–1953). He wrote for a corporate magazine of Humble Oil from 1953 to 1955, then in 1956 began a daily column for the *Houston Post.* He has also taught journalism at Sam Houston State University. Hale has been an active author; most of his books are about Texas.

BOOKS: *Turn South at the Second Bridge* (Garden City, N.Y., 1965); *Bonney's Place* (Garden City, N.Y., 1972); *Texas out Back* (Austin, Tex., 1973); *Addison* (Garden City, N.Y., 1979); *A Smile from Katie Hattan and Other Natural Wonders* (Bryan, Tex., 1982); *Miracles out of a '22 Chevy* (N.p., 1983); *Easy Going* (Bryan, Tex., 1983); *One Man's Christmas* (Bryan, Tex., 1984); *Paper Hero* (Fredericksburg, Tex., 1986); *Texas Chronicles* (Fredericksburg, Tex., 1989).

Halpern, Frances (20 Aug. 1935–   ). Frances Halpern's column "Words and Images" has appeared weekly in the *Los Angeles Times* since 1992. She is also host of an interview/commentary show, "Literary Lunch with Fran Halpern," on KTMS radio in Santa Barbara/Ventura, California.

Halpern was born in New York City. She studied at the American Academy of Dramatic Arts and took courses at New York University, though she refers to herself as basically an autodidact.

For four years she was on the staff of the *Palos Verdes Peninsula News,* first as general assignment and political reporter, then as editor of the Profile section. Her first column, "Bookmarks," was published in the *Los Angeles Herald Examiner* (1981–1986) and in the *Los Angeles Daily News* (1986–1991). Her present column in the *Times* concentrates on literary people and events and runs in the Ventura Life section. Halpern has also free-lanced for such periodicals as *Seventeen, Westways, Womensport, Los Angeles Magazine, Valley Magazine, Reeves Journal,* and *Grit.*

Hamblin, Ken (22 Oct. 1940–   ). Ken Hamblin, who began writing his op-ed column for the *Denver Post,* is now distributed by the New York Times Syndicate.

Hamblin was born in Brooklyn, New York, the son of West Indian immigrants. He began his career as a *Detroit Free Press* photographer and later became a host/producer at Detroit's public television station WTVS. Next he became a radio talk-show host in Denver, Colorado, after which he began writing his column.

Hamblin's column is generally conservative. Unlike many of his fellow African-American columnists, he opposes gun control, is critical of our present welfare system, and supports capital punishment.

Hamill, Pete (24 June 1935–   ). Pete Hamill has written columns since 1965 for the *New York Post,* the *New York Daily News,* the *Village Voice,* and *Newsday.*

Hamill was born in Brooklyn, New York. He studied at Pratt Institute (1955–1956, 1957–1958) and Mexico City College (1956–1957) after serving in the navy from 1952 to 1954. Prior to his military service, he was a sheetmetal worker in the Brooklyn Navy Yard (1951–1952).

Hamill left college to work in advertising in New York City. He became a *New York Post* reporter (1960–1963) and during 1964–1965 was a contributing editor for *Saturday Evening Post.* He began a political column for the *New York Post* that ran from 1965 to 1974, with a break in 1966 to report from Vietnam and a year off (1968) for free-lancing. He wrote a Washington column for *Newsday* and did a column for the *New York Daily News* (1977–1979), after which he began a *Village Voice* column. Hamill became editor of the *New York Post* and by late 1994 was once again a columnist for *Newsday.*

Hamill was singled out by Vice President Spiro Agnew in 1970 for his comments critical of the Nixon administration. Hamill has published two collections of his columns and has authored a number of novels. He has also contributed to numerous magazines.

BOOKS: *A Killing for Christ* (New York, 1968); *Doc* (New York, 1971); *Irrational Ravings* (New York, 1971); *The Gift* (New York, 1973); *Flesh and Blood* (New York, 1977); *Fighters* (Garden City, N.Y., 1978); *Dirty Laundry* (New York, 1978); *The Deadly Piece* (New York, 1979); *The Invisible City: A New York Sketchbook* (New York, 1980); *The Guns of Heaven* (New York, 1984); *Loving Women* (New York, 1989); *Tokyo Sketches: Short Stories* (Tokyo, 1992); *The Drinking Life: A Memoir* (Boston, 1994).

Hapgood, Hutchins (21 May 1869–18 Nov. 1994). Gentleman-columnist Hutchins Hapgood did columns for the *New York Globe* and *New York Sun* in the early 1900s.

Hapgood was born in Chicago, the son of a lawyer/industrialist. He studied for one year at the University of Michigan; received the B.A. at Harvard, where he earned Phi Beta Kappa honors, in 1892; and spent the following two years traveling and studying at universities in Berlin and Freiburg in Germany. During 1896–1897, he did graduate work at Harvard, earning the A.M. in 1897.

After earning his master's degree, Hapgood became a reporter for the *New York Commercial Advertiser* under city editor Lincoln Steffens. Hapgood's specialties became art and the immigrants who poured into New York's Lower East Side around the turn of the century. Hapgood moved to the *New York Morning Telegraph* and next was drama critic for the *Chicago Evening Post.* He alternated newspaper jobs with trips to Italy, returning to write editorials and dramatic criticism for the *New York Evening Post.* In 1903 he joined the *New York Globe,* where he began his column.

Hapgood's great love was the theater. He was one of the charter members of the Provincetown [Massachusetts] Players in 1915, and his involvement in theater is documented at length in his autobiography, *A Victorian in the Modern World* (1939). He authored a number of additional books, as well, including a collection of his precolumn immigrant sketches, *The Spirit of the Ghetto* (1902).

BOOKS: *Paul Jones* (Boston and New York, 1901); *The Spirit of the Ghetto: Studies of the Jewish Quarter in New York* (New York, 1902); *The Autobiography of a Thief* (New York, 1903); *The Spirit of Labor* (New York, 1907); *An Anarchist Woman* (New York, 1909); *A Victorian in the Modern World* (New York, 1939).

Harden, Michael William (8 Aug. 1946–   ). Mike Harden was a columnist for the *Columbus* [Ohio] *Citizen-Journal* from 1981 to 1983 and at the *Columbus Dispatch* since 1983.

Harden was born in Columbus, Ohio, and received the B.A. in journalism at Ohio State University in 1973.

From 1975 to 1978 Harding was a contributing editor for *Columbus Monthly* and from 1978 to 1979, associate editor of *Ohio Magazine.* His column, "In Essence," is a mix of personal observations, humor, and profiles. Harden is also active in theater; he wrote and starred in the play *Please Don't Hold the Dog up to the Casket,* which was presented at the Thurber Theatre at Ohio State University in 1990. He has also published five paperbook book collections of his columns.

BOOKS: *First Gathering* (Columbus, Ohio, 1982); *Playing Favorites* (Columbus, Ohio, 1984); *Homegrown* (Columbus, Ohio, 1986); *Heartland Journal* (Columbus, Ohio, 1988); *Among Friends: The Best of Mike Harden* (Columbus, Ohio, 1994).

Harper, Charles Howard (9 March 1928–   ). Charley Harper is a country columnist/essayist whose work is carried by various New England weeklies. His weekly column "Ms. Plunkitt's Report" has appeared since 1990.

Harper was born in Rehoboth, Massachusetts. He received the B.S. in education from Boston University in 1952 but decided against a career in teaching in favor of corporate personnel work, which he did for thirty-five years. He became a columnist for the Nanlo newspaper group in New England; his column was titled "The Voice." He has contributed pseudonymous pieces to the *Boston Globe* and has written for Boston television stations WLVI and WBZ.

"Ms. Plunkitt's Report" is written for the *Westborough* [Massachusetts] *News* and features an array of fictitious characters through whom Harper comments on, in his words, "politics, morals, mores, historical events, books, movies, sports, religion, life, death." He describes himself as the typical country columnist.

Harris, Joel Chandler (9 Dec. 1848–3 July 1908). Southern folklorist Joel Chandler Harris, creator of the Uncle Remus tales of life on the antebellum plantation, was also a columnist for two Georgia newspapers from 1870 to 1900.

He was born in Eatonton, Georgia, and attended the Eatonton Academy for Boys. At age fourteen, he answered a help-wanted ad and in March 1862 became printer's devil to Joseph Addison Turner on his unusual plantation newspaper, the *Countryman.* When that paper ceased publication in spring 1866, Harris found work as a typesetter on the *Macon* [Georgia] *Telegraph,* where he also reviewed books and magazines and wrote short, humorous snippets. After roughly half a year, he took a new job as personal secretary to William Evelyn, publisher of the *Crescent Monthly,* a New Orleans magazine. In May 1867 he returned to Georgia and another typesetting job, this time on the weekly *Monroe Advertiser* in Forsyth. There he began writing humorous sketches of Georgia life that in autumn 1870 earned him the associate editorship of the *Savannah Morning News* under William Tappan Thompson. Here he began his first column, initially titled "State Affairs" and later altered to "Affairs of Georgia." In this column he playfully mined odd items culled from the smaller papers of the state. By the end of his six years on the *Morning News,* Harris had arrived as an established humorist.

Harris left Savannah because of an outbreak of yellow fever in August 1876 and in November of that year, at age twenty-seven, was hired as associate editor of the state's premier newspaper, the *Atlanta Constitution,* under editor Evan Howell. The paper's other associate editor was Henry W. Grady. Again Harris wrote a column, "Roundabout in Georgia." He also began writing dialect sketches in which his character Remus made his first appearance, as well as editorials, features, and book reviews for the *Constitution.* He credited an article in *Lippincott's* magazine on black Southern folklore with inspiring him to try to set down and convey the tales and dialect he had absorbed from his years of plantation upbringing. His first book, *Uncle Remus: His Songs and His Sayings,* appeared in 1880.

Harris's books flowed mainly from his newspaper writing. Most of his work was intended for adult readers, but some of his books were written for children. His stories reached new audiences in such papers as the *Boston Globe, New York Sun, San Francisco Examiner,* and *Louisville Courier-Journal,* and by the 1890s, he had become a widely admired literary figure. In 1899 he did a series on Civil War espionage and blockade running for the *Saturday Evening Post,* and in autumn 1900 he left the *Constitution* to devote full-time effort to his books and magazine articles.

His reputation received a boost in October 1905, when President Theodore Roosevelt visited Atlanta, singled Harris out for special praise, and invited him to the White House. Harris's final literary venture was a new periodical, *Uncle Remus's Magazine.* Harris served as editor, talked into the project by his son, Julian, one of the magazine's backers. Harris wrote an editorial and a political article for each issue and wrote several Uncle Remus stories for it, as well. The magazine, which was first published in June 1907, gained the largest circulation of any southern magazine but soon declined after the elder Harris's death in July 1908.

Harris's writing was marked by optimism, warmth, and perceptive interpretation of the patriarchal society of the Old South.

BOOKS: *Uncle Remus: His Songs and His Sayings* (New York, 1880); *Nights with Uncle Remus: Myths and Legends of the Old Plantation* (Boston, 1883); *Mingo and Other Sketches in Black and White* (Boston, 1884); *Free Joe and Other Georgian Sketches* (New York, 1887); *Daddy Jake the Runaway and Short Stories Told After Dark* (New York, 1889); ed., *Life of Henry W. Grady* (New York, 1890); *Balaam and His Master and Other Sketches and Stories* (Boston and New York, 1891); *A Plantation Printer: The Adventures of a Georgia Boy During the War* (London, 1892); *Uncle Remus and His Friends* (Boston and New York, 1892); *Little Mr. Thimblefinger and His Queer Country* (Boston and New York, 1894); *Mr. Rabbit at Home: A Sequel to Little Mr. Thimblefinger and His Queer Country* (Boston and New York, 1894); *Mr. Rabbit at Home: A Sequel to Little Mr. Thimblefinger and His Queer Friends* (Boston and New York, 1895); *The Story of Aaron (So Named) the Son of Ben Ali* (Boston and New York, 1896); *Stories of Georgia* (New York, 1896); *Sister Jane: Her Friends and Acquaintances* (Boston and New York, 1896); *Aaron in the Wildwoods* (Boston and New York, 1897); *Tales of the Home Folks in Peace and War* (Boston and New York, 1898); *The Chronicles of Aunt Minervy Ann* (New York, 1899); *Plantation Pageants* (Boston and New York, 1899); *On the Wing of Occasions* (New York, 1900); *The Making of a Statesman and Other Stories* (New York, 1902); *Gabriel Tolliver: A Story of Reconstruction* (New York, 1903); *Wally Wanderoon and His Story-Telling Machine* (New York, 1903); *A Little Union Scout* (New York, 1903); *The Tar-Baby and Other Rhymes of Uncle Remus* (New York, 1904); *Told by Uncle Remus: New Stories of the Old Plantation* (New York, 1904); *Uncle Remus and Brer Rabbit* (New York, 1907); *The Bishop and the Booger-Man* (New York, 1907); *The Shadow Between His Shoulder-Blades* (Boston, 1909); *Uncle Remus and the Little Boy* (Boston, 1910); *Uncle Remus Returns* (Boston and New York, 1918); *The Witch Wolf: An Uncle Remus Story* (Cambridge, Mass., 1921); *The Complete Tales of Uncle Remus,* comp. by Richard Chase (Boston, 1955).

REFERENCES: R. Bruce Bickley, Jr., *Joel Chandler Harris* (Boston, 1978); Stella Brewer Brookes, *Joel Chandler Harris—Folklorist* (Athens, Ga., 1950); Paul M. Cousins, *Joel Chandler Harris: A Biography* (Baton Rouge, La., 1968); Julian Collier Harris, *The Life and Letters of Joel Chandler Harris* (Boston, 1918); Julian Collier Harris, *Joel Chandler Harris as Editor and Essayist* (Chapel Hill, N.C., 1931); Alvin P. Harlow, *Joel Chandler Harris: Plantation Storyteller* (New York, 1941); William Bradley Strickland, ''A Check List of the Periodical Contributions of Joel Chandler Harris (1848–1908),'' *American Literary Realism* 9 (Summer 1976): 207–229; Robert Lemuel Wiggins, *The Life of Joel Chandler Harris, from Obscurity in Boyhood to Fame in Early Manhood* (Nashville, Tenn., 1918).

Harris, Sydney Justin (14 Sept. 1917–7 Dec. 1986). English-born, American-bred Sydney Harris is remembered for his philosophical general column ''Strictly Personal,'' which appeared from 1944 to 1986.

Harris was born in London in 1917 but went with his family to the United States in 1922. He never finished college but attended the University of Chicago and Central College in that same city. He worked for the *Chicago Herald-Examiner* and the *Chicago Daily Times* (1934–1936), then at age twenty founded and edited (1937–1938) a Chicago opinion magazine, the *Beacon,* which employed Saul Bellow as an assistant editor. From 1939 to 1941 he worked in public relations for the city of Chicago.

Harris was a reporter and feature writer for the *Chicago Daily News* from 1941 to 1944, then in 1944 launched his column, "Strictly Personal," which was picked up by Publishers Hall Syndicate. He also began a long run as the *Daily News* drama critic in 1945. He continued his column under the same title after going with the *Chicago Sun Times* in 1978; his column was then syndicated by Field Enterprises to roughly two hundred papers.

Harris's former associate Saul Bellow characterized the Harris style as marked by "civilized lucidity." His column was one of social commentary and seldom addressed partisan politics. He was a skillful creator of aphorisms regarding human nature and human foibles, and his main object, he said, was to help his readers to think with clarity. The many unusual topics he chose for his concise essay-style columns included the arrogance of ignorance, aristocracy and democracy, and keeping friendships in repair.

Harris was honored with several honorary degrees, was inducted into the Chicago Journalism Hall of Fame, and every three or four years collected his columns into books—a dozen in all.

BOOKS: *Strictly Personal* (Chicago, 1953); *Majority of One* (Boston, 1957); *Last Things First* (Boston, 1961); *On the Contrary* (Boston, 1964); *Leaving the Surface* (Boston, 1967); *The Authentic Person: Dealing with Dilemma* (Niles, Ill., 1972); *For the Time Being* (Boston, 1972); *Winners and Losers* (Allen, Tex., 1973); *The Best of Sydney J. Harris* (Boston, 1976); *Would You Believe?* (Niles, Ill., 1979); *Pieces of Eight* (Boston, 1982); *Clearing the Ground* (Boston, 1986).

Harsch, Joseph Close (25 May 1905–   ). Joseph Harsch was a foreign affairs columnist for the *Christian Science Monitor* since 1952.

Harsch was born in Toledo, Ohio. He received a B.A. from Williams College in 1927 and an A.B. from Corpus Christi College, Cambridge, in 1929.

From 1929 to 1943 Harsch was a Washington, D.C., correspondent for the *Christian Science Monitor*. From 1939 to 1941 he wrote for that paper from Rome and Berlin, and from 1943 to 1949 he was a commentator for CBS. He worked as an NBC commentator (1953–1967), senior European correspondent (1957–1965), and diplomatic correspondent (1965–1967). In 1967 he made a clean sweep of the major networks by becoming a commentator for ABC (1967–1971). In 1971 he returned to newspapering as chief editorial writer for the *Monitor*. Harsch was granted an honorary M.A. by Williams College and also received the designation Commander of the Order of the British Empire.

BOOKS: *Pattern of Conquest* (Garden City, N.Y., 1941); *The Curtain Isn't Iron* (Garden City, N.Y., 1950); *At the Hinge of History: A Reporter's Story* (Athens, Ga., 1993).

Hastings, James Syme (3 June 1870–3 June 1921). Writing as "Luke McLuke" in his syndicated column "Bits of Byplay," the *Cincinnati Enquirer's* James Hastings became a well-known humorist.

Hastings was born in Lowell, Massachusetts, and attended McGill University. He edited a newspaper titled *Uncle Sam* in Cumberland, Maryland, and during the Spanish-American War was a correspondent for the *Washington Times.* He joined the *Enquirer* in 1900 as exchange editor and began his own column in December 1911. The column enjoyed national syndication.

Haught, Robert L. (20 May 1930–   ). Robert Haught writes a weekly humor column, "Potomac Junction," out of the Washington bureau of the *Daily Oklahoman.* He is also an editorial writer for that paper.

Haught was born in Lawton, Oklahoma. He received the B.A. in journalism (1954) and the M.A. in public administration (1972) from the University of Oklahoma in Norman. He had earlier attended Southwestern State College (1949–1950, 1952) and has since done postgraduate work at American University in Washington, D.C.

From 1954 to 1963 Haught was a staff correspondent, and later a bureau manager, for United Press International. Concurrently, he wrote "Only in Oklahoma," a weekly humor column, plus a weekly business column.

He was press secretary, and later press agency head, under Oklahoma governor Henry Bellmon; in this position he produced the column "Plainly Speaking," which appeared under the governor's byline. From 1969 to 1981 he was press secretary and administrative assistant to Sen. Henry Bellmon, and for the latter part of 1981, administrative assistant to Senator Charles Mathias. He then founded and ran an editorial service, Haught Associates (1981–1987), and published two newsletters: "The Political Communicator" and "Sunbelt Monthly." He has been an editorial writer for the *Daily Oklahoman* since 1987. His column has appeared since 1989; he describes it as "a breezy, often satirical, report on events in the nation's capital."

BOOKS: Ed., *Giants of Management* (Washington, D.C., 1985); principal writer, *Space: America's New Competitive Frontier* (Washington, D.C., 1987).

Hearn, Patricio Lafcadio Tessima Carlos (27 June 1850–26 Sept. 1904). Lafcadio Hearn, mainly remembered as a literary figure who wrote about Japan, honed his writing skills as a columnist for the *New Orleans Item* in the late 1870s and early 1880s.

Hearn was born on the Greek island of Lafcadio, learned French at a Catholic school in Paris, and attended St. Cuthbert's school in England and another Jesuit school in Rouen, France. When funds ran out, he set off for Cincinnati, Ohio, where he had relatives. On the way, he spent two years in New York City, working as a typesetter for a commercial paper called the *Trade List.* Reaching Cincinnati in 1872, he was hired as a reporter/feature writer by the *Cincinnati Enquirer.* With a friend, he founded a short-lived journal of satire titled *Ye Giglampz: A Weekly Illustrated Journal.* He worked for the *Cincinnati Commercial* in 1876–1877, then became associate editor of the *New Orleans Item* (1978–1981). In a city as exotic as his own background, Hearn had a column, translated and republished French literature and French-language items from various Louisiana papers, and wrote a number of purposefully weird short stories. He published in *Century* and *Harper's* and wrote his first novel, *Chita* (1889). *Harper's* sent him to the island of Martinique to write about the Indies. After two years *Harper's* posted him to Japan, where he lived for the remainder of his life.

Hearn cut his ties with *Harper's,* took Japanese citizenship, changed his name to Koizumi Yakumo, and took an editing job with the *Kobe Chronicle.* He also taught English in a school in Matsue, then at another school on the island of Kyushu (1891–1894). Finally, he was an English professor at the Imperial University in Tokyo (1896–1903). He again indulged his fondness for eerie, Poe-like writing in a number of books that made use of Japanese folktales and legends.

BOOKS: *Stray Leaves from Strange Literature* (Boston, 1884); *Some Chinese Ghosts* (Boston, 1887); *Chita: A Memory of Last Island* (New York, 1889); *Two Years in the French West Indies* (New York, 1890); *Youma: The Story of a West-Indian Slave* (New York, 1890); *Glimpses of Unfamiliar Japan,* 2 vols. (Boston and New York, 1894); *"Out of the East": Reveries and Studies in New Japan* (Boston and New York, 1895); *Kokoro: Hints and Echoes of Japanese Inner Life* (Boston and New York, 1896); *Gleanings in Buddha-Fields: Studies of Hand and Soul in the Far East* (Boston and New York, 1897); *Exotics and Retrospectives* (Boston, 1899); *In Ghostly Japan* (Boston, 1899); *Shadowings* (Boston, 1900); *A Japanese Miscellany* (Boston, 1901); *Kotto: Being Japanese Curios, with Sundry Cobwebs* (New York and London, 1902); *Kwaidan: Stories and Studies of Strange Things* (Boston and New York, 1904); *Japan: An Attempt at Interpretation* (New York and London, 1904); *The Romance of the Milky Way and Other Stories* (Boston and New York, 1905); *Letters from the Diary of an Impressionist: Early Writings* (Boston and New York, 1911); *Fantastics and Other Fancies,* ed. by Charles W. Hutson (Boston and New York, 1914); *Karma,* ed. by Albert Mordell (New York, 1918); *Essays in European and Oriental Literature,* ed. by Albert Mordell (New York, 1923); *Creole Sketches,* ed. by Charles Hutson (Boston and New York, 1924); *An American Miscellany: Articles and Stories,* 2 vols., ed. by Albert Mordell (New York, 1924); *Occidental Gleanings: Sketches and Essays,* ed. by Albert Mordell (New York, 1925); *Editorials,* ed. by Charles Hutson (Boston and New York, 1926); *Essays on American Literature,* ed. by Sanki Ichikawa (Tokyo, 1929); *Barbarous Barbers and Other Stories,* ed. by Ichiro Nishizaki (Tokyo, 1939); *Buying Christmas Toys and Other Essays,* ed. by Ichiro Nishizaki (Tokyo, 1939); *Literary Essays,* ed. by Ichiro Nishizaki (Tokyo, 1939); *The New Radiance and Other Scientific Sketches,* ed. by Ichiro Nishizake (Tokyo, 1939); *Oriental Articles,* ed. by Ichiro Nishizake (Tokyo, 1939); *The Buddhist Writings of Lafcadio Hearn,* ed. by Kenneth Rexroth (Santa Barbara, Calif., 1977).

REFERENCES: Elizabeth Bisland, *The Life and Letters of Lafcadio Hearn,* 2 vols. (Boston and New York, 1906); George M. Gould, *Concerning Lafcadio Hearn* (Philadelphia, 1908); Arthur E. Kunst, *Lafcadio Hearn* (New York, 1969); Elizabeth Stevenson, *Lafcadio Hearn* (New York, 1961); Edward Larocque Tinker, *Lafcadio Hearn's American Days* (New York, 1924); Beongcheon Yu, *An Ape of the Gods: The Art and Thought of Lafcadio Hearn* (Detroit, 1964).

Hearst, William Randolph (29 April 1863–14 Aug. 1951). William Randolph Hearst, one of the best known of all U.S. newspaper owners and builder of a vast media empire, wrote a column, "In the News," which initially appeared on the front page of the *Los Angeles Examiner* in March 1940, then was used by all the Hearst papers until 1942.

Hearst was born in San Francisco, California, the son of an enormously wealthy miner and land speculator. Hearst attended Harvard University, starting in 1882, and was business manager of the *Harvard Lampoon,* but was expelled after his junior year because of practical jokes he had played on the school's faculty. He worked as a reporter for Joseph Pulitzer's innovative and successful *New York World* during 1885, then in 1887 talked his father into giving him the small, sagging *San Francisco Examiner.* Using family money, he built this paper into what he termed "the monarch of the dailies." Under Hearst, it became sensationalistic but successful. In 1895 Hearst bought the *New York Morning Journal,* the paper that had been founded by Joseph Pulitzer's brother, Albert, and entered into aggressive competition with the *World.*

Hearst extended his ownership of newspapers, eventually acquiring around thirty, plus radio stations; national magazines such as *Cosmopolitan, Harper's Bazaar, House Beautiful,* and *Good Housekeeping;* motion picture companies; the International News Service, the International News Reel Corporation, and King Features Syndicate. At their peak, the Hearst companies had roughly thirty-one thousand employees and an audience of many millions. It is perhaps surprising that having become one of the most powerful mass media owners of all time, Hearst would want to write a column of his own, but after the death of his editor/columnist Arthur Brisbane, he was unable to find a suitable replacement for the front-page Brisbane column, "Today," and decided to do it himself. According to longtime Hearst employee and confidant Edmond Coblentz, Hearst did all of his own writing for the column, unlike many celebrity columnists since, doing most of his writing late at night. Joseph Connolly, head of King Features, wanted to syndicate the column more widely, but Hearst himself preferred to have it appear only in his own chain. The column was general in content and often quite witty. Once asked why such a busy man would choose to write a column, Hearst replied that he really didn't know, saying, "I suppose I have the bear by the tail."

BOOKS: *Editorials from the Hearst Newspapers* (New York, 1914); *Let Us Promote the World's Peace* (New York, 1915); *The Obligations and Opportunities of the United States in Mexico and in the Philippines* (New York, 1916); *Truths About the Trusts* (Rahway, N.J., 1916); *On the Foreign War Debts* (N.p., 1931); *Selections from the Writings and Speeches of William Randolph Hearst,* ed. by E. F. Tompkins (San Francisco, 1948); *William Randolph Hearst: A Portrait in His Own Words* (New York, 1952).

REFERENCES: Rodney P. Carlisle, *Hearst and the New Deal: The Progressive as Reactionary* (New York, 1979); Oliver Carlson and Ernest Bates, *Hearst: Lord of San Simeon* (Westport, Conn., 1936); Roy Everett Littlefield III, *William Randolph Hearst: His Role in American Progressivism* (Washington, D.C., 1980); Ferdinand Lundberg, *Imperial Hearst* (New York, 1936); Mrs. Fremont Older, *William Randolph Hearst, American* (New York, 1936); John Tebbel, *The Life and Good Times of William Randolph Hearst* (New York, 1952); John K. Winkler, *William Randolph Hearst: A New Appraisal* (New York, 1955); W. A. Swanberg, *Citizen Hearst* (New York, 1961).

Hecht, Ben (28 Feb. 1894–18 April 1964). Ben Hecht is most remembered as coauthor of the play *The Front Page* but also was a successful columnist for the *Chicago Daily News* and years later, for the New York paper *PM.*

Hecht was born in New York City, the son of Russian Jewish immigrants. He moved with his family to Racine, Wisconsin, and graduated from high school there. In 1910 he withdrew from the University of Wisconsin just three days after his arrival there and instead took a low-paid job running down photos of criminals and their victims for the *Chicago Journal.* Eventually he was allowed to write for the *Journal* and in 1914 was hired by the *Chicago Daily News,* where he worked until 1923 as reporter, foreign correspondent, and columnist. His column, launched in June 1921, specialized in human interest stories and earned him a national reputation after the 1922 publication of a collection of these columns in book form. A novel he published in 1922 resulted in an obscenity suit, which Hecht lost, and in 1923 he left the *Daily News* to cofound, with publisher Pascal Covici, an irreverent tabloid, the *Chicago Literary Times,* which folded in the following year.

In 1925 he left journalism for a career in play and screenplay writing. The highly successful play *The Front Page,* coauthored with Charles MacArthur, opened on Broadway in 1928 and was made into a movie in 1931. Hecht enjoyed a long and highly profitable career in Hollywood, winning an Oscar in 1927 for his film *Underworld* and in 1935 for *The Scoundrel,* which he cowrote with MacArthur. In 1940 he became a columnist for *PM,* writing on urban affairs and the activities of the Nazi party in Europe. He returned to Hollywood and screenwriting the following year.

BOOKS: With Kenneth S. Goodman, *The Wonder Hat* (New York, 1920); with Kenneth Goodman, *The Hero of Santa Maria* (New York, 1920); *Erik Dorn* (New York, 1921); *1001 Afternoons in Chicago* (Chicago, 1922); *Gargoyles* (New York, 1922); *Fantazius Mallare: A Mysterious Oath* (Chicago, 1922); *The Florentine Dagger: A Novel for Amateur Detectives* (New York, 1923); with Maxwell Bodenheim, *Cutie, A Warm Mamma* (Chicago, 1924); *Humpty Dumpty* (New York, 1924); *Tales of Chicago Streets* (Girard, Kan., 1924); *Broken Necks and Other Stories* (Girard, Kan., 1924); *The Kingdom of Evil: A Continuation of the Journal of Fantazius Mallare* (Chicago, 1924); with Kenneth Goodman, *The Wonder Hat and Other One-Act Plays* (New York and London, 1925); *Count Bruga* (New York, 1926); *Broken Necks* (Chicago, 1926); *Infatuation and Other Stories of Love's Misfits* (Girard, Kan., 1927); *The Unlovely Sin and Other Stories of Desire's Pawns* (Girard, Kan., 1927); *Jazz and Other Stories of Young Love* (Girard, Kan., 1927); *Christmas Eve* (New York, 1928); with Charles MacArthur, *The Front Page* (New York, 1928); *A Jew in Love* (New York, 1931); *The Champion from Far Away* (New York, 1931); with Gene Fowler, *The Great Magoo* (New York, 1933); *Actor's*

Blood (New York, 1936); *To Quito and Back* (New York, 1937); *A Book of Miracles* (New York, 1939); with Charles MacArthur, *Fun to Be Free, Patriotic Pageant* (New York, 1941); with Charles MacArthur, *Ladies and Gentlemen* (New York, 1941); *1001 Afternoons in New York* (New York, 1941); *I Hate Actors!* (New York, 1944); *A Guide for the Bedevilled* (New York, 1944); *The Collected Stories of Ben Hecht* (New York, 1945); *A Flag Is Born* (New York, 1946); *A Child of the Century* (New York, 1954); *Charlie: The Improbable Life and Times of Charles MacArthur* (New York, 1957); *The Sensualists* (New York, 1959); *Perfidy* (New York, 1961); *Gaily, Gaily* (Garden City, N.Y., 1963); *Letters from Bohemia* (Garden City, N.Y., 1964).

REFERENCES: Marvin Felheim, "Tom Sawyer Grows Up: Ben Hecht as a Writer," *Journal of Popular Culture* 9 (Spring 1976): 908–915; Doug Fetherling, *The Five Lives of Ben Hecht* (Toronto, 1977); Chaim Lieberman, *This Man and His "Perfidy"* (New York, 1964); Abe C. Ravitz, "Ballyhoo, Gargoyles and Firecrackers: Ben Hecht's Aesthetic Calliope," *Journal of Popular Culture* 1 (Summer 1967): 37–51.

Heinemann, Jennifer Howe (12 Oct. 1962–   ). Jennifer Heinemann, whose column appears with her maiden name, Jennifer Howe, as its byline, has written a general column for the *Kansas City Star* since 1992.

She was born in Sioux City, Iowa, and earned her B.J. from the University of Missouri—Columbia, in 1985.

Heinemann's first job was as a feature writer for the *Winston-Salem* [North Carolina] *Journal* (1985–1987). She spent the next two years as a reporter for the *Examiner* in Independence, Missouri, and in 1989 she was hired as a feature writer by the *Kansas City Star*. Her column appears on the Metropolitan section front and is concerned with the people and issues of her city.

Heitman, James Daniel (31 Jan. 1964–   ). Danny Heitman has written the "At Random" general column for the *Morning Advocate* in Baton Rouge, Louisiana, since 1990.

Heitman was born in Hammond, Louisiana, and received the B.A. in liberal arts in 1986 from Southeastern Louisiana University.

From 1982 to 1985, Heitman was a reporter and editor for the *Ponchatoula Enterprise* in Ponchatoula, Louisiana. He was a regional correspondent for the *Morning Advocate* during 1985 and 1986, and from 1986 to 1987, environmental writer for the *State-Times* in Baton Rouge. He was the *State-Times*'s art critic from 1987 to 1990.

The topics addressed in Heitman's column vary widely—in his words, "from the war in Bosnia to singing in the shower."

Hellinger, Mark John (21 March 1903–21 Dec. 1947). Mark Hellinger is chiefly remembered as a Hollywood producer and as the first Broadway columnist, but he also wrote and edited a more general column and page on Sundays in the *New York Mirror*.

Hellinger was born in New York City and attended the city's public schools.

He was expelled from Townsend Harris High School for organizing a student strike, after which he became a waiter at a nightspot in Greenwich Village. He began writing songs and direct-mail advertising copy, then began writing for a theatrical weekly, *Zit's*. In 1923 he was hired by the New York *Daily News* as a reporter. Six months later he was given an existing column, "About Town," which he converted from a woman's feature into the first column to specialize in news and tales of Broadway. He attracted extra attention via a literary ploy used earlier by Mark Twain and his rival reporter Clement Rice ("The Unreliable")—the "feud." Hellinger's "adversaries" were the entertainer Rudy Vallee and the New York sportswriter Paul Gallico.

In 1930 Hellinger left the *News* for a far higher salary with the New York *Daily Mirror,* a deal sweetened by having his column syndicated by King Features. Eventually, he cut his Broadway column from daily to thrice weekly and began his Sunday page, "All in a Day," for the *Mirror*. On it he used short stories; jokes; his comments on various plays, movies, and books; sports predicitons; and comments on the political scene. He also appeared in vaudeville and had his own radio program, "Penthouse Party." He spent 1933 and 1934 traveling abroad, sending back columns from each destination. He also wrote plays and musicals and in 1937 moved to Hollywood as a Warner Brothers writer and producer. He produced numerous movies, the most memorable of which is probably *High Sierra,* starring Humphrey Bogart. In 1941 he switched to Twentieth Century Fox but returned to Warner the following year. In 1944 he left Hollywood for one year to work as a war correspondent for the Hearst papers, then he returned to form his own movie company, Mark Hellinger Productions. Despite his work in movies, Hellinger continued writing his Sunday column until his death.

BOOKS: *Moon over Broadway* (New York, 1931); *The Ten Million* (New York, 1934).

REFERENCES: James Bishop, *The Mark Hellinger Story* (New York, 1952).

Hemingway, Sam (?–). Sam Hemingway writes a general/political/investigative column for Vermont's *Burlington Free Press.*

Hemingway attended Syracuse University as a magazine journalism major in the 1960s. From 1971 to 1974 he was editor of the *Lamoille County Weekly* in Johnson, Vermont. After two years at the Journalism Institute at Johnson State College, he became a reporter for the *Burlington Free Press.* In 1980 he became editor of this paper's Sunday magazine. After stints as day editor (1983–1984) and city editor (1984–1989), he began his column in 1989. It appears three times weekly.

Hempstone, Smith, Jr. (1 Feb. 1929–). Smith Hempstone wrote a nationally syndicated column, "Our Times," from 1970 to 1989.

Hempstone was born in Washington, D.C. He attended George Washington University (1946–1947) and graduated with honors from the University of the

South in 1950. He served in the Marine Corps from 1950 to 1952 and did graduate work at Harvard University in 1964–1965 as a Nieman Fellow.

Hempstone did radio rewrite for the Associated Press in Charlotte, North Carolina, in 1952, then was a *Louisville* [Kentucky] *Times* reporter in 1953. He did rewrite for *National Geographic* in 1954 and reported for the *Washington Star* in 1955–1956. From 1956 to 1960 he was a Fellow of the Institute of Current World Affairs in Africa.

Hempstone then joined the staff of the *Chicago Daily News* as a foreign correspondent, first in Africa (1961–1964) then in Latin America (1965). He was a *Washington Star* foreign correspondent in Latin America in 1966 and in Europe in 1967–1969. He then became the *Star*'s associate editor and editorial page chief (1970–1975). He was executive editor of the *Washington Times* (1982–1984) and that paper's editor in chief (1984–1985). In 1989 he was named ambassador to Kenya by President George Bush. Hempstone had lived there for several years and could speak Swahili.

Hempstone's views are, on balance, conservative. He has contributed to *Atlantic, U.S. News and World Report,* and other magazines and has authored seven books, some of which concern Africa.

BOOKS: *Africa, Angry Young Giant* (New York, 1961); *The New Africa* (London, 1961); *Rebels, Mercenaries, and Dividends: The Katanga Story* (New York, 1962); *Katanga Report* (London, 1962); *A Tract of Time* (Greenwich, Conn., 1966); *In the Midst of Lions* (New York, 1968); *STA: An Illustrated History of St. Albans School* (N.p., 1981).

Henderson, Michael Douglas (15 March 1932–). Michael Henderson is a freelance columnist for the *Lake Oswego Review* in Lake Oswego, Oregon.

Henderson was born in London, England. He immigrated to the United States in 1978 and became a newspaper columnist after first working in radio and television. He was moderator of ''World Press in Review'' on KOAP-TV in Portland, Oregon, from 1979 to 1981, then was a KBOO radio commentator in that city starting in 1981. He began working in public radio in Oregon in 1987 and has written five books.

BOOKS: *From India with Hope* (London, 1972); *Experiment with Untruth: India Under Emergency* (Columbia, Mo., 1977); *A Different Accent* (Richmond, Va., 1985); *On History's Coat-Tails* (Richmond, Va., 1988); *Hope for a Change* (Salem, Ore., 1991).

Hendren, Ron (3 Aug. 1945–). Ron Hendren began writing the syndicated column ''In Washington'' in 1972.

Hendren was born in Pinehurst, North Carolina, and received the B.A. from the University of North Carolina at Chapel Hill in 1967.

Hendren got into the columnist business by way of politics. He was an assistant to Sargent Shriver in 1969, to Sen. Stephen M. Young in 1970, and to Sen. B. Everett Jordan in 1971. In 1972 he began his column.

Hendren was a visiting lecturer at the University of Maryland in 1976–1977 and in 1976 began as a commentator on WRC-TV in Washington on ''About

Washington.'' He also worked as a commentator for KQED-TV in San Francisco, starting in 1978.

Hentoff, Nathan Irving (10 June 1925–   ). Nat Hentoff is known for his work for the *New Yorker* since 1960 and for his two columns: in the *Village Voice* since 1957 and the *Washington Post* since 1984.

Hentoff was born in Boston. He received the B.A., with highest honors, in 1946 from Northeastern University and did graduate study at Harvard University (1946) and as a Fulbright Fellow at the Sorbonne in 1950.

From 1944 to 1953 he was an announcer, writer, and producer for radio station WMEX in Boston. Hentoff was associate editor of *Downbeat* magazine from 1953 to 1957 and was a cofounder and coeditor of *The Jazz Review* (1958–1960), after which he became a *New Yorker* staff writer. He has been a prolific author and editor of books whose interests at first centered on jazz, then began to shift to social concerns such as education, race relations, and censorship. He has written an autobiography, *Boston Boy*, and novels in addition to nonfiction. Hentoff is a liberal with a strong sense of empathy with the underdog. His weekly *Post* column now focuses on the freedoms guaranteed Americans by the Bill of Rights. It was syndicated by Copley News Service until mid-1992, when Hentoff went with Newspaper Enterprise Association.

BOOKS: Ed. with Nat Shapiro, *Hear Me Talkin' to Ya: The Story of Jazz by the Men Who Made It* (New York, 1955); ed. with Nat Shapiro, *The Jazz Makers* (New York, 1957); ed. with Albert J. McCarthy, *Jazz: New Perspectives on the History of Jazz* (New York, 1959); *The Jazz Life* (New York, 1961); *Peace Agitator* (New York, 1963); *The New Equality* (New York, 1964); *Jazz Country* (New York, 1965); *Call the Keeper* (New York, 1966); *Our Children Are Dying* (New York, 1966); ed., *The Essays of A. J. Muste* (Indianapolis, 1967); *Journey into Jazz* (New York, 1968); *I'm Really Dragged but Nothing Gets Me Down* (New York, 1968); *A Doctor Among the Addicts* (New York, 1968); *Onwards* (New York, 1968); *A Political Life: The Education of John V. Lindsay* (New York, 1969); *In the Country of Ourselves* (New York, 1971); *Jazz Is* (New York, 1976); *This School Is Driving Me Crazy* (New York, 1976); *Does Anybody Give a Damn? Nat Hentoff on Education* (New York, 1977); *The First Freedom: A Tumultuous History of Free Speech in America* (New York, 1980); ed. with Albert J. McCarthy, *Jazz* (London, 1977); *Does This School Have Capital Punishment?* (New York, 1981); *Blues for Charlie Darwin* (New York, 1982); *The Day They Came to Arrest the Book* (New York, 1982); *The Man from Internal Affairs* (New York, 1985); *Boston Boy* (New York, 1986); *American Heroes: In and Out of School* (New York, 1987); *John Cardinal O'Connor: At the Storm Center of a Changing American Catholic Church* (New York, 1988); *Free Speech for Me—but Not for Thee: How the American Left and Right Relentlessly Censor Each Other* (New York, 1992).

Herling, John (14 April 1907–   ). John Herling, mainly known as publisher of *John Herling's Labor Letter* since 1947, was also a columnist with the National Newspaper Syndicate during the 1950s.

Herling was born in New York City. From 1930 to 1934 he served as executive secretary of the League for Democracy's Emergency Committee for Strikers. In 1935 he was assistant editor of United Features Syndicate and from 1936 to 1937, Washington correspondent for the *Milwaukee Leader.* He worked in Washington, D.C., for Time, Inc., in 1937 and was publicity director for March of Time, in 1937–1938. In 1939–1940 he was director of the Children's Crusade for Children and from 1940 to 1941 assistant secretary of the New School for Social Research. From 1941 to 1946 Herling was director of labor and social relations for the Office of Inter-American Affairs. He was a European correspondent for various newspapers in 1946, then began his newsletter in 1947. In 1953 he began his syndicated column, which addressed both labor and general topics. Herling also lectured abroad for the U.S. State Department and wrote free-lance for magazines.

BOOKS: With Morris Shapiro, *The Terzani Case: An Account of a Labor Battle Against a Fascist Frame-Up* (New York, 1934); with Maurice Goldbloom, Joel Seidman, and Elizabeth Yard, *Strikes Under the New Deal* (Katonah, N.Y., 1935); *The Great Price Conspiracy: The Story of the Antitrust Violations in the Electrical Industry* (Washington, D.C., 1962); *Labor Unions in America* (New York, 1964); *Right to Challenge: People and Power in the Steelworkers Union* (New York, 1972).

Hernandez, Roger (?–   ). Roger Hernandez writes a weekly Hispanic issues column syndicated by King Features.

Hernandez was born in Cuba and moved to the United States in 1965 when his parents were exiled by the Castro regime. Hernandez is a graduate of Rutgers University. His journalistic background includes jobs as news editor for New Jersey public television and for WWOR-TV. He has contributed to *Washington Journalism Review, Vista, New Jersey Monthly, Hispanic Business,* and the Spanish and French editions of *Reader's Digest,* and he is an adjunct journalism faculty member at two institutions: Fairleigh Dickinson University and Bloomfield College, both in New Jersey.

Hesselberg, George Roy (2 Feb. 1951–   ). George Hesselberg has been a columnist and reporter for the *Wisconsin State Journal* in Madison, Wisconsin, since 1987.

Hellesberg was born in La Crosse, Wisconsin. He earned the B.A. in journalism from the University of Wisconsin—Madison in 1973, then during 1974 and 1975 studied language and phonetics at the University of Oslo in Norway.

He began as an unpaid sportswriter for the *Bangor Independent* in Bangor, Wisconsin, in the 1960s. While in college he was reporter, and later fine arts editor and city editor, for the *Badger Herald* in Madison and in 1972 also reported for the *Daily Cardinal* in Madison. From 1972 to 1974 he wrote for the *Wisconsin State Journal* in Madison, and while studying in Oslo in 1974 and 1975, worked as proofreader and copy editor for the Norwegian Council for Research. Concurrently, he performed the same duties for the Norwegian State Department's Press and Culture Division.

During 1977 Hesselberg free-lanced for the *Isthmus* in Madison and served briefly as a reporter for a Madison weekly, the *Press Connection.* He joined the *Wisconsin State Journal* in 1977 as a reporter and began his column in 1987. Hesselberg, who collects umbrellas, is a frequent award winner and has published one collection of his columns.

BOOKS: *Paint Me Green and Call Me Fern—or, How to Walk with Your Hands in Your Pockets* (Madison, Wis., 1991).

Hiaasen, Carl (12 March 1953–). Carl Hiaasen is a hard-hitting Metro columnist for the *Miami Herald* and the author of hot-selling, comedic murder mysteries set in his native South Florida.

Hiaasen (pronounced HIYA-sun) was born in Fort Lauderdale. He attended Emory University for two years, then transferred to the University of Florida, where he received the B.S. in journalism in 1974.

After college, Hiaasen was hired as a general assignment reporter by *Cocoa Today,* which has been renamed *Florida Today.* In 1975 he began writing for that paper's Sunday magazine, then in 1976 was hired by the *Miami Herald* to work in its Broward County bureau. He soon was moved to the Miami city desk and from there to the *Herald*'s Sunday magazine. Next he became part of an investigative unit that wrote about drug dealers, incompetent or dishonest physicians, unprincipled developers, smuggling, and other assorted topics from South Florida's substantial underside. Five years later, in 1985, he began writing his hard-hitting column. In it he continues to hammer away at the exploitation of his region's ecology and the general crime and sleaze that seem to accompany tourism in exotic settings. His first three books were coauthored, his last four written solo.

BOOKS: With William D. Montalbano, *Powder Burn* (New York, 1981); with William D. Montalbano, *Trap Line* (New York, 1982); with William D. Montalbano, *A Death in China* (New York, 1984); *Tourist Season* (New York, 1986); *Double Whammy* (New York, 1987); *Skin Tight* (New York, 1989); *Native Tongue* (New York, 1991).

REFERENCES: Joanne Kenen, "Carl of the Wild," *American Journalism Review* (October 1993): 25–29; Mike Thomas, "Cruising for Trouble," *Florida Magazine* (4 August 1991): 8, 10–12.

Hibbs, Benjamin Smith (23 July 1901–30 March 1975). Ben Hibbs, editor of the *Saturday Evening Post* for two decades, was, early in his career, a columnist for the Arkansas City (Kansas) *Traveler.* His columns and editorials were reprinted by various Kansas papers, including the *Emporia Gazette* under the editorship of William Allen White.

Hibbs was born in the small community of Fontana, Kansas, and grew up in another tiny Kansas town, Pretty Prairie. He received the A.B. in journalism from the University of Kansas in 1923 after being inducted into Phi Beta Kappa. He was editor of the *Daily Kansan,* the university's student paper.

Hibbs became news editor of the Fort Morgan (Colorado) *Times* in 1923, then returned to his native state the following year as news editor of the *Daily Tribune* in Pratt. In 1924 he taught journalism and English at Hays State College, an experience not to his liking. After two years of teaching, he became editor and manager of the *Goodland* [Kansas] *News Republic* (1926–1927), then moved to be managing editor of the Arkansas City (Kansas) *Daily Traveler,* where his writing began to attract attention. His columns and editorials were said to be clever and optimistic.

Hibbs became associate editor of the national magazine *Country Gentleman* (1929–1940). Later he was this magazine's fiction editor, and, from 1940 to 1942, its editor. He was editor of the *Saturday Evening Post* from 1942 to 1962, having replaced Wesley Stout in that position. After retiring from the *Post,* he was a senior editor for *Reader's Digest* (1963–1972).

BOOKS: *Two Men on a Job: A Behind-the-Scenes Story of a Rowdy Genius and His Mentor* (Philadelphia, 1938); ed., *Great Stories from the Saturday Evening Post* (New York, 1948); ed., *White House Sermons* (New York, 1972); ed., *A Michener Miscellany, 1950–1970* (London, 1975).

REFERENCES: Deryl R. Leaming, *A Biography of Ben Hibbs,* Ph.D. Dissertation, Syracuse University, 1969; B. R. Manago, *The Saturday Evening Post Under Ben Hibbs, 1942–1961,"* Ph.D. Dissertation, Northwestern University, 1968.

Higgins, Marguerite (3 Sept. 1920–3 Jan. 1966). Marguerite Higgins, the first woman to win a Pulitzer Prize for war correspondence, wrote a thrice-weekly syndicated Washington column for *Newsday.*

Higgins was born in Hong Kong and grew up in Oakland, California. She earned the B.A. in French from the University of California at Berkeley in 1941 and the M.S. in journalism from Columbia University in 1942. During college she wrote for the school paper, the *Daily Californian,* and did summer work with the *Vallejo Times Herald.* While at Columbia, she was a stringer for the *New York Herald Tribune.* She remained with that paper from 1942 to 1963. In 1944 she worked as a war correspondent, in 1947 as Berlin bureau chief, and in 1950 as bureau chief in Tokyo. She was a Washington correspondent between the end of World War II and the Korean conflict, when she again worked as a war correspondent, winning the Pulitzer in 1951.

In 1963 Higgins left her former employer for *Newsday* and began her column, which was syndicated to roughly ninety papers. Her final assignment was covering Vietnam, where she died of a tropical disease at age forty-five.

BOOKS: *War in Korea: The Report of a Woman Combat Correspondent* (Garden City, N.Y., 1951); *News Is a Singular Thing* (Garden City, N.Y., 1955); *Red Plush and Black Bread* (New York, 1955); *Jessie Benton Freamont* (Boston, 1962); with Peter Lisagor, *Overtime in Heaven: Adventures in the Foreign Service* (Garden City, N.Y., 1964); *Our Vietnam Nightmare* (New York, 1965).

REFERENCES: Kathleen Kearney Keeshen, *Marguerite Higgins: Journalist, 1920–1966,* Ph.D. Dissertation, University of Maryland, 1983; Antoinette May, *Witness to War: A Biography of Marguerite Higgins* (New York, 1983).

Hill, Robert Spear, Jr. (21 Nov. 1942–   ). Bob Hill writes a thrice-weekly
Metro column for the *Louisville Courier Journal.*

Hill was born in Paterson, New Jersey. He received the B.C. (Bachelor of
Commerce) degree in 1964 at Rice University, where he was on the basketball
team. After brief graduate work at the University of Houston and Northern
Illinois University, he worked from 1967 to 1969 for a biweekly paper, then
moved to Rockford, Illinois, and the *Morning Star.* Hill was with the *Star* from
1969 to 1975 and did his first column there.

He was hired by the *Louisville Courier Journal* as a general assignment reporter in 1975 and after two years became the paper's Kentucky columnist.
Thereafter, he was Metro columnist for the *Louisville Times* until it folded in
1987, when he assumed his present job.

Hill is treasurer of the National Society of Newspaper Columnists, has edited
two gardening almanacs, and has authored three books, with a fourth expected
out in 1995. His columns are often whimsical: everything from eulogies for cars
and washing machines that have finally died to a poem about a water-skiing
squirrel.

BOOKS: *Survivors: The History of Depression and Manic Depression* (Louisville, 1988);
The Amazing Basketball Book (Louisville, 1989); *Old Friends: The Best of Bob Hill*
(Louisville, 1991).

Hoagland, Jim (22 October 1940–   ). Two-time Pulitzer Prize winner Jim
Hoagland has written a twice-weekly foreign affairs column for The Washington
Post Writers Group since 1986. He has been with the *Washington Post* since
1966 and is also the paper's associate editor and senior foreign correspondent.

Hoagland was born in Rock Hill, South Carolina. He is a cum laude graduate
of the University of South Carolina.

In 1969 Hoagland was named the *Post*'s African correspondent, working out
of Nairobi, Kenya. He wrote about racial strife in southern Africa, covering the
Portuguese colonial wars in Angola, Guinea, and Mozambique in addition to
detailing the practice of apartheid in South Africa. He won the Pulitzer for
international reporting in 1971 for his work on apartheid; his ten-part series on
this topic was published in 1972 as a book, *South Africa: Civilizations in Conflict.* Later work on this story led to denunciation and visa refusal by the South
African government.

Hoagland covered the Middle East out of Beirut from 1972 to 1976, when
he moved to Paris to cover France, Italy, and Spain. He returned to Washington
in 1978 as the *Post*'s diplomatic correspondent and became foreign news editor
in 1979. In 1991 he was awarded his second Pulitzer, this time for commentary.

BOOKS: *South Africa: Civilizations in Conflict* (Boston, 1972).

Holbert, Robert D., Jr. (27 September 1967–   ). Columnist/reporter Rob
Holbert has written "The Rostrum," a twice-weekly opinion column, for the
Mississippi Press (Pascagoula, Mississippi) since 1989.

Holbert received the B.A. in communications in 1989 from Spring Hill College in Mobile, Alabama, and the M.A. in communications from Loyola University in 1992.

From November 1989 to August 1990 he wrote "The Rostrum" and did both hard news and features for the *Mississippi Press*. While attending graduate school, Holbert free-lanced shipping stories for the *Daily Shipping Guide* in New Orleans (1991–1992) and during 1992, also wrote for the biweekly *L'Observateur* in that city. He rejoined the *Mississippi Press* in December 1992. Holbert's columns often take a humorous approach.

Hopkins, John Christian (6 July 1960–   ). John Hopkins is a member of the Narragansett Indian Tribal Council, assistant features editor of the *Norwich* [Connecticut] *Bulletin,* and a columnist syndicated by Gannett News Service.

Hopkins was born in Westerly, Rhode Island, and received the B.A. in 1987 from the University of Rhode Island.

From 1987 to 1988 he was a reporter for the *New London* [Connecticut] *Day*. From 1988 to 1990 he was a reporter/columnist for the *Fall River* [Massachusetts] *Herald News* and from 1990 to 1993 a reporter/columnist for the *Fort Myers* [Florida] *News-Press*. He became a Gannett columnist in 1992 and in 1993 returned to New England as the *Norwich Bulletin*'s assistant features editor. The title of his column is "Native Perspectives." He considers his column a cross between personal and general interest.

Hopper, Hedda (2 June 1890–1 Feb. 1966). Hedda Hopper is remembered for her Hollywood gossip column that was syndicated by Chicago Tribune-New York News from 1936 to 1966.

She was born Elda Furry in Hollidaysburgh, Pennsylvania, and studied voice at the Carter Conservatory in Pittsburgh. Though born into a Quaker family, she became a chorus girl and from 1909 to 1966 played supporting roles in dozens of silent movies and "talkies." After marrying actor De Wolf Hopper, she changed her given name to Hedda after consulting a numerologist.

As a Hollywood columnist, the flamboyant Hopper was known for her exposés of the peccadillos of the film community, for the outlandish hats she wore, and for her feud with rival columnist Louella Parsons. Hopper became increasingly political-minded toward the latter part of her writing career and was an outspoken anticommunist. She also did radio work, appeared on television on "The Art Linkletter Show," and published two books.

BOOKS: *From Under My Hat* (Garden City, N.Y., 1952); with James Brough, *The Whole Truth and Nothing But* (New York, 1963).

Howe, Gene Alexander (22 March 1886–24 June 1952). Gene Howe, son of the more famous Ed Howe (the "Sage of Potato Hill"), wrote an unusual column titled "The Tactless Texas" for his newspaper, the *Amarillo* [Texas] *Globe-News.*

Howe was born in Atchison, Kansas; his formal education was limited to the public schools in Atchison. After Gene Howe was expelled from high school, his father put him to work at the elder Howe's paper, the *Atchison Globe,* as a reporter and typesetter. His father fired him after a drinking incident, and Gene Howe found work as a reporter for the Portland *Oregonian.* After four years of hard work and frugality, Howe was summoned back to the Atchison paper by his father, who eventually, in 1911, allowed his son to buy the *Globe.* In 1924 the younger Howe founded the *Amarillo Globe,* and in 1926 he purchased an older paper, the *Amarillo News,* consolidating the two papers into the *Globe-News.*

Howe wrote for his Amarillo paper a curious column, adopting the pen name Kernel Erasmus Rookus Tack and generally casting himself as a rustic bumbler. The column was used to brag about the attributes of Amarillo and the Texas Panhandle in general, to locate lost pets, to help people find jobs, and even to arrange marriages for lonesome cowboys. Howe would submit each column to a committee of staffers to ensure that it was sufficiently nutty and exaggerated. He resigned as the *Globe-News*'s editor in 1936 to spend more time on his column.

Howe also owned at least ten other papers, such as the Lubbock (Texas) *Avalanche,* the *Lubbock Journal,* and the *Falls City* [Nebraska] *Journal,* plus radio stations in Amarillo, San Antonio, and Weslaco, Texas.

BOOKS: *Them Texans, by Kernel Erasmus Tack, the Tactless Texan* (Amarillo, Tex., 1930).

Howe, Jennifer (10 Dec. 1962–   ). Jennifer Howe has been a general interest columnist for the *Kansas City Star* since 1992.

Howe was born in Sioux City, Iowa. She holds a bachelor's in journalism from the University of Missouri (1985) and broke into the business as a feature writer for the *Winston-Salem* [North Carolina] *Journal* (1985–1987). From 1987 to 1989 she was a reporter for the *Examiner* in Independence, Missouri. She joined the *Kansas City Star* as a feature writer in 1989. Her column focuses on the people, places, issues, and events of the Kansas City area.

Hubbard, Frank McKinney (1 Sept. 1868–26 Dec. 1930). Kin Hubbard, while not a columnist in every sense of the word, was syndicated to more than three hundred newspapers between 1910 and 1930. His syndicated feature contained his own cartoon drawing plus humorous written comments in epigrammatic or dialog form.

Hubbard was born into a newspaper family in Bellefontaine, Ohio. His father, Thomas Hubbard, was owner of the *Examiner* in that town. Kin Hubbard ended his formal education midway through the seventh grade and learned printing at his father's paper. He also organized and acted in minstrel shows prior to taking a job as a sketch artist for the *Indianapolis News* in 1910. Fired after three years, he found a second job sketching for the *Cincinnati Tribune* and a third at the *Mansfield* [Ohio] *News*. He returned to the *Indianapolis News* in 1901 and in late 1904 began drawing a rural idler named Abe Martin (after having considered Steve Martin and other variations). Beneath these drawings, which ran daily on the *News*'s back page, appeared several lines of copy couched in hayseed dialect. As time went by, Hubbard added a whole community of neighbors, ostensibly from the same Brown County vicinity as Abe. Starting in 1906, he collected this material into books, proceeding at the rate of one a year until his death. Hubbard signed with a syndicate in 1910 and in 1916 changed syndicates and made, he said, more money than he had ever supposed there was. In October 1911 he added a longer weekly feature, "Short Furrows," done in the same crackerbarrel humor style.

Hubbard's syndicated feature was used to satirize human foibles and people and events in the news. Despite the homespun spelling and butchered syntax, his "sayings" retain some of their appeal: "It's purty hard t' be efficient without bein' obnoxious." "Th' first thing t' turn Green in th' spring is th' Christmas jewelry." "Somehow sickness or a late train never seems t' keep a tiresome speaker from fillin' a date." Hubbard, who refused invitations to go on the lecture circuit, was admired by contemporaries as diverse as James Whitcomb Riley, Brander Matthews, and fellow humorist Will Rogers.

BOOKS: *Abe Martin of Brown County, Indiana* (Indianapolis, 1906); *Abe Martin's Almanack* (Indianapolis, 1907); *Abe Martin's Brown County Almanac* (Indianapolis, 1909); *Brown County Folks* (Indianapolis, 1910); *Short Furrows* (Indianapolis, 1911); *Abe Martin's Primer* (Indianapolis, 1914); *Back Country Folks* (Indianapolis, 1914); *Abe Martin's Sayings and Sketches* (Indianapolis, 1915); *New Sayings by Abe Martin* (Indianapolis, 1916?); *Abe Martin's Back Country Sayings* (Indianapolis, 1917); *Abe Martin on the War and Other Things* (Indianapolis, 1918?); *Abe Martin's Home-Cured Philosophy* (Indianapolis, 1919); *Abe Martin, the Joker on Facts* (Indianapolis, 1920); *On Advertisin', by Abe Martin* (Indianapolis, 1920); *Fifty-Two Weeks of Abe Martin* (Indianapolis, 1924); *Abe Martin on Things in General* (Indianapolis, 1925?); *Abe Martin, Hoss Sense and Nonsense* (Indianapolis, 1926); *Abe Martin's Wise Cracks and Skunk Ridge Papers* (Indianapolis, 1927?); *Abe Martin's Barbed Wire* (Indianapolis, 1928); *Abe Martin's Town Pump* (Indianapolis, 1929); ed. with others, *A Book of Indiana* (Indianapolis, 1929); *Abe Martin's Broadcast* (Indianapolis, 1930); *Abe Martin's Wisecracks,* ed. by E. V. Lucas (London, 1930); *The Hoosier Humor of Kin Hubbard,* comp. by Jack A. Stroube (Hallux, 1970); *The Best of Kin Hubbard,* ed. by David S. Hawes (Bloomington, Ind., 1984); *Comments of Abe Martin and His Neighbors* (Indianapolis, n.d.); *These Days* (Indianapolis, n.d.).

REFERENCES: Fred C. Kelly, *The Life and Times of Kin Hubbard, Creator of Abe Martin* (New York, 1952); Blanche Stillson and Dorothy Ritter Russo, *Abe Martin-Kin Hubbard . . . a Checklist* (Indianapolis, 1939); Norris W. Yates, *The American Humorist: Conscience of the Twentieth Century* (Ames, Iowa, 1964): 100–112.

Huddleson, Thomas M. (14 March 1949–   ). Tom Huddleson writes personal columns under two titles for the *Alliance Times-Herald* in Alliance, Nebraska. The titles are "Cantankerously Speaking" and "Strictly Personal."

Huddleson was born in Philadelphia. He holds the B.A. in English from Kutztown State College and the M.A. in English from Purdue University. From 1980 to 1990 he was employed by the *Nebraska Signal.* He joined the Alliance paper in 1991.

Hughes, Alice (circa 1899–20 June 1977). Alice Hughes wrote two columns for women, "A Woman's New York" and "You Can Be Beautiful," which appeared first in the *New York World-Telegram,* then in the *New York American.* Both were syndicated by King Features.

Hughes was born in White Plains, New York; grew up in New Hampshire; and was a graduate of Columbia University's journalism program. For six months she was a manuscript reader for *Detective Story Magazine,* after which, in 1923, she wrote an advice column titled "Mary Jane's Household Guide" for the *New York American.* The column did not catch on, and she left the paper to work in advertising for Macy's, where she became head of the store's apparel advertising.

Her column "A Woman's New York" was a highly popular combination of shopping tips, fashion hints, merchandising history, and human interest copy centering on the city's stores. Hughes traveled extensively and filed stories about the lives of women in other countries. She died at age seventy-eight.

REFERENCES: Ishbel Ross, *Ladies of the Press* (New York, 1974): 393–395.

Hughes, James Langston (1 Feb. 1902–22 May 1967). Langston Hughes, one of the outstanding literary voices of the twentieth century, wrote a witty, insightful column for the black weekly *Chicago Defender* from 1942 until 1965.

Hughes was born in Joplin, Missouri, but spent much of his early life in Lawrence, Kansas. He went to high school in Cleveland, Ohio, reading Carl Sandburg and writing his own poetry for the school magazine, as well as editing the school yearbook. After graduation from high school in 1920, he spent a little more than a year living in Mexico with his father, then spent 1921 and 1922 at Columbia University. Not happy there, he dropped out of school and worked on freighters on voyages to West Africa and to Europe. He left the ship *McKeesport* in the Netherlands and traveled to Paris, where he worked as a doorman at nightclubs where American jazz was played and as a cook at the Grand Duc Café. After further travel in Spain and Italy, he returned to the United States in the autumn of 1924, working in a laundry and as a hotel busboy until he met writer Vachel Lindsay, who encouraged him to pursue a literary career. In 1926 he became a student at Lincoln University and graduated in 1929. By that time he was already an established figure in the Harlem Renaissance, a literary movement through which New York intellectuals, black and white, encouraged the work of black writers.

When the Harlem Renaissance movement began to go out of vogue around 1930, Hughes's work took on a sharper edge regarding race relations. He and other African Americans went to the Soviet Union in 1932 intending to make a film that would point out the racial injustices so abundant in the United States. He was put off, however, by the regimentation of Soviet society, where even jazz music was banned, and returned home. He became highly involved in black theater in the mid-1930s after his play *Mulatto* appeared on Broadway. He helped found the Suitcase Theatre in New York in 1938, the New Negro Art Theater in Los Angeles in 1939, and the Skyloft Players in Chicago in 1941.

While continuing to produce poetry and short stories, Hughes in 1937 broke into journalism as the Madrid correspondent for the *Baltimore Afro-American*, covering the Spanish Civil War. Then in 1942 he began writing a column for the *Chicago Defender;* some of this work also appeared in the *New York Post.* His seriocomic column hit its stride in January 1943 when he began writing dialog sketches featuring the literary characters Jesse B. Semple (later shortened to ''Simple''), who represented poor, hard-pressed blacks in general, and his friend Boyd, a voice of the more hopeful middle-class black community. Through these fictitious spokesmen, Hughes was able to get at the difficulties of being black in a white-dominated society without appearing either preachy or angry. These columns made use of irony in dealing obliquely with a wide range of social problems, though some black leaders were unhappy with the black street dialect Hughes used and with the presentation of blacks in stereotypical roles. These columns, which have been collected into five books, continued to take the ''laugh to keep from crying'' approach to examining racial intolerance until the protest era of the 1960s rendered them outdated. The last of these columns appeared in 1965.

Hughes was a remarkably prolific writer, turning out more than fifty books and writing for innumerable periodicals, including *Saturday Review of Literature, Scribner's, Nation, Phylon, Esquire, Negro Digest,* and *Negro Quarterly.* He was also a frequent public speaker and traveled abroad under the auspices of the U.S. State Department in his later years. His insightful social realism will probably ensure him an enduring place among the finest black writers of his century.

BOOKS: *The Weary Blues* (New York, 1926); *Fine Clothes to the Jew* (New York, 1927); *Not Without Laughter* (New York and London, 1930); *Dear Lovely Death* (Amenia, N.Y., 1931); *The Negro Mother and Other Dramatic Recitations* (New York, 1931); *The Dream Keeper and Other Poems* (New York, 1932); *Scottsboro Limited: Four Poems and a Play in Verse* (New York, 1932); with Arna Bontemps, *Popo and Fifina: Children of Haiti* (New York, 1932); *A Negro Looks at Soviet Central Asia* (Moscow and Leningrad, 1934); *The Ways of White Folks* (New York, 1934); *A New Song* (New York, 1938); *The Big Sea: An Autobiography* (New York and London, 1940); *Shakespeare in Harlem* (New York, 1942); *Freedom's Plow* (New York, 1943); *Jim Crow's Last Stand*

(Atlanta, 1943); *Lament for Dark Peoples and Other Poems* (N.p., 1944); *Fields of Wonder* (New York, 1947); *One-Way Ticket* (New York, 1949); *Troubled Island* (New York, 1949); *Simple Speaks His Mind* (New York, 1950); *Montage of a Dream Deferred* (New York, 1951); *Laughing to Keep from Crying* (New York, 1952); *The First Book of Negroes* (New York, 1952); *Simple Takes a Wife* (New York, 1953); *The Glory Round His Head* (New York, 1953); *Famous American Negroes* (New York, 1954); *The First Book of Rhythms* (New York, 1954); *The First Book of Jazz* (New York, 1955); *Famous Negro Music Makers* (New York, 1955); *The Sweet Flypaper of Life* (New York, 1955); *The First Book of the West Indies* (New York, 1956); *I Wonder As I Wander: An Autobiographical Journey* (New York and Toronto, 1956); with Milton Meltzer, *A Pictorial History of the Negro in America* (New York, 1956); *Simple Stakes a Claim* (New York and Toronto, 1957); *The Langston Hughes Reader* (New York, 1958); *Famous Negro Heroes of America* (New York, 1958); *Tambourines to Glory* (New York, 1958); *Selected Poems of Langston Hughes* (New York, 1959); *Simply Heavenly* (New York, 1959); *The First Book of Africa* (New York, 1960); *The Best of Simple* (New York, 1961); *Ask Your Mama: 12 Moods for Jazz* (New York, 1961); *The Ballad of the Brown King* (New York, 1961); *Fight for Freedom: The Story of the NAACP* (New York, 1962); *Something in Common and Other Stories* (New York, 1963); *Five Plays by Langston Hughes,* ed. by Webster Smalley (Bloomington, Ind., 1963); *Simple's Uncle Sam* (New York, 1965); *The Panther and The Lash* (New York, 1967); with Milton Meltzer, *Black Magic: A Pictorial History of the Negro in American Entertainment* (Englewood Cliffs, N.J., 1967); *Black Misery* (New York, 1969); *Good Morning Revolution: Uncollected Social Protest Writings by Langston Hughes,* ed. by Faith Berry (New York, 1973).

REFERENCES: Richard K. Barksdale, *Langston Hughes: The Poet and His Critics* (Chicago, 1977); Faith Berry, *Langston Hughes: Before and Beyond Harlem* (Westport, Conn., 1983); Donald C. Dickinson, *A Bio-Bibliography of Langston Hughes, 1902– 1967* (Hamden, Conn., 1967); James Emanuel, *Langston Hughes* (New York, 1967); Nathan Huggins, *Harlem Renaissance* (New York, 1971); Blyden Jackson, "A Word About Simple," *CLA Journal* 11 (June 1968): 310–318; Milton Meltzer, *Langston Hughes: A Biography* (New York, 1968); Elizabeth P. Myers, *Langston Hughes: Poet of His People* (Champaign, Ill., 1970); Therman B. O'Daniel, ed., *Langston Hughes: Black Genius* (New York, 1971); Arnold Rampersad, *The Life of Langston Hughes; Volume I: 1902–1941: I, Too, Sing America* (New York, 1986).

Huglin, Henry Charles (6 Aug. 1915–   ). Air Force Brigadier General Henry Huglin wrote a column, "Affairs of Nations," that was begun in 1972.

Huglin was born in Fairfield, Iowa. He received the B.S. in 1938 from the U.S. Military Academy at West Point, entering active duty immediately after graduation. He commanded a bomber group during World War II and was then assigned to NATO; he retired in 1964. Huglin was a self-syndicated columnist and photographer, working out of Santa Barbara, California.

Hunt, Haroldson Lafayette (17 Feb. 1889–29 Nov. 1974). Self-made oil billionaire H. L. Hunt of Texas wrote a column starting in 1964 that appeared mainly in weekly papers in the Sun Belt. The column's focus was what was wrong in America and what, according to its writer, needed to be done to improve the situation.

Hunt was born on a farm near Vandalia, Illinois; learned to read by age three; but only completed the fifth grade. In his youth, Hunt worked as a farmer, cowboy, mule skinner, and lumberjack until 1911, when he began to speculate in cotton and timber in Louisiana. In the 1920s he entered the oil business in Arkansas, Oklahoma, and Louisiana, and in the 1930s he bought the oil leases in East Texas that produced the bulk of his enormous fortune, which was said to be between $2 and $3 billion, giving him a weekly income of more than $1 million.

Hunt kept strictly to his business ventures until around 1950, by which time he had developed a desire to pass along his economic/political ideas to the public. In 1951 he established the Facts Forum, which produced and distributed radio and television programs of a conservative slant. It also underwrote the publication of conservative books. He closed Facts Forum in late 1956 and in 1958 started a new foundation, Life Line, which had similar aims and operations. His own column was launched in 1964; his column writings make up the content of four of his dozen books, all published by his own publishing concerns, a part of HLH Products Company. Another outlet for his ideas was the daily fifteen-minute radio commentary "Life Line."

BOOKS: *Alpaca* (Dallas, 1960); *Why Not Speak?* (Dallas, 1964); *Hunt for Truth* (Dallas, 1965); *HLH Columns* (Dallas, 1966); *Alpaca Revisited* (Dallas, 1967); *Right of Center: A Collection of Thought-Provoking Newspaper Columns* (Dallas, 1971); *Hunt Heritage: The Republic and Our Families* (Dallas, 1973); *H. L. Hunt Early Days* (Dallas, 1973); *Old Letters-to-the-Editor from H. L. Hunt* (Dallas, n.d.); *Right of Average* (Dallas, n.d.); *Fabians Fight Freedom* (Dallas, n.d.); *Constructively, H. L. Hunt* (Dallas, n.d.).

I

Iacocca, Lido Anthony (15 Oct. 1924–). One of America's business demigods, former Chrysler CEO Lee Iacocca writes a column of commentary on business, government, and social issues that is distributed by the Los Angeles Times Syndicate.

Iacocca was born in Allentown, Pennsylvania, to Italian immigrant parents. He earned the B.S. in engineering from Lehigh University in 1945 and the M.E. from Princeton University in 1946, after which he was hired by Ford Motor Company as a management trainee. He began in sales, was helped along by general manager Robert S. McNamara, and moved steadily up the corporate ladder, serving as the company's president from 1970 to 1978. He is credited with having developed the sporty and highly popular Ford Mustang.

Iacocca became president of Chrysler Corporation in 1978 and CEO in 1979. Two unblushing books about his successes plus articles he has contributed to such periodicals as *Fortune* and *U.S. News and World Report* have helped make him one of the most famous and recognized individuals in U.S. business.

BOOKS: With William Novak, *Iacocca: An Autobiography* (New York, 1984); with Sonny Kleinfield, *Talking Straight* (New York, 1988).

Ickes, Harold Le Claire (15 March 1874–3 Feb. 1952). Harold Ickes was one of those individuals who became a syndicated columnist after retirement. He had been a journalist, attorney, and political figure whose highest office was Secretary of the Interior under Franklin Roosevelt (1933–1946). His scandal-free management of the billions spent by the Public Works Administration earned him the nickname ''Honest Harold.''

Ickes was born in Frankstown Township in Pennsylvania. At age sixteen he moved with his mother to Chicago; he received the B.A. from the University of Chicago in 1897, after which he worked for several years for the *Chicago Chronicle* and the *Chicago Tribune*. He began as a sportswriter and switched to political reporting. He returned to the University of Chicago for law school, receiving the J.D. in 1907 and practicing law until 1932. During these years he contributed to various magazines and newspapers and wrote nine books, two of which were indictments of the American press. It is ironic that before he became a columnist, he was well known for criticizing columnists, calling them "calumnists" and gossip mongers.

BOOKS: *The New Democracy* (New York, 1934); *Back to Work: The Story of WPA* (New York, 1935); *America's House of Lords: An Inquiry into the Freedom of the Press* (New York, 1939); *The Third Term Bugaboo: A Cheerful Anthology* (Washington, D.C., 1940); ed., *Freedom of the Press Today: A Clinical Examination by 28 Specialists* (New York, 1941); *The Autobiography of a Curmudgeon* (New York, 1943); *Fightin' Oil* (New York, 1943); *The Secret Diary of Harold L. Ickes,* 3 vols. (New York, 1953–1954).

Irvine, Reed John (29 Sept. 1922–   ). Known primarily as cofounder of the organizations Accuracy in Media and Accuracy in Academia, Reed Irvine also writes a syndicated column, "Accuracy in Media."

Irvine was born in Salt Lake City, Utah. He made Phi Beta Kappa at and received the B.A. from the University of Utah in 1942, did graduate study at the University of Colorado (1943–1944) and at the University of Washington (1949), and was a Fulbright Scholar at Oxford University, which awarded him the B.Litt. in 1951. From 1946 to 1948 he was a translator and investigator in Tokyo for the War Department.

After leaving Oxford, Irvine worked as a Federal Reserve System economist and adviser on international finance from 1951 to 1977. He cofounded Accuracy in Media in 1969 and was its head from 1971. He cofounded Accuracy in Academia in 1985. He has published three books, all critical of the U.S. mass media.

BOOKS: *Media Mischief and Misdeeds* (Chicago, 1984); ed., *The Secret Censors* (Washington, D.C., 1986); with Cliff Kincaid, *Profiles of Deception: How the News Media Are Deceiving the American People* (Smithtown, N.Y., 1990).

Ives, Mike (24 Dec. 1940–   ). Longtime readers of the *Roanoke Times and World News* still talk about former columnist Mike Ives, who wrote for that paper from July 1968 to February 1979.

Ives was born in Washington, D.C., and grew up in Arlington, Virginia. He graduated from Roanoke College in Salem, Virginia, after attending that institution off and on for nine years and then served in Vietnam.

Ives wrote sports in Lynchburg, Virginia, before going to Roanoke to write "My Turn," his iconoclastic thrice-weekly column that chronicled the seamy adventures of such beer-drinking, pool-shooting "good ole boys" as trucker Wild Turkey, pool sharks Bigfoot and Big Rich, and a bearlike, bearded friend of Ives's known to readers by the euphonious name Wild Lyle DeWilde.

Most columnists who write about this life-style merely write about it; Ives came to live it. In 1979 he left the Roanoke paper and headed west. He wrote for the *Phoenix New Times* in Arizona in the mid-1980s, then abandoned writing to earn his living as a pool player. He moved to Bradenton, Florida, in 1986, and when he isn't playing pool, he sails on his boat, the *Gypsy Rose*. A fellow Roanoke staffer, John Pancake, once wrote that trying to describe Mike Ives was similar to being a mosquito in a nudist colony: "You just don't know where to start."

BOOKS: *Give Me a Break: Buy This Book* (Roanoke, Va., 1976).

Ivins, Molly (1944?–). Molly Ivins has been a Texas columnist since 1980 and is known for her incisive wit.

Ivins was born in Houston, Texas. She earned the B.A. from Smith College and the M.A. in journalism from Columbia University. She also studied for a year at the Institute of Political Science in Paris, France.

As a journalist, she has worked for the *Houston Chronicle* and the *Minneapolis Star Tribune*. From 1970 through 1976 she was a reporter for the *Texas Observer*, then was a *New York Times* reporter in 1976–1977 and head of the *Times*'s Denver bureau, 1977–1980. She became a columnist for the *Dallas Times Herald* in 1980. She has since moved to the *Ft. Worth Star-Telegram* and is handled by Creators Syndicate. The iconoclastic Ivins has been quoted to the effect that politicians, her usual target, live in a journalistic free-fire zone. Her commentaries also address anything interesting that sets Texas apart, country music, and feminism. She has done a column for *Ms.* magazine and has written free-lance for other periodicals, including *Progressive, Mother Jones,* and *Nation*. In addition, she has often appeared on the McNeil/Lehrer show and on public radio.

BOOKS: *Molly Ivins Can't Say That, Can She?* (New York, 1991); *Nothin' but Good Times Ahead* (New York, 1993).

J

Jackson, Derrick Z. (?–). Derrick Jackson has been a *Boston Globe* columnist since 1988.

Jackson grew up in Milwaukee, Wisconsin, and is a University of Wisconsin in Milwaukee graduate. His first job was writing sports for the *Milwaukee Courier,* a black weekly. He was also a sportswriter for the *Milwaukee Journal* during high school. From 1976 to 1978 he covered sports for the *Kansas City Star* and thereafter was a *Newsday* reporter prior to becoming a *Globe* columnist. He was a 1983 Nieman Fellow.

Jackson, Jesse Louis (8 Oct. 1941–). Prominent spokesman for black America Jesse Jackson writes a column that is handled by the Los Angeles Times Syndicate.

Jackson was born in Greenville, South Carolina. He attended the University of Illinois on an athletic scholarship in 1959–1960 but transferred to North Carolina A & T State University, where he received the B.A. in sociology and economics in 1964. While a student, he participated in sit-in demonstrations and protest marches in Greensboro. After graduation, he worked for North Carolina governor Terry Sanford and in 1965 enrolled in the Chicago Theological Seminary. Jackson became a protégé of the Reverend Martin Luther King, Jr., and left the seminary to head the Chicago branch of a King program known as Operation Breadbasket. Jackson was ordained a Baptist minister in June 1968 and learned the art of oratory from Dr. King.

Jackson has maintained high visibility since that time, heading Operation PUSH (People United to Serve Humanity) and the National Rainbow Coalition. He has been a forceful advocate of black economic betterment and black pride and also favors granting statehood to Washington, D.C. He has been seen frequently on television and has authored or coauthored three books.

BOOKS: With Elaine Landau, *Black in America: A Fight for Freedom* (New York, 1973); *Straight from the Heart,* ed. by Roger D. Hatch and Frank E. Watkins (Philadelphia, 1987); *A Time to Speak: The Autobiography of the Reverend Jesse Jackson* (New York, 1987).

Jarrett, Vernon D. (19 June 1921–   ). Vernon Jarrett worked for three Chicago newspapers and did editorial page columns for the last two: the *Tribune* and the *Sun-Times.*

Jarrett was born in Saulsbury, Tennessee. He received the B.A. from Knoxville College and did further study in journalism at Northwestern University, in television at the University of Kansas City, and in urban sociology at the University of Chicago.

In 1946 Jarrett became a reporter for the *Chicago Defender.* In 1970 he became a thrice-weekly columnist for the *Chicago Tribune,* and in 1983 he switched to the *Chicago Sun-Times,* where he again wrote an editorial page column specializing in urban politics and race relations. He also was host of the WJPC radio show "The Vernon Jarrett Report" and producer/host of a Sunday morning interview show on WLS-TV, "Black on Black." As such, he was one of the first African-American newsmen to be successful in both print and broadcast journalism. Jarrett was president of the National Association of Black Journalists from 1977–1979.

Johnson, Haynes Bonner (9 July 1931–   ). Haynes Johnson is a longtime political columnist with the *Washington Post.* He also won a Pulitzer Prize in 1964 for his reporting of civil rights demonstrations in Selma, Alabama.

Johnson was born in New York City. He earned the B.J. from the University of Missouri in 1952 and the M.S. from the University of Wisconsin in 1956. He was an army officer from 1952 to 1955.

In 1956–1957 he was a reporter for the Wilmington (Delaware) *News-Journal.* He was reporter, rewrite man, assistant city editor, and national assignments editor for the *Washington Star* from 1957 until 1969, then signed on with the *Washington Post* as a national correspondent. From 1973 to 1977 he was the *Post*'s assistant managing editor and began his column in 1977. He is known for his coverage of such stories as the CIA's Bay of Pigs invasion of Cuba, his commentary of former president Jimmy Carter's inability to deal productively with Congress, and his comments on the unreality of the Reagan administration. Johnson has also appeared as a commentator on the PBS show "Washington Week in Review" and on NBC's "Today Show."

Johnson and his father, Malcolm Malone Johnson, are the only father-son winners of the Pulitzer Prize. M. M. Johnson's prize was awarded in 1948 for his *New York Sun* coverage of waterfront crime in New York.

BOOKS: *Dusk at the Mountain: The Negro, the Nation, and the Capital: A Report on Problems and Progress* (Garden City, N.Y., 1963); with Manuel Artime and others, *The Bay of Pigs: The Leaders' Story of Brigade 2506* (New York, 1964); with Bernard M. Gwertzman, *Fulbright: The Dissenter* (Garden City, N.Y., 1968); with George C. Wilson and others, *Army in Anguish* (New York, 1972); with Nick Kotz, *The Unions* (New York, 1972); *Lyndon* (New York, 1973); *The Working White House* (New York, 1975); *In the Absence of Power: Governing America* (New York, 1980); with Howard Simons, *The Landing* (New York, 1986); *Sleepwalking Through History: America in the Reagan Years* (New York, 1991).

Johnson, Philander Chase (6 Feb. 1866–18 May 1939). Humorist Philander Johnson is remembered for his column ''Postscripts'' in the *Washington Post* and his later *Washington Star* column ''Shooting Stars.''

Johnson was born in Wheeling, West Virginia. In the early part of his career, he contributed to the humor and literary sections of the *Merchant Traveler* in Chicago and the Washington (D.C.) *Critic*. In addition to his columns, he also wrote editorials and reviews for the *Post* and *Star*. His columns contained both prose and verse humor.

BOOKS: *Sayings of Uncle Eben* (Washington, D.C., 1896); *Now-a-Day Poems* (Washington, D.C., 1900); *Songs of the G.O.P.* (Washington, D.C., 1900); *Senator Sorghum's Primer of Politics* (Upper Saddle River, N.J., 1906).

Johnson, Rheta Grimsley (30 Nov. 1953–   ). A rising star among local columnists now in syndication, Rheta Johnson writes for the *Atlanta Journal Constitution* and is syndicated by United Feature Syndicate.

Johnson was born in Colquitt, Georgia. She received the B.A. in journalism from Auburn University in 1975. She and a friend founded a weekly paper on Georgia's St. Simon's Island. She also worked for the *Auburn* [Alabama] *Bulletin*, the *Birmingham* [Alabama] *News*, and United Press International before signing on with the *Memphis* [Tennessee] *Commercial Appeal* in 1980, working in its bureaus in Greenville, Tupelo, and Jackson, Mississippi. Her column was distributed to about three hundred papers by the Scripps-Howard News Service.

Johnson was hired as a general columnist by the *Atlanta Journal Constitution* in June 1994, after the death of that paper's popular columnist Lewis Grizzard. She has authored two books: a collection of her columns and a biography of the cartoonist Charles Schulz.

BOOKS: *America's Faces* (Memphis, Tenn., 1987); *Good Grief: The Story of Charles M. Schulz* (New York, 1989).

Jones, Jenkin Lloyd (1 Nov. 1911–   ). Jenk Jones, who inherited the *Tulsa Tribune* from his father, wrote a syndicated weekly column, ''An Editor's Outlook,'' at that paper for roughly thirty years. The column was handled by the Los Angeles Times Syndicate and ended in September 1992 with the death of the *Tribune* itself.

Jones was born in Madison, Wisconsin. The family moved to Oklahoma in 1919 when Richard Lloyd Jenkins purchased the *Tulsa Daily Democrat,* which he rechristened the *Tulsa Tribune.* Jenk Jones received the Ph.B. from the University of Wisconsin in 1933 and became a reporter for his father's paper. He was promoted to managing editor in 1936, to associate editor in 1938, and to editor in 1941 when his father relinquished that position. He served as a navy communications officer in the Pacific from 1944 to 1946 and took over as publisher in 1963 on Richard Jenkins's death.

Jones was active in setting up the Navy's Office of Analysis and Review in 1953, was president of the American Society of Newspaper Editors in 1956, and in 1969 was president of the U.S. Chamber of Commerce. He was a frequent traveler and reportedly had visited one hundred twenty nations plus both Poles by the time of his retirement at age eighty.

BOOKS: *The Changing World: An Editor's Outlook* (New York, 1964).

REFERENCES: Bob Foresman, "Globe-Trotter from Tulsa," *Editor and Publisher* 89 (28 April 1956): 23, 140.

K

Kalson, Sally (21 Oct. 1950–   ). Sally Kalson has been a weekly columnist and staff writer for the *Pittsburgh Post-Gazette* since 1983.

Kalson was born in Pittsburgh and in 1972 received the B.A. in speech and communications from the University of Pittsburgh.

Her first job was as a staff writer for the *Jewish Chronicle* of Pittsburgh (1972–1974). In 1977–1978 she was assistant editor of *Pittsburgher Magazine,* and in 1979–1980, associate editor of *Pennsylvania Illustrated Magazine.* Kalson taught journalism from 1981 to 1983 at Chatham College, after which she joined the *Post-Gazette.* Her column is a mix of personal and political commentary and social satire. Frequent themes are the courts, politicians, national scandals, fashion, the media, the sexes, and parenthood. Kalson has also freelanced articles to the *New York Times Magazine* and from 1990 to 1993 she was an evening news commentator on KDKA-TV in her city.

Kane, Eugene (15 May 1956–   ). Eugene Kane is a columnist as well as a feature writer and entertainment reporter for the *Milwaukee Journal.*

Kane grew up in Philadelphia and earned the B.A. in journalism at Temple University in 1980 after interning at the *Philadelphia Bulletin.* In 1981 he joined the *Journal* in Milwaukee as a general assignment reporter. He has since covered the federal courts and has held the suburban affairs beat. He was a Poynter Institute Fellow in 1987 and in 1984 was a founding member of the Wisconsin Black Media Association. His columns frequently display a gentle, likable wit.

Karnow, Stanley (4 Feb. 1925–   ). Stanley Karnow, known for his foreign correspondence with an Asian specialty, has written columns for the Des Moines Register & Tribune Syndicate, King Features, and *Le Point* in Paris, France.

Karnow was born in New York City and served with the Army Air Forces from 1943 to 1946. His A.B., in 1947, was from Harvard University. He did further study at the Sorbonne (1947–1948) and at the Ecole des Sciences Politiques (1948–1949).

From 1950 to 1957 he was a *Time* correspondent in Paris. He was North Africa bureau head (1958–1959) and Hong Kong bureau chief (1959–1962) for Time-Life. He worked for *Time* in New York City, 1962–1963, then was the *Saturday Evening Post*'s Far East correspondent from 1963 to 1965. He served in the same capacity for the *Washington Post* (1965–1971) and handled diplomatic news for the *Post* in 1971–1972.

Karnow worked briefly for NBC News (1972–1973), then returned to the print media as associate editor of *New Republic* from 1973 to 1975. His syndicated Register & Tribune column began in 1974, and his King Features column ran from 1975 to 1987. In 1975 he began working for public television, and from 1975 to 1986 he was editor in chief of International Writers Service in Washington, D.C.

Karnow also wrote for the *London Observer* from 1961 to 1965 and did a *Le Point* column from 1976 to 1983. His six books deal with the politics of various Asian countries.

BOOKS: *Southeast Asia* (New York, 1962); *Bitter Seeds: A Farmer's Story of Revolution in China* (Hong Kong, 1964); *Mao and China: Inside China's Cultural Revolution* (New York, 1972); *Vietnam: A History* (New York, 1983); *In Our Image: America's Empire in the Philippines* (New York, 1989); with Nancy Yoshihara, *Asian Americans in Transition* (New York, 1992).

Kee, Lorraine (25 May 1959–   ). Lorraine Key's unusual column for the *St. Louis Post-Dispatch* combines social and political issues with sports.

Kee was born in Lake Charles, Louisiana. Her B.S. in communications was earned at Fort Hays State University.

After student internships at the *Kansas City Star* and *Wichita Eagle-Beacon,* she was a reporter for the Springfield Newspapers in Springfield, Missouri, from 1984 to 1987. She was with the *Hartford Courant* in Connecticut from 1987 to 1989 prior to joining the *Post-Dispatch.*

Kelly, Florence Finch (27 March 1858–17 Dec. 1939). Florence Kelly wrote three columns: "The Woman's Hour" in the early 1880s for the *Boston Globe,* a column for the *Los Angeles Times* in 1899, and a column in the *New York Times Book Review* starting in 1906.

She was born Florence Finch on a farm near Girard, Illinois. She attended high school in Paoli, Kansas; taught for two years before entering college; and in 1881 graduated from the University of Kansas. She was hired by the *Boston Globe* a few months after her graduation and did news reporting, society news, art criticism, editorials, a series of stories on American humorists, and her woman's column. She left the *Globe* to work on the *Morning Telegram* in Troy,

New York, then married Allen Kelly, with whom she had worked at the *Globe.* The two founded a short-lived newspaper, the *Lowell Bell,* in Lowell, Massachusetts.

She worked briefly at the *San Francisco Examiner* and in 1899 was a columnist and literary editor of the *Los Angeles Times.* In 1906 she was hired by the *New York Times Book Review,* for which she wrote a column, and in addition, wrote interview stories and other features for the *Times.* Kelly wrote ten books, several of which were novels.

BOOKS: *Frances: A Story for Men and Women* (New York, 1889); *On the Inside* (New York, 1890); *With Hoops of Steel* (Indianapolis, 1900); *Rhoda of the Underground* (New York, 1909); *The Delafield Affair* (Chicago, 1909); *Emerson's Wife and Other Western Stories* (Chicago, 1911); *The Fate of Felix Brand* (Philadelphia, 1913); *What America Did: A Record of Achievement in the Prosecution of the War* (New York, 1919); *The Dixons: A Story of American Life Through Three Generations* (New York, 1921); *Flowing Stream: The Story of Fifty-Six Years in American Newspaper Life* (New York, 1939).

Kempton, James Murray (16 Dec. 1918–). Murray Kempton has written a column for *Newsday* since 1981. Prior to that time, he was a columnist for the *New York Post,* the *New York World-Telegram and Sun,* and *New Republic.*

Kempton was born in Baltimore, Maryland. A history/political science major at Johns Hopkins University, he received the B.A. in 1939, then worked for nearly a year as a welfare investigator in his home city. Next he was an organizer of the Non-Communist American Youth Congress in New York City and an organizer for the International Ladies Garment Workers Union. He became publicity director for the American Labor party in 1941, and in 1942 he entered journalism as a labor reporter for the *New York Post.* Two years of army combat duty in the Pacific interrupted his journalistic career, and from 1946 to 1947 he was a *Wilmington* [North Carolina] *Star* reporter. He returned to the *Post* in 1947 as assistant to Victor Riesel, the paper's labor editor/columnist.

Kempton assumed Riesel's place in 1949 and wrote his *Post* column until 1963, broadening the column's focus to include civil rights and foreign affairs. (Some years later, in 1968, Kempton was convicted of disorderly conduct for taking part in an antiwar demonstration.) He became a columnist for the liberal weekly magazine *New Republic* in 1963, continuing the column for about eighteen months, then in September 1964 began a column in the *New York World-Telegram and Sun.* When that paper folded in 1966, he resumed his *Post* column, writing it until 1969. In that same year he began contributing regularly to the *New York Review of Books,* and in 1970 he became a CBS commentator on the "Spectrum" show.

Kempton, who won a Pulitzer Prize in 1985, enjoys a strong reputation as a verbal stylist and has contributed innumerable articles to such magazines as *Esquire, Harper's,* and *Atlantic Monthly* and has authored four books.

BOOKS: *Part of Our Time: Some Monuments and Ruins of the Thirties* (New York, 1955); *America Comes of Middle Age: 1950–1962* (New York, 1963); *The Briar Patch: The*

People of the State of New York v. Lumumba Shakur et al. (New York, 1973); *Rebellions, Perversities, and Main Events* (New York, 1994).

Kennedy, Mark K. (30 May 1958–   ). Mark Kennedy writes the "Life Stories" column for the *Chattanooga* [Tennessee] *Times.*

Kennedy was born in Columbia, Tennessee, and in 1980 received the B.S. in journalism from Middle Tennessee State University.

From 1980 to 1982, he was sports editor for the *Cleveland Daily Banner.* He joined the *Chattanooga Times* as columnist and reporter in 1982. His column presents human-interest narratives.

Kenny, Nicholas Napoleon (3 Feb. 1895–14 Dec. 1975). Writer of the syndicated *New York Mirror* column "Nick Kenny Speaking" (1930–1963), Kenny had also written columns for New Jersey's *Bayonne Times* in the early 1920s and the *Sarasota* [Florida] *Herald Tribune* (1963–1975). His columns usually combined light verse in the Edgar A. Guest vein with humorous comments, jokes, and observations about radio programs.

Kenny was born in the Queens area of New York City. After only three months of high school, he joined the navy (1911–1918), where he gained much of his education by reading in ships' libraries; he was also in the Merchant Marine (1918–1920).

Kenny was with the *Bayonne Times* from 1920 to 1923 as a sportswriter, rewrite man, and writer of the column "Getting an Earful." He worked briefly on the *Boston American* (1923–1924) and the *New York Journal* (1924–1927), then went with the *New York Daily News* (1927–1930). In 1930 he began his radio-oriented column for the *New York Mirror,* continuing it until the paper closed in 1963. He then moved to Sarasota and began writing a new column for the *Herald Tribune,* which he continued until his death at age eighty.

Kenny is also remembered as a writer of song lyrics. His first big hit, "Gold Mine in the Sky," is largely forgotten today but enabled Kenny and his brother to form their own publishing house, Gold Mine in the Sky Publishing Company. As a songwriter, Kenny is probably best remembered for "Love Letters in the Sand," which the singer Pat Boone made a gold record. Kenny also published a half dozen books.

BOOKS: *The Navy in Rhyme* (New York, 1929); *Getting an Earful* (New York, 1932); *Favorite Poems, Day unto Day* (Garden City, N.Y., 1943); with others, *How to Write, Sing and Sell Popular Songs* (New York, 1946); *More Poems* (Garden City, N.Y., 1948); *Poems to Inspire* (Minneapolis, 1959).

Kent, Frank Richardson (1 May 1877–14 April 1958). Frank Kent was one of America's earliest and most influential political columnists. His column ran in the *Baltimore Sun* from 1922 until 1958.

Kent was born in Baltimore, Maryland. His given name was originally Francis rather than Frank. He attended the public schools of Baltimore and studied at the Maryland Agricultural College for a short time before taking a job writing about sports for the *Columbus* [Georgia] *Enquirer Sun.* In 1897 he returned to his hometown to become a reporter for the *Baltimore American.* Then in January 1900 he went over to the *Baltimore Sun,* first as a police reporter, next as city hall reporter. Kent left the *Sun* for one year, 1909, to work as secretary/treasurer of the Maryland Agricultural College, which now is the University of Maryland. He returned to the *Sun* as its Washington correspondent and was soon promoted to managing editor. He held this job until 1921, when he became the paper's London correspondent and was also named vice president of the *Sunpapers'* parent company, the A. S. Abell Company.

Kent's long career as a political columnist began in 1922 on the *Sun's* front page. He began using the column title "The Great Game of Politics" in February 1923. In 1934 the McNaught Syndicate distributed the column to roughly 140 other papers, and in the 1940s Kent dropped the column title. With his competitors David Lawrence and Mark Sullivan, Kent was one of the pioneers of the syndicated political column in the pre–Walter Lippmann era. Kent's work was marked by a gentlemanly formality, yet he was a thoroughgoing critic of President Franklin Roosevelt and New Deal policy. Kent's column ran daily until 1947, after which it appeared weekly until January 1958, about four months prior to his death. He authored seven books, mainly about politics, and coauthored one on the history of the *Sunpapers.*

BOOKS: *The Story of Maryland Politics* (Baltimore, 1911); *The Great Game of Politics* (Garden City, N.Y., 1923); *The Story of Alexander Brown & Sons* (Baltimore, 1925); *The Democratic Party: A History* (New York and London, 1928); *Political Behavior* (New York, 1928); *Without Gloves* (New York, 1934); *Without Grease* (New York, 1936); with Gerald W. Johnson, H. L. Mencken and Hamilton Owens, *The Sunpapers of Baltimore,* 1837–1937 (New York, 1937).

REFERENCES: Charles Fisher, *The Columnists* (New York, 1944): 197–209.

Kerbel, Barbara (30 June 1946–). A promising newcomer is Barbara Kerbel, director of corporate communications for CMP Publications in New York City. Kerbel's column, picked up in late summer 1994 by the Los Angeles Times Syndicate, is aimed at working women.

Kerbel is writing especially to women trying to climb the corporate ladder "with a child hanging on each leg," in other words, working mothers. More often than not, she deals with the challenges of the working homemaker in a humorous fashion, covering such topics as office relationships, child care, and hanging on to a sense of self in the face of the conflicting demands of home and work.

Kershner, James E. (17 Aug. 1953–). Jim Kershner writes a general/humor column for the *Spokesman-Review* in Spokane, Washington.

Kershner was born in Denver, Colorado. He received the B.A. in history from Lewis & Clark College in Portland, Oregon, in 1975. His first experience as a humorous columnist was with the college paper, the *Pioneer Log*, for which he wrote a column headed "Dear Mom—A Freshman's Letter Home."

From 1975 to 1978 Kershner worked as a reporter and photographer for the *Cody Enterprise* in Cody, Wyoming. For the following decade, 1978–1989, he was reporter, entertainment editor, and columnist for the *Valley Daily News* in Kent, Washington. Since 1989 he has been a reporter and columnist with the Spokane *Spokesman-Review*.

Kessler, Merle Bruce (1 Oct. 1949–   ). Merle Kessler is the creator of Ian Shoales, humor columnist for the *San Francisco Examiner*, who is syndicated by the Newspaper Enterprise Association.

Kessler was born in Milbank, South Dakota. He earned the B.A. in 1971 at St. Cloud State College and dual M.F.A. degrees in fiction and playwriting in 1974 at the University of Iowa.

After graduation, Kessler became a partner in the Duck's Breath Mystery Theatre in San Francisco and coowner of a production company, Civilized Entertainments. The Duck's Breath Mystery Theatre was a satiric feature on National Public Radio's "All Things Considered" in the early 1980s, and here Ian Shoales was born. The Shoales persona was that of a grumpy social critic. The fictitious cynic has also appeared on National Public Radio's (NPR's) "Morning Edition," on KQED-FM's "West Coast Weekend," and on ABC-TV's "Nightline" and "World News Now."

The versatile Kessler is also the creator of "Ask Dr. Science" and has written various other productions, such as the comedies "Dead Pan Alley," "Table for One," and "Don't Even Think of Parking Here."

In addition to his column and contributions to such periodicals as the *Washington Post* and *Mademoiselle,* Kessler has published four humor books.

BOOKS: *I Gotta Go* (New York, 1985); with Dan Coffey, *The Official Dr. Science Big Book of Science* (Chicago, 1986); *Ian Shoales' Perfect World* (New York, 1988); with Dan Coffey, *Dr. Science's Book of Shocking Domestic Revelations* (New York, 1993).

Ketcham, Diane Elizabeth (?–   ). Diane Ketcham writes two columns about Long Island for the *New York Times.*

Ketcham was born in Brooklyn and was reared in Port Washington, New York. She attended Miami University in Oxford, Ohio, for three years as a theatre/radio/television/film major, then switched to SUNY—Stonybrook, where she completed her B.A. She also received the M.A. in communication from New York Institute of Technology in 1978.

From 1977 to 1983, Ketcham worked in Washington, D.C., as press secretary and chief of staff for Congressman Thomas J. Downey. She syndicated her first column, "Words by Wire," to more than twenty major newspapers during 1983 and 1984, then later in 1984 became a *New York Times* feature writer. Her career as a Long Island columnist for the *Times* began in 1985. "About Long

Island'' is a general interest feature column, and "The Long Island Journal" is an offbeat items column noted for its humor.

The winner of many awards for her column writing, she has also written for *New York* magazine, *Fact Magazine,* and other periodicals and is a weekly panelist on "The 21 Edition," a public television news program produced by WLIW-TV. She has written one book, which is about Long Island, and she is a member of the National Society of Newspaper Columnists.

BOOKS: *Long Island, Shores of Plenty* (Northridge, Calif., 1988).

Kilgallen, Dorothy Mae (3 July 1913–8 Nov. 1965). Perhaps best remembered as a panelist on the early television show "What's My Line," Dorothy Kilgallen was twice a columnist for the *New York Journal-American.*

Kilgallen was born in Chicago, the daughter of the accomplished reporter James Lawrence Kilgallen. She moved with her family to Wyoming, Indiana, back to Chicago, and finally New York City. Her formal education past high school was limited to one academic year, 1930–1931, at the College of New Rochelle, which she left for a reporting job on the *New York Evening Journal.* In 1936 she was given the Nellie Bly–like assignment of traveling around the world—this time by air. She made the trip in twenty-four days and returned a minor celebrity. After a brief stint on the West Coast as the *Journal-American*'s Hollywood columnist, she returned to New York, went to London to write about the coronation of George VI, then in 1938 began writing a new column, "The Voice of Broadway," as the first woman columnist to cover the Broadway scene. The column was distributed by King Features Syndicate.

She became a radio personality on CBS in 1941 as host of the weekly "Voice of Broadway." She and her husband, Dick Kollman, collaborated on the show "Breakfast with Dorothy and Dick" until 1945, and in 1947 she did "Star Time" for ABC. From 1949 to 1965 she appeared on "What's My Line" and was also on the little-remembered show "Leave It to the Girls." Kilgallen authored two books.

BOOKS: *Girl Around the World* (Philadelphia, 1936); *Murder One* (New York, 1967).

REFERENCES: Lee Israel, *Kilgallen* (New York, 1979); Ishbel Ross, *Ladies of the Press* (New York, 1974): 240–245.

Kilpatrick, James Jackson, Jr. (1 Nov. 1920–   ). A courtly, stylish southern writer of the old school, now in semiretirement, James J. Kilpatrick has been a nationally syndicated conservative columnist since 1964.

Kilpatrick, or "Kilpo," as he is known among journalists, was born not in the South, the region with which he is identified, but in Oklahoma City. He was an *Oklahoma City Times* copyboy at age thirteen, was editor of his high school newspaper, and received the B.J. from the University of Missouri in 1941. During college, he worked summers for the *Oklahoma City Times* and during the school year was a staff photographer for the public relations office at Stephens College, a woman's school in Columbia, Missouri.

After graduation, Kilpatrick found a reporting job at the *Richmond* [Virginia] *News Leader* under its legendary editor, historian Douglas Southall Freeman. In 1949 Kilpatrick became the paper's chief editorial writer, and when Freeman retired in June 1951, he made Kilpatrick his successor. Editor of a major southern paper at age thirty, Kilpatrick continued to write: editorials, reviews, and investigative news stories. In hindsight, the most difficult thing he has had to live down from this period has been his initial opposition to racial integration after the 1954 Supreme Court decision in *Brown* v. *Board of Education.*

His stylish writing, however, was noticed, and in 1964 Harry Elmlark of the Washington Star syndicate approached him about moving to Washington to write a column. *Newsday* made a second offer that allowed him to try a column without so drastic a change: remaining editor of the *News Leader* and writing a column from Richmond. He accepted the *Newsday* proposal, and his column was a hit—so much so that in 1966 Elmlark finally persuaded him to give up the editorship and move to D.C. Kilpatrick also wrote for *Nation's Business* and was a contributing editor to *National Review* from 1964 to 1968.

Kilpatrick's political opinion column, "A Conservative View," was handled for many years by Universal Press Syndicate. It appeared in as many as 450 papers, giving him a longer reach than most political columnists. He has spoken out in favor of gun control, against prayer in public schools, and, for many years now, against racial discrimination. Among modern columnists, his use of simile and metaphor is probably unmatched. His readers were especially fond of the lighter columns he occasionally wrote, datelined Scrabble, Virginia (even though he actually lived in nearby Woodville). In a courtly, poetic style that was the print equivalent of a Charles Kuralt "On the Road" segment for television, Kilpatrick told readers about the wildlife and weather of Virginia's semimountainous hunt country, often managing to work in a subtle political message at the same time. These columns ceased when he and his wife moved to the warmer climate of Charleston, South Carolina, in the late 1980s.

Kilpatrick now writes two weekly columns for Universal, "Covering the Courts," and "The Writer's Art," a column about writing that competes with William Safire's "On Language." In addition, he appeared as a regular on television's "Agronsky & Co.," often debating fellow columnist Carl Rowan. The show that made him most recognized to American viewers, however, was "60 Minutes" on CBS, for which he and liberal columnist Shana Alexander did a debate segment called "Point, Counterpoint." He has been one of the lecture circuit crowd who is actually worth the $5,000–$10,000 an hour price and has written a number of books—on writing, the South, and politics.

BOOKS: Ed. with Louis D. Rubin, Jr., *The Lasting South: Fourteen Southerners Look at Their Home* (Chicago, 1957); *The Sovereign States: Notes of a Citizen of Virginia* (Chicago, 1957); *The Smut Peddlers* (New York, 1960); *The Southern Case for School Segregation* (New York, 1962); *The Foxes' Union* (McLean, Va., 1977); with Eugene J.

McCarthy, *A Political Bestiary* (New York, 1978); with William A. Bake, *The American South: Four Seasons of the Land* (Birmingham, Ala., 1980); *The Writer's Art* (Kansas City, Mo., 1984); *The Ear Is Human: A Handbook of Homophones and Other Confusions* (Kansas City, Mo., 1985); *A Bestiary of Bridge* (Kansas City, Mo., 1986); *Fine Print: Reflections on the Writing Art* (Kansas City, Mo., 1993).

REFERENCES: Neil A. Grauer, *Wits and Sages* (Baltimore and London, 1984): 179–193.

Kintner, Robert E. (12 Sept. 1909–23 December 1980). Robert Kintner, in partnership with Joseph Alsop, Jr., wrote a political column out of Washington, D.C., titled "The Capitol Parade," which was distributed by the North American Newspaper Alliance. He later went into the management side of broadcasting, rising rapidly to become president and board chairman of ABC.

Kintner was born in Stroudsburg, Pennsylvania. He earned the B.A. from Swarthmore College in 1931.

After college, Kintner became a financial reporter for the *New York Herald Tribune* and later wrote a column for that paper. During 1937–1941, he and Joseph Alsop, Jr., who also was employed by the *Herald Tribune,* collaborated in writing a column of insider information from the nation's capital; the column appeared in nearly one hundred newspapers. They also wrote two books together just prior to World War II. Kintner volunteered for military service and served in the army until 1944.

During his years as a newspaper columnist, Kintner had become acquainted with Edward Noble, who later bought and ran the American Broadcasting Company. Noble hired Kintner in 1944 as a vice president in public relations. In 1950 Kintner was named president of the network. In 1966 he became board chairman, and during 1966–1967 he was an adviser/assistant to President Lyndon Johnson. Kintner also wrote for various magazines, including *Life* and *Saturday Evening Post.*

BOOKS: With Joseph Alsop, Jr., *Men Around the President* (New York, 1939); with Joseph Alsop, Jr., *American White Paper: The Story of American Diplomacy and the Second World War* (New York, 1940).

Kirkpatrick, Jeane Duane Jordan (19 Nov. 1926–   ). Political figure/educator Jeane Kirkpatrick's column has been syndicated by the Los Angeles Times Syndicate since 1985.

She was born Jeane Jordan in Duncan, Oklahoma. She earned the A.B. from Barnard College in 1948 and the M.A. (1950) and Ph.D. (1967) from Columbia University. In addition, she did graduate study at the Institut de Science Politique of the University of Paris.

She began her career as a State Department researcher (1951–1952), then was a research associate at George Washington University (1954–1956). Kirkpatrick was a researcher for the Fund for the Republic (1956–1957), then in 1962 began a long tenure as a government professor at Georgetown University. She became a public figure as U.S. representative to the United Nations (1981–1985) and launched her column thereafter. Her specialty is foreign policy. She has also authored eight books on politics.

BOOKS: *The Strategy of Deception: A Study in World-Wide Communist Tactics* (New York, 1963); *Leader and Vanguard in Mass Society: A Study of Peronist Argentina* (Cambridge, Mass., 1971); *Political Woman* (New York, 1974); with Warren E. Miller, *The New Presidential Elite: Men and Women in National Politics* (New York, 1976); *Dictatorships and Double Standards: Rationalism and Reason in Politics* (New York, 1982); *The Reagan Phenomenon, and Other Speeches on Foreign Policy* (Washington, D.C., 1983); *Legitimacy and Force* (New Brunswick, 1988); *The Withering Away of the Totalitarian State—and Other Surprises* (Washington, D.C., 1990).

Kissinger, Henry Alfred (27 May 1923–   ). Nobel Peace Prize winner and former U.S. secretary of state Henry Kissinger writes a column on international relations for the Los Angeles Times Syndicate.

Kissinger was born Heinz Alfred Kissinger in Fuerth, Germany. He emigrated with his family to the United States in 1938 and became a U.S. citizen in 1943. He took evening accounting courses at New York's City College in 1941 while holding a day job at a shaving brush factory. He was drafted into the army in 1943 and served as an interpreter and interrogator in counterintelligence. At war's end in 1945, Kissinger, who had anglicized his name to Henry, took charge of municipal reorganization of the German town of Krefeld.

In 1946 he obtained a scholarship to Harvard University, where he made Phi Beta Kappa and received the B.A., summa cum laude, in 1950. During the following year he became director of the university's foreign student project, which became known as the Harvard International Seminar, and headed the program until 1969. He also earned the M.A. in 1952 and the Ph.D. in 1954 at Harvard, where he remained as a faculty member through 1971. From 1969 to 1974 he was also director of the National Security Council, and from 1969 to 1974, an assistant to President Richard Nixon. Kissinger was secretary of state from 1973 to 1977, after which he became a professor at Georgetown University and chairman of Kissinger Associates, Inc.

Kissinger was *Time* magazine's "Man of the Year" in 1972 and in 1973 won the Nobel Peace Prize. He has also authored, coauthored, or edited several books, mainly on foreign policy topics.

BOOKS: *A World Restored: Castlereagh, Metternich and the Restoration of Peace* (Boston, 1957); *Nuclear Weapons and Foreign Policy* (New York, 1957); *The Necessity for Choice: Prospects of American Foreign Policy* (New York, 1961); *The Troubled Partnership: A Reappraisal of the Atlantic Alliance* (New York, 1965); ed., *Problems of National Security: A Book of Readings* (New York, 1966); *American Foreign Policy: Three Essays* (New York, 1969); *White House Years* (Boston, 1979); *For the Record: Selected Statements 1977–1980* (Boston, 1981); *Years of Upheaval* (Boston, 1982); *American Foreign Policy: A Global View* (New York, 1982); *Observations: Selected Speeches and Essays, 1982–1984* (Boston, 1985); with McGeorge Bundy, *The Dimensions of Diplomacy* (New York, 1989).

REFERENCES: Gary Allen, *Kissinger* (Seal Beach, Calif., 1976); Ralph Blumenfeld, et al. *Henry Kissinger: The Private and Public Story* (New York, 1974); Henry Brandon, *The Retreat of American Power* (New York, 1973); Peter Kickson, *Kissinger and the Meaning of History* (Cambridge, Mass., 1978); Marvin Kalb and Bernard Kalb, *Kissinger* (Boston, 1974); Roger Morris, *Uncertain Greatness: Henry Kissinger and American Foreign Policy* (New York, 1977); John G. Stoessinger, *Henry Kissinger: The Anguish of Power* (New York, 1976).

Kleinberg, Howard (23 Oct. 1932–   ). Howard Kleinberg currently wears two hats: national columnist for Cox Newspapers and local columnist for the *Miami Herald.*

Kleinberg was born in New York City but graduated from Miami Senior High School in 1951. He was a longtime employee of the *Miami News* (1950–1988), where he served as sportswriter, sports editor, news editor, managing editor, and finally the paper's last editor until it folded on 31 December 1988.

Kleinberg became national columnist for Cox in 1989 and as such has his general interest column on national and international affairs distributed by the New York Times News Service. In 1990 he also became a local columnist for the *Miami Herald,* in which capacity he comments on local issues in terms of a historical perspective of South Florida.

BOOKS: *Miami: The Way We Were* (Miami, 1985); *The Great Florida Hurricane and Disaster* (Miami, 1993); *Miami Beach, a History* (Miami, 1994).

Klobuchar, Jim (9 April 1928–   ). The *Minneapolis Star and Tribune* has employed witty columnist Jim Klobuchar for nearly twenty-five years.

Klobuchar is a native of Ely, Minnesota, and is a graduate of the University of Minnesota. He began his career with a seven-year job as a reporter for the Associated Press. Since that time he has worked on newspapers and has also hosted radio and television programs in his city. He has written eleven books, including a biography of football great Fran Tarkenton. His is a general column, but he frequently deals, in a humorous fashion, with sports and the outdoors.

BOOKS: *The Zest and Best of Klobuchar* (Minneapolis, 1967); *The Playbacks of Jim Klobuchar* (Minneapolis, 1969); *True Hearts and Purple Hearts: An Unauthorized Biography of a Football Team* (Minneapolis, 1970); *Will America Accept Love at Halftime? Or How to Survive Pro Football Sunday* (Minneapolis, 1972); *Where the Wind Blows Bittersweet* (Wayzata, Minn., 1975); *Tarkenton* (New York, 1976); *Will the Vikings Ever Win the Sugar Bowl?* (New York, 1977); *Eight Miles Without a Pothole* (Minneapolis, 1986); *High and Inside* (Stillwater, Minn., 1987); *When We Reach for the Sun* (Stillwater, Minn., 1987); *Wild Places and Gentle Breezes* (Stillwater, Minn., 1990).

Knapp, George (?–   ). *Las Vegas Sun* columnist George Knapp is unusual in that he entered print journalism from a career in television.

Knapp holds a master's degree in communications from the University of the Pacific, where he also taught public speaking and directed forensics. His first job in Las Vegas was driving a taxi, after which he got into television by an unusual route: as an assistant set carpenter. He became a part-time studio cameraman at KLVX-TV, the PBS affiliate in Las Vegas, and eventually became a TV reporter.

Switching to CBS affiliate KLAS-TV, he was chief investigative reporter, news anchor, talk show host, and producer. He is still with KLAS in addition to writing his column, which he launched in 1990 after spending two years as a contributing editor to *Las Vegas Magazine*. Knapp has also taught journalism at the University of Nevada, Las Vegas. His columns often deal with the sleaze and glitz of his city.

Knebel, Fletcher (1 Oct. 1911–April 1993). Fletcher Knebel (pronounced Kuh-nabul) wrote the syndicated column "Potomac Fever" for Cowles Publications from 1951 to 1964. He is also remembered as coauthor of the Cold War best-seller *Seven Days in May* (1962).

Knebel was born in Dayton, Ohio. He earned Phi Beta Kappa honors and received the B.A. from Miami University of Ohio in 1934 and later that year became a reporter for the *Coatesville* [Pennsylvania] *Record*. He moved to the *Chattanooga News* still later in 1934, and in 1935 he took a reporting job at the Toledo (Ohio), *News-Bee*. He was a reporter for the *Cleveland Plain Dealer* in 1936 and was that paper's Washington correspondent from 1937 to 1950, with time out for navy service from 1942 to 1945.

Knebel's column satirized items in the news. He also became known for his *Look* magazine profiles of John F. Kennedy and other political figures. After ending his column in 1964, Knebel moved to Hawaii and worked as a freelance writer. He authored and coauthored a number of books, mainly novels.

BOOKS: With Charles W. Bailey, *No High Ground* (New York, 1960); with Charles W. Bailey, *Seven Days in May* (New York, 1962); with Charles W. Bailey, *Convention* (New York, 1965); *Night of Camp David* (New York, 1965); *Zinzin Road* (Garden City, N.Y., 1966); *Vanished* (Garden City, N.Y., 1968); *Trespass* (Garden City, N.Y., 1969); *Dark Horse* (Garden City, N.Y., 1972); *The Bottom Line* (Garden City, N.Y., 1974); *Dave Sulkin Cares!* (Garden City, N.Y., 1978); *Crossing in Berlin* (Garden City, N.Y., 1981); *Poker Game* (Garden City, N.Y., 1983); *Sabotage* (Garden City, N.Y., 1986); *Before You Sue* (New York, 1987).

Knight, John Shively (26 Oct. 1894–16 June 1981). John S. Knight, who controlled one of America's most powerful newspaper chains, wrote a personal column, "The Editor's Notebook," for his papers from 1933 until his retirement in 1975.

Knight was born in Bluefield, West Virginia, the son of C. L. Knight, who became owner of the *Akron* [Ohio] *Beacon-Journal*. The younger Knight attended Cornell University for three years, then joined the U.S. Army in 1917 and saw action in France. After the war, he worked as a reporter for his father's paper. Dissatisfied with his writing skill, he preferred to use the pen name Walker. In 1925, however, he was made managing editor, and in 1933, editor. He became publisher upon his father's death in 1933. He began building his newspaper empire in that same year with the purchase of the *Massillon* [Ohio] *Independent.* In 1937 he bought the most profitable of all his properties, the *Miami Herald;* in 1940 the *Detroit Free Press;* and in 1944 the *Chicago Daily News.* He continued buying and selling newspapers from that time and in July 1974 bought the Ridder chain of nineteen papers, changing the name of his own chain (he insisted on using the word *group* instead) to Knight-Ridder. He was a proponent of individual editorial autonomy for the papers he controlled and was politically conservative. He was a longtime critic of foreign aid and was critical of U.S. involvement in Vietnam before it was "patriotic" to take that position.

Knight won a Pulitzer Prize in 1968 for editorial writing, plus innumerable other awards and recognitions. Beginning in December 1936, his "Editor's Notebook" column began to appear on the front pages of all his papers; in this, he provided a personal touch that most other large newspaper chains lacked.

In 1943 Knight became director of the U.S. Office of Censorship in London during World War II. He was twice president of the American Society of Newspaper Editors and helped establish the Inter American Press Association.

REFERENCES: Frank Angelo, *On Guard: A History of the Detroit Free Press* (Detroit, 1981); Eugene L. Meyer, "The Knights Invade Philadelphia," *Columbia Journalism Review* 10 (May/June 1971): 44–49; Nixon Smiley, *Knights of the Fourth Estate: The Story of the Miami Herald* (Miami, 1974).

Koch, Edward Irving (12 Dec. 1924–). Former New York City mayor Ed Koch writes a weekly *New York Post* column that is distributed by United Feature Syndicate.

Koch was born in New York City. He studied at City College, served as a combat infantryman in World War II, and received the LL.B. from New York University in 1948. After passing the New York bar in 1949, Koch operated his own law practice from 1949 to 1964. From 1965 to 1969 he was senior partner in the firm of Koch Lankenau Schwartz & Kovner. He was a member of the New York City Council during 1967–1968 and from 1969 to 1972 was a New York congressman. Koch served as mayor from 1978 to 1989, then in 1990 became a partner in the firm of Robinson Silverman Pearce Aronsohn and Berman.

Koch's column more often than not deals with urban cultural and political issues. The colorful ex-mayor has also coauthored several books about his experiences.

BOOKS: With Daniel Paisner, *Citizen Koch: An Autobiography* (New York, 1973); *How'm I Doing? The Wit and Wisdom of Ed Koch,* ed. by Mel Shestack and Sayre Ross (New York, 1981); with William Rauch, *Mayor* (New York, 1984); with William Rauch, *Politics* (New York, 1985); with John Cardinal O'Connor, *His Eminence and Hizzoner: A Candid Exchange* (New York, 1989); with Leland T. Jones, *All the Best: Letters from a Feisty Mayor* (New York, 1990).

Kohler, Saul (4 Oct. 1928–). Saul Kohler wrote a weekly political column, "The Presidency," which was begun for Newhouse Newspapers in 1971.

Kohler was born in New York City and received the A.B. from Brooklyn College in 1956.

He began his career as a general assignment reporter for the *Philadelphia Inquirer* (1956–1962); he was the *Inquirer*'s Harrisburg bureau chief from 1962 to 1968 and Washington bureau chief in 1968–1969. In 1970 he served as Sen. Hugh Scott's press secretary, then began his column for Newhouse.

Kohlmeier, Louis Martin, Jr. (17 Feb. 1926–). Pulitzer Prize–winning reporter Louis Kohlmeier began writing a Washington, D.C., column for the Chicago Tribune–New York News Syndicate in 1973.

Kohlmeier was born in St. Louis, Missouri; received the B.J. from the University of Missouri in 1950; and served in the U.S. Army from 1950 to 1952.

He was a *Wall Street Journal* staff writer from 1952 to 1957, first stationed in St. Louis, then in Chicago. He was hired as a reporter by the *St. Louis Globe-Democrat* (1957–1960), then returned to report for the *Wall Street Journal* (1960–1972). His Pulitzer was awarded in 1964 for a story involving then-president Lyndon Johnson and his wife's broadcast interests and possible favorable treatment given them by the Federal Communications Commission.

BOOKS: *The Regulators: Watchdog Agencies and the Public Interest* (New York, 1969); *God Save This Honorable Court* (New York, 1972); ed. with Jon G. Udell and Laird B. Anderson, *Reporting on Business and the Economy* (Englewood Cliffs, N.J., 1981).

Kondracke, Morton (28 April 1939–). Morton Kondracke was a *Wall Street Journal* columnist from 1981 to 1985 and now writes a political column for United Feature Syndicate. He also did a column titled "Pennsylvania Avenue" for the Washington, D.C., paper *Roll Call.*

Kondracke was born in Chicago. He received the A.B. from Dartmouth College in 1960 and was a Nieman Fellow at Harvard University (1973–1974). He served in the U.S. Army in 1960–1963.

He entered journalism in 1963 as a general assignment reporter for the *Chicago Sun-Times;* became bureau chief in Springfield, Illinois, in 1965; and moved to that paper's Washington, D.C., bureau in 1968. In 1976 he became executive editor of *New Republic* magazine. He was chief of *Newsweek*'s Washington bureau for 1985–1986, then returned to *New Republic* as senior editor in 1986.

Also active in broadcast news work, Kondracke was a National Public Radio commentator on "All Things Considered" (1978–1980), a panel member on television's "The McLaughlin Group" (1981–present), and has appeared on "This Week with David Brinkley." He has also had his own show on WRC-AM radio and has appeared on various other radio and television news/commentary shows. His politics appear to have progressed from liberal to conservative to moderate.

Kornheiser, Anthony I. (13 July 1948–). The versatile Tony Kornheiser has been a sports columnist for the *Washington Post* since 1979 and in 1989 began writing a humor column as well.

Kornheiser was born in New York City and in 1970 received the B.A. in English and social sciences from Harpur College of the State University of New York.

He began his career as a *Newsday* reporter (1970–1975), then was a *New York Times* sports reporter and weekly rock music columnist from 1976 to 1979. He joined the *Post* in 1979 as a reporter/feature writer/columnist. Kornheiser has won numerous awards for his sportswriting and has also been active in broadcasting. From 1988 to 1990 he cohosted the WMAL-Radio show "Out of Bounds" and from 1988 to 1990 was host of the "Tony Kornheiser Show" on WJLA-TV in Washington, D.C. He has, in addition, written freelance for *Sports Illustrated, Rolling Stone, New York, Cosmopolitan,* and other magazines and has written a book, *The Baby Chase,* about the difficult process of adoption.

BOOKS: *The Baby Chase* (New York, 1983).

Kraft, Joseph (4 Sept. 1924–10 Jan. 1986). Joseph Kraft wrote a liberal political column from 1963 until his death in 1986.

Kraft was born in South Orange, New Jersey, and grew up in New York City. He received the A.B. from Columbia University in 1947 and did graduate study at Princeton University from then until 1951. In this same year he studied briefly at the Sorbonne in Paris.

His first newspaper experience was as a teenage part-time contributor of sports stories for the *New York World-Telegram.* He joined the army in 1943 and spent World War II as a cryptographer and translator. Once his formal education was completed, he considered becoming a history professor but instead took a temporary writing job with the *Washington Post.* In 1952 he joined the *New York Times* to write a weekly news analysis titled "News of the Week in Review." He remained with the *Times* until 1957, when he left the paper to write for *Saturday Evening Post.* In 1960 he became a foreign affairs adviser to presidential candidate John F. Kennedy and in 1962 was a speech writer for Kennedy and for Secretary of State George Ball. He worked as Washington correspondent for *Harper's* magazine (1962–1965) and wrote "Letters from Far Off Places" for *New Yorker.*

Kraft's column was launched in 1963 for the *Washington Star.* He self-syndicated it, then had it picked up by Field Newspaper Syndicate. Two years before his death, Kraft affiliated with the *Los Angeles Times.* At its peak, the column appeared in about two hundred newspapers.

BOOKS: *The Struggle for Algeria* (Garden City, N.Y., 1961); *The Grand Design: From Common Market to Atlantic Partnership* (New York, 1962); *Profiles in Power: A Washington Insight* (New York, 1966); *The Chinese Difference* (New York, 1973).

Kramer, Hilton (25 March 1928–   ). Veteran art critic Hilton Kramer stirred up a hornet's nest in 1993 with what appears to be a unique column—one that attacks "political correctness" by directly criticizing his former employer, the *New York Times*. His column, "Timeswatch," appears in the *New York Post*.

Kramer was born in Gloucester, Massachusetts. His B.A. is from Syracuse University (1950), and he has also studied at the New School for Social Research (1950), Columbia University (1950–1951), Harvard University (1951), and Indiana University (1951–1952).

Kramer was associate editor and features editor of *Arts Digest* (1954–1955), then managing editor (1955–1958) and editor (1958–1961) of *Arts Magazine*. Next he worked as art critic of *Nation* (1962–1963) and as critic and associate editor of *New Leader* (1964–1965). He was with the *New York Times* from 1965 to 1982 and became that paper's chief art critic, then resigned to found and edit *New Criterion,* an arts monthly.

Kramer's *Post* column does not limit itself to *Times* arts coverage, but criticizes virtually every aspect of what its writer sees as the slavishly liberal leanings of the nation's "newspaper of record." Kramer's own critics have called him, among other things, a "walking right-wing cause." He has also been a frequent contributor to *New Republic, Commentary, Partisan Review,* and other journals of commentary.

BOOKS: Ed., *The Turn of the Century* (New York, 1957); ed., *Romantic Art* (New York, 1958); ed., *Perspectives on the Arts* (New York, 1961); *The Age of the Avant-Garde: An Art Chronicle of 1956–1972* (New York, 1973); *The Revenge of the Philistines: Art and Culture, 1972–1984* (New York, 1985); ed., *The New Criterion Reader: The First Five Years* (New York, 1988).

Krauss, Robert G. (14 Jan. 1924–   ). Bob Krauss has been a local columnist for the *Honolulu Advertiser* since 1953.

Krauss was born in Plainview, Nebraska. He received the B.A. from the University of Minnesota in 1950 after seeing active navy duty in the Pacific theater in World War II.

Krauss was a reporter for the *Watertown* [South Dakota] *Public Opinion* from 1950 to 1951, then joined the *Honolulu Advertiser* as a general assignment reporter. He is now columnist and senior reporter for this paper. During his long career, he has covered statehood for Hawaii (1959) and the war in Vietnam. He has covered stories from roughly thirty-five Pacific islands and atolls, has accompanied archaeological expeditions, and has sailed in a double-hulled voyaging canoe to retrace the ancient Polynesians' migration routes.

BOOKS: *Here's Hawaii* (New York, 1960); *Travel Guide to the Hawaiian Islands* (New York, 1963); with William P. Alexander, *Grove Farm Plantation: The Biography of a Hawaiian Sugar Plantation* (Palo Alto, Calif., 1965); *High-Rise Hawaii* (New York, 1969); ed., *A Child's History of Hawaii* (Norfolk Island, Australia, 1973); with Edward J. McGrath and Kenneth M. Brewer, *Historic Waianae: A Place of Kings* (Norfolk Island, Australia, 1973); *The Island Way* (Norfolk Island, Australia, 1975); *Kauai* (Norfolk Island, Australia, 1979); with Kenneth M. Brewer, *An Island Heritage Book* (Waianae

Coast, Hawaii, 1979); *McInerny* (Honolulu, 1981); *South Seas Adventures of Kenneth Emory* (Honolulu, 1988); *Hawaii, Tides of Change* (Aiea, Hawaii, 1989); *Our Hawaii: The Best of Bob Krauss* (Aiea, Hawaii, 1990); *Birth by Fire: A Guide to Hawaii's Volcanoes* (Aiea, Hawaii, 1992).

Krauthammer, Charles (13 March 1950–   ). Charles Krauthammer has been a weekly syndicated columnist with the *Washington Post* since 1985. He won a Pulitzer Prize in 1987 for his commentary on politics and society in general.

Krauthammer was born in New York City. His educational background is unusual for a political/social columnist. He holds a B.A. in political science from McGill University (1970); furthered his study of politics at Balliol College, Oxford, during 1970–1971; and then reversed direction to study medicine and received the M.D. degree from Harvard in 1975. He worked at Massachusetts General Hospital in Boston from 1975 to 1978; worked in Washington, D.C., for the Mental Health Administration (1978–1980); and became board certified in psychiatry in 1984.

Krauthammer's career changed again in 1980, when he became a speech writer for Vice President Walter Mondale, after which he was hired as associate editor of *New Republic* (1981–1982). He was senior editor of that magazine from 1982 to 1988 and since then been a contributing editor. He began writing essays for *Time* in 1983 and began his column in 1985 at the *Post*.

BOOKS: *Cutting Edges: Making Sense of the Eighties* (New York, 1985).

Krock, Arthur (16 Nov. 1886–12 April 1974). One of the pioneers of the American political column, Arthur Krock was a columnist for the *New York Times* from 1927 until 1966.

Krock was born in Glasgow, Kentucky, and later moved with his family to Chicago. He briefly attended Princeton in 1904, but family financial difficulties caused him to return home. He completed his A.A. at Chicago's Lewis Institute in 1907.

From 1907 to 1910 Krock was a general assignment reporter for the *Louisville Herald,* then spent two years as a night editor for the Associated Press in that same city. He became Washington correspondent for the *Louisville Times* in 1910 and in 1911 also served the *Louisville Courier-Journal* in the same capacity. He returned to Louisville and was managing editor of these jointly owned papers from 1915 to 1919, and from 1919 to 1923 was editor in chief of the *Times.* In 1923 he joined the *New York World* under editor Herbert Bayard Swope and was eventually promoted to assistant to the publisher.

Krock was hired by *New York Times* publisher Adolph Ochs as an editorial writer (1927) and became the *Times*'s Washington correspondent in 1931. The following year he began writing his column "In the Nation" for the *Times*'s editorial page. Called by some "the ultimate insider," the dignified Krock garnered four Pulitzers (he turned down the 1950 prize to avoid possible conflict of interest) and published many scoops. He was a conservative, a supporter of Eisenhower, and a critic of Kennedy, as he had been of Franklin Roosevelt.

BOOKS: Ed., *The Editorials of Henry Watterson* (New York, 1923); *In the Nation, 1932–1966* (New York, 1966); *Memoirs: Sixty Years on the Firing Line* (New York, 1968); *The Consent of the Governed and Other Deceits* (Boston, 1971); *Myself When Young: Growing Up in the 1890s* (Boston, 1973).

REFERENCES: "Grand Old Man," *Time* 103 (22 April 1974): 61; Charles J. V. Murphy, "Unforgettable Arthur Krock," *Reader's Digest* 107 (March 1975): 101.

Kuhn, Irene Corbally (15 Jan. 1900–   ). Irene Kuhn was a syndicated columnist with King Features from 1953 to 1969 and with Columbia Features from 1970.

Kuhn was born Irene Corbally in New York City. She studied stenography at a New York business school, then held several secretarial jobs before attending Marymount College and Columbia University.

In 1919 she became a reporter for the *Syracuse Herald,* then in 1920 moved back to New York City for a reporting job on the city's new tabloid, the *Daily News.* Cost-cutting measures ended this job, and in 1921 she moved to Paris, France, as an advertising copywriter. Later that same year she was hired by the Paris edition of the *Chicago Tribune,* and when its fashion editor, Rosemary Carr, resigned to marry the poet Stephen Vincent Benet, Corbally replaced her. In 1922 she relocated in Shanghai, where she met and married fellow reporter Bert Kuhn and wrote for the Shanghai *Evening Star.* Kuhn took a leave of absence to work for parts of 1929–1930 with the *Honolulu Star Bulletin,* then returned to her job in China, where in 1924 she also became the first announcer for Shanghai's earliest radio station, KRC.

After her husband's death, Kuhn returned to New York for two years as a reporter for the *Sun,* from which she went back to her job on the *Honolulu Star-Bulletin.* She next wrote scenarios and publicity for MGM, Twentieth Century-Fox, and Paramount in Hollywood (1931–1933), and in 1933 she became a feature writer for the *New York World-Telegram.* She worked as a foreign correspondent for the International News Service and wrote for *Stars and Stripes* (the China edition), the *New York Mirror,* and the *New York Daily News* prior to beginning her column, "It's My Opinion," for King Features in 1953. In 1970 she switched her column to Columbia Features.

Kuhn was a commentator with Mutual Broadcasting System (1938–1939), then went to work for NBC in 1940 and conducted her own radio "column," "Irene Kuhn's Feature Page." She was the first newsperson to broadcast out of Shanghai when it was liberated in 1945 and the first woman to broadcast from a U.S. warship. She also contributed to numerous magazines, including *Reader's Digest, Good Housekeeping, Town and Country,* and *Cosmopolitan,* and was travel editor of *American Labor Magazine.*

BOOKS: *Assigned to Adventure* (New York, 1938); with Raymond J. DeJaegher, *The Enemy Within: An Eyewitness Account of the Communist Conquest of China* (Garden City, N.Y., 1952).

Kupcinet, Irv (31 July 1912–). Irv Kupcinet has written his "Kup's Column" for the *Chicago Sun-Times* since 1943 and in the *Chicago Daily Times* prior to that.

Kupcinet was born in Chicago. He attended Northwestern University from 1930 to 1932 but received his A.B. from the University of North Dakota in 1935. In that same year he was named to the College All-Star team, after which he played pro football with the Philadelphia Eagles. His career as an athlete was cut short by a shoulder injury, and later in 1935 he became a sportswriter for the *Chicago Daily Times*. The exact date his column began is unclear, but Kupcinet's focus gradually turned from sports to more general topics, and "Kup's Column" been described by some as a gossip column, though its content has been more varied than that label would suggest. When the *Daily Times* merged with the *Sun* in 1943, Kup remained as a popular columnist, and on January 18, 1993, he celebrated his column's fiftieth anniversary with the *Sun-Times*. The column appeared six days a week until February 1993, when its frequency was cut to five days a week. Kupcinet has also been a radio sports announcer, and from 1959 to 1986 the gregarious columnist hosted his own television program, "Kup's Show," which won an Emmy in 1960. He is a founding member of the Chicago Newspaper Guild and is one of the only columnists to have had a bridge named after him (in 1986, when the Wabash Avenue Bridge was renamed the Irv Kupcinet Bridge).

BOOKS: *Kup: A Man, an Era, a City* (Chicago, 1988).

REFERENCES: Mark Fitzgerald, "Chicago Still His Oyster," *Editor and Publisher* (6 March 1993): 16–17.

Kuralt, Charles Bishop (10 Sept. 1934–). Beloved television host and feature correspondent, Charles Kuralt began his career as a newspaper reporter and columnist for the *Charlotte* [North Carolina] *News*.

Kuralt was born in Wilmington, North Carolina, and earned the B.A. from the University of North Carolina, Chapel Hill, in 1955. He was a reporter/general columnist for the Charlotte paper from 1955 to 1957, then became a writer for CBS News. In 1959 he began his acclaimed human interest show "On the Road," on which he, a cameraman, a soundman, and an electrician drove the back roads of America in search of the unusual. He also hosted various CBS specials and the shows "Eyewitness to History" and "CBS Sunday Morning" before retiring in 1994. Kuralt is a seven-time Emmy winner.

BOOKS: *To the Top of the World: The Adventures and Misadventures of the Plaisted Polar Expedition* (New York, 1968); *Dateline America* (New York, 1979); *On the Road with Charles Kuralt* (New York, 1985); with Loomis McGlohon, *North Carolina Is My Home* (Chester, Conn., 1986); with Irwin Glusker, *Southerners: Portrait of a People* (Birmingham, Ala., 1986); *A Life on the Road* (New York, 1990).

L

Lambro, Donald Joseph (24 July 1940–). Donald Lambro has been a conservative Washington columnist for United Feature Syndicate since 1980. The primary targets of his commentary are public policy and economic issues.

Lambro was born in Wellesley, Massachusetts. He holds the B.A. from Boston University (1963).

Before entering newspaper journalism, he was an editor with Young Americans for Freedom (1963–1964), a writer for the Republican National Committee (1964), and vice president of the political consulting firm Richard A. Viguerie in Falls Church, Virginia.

Lambro free-lanced during 1966–1967, then was employed by United Press International as Hartford, Connecticut, statehouse correspondent from 1968 to 1970, when he moved to the D.C. bureau. After ten years, he launched his column, in which he has been an outspoken critic of government waste. He has contributed to various magazines: *Washingtonian, Reader's Digest, National Review,* and others.

BOOKS: *The Federal Rathole* (New Rochelle, N.Y., 1975); *The Conscience of a Young Conservative* (New Rochelle, N.Y., 1976); *Fat City: How Washington Wastes Your Taxes* (South Bend, Ind., 1980); *Washington—City of Scandals: Investigating Congress and Other Big Spenders* (Boston, 1984); *Land of Opportunity: The Entrepreneurial Spirit in America* (Boston, 1986).

Lane, Mark R. (7 Jan. 1956–). Mark Lane has been writing a column of humorous social commentary for the Daytona Beach (Florida) *News-Journal* since 1988.

Lane was born in Long Beach, California, and grew up in Florida. He holds the B.A. (1976) and the M.A. (1979) from Boston University.

He has, he says, "followed something of a nineteenth century career path," remaining with the same paper for which he was a copyboy at age sixteen. He worked for the *News-Journal* from 1972 to 1973 and from 1980 to the present. He has been an editorial writer since 1986, associate editor since 1992. His column has been distributed by Cox News Service since 1991.

Lardner, Ringgold Wilmer (6 March 1885–25 Sept. 1933). Ring Lardner spent much of his working life as a sportswriter but is mainly remembered as a humorist. His best known column was "In the Wake of the News," which he wrote for the *Chicago Tribune* from 1913 to 1919; it was, for the most part, a sports column, but of an unusual sort. He reported on World War I from Europe, altering his column's title to "In the Wake of the War." After the peace, he began another column for the Bell Syndicate (1919–1927).

Lardner was born in Niles, Michigan. He was educated at home in his early years, finished Niles High School, and spent a term at the Armour Institute in Chicago, where he considered studying engineering. Instead, he worked at a series of jobs, including being a meter reader for the Niles Gas Company, before becoming sports editor (and sports reporter, court reporter, and drama critic) for the *South Bend Times*. From there he moved to Chicago as sports reporter for the *Chicago Inter Ocean,* the *Chicago Examiner,* and the *Chicago Tribune,* all from 1907 to 1910. At the *Tribune* he began to featurize his sportswriting, lacing it with humor.

Lardner became managing editor of the *Sporting News* in St. Louis in 1910 and inserted vernacular dialogue into his stories. In February of the following year he moved to Boston as sports editor of the *Boston American.* He resigned later that year in protest of the firing of his brother, Rex; he worked next as a copyreader for the *Chicago American* and later as a sportswriter for the *Chicago Examiner.* Here he introduced verse into his sports writing and also wrote sports-connected parodies of popular songs. The column "In the Wake of the News," which had been started for the *Tribune* by Hugh E. Keogh, was taken over by Lardner on Keogh's death and was written by him from 1913 to 1919, with time out in 1917 for Lardner's wartime substitute column from Europe. In 1919 he moved to New York City and wrote a sports column for the Bell Syndicate. A "Wake of the News" standout was a series Lardner called "The Pennant Pursuit," in which he poked fun at Americans' penchant for making heroes of sports stars. He also began writing for the *Saturday Evening Post* and contributed to *Collier's, Cosmopolitan, Liberty,* and other magazines. In 1932, the year before he died, he wrote several autobiographical pieces for the *Saturday Evening Post.* He also did a series about radio, "Over the Waves," for *New Yorker.*

His humor writing, with its short character sketches and dialogue, became extremely popular. Ernest Hemingway was among his admirers. "In the Wake of the News" was syndicated to around 150 newspapers, and Lardner became one of the nation's best known humorists. Many of his two dozen books were collections of his newspaper and magazine writing.

BOOKS: *March 6th: The Home Coming of Charles A. Comiskey, John J. McGraw, and James J. Callahan* (Chicago, 1914); *Bib Ballads* (Chicago, 1915); *You Know Me Al* (New York, 1916); *Gullible's Travels, Etc.* (Indianapolis, 1917); *My Four Weeks in Europe* (Indianapolis, 1918); *Treat 'Em Rough* (Indianapolis, 1918); *The Real Dope* (Indianapolis, 1919); *Own Your Own Home* (Indianapolis, 1919); *Regular Fellows I Have Met* (Chicago, 1919); *The Young Immigrunts* (Indianapolis, 1920); *Symptoms of Being 35* (Indianapolis, 1921); *The Big Town* (Indianapolis, 1921); *Say It with Oil* (New York, 1923); *How to Write Short Stories* (with Samples) (New York, 1924); *What of It?* (New York, 1925); *The Love Nest and Other Stories* (New York, 1926); *The Story of a Wonder Man* (New York, 1927); *Round Up: The Stories of Ring W. Lardner* (New York, 1929); with George S. Kaufman, *June Moon* (New York, 1930); *Lose with a Smile* (New York, 1933); *First and Last,* ed. by Gilbert Seldes (New York, 1934); *Shut Up, He Explained,* ed. by Babette Rosmond and Henry Morgan (New York, 1962); *Some Champions: Sketches and Fiction by Ring Lardner,* ed. by Matthew J. Bruccoli and Richard Layman (New York, 1976); *Ring Lardner's You Know Me Al: The Comic Strip Adventures of Jack Keefe* (New York, 1979).

REFERENCES: Donald Elder, *Ring Lardner, A Biography* (Garden City, N.Y., 1956); Elizabeth Evans, *Ring Lardner* (New York, 1979); Otto Friedrich, *Ring Lardner* (Minneapolis, Minn., 1965); Ring Lardner, Jr., *The Lardners: My Family Remembered* (New York, 1976); Walton R. Patrick, *Ring Lardner* (New York, 1963); Jonathan Yardley, *Ring: A Biography of Ring Lardner* (New York, 1977).

Larsen, Leonard (24 Aug. 1926–   ). Leonard Larsen writes a national affairs column out of Washington, D.C., for the Scripps-Howard News Service; he was a *Denver Post* columnist from 1971 until retiring from that paper in 1987.

Larsen was born in Denver, Colorado, and attended the University of Colorado; he dropped out in 1950 in favor of beginning a newspaper career. he began as a *Denver Post* copyboy, then three months later began reporting. He was the paper's D.C. bureau chief as well as its columnist from 1971 to 1987.

Although Larsen's usual subject matter is the national political scene, he sometimes delves into organized religion and occasionally selects lighter, more whimsical topics.

Larson, Douglas L. (10 Feb. 1926–   ). Few columnists have been at it for forty years, as has Doug Larson, who writes a daily column for the *Green Bay* [Wisconsin] *Press-Gazette* and a weekly column for the *Door County* [Wisconsin] *Advocate.*

Larson was born in Sturgeon Bay, Wisconsin. He received the B.A. from Carroll College in Waukesha, Wisconsin, in 1951. He wrote his first column while working as columnist/reporter/photographer for the *Door County Advocate* (1953–1964). From 1964 to 1988, he was a columnist and, successively, copy editor, makeup editor, state editor, and city editor for the *Green Bay Press-Gazette.* Larson continued writing this daily column after his retirement from the paper in 1988. It appears under his name in the *Press-Gazette* but under the title ''Senator Soaper Says'' in the other papers to which it is syndicated by

United Feature. It is regarded as a continuation of the column of the same title started earlier by Bill Vaughn of the *Kansas City Star*. Larson has written it since 1980.

Lasky, Victor (7 Jan. 1918–). Victor Lasky wrote a conservative news column for the North American Newspaper Alliance for many years, beginning in 1962.

Lasky was born in Liberty, New York. He received the B.A. from Brooklyn College in 1940. Enticed into journalism by the movie *The Front Page,* he became a copyboy for the *New York Journal* while he was in college.

Lasky was a reporter for the *Chicago Sun* from 1941 to 1942, and during World War II was a correspondent for *Stars and Stripes* (1942–1946). From 1947 to 1950 he was a reporter and rewrite man for the *New York World-Telegram and Sun*. In 1951 he made an abrupt career change, becoming a screen writer for Metro-Goldwyn-Mayer in California (1951–1952), after which he wrote for RKO General Teleradio in New York City (1955–1956). From 1956 to 1961 he was a press officer with Radio Liberty. Lasky was also the best-selling author of several rapidly produced political biographies.

BOOKS: With Ralph de Toledano, *Seeds of Treason* (Chicago, 1950); ed., *The American Legion Reader* (New York, 1953); *John F. Kennedy: What's Behind the Image?* (Washington, 1960); *J.F.K.: The Man and the Myth* (New York, 1963); *The Ugly Russian* (New York, 1965); *Robert F. Kennedy: The Myth and the Man* (New York, 1968); with George Murphy, *"Say . . . Didn't You Used to Be George Murphy?"* (New York, 1970); *Arthur J. Goldberg: The Old and the New* (New Rochelle, N.Y., 1970); *It Didn't Start with Watergate* (New York, 1977); *Jimmy Carter, the Man and the Myth* (New York, 1979); *Never Complain, Never Explain: The Story of Henry Ford II* (New York, 1981).

Laurant, Robert Darrell (15 Oct. 1947–). Darrell Laurant has written a local column for the Lynchburg (Virginia) *News & Daily Advance* since 1981. The column appears three times weekly.

Laurant was born in Sanford, North Carolina, and spent much of his youth in Syracuse, New York. In 1970 he received the B.A. in history from Belmont Abbey College outside Charlotte, North Carolina. The degree prepared him well, he tells people, for his first job—as a Howard Johnson's restaurant dishwasher. He is also one of very few columnists to have been employed as a Ferris wheel operator.

He made his start in journalism as a general assignment reporter for the *West Columbia-Cayce Journal* in West Columbia, South Carolina. He became a sportswriter for the Charleston (South Carolina) *News & Courier* in 1974–1975, then in 1976 served as editor of *South Carolina Sport Magazine*. He moved to Lynchburg and the *News & Advance* in 1977 as a sportswriter and became executive sports editor in 1980. Laurant assumed his present duties as columnist in 1981.

BOOKS: *Mom Never Told Me About Chitlins* (Lynchburg, Va., 1983); *If It Ain't Broke, Don't Fix It* (Lynchburg, Va., 1986); with Bob Wimer, *We're Still Here* (Lynchburg, Va., 1989); *Even Here: A Small Virginia Community, A Violent Decade* (Lynchburg, Va., 1992).

Lawrence, David (25 Dec. 1888–11 Feb. 1973). David Lawrence was a syndicated political columnist from 1919 until his death in 1973. He also founded and published the news magazine *U.S. News & World Report.*

Lawrence was born on Christmas Day in Philadelphia, the son of a tailor. The family moved to Buffalo, New York, where the young Lawrence worked part-time as a photographer and reporter for the *Buffalo Express* while he attended school. While a student at Princeton, he was an Associated Press reporter and a stringer for a reported seventeen newspapers. His first great scoop was in breaking the story of the death of former president Grover Cleveland, who had lived at that time in Princeton.

After graduation in 1910, Lawrence was employed at the Associated Press's (AP's) Philadelphia bureau. Within a year he moved to the wire service's Washington bureau, and in December 1915, he took a new position as the *New York Evening Post*'s Washington correspondent. In 1919 he began a political column for the *Post,* then founded and began writing for the Consolidated Press Association. Lawrence was one of the earliest U.S. columnists to concentrate almost exclusively on politics and probably the first to syndicate by wire instead of by mail.

In 1926 he became a publisher with the founding of a newspaper, the *United States Daily,* that provided thorough coverage of Washington political news, and later, state news. He became one of the first radio news commentators in 1929 with his Sunday broadcast, "Our Government" on NBC; the program aired until 1933. He also wrote for *Saturday Evening Post, Century, Scribner's,* and other magazines.

In 1931 Lawrence made an unsuccessful bid to buy the *Washington Post.* Failing at this, he divested himself of the Consolidated News Service in 1933 and converted his daily paper into a weekly, the *United States News.* The periodical was changed into a magazine of national news in 1940. In 1946 he launched a second magazine, *World Report,* to expand his attention to international news. The two magazines were merged in 1948 into *U.S. News & World Report,* for which Lawrence also wrote a column. By this time he was said to be the only active U.S. columnist to own a yacht.

Lawrence was politically conservative: a spokesman for capitalism and U.S. industry, an outspoken critic of Roosevelt's New Deal, an anticommunist, a believer in tradition. Critics accused him of blind support of the powers that be, and one of his worst bits of punditry was in predicting just after the stock market crash of 1929 that recovery would be swift. His conservatism became predictable toward the end of his life, yet he had staying power. His final column was written just hours before his death in 1973.

BOOKS: *The Truth About Mexico* (New York, 1917); *The True Story of Woodrow Wilson* (New York, 1924); *The Business Man and His Government* (Washington D.C., 1929); *The Other Side of Government* (New York, 1929); *Industry's Public Relations* (New York, 1930); *Beyond the New Deal* (New York and London, 1934); *Stumbling into Socialism and the Future of Our Political Parties* (New York and London, 1935); *Nine Honest Men* (New York and London, 1936); *Supreme Court or Political Puppets? Shall the Supreme Court Be Free or Controlled by a Supreme Executive?* (New York and London, 1937); *Who Were the Eleven Million?* (New York and London, 1937); *Diary of a Washington Correspondent* (New York, 1942); *The Editorials of David Lawrence,* 6 vols. (Washington, D.C., 1970).

REFERENCES: "The Durable Wilsonian," *Time* 46 (26 February 1973): 46; Charles Fisher, *The Columnists* (New York, 1944): 278–284; Arthur Krock, "Unforgettable David Lawrence," *Reader's Digest* 104 (January 1974): 75–79; John C. O'Brien, "Custodian of the New Freedom," in *Molders of Opinion,* ed. by David Bulman (Milwaukee, 1945): 121–131.

Lederer, Esther Pauline (4 July 1918–   ). Writing as advice columnist "Ann Landers," Eppie Lederer is syndicated by Creators Syndicate to roughly twelve hundred newspapers.

Born Esther Pauline Friedman in Sioux City, Iowa, she is the twin of fellow advice columnist Pauline Phillips, better known as "Dear Abby." The twins majored in journalism and minored in psychology at Morningside College in Sioux City from 1936 to 1939, collaborating on a gossip column, "PEEP," in the school paper, but dropped out of college to be married in a double ceremony. Lederer began her life as an advice columnist in 1955 at the *Chicago Sun-Times* when she was selected to replace the late Ruth Crowley, a nurse who was the original "Ann Landers." Lederer's version of the column, which appeared in October 1955, immediately proved popular. It was at first distributed through the Sun-Times Syndicate, then by Publishers-Hall, the Los Angeles Times Syndicate, and, starting in 1990, Creators Syndicate.

Readers who write in more often than not ask questions regarding sex. In giving her replies, Lederer often consults psychiatrists, medical specialists, lawyers, and members of the clergy. Like her sister, she has enormous drawing power. For example, a mention in 1990 of an organization called Canine Companions for Independence brought that organization donations of roughly $250,000. She has helped many charities and other worthy causes and has garnered considerable recognition, including at least twenty-five honorary degrees. Lederer has published eight advice books.

BOOKS: *Since You Ask Me* (Greenwich, Conn., 1961); *Ann Landers Talks to Teen-Agers About Sex* (New York, 1963); *Ann Landers' New Bride's Guide* (Chicago, 1963); *Ann Landers Says* (Englewood Cliffs, N.J., 1966); *Dear Ann Landers* (Chicago, 1967); *Straight Dope on Drugs* (Chicago, 1972); *Ann Landers Speaks Out* (Greenwich, Conn., 1975); *The Ann Landers Encyclopedia A to Z: Improve Your Life Emotionally, Medically, Sexually, Socially, Spiritually* (New York, 1978).

REFERENCES: Richard Weiner, *Syndicated Columnists,* 3rd Ed. (New York, 1979): 103–113.

Leo, John (16 June 1935–   ). Conservative columnist John Leo's weekly "On Society" column for *U.S. News and World Report* is syndicated nationally by Universal Press Syndicate. He is perhaps the nation's leading foe of "political correctness."

Leo was born in Hoboken, New Jersey. He attended the University of Toronto and completed his studies in 1957.

Leo began his career as a reporter for the *Bergen Record* in Hackensack, New Jersey, where he later became editor (1957–1960). He coedited, then edited the *Catholic Messenger* in Davenport, Iowa (1960–1963) and was associate editor of *Commonweal* from 1963 to 1969. From 1964 to 1967 he also wrote a column for the *National Catholic Reporter.* Leo was a reporter for the *New York Times* (1969–1972), deputy administrator of the New York City Environmental Protection Administration (1969–1972), book editor for *Trans-Action* [now *Society*] *Magazine* (1972–1973), press clips columnist for the *Village Voice* in 1973 and from 1974 to 1988 associate editor, then senior writer for *Time* magazine. He began writing his column for *U.S. News and World Report* in 1988; it was syndicated by Universal Press Syndicate in 1991. Leo is also on the board of *Columbia Journalism Review.*

BOOKS: *How the Russians Invented Baseball and Other Essays* (New York, 1989); *Two Steps Ahead of the Thought Police* (New York, 1994).

Leo, Peter Andrew (8 March 1943–   ). Peter Leo has been a humor columnist for the *Pittsburgh Post-Gazette* since January 1981.

Leo was born in Teaneck, New Jersey. He earned the B.A. in English and philosophy from St. Michael's College of the University of Toronto in 1966 and the M.A. in American Studies from New York University in 1967.

Leo began his career in 1970 as a broadcast news reporter for the Associated Press. He was a reporter for the Greensboro (North Carolina), *Record* in 1971–1972 and for the Wilmington (Delaware), *News-Journal* from 1973 until 1978. He has been with the *Pittsburgh Post-Gazette* since 1978, first as a reporter, then as assistant city editor, finally as columnist.

Leonard, Baird (1889–23 Jan. 1941). Baird Leonard, whose married name was Mrs. Harry St. Clair Zogbaum, wrote a daily column for the *New York Morning Telegraph* for a decade.

Leonard also did dramatic criticism for the original *Life* magazine and wrote light verse for various periodicals. She authored one book, *Simple Confessions* (1930), and edited a sort of handbook for women, *Cora Scovil's Lady's Book* (1940). After marrying architech Harry Zogbaum, she continued to write under her maiden name.

BOOKS: *Simple Confessions* (New York, 1930).

Leonard, John (25 Feb. 1939–   ). Once derided in *Atlantic* as "the Erma Bombeck of the Upper East Side," modest John Leonard is the author of "Private Lives," a *New York Times* column about daily life in the big city.

Leonard was born in Washington, D.C. He studied at Harvard from 1956 to 1958 and received the B.A. from the University of California at Berkeley in 1962. He interned at *National Review* in 1959–1960.

After graduation, Leonard reviewed books and did literary programming at radio station KPFA in Berkeley. He spent 1964–1967 as a publicity writer in Boston, then joined the *New York Times,* serving as a book reviewer from 1969 to 1970 and as book review editor from 1971 to 1976. From 1977 to 1983 he was the paper's cultural critic and wrote his "Private Lives" column. He has published a collection of these columns, *Private Lives in the Imperial City* (1979), plus six more books.

BOOKS: *The Naked Martini* (New York, 1964); *Wyke Regis* (New York, 1966); *Crybaby of the Western World* (Garden City, N.Y., 1969); *Black Conceit* (Garden City, N.Y., 1973); *This Pen for Hire* (Garden City, N.Y., 1973); *Private Lives in the Imperial City* (New York, 1983); *The Last Innocent White Man in America, and Other Writings* (New York, 1993).

Leonard, Mike (7 Oct. 1954–   ). Mike Leonard has been the featured general columnist for the Bloomington (Indiana) *Herald-Times* since 1984.

Leonard was born in New Castle, Indiana, and grew up in the nearby town of Greenfield. He was an honor graduate of Ball State University, where he double-majored in journalism and English.

From his first job, assistant editor of the *Carroll County Comet* in Flora, Indiana, Leonard moved to Bloomington and the *Herald-Telephone,* now the *Herald-Times,* as its education writer. He later covered the regional beat and for ten years wrote a pop music column. He is also a part-time newswriting instructor at Indiana University's Ernie Pyle School of Journalism.

Lerner, Maxwell Alan (20 Dec. 1902–5 June 1992). One of the important academic, liberal journalists and authors of the 1930s–1970s, Max Lerner wrote columns for the *New York Star, New York Post,* and the New York Post–Los Angeles Times Syndicate.

He was born Mikhail Lerner in Ivenitz, Minsk, Russia. His family immigrated to the United States in 1907; they lived first in New York City and later in New Haven, Connecticut. His B.A. at Yale, in 1923, was in English literature, social theory, and economics. He remained another year to study law, earned the A.M. from Washington University in St. Louis, and in 1927 received the Ph.D. at the Robert Brookings Graduate School of Economics and Government.

Lerner was assistant editor, then managing editor of the *Encyclopedia of Social Sciences* from 1927 to 1932. From 1932 to 1936 he taught social science at Sarah Lawrence College; he lectured in government at Harvard in 1935–1936 and taught in the Harvard summer program from 1934 to 1941. In 1936 he became an editor/writer for the *Nation*, after which he taught political science at Williams College from 1938 to 1943. He was editorial director of *PM* and a radio commentator from 1943 to 1948.

During 1948–1949 Lerner wrote a column for the *New York Star*. He switched to the *Post* in 1949, and his column was picked up by the New York Post and Los Angeles Times Syndicate. He also became a member of the American civilization faculty at Brandeis University in 1948 and was Graduate School dean of that institution from 1954 to 1956. He also wrote for a variety of opinion journals and was an active author/editor of books on American politics and civilization.

BOOKS: *It Is Later Than You Think* (New York, 1938); *Ideas Are Weapons: The History and Uses of Ideas* (New York, 1939); *Ideas for the Ice Age: Studies in a Revolutionary Era* (New York, 1941); ed., *The Mind and Faith of Justice Holmes* (New York, 1943); *Public Journal: Marginal Notes on Wartime America* (New York, 1945); ed., *The Portable Veblen* (New York, 1948); *Actions and Passions: Notes on the Multiple Revolution of Our Time* (New York, 1949); *America as a Civilization: Life and Thought in the U.S. Today* (New York, 1957); *The Unfinished Country: A Book of American Symbols* (New York, 1959); ed., *Essential Works of John Stuart Mill* (New York, 1961); *The Age of Overkill: A Preface to World Politics* (New York, 1962); *Education and a Radical Humanism* (Columbus, Ohio, 1962); ed. with J. P. Mayer, *Democracy in America* (Lexington, Ky., 1965); *Tocqueville and American Civilization* (New York, 1969); *Values in Education* (New York, 1976); *Ted and the Kennedy Legend: A Study in Character and Destiny* (New York, 1980); *Wrestling with the Angel: A Memoir of My Triumph over Illness* (New York, 1990); *Magisterial Imagination: Six Masters of the Human Sciences*, ed. by Robert Schmuhl (New Brunswick, N.J., 1994); *Nine Scorpions in a Bottle: Great Judges and Cases of the Supreme Court*, ed. by Richard Cummings (New York, 1994).

Levendosky, Charles Leonard (4 July 1936–). Charles Levendosky is editorial page editor and general columnist for the Casper, (Wyoming) *Star-Tribune* and has been his state's poet laureate since 1988.

Levendosky was born not in the wide open spaces of the West, but in the Bronx, New York. His academic degrees are a B.S. in physics (1958) and a B.A. in math (1960), both from the University of Oklahoma, and an M.A. in secondary education (1963) from New York University. After two years in the U.S. Army (1961–1962), he taught high school math and science in St. Croix, U.S. Virgin Islands (1963–1965); tutored English at Kyoto University in Japan (1965–1966); and taught high school in New York City (1966–1968). From 1967 to 1972 he was an assistant professor of English at New York University, and he taught in the Poetry in the Schools program in New York, Georgia, and New Jersey in 1971 and 1972. In the summers of these two years, he was poet in residence at Georgia Southern College. For the decade 1972–1982, he was poet in residence for the Wyoming Council on the Arts, after which he joined the *Star-Tribune*. His columns have been reprinted in numerous newspapers around the nation. He has been on the advisory board of *New York Quarterly* and has contributed poems and reviews to *Poetry in Review, Parnassus,* and other magazines and has published eight books of poetry.

BOOKS: *Perimeters* (Middletown, Conn., 1970); *Small Town America* (Statesboro, Ga., 1975); *Words and Fonts* (Statesboro, Ga., 1975); *Aspects of the Vertical* (Norman, Okla., 1978); *Distances* (Story, Wyo., 1980); *Wyoming Fragments* (Cody, Wyo., 1981); *Nocturnes* (Story, Wyo., 1982); *Hands and Other Poems* (Norman, Okla., 1986).

REFERENCES: Herbert N. Foerstel, *Surveillance in the Stacks* (Westport, Conn., 1991); Daniel Jussim, *Drug Tests and Polygraphs* (New York, 1987).

Levey, Robert Frank (2 June 1945–). Bob Levey writes the general column "Bob Levey's Washington" for the *Washington Post.*

Levy is a native of New York City and received a B.A. from the University of Chicago in 1966. He began his career as a general assignment reporter for the *Albuquerque Tribune* (1966–1967), then joined the *Washington Post,* where he served as reporter and editor from 1967 until 1981, the year he began writing his column.

BOOKS: *Sillygisms* (New York, 1988).

Lewis, Charles Bertrand (15 Feb. 1842–21 Aug. 1924). Journalist C. B. Lewis became nationally famous as an early humor columnist by writing as his literary character "M. Quad" for the *Detroit Free Press.* Later in his career he wrote a humor column for the *New York World* and *Evening World.*

Lewis was born in Liverpool, Ohio. He learned printing during his teens and was a graduate of Michigan State Agricultural College. Lewis was a private in the Union Army, after which he worked as a printer for papers in Pontiac and Lansing, Michigan. His career as a humorist began after he was hurt by a boiler explosion on an Ohio River steamboat. His subsequent story, "How It Feels to Be Blown Up," published in the *Lansing Jacksonian,* got him a reporting job for the *Detroit Free Press* in 1869. Lewis's humor articles were extremely popular. He was somewhat unusual compared to many of the other humor columnists of the day in that he did not rely on dialect, though he did dabble in this form later in his career. Like most of his contemporary humorists, he mined his work to publish books—twenty of them. Some of this writing was for the stage.

Lewis took M. Quad to the *New York World* in 1891 and wrote six zany columns a week until his death.

BOOKS: *The Hunter's Vision: The Search for the Cave of Gold* (Boston, 1872); *Bugler Ben: Or The Scout of the Delaware* (New York, 1872); *Mad Dan, the Spy of 1776* (New York, 1873); *Goaks and Tears* (Boston, 1875); *Quad's Odds* (Detroit, 1875); *Bessie Baine: Or The Mormon's Victim* (Boston, 1876); *Ben and Dot: A Comedy in Three Acts* (Detroit, 1879); *Deacon Jackson: A Comedy in Four Acts* (Detroit, 1879); *Bijah: A Comedy in One Act and Three Scenes* (Detroit, 1880); *Brother Gardner's Lime-Kiln Club* (Chicago, 1882); *Sawed-Off Sketches* (New York, 1884); *Field, Fort and Fleet*

(Detroit, 1885); *Sparks of Wit* (Detroit, 1885); *Under Five Lakes* (New York, 1886); *Tennessee: A Three Cast Play in One Act* (Brooklyn, N.Y., 1898); *Mr. and Mrs. Bowser and Their Varied Experiences* (New York, 1899); *Trials and Troubles of the Bowser Family* (New York, 1899); *The Life and Troubles of Mr. Bowser* (Chicago, 1902); *The Humorous Mr. Bowser* (New York, 1911).

REFERENCES: William Clemens, *Famous Funny Fellows* (Cleveland, 1882): 41–48.

Lewis, Claude Aubrey (14 Dec. 1934–   ). *Philadelphia Inquirer* columnist Claude Lewis formerly wrote a column for the *Philadelphia Bulletin.*

Lewis was born in New York City and attended City College. In 1952 he went to work as an office boy for *Newsweek,* moving up to teletype operator in 1957, to teletypesetter in 1958, to editorial assistant/reporter in 1959, and to assistant sports editor in 1962. During 1964–1965 he was on the city desk of the *New York Herald-Tribune,* after which he worked for ABC-TV in Philadelphia as a writer and reporter. He next worked for Westinghouse Broadcasting Company in the same city and in 1967 began writing his *Bulletin* column. In 1975 he became the *Bulletin*'s associate editor.

In 1982 Lewis founded a weekly tabloid for a national black audience, the *National Leader.* He later began his column for the *Inquirer.* Lewis is active with the National Association for the Advancement of Colored People (NAACP) and the Congress on Racial Equality. He specializes in writing about issues of interest to the African-American community and has published three books.

BOOKS: *Adam Clayton Powell* (Greenwich, Conn., 1963); *Cassius Clay: A No-Holds-Barred Biography of Boxing's Most Controversial Champion* (New York, 1965); *Benjamin Banneker: The Man Who Saved Washington* (New York, 1970).

Lewis, Dorothy Roe (18 May 1904–24 March 1985). Dorothy Roe (the name under which she wrote) was four times a columnist, the last time for the Chicago Tribune–New York News Syndicate from 1960 to 1971.

She was born Dorothy Roe in Alba, Missouri, and received the B.J. from the University of Missouri in 1925.

Roe began as a reporter for the *El Dorado* [Arkansas] *Daily News* (1925–1926). Next she wrote a shopping column and wrote features for the *Los Angeles Examiner* (1926–1927); after that she wrote a Wall Street column in New York for the *New York Daily Investment News* (1927–1929).

From 1930 to 1937 she was a columnist/feature writer for Universal Service in New York, and during 1939 and 1940 she and her husband coedited and published the *Burlington* [New Jersey] *Enterprise.* She was assistant women's editor for King Features Syndicate in 1940–1941 and women's editor of the Associated Press from 1941 to 1960. Her column for the Chicago Tribune–New York News Syndicate ran from 1960 to 1971, and in 1964 she joined the journalism faculty of the University of Missouri.

BOOKS: Ed., *Talking Through My Hats* (New York, 1946); *Here's Looking at You: The Modern Slant on Smartness for the Junior Miss* (New York, 1948); with Ruth Nichols,

Wings for Life (Philadelphia, 1957); *The Trouble with Women Is Men* (Englewood Cliffs, N.J., 1961); ed., *Glamour Book* (Philadelphia, 1966).

Lewis, Flora (circa 1920–   ). Based in Paris, France, Flora Lewis writes a weekly international issues column for the New York Times Syndicate.

Lewis was born in Los Angeles and received the B.A. in 1941 at the University of California, Los Angeles, where she was a member of Phi Beta Kappa. She earned the M.S. from Columbia University in 1942.

Lewis began her career in her home city as a reporter for the *Los Angeles Times* (1941). After finishing her graduate degree, she was an Associated Press (AP) reporter in New York, Washington, and London (1942–1946), then spent almost a decade free-lancing for *Time,* the *New York Times Magazine,* the *Observer,* the *Economist,* and other periodicals on both sides of the Atlantic.

She worked as an editor for McGraw-Hill in 1955, and from 1958 to 1966 she was *Washington Post* bureau chief in Bonn, London, and New York City. Lewis wrote a syndicated column out of Paris for *Newsday* from 1967 to 1972, then from 1972 to 1980 was the *New York Times* bureau head in Paris. She worked as the *Times*'s European diplomatic correspondent from 1976 to 1980 and was that paper's foreign affairs columnist from 1980 to 1990 before beginning her present weekly international issues column. She has written five books.

BOOKS: *A Case History of Hope: The Story of Poland's Peaceful Revolutions* (Garden City, N.Y., 1958); *Red Pawn: The Story of Noel Field* (Garden City, N.Y., 1965); *One of Our H-Bombs Is Missing* (New York, 1967); *Europe: A Tapestry of Nations* (New York, 1987); *Europe: Road to Unity* (New York, 1992).

Lewis, Fulton, Jr. (30 April 1903–20 Aug. 1966). Probably best known for his news commentaries for Mutual Radio from 1937 until his death, Fulton Lewis, Jr., also wrote two syndicated columns. The first was "The Washington Sideshow" (1933–1936), the second, "Fulton Lewis Says" (1944–1945).

Lewis was born in Washington, D.C. He studied at the University of Virginia for two years (1923–1924); he wrote the "Cavalier Song," after which the school's sports teams are named. He left the university in 1924 to become a fishing columnist and reporter for the *Washington* [D.C.] *Herald.* He was named this paper's city editor in 1927 but left the next year to work as assistant Washington bureau head of Universal News Service. He became bureau chief and from 1933 to 1936 wrote the first of his two syndicated political columns, which King Features placed in roughly sixty papers.

In autumn 1937 Lewis left Universal to become a radio commentator on station WOL, the Mutual station in Washington. Within two months, his nightly commentaries went national and were carried by as many as 150 stations. Lewis rejoined King Features as a columnist and wrote "Fulton Lewis Says" during 1944 and 1945. He also wrote a five-times-weekly column titled "Washington Report."

Lewis was an isolationist and a true right-winger, supporting Sen. Joseph

McCarthy and, later, Barry Goldwater and targeting Franklin Roosevelt's New Deal and Harry Truman's Fair Deal politics. He contributed to numerous magazines, founded the Radio Correspondents Association, and served as its first president. Lewis was instrumental in opening the Senate press gallery to radio reporters.

REFERENCES: Irving E. Fang, *Those Radio Commentators!* (Ames, Iowa, 1977).

Lewis, Joseph Anthony (27 March 1927–   ). Two-time Pulitzer Prize winner Anthony Lewis has written a liberal column for the *New York Times* since 1969.

Lewis was born in New York City. He received the A.B. from Harvard University in 1948 and was a Nieman Fellow there in 1956–1957.

Lewis held a desk job at the *New York Times* from 1948 to 1952 and in 1952 worked for the Democratic National Committee as a researcher. He was a reporter for the *Washington Daily News* from 1952 to 1955, then returned to the *New York Times* in 1955; there he covered the Supreme Court and the Department of Justice for the paper's Washington bureau. From 1964 to 1972 Lewis was chief of the *Times*'s London bureau. Since 1960 he has written a column, titled "At Home Abroad" while he was in residence in London and "Abroad at Home" when living in West Tisbury, Massachusetts. He has also lectured at Harvard and at Columbia University. Lewis's work often centers on constitutional issues.

BOOKS: *The Supreme Court: Process and Change* (Ames, Iowa, 1963); *Gideon's Trumpet* (New York, 1964); *The Supreme Court and How It Works* (New York, 1966); *Make No Law: The Sullivan Case and the First Amendment* (New York, 1991).

Lewis, Lillian Alberta (1861–?). Lillian Lewis, author of the "They Say" column in the *Boston Advocate* from 1889 to 1895, became one of the first black women to be employed by a white newspaper in 1895 when she was hired as a stenographer and writer for the *Boston Herald*.

Lewis was born in Boston in a home that had been on the "underground railroad" and is thought to have been the daughter of a runaway slave. She studied at Bowdoin Grammar School and Boston's Girls High School in the 1870s.

In 1889 Lewis became a columnist for an African-American paper, the *Boston Advocate*. Her column presented the views of a diverse population that had little voice in the mainstream papers. She signed her column "Bert Islew." In 1893 she became the paper's society editor. Lewis also wrote for another black paper, the *Richmond Planet* in Virginia, and was a regular correspondent for a black monthly magazine, *Our Women and Children*. It is thought that she was a reporter for the *Boston Herald* until 1901.

REFERENCES: I. Garland Penn, *The Afro-American Press and Its Editors* (Springfield, Mass., 1891).

Lileks, James (9 August 1958–). Humor columnist James Lileks (pronounced LYE-liks) has been syndicated by the Newhouse News Service since 1990.

Lileks was born in Fargo, North Dakota, and attended the University of Minnesota, where he wrote a humor column for the campus paper. After graduation, he was a columnist/feature writer/food critic for the Minneapolis weekly paper *City Pages.* He joined the staff of the *Pioneer Press* in St. Paul, Minnesota, in 1987 as a feature writer.

Lileks writes two columns a week. His Tuesday column is usually about a national political topic, his Wednesday offering for the *Pioneer Press* on something humorous. He has engaged in a mock feud with fellow humor columnist Dave Barry. Examples of his work include a script for ''every State of the Union address ever given'' and a satirical cry of outrage over a New York jury award that gave $4.3 million to a man who had beaten and robbed an elderly subway rider and was shot by police while trying to escape the scene of the crime. Correct police procedure, Lileks wrote, apparently would have been to run after the fleeing felon, who had probably had an unfortunate upbringing, shouting, ''I understand!'' The young humorist, who now works out of Minneapolis, Minnesota, has authored three humor books.

BOOKS: *Falling Up the Stairs* (New York, 1988); *Notes of a Nervous Man* (New York, 1991); *Fresh Lies* (New York, 1994).

REFERENCES: Chris Lamb, ''Humorist Holds His Own in Newspapers,'' *Editor and Publisher* (5 June 1993): 34–35.

Lilly, Doris (26 Dec. 1926–9 Oct. 1991). Doris Lilly, who did a society column for the *New York Post* and another column for the *New York Daily Mirror,* specialized in celebrity coverage. Her work was distributed by the McNaught Syndicate.

Lilly was born in South Pasadena, California, and attended the public schools of Santa Monica. Before becoming a columnist, she was a movie actress as part of the Cecil B. DeMille stable. She later worked as *Town and Country*'s beauty editor and as a press agent.

In addition to her columns, she contributed to *Ladies' Home Journal, Cosmopolitan,* and *McCall's* and wrote film scripts. The much-traveled Lilly broke into the literary market as author of *How to Meet a Millionaire* (1951), which was made into a movie starring Marilyn Monroe. In keeping with upper-echelon golddigging trends, she wrote a later version, *How to Meet a Billionaire* (1984).

BOOKS: *How to Meet a Millionaire* (New York, 1951); *How to Make Love in Five Languages* (Indianapolis, 1965); *Those Fabulous Greeks: Onassis, Niarchos and Livanos* (New York, 1970); *How to Meet a Billionaire* (New York, 1984).

Lindley, Ernest Kidder (14 July 1899–1979). Ernest K. Lindley was a *Washington Post* political columnist from 1938 to 1943 and with the Des Moines

Register and Tribune Syndicate from 1938 to 1952. He is also remembered for his "Washington Tides" in *Newsweek* magazine from 1937 to 1961.

Lindley was born in Richmond, Indiana, and grew up mainly in Bloomington. He studied at the University of Kansas and at the University of Indiana (1916–1917), dropped out for service in the army during World War I, then completed his degree in 1920, Phi Beta Kappa, at the University of Idaho. Next he was a Rhodes Scholar at Oxford, where he studied modern history and economics and received an English B.A. in 1923.

In 1924 Lindley began working as a reporter for the *Beacon* in Wichita, Kansas; he left after a few months to join the reporting staff of the *New York World,* where he worked until that paper closed in 1931. He was a political reporter for the *New York Herald Tribune* from 1931 to 1937, working in that paper's Washington bureau from 1933. From 1937 to 1961 he was head of *Newsweek*'s Washington bureau; concurrently, from 1938 to 1943, he was a political columnist for the *Washington Post,* chosen by publisher Eugene Meyer. His column was continued with the Register and Tribune Syndicate until 1952, and Lindley was also a broadcast commentator from 1938 to 1961, after which he spent nearly a decade working for the U.S. State Department.

Lindley was an early admirer of Franklin Roosevelt, reporting on him for the *World* after his election as governor of New York State. He has been described as President Roosevelt's "reporter/confidant" and was generally regarded as a conscientious, reliable columnist of generally liberal bent whose work was marked by accuracy and fairness. Lindley authored or coauthored five books.

BOOKS: *Franklin D. Roosevelt: A Career in Progressive Democracy* (Indianapolis, 1931); *The Roosevelt Revolution* (New York, 1933); *Half Way with Roosevelt* (New York, 1936); with Betty Lindley, *A New Deal for Youth: The Story of the National Youth Administration* (New York, 1938); with Forrest Davis, *How War Came, an American White Paper: From the Fall of France to Pearl Harbor* (New York, 1942).

REFERENCES: Charles Fisher, *The Columnists* (New York, 1944): 290–295.

Lindley, Mary Ann (4 Aug. 1947–   ). Mary Ann Lindley has written columns since 1974 and is currently a general interest columnist for Florida's *Tallahassee Democrat.*

Lindley was born in King City, Missouri, and received the B.J. from the University of Missouri in 1969.

She began her career as arts editor and assistant wire editor for the *Tallahassee Democrat* (1969–1973). From 1973 to 1978 she worked as a bureau chief, political reporter, and columnist at the Florida Capitol Bureau of the New York Times Affiliated Newspaper Group, then was state desk editor for the *Miami Herald* (1978–1979). She has been with the *Tallahassee Democrat* since 1979, for the first four years as columnist and editorial writer, as full-time columnist thereafter. Her general interest column has appeared three times a week since 1984.

REFERENCES: David Astor, "Variety Is Spice of Journalism Life for Her," *Editor and Publisher* (22 June 1991): 30.

Lindsay, Rae (?–   ). Rae Lindsay began writing a twice-weekly syndicated column, "First Person Singular," in 1978.

Lindsay was born Rae Baldanza in Garfield, New Jersey. She holds the B.A. from Wellesley College.

Lindsay's career began at *Seventeen* magazine, where she was assistant publicity director from 1959 to 1961. She and her husband, Alexander Lindsay, owned and ran a New York City public relations firm, Lindsay & Gray, from 1961 to 1972. She then worked as a senior publicist for Macmillan Publishing in 1978–1979. Since that time she has been president of R & R Writers/Agents Inc., a literary agency in Englewood Cliffs, New Jersey. In addition to her column, Lindsay has contributed to numerous magazines and has written or cowritten eight books, perhaps the most significant of which is *Alone and Surviving*, which examined the problems faced by widows.

BOOKS: *International Party Cookbook* (New York, 1973); *The Pursuit of Youth* (New York, 1976); *Alone and Surviving* (New York, 1977); *Sleep and Dreams* (New York, 1978); *The Left-Handed Book* (New York, 1980); with George Michael, *Secrets for Beautiful Hair* (Garden City, N.Y., 1981); with George Michael, *George Michael's Complete Hair Care for Men* (Garden City, N.J., 1983); with Dianne Rowe, *How to Be a Perfect Bitch* (Piscataway, N.J., 1983).

Lippincott, Sara Jane Clarke (23 Sept. 1823–20 April 1904). Better known by her pen name, Grace Greenwood, Sara Lippincott was a pioneering newswoman in the nation's capital for decades before becoming a columnist for the *New York Independent* (1892–1904).

She was born Sara Jane Clarke in Pompey, New York. Her family also lived in Fabius and Rochester, New York, and New Brighton, Pennsylvania. Her formal education was limited to eight years in the Rochester public schools.

When the Clarke family moved to New Brighton in 1842, Sara contributed letters signed "Grace Greenwood" to the *New York Mirror,* as well as to such magazines as *Sartain's, Graham's, Saturday Evening Post,* and *Godey's Lady's Book.* She was hired as editor of another of Godey's periodicals, the *Lady's Dollar Newspaper,* in 1949 but was sacked the following year for an article supporting the abolition of slavery that she had written for *National Era.* She was then hired by the editor of that antislavery periodical, Gamaliel Bailey, and she also became Washington correspondent for *Saturday Evening Post.* Her "Washington Letters" feature in the *Post* continued until 1897. In addition, 1850 saw the publication of her first book, *Greenwood Leaves,* a compilation of her magazine and newspaper writing. It sold well, and twenty-four other books followed throughout the 1800s.

In 1852 she traveled to Europe; she interviewed Browning, Dickens, and Thackeray and sent her dual employers travel pieces as well. She married Leander K. Lippincott in 1853, and the couple founded *Little Pilgrim,* a children's magazine, for which Sara, as Grace Greenwood, was editor and did most of the writing, but which also carried the work of Alcott, Longfellow, and Whittier. The magazine was a casualty of the Civil War, finally folding in 1875.

Sara Lippincott became active on the lecture circuit, speaking in favor of suffrage and pay equity for women, fair treatment of the American Indian, prison reform, and an end to slavery and capital punishment. In 1870 she moved to Washington and worked as a reporter for the *New York Times,* the *New York Tribune,* and other papers. She kept up her magazine writing, as well, contributing to *Ladies' Home Journal, Hearth and Home,* and other publications. She made two trips to Europe in the late 1870s, writing for the *New York Times* and the *New York Independent,* the paper for which she wrote a column from 1892 until just before her death at age eighty.

Lippincott's flowery and sentimental style, so popular during the late 1800s, prevents her being considered an important literary figure, but she was indeed a trailblazer among women journalists. She appears to have been the second woman Washington correspondent, after Jane Swisshelm.

BOOKS: *Greenwood Leaves* (Boston, 1850); *History of My Pets* (Boston, 1851); *Poems* (Boston, 1851); *Recollections of My Childhood, and Other Stories* (Boston, 1952); *Greenwood Leaves, Second Series* (Boston, 1854); *Haps and Mishaps of a Tour in Europe* (Boston, 1854); *Merrie England* (Boston, 1855); *A Forest Tragedy, and Other Tales* (Boston, 1856); *Stories and Legends of Travel and History, for Children* (Boston, 1857); *Old Wonder-Eyes and Other Stories for Children* (New York, 1957); *Stories from Famous Ballads for Children* (New York, 1859); *Nelly, the Gipsy Girl* (New York, 1863); *Stories of Many Lands* (New York, 1866); *Records of Five Years* (Boston, 1867); *Stories and Sights of France and Italy* (Boston, 1867); *Bonnie Scotland* (Boston, 1872); *New Life in New Lands: Notes of Travel* (New York, 1872); *Heads and Tales: Studies and Stories of Pets* (New York, 1874); *Emma Abbott, Prima Donna* (New York, 1878); with Rossiter W. Raymond, *Treasures from Fairy Land* (New York, 1879); *Queen Victoria: Her Girlhood and Womanhood* (New York, 1883); *Some of My Pets* (New York, 1884); *Stories for Home-Folks, Young and Old* (New York, 1884); *Stories and Sketches* (New York, 1892); *Europe: Its People and Princes—Its Pleasures and Palaces* (Philadelphia, n.d.).

REFERENCES: Joseph Lyman, "Grace Greenwood—Mrs. Lippincott," in *Eminent Women of the Age,* ed. by James Parton and others (New York, 1869): 147–163; Barbara Welter, "Sara Jane Lippincott," in *Notable American Women, 1607–1950,* ed. by Edward T. James (Cambridge, Mass., 1971): 407–409.

Lippmann, Walter (23 Sept. 1889–14 Dec. 1974). America's prototypical political pundit, Walter Lippmann was a syndicated columnist from 1931 to 1971.

Lippmann was born in New York City. He earned his A.B., cum laude, from Harvard University in 1909 and remained one more year to do graduate study. He studied under Professor George Santayana and became a friend of William James.

After Harvard, he was a cub reporter for the *Boston Common* until July 1910, when he became an assistant to the famous muckraking journalist Lincoln Steffens, who at that time was working on an investigative series for *Everybody's Magazine*. When the series was completed and Steffens had moved on, Lippmann remained with the magazine as a subeditor. Then in 1912 he spent four months working as secretary to the socialist mayor of Schenectady, New York, the Reverend George T. Lunn.

During 1913 and 1914 Lippmann published the first two of his more than forty books and joined the *New Republic* as that new magazine's associate editor. One of his initial assignments was a trip to Europe to recruit writers. He remained with the magazine until 1922, with time out in 1917 to serve as assistant to Secretary of War Newton D. Baker and to work as one of the writers of President Woodrow Wilson's Fourteen Points. From 1918 to 1919 he was a captain in Army Intelligence, attached to Gen. John J. Pershing's staff. In 1920 he began writing a column for the magazine *Vanity Fair;* he continued the column until 1934.

In January 1922 he joined the *New York World*'s editorial page staff under its editor, Frank Cobb. Here he wrote a reported twelve hundred editorials, and on Cobb's death in 1923, Lippmann became editorial page editor. Under his leadership, the *World*'s editorial page enjoyed a reputation as the nation's most intellectual. Part of his arrangement with the *World* was that he would have three months off a year to work on his books and magazine articles. In 1929 Lippmann became the paper's executive editor, but in February 1931 the paper was sold to Scripps-Howard and was combined with the *Telegram*. Lippmann had several attractive offers and chose to write a column for the *New York Herald Tribune*. His new column, "Today and Tomorrow," first appeared in September 1931. It was eventually syndicated to some two hundred papers and was continued until 1962. From 1963 to 1967 Lippmann was syndicated by the Washington Post and Los Angeles Times syndicates to roughly 275 papers, and from 1962 to 1971 he was a fortnightly columnist for *Newsweek*.

Lippmann was an admirer of Franklin Roosevelt, a supporter of the United Nations, a critic of Sen. Joseph McCarthy, a lukewarm supporter of Dwight Eisenhower, a close adviser of John F. Kennedy, and an opponent of Lyndon Johnson and that president's decision to involve the United States more deeply in Vietnam. Lippmann's commentary about America's relations with the Soviet Union won him two Pulitzer Prizes, in 1958 and 1962. Of all the Washington press corps, Lippmann was regarded as the premier insider, courted by the powerful, a journalist of great prominence. His work, careful and balanced, was of considerable intellectual caliber but made for heavy, tedious reading. He was probably more carefully read by the powerful than by the everyday newspaper subscriber, yet his long and dignified career earned Lippmann the status of pundit and journalistic statesman.

BOOKS: *A Preface to Politics* (New York, 1913); *Drift and Mastery* (New York, 1914); *The Stakes of Diplomacy* (New York, 1915); *The World Conflict in Its Relation to Amer-*

ican Democracy (Washington, D.C., 1917); *The Political Scene: An Essay on the Victory of 1918* (New York, 1919); *Liberty and the News* (New York, 1920); *France and the European Setting* (New York, 1922); *Public Opinion* (New York, 1922); *Mr. Kahn Would Like to Know* (New York, 1923); *The Phantom Public* (New York, 1925); *H. L. Mencken* (New York, 1926); *Men of Destiny* (New York, 1927); *American Inquisitors: A Commentary on Dayton and Chicago* (New York, 1928); *A Preface to Morals* (New York, 1929); *Notes on the Crisis* (New York, 1931); with others, *The United States in World Affairs,* 2 vols. (New York, 1932–1933); *Interpretations, 1931–1932,* ed. by Allan Nevins (New York, 1932); *A New Social Order* (New York, 1933); *The Method of Freedom* (New York, 1934); *Self-Sufficiency* (Worcester, Mass., 1934); *The New Imperative* (New York, 1935); *Interpretations, 1933–1935,* ed. by Allan Nevins (New York, 1936); ed. with Allan Nevins, *A Modern Reader: Essays on Present-Day Life and Culture* (Boston and New York, 1936); *An Inquiry into the Principles of the Good Society* (Boston, 1937); *The Supreme Court: Independent or Controlled?* (New York and London, 1937); *Some Notes on War and Peace* (New York, 1940); *U.S. Foreign Policy: Shield of the Republic* (Boston, 1943); *U.S. War Aims* (Boston, 1944); *In the Service of Freedom* (New York, 1945); *The Cold War: A Study in U.S. Foreign Policy* (New York 1947); *Commentaries on Far Eastern Policy* (New York, 1950); *Isolation and Alliances: An American Speaks to the British* (Boston, 1952); *Public Opinion and Foreign Policy in the United States* (London, 1952); *Essays in the Public Philosophy* (Boston, 1955); *America in the World Today* (Minneapolis, 1957); *The Communist World and Ours* (Boston, 1959); *The Confrontation* (Stamford, Conn., 1959); *The Coming Tests with Russia* (Boston, 1961); *The Nuclear Era: A Profound Struggle* (Chicago, 1962); *Western Unity and the Common Market* (Boston, 1962); *The Essential Lippmann: A Political Philosophy for Liberal Democracy,* ed. by Clinton Rossiter and James Lave (New York, 1963); *A Free Press* (Copenhagen, 1965); *Conversations with Walter Lippmann* (Boston, 1965); *Early Writings* (New York, 1970).

REFERENCES: Marquis Childs and James Reston, eds., *Walter Lippmann and His Times* (New York, 1959); Charles Fisher, *The Columnists* (New York, 1944): 69–86; Richard H. Rovere, "Walter Lippmann," *American Scholar* 44 (Autumn 1975): 585–603; Ronald Steel, *Walter Lippmann and the American Century* (Boston, 1980); David Elliott Weingast, *Walter Lippmann, a Study in Personal Journalism* (New Brunswick, N.J., 1949).

Lisagor, Peter Irvin (5 Aug. 1915–10 Dec. 1976). Probably most remembered for his frequent appearances on television's "Meet the Press" and "Washington Week in Review," Peter Lisagor was also the longtime Washington bureau head of the *Chicago Daily News* and for a time wrote a syndicated political column.

Lisagor was born in Keystone, West Virginia. He attended Northwestern University in 1933 and in 1939 received the B.A. from the University of Michigan.

Lisagor began his career writing about sports for the *Chicago Daily News* (1939–1941). In 1941 he went with United Press but left in 1942 to enlist in the army. He worked as managing editor of the *Stars and Stripes* London edition in 1944 and 1945, then was that paper's editor in Paris in 1945. When his enlistment was up, Lisagor became news editor of the *Paris Post* but returned home later in 1945 to become a news reporter for the *Chicago Daily News.* He became that paper's UN correspondent in 1949 and from 1950 to 1959 was its diplomatic correspondent in Washington, and bureau head in 1959. With columnist Marguerite Higgins, he wrote an account of various Foreign Service exploits, *Overtime in Heaven.*

BOOKS: With Marguerite Higgins, *Overtime in Heaven* (Garden City, N.Y., 1964).

Lockman, Norman Alton (11 July 1938–). Norman Lockman has been associate editor of the editorial department of the *News Journal* in Wilmington, Delaware, since 1990 and writes a liberal column that is syndicated by Gannett News Service.

Lockman was born in Kennett Square, Pennsylvania. He attended Penn State University from 1957 to 1959. He served in the Air Force from 1961 to 1965 and in 1964 attended the Department of Defense School of Journalism.

Lockman was a columnist for the *Kennett News* from 1965 to 1968, then reporter for the Wilmington *News Journal* from 1969 to 1975. He worked for the *Boston Globe* from 1975 to 1984, where he was part of a seven-person team that won the Pulitzer Prize for special local reporting in 1984. In 1984 he returned to the Wilmington paper as managing editor.

The versatile Lockman has also worked as an announcer for WCOJ in Coatesville, Pennsylvania (1965–1966); hosted a talk show on Wilmington's WILM; and served in the mid-1970s as a panelist on National Educational Television's "Black Perspective on the News." More recently he has been a weekly news panelist on WHYY-TV in the Wilmington/Philadelphia market.

Lofgren, Merle E. (5 March 1926–). Merle Lofgren is the longtime publisher, editor, and columnist for the weekly *McLaughlin Messenger* in McLaughlin, South Dakota.

In 1950, Lofgren graduated from South Dakota State College in Brookings, borrowed a $1,000 down payment, and bought a weekly paper in McIntosh, South Dakota. Since that time he has owned and run weekly papers, serving, he says, as "editor, publisher, society editor, sports editor, editorial writer, janitor, bookkeeper, and machinist—mostly all at the same time." The last of his many jobs before the *Messenger* goes to bed is writing his column, "Top of the Hill," which in former years he keyed directly on a Linotype. Lofgren's column also appears in another South Dakota paper, the *Corson County News.* Lofgren has also spent four years as a member of his state's House of Representatives.

Lord, Mary Grace (18 Nov. 1955–). M. G. Lord is both a columnist and an editorial cartoonist for *Newsday* and for Copley News Service.

Lord was born in La Jolla, California. She holds the B.A., cum laude, from Yale University (1977). Encouraged by cartoonists Bill Mauldin and Garry Trudeau, she decided to take up cartooning, working first as a staff artist for the *Chicago Tribune* (1977–1978), then as *Newsday*'s first woman cartoonist (since

1978). Her cartooning was handled by Universal Press Syndicate from 1981 to 1983 and by the Los Angeles Times Syndicate from 1984 to 1989. She took leave during 1986–1987 as a Resident Fellow in Humanities at the University of Michigan and while there decided to begin writing a column.

Her wry column, unusual in that she herself illustrates it, appears in *Newsday* and has been syndicated since 1989 by Copley News Service. She has two books to her credit, the first a collection of her cartoons, the second a humorous book attacking prigs. She has also contributed to *GQ, Nation, Savvy Woman,* and other magazines.

BOOKS: *Mean Sheets* (Boston, 1982); *Prig Tales* (New York, 1990).

Lubell, Samuel (3 Nov. 1911–16 Aug. 1987). Samuel Lubell, an authority on public-opinion reporting, wrote a column for United Feature Syndicate (1952–1966) and before that for the *Washington Post* (1936).

Lubell was born in or near Sosnowiec, Poland, in 1911. His exact birth date was not officially recorded, and when he began the first grade and discovered he needed a birthday, Lubell chose November 3 because it was an election day. He immigrated to America in 1913, settling in New York City. Lubell studied at City College from 1927 to 1931, then went to Columbia University, where he received the B.S. in journalism in 1933.

Lubell began his career writing obituaries for the *Long Island Daily Press.* He moved to the *Washington Post* in 1936 as reporter, military editor, and columnist ("Federal Diary"). He worked on the copy desk and was labor editor of the *Richmond Times-Dispatch* in Virginia during most of 1937, then became a reporter and rewrite man for the *Washington Herald.* Later in 1938 he traveled and wrote free-lance, contributing often to the *Saturday Evening Post.*

Starting in December 1941 he was a writer for the Office of Facts and Figures, which was renamed the Office of War Information. He assisted the director of the Office of Economic Stabilization and was also an assistant to Bernard Baruch. In 1946 he was a war correspondent for the *Saturday Evening Post* and for the *Providence* [Rhode Island] *Journal.* He also free-lanced for *Nation, Current History, Harper's, American Mercury,* and other periodicals. In 1948 Lubell was assigned by the *Saturday Evening Post* to study Harry Truman's White House victory, which gave his career a new direction that lasted for the remainder of his life. He studied voter patterns and voter demographics, doing voter interviews that enabled him to predict future elections with considerable accuracy. Supported by Guggenheim grants, he wrote a number of books on American politics. He wrote a column from 1952 to 1966 that appeared in about 130 papers.

Lubell spent parts of the last two decades of his working life teaching—at Columbia University (1952–1966), the University of Connecticut (1976), and the University of California at Irvine (1981).

BOOKS: *The Future of American Politics* (New York, 1952); *The Revolution in World Trade and American Economic Policy* (New York, 1955); *Revolt of the Moderates* (New

York, 1956); *White and Black: Test of a Nation* (New York, 1964); *The Future While It Happened* (New York, 1973).

Lyons, Leonard (10 Sept. 1906–7 Oct. 1976). Leonard Lyons wrote the syndicated Broadway column "The Lyons Den" from 1934 to 1974.

He was born Leonard Sucher on the Lower East Side of New York City, the son of immigrant parents. His mother went to school at age sixty in order to be able to read his column. He himself was a graduate of City College (1925) and the St. John's University College of Law (1928). Lyons practiced corporate law with a Wall Street firm, Armstrong, Keith & Kern, from 1929 to 1934, then opened his own independent practice. Even after starting his successful column, he kept up an active interest in the law. He interviewed several justices of the U.S. Supreme Court and from 1954 to 1968 was a special assistant attorney general for New York.

Lyons began his newspaper work by contributing occasional items to Walter Winchell, Mark Hellinger, and other columnists whose work he admired. He was given his start in 1934 by David Stern, publisher of the *New York Post,* and was also supported by Winchell, who helped his new competitor get on with Winchell's own syndicate, King Features, and who also suggested the title for Lyons's column. After clashing with King Features's owner, William Randolph Hearst, over the film *Citizen Kane,* Lyons moved to the New York Post Syndicate, which merged with Publishers Newspaper Syndicate in 1975 and became Publishers-Hall. The syndicate had another name change in 1975 when it became the Field Newspaper Syndicate.

Like the other Broadway columnists, Lyons worked mainly at night. He made the rounds of chi-chi cocktail parties, theater openings, and the Stork Club, the Plaza, the Cotton Club, Sardi's, the Four Seasons, the Algonquin, and other similar haunts of celebrity. He avoided writing about scandal, divorces, and the like, preferring to find the positive and the humorous in celebrity news. His attention went beyond show business into the realms of the literary, the artistic, and even the political. "The Lyons Den" appeared in roughly one hundred papers and ended on 20 May 1974.

REFERENCES: Charles Fisher, *The Columnists* (New York, 1944): 263–269; Richard Weiner, *Syndicated Columnists* (New York, 3rd Ed. 1979): 131–135.

M

Mallon, Paul Raymond (5 Jan. 1901–30 July 1950). Paul Mallon's syndicated Washington column "News Behind the News" was published from 1932 to 1947.

Mallon was born in Matton, Illinois. He attended the University of Louisville (1918–1919) and the University of Notre Dame (1919–1920).

Mallon began as a reporter for the *Louisville Courier-Journal* in 1918, then worked for the *Louisville Herald-Post* and the *South Bend* [Indiana] *News-Times*. He went with the United Press in 1920, first in New York, then from 1923 to 1932 as a political correspondent in Washington, D.C. In 1929, Mallon published the results of two secret Senate roll calls on nominations to federal offices, which contributed to the discontinuance of that practice.

Mallon's column began in 1932 and appeared in from 250 to 300 papers. His outlook was of the "whatever is, is wrong" school of thought as regarded the federal government. The columnist authored two books.

BOOKS: *The Ease Era: The Juvenile Oligarchy and the Educational Trust* (Grand Rapids, Mich., 1945); *Practical Idealism* (Boston, 1946).

REFERENCES: Charles Fisher, *The Columnists* (New York, 1944): 284–290.

Malveaux, Julianne Marie (22 Sept. 1953–). Julianne Malveaux began her career as a columnist in 1981, writing for the *San Francisco Sun Reporter,* and now does a twice-weekly column syndicated by King Features.

Malveaux was born in San Francisco. She received the A.B. from Boston College in 1974 and both the M.A. (1975) and the Ph.D. (1980) from Massachusetts Institute of Technology. Her field of study was economics.

During 1987–1988 she was a junior staff economist for the White House Council of Economic Advisers and from 1978 to 1980, a research fellow with the Rockefeller Foundation in New York City. She taught economics at the New School for Social Research in 1980–1981 and at San Francisco State University in 1981–1985. Since 1985 she has been on the faculty of the University of California, Berkeley, where she is in the Department of Afro-American Studies.

As a columnist Malveaux has been concerned with lingering barriers to working women and the backlash that has followed the progress they have made. One of her two weekly columns for King Features addresses politics; the other is more business-oriented. Among the papers that carry her column are the *Philadelphia Inquirer, Denver Post, Los Angeles Times, San Francisco Examiner, Portland Oregonian, Detroit News,* and *Seattle Post-Intelligencer.* She is also a contributing editor to *Essence,* has written often for *Ms.* and *USA Today,* and is a panelist on the PBS show "To the Contrary." She has been coauthor/coeditor of two books.

BOOKS: With Linda Datcher, *Black Women in the Labor Force* (Cambridge, Mass., 1980); ed. with Margaret Simms, *Slipping Through the Cracks: The Status of Black Women* (New Brunswick, N.J., 1986).

Mankiewicz, Frank Fabian (16 May 1924–   ). Journalist/lawyer/politician/broadcasting executive Frank Mankiewicz cowrote a political column with Tom Braden (1968–1971) and wrote a solo column for The *Washington Post* from 1976 to 1977.

Mankiewicz was born in New York City. He received the A.B. from the University of California at Los Angeles in 1947 and the M.S. from Columbia University in 1948, after which he worked for newspapers in Washington, D.C., and Los Angeles until 1952. He studied law at the University of California at Berkeley, earning the LL.B. in 1955 and practicing law in Beverly Hills from 1955 to 1961.

He was director of the U.S. Peace Corps in Lima, Peru, 1962–1964, then returned to Washington as regional director for Latin America, 1964–1966. He served as press secretary for Sen. Robert Kennedy from 1966 to 1968, wrote his Washington column and did commentary on WTOP-TV with Braden until 1971, then during 1971–1972 was campaign director for George McGovern. After McGovern's decisive defeat, Mankiewicz spent time on book and magazine writing, wrote a column for the *Washington Post* in 1976, then in 1977 became president of National Public Radio, strengthening its news operation and boosting its audience before resigning over budget cuts in 1983. Thereafter he was involved in public relations work.

Mankiewicz ran unsuccessfully for the California legislature in 1950 and for Congress in 1976. He is remembered as one of Richard Nixon's most outspoken critics, and as a columnist, he was known for the incisive wit and sudden flashes of whimsy with which he enlivened his serious subject matter.

BOOKS: *Perfectly Clear: Nixon from Whittier to Watergate* (New York, 1973); *Nixon's Road to Watergate* (London, 1973); *U.S. v. Richard M. Nixon: The Final Crisis* (New York, 1975); with Kirby Jones, *With Fidel: A Portrait of Castro and Cuba* (Chicago,

1975); with Joel Swardlow, *Remote Control: Television and the Manipulation of American Life* (New York, 1978).

Manning, Marie (22 June 1873?–28 Nov. 1945). Writing as "Beatrice Fairfax," Marie Manning was one of the early queens of the lovelorn personal advice column in 1898 while working for the *New York Journal.*

She was born in Washington, D.C., of English parents and attended private schools in that city as well as in New York and London. At age twenty she met the *New York World's* Arthur Brisbane, who hired her soon thereafter. An exclusive interview with ex-president Grover Cleveland ensured her success at the *World.*

Manning followed her mentor Brisbane to Hearst's *New York Journal* in 1898. Here she and two other women reporters shared a small office known at the paper as the "hen coop," from which they handled the women's page and added the female angle to other stories, including murder trials. Soon after the end of the Spanish-American War, Brisbane brought to the "hen coop" three letters from women who had written to the paper about personal problems. Manning suggested the creation of a separate department to reply to such letters and chose the name "Beatrice Fairfax" after Dante's Beatrice combined with Fairfax, the Virginia community where her family owned property. The successful column was soon syndicated by King Features Syndicate to around two hundred papers.

Although it has been remarked that Marie Manning's column grew out of the sob-sister stories of Annie Laurie (Hearst writer Winifred Black), Manning's technique was much less weepy and more commonsensical. The popularity of the column can be attributed in part to the way it involved readers as participants, not just passive readers. Manning received a reported fourteen hundred letters a day. She also did celebrity interviews and other stories for the *Journal* under her own name, contributed to magazines, and began writing books.

Manning married Herman Gasch in June 1905 and retired from day to day journalism. The Beatrice Fairfax column was handled by a succession of other women writers, among them Lilian Lauferty, until the stock market crash of 1929 caused Marie Manning Gasch to return and take it over once again. She also wrote women's angle stories out of Washington for Hearst's International News Service and took part in Eleanor Roosevelt's women's-only press conferences. Manning Gasch wrote and spoke for the causes of early feminism and was a charter member of the Women's National Press Club and the Newspaper Women's Club.

BOOKS: *Lord Allingham, Bankrupt* (New York, 1902); *Judith of the Plains, a Novel* (New York, 1903); *Personal Reply* (Philadelphia, 1943); *Ladies Now and Then, by Beatrice Fairfax* (New York, 1944).

Marable, Manning (13 May 1950–). University professor Manning Marable writes a weekly column, "Along the Color Line," which he provides without fee to black newspapers and radio stations.

Marable was born in Dayton, Ohio. He received the A.B. in American history from Earlham College in 1971, the M.A. from the University of Wisconsin, Madison, in 1972, and the Ph.D. in American history from the University of Maryland in 1976.

Marable began his teaching career at Smith College (1974–1976) and has taught political science, economics, history, sociology, and black studies at a number of other schools: Tuskegee University (1976–1978), University of San Francisco (1979), Cornell University (1979–1982), Fisk University (1982–1983), Colgate University (1983–1986), Purdue University (1986–1987), Ohio State University (1987–1989), University of Colorado at Boulder (1989–1993), and, since 1993, Columbia University. He refers to himself as a democratic socialist and an activist and has written books, scholarly journal articles, and magazine articles dealing with the effects of race and class throughout history. His main thesis is that class distinctions rather than race account for most intolerance and inequality in today's society.

BOOKS: *From the Grassroots: Essays Toward Afro-American Liberation* (Boston, 1980); *Blackwater: Historical Studies in Race, Class Consciousness, and Revolution* (Dayton, Ohio, 1981); *How Capitalism Underdeveloped Black America* (Boston, 1983); *Race, Reform and Rebellion: The Second Reconstruction in Black America, 1945–1982* (London, 1984); *Black American Politics: From the Washington Marches to Jesse Jackson* (London, 1985); *W.E.B. DuBois, Black Radical Democrat* (Boston, 1986); *The Crisis of Color and Democracy: Essays on Race, Class, and Power* (Monroe, Me., 1992).

REFERENCES: Michele N-K Collison, "You Can't Outgrow New York," *Chronicle of Higher Education* (20 October 1993): A15–17.

Margolis, Jon (25 Sept. 1940–   ). Jon Margolis is a columnist and writer at large for the *Chicago Tribune.*

Margolis was born in Trenton, New Jersey, and in 1962 received a bachelor's degree in history from Oberlin College.

His newspaper career was launched when he worked as a copyboy for the *New York Daily Mirror.* He then held a succession of reporting jobs: the *Bergen Record* in Hackensack, New Jersey (1963–1964), the *Miami Herald* (1964–1965), the *Concord Monitor* in New Hampshire (1965–1966), and *Newsday* (1969–1973). From 1969 until 1973 he was *Newsday*'s Albany bureau chief, and from 1973 to 1989 he was chief national political correspondent for the Washington bureau of the *Chicago Tribune.* From January 1989 to September 1990 he was a sports columnist for the *Tribune* before beginning his general column. At times he has used the column title "in the wake of the news." Margolis has also free-lanced for *Esquire, New York Magazine,* the *New Republic, Regardie's,* and *Ms.*

BOOKS: *How to Fool Fish with Feathers, an Incompleat Guide to Fly Fishing* (New York, 1993).

Markey, Judy (?–   ). Judy Markey has been writing a humor column that centers on domestic foibles since 1982. It was handled until late 1994 by United Feature Syndicate.

Markey's thrice-weekly column originated at the *Chicago Sun-Times* and appeared in roughly twenty-five papers. It was first syndicated in 1982 by the North America Syndicate. Prior to starting her column, Markey had free-lanced for *Woman's Day, Cosmopolitan,* and other magazines. She now appears regularly on WGN radio in Chicago and has also been a guest on television's "Oprah Winfrey Show," "Good Morning America," and "Donohue." She has published two collections of her columns.

BOOKS: *How to Survive Your High School Reunion—and Other Mid-Life Crises* (Chicago, 1984); *You Only Get Married for the First Time Once* (New York, 1988).

Markgraf, Richard (17 Feb. 1935–   ). Denison University Professor Emeritus Richard Markgraf self-syndicates a weekly humor column entitled "Blundering On."

Markgraf was born in La Crosse, Wisconsin, and received the B.S (1956), M.S. (1957), and Ph.D. (1960) in communications and theater from the University of Wisconsin at Madison.

Markgraf's teaching career began at Wesleyan University in Connecticut, where he was a professor of English from 1959 until 1966. From 1966 until his retirement in 1990, he was a professor of communications at Denison. He had written free-lance for various papers throughout the United States, and his column appears in papers in California, Illinois, and Michigan.

Marquis, Donald Robert Perry (29 July 1878–29 Dec. 1937). One of the funniest writers of all time, Don Marquis (pronounced MAR-kwis) wrote columns for the *New York Evening Sun* (1912–1922) and the *New York Tribune* and *Herald Tribune* (1922–1925).

Marquis was born in Walnut, Illinois. After high school, he briefly attended Knox College in Galesburg, Illinois, in 1898. In his youth he worked in a pharmacy, plucked chickens, was a railroad section hand, and taught school before breaking into journalism with an Illinois weekly. He was a printer and was allowed to write an unpaid column, which he wanted to do because of his admiration for the early columnists George Ade and Eugene Field. In 1900 he worked for a year with the Census Bureau in Washington, D.C., reporting for the *Washington Times* in his spare time. He moved to Philadelphia hoping to become a columnist there, but when his plan failed, he went in 1902 to Atlanta as associate editor of the *Atlanta News*. In 1904 he became an editorial writer for the *Atlanta Journal* and became friends with Joel Chandler Harris. He left the paper in 1907 to work as associate editor of *Uncle Remus's Magazine,* to which Harris had lent his name and support.

After Harris's death, Marquis relocated in 1909 to New York City, worked briefly for a news service and as a rewrite man for the *American,* and was a reporter and rewrite man on the *Brooklyn Daily Eagle.* In 1912 he became editor of the *New York Sun*'s magazine page and soon was allowed to try a column, though it was unsigned and run under the plain head "Notes and Comment." The following year, he was given a bylined column, "The Sun Dial," for which three years later he created his most lasting character, archy the cockroach. Along with mehitabel the promiscuous alley cat and archy's critic, freddy the rat, the "insect Voltaire" was Marquis's way of satirizing the roaring twenties.

Marquis created two more literary characters: Hermione (and her little group of serious thinkers), his means of needling superficial "intellectuals," and Clem Hawley (the Old Soak), his voice in speaking out against Prohibition. Marquis published a number of successful books of humor, and his play *The Old Soak* was a hit on Broadway in 1922. He switched that same year to the *New York Tribune,* later merged and renamed the *Herald Tribune,* where his column appeared six days a week and was titled "The Lantern." The *Tribune* column was syndicated to about twenty other papers. The strain of deadlines six days a week weighed heavily on Marquis, and in 1925 he quit newspaper journalism for good to concentrate on his books and plays, and later Hollywood movies. Hardly overwhelmed by the glamour of Hollywood, in typical Marquis style he dubbed California "a country that has never been thought in."

BOOKS: *Danny's Own Story* (Garden City, N.Y., 1912); *Dreams and Dust* (New York and London, 1915); *The Cruise of the Jasper B.* (New York and London, 1916); *Hermione and Her Little Group of Serious Thinkers* (New York and London, 1916); *Prefaces* (New York and London, 1919); *Carter, and Other People* (New York and London, 1921); *Noah an' Jonah an' Cap'n John Smith, a Book of Humorous Verse* (New York and London, 1921); *The Old Soak, and Hail and Farewell* (Garden City, N.Y. and Toronto, 1921); *Sonnets to a Red-Haired Lady (by a Gentleman with a Blue Beard) and Famous Love Affairs* (Garden City, N.Y., 1922); *The Revolt of the Oyster* (Garden City, 1922); *Poems and Portraits* (Garden City N.Y. and Toronto, 1922); *The Old Soak's History of the World* (Garden City, N.Y., 1924); *The Dark Hours, Five Scenes from History* (Garden City, N.Y., 1924); with Christopher Morley, *Pandora Lifts the Lid* (New York, 1924); *Words and Thoughts, A Play in One Act* (New York and London, 1924); *The Awakening, and Other Poems* (London, 1925); *The Old Soak: A Comedy in Three Acts* (New York and London, 1926); *The Almost Perfect State* (Garden City, N.Y., 1927); *Out of the Sea: A Play in Four Acts* (Garden City, 1927); *Archy and Mehitabel* (Garden City, N.Y., 1927); *Love Sonnets of a Cave Man and Other Verses* (Garden City, N.Y., 1928); *When Turtles Sing, and Other Unusual Tales* (Garden City, N.Y., 1928); *A Variety of People* (Garden City, N.Y., 1929); *Off the Arm* (Garden City, N.Y., 1930); *Archys Life of Mehitabel* (Garden City, N.Y., 1934); *Chapters for the Orthodox* (Garden City, 1934); *Master of the Revels: A Comedy in Four Acts* (Garden City, N.Y., 1934); *Archy Does His Part* (Garden City, N.Y., 1935); *Her Foot Is on the Brass Rail* (New York, 1935); *Sun Dial Time* (Garden City, N.Y., 1936); *Sons of the Puritans* (Garden City, N.Y., 1939); *the lives and times of archy and mehitabel* (New York, 1940); *The Best of Don Marquis,* ed. by Christopher Morley (Garden City, N.Y., 1946); *Everything's Jake* (Tacoma, Wash., 1978).

REFERENCES: Edward Anthony, *O Rare Don Marquis* (Garden City, N.Y., 1962); Hamlin Hill, "Archy and Uncle Remus: Don Marquis's Debt to Joel Chandler Harris," *Georgia Review* (Spring 1961): 78–87; Rollin Kirby, "Don Marquis: Delayed Elizabethan," *American Mercury* 64 (March 1947): 337–340; Norris Yates, "The Many Masks of Don Marquis," *The American Humorist: Conscience of the Twentieth Century* (Ames, Iowa, 1964): 195–216.

Marshall, Marguerite Mooers (9 Sept. 1887–1964). Marguerite Mooers Marshall was a columnist for two New York City dailies from 1922 until 1945.

Marshall was born Marguerite Mooers in Kingston, New Hampshire. She was awarded the A.B. from Tufts University in 1907, finishing in three years and qualifying for Phi Beta Kappa. She briefly taught English at Westbrook Seminary in Portland, Maine, at the same time writing without pay for the *Portland Press*. She was hired by the *Boston Herald* in 1908, and in 1909 moved to New York City and a job with the *Sunday World*. She shifted to the *Evening World* in 1910, writing celebrity interview stories and other features for roughly a decade. Her column "The Woman of It" was launched in 1922; in it she addressed the myriad personal relationships of women. Marshall joined the *New York Journal* in 1931 and changed the title of her column to "Just Like a Woman." She remained with the *Journal* until 1937, then was picked up by King Features Syndicate, which distributed her column until 1945. She also continued to report and write feature articles, free-lanced both prose and verse to magazines, and wrote novels.

BOOKS: *The Drift* (New York, 1911); *None but the Brave: A Novel of Recovery* (Garden City, N.Y., 1934); *Salt of the Earth* (New York, 1935); *Not in Our Stars* (New York, 1937); *Land of Their Fathers* (New York, 1938); *Her Soul to Keep* (Philadelphia, 1940); *Nurse into Woman* (Philadelphia, 1941); *Arms and the Girl* (Philadelphia, 1942); *Wilderness Nurse* (Philadelphia, 1949); with Sidney W. Dean, *We Fell in Love with Quebec* (Philadelphia, 1950); *The Longest Way Round* (Philadelphia, 1951); *Nurse with Wings* (Philadelphia, 1952); *One Man Loved* (Philadelphia, 1952).

REFERENCES: Ishbel Ross, *Ladies of the Press* (New York, 1974): 94–96.

Martin, Judith Sylvia (13 Sept. 1938–). Judith Martin has written the weekly personal advice column "Miss Manners" for United Feature Syndicate since 1978.

Born Judith Perlman in Washington, D.C., she received the B.A. from Wellesley College in 1959. She became a reporter for the *Washington Post* in 1960, specializing in society and cultural stories. In addition to her column, she has been critic at large for the magazine *Vanity Fair*. The emphasis of her column is somewhat different from those of such predecessors as Emily Post or Amy Vanderbilt in that it is less concerned with "faux-European manners" and more attuned to the much changed conventions of present-day America. Her more light-hearted approach to manners is reflected in the title of one of her books: *Miss Manners' Guide to Excruciatingly Correct Behavior.*

BOOKS: *The Name on the White House Floor, and Other Anxieties of Our Times* (New York, 1972); *Miss Manners' Guide to Excruciatingly Correct Behavior* (New York, 1982); *Gilbert, a Comedy of Manners* (New York, 1982); *Miss Manners' Guide to Rearing Perfect Children* (New York, 1984); *Common Courtesy: In Which Miss Manners Solves the Problem That Baffled Mr. Jefferson* (New York, 1985); *Style and Substance: A Comedy of Manners* (New York, 1986); *Miss Manners' Guide for the Turn-of-the-Millennium* (New York, 1989).

Martinez, Al (21 July 1929–   ). Al Martinez has been a columnist for the *Los Angeles Times* since 1984.

Martinez was born in Oakland, California. He attended San Francisco State University and the University of California, Berkeley. He was a sniper, rifleman, and combat correspondent in the U.S. Marine Corps from 1950 to 1952.

From 1952 to 1955 Martinez was a reporter/feature writer for the Richmond (California) *Independent.* Moving to the Oakland *Tribune,* he worked as military writer, feature writer, and columnist through 1971, when he took a job as reporter and feature writer for the *Los Angeles Times*'s Metro section. He became a columnist for the Valley edition and Westside section from 1984 to 1988, and since 1988 he has written a general column for the Metro section. His column is sometimes serious, straight commentary, at other times satirical.

Martinez has also written for television entertainment shows and movies. He has been a scriptwriter for MGM-TV, Lorimar Productions, and Columbia-TV.

BOOKS: *Rising Voices* (New York, 1974); *Jigsaw John* (Los Angeles, 1978); *Ashes in the Rain* (Berkeley, Calif., 1989); *Dancing Under the Moon* (New York, 1992).

Mathews, Garret (23 Sept. 1949–   ). Garret Mathews has been a columnist since 1973. He is currently a daily general/humor columnist for the *Evansville* [Indiana] *Courier.*

Mathews was born in Covington, Virginia, and received the B.S. in economics from Virginia Polytechnic Institute and State University in 1971.

Mathews worked at the Bluefield (West Virginia) *Daily Telegraph* from 1972 until 1987 and at various times was copy editor, news editor, sports editor, and columnist. He joined the *Evansville Courier* in 1987.

BOOKS: *Folks* (Bluefield, W. Va., 1979); *Folks II* (Bluefield, W. Va., 1984).

Mathis, Deborah (24 Aug. 1953–   ). Deborah Mathis, who in 1993 joined Gannett News Service to cover the White House, writes a twice-weekly column syndicated by Tribune Media Services.

Mathis first wrote a column at the *Arkansas Gazette* in Little Rock and also spent roughly a decade in that city as a television anchor/reporter. She did similar television work in Washington, D.C., from 1974 to 1976. Prior to joining Gannett News Service, she was a member of the editorial board of the *Jackson* [Mississippi] *Clarion-Ledger.* Mathis writes about a wide range of topics and attempts to discover and write about what newspaper readers appear to be thinking.

Maupin, Armistead (13 May 1944–). Armistead Maupin's fame as a writer derives mainly from a series of six novels, "Tales of the City," which tell the stories of the people who live in a San Francisco rooming house; the books are extensions of Maupin's column of the same title that appeared in the *San Francisco Chronicle* in 1976–1977.

Maupin was born Armistead Jones in Raleigh, North Carolina. He later adopted his mother's maiden name. He was an English major at the University of North Carolina (UNC) at Chapel Hill, where he wrote a humor column for the *Daily Tarheel.* After graduation in 1966, he put in an unhappy year at the UNC School of Law, then joined the navy in 1967. He served in Vietnam until 1970, then returned to help build housing for that country's disabled veterans.

In 1970–1971 Maupin was a reporter for the *Charleston* [South Carolina] *News and Courier,* then took a job in San Francisco with the Associated Press. He spent 1973 as a public relations account executive, then was a reporter/ columnist for the San Francisco edition of *Pacific Sun* in 1974, the year he publicly identified himself as gay. In 1975 he was the publicist for his city's opera company, then the following year became a columnist for the *Chronicle.* His "Tales of the City" column proved popular. It featured well-known local settings and described the city's variety of life-styles, yet its popularity probably derived mainly from its witty style and the way it avoided an "us versus them" approach in dealings between gays and straights. Acceptance was Maupin's main message. His reputation as a writer was cemented by his subsequent series of novels, the central character of which is Anna Madrigal, the transsexual keeper of a rooming house on Barbary Lane.

BOOKS: *Tales of the City* (New York, 1978); *More Tales of the City* (New York, 1980); *Further Tales of the City* (New York, 1982); *Babycakes* (New York, 1984); *Significant Others* (New York, 1987); *Sure of You* (New York, 1989); *28 Barbary Lane* (New York, 1990); *Back to Barbary Lane* (New York, 1991); *Maybe the Moon* (New York, 1992).

REFERENCES: Chuck Allen, "Armistead Maupin," *Frontiers* 3 (November 1989): 18–21; Frances Fitzgerald, *Cities on a Hill* (New York, 1981): 25–119; Tom Spain, "A Talk with Armistead Maupin," *Publisher's Weekly* (20 March 1987): 53–54.

Maxwell, Bill (16 Oct. 1945–). Columnist Bill Maxwell has been with three Florida papers: the *Tampa Tribune* (1986–1988), the *Gainesville Sun* (1988–1994), and the *St. Petersburg Times* (since July 1994).

Maxwell was born in Fort Lauderdale, Florida, and also spent parts of his youth in Crescent City, Florida, and in Chicago. His father was a migrant farm worker, and until age sixteen, Maxwell also worked the fields. He attended Wiley College in Marshall, Texas, for two years; joined the Marine Corps; then graduated summa cum laude with an English major from Bethune-Cookman College in Daytona Beach. He completed the M.A. in English in 1974 at the

University of Chicago and has been a doctoral student at the University of Florida.

Maxwell's *Tampa Tribune* column was syndicated to seven other papers, and his weekly column in the *Sun* was handled by the New York Times Syndicate. His weekly column for the *St. Petersburg Times* appears in the Sunday Perspective section, and Maxwell also writes editorials. His work background also includes experience as a labor organizer and as a tenured English instructor at Santa Fe Community College near Gainesville.

Maxwell, Elsa (24 May 1883–1 Nov. 1963). Elsa Maxwell was a daily columnist during World War II for Press Alliance, Inc., although she is probably more often remembered for her motion picture roles and for her prowess as a nightclub owner and party hostess.

Maxwell was born in Keokuk, Iowa—in an opera box. The family moved to California, and Elsa attended Miss West's school in San Francisco. She was publicly exhibited as a musical prodigy, able to play and compose without benefit of music lessons. After studying at the University of California and at the Sorbonne in Paris, she began a varied career as a songwriter, golf course designer, organizer of motor boat races, and owner of hotels, clubs, and restaurants in such glamorous locations as Monte Carlo and Venice. She developed a reputation as the leader of European café society in the 1920s. She relocated to Hollywood in 1938, gave fabulous parties, and appeared in various films.

In 1942 Maxwell began her own radio program, "Elsa Maxwell's Party Line," and in 1943 she appeared in New York as a nightclub performer. She also began writing her column around this time; it was, in the main, a gossip column, although she often worked in war-related material of a more serious nature. She also authored five books, including an autobiography that appeared in 1954.

BOOKS: *Elsa Maxwell's Etiquette Book* (New York, 1951); *R.S.V.P.: Elsa Maxwell's Own Story* (Boston, 1954); *I Married the World* (London, 1955); *How to Do It: Or The Lively Art of Entertaining* (Boston, 1957); *The Celebrity Circus* (New York, 1963).

Maynard, Robert Clyve (17 June 1937–17 August 1993). One of the best known African-American journalists and former owner of the *Oakland* [California] *Tribune,* Robert Maynard wrote a twice-weekly column for Universal Press Syndicate.

Maynard was born in Brooklyn, New York, the son of an immigrant from Barbados. He dropped out of high school at age sixteen and became a Greenwich Village writer. Maynard was self-taught, aided by a photographic memory. He attended Harvard University in 1966 as a Nieman Fellow, and in 1992, when his daughter, Dori, also became a Nieman Fellow, the Maynards became the only father-daughter pair ever to participate in this prestigious program.

Maynard began his career in 1956 as a reporter for the *Afro-American News* in Baltimore, Maryland. From 1961 to 1967 he reported for the York (Pennsylvania) *Gazette and Daily.* He then joined the *Washington Post,* where he was that paper's first black full-time national correspondent (1967–1972), associate editor and ombudsman during Watergate (1972–1974), and editorial writer (1974–1977).

Maynard founded the nonprofit Institute for Journalism Education in Berkeley, California, in 1977 and directed it until becoming editor, publisher, and president of the *Oakland Tribune* in 1979. As such, he was the first black owner of a large U.S. metropolitan newspaper. Maynard led the way in ensuring that his newspaper's staff reflected the considerable ethnic diversity of the geographical area it served. He began writing a twice-weekly column in the 1980s and has also worked as a commentator on "This Week with David Brinkley" and the "MacNeil/Lehrer News Hour."

Maynard and his wife, former *New York Times* reporter Nancy Hicks Maynard, sold the *Tribune* in 1992 after Maynard had been diagnosed with prostate cancer. Maynard's achievements have been recognized by eight honorary doctorates. He died at age 56.

McAllister, R. Ray (14 April 1952–   ). Ray McAllister has written a thrice-weekly general column for the *Richmond* [Virginia] *Times-Dispatch* since November 1988.

McAllister was born in Philadelphia and in 1974 earned the B.A. in journalism from Pennsylvania State University. During the summers of 1973 and 1974, he was a student intern on the *Philadelphia Inquirer* and the *Philadelphia Bulletin.*

After graduation McAllister became a general assignment reporter for the *Richmond Times-Dispatch.* He has since covered police, labor, and the state and federal courts. He has also been a member of an investigative team and a legal affairs team for his paper. McAllister often applies the humorous touch to his column and has appeared on both radio and television as a commentator.

McCabe, Charles Raymond (24 Jan. 1915–30 April 1983). Charles McCabe wrote a syndicated column out of the *San Francisco Chronicle.* His column dates from 1958.

McCabe was born in New York City and studied at Manhattan College. He was a reporter for the *New York American* starting in 1937, after which he worked in public relations, was in the navy, and was a World War II war correspondent with United Press. He also worked as managing editor of the *Puerto Rico World Journal.*

McCabe's column was originally titled "Fearless Spectator" but was retitled "Himself" in the 1960s. He wrote or edited five books.

BOOKS: Ed., *Damned Old Crank, a Self-Portrait of E. W. Scripps* (New York, 1951); *The Fearless Spectator* (San Francisco, 1970); *Tall Girls Are Grateful: Wry Commentaries on the Female of the Species* (San Francisco, 1973); *The Good Man's Weakness* (San Francisco, 1974); *The Charles McCabe Reader* (San Francisco, 1984).

McCann, Dennis (25 July 1950–   ). Dennis McCann has written a general interest/local news column for the *Milwaukee Journal* since 1987.

McCann was born in Janesville, Wisconsin, and was awarded the J.B.A. degree from the University of Wisconsin in Madison in 1974.

After a brief experience in broadcast news work, McCann was a reporter for the *Janeville Gazette* (1976–1977), then moved to the Arlington Heights (Illinois) *Herald* in 1978. In 1979 he returned to the Janeville paper and worked until 1983 in its state capital bureau in Madison. Later that same year he moved to the *Milwaukee Journal*'s Madison bureau. He later worked for the *Journal* as an agriculture reporter, fill-in government reporter, and state roving reporter. In 1987 he began a column for the Sunday magazine section and after two years, moved to Milwaukee and launched his present thrice-weekly column.

McCarthy, Dennis (26 November 1944–   ). Dennis McCarthy is a *Los Angeles Daily News* general columnist who believes in the need for columnists to do good reporting as opposed to becoming inner-directed.

McCarthy is a 1972 graduate of California State University, Northridge. He reported for several Southern California papers prior to taking his present job in 1984. His column formerly ran five days a week and now appears four days. His work is strong on human interest value.

McCarthy, Eugene Joseph (29 March 1916–   ). Eugene McCarthy, best known to the nation as a liberal politician who twice ran for the U.S. presidency, has written a syndicated political column since 1977.

McCarthy was born in Watkins, Minnesota. His B.A. is from St. John's University in 1935, his M.A. from the University of Minnesota in 1941.

McCarthy began his work life with ten years of teaching, first in Minnesota and North Dakota high schools (1935–1940, and 1945), then as an economics and education instructor at St. John's University (1940–1942). He was a civilian code breaker for U.S. Military Intelligence during 1943–1944, then taught economics and sociology at the College of St. Thomas, 1946–1948. McCarthy represented Minnesota in the U.S. House of Representatives from 1949 to 1958, then in the Senate from 1958 to 1970. He was the Democratic party's candidate for president in 1968 and ran again as an independent in 1970. From 1973 to 1974 he was the Adlai Stevenson Professor of Political Science at the New School for Social Research. Since that time he has concentrated mainly on writing: his column since 1977, poetry, and books about the political scene.

BOOKS: *Frontiers in American Democracy* (Cleveland, 1960); *Crescent Dictionary of American Politics* (New York, 1962); *A Liberal Answer to the Conservative Challenge* (New York, 1964); *The Limits of Power: America's Role in the World* (New York, 1967); *The Year of the People* (New York, 1969); *Other Things and the Aardvark* (New York, 1970); *The Hard Years: A Look at Contemporary America and American Institutions* (New York, 1975); *Mr. Raccoon and His Friends* (Chicago, 1977); *America Revisited: 150 Years After Tocqueville* (New York, 1978); with James J. Kilpatrick, *A Political*

Bestiary (New York, 1978); *Ground Fog and Night: Poems* (New York, 1979); *The Ultimate Tyranny: The Majority over the Majority* (New York, 1980); *Gene McCarthy's Minnesota* (Minneapolis, 1982); *Complexities and Contraries: Essays of Mild Discontent* (New York, 1982); *The View from Rappahannock* (McLean, Va., 1984); *Up 'Til Now: A Memoir* (San Diego, 1987); *Required Reading* (San Diego, 1988); *The View from Rappahannock II* (McLean, Va., 1989).

REFERENCES: Arthur Herzog, *McCarthy for President* (New York, 1970).

McClatchy, Charles Kenny (1 Nov. 1858–27 April 1936). C. K. McClatchy, owner of the McClatchy Newspapers chain in central California, wrote a column for his papers from 1883 until 1936.

McClatchy was born in Sacramento, the son of James McClatchy, who had worked for Horace Greeley on the *New York Tribune* then founded the *Sacramento Bee* in 1857. The younger McClatchy attended Santa Clara College but left without a degree in 1875 to become a reporter for his father's paper. He assumed ownership of this paper on his father's death in 1883. Years later he began acquiring other papers for his "Bee" chain, starting with the *Fresno Bee* in 1922. He bought the *Sacramento Star* in 1925, renaming it the *Sacramento Bee,* and in 1927 his next purchase, the *Modesto News-Herald,* became the *Modesto Bee.* He also was the earliest newspaper publisher on the West Coast to run radio stations, which were located in four California cities plus Reno, Nevada.

From 1883 to 1897 McClatchy's column was simply titled "Notes"; from 1897 to 1936 it appeared as "Private Thinks." His wide-ranging columns covered politics, economics, and social issues. McClatchy was a moderate who spoke out against organized crime, concentration of industrial ownership, the Ku Klux Klan, and the political involvement of big railroads. He favored women's suffrage, a minimum wage, antitrust legislation, and conservation of natural resources. His crusade against organized crime won the *Bee* a Pulitzer Prize in 1934.

BOOKS: *Private Thinks by C. K. and Other Writings of Charles K. McClatchy* (New York, 1936).

REFERENCES: Bernard A. Shepard, *C. K. McClatchy and the Sacramento Bee,* Ph.D. Dissertation, Syracuse University, 1960.

McCormack, Patricia Seger (1927–   ). Patricia McCormack was a columnist with United Press International starting in 1959.

She was born Patricia Seger in Pittsburgh, Pennsylvania, and was a 1949 graduate of the University of Pittsburgh. From 1952 to 1957 she was health and welfare editor of the *Pittsburgh Sun Telegraph* and in 1957 was medical science editor of International News Service.

McCormick, Anne O'Hare (16 May 1880–29 May 1954). Anne O'Hare Mc-Cormick, who wrote a foreign affairs column titled "In Europe" and later, simply "Abroad" for the *New York Times,* was the first woman member of the *Times*'s editorial board and the first woman journalist to win a Pulitzer Prize.

She was born Anne Elizabeth O'Hare in Wakefield, Yorkshire, England, and left with her family to settle in Columbus, Ohio. She received the B.A. in 1898 from St. Mary's Academy near Columbus. After her father had business problems and deserted the family, she and her mother moved to Cleveland, where both found work on the *Catholic Universe Bulletin.* She was associate editor and her mother became a columnist and editor of the women's section. After marrying Francis McCormick in 1910, she left the *Bulletin* but published poetry in *Bookman* and *Smart Set* and free-lanced articles to *Atlantic Monthly, Reader,* and other magazines. She began writing for the *New York Times* in 1920 while traveling in Europe with her husband, an importer. She became a *Times* regular in 1922, working as a foreign correspondent until 1954. In this capacity she interviewed most of the major world leaders of the pre–World War II era, including Hitler, Mussolini, Chamberlain, Churchill, Roosevelt, Pope Pius XI, and Pope Pius XII.

McCormick became a member of the *Times*'s editorial board in 1936, and the following February, her column "In Europe" began appearing three times weekly. Later the title was changed to "Abroad." She continued the column until her death in 1954. Her Pulitzer Prize came in 1937 for her work as a foreign correspondent. The quiet, unassuming McCormick received many, many other awards and tokens of recognition.

BOOKS: *St. Agnes Church, Cleveland, Ohio: An Interpretation* (N.p., 1920); *The Hammer and the Scythe: Communist Russia Enters the Second Decade* (New York, 1928); *Ourselves and Europe* (Poughkeepsie, N.Y., 1941); *The World at Home: Selections from the Writings of Anne O'Hare McCormick,* ed. by Marion Turner Sheehan (New York, 1956); *Vatican Journal, 1921–1954,* ed. by Marion Turner Sheehan (New York, 1957).

REFERENCES: L. C. Fray, "McCormick of the Times," *Current History* 50 (July 1939): 27–64; Helen Walker Homan, "Anne O'Hare McCormick: An Appreciation," *Catholic World* 180 (October 1954): 42–48; Ishbel Ross, *Ladies of the Press* (New York, 1936): 360, 366–369.

McCormick, Elsie (?–   ). Much traveled reporter Elsie McCormick was chosen to replace Heywood Broun as columnist for the *New York World* after Broun's death in December 1939.

McCormick was born in San Francisco and contributed a column of school news to the *San Francisco News* when she was eleven. During her time in the public schools and at the University of California, she wrote for the *San Francisco Bulletin,* and after college, she became the first woman courthouse reporter for the *Oakland Post-Enquirer.*

She moved to New York City after a year and found a job as publicist for the Interchurch World Movement. Her world travels began when she was sent to France and Italy to write about that organization's efforts there after World War I. Soon thereafter, she was sent to China by the same organization—the first of many trips to that country. She wrote a column in the *China Press* for roughly a year, traveling into the interior of China plus excursions to Korea, Japan, and the Philippines. One of her more unusual adventures was a trip into Shantung province to locate a Confucian duke who reputedly was the seventy-seventh-generation descendant of Confucius. She found him but could not get an interview. The duke was two years old. McCormick published at least two books about her travel observations. She eventually returned to New York and worked as a features writer for the *New York World* for about a year before beginning her column at the end of 1939.

BOOKS: *Audacious Angles on China* (Shanghai, 1922); *The Diary of a Shanghai Baby* (Shanghai, 1940).

REFERENCES: Ishbel Ross, *Ladies of the Press* (New York, 1974): 381–384.

McCrary, John Reagan (13 Oct. 1910–   ). Tex McCrary and his glamorous wife Jinx Falkenburg wrote a widely syndicated *New York Herald Tribune* column for two years, beginning in September 1949. They were also radio performers and pioneers in the new medium of television.

McCrary was born to a politically prominent family in Calvert, Texas. He graduated from Phillips Exeter Academy in 1928 and from Yale University, with a degree in architecture, in 1932. Instead of seeking a job in his field of study, McCrary became a copyboy for the *New York World-Telegram* in 1932, soon moving up to cub reporter. He next was a reporter, columnist, and editorial writer for the *New York Mirror* under editor Arthur Brisbane, then in 1936 became editor of the *Literary Digest*. After that magazine's much-publicized death, he returned to the *Mirror* as assistant to the editor.

McCrary was a combat photographer and a public relations officer for the Army Air Forces during World War II, then returned home to edit the *American Mercury*. He and his second wife, Jinx Falkenburg, then the nation's highest-paid fashion model, began an early morning radio show, "Hi Jinx," over WEAF in April 1946. The program combined entertainment with interviews and serious discussion of hard news. The couple made the jump to television in March 1947 with a Sunday night interview show called "At Home" and soon added a daytime program, "Home Service Club," which combined news with patter and household hints. During the summers of 1947 and 1948, they added a new radio show, "Meet Tex and Jinx," as an off-season replacement for the legendary "Duffy's Tavern." In March 1949, they began yet another television show, "Preview," a sort of ancestor of today's TV magazine shows. Apparently ahead of its time, the show folded in September of that same year.

In September 1949, the couple launched "New York Close-Up," a daily column in the *New York Herald Tribune* that presented personality profiles of both famous and obscure New Yorkers. They later added a second column for *Variety* that covered the world of radio and television.

Tex McCrary took a leave of absence from his radio and television work in

1952 in order to campaign for Dwight Eisenhower. He authored one book, which was about the Eighth Air Force during World War II.

BOOKS: *First of the Many: A Journal of Action with the Men of the Eighth Air Force* (New York, 1944).

REFERENCES: Jinx Falkenburg, *Jinx* (New York, 1951).

McCutcheon, John Tinney, Jr. (8 Nov. 1917–   ). John T. McCutcheon had a forty-two-year career at the *Chicago Tribune* and is perhaps most remembered for having been in charge of the "A Line o' Type or Two" column.

McCutcheon was born in Chicago. He received the B.B. from Harvard University in 1939.

After graduation from Harvard, McCutcheon worked for a year (1939–1940) as a reporter for the City News Bureau of Chicago, then joined the *Tribune* as a reporter in 1940–1941. He served in the U.S. Navy, then returned to his *Tribune* reporting job (1946–1951). During the years 1951–1957 he handled the "Line o' Type" column, then began writing editorials in 1957. He was named editor of the *Tribune*'s editorial page in 1971 and held that position until his retirement in 1982. He also wrote another column from 1967 to 1970.

McEnroe, Colin (15 Oct. 1954–   ). Colin McEnroe of the *Hartford Courant* writes a humor column that is distributed by Erwenter Quality Features Syndicate.

McEnroe is a Hartford native. He received the B.A., with honors, from Yale University in 1976 and since that time has been employed by the *Courant*. He first worked as a reporter and began writing his column in 1976. He was handled during 1985–1986 by the Los Angeles Times–Washington Post Wire Service and by Universal Press Syndicate from 1986 to 1988. McEnroe was one of the founders of the Erwenter syndicate. He has also worked for the *Courant* as religion editor, critic, and political writer and has authored two humor books.

BOOKS: *Swimming Chickens and Other Half-Breasted Accounts of the Animal World* (Garden City, N.Y., 1987); *Lose Weight Through Great Sex with Celebrities (the Elvis Way)* (New York, 1989).

McGill, Ralph Waldo Emerson (5 Feb. 1898–3 Feb. 1969). Pulitzer Prize–winning editor/columnist Ralph McGill wrote various columns from the 1920s until his death in 1969. The column for which he is most remembered was "One Word More," which appeared on the editorial page of the *Atlanta Constitution* from 1938 to 1969.

McGill was born on a farm located between the towns of Daisy and Soddy, Tennessee, and grew up largely in Chattanooga. He attended Vanderbilt University in 1917, dropping out to enlist in the Marine Corps, then returning to Vanderbilt, where he wrote for the school newspaper, started a campus humor periodical, and worked as copyboy and part-time sports reporter for the *Nashville*

Banner. He was expelled from the university because of a prank and a column critical of the administration and hence never completed his degree.

McGill spent seven years as a reporter at the *Banner,* for which he also wrote a humor column titled "I'm the Gink." In 1929 he was hired by the *Atlanta Constitution* as assistant sports editor and sports reporter. Here he wrote a new column, "Break o' Day," which appeared on the sports page but dealt with more than sports. He became executive editor of the paper in 1938 and used his new daily column, "One Word More," to combat the Ku Klux Klan and to attempt to promote racial understanding and harmony. This column was syndicated by the North American Newspaper Alliance, and in 1958 McGill won the Pulitzer. His title was changed to editor in chief (1942–1960), and from 1960 to 1969 he was listed as publisher. In 1942 his column began appearing on the *Constitution*'s front page. McGill also wrote several books and contributed articles to such magazines as *Atlantic, Saturday Review,* and *Look.*

BOOKS: With Thomas C. David, *Two Georgians Explore Scandinavia: A Comparison of Education for Democracy in Northern Europe and Georgia* (Atlanta, 1938); *Israel Revisited* (Atlanta, 1950); *The Fleas Come with the Dog* (Nashville, 1954); *A Church, a School* (Nashville, 1959); *The South and the Southerner* (Boston, 1963); *The Best of Ralph McGill: Selected Columns* (Atlanta, 1980).

REFERENCES: Calvin McLeod Logue, *Ralph McGill, Editor and Publisher,* 2 vols. (Durham, N.C., 1969); Harold H. Martin, *Ralph McGill, Reporter* (Boston, 1973).

McGrory, Mary (22 Aug. 1918–   ). Pulitzer Prize–winning columnist Mary McGrory writes out of Washington, D.C., for Universal Press Syndicate.

She was born in Boston, Massachusetts, and received the A.B. in 1939 at Emmanuel College.

McGrory was a picture cropper for the Boston publisher Houghton Mifflin from 1939 to 1942. She took a secretarial job at the *Boston Herald Traveler* in 1942 and worked her way into book reviewing. From 1947 to 1954 she was a book reviewer/feature writer for the *Washington Evening Star,* which gave her a column toward the end of that period. She became a known quantity in Washington during the Kennedy administration. McGrory made President Richard Nixon's enemies list and won the Pulitzer in 1974 for her columns on Watergate. She joined the *Washington Post* as a thrice-weekly columnist in 1981 and was picked up by Universal. Hers is a reportorial style of column writing—long on observation, short on ruminative punditry. Her column has appeared in as many as 225 papers.

REFERENCES: Barbara Belford, *Brilliant Bylines* (New York, 1986): 270–283.

McIntyre, Oliver Odd (18 Feb. 1884–14 Feb. 1938). O. O. McIntyre's reputation was made with his syndicated column "New York Day by Day," which was handled by the McNaught syndicate and appeared in more than 375 papers.

McIntyre was born in Plattsburg, Missouri, and grew up in Gallipolis, Ohio.

He did poorly in school, though he apparently published a school paper. He became a typesetter and reporter for the *Gallipolis Journal,* then for two years attended Barlett's Business College in Cincinnati. In 1904 he was hired as a reporter by the *East Liverpool* [Ohio] *Morning Tribune.* His next job was police reporter for the *Dayton Herald;* he soon added the duties of city editor. By 1907 he was managing editor, city editor, and also telegraph editor of that paper. McIntyre's next move in that same year was to the *Cincinnati Post* as telegraph editor, later city editor, under managing editor Ray Long. He showed a proclivity for featurizing the news and began to build a reputation as a humorist.

Ray Long had changed jobs and was made editor of *Hampton's* magazine, and in 1911, he hired McIntyre as his assistant. When the magazine went out of business, McIntyre became a copy editor for the *New York Evening Mail.* He became city editor and directed coverage of the *Titanic* disaster for that paper. Fired for his poor spelling, he began writing sketches of New York from the perspective of a small-town boy and became publicist for the Majestic hotel. His sketches caught on, and in 1922 he had converted them into a highly popular syndicated column and also did a monthly column for *Cosmopolitan* magazine. He continued both columns until his death. His columns captured the city dwellers' nostalgia for their less urban roots and were so successful that shy but dapper McIntyre, whose middle name was pronounced "Udd," lived on Park Avenue and had a chauffeur. He is said to have received as many as three thousand letters a week from his readers.

BOOKS: *White Light Nights* (New York, 1924); *Twenty-Five Selected Stories of O. O. McIntyre* (New York, 1929); *Another "Odd" Book: 25 Selected Stories of O. O. McIntyre* (New York, 1932); *The Big Town* (New York, 1935).

REFERENCES: J. Bryan III, "Gallipolis Boy Makes Good," in *Post Biographies of Famous Journalists,* ed. by John E. Drewry (Athens, Ga., 1942); Charles B. Driscoll, *The Life of O. O. McIntyre* (New York, 1938).

McManus, Michael J. (11 June 1941–). Mike McManus currently writes a self-syndicated ethics and religion column for roughly ninety newspapers; from 1977 to 1991 he wrote and self-syndicated a political/economic column titled "The Northern Perspective" for around seventy papers. The main focus of the latter column was the section of the nation known as the Rust Belt.

McManus was born in Springfield, Ohio. He received the A.B. from Duke University in 1963. While attending Duke, he wrote for the *Durham Morning Herald,* and during the years 1961–1963 he also wrote stories for the *Stamford Advocate* and the *Middletown Times-Herald.*

From 1964 to 1968 he was a correspondent for *Time* magazine in Buenos Aires and in Washington. During the years 1969–1977 his interests turned to television. He created and was director of a series of multimedia "town meetings," such as "Choices for '76," which won him an Emmy. From 1990 to 1993 McManus was a commentator for "Family News in Focus," a widely syndicated news show for Christian radio. He currently works out of Bethesda, Maryland.

BOOKS: *Marriage Savers* (Grand Rapids, Mich., 1993); *50 Practical Ways to Take Our Kids Back from the World* (Wheaton, Ill., 1993).

McMullen, Catherine Olson (20 Aug. 1952–). Cathy McMullen, who wrote as Cathy Mauk until her recent marriage, has written a general life-style column for the *Forum* of Fargo, North Dakota, since 1985.

McMullen was born in Moorhead, Minnesota; spent four years in the U.S. Navy; and in 1981 received the B.S. from Moorhead State University.

She has worked as a feature writer at the *Forum* since 1981. McMullen reports receiving considerably more reader responses from her columns than from her feature articles, which she interprets as evidence that newspaper readers "hunger for a human voice in the newspaper."

McNally, Joel (4 March 1944–). Joel McNally has written the satirical column "The Innocent Bystander" for the *Milwaukee Journal* since 1978.

McNally was born in Indianapolis, Indiana, and grew up in Union City, Indiana. He is a journalism and sociology graduate of Indiana University. He has also had a graduate fellowship at Northwestern University's Urban Journalism Center.

He began as a reporter, copy editor, and makeup editor for the *Chicago Tribune*'s suburban news sections. He then joined the *Journal* in 1968 as a reporter, covering city hall, labor, and politics. His column's satire is aimed at both local and national issues, and he also writes features and reviews for the paper's arts and entertainment sections.

Means, Marianne Hansen (13 June 1934–). Marianne Means has been a political columnist for King Features Syndicate since 1965.

Means was born in Sioux City, Iowa. She received the B.A. from the University of Nebraska in 1956 and the J.D. from George Washington University in 1977.

Her career began at the *Dakota County Star* in South Sioux City, where she was a reporter in 1954. She was a copy editor at the *Lincoln Journal* in Lincoln, Nebraska, from 1955 to 1957, then was woman's editor of the *Northern Virginia Sun* in Arlington, Virginia, 1957–1959. Means was Washington bureau correspondent for the Hearst papers, 1959–1961, then White House correspondent, 1961–1965. She has also been a commentator on "Spectrum" on CBS radio and has appeared often on various other radio and television public affairs programs.

BOOKS: *The Woman in the White House* (New York, 1963).

Mecham, Evan (1924–   ). Evan Mecham, impeached in 1988 as governor of Arizona, began writing a conservative political column titled "Common Sense" in February 1993.

Mecham has also had his say via one book, several newsletters, and his own tabloid, the *Impeachment Journal.* He considered starting a new Phoenix daily to be called *Arizona Newsday* but instead launched his column, which appears in small western papers. The column first appeared in February 1993 in a La Paz County weekly, the *Gem.* The column is available free of charge.

Since his impeachment, Mecham has lost a 1990 run for another term as governor and was defeated by incumbent John McCain in a campaign for the U.S. Senate. Mecham is anti–health care reform, anti–gay rights, and antiwelfare. He sees no good in the Clinton administration and is firmly convinced that the country has "gone to the dogs." He also finds little to admire in the U.S. press.

From 1963 to 1965, Mecham was publisher of the *Evening American,* a Phoenix daily whose motto was "A Straight-Shootin' Newspaper." He also wrote a column for that paper and, in addition, was a radio talk show host in Phoenix.

BOOKS: *Come Back America* (Glendale, Ariz., 1982).

REFERENCES: Walt Jayroe, "His Pulpit: The Newspaper," *Editor and Publisher* (17 July 1993): 12–13.

Meeks, Larry M. (?–   ). Larry Meeks writes the column "Ethically Speaking," which examines ethical issues from a minority viewpoint. He is handled by Creators Syndicate.

Meeks, who lives in Sacramento, California, holds a B.S. in behavioral science and community planning from the University of California, Irvine; a master's of public administration from Golden State University; and a doctorate of divinity from Trinity University. He was an army officer and served in Vietnam.

From 1983 to 1991 Meeks was director of the Office of Statewide Health Planning and Development for California, and he has taught at Golden State University in San Francisco. He began writing his column in 1991 and does two shows for radio station KFBK in Sacramento: "Ethnic Almanac" and the talk show "Inside Sacramento." He is active in his city's chapter of the National Association for the Advancement of Colored People (NAACP) and in many other organizations.

Melone, Mary Jo (15 Sept. 1952–   ). Mary Jo Melone is a Metro page columnist for the *St. Petersburg Times* in Florida. Her column deals with people, events, and politics in Tampa and the Tampa Bay area.

Melone was born in Philadelphia. She earned the A.B. cum laude in 1974 at Barnard College, majoring in political science. In 1989 she was a journalism fellow at Duke University.

Before becoming a newspaper columnist, Melone worked for nearly a decade in radio. She was a reporter/announcer for DYW Newsradio in Philadelphia from 1974 to 1983, then joined the *Times* as a general assignment reporter. Her thrice-weekly column has appeared since November 1987, and she does occasional commentaries on Tampa's radio station WUSF-FM.

Memminger, Charles Gustavus (5 Jan. 1954–   ). Charles Memminger writes a thrice-weekly humor column, "Honolulu Lite," for the *Honolulu Star-Bulletin.*

Memminger was born in Tampa, Florida. He earned the B.A. from Oregon State University in 1976. He began his career at the *Wheeling Intelligencer* (1977); spent 1978–1980 working at the *Pacific Daily News* in Agana, Guam; and has been at the *Star-Bulletin* since 1980.

Memminger's columns have been distributed via the New York Times News Service to other papers. He has also been a guest columnist in *Newsweek's* "My Turn" feature in *Omni* magazine's "Last Word."

Mencken, Henry Louis (12 Sept. 1880–29 Jan. 1956). One of America's truly unusual literary figures, H. L. Mencken wrote a variety of columns for four newspapers.

Mencken was born in—and remained in—Baltimore. His formal education consisted of graduation from Friedrich Knapp's Institute, a private school for boys and girls in Baltimore, and in 1896, at age fifteen, from Baltimore Polytechnic Institute, where he had combined concentrations in journalism and chemistry. He worked for his family's cigar factory until summer 1899, when he became a staff writer for the *Baltimore Morning Herald.*

For seven years he reported for this paper, covering the police beat, city hall, and the waterfront district and doubling as a drama critic. He became Sunday editor in 1901, city editor in 1903. The paper became the *Evening Herald* in 1904, and Mencken was promoted to managing editor; he became editor in January 1906, half a year before the paper folded. During his rise through the *Herald's* ranks, Mencken also worked as a columnist. His earliest column, "Rhymes and Reason," was launched in 1900 in the Sunday edition. He used other column titles during his years on the *Herald:* "Terse and Terrible Texts," "Knocks and Jollies," Untold Tales," and "Baltimore and the Rest of the World." He also contributed to other papers, such as the *Philadelphia Inquirer, New York Telegram,* and *New York Sun,* and sold short stories to *Munsey's, Frank Leslie's Popular Monthly,* and other magazines.

In July 1906 Mencken went to work as Sunday editor for the *Baltimore Sun.* He was a reviewer and editorial writer and became associate editor in April 1910. In addition to writing two editorials a day, he began a new column, signed merely "H.L.M." A year later he began his column "The Free Lance," in which he adopted a more iconoclastic approach, skewering boobs, balderdash, and buncombe of every variety. His use of hyperbole and frequent exclamation marks made the column famous, or infamous, depending on the reader. His column was frequently quoted in other U.S. newspapers.

From 1914 to 1923 Mencken coedited a sophisticated magazine, *Smart Set,* with theater critic George Jean Nathan. Here Mencken established himself as a leading American literary critic, reviewing some two thousand books during these years.

Mencken's column was dropped by the *Sun* in October 1915 after the columnist's defense of the sinking of the ship *Lusitania* by a German submarine. He continued writing for the paper and was sent to Germany as a foreign correspondent in January 1917, but he resigned in March of that year, going to work as a thrice-weekly columnist for the *New York Evening Mail.* His famous column, ''The Sahara of the Bozart,'' in which he ridiculed the American South as a cultural desert, appeared in the *Mail* in November 1917. The *Mail's* pro-German bias brought its demise in 1918, and in the following year, Mencken was rehired by the *Baltimore Sun,* this time as editorial adviser. He started a new *Sun* column, the ''Monday Articles,'' which lasted until 1938. From 1924 to 1928 he also wrote columns for the *Chicago Tribune.*

Mencken and Nathan parted company with *Smart Set* in 1923 and with the backing of publisher Alfred Knopf founded another magazine, the *American Mercury.* Nathan wrote on the theater; Mencken was editor and wrote on the literary scene, politics, and America's social milieu. A major assignment for Mencken was covering the Scopes trial in 1925; there he was able to describe ''boobus Americanus'' in one of its most flagrant manifestations. His curmudgeonly reign at the *Mercury* ended in December 1933, after which he wrote for the *New York American* (July 1934–May 1935).

Mencken also wrote roughly forty books, edited others, and wrote for such magazines as *New Yorker, Atlantic Monthly, New Republic, Harper's, Outlook,* and *Forum.*

BOOKS: *Ventures into Verse* (Baltimore, 1903); *George Bernard Shaw: His Plays* (Boston and London, 1905); *The Philosophy of Friedrich Nietzsche* (Boston, 1908); *Man Versus the Man* (New York, 1910); *A Book of Burlesques* (New York, 1916); *A Little Book in C Major* (New York, 1916); *A Book of Prefaces* (New York, 1917); *Damn! A Book of Calumny* (New York, 1918); *In Defense of Women* (New York, 1918); *The American Language* (New York, 1919); *Prejudices: First Series* (New York, 1919); *Heliogabalus: A Buffoonery in Three Acts* (New York, 1920); *Prejudices: Second Series* (New York, 1920); *Prejudices: Third Series* (New York, 1922); *Prejudices: Fourth Series* (New York, 1924); ed., *Americana* (New York, 1925); *Selected Prejudices* (London, 1926); *Notes on Democracy* (New York, 1926); *Prejudices: Fifth Series* (New York, 1926); *Prejudices: Sixth Series* (New York, 1927); *James Branch Cabell* (New York, 1927); *Selected Prejudices: Second Series* (London, 1927); ed., *Menckeniana: A Schimpflexicon* (New York, 1928); *Treatise on the Gods* (New York and London, 1930); *Making a President* (New York, 1932); *Treatise on Right and Wrong* (New York, 1934); with others, *The Sunpapers of Baltimore, 1837–1937* (1937); *Happy Days, 1880–1892* (New York, 1940); *Newspaper Days, 1899–1906* (New York, 1941); ed., *A New Dictionary of Quotations on Historical Principles from Ancient and Modern Sources* (New York,

1942); *Heathen Days,* 1890–1936 (New York, 1943); *Christmas Story* (New York, 1946); *A Mencken Chrestomathy* (New York, 1949); *The Vintage Mencken,* ed. by Alistair Cooke (New York, 1955); *A Carnival of Buncombe,* ed. by Malcolm Moos (Baltimore, 1956); *Minority Report: H. L. Mencken's Notebooks* (New York, 1956); *The Bathtub Hoax, and Other Blasts and Bravos from the Chicago Trubune,* ed. by Robert McHugh (New York, 1958); *H. L. Mencken on Music,* ed. by Louis Cheslock (New York, 1961); *The American Scene: A Reader,* ed. by Huntington Cairns (New York, 1965); *H. L. Mencken's Smart Set Criticism,* ed. by William H. Nolte (Ithaca, N.Y., 1968); *The Young Mencken: The Best of His Work,* ed. by Carl Bode (New York, 1973); *A Gang of Pecksniffs, and Other Comments on Newspaper Publishers, Editors and Reporters,* ed. by Theo Lippman, Jr. (New Rochelle, N.Y., 1975); *Mencken's Last Campaign: H. L. Mencken on the 1948 Election,* ed. by Joseph C. Goulden (Washington, D.C., 1976); *A Choice of Days,* ed. by Edward L. Galligan (New York, 1980).

REFERENCES: Charles Angoff, *H. L. Mencken: A Portrait from Memory* (New York, 1956); Carl Bode, *Mencken* (Carbondale, Ill., 1969); John Dorsey, ed., *On Mencken* (New York, 1980); Charles A. Fecher, *Mencken: A Study of His Thought* (New York, 1978); Isaac Goldberg, *The Man Mencken* (New York, 1925); Edgar Kemler, *The Irreverent Mr. Mencken* (Boston, 1950); William Manchester, *Disturber of the Peace: The Life of H. L. Mencken* (New York, 1950); Sara Mayfield, *The Constant Circle: H. L. Mencken and His Friends* (New York, 1968); M. K. Singleton, *H. L. Mencken and the American Mercury Adventure* (Durham, N.C., 1962); Douglas C. Stenerson, *H. L. Mencken: Iconoclast from Baltimore* (Chicago, 1971).

Messick, Henry Hicks (14 Aug. 1922–   ). Hank Messick's work usually deals with a different meaning of the term *syndicate*: his writing as a columnist, investigative reporter, and book author often addressed organized crime.

Messick was born in Happy Valley, North Carolina. He holds a B.A. from the University of North Carolina (1947) and an M.A. from the University of Iowa (1948).

Messick worked as an English professor for Colorado Agricultural and Mechanical College (now renamed Colorado State University) from 1948 to 1951, then from 1951 to 1957 reported for a succession of North Carolina newspapers: the *Waynesville Mountaineer, Durham Herald,* and *Raleigh Times.* He was an investigative reporter for the Louisville (Kentucky) *Courier-Journal* from 1957 to 1963 and a researcher for the Ford Foundation at the University of Louisville from 1963 to 1965. In 1965–1966 he wrote for the *Miami Herald,* and in 1969–1970 he wrote a column for the *Miami Beach Sun.* Messick has been a prolific author of books.

BOOKS: *The Silent Syndicate* (New York, 1967); *Syndicate in the Sun* (New York, 1968); *Syndicate Wife: The Story of Ann Drahmann Coppola* (New York, 1968); *Syndicate Abroad* (New York, 1969); *Secret File* (New York, 1969); *Lansky* (New York, 1971); *John Edgar Hoover: An Inquiry into the Life and Times of John Edgar Hoover and His Relationship to the Continuing Partnership of Crime, Business, and Politics* (New York, 1972); with Bob Goldblatt, *The Mobs and the Mafia: The Illustrated History of Organized Crime* (New York, 1972); *The Beauties and the Beasts: The Mob in Show Business* (New York, 1973); with Joseph L. Nallis, *The Private Lives of Public Enemies* (New

York, 1973); *Gangs and Gangsters: The Illustrated History of Gangs from Jesse James to Murph the Surf* (New York, 1974); *Kidnapping: The Illustrated History* (New York, 1974); with Joseph Barboza, *Barboza* (New York, 1975); *King's Mountain: The Epic of the Blue Ridge "Mountain Men"* (Boston, 1976); with Burt Goldblatt, *The Only Game in Town: An Illustrated History of Gambling* (New York, 1976); *The Politics of Prosecution* (Ottawa, Ill., 1978); *Of Grass and Snow: The Secret Criminal Elite* (Englewood Cliffs, N.J., 1979); *Desert Sanctuary* (Albuquerque, N. Mex., 1987).

Metz, Russell L. (25 Feb. 1919–). Russ Metz is publisher and columnist at the weekly Bath County *News-Outlook* in Owingsville, Kentucky. His column is self-syndicated to roughly fifty papers in the South and Midwest.

Metz was born in Tell City, Indiana, and lists himself as a "Tell City High School graduate (barely)." He fought in World War II for the Royal Canadian Air Force (1940–1941) and the U.S. Air Force (1941–1945).

His newspaper career started at the Cannelton *Telephone* and the Boonville *Enquirer,* both in Indiana, where after a four-year apprenticeship he became a journeyman printer and Linotype operator. From 1950 until 1960 he was managing editor of the Salem (Indiana), *Leader,* after which he purchased the Bath County *News-Outlook.* From 1968 to 1974 he was also publisher and general manager of Cynthiana Publishing in Cynthiana, Kentucky, printing one daily and seventeen weeklies. In 1974 and 1975 Metz was executive editor of Landmark Community Newspapers, Inc.

Metz was cofounder in 1968 of the Kentucky Weekly Newspaper Association; was the 1981 president of the Kentucky Press Association; has been president of the Chamber of Commerce in both Salem, Indiana, and Owingsville, Kentucky; and in 1990 was named to the Kentucky Journalism Hall of Fame. His son, Ken. E. Metz, now edits the *News-Outlook.* In a 1991 interview in *Editor and Publisher,* Metz mentioned that he had written more than twenty-three hundred columns during his long career. His column is mainly given to humor. It formerly appeared under the title "The Pied Typer" and now simply appears under "Russ Metz."

REFERENCES: Tom Riordan, "Russ Metz," *Editor and Publisher* (27 July 1991): 16–17.

Meyer, Ernest Louis (1892–1952). Ernest L. Meyer was a *New York Post* columnist from 1935 to 1941. His work appeared under two column titles: first "Making Light of the Times," later "As the Crow Flies."

Meyer was born in Denver, Colorado, and grew up in Milwaukee, Wisconsin. He attended the University of Wisconsin, where he edited the campus literary magazine.

Meyer wrote and set type for the *Warden Herald* in Washington state before becoming a police reporter for the *Daily News* in Chicago. From 1920 to 1935 he was managing editor, telegraph editor, and columnist ("Making Light of the Times") for the *Capital Times* in Madison, Wisconsin. He then signed on with the *New York Post,* where his column appeared as "As the Crow Flies" until

1941. His column was a whimsical mixture of prose and verse. Meyer's son, Karl E. Meyer, compiled the 1990 book *Pundits, Poets, and Wits: An Omnibus of American Newspaper Columnists.*

BOOKS: *Making Light of the Times* (Madison, Wis., 1928); *"Hey! Yellowbacks!" The War Diary of a Conscientious Objector* (New York, 1930); *Bucket Boy: A Milwaukee Legend* (New York, 1947).

REFERENCES: Karl E. Meyer, *Pundits, Poets, and Wits: An Omnibus of American Newspaper Columnists* (New York, 1990).

Milloy, Courtland (?–   ). Courtland Milloy has written a *Washington Post* column since 1985.

He was born in Shreveport, Louisiana, and is a 1973 graduate of Southern Illinois University. Before going to the *Post* in 1975, Milloy was a police and court reporter for the *Miami Herald.* He worked the same beat for the *Post* until 1983, when he began writing a weekly column. The column began to appear twice weekly in 1985. Milloy is a member of the Trotter Group.

Minor, Wilson Floyd (17 May 1922–   ). Former New Orleans *Times-Picayune* reporter Bill Minor began self-syndicating his political column "Eyes on Mississippi" in 1976 and is now carried by roughly fifty Mississippi papers.

Minor was born in Hammond, Louisiana, and earned the B.S. in journalism from Tulane University in 1922. He was a cub reporter for the *Bogalusa Enterprise,* spent World War II on a destroyer in the Pacific, then worked as a general assignment reporter for the *Times-Picayune* in 1946–1947. He was this paper's state capital correspondent from 1947 to 1976. He was editor and publisher of the short-lived weekly *Capital Reporter* in Jackson, Mississippi, in 1976. In addition to writing his column, Minor works as a commentator on Jackson's WLBT-TV.

REFERENCES: George T. Wilson, "Minor's Major Beat Has Been Civil Rights," *Editor and Publisher* (21 July 1990): 38.

Mitchard, Jacqueline Gay (10 Dec. 1952–   ). Jacqueline Mitchard became a feature columnist for the Life/Style section of the *Milwaukee Journal* in 1984. She continues her column, though she left full-time newspapering to work as a speech writer for Donna Shalala, secretary of health and human services in the Clinton administration.

Mitchard grew up in Chicago and received her bachelor's degree in American literature and secondary education in 1973 from Rockford College. She taught for one year, then was hired as a staff writer for a small chain of weekly newspapers in the Chicago area. She became a columnist and feature writer for the *Capital Times* in Madison, Wisconsin, in 1979 and began in the same capacities for the *Milwaukee Journal* in 1984. She has written a second column, "The Rest of Us," for fourteen years for various Wisconsin papers and is a contributing editor of *Parenting* magazine. She also contributes to *Money* and *TV Guide* and has written two books.

BOOKS: *Mother Less Child* (New York, 1985); *Jane Addams: Pioneer in Social Reform and Activist for World Peace* (Milwaukee, 1991).

Mitchell, Henry Clay, II (24 Nov. 1923–12 Nov. 1993). Henry Mitchell wrote two columns for the *Washington Post:* a gardening column titled "Earthman," which he launched in 1973, and the general column "Any Day," which dates from 1976.

Mitchell was born in Washington, D.C., but grew up in Memphis, Tennessee. He attended the University of Virginia in 1941–1942, then served as a radar operator for the Army Air Forces on an island near New Guinea. He reentered the University of Virginia but left in 1948 to work as a farm laborer on a cotton plantation. He was a copyboy on the *Washington Evening Star* during 1949–1950, and in 1951 he became a reporter for the Memphis *Commercial Appeal.* He remained there as reporter and critic until 1966, after which he was editor of two magazines, *Resorts Management* and *Delta Review.*

The *Washington Post* hired Mitchell as a copy editor in 1970, and in 1973 he began his popular gardening column, adding the general column three years later. Mitchell was a member of the Royal Horticultural Society in London and published three books, two of which are collections of his columns.

BOOKS: *The Essential Earthman: Henry Mitchell on Gardening* (Bloomington, Ind., 1981); with photographer Derry Moore, *Washington, Houses of the Capital* (New York, 1982); *One Man's Garden* (Boston, 1992).

Molloy, Paul George (4 July 1924–   ). Paul Molloy was a columnist for the Memphis (Tennessee) *Commercial Appeal* from 1953 to 1957 and thereafter a radio/television critic for the *Chicago Sun-Times.*

Molloy was born in Winnipeg, Manitoba, Canada. He received the B.A. at the University of Manitoba in 1941, came to the United States in 1950, and became a U.S. citizen in 1956.

Molloy's first newspaper job was with the *Montreal Herald* (1941–1945). From 1946 to 1950 he was with United Press International in Quebec City and in Winnipeg. Molloy became a feature writer at the *Tulsa* [Oklahoma] *Daily-Tribune* for 1950–1951, then was a writer and editor for *Time* magazine in New York City (1951–1953). He has authored four books and has contributed to a number of magazines.

BOOKS: *And Then There Were Eight* (Garden City, N.Y., 1961); *A Pennant for the Kremlin* (Garden City, N.Y., 1964); *All I Said Was . . .* (New York, 1966); *Where Did Everybody Go?* (Garden City, N.Y., 1981).

Montini, E. J. (25 November 1954–   ). E. J. (Ed) Montini is a witty *Arizona Republic* columnist unusually adept at satire.

Montini was born in Pittsburgh, Pennsylvania, and is a graduate of Pennsylvania State University. He held newspaper jobs in Pennsylvania and New Jersey prior to becoming the *Republic's* news columnist in 1986.

Morehouse, Ward (24 Nov. 1897–7 Dec. 1966). Ward Morehouse wrote the column "Broadway After Dark" at the *New York Sun;* the column appeared in several newspaper chains. Morehouse was also a drama critic and playwright.

He was born in Savannah, Georgia, and briefly attended Georgia College. Still in his teens, he became a reporter/sportswriter for the *Savannah Press,* then in 1918 became a reporter for the *Atlanta Journal.* His next move was to New York City as a *Tribune* rewrite man, later as assistant night city editor. He gravitated to theater reviewing and for about five years held two full-time jobs: with the *Tribune* and with the *Brooklyn Times.* In 1926, he joined the *New York Sun* and launched his Broadway column.

Morehouse wrote a number of plays that appeared on Broadway and that were made into movies. His plays include *Gentlemen of the Press* and *Miss Quis.* He authored five books, including the autobiographical *Just the Other Day* (1953).

BOOKS: *Forty-Five Minutes past Eight* (New York, 1939); *American Reveille: The United States at War* (New York, 1942); *George M. Cohan: Prince of the American Theater* (Philadelphia, 1943); *Matinee Tomorrow; Fifty Years of Our Theater* (New York, 1949); *Just the Other Day: From Yellow Pines to Broadway* (New York, 1953).

Morgan, Edward Paddock (23 June 1910–27 Jan. 1993). Although mainly remembered as a broadcaster, Edward P. Morgan did a column for the Newsday Syndicate from 1966 to 1971.

Morgan was born in Walla Walla, Washington, and grew up in the Snake River region of Idaho. He attended the private Intermountain Institute in Weiser, Idaho, and attended Whitman College in Walla Walla, majoring in political science, working for the campus paper, the *Pioneer,* and writing on campus affairs for the Spokane *Spokesman-Review.* He graduated in 1932, cum laude and Phi Beta Kappa.

Morgan accepted a job as an unpaid sports reporter for the *Seattle Star* in 1932 while doing graduate study in political science and journalism at the University of Washington in Seattle. In 1922 he was a police reporter and assistant city editor for the *Seattle Star.* The following year he left the paper to work as a United Press correspondent, and in 1943 he was a *Chicago Daily News* roving correspondent, reporting war news out of Europe. In 1946 he became a foreign correspondent and associate editor of *Collier's* magazine, writing out of Europe and the Middle East. From 1948 to 1950 he free-lanced from Paris.

Morgan's first radio experience was a brief report of an eruption of Mauna Loa, made from a Honolulu station in the 1930s. He also did limited broadcasting for BBC while working in London during World War II. His career as a radio personality did not blossom until 1950, when he returned to the United

States and worked with Edward R. Murrow on "This I Believe," which aired on the CBS station WCAU in Philadelphia. He was news director of CBS in 1954 but liked on-air work better and in 1955 went with ABC. In 1957 he began his nightly "Edward P. Morgan and the News," a mix of news and comment. Other ABC programs on which he appeared through 1975 were "Open Hearing," "Editor's Choice," and "Issues and Answers."

Toward the end of his long career, he worked with public television in its early years. Morgan wrote for numerous magazines, including *Esquire, New Republic, Progressive,* and *Saturday Evening Post.*

BOOKS: Edited with Edward R. Murrow, *This I Believe* (New York, 1952); *Clearing the Air* (Washington, D.C., 1963).

Morgan, Neil Bowen (27 Feb. 1924–   ). *San Diego* [California] *Evening Tribune* columnist Neil Morgan began his general column in 1950. In 1958 it was picked up by the Copley News Service.

Morgan was born in Smithfield, North Carolina, and received the A.B. from Wake Forest College in 1943.

His first job was reporting for the *News & Observer* in Raleigh, North Carolina (1942–1943). He served in the U.S. Navy from 1943 to 1946, after which he became a reporter for the *San Diego Daily Journal* (1946–1950). He became a columnist for the *Evening Tribune* in 1950, travel editor in 1976, and associate editor in 1978.

Morgan has authored several books, mostly about his city and region, and has written for such magazines as *Esquire, Redbook, Reader's Digest,* and *Town and Country.*

BOOKS: *My San Diego* (San Diego, 1951); *Crosstown* (San Diego, 1953); *Know Your Doctor* (Boston, 1953); *Westward Tilt* (New York, 1963); *The Pacific States* (New York, 1967); *The California Syndrome* (Englewood Cliffs, N.J., 1969); with Robert M. Witty, *Marines of the Margarita* (San Diego, 1970); with Judith Morgan, *Island in the Coast: Notes on the Random Encounters of Men and Nature Along a Wild Sonoma Shore* (Sonoma County, Calif., 1974); with Tom Blair, *Yesterday's San Diego* (Miami, Fla., 1976); with Judith Morgan, *California's North Coast: Redwoods, Rain, and Lots of Room* (Washington, D.C., 1977); *Above San Diego: A New Collection of Historical and Original Aerial Photographs of San Diego* (San Francisco, 1990).

Morley, Christopher Darlington (5 May 1890–28 March 1957). Although his reputation rests mainly on his accomplishments as a prolific novelist, essayist, and poet, Morley wrote a column for the *Philadelphia Public Ledger* in 1917, the column "Bowling Green" for the *New York Evening Post* from 1920 to 1923, and a longer-lasting column for the *Saturday Review of Literature* (1924–1941).

Morley was born in Haverford, Pennsylvania, and spent part of his youth in Baltimore. He received the B.A. in 1910 from Haverford College, where he wrote for the *Haverfordian* and made Phi Beta Kappa, and he studied history as a Rhodes Scholar at New College, Oxford, from 1910 to 1913.

His first job was with the publisher Doubleday, Page and Company, the company that would publish most of his books. He became a *Ladies' Home Journal* editor in 1917 and in this same year did a column for the *Philadelphia Public Ledger*. In 1920 he moved to New York City and launched "The Bowling Green," the *New York Evening Post* column, which he moved to the *Saturday Review of Literature* in 1924. In 1934 he used this column to publicize the Baker Street Irregulars, an organization of Sherlock Holmes fanciers that Morley himself founded. He also wrote the column "Trade Winds" for the *Review* until 1939. His columns sometimes promoted promising young writers; examples are Joseph Conrad and Sherwood Anderson.

Morley was a judge for the Book of the Month Club, starting in 1926, and edited an edition of *Bartlett's Familiar Quotations* between 1934 and 1937.

BOOKS: *The Eighth Sin* (Oxford, England, 1912); *Parnassus on Wheels* (Garden City, N.Y., 1917); *Songs for a Little House* (New York, 1917); *Shandygaff* (Garden City, N.Y., 1918); *The Rocking Horse* (New York, 1919); *The Haunted Bookshop* (Garden City, N.Y., 1919); with Bart Haley, *In the Sweet Dry and Dry* (New York, 1919); *Mince Pie* (New York, 1919); *Travels in Philadelphia* (Philadelphia, 1920); *Kathleen* (Garden City, N.Y., 1920); *Hide and Seek* (New York, 1920); *Pipefuls* (Garden City, N.Y., 1920); *Tales from a Rolltop Desk* (Garden City, N.Y., 1921); *Chimneysmoke* (New York, 1921); ed., *Modern Essays* (New York, 1921); *Plum Pudding* (Garden City, N.Y., 1922); *Translations from the Chinese* (New York, 1922); *Where the Blue Begins* (Garden City, N.Y., 1922); *The Power of Sympathy* (Garden City, N.Y., 1923); *Parson's Pleasure* (New York, 1923); *Inward Ho!* (Garden City, N.Y., 1923); *Conrad and the Reporters* (Garden City, N.Y., 1923); with Don Marquis, *Pandora Lifts the Lid* (New York, 1924); *One-Act Plays* (Garden City, N.Y., 1924); *Religio Journalistici* (Garden City, N.Y., 1924); ed., *Modern Essays, Second Series* (New York, 1924); ed., *The Bowling Green: An Anthology of Verse* (Garden City, N.Y., 1924); *Hostages to Fortune* (Haverford, Pa., 1925); *Thunder on the Left* (Garden City, N.Y., 1925); *The Romany Stain* (Garden City, N.Y., 1926); *Good Theatre* (Garden City, N.Y., 1926); *The Arrow* (Garden City, N.Y., 1927); *Pleased to Meet You* (Garden City, N.Y., 1927); *I Know a Secret* (Garden City, N.Y., 1928); *Toulemonde* (Garden City, N.Y., 1928); *Off the Deep End* (Garden City, N.Y., 1928); *Really, My Dear* (New York, 1928); *Seacoast of Bohemia* (Garden City, N.Y., 1929); with Ogden Nash and others, *Born in a Beer Garden, or, She Troupes to Conquer* (New York, 1930); *Rudolph and Amina, or, The Black Crook* (New York, 1930); *John Mistletoe* (Garden City, N.Y., 1931); *Swiss Family Manhattan* (Garden City, N.Y., 1932); *Ex Libris Carissimis* (Philadelphia, 1932); *Human Being* (Garden City, N.Y., 1932); *Mandarin in Manhattan* (Garden City, N.Y., 1933); *Shakespeare and Hawaii* (Garden City, N.Y., 1933); *Internal Revenue* (Garden City, N.Y., 1933); *Hasta la Vista: A Postcard from Peru* (Garden City, N.Y., 1935); *Christopher Morley's Briefcase* (Philadelphia, 1936); *Streamlines* (Garden City, N.Y., 1936); *The Trojan Horse* (Philadelphia, 1937); *History of an Autumn* (Philadelphia and New York, 1938); *Letters of Askance* (Philadelphia and New York, 1939); *Kitty Foyle* (Philadelphia and New York, 1939); *Thorofare* (New York, 1942); *The Middle Kingdom: Poems, 1929–1944* (New York, 1944); *Spirit Level and Other Poems* (Cambridge, Mass., 1946); *The Old Mandarin, More Transla-*

tions from the Chinese (New York, 1947); *The Man Who Made Friends with Himself* (Garden City, N.Y., 1949); *The Ironing Board* (Garden City, N.Y., 1949); with William Rose Benet, *Poetry Package* (New York, 1950); *The Ballad of New York, New York, and Other Poems, 1930–1950* (Garden City, N.Y., 1950); *Gentleman's Relish* (New York, 1955); ed. by Jon Bracker, *Bright Cages: Selected Poems and Translations from the Chinese* (Philadelphia, 1965); ed. by Herman Abromson, *Prefaces Without Books: Prefaces and Introductions to Thirty Books* (Austin, Tex., 1976).

REFERENCES: Babette Hughes, *Christopher Morley, Multi ex Uno* (Seattle, 1927); Alfred P. Lee, *A Bibliography of Christopher Morley* (Garden City, N.Y., 1935); Guy R. Lyle and H. Tatnall Brown, Jr., *A Bibliography of Christopher Morley* (Washington, D.C., 1952); Helen Oakley, *Three Hours for Lunch, The Life and Times of Christopher Morley* (Searingtown, 1976); Mark I. Wallach and Jon Bracker, *Christopher Morley* (Boston, 1976).

Morris, Bob (1949–   ). Bob Morris began writing a column in the *Fort Myers* (Florida) *News-Press* in 1978 and later was a columnist for the *Orlando Sentinel.*

Morris was born in Leesburg, Florida. He attended the University of Florida but left without a degree and lived for half a year on an Israeli kibbutz. Returning to Florida, he signed on as a reporter for the Fort Myers paper and later worked for the *Orlando Sentinel.* Though no longer a full-time columnist, he still contributes his column "Florida Byways" to various Florida papers. He frequently uses his column to poke fun at tourists, especially those from Ohio. His work is often humorous but sometimes is of the more emotional human interest type.

BOOKS: *True Floridians and Other Passing Attractions* (St. Petersburg, Fla., 1981); *Greetings from Florida* (St. Petersburg, Fla., 1982).

Mortimer, Frederick Craig (17 Sept. 1857–27 Jan. 1936). Frederick Mortimer wrote the "Topics of the Times" column for the *New York Times* from 1896 until his retirement in 1926.

Mortimer was born in Waterville, Maine. He received the A.B. from Colby College in 1881, then was hired by the Rochester (New York) *Democrat and Chronicle.* He became assistant city editor of that paper, then took the identical job at the *New York Times.*

In 1896 Mortimer took over a column that had been initiated in the 1860s by William Livinston Alden. Mortimer changed the column title from "Minor Topics" to "Topics of the Times," continuing, as Alden had to offer commentary on news events. The popular column was continued by Simeon Strunsky after Mortimer's retirement. Mortimer also selected the verse that in that era still appeared on the *Times's* editorial page, and he was known for his expertise in medical and scientific news. Colby College awarded him an honorary M.A. degree in 1932.

Moskowitz, Gary (?–   ). Martial arts instructor and former New York City police officer Gary Moskowitz writes an unusual column titled "On the Streets," which he self-syndicates out of Flushing, New York.

Moskowitz has also worked as a high school teacher and social worker. He is president of Barzel Security Systems and founded the Violence Prevention Institute. He has done consulting for the film industry and has hosted a cable TV talk show. His column deals with criminal behavior and crime prevention and sometimes delves into racial tensions, terrorism, and drug abuse. The column originated in the *Jewish Press.*

Mossell, Gertrude Bustill (3 July 1855–21 Jan. 1948). An early African-American woman columnist of note was Gertrude Mossell, who wrote columns for the *New York Age* and four Philadelphia papers.

Mossell was born Gertrude Bustill in Philadelphia. She was a graduate of the Vaux Consolidated Grammar School in that city in 1872. Her valedictory address was published in the *Christian Recorder.*

She taught for seven years in the public schools of Camden, New Jersey; Philadelphia; and Frankfort, Kentucky, then became women's editor for the *New York Freeman* and the *Philadelphia Echo.* Her column in the *New York Age* began in 1885, and her columns also appeared in the *Philadelphia Times,* the Philadelphia *Independent,* and the Philadelphia *Press Republican.* Mossell, by this time married to a Philadelphia physician, specialized in topics relating to race and women's issues, especially suffrage, which she favored. She often signed her work N. F. Mossell.

Mossell helped edit the *Lincoln Alumni Magazine,* wrote two books, and contributed to the *A.M.E. Church Review,* the magazine *Our Women and Children,* two midwestern newspapers, the *Indianapolis World,* and *Indianapolis Freeman.* She advised publishers of black newspapers to increase their visibility by having them sold on the streets by newsboys rather than merely by subscription.

BOOKS: *The Work of Afro-American Women* (Philadelphia, 1894); *Little Dansie's One Day at Sabbath School* (Philadelphia, 1902).

REFERENCES: I. Garland Penn, *The Afro-American Press and Its Editors* (New York, 1891); Roger Streitmatter, *Raising Her Voice: African-American Women Journalists Who Changed History* (Lexington, Ky., 1994): 37–48.

Mowrer, Edgar Ansel (8 March 1892–2 March 1977). Edgar Mowrer was a syndicated columnist with the *New York Post* from 1943 until 1969.

He was born in Bloomington, Indiana, and grew up in Chicago. Mowrer enrolled at the University of Michigan, transferred in 1910 to the University of Chicago, took time out in 1911–1912 to study in Paris at the Sorbonne, then returned to finish his B.A. at the University of Michigan in 1913. He returned to Paris and helped his brother, Paul Mowrer, who headed the *Chicago Daily News* bureau there, to cover some of the early battles of World War I. Instead of the literary career he had envisioned, Edgar Mowrer became a foreign correspondent for the *Daily News.* He won a Pulitzer Prize in 1932 for his dispatches, which appeared in book form just prior to Hitler's rise to power. He was elected president of the Foreign Press Association in the following year. Based in Paris, he covered the Spanish Civil War. In 1940–1941 he wrote for the *Daily News* out of Washington, D.C., and was deputy director of the U.S. Office of Facts and Figures, then interim director of operations for the Office of War Information for the Pacific area. In 1943 he became a columnist at the *New York Post,* a job he held until 1969. From 1957 until 1969 he was also editor in chief of the monthly *Western World.*

Mowrer's forthright commentary got him expelled from Germany, Italy, and the Soviet Union. Throughout his career he was a frequent contributor of magazine articles to such periodicals as *Forum, Nation, Harper's, Foreign Affairs, Saturday Review, Collier's,* and *National Review.* He authored thirteen books.

BOOKS: *Immortal Italy* (New York and London, 1922); *This American World* (New York, 1928); *Sinon: Or the Future of Politics* (London, 1930); *Germany Puts the Clock Back* (New York, 1933); *The Dragon Wakes: A Report from China* (New York, 1939); with Marthe Rajchman, *Global War: An Atlas of World Strategy* (New York, 1943); *Our State Department and North Africa* (Chicago, 1943); *The Nightmare of American Foreign Policy* (New York, 1949); *Challenge and Decision: A Program for the Times of Crisis Ahead, for World Peace Under American Leadership* (New York, 1950); *A Good Time to Be Alive* (New York, 1959); *An End to Make-Believe* (New York, 1961); *Triumph and Turmoil: A Personal History of Our Time* (New York, 1970); with Lilian T. Mowrer, *Umano and the Price of Lasting Peace* (New York, 1973).

REFERENCES: Stuart W. Little, ''Mowrer's Great Events,'' *Saturday Review* 51 (14 September 1968): 145; Lilian Thompson Mowrer, *Journalist's Wife* (New York, 1937).

Murchison, William P. (3 Feb. 1942–   ). William Murchison writes the column ''Main Street U.S.A.'' He has been based at the *Dallas Morning News* since 1973 and is distributed by Creators Syndicate.

Murchison was born in Corsicana, Texas. He studied U.S. and British history and received the B.A. in 1963 from the University of Texas and the M.A. in 1964 from Stanford University.

From 1964 to 1966 he was with the *Corsicana Daily Sun;* he wrote for the *Dallas Times Herald* from 1966 to 1973. He has also contributed to such periodicals as *National Review,* the *Wall Street Journal, American Spectator,* and *Texas Lawyer.*

N

Nachman, Gerald Weil (13 Jan. 1938–). Gerald Nachman has been a columnist since the early 1960s and is known mainly for his humor copy.

He was born in Oakland, California. He received the A.A. from Merritt College in 1958 and the B.A. from San Jose State University in 1960. He began working for the *San Jose Mercury* while still in school. From 1960 to 1963 he wrote a humor column and was a television reviewer for the *Mercury,* then moved to New York City as a *New York Post* feature writer (1964–1966). He returned to California in 1966 as columnist and film critic for the *Oakland Tribune,* then retraced his steps in 1972 to become a feature writer and TV critic for the *New York Daily News.* He is most widely known for the syndicated general humor column he wrote from 1973 to 1979, which at times appeared thrice weekly, at other times twice weekly. The column was titled ''The Single Life'' and was handled by the Universal Press Syndicate. Nachman joined the *San Francisco Chronicle* in 1979 as a columnist and theater critic.

Nachman has published four books and has contributed to such magazines as *Esquire, Cosmopolitan, Saturday Review,* and *Newsweek.*

BOOKS: *The Portable Nachman* (San Jose, Calif., 1960); *Playing House* (Garden City, N.Y., 1978); *Out on a Whim: Some Very Close Brushes with Life* (Garden City, N.Y., 1983); *The Fragile Bachelor* (Berkeley, Calif., 1989).

Naness, Barbara (15 Aug. 1950–). Humor columnist Barbara Naness, news editor of the *Staten Island* [New York] *Register,* self-syndicates ''In a Nutshell.''

Naness was born in Brooklyn, New York. She began work as a free-lance contributor to various newspapers and magazines. Naness was a general assignment reporter for the *Register* from September 1983 to February 1990, when she became that paper's assistant news editor. Her column first appeared in the

Register in February 1984; she began self-syndicating it in 1988. She was named news editor in February 1994.

Nash, Jay Robert (26 Nov. 1937–   ). Most American newspapers are accused of being preoccupied with crime. Robert Nash, who might be called a professional observer of crime, wrote the column "Crime in America" for King Features during part of the 1990s.

Nash was born in Indianapolis, Indiana. He received his B.A. in 1958 at the University of Paris, then returned home to become editor of the *Milwaukee Literary Times* (1960–1962) and of the *Antioch* [Illinois] *News* (1961–1962). He also edited and published the *Literary Times* in Chicago from 1961 to 1970, edited *American Trade Magazines* in Chicago (1962–1966), and edited both *FM Guide* and *ChicagoLand* from 1967 to 1970. He then wrote free-lance and has been president of two book publishing firms since the early 1980s, CineBooks and Crime Books, Inc. His own books, mainly on crime or crime-related topics, make a long list.

BOOKS: *Dillinger: Dead or Alive?* (Chicago, 1970); *Citizen Hoover* (Chicago, 1972); *Bloodletters and Badmen: A Narrative Encyclopedia of American Criminals from the Pilgrims to the Present* (New York, 1973); *On All Fronts* (Western Springs, Ill., 1974); *Darkest Hours: A Narrative Encyclopedia of Worldwide Disasters from Ancient Times to the Present* (Chicago, 1976); *Hustlers and Con Men* (New York, 1976); *Among the Missing: An Anecdotal History of Missing Persons from 1800 to the Present* (New York, 1978); *Murder, America: Homicide in the United States from the Revolution to the Present* (New York, 1980); *Almanac of World Crime* (Garden City, N.Y., 1981); *Crime Movie Quiz Book* (New York, 1981); *The True Crime Quiz Book* (New York, 1981); *A Crime Story* (New York, 1981); *People to See: An Anecdotal History of Chicago's Makers and Breakers* (Piscataway, N.J., 1981); *The Dark Fountain: A Novel of Horror* (New York, 1982); *The Innovators* (Chicago, 1982); *Zanies: The World's Greatest Eccentrics* (Piscataway, N.J., 1982); *The Dillinger Dossier* (Highland Park, Ill., 1983); *Murder Among the Mighty: Celebrity Slayings That Shocked America* (New York, 1983); *Open File: A Narrative Encyclopedia of the World's Greatest Unsolved Crimes* (New York, 1983); *The Toughest Movie Quiz Book Ever* (Chicago, 1983); *Jay Robert Nash's Crime Chronology: A Worldwide Record, 1900–1983* (New York, 1984); *The Mafia Diaries* (New York, 1984); *The Motion Picture Guide* (Chicago, 1985); with Stanley Ralph Ross, *The CineBooks Motion Picture Guide* (New York, 1986); ed., *Encyclopedia of World Crime*, 6 vols. (Wilmette, Ill., 1989–1990).

Neilan, Edward (24 July 1932–   ). Edward Neilan has written three columns since 1974, most recently a self-syndicated column on Asian affairs written from Toyko while working as the *San Francisco Chronicle*'s chief correspondent for Japan.

Neilan was born in Torrance, California. He received the B.A. in journalism and political science from the University of Southern California in Los Angeles and has studied at the Institute of International Education at the University of London and the East-West Center at the University of Hawaii.

From 1960 to 1962 he was special correspondent in Toyko for the *Christian Science Monitor,* from 1962 to 1969 the China and Southeast Asia correspondent in Hong Kong for Copley News Service. Neilan served as State Department correspondent at Copley's Washington bureau (1969–1976) and in 1976 founded the *Asia Mail,* which he edited and published through 1979, the year he became president, publisher, and editor of the *Alexandria Gazette,* at that time one of the two or three oldest dailies in the nation. In 1982 he became foreign editor of the *Washington Times* and in 1986, Northeast Asia bureau chief for the same paper. In 1992 he assumed his present position with the *San Francisco Chronicle.*

Neilan's first column was "Asia Memo," written for the Copley News Service from 1974 to 1982. His second, "Perspectives on the World," appeared in the *Washington Times* from 1984 to 1986, and his third has been self-syndicated out of Toyko since 1992. His columns have appeared in many papers around the world, including the *Tokyo Shimbun,* the *Japan Times,* the *Korea Herald,* the *Jakarta Post,* the *Wellington Evening Post,* the *Johannesburg Star,* and Chile's *El Murcurio.*

Nelson, Lars-Erik (15 Oct. 1941–). Lars-Erik Nelson writes a liberal political/economics/foreign affairs column that since 1993 has been based at *Newsday* and syndicated by the Los Angeles Times Syndicate. Prior to that time it was handled by Tribune Media Services.

Nelson was born in New York City and received his A.B. from Columbia University in 1963.

From 1959 to 1963 he was an editorial assistant at the *New York Herald Tribune* and during 1963–1964 was a Russian translator for *Current Digest.* He next worked as a rewrite man for the Hackensack (New Jersey) *Record* (1965–1966), and from 1966 to 1977 was a Reuters correspondent in London, Moscow, Prague, and Washington, D.C. He wrote for *Newsweek* from 1977 to 1979 and was Washington bureau chief and columnist for the *New York Daily News* from 1979 to 1993, when he joined the staff of *Newsday.* His column appears three times a week.

Newberry, Robert Curtis (20 Feb. 1945–). Robert C. Newberry has written his present column for the *Houston Post* since 1987.

Newberry was born in Port Arthur, Texas, and received the B.A. from the University of Houston in 1967. Before graduation he served as editor of *Sports World* (1964–1965) and as sports editor of the *Houston Informer.*

Working as a *Houston Post* reporter from 1967 to 1972, he was given a variety of beats: city government, police, state news, and sports. He was a copy editor from 1972 to 1980 and assistant news editor from 1980 to 1986, during which years he also wrote feature stories, book reviews, and a weekly column. Since 1987 Newberry has been an editorial writer and thrice-weekly columnist. He pays special attention to issues of importance to the black community and is a member of the National Association of Black Journalists, the Houston Association of Black Journalists, and the Professional Journalism Society Sigma Delta Chi.

Newhouse, Nancy R. (?–   ). Nancy Newhouse has conducted the "Hers" column in the *New York Times* since 1977.

Newhouse was born in Bellingham, Washington, and received the B.A. from Vassar College in 1958.

Her professional background includes senior editor positions at two magazines, *New York Magazine* (1970–1975) and *House & Garden* (1976). Newhouse became style editor and travel editor for the *New York Times* in 1976. In 1977 the "Hers" column, by and about women, but written to be of interest to both sexes, began as a weekly column in the news pages, then switched to the Sunday magazine two times monthly.

BOOKS: *Hers, Through Women's Eyes* (New York, 1985).

Nicholas, Jonathan (25 June 1949–   ). Jonathan Nicholas has been a general interest columnist for the *Oregonian* in Portland since 1982.

Nicholas was born in Merthyr, Tydfil, Wales. He holds the bachelor of social studies degree with joint honors in sociology and political science from the University of Bristol in England (1971). Nicholas refers to his column as "the conscience of Oregon."

Noel, Don O., Jr. (27 Nov. 1931–   ). *Hartford Courant* political columnist Don Noel writes a thrice-weekly column.

Noel was born in Elizabeth, New Jersey, and received a B.A. in American studies from Cornell University in 1954.

For nearly two decades Noel worked for the *Hartford Times,* as reporter (1958–1967), assistant managing editor (1968–1969), editorial page editor (1969–1975), and editor (1974–1975). He then switched media and from 1975 until 1985 was senior correspondent for WFSB-TV 3 in Hartford. In 1985 he returned to newspapering as a columnist for the *Courant.* In 1963 Noel shared in a Pulitzer for the Gannett Group's story "Road to Integration," and in 1966–1967 he was an Alicia Patterson Fellow.

North, Marjorie Mary (21 Oct. 1945–   ). Marjorie North has written a column titled "Let's Talk" for the Sarasota (Florida) *Herald-Tribune* since 1985.

North was born in Mt. Clemens, Michigan, and attended Wayne State University for three years.

She began her career as features editor of the Elizabeth City (North Carolina) *Daily Advance* (1965–1969). From 1977 to 1978 she was news editor, then managing editor of the Brandon (Florida) *News.* and from 1978 to 1979 city editor of the *Leesburg* [Florida] *Commercial.* She joined the *Sarasota Herald-*

Tribune in 1979 as metro editor, was features editor from 1981 to 1985, and began her daily column in 1985. "Let's Talk" focuses on people and on human interest topics.

BOOKS: *Sarasota: A City for All Seasons* (Sarasota, Fla., 1994).

North, Oliver Laurence (7 Oct. 1943–   ). Oliver North is one of those politicians who make use of a syndicated newspaper column to further their political ends. His conservative column is handled by Creators Syndicate.

North was born in San Antonio, Texas. He attended the State University of New York as an English major during 1961–1963. He was admitted to the Naval Academy in 1963, had to delay his studies as a result of an automobile accident, then graduated in 1968 and went immediately to Vietnam, where he served with distinction. From 1970 to 1974 he taught guerrilla tactics at Quantico, then ran a jungle warfare school in Okinawa for the remainder of 1974. From 1975 to 1978 he was a policy analyst at Marine headquarters in Washington, D.C. He was stationed at Camp Lejeune from 1978 to 1980 and spent 1980–1981 at the Command and Staff College in Newport, Rhode Island.

North's rise to prominence began in 1981 when he was assigned to the National Security Council in Washington. He became a Central American specialist during the Reagan administration and apparently originated the idea of overcharging the Iranians for U.S. arms and secretly giving the profits to the Nicaraguan Contras. He was indicted on various counts of conspiring to defraud the government in March 1988 and in 1989 resigned from the Marine Corps to become cofounder of Guardian Technologies in Virginia, a company that makes body armor. In May of that year he was found guilty of obstructing Congress, illegally destroying documents, and accepting an illegal gratuity, but in July 1990 his convictions were reversed or set aside by a federal appeals court. The appeals court was supported by the U.S. Supreme Court in 1991, and special prosecutor Lawrence Walsh dropped all charges against North.

North has emerged from this controversy as one of the 1990s' most colorful figures. Many liberals view him as an opportunistic scoundrel, but conservatives are more likely to see him as a sort of can-do latter-day cowboy who isn't afraid to shoot it out with the Establishment. Either way, he stands out vividly from the usual herd of middle-aged white men in dark suits that dominates American politics, and in 1994 ran a strong race for a Senate seat to represent Virginia. His column argues for mother, God, and country; assails high taxes and government waste; and is music to the ears of the National Rifle Association. The enterprising North has four books to his credit.

BOOKS: *Taking the Stand: The Testimony of Lieutenant Colonel Oliver L. North* (New York, 1987); *The Found Poetry of Lt. Col. Oliver L. North,* comp. by John W. Hart III (Woodland Hills, Calif., 1989); with William Novak, *Under Fire: An American Story* (New York, 1991); with David Roth, *One More Mission: Oliver North Returns to Vietnam* (Grand Rapids, Mich., 1993).

REFERENCES: Ben Bradlee, Jr., *Guts and Glory: The Rise and Fall of Oliver North* (New York, 1988).

Novak, Michael (9 Sept. 1933–). High-powered academic and politically well connected Michael Novak was a syndicated newspaper columnist from 1976 to 1989. Since 1989 he has been a columnist for *Forbes* magazine. He also cofounded *Crisis* magazine in 1982.

Novak was born in Johnstown, Pennsylvania. His A.B., summa cum laude, was from Stonehill College in 1956; his B.T., cum laude, from Rome's Gregorian University in 1958; and his M.A. from Harvard University in 1965. He also studied at Catholic University from 1958 to 1960.

Novak began his academic career as a humanities professor at Stanford University (1965–1968). He taught religion and philosophy at the State University of New York (1968–1973), was provost of Disciplines College (1969–1971), and was associate director of humanities for the Rockefeller Foundation (1973–1974). He was a religion professor at Syracuse University from 1977 to 1979 and has held numerous visiting professorships in addition to work with the United Nations.

Novak was an adviser to and speech writer for R. Sargent Shriver in 1970 and 1972 and did similar work for Edmund Muskie in 1971. He was part of George McGovern's campaign organization in 1972. He has been a prolific author of books and has written widely for scholarly journals and such other periodicals as *Harper's, New Republic, Commentary,* and *Commonweal.* He has served on the editorial boards of *National Review, Motive,* the *World,* and other periodicals. He is one of America's leading Roman Catholic intellectuals and is known for his support of cultural diversity.

BOOKS: *The Tiber Was Silver* (Garden City, N.Y., 1961); *The Experience of Marriage* (New York, 1964); *A New Generation, American and Catholic* (New York, 1964); *The Open Church* (New York, 1964); *A Lay View of the World We Live In* (Stanford, Calif., 1966); *Belief and Unbelief: A Philosophy of Self-Knowledge* (London, 1967); *A Time to Build* (New York, 1967); with Robert McAfee Brown and Abraham J. Heschel, *Vietnam: Crisis of Conscience* (New York, 1967); *American Philosophy and the Future: Essays for a New Generation* (New York, 1968); *A Theology for Radical Politics* (New York, 1969); *The Experience of Nothingness* (New York, 1970); *Naked I Leave: A Novel* (New York, 1970); *Ascent of the Mountain, Flight of the Dove* (New York, 1971); *Politics: Realism and Imagination* (New York, 1971); *All the Catholic People: Where Did All the Spirit Go?* (New York, 1971); *A Book of Element: Reflections on Middle-Class Days* (New York, 1972); *The Rise of the Unmeltable Ethnics: Politics and Culture in the Seventies* (New York, 1972); *Choosing Our King: Powerful Symbols in Presidential Politics* (New York, 1974); *The Joy of Sports* (New York, 1976); *Further Reflections on Ethnicity* (Middletown, Pa., 1977); *The Guns of Lattimer: The True Story of a Massacre and a Trial* (New York, 1978); ed. with Keith P. Dyrud and Rudolph J. Vecoli, *The Other Catholics* (New York, 1978); ed., *Capitalism and Socialism: A Theological Inquiry* (Washington, D.C., 1979); *The Family, America's Hope* (Rockford, Ill., 1979); with William Petersen and Philip Gleason, *Concepts of Ethnicity* (Cambridge, Mass., 1980);

ed., *Democracy and Mediating Structures* (Washington, D.C., 1980); ed., *Liberation South, Liberation North* (Washington, D.C., 1981); *The Spirit of Democratic Capitalism* (New York, 1982); *Confession of a Catholic* (San Francisco, 1983); *Moral Clarity in the Nuclear Age* (Nashville, Tenn., 1983); *Freedom with Justice* (San Francisco, 1984); *Will It Liberate?* (New York, 1986); *Human Rights and the New Realism* (New York, 1986); *Character and Crime: An Inquiry into the Causes of the Virtue of Nations* (Notre Dame, Ind., 1986); *Free Persons and the Common Good* (Lanham, Md., 1989); *This Hemisphere of Liberty: A Philosophy of the Americas* (Washington, D.C., 1990); *The Catholic Ethic and the Spirit of Capitalism* (New York, 1993).

Novak, Robert David Sanders (26 Feb. 1931–   ). Robert D. Novak is a political columnist for Creators Syndicate and is also known for the Washington columns, books, and series of reports he has cowritten with Rowland Evans, Jr.

Novak was born in Joliet, Illinois, and studied at the University of Illinois from 1948 to 1952. Novak's first newspaper job was as a reporter for the *Joliet Herald-News* in Illinois in 1948. While a college student, he also worked for the *Champaign-Urbana Courier* (1951–1952). From 1954 to 1958 he was an Associated Press writer in Lincoln and Omaha, Nebraska; Indianapolis; and Washington, D.C. He worked as D.C. correspondent for the *Wall Street Journal* from 1958 to 1963.

From 1963 to 1966 Novak wrote the Washington column "Inside Report" for the New York Herald Tribune Syndicate, and his column cowritten with Evans was handled by Publisher's Hall Syndicate from 1966.

Novak has worked as a roving editor for *Reader's Digest* and has written for *Esquire, New Republic, National Observer,* and the *Economist.* In addition, he has been a broadcast commentator since the early 1960s. He and Evans issued the *Evans-Novak Political Report,* starting in 1967; the *Evans-Novak Tax Report,* beginning in 1985; and the *Evans-Novak Japan Report* (1989–1992). Novak has authored or coauthored four books on politics and politicians.

BOOKS: *The Agony of the G.O.P.* (New York, 1965); with Rowland Evans, *Lyndon B. Johnson: The Exercise of Power: A Political Biography* (New York, 1966); with Rowland Evans, *Nixon in the White House: The Frustration of Power* (New York, 1971); with Rowland Evans, *The Reagan Revolution* (New York, 1981).

Nye, Edgar Wilson (25 Aug. 1850–22 Feb. 1896). One of the great American humorists of the latter half of the 1800s, Bill Nye wrote columns for Wyoming's *Laramie Boomerang* (1881–1883) and the *New York World* (1887–1896).

He was born in Shirley, Maine, and with his family moved several times— to Buffalo, New York, and to three Wisconsin cities: Milwaukee, Madison, and Hudson. His formal education was limited to a few weeks in a Hudson school and a year at a military academy in River Falls, Wisconsin. He took jobs as a farmer, miller, teacher, and law clerk. Then in 1876 he began writing for the *Hudson Star* and the *Chippawa Falls Weekly Herald.* Unhappy with his work, he traveled westward until his funds ran out—in Cheyenne in Wyoming Territory. There in May 1876 he found a reporting job with the *Sentinel* in the neighboring town of Laramie. Like so many other humor writers who began in newspapering, he was a poor, undisciplined reporter but became popular through the comic twists he gave stories. Today's readers, while recognizing Nye's gift for doing humor copy, would likely find his work full of stereotypes: of Indians, tenderfeet from the effete East, and the like.

Nye combined journalism with civic duties by becoming, in this order, a justice of the peace, a notary public, a U.S. land commissioner, and the postmaster of Laramie. He also read the law, passed the bar examination, and practiced law in Laramie. During the same period, he began writing for the *Denver Tribune* and the *Cheyenne Sun,* later adding the *Detroit Free Press* and the humor magazines *Texas Siftings* and *Puck.*

In 1881 he and some of his fellow Republicans started their own newspaper in answer to the *Laramie Times,* a Democratic sheet. Nye, who was editor, named the paper for his mule, Boomerang. His daily column in the *Laramie Boomerang* gave the little paper far more than local fame. It enjoyed subscriptions from every state and a few other nations and was on the exchange list of many larger papers. Nye soon had a national reputation as a humorist but developed meningitis and was advised to move to a milder climate for his health. He left the *Boomerang* in 1883 and went home to Hudson, Wisconsin for three years of rest. During this period he began writing regularly for the *Boston Globe,* and in 1885 he went on the lecture circuit, at which he was a great success. In 1886 he teamed with the poet James Whitcomb Riley; the two lectured together until 1890. Nye wrote two successful Broadway plays and in 1887 moved to New York City to begin a column for the *New York World.* Because of health problems, he left New York in March 1891 and moved to Asheville, North Carolina. He kept up a column in the *Sunday World* and, via the American Press Humor Association, syndicated it to around seventy papers.

Nye built a large frame house next to the fabulous Biltmore estate outside Asheville and in typical Nye fashion wrote in his column about his "farmer neighbor," G. W. Vanderbilt II. His columns and other humorous writings have worn better than those of many of his contemporaries, who wrote in hayseed dialect and poked fun at passing political events. Nye's themes were often of the timeless sort, addressing the human condition.

BOOKS: *Bill Nye and Boomerang* (Chicago, 1881); *Forty Liars, and Other Lies* (Chicago, 1882); *Boomerang Shots* (London and New York, 1884); *Hits and Skits* (London and New York, 1884); *Baled Hay: A Drier Book than Walt Whitman's "Leaves o' Grass"* (Chicago and New York, 1884); *Bill Nye's Cordwood* (Chicago, 1887); *Remarks* (Chicago, 1887); with James Whitcomb Riley, *Nye and Riley's Railway Guide* (Chicago, 1888); *Bill Nye's Chestnuts Old and New: Latest Gathering* (Chicago and New York, 1888); *Bill Nye's Thinks* (Chicago, 1888); *An Aristocrat in America* (New York, 1888); *An Almanac for 1891* (New York, 1890); *Bill Nye's Red Book* (Chicago, 1891); *Sparks from the Pen of Bill Nye* (Chicago and New York, 1891); *Bill Nye's History of the United States* (Philadelphia, 1894); *Bill Nye's History of England from the Druids to the Reign of Henry VIII* (Philadelphia, 1896); *A Guest at the Ludlow and Other Stories* (Indian-apolis and Kansas City, 1897); *Bill Nye, His Book* (Chicago, 1900); *Bill Nye's Western Humor,* ed. by T. A. Larson (Lincoln, Neb., 1968); *Bill Nye's Grim Jokes* (Chicago, n.d.).

REFERENCES: Walter Blair, *The Background of Bill Nye in American Humor,* Ph.D. Dissertation, University of Chicago, 1931; Diane Elissa Heestand, *The Writing of Bill Nye in Laramie,* M.A. Thesis, University of Wyoming, 1968; David B. Kesterson, *Bill Nye* (Edgar Wilson Nye) (Boston, 1981); Kesterson, *Bill Nye: The Western Writings* (Boise, Idaho, 1976); Frank Wilson Nye, *Bill Nye: His Own Life Story* (New York, 1926).

O _____

O'Brian, Jack (1921–). Jack O'Brian's column "Voice of Broadway" was handled by the King Features Syndicate beginning in 1967.

O'Brian's newspaper career began at the *Buffalo* [New York] *Times* in 1939. In 1940 he relocated to the *New York World-Telegram* but later that same year returned to Buffalo and the *Courier-Express.* Then, in 1943, he joined the Associated Press as a columnist/critic, and in 1949 he became a columnist for the *New York Journal-American.* He continued this column until 1967, when he began the Broadway column for King Features. He wrote one book.

BOOKS: *The Great Godfrey* (New York, 1951).

O'Hara, John Henry (31 Jan. 1905–11 April 1970). John O'Hara's fame rests solidly on his short stories and novels, but he also had considerable experience at column writing. He wrote two newspaper columns, three magazine columns, and, as "Franey Delaney," a radio column.

O'Hara was born in Pottsville, Pennsylvania. His formal education was limited to study at Niagara Preparatory School in Niagara Falls, New York.

In his youth, O'Hara apparently worked as a reporter in Pottsville, then in 1927 went to Chicago, where he held a variety of menial jobs, none of which involved writing. He relocated to New York City and worked as night rewrite man for the *New York Daily Mirror,* movie critic for the *New York Morning Telegraph,* radio columnist using the air name "Franey Delaney," and secretary to the columnist Heywood Broun.

O'Hara also worked as managing editor of the *Pittsburgh* [Pennsylvania] *Bulletin-Index,* was a Warner Brothers press agent, and from 1934 through the mid-1940s was a film writer.

His newspaper columns were "Sweet and Sour," a weekly feature in the

Trenton [New Jersey] *Sunday Times-Advertiser* (December 1953–June 1954), and the weekly "My Turn" in *Newsday* (October 1964–October 1965). His magazine columns were "Entertainment Week," appearing weekly in *Newsweek* (July 1940–February 1942), "Appointment with O'Hara," weekly in *Collier's* (February 1954–September 1956), and "The Whistle Stop," monthly in *Holiday* (September 1966–May 1967).

O'Hara's columns pale, of course, in comparison to his roughly four hundred short stories and fifteen novels, which made him one of the most popular writers of his time.

BOOKS: *Appointment in Samarra* (New York, 1934); *The Doctor's Son and Other Stories* (New York, 1935); *Butterfield 8* (New York, 1935); *Hope of Heaven* (New York, 1939); *Files on Parade* (New York, 1939); *Pal Joey* (New York, 1940); *Pipe Night* (New York, 1945); *Here's O'Hara* (New York, 1946); *Hellbox* (New York, 1947); *A Rage to Live* (New York, 1949); *All the Girls He Wanted and Other Stories* (New York, 1949); *The Farmers Hotel* (New York, 1951); *Sweet and Sour* (New York, 1954); *Ten North Frederick* (New York, 1955); *A Family Party* (New York, 1956); *Selected Short Stories of John O'Hara* (New York, 1956); *The Great Short Stories of John O'Hara* (New York, 1956); *From the Terrace* (New York, 1958); *Ourselves to Know* (New York, 1960); *Sermons and Soda-Water,* 3 vols. (New York, 1960); *Five Plays* (New York, 1961); *Assembly* (New York, 1961); *The Big Laugh* (New York, 1962); *The Cape Cod Lighter* (New York, 1962); *Elizabeth Appleton* (New York, 1963); *The Hat on the Bed* (New York, 1963); *49 Stories* (New York, 1963); *The Horse Knows the Way* (New York, 1964); *The Lockwood Concern* (New York, 1965); *My Turn* (New York, 1966); *Waiting for Winter* (New York, 1966); *The Instrument* (New York, 1967); *And Other Stories* (New York, 1968); *Lovey Childs: A Philadelphian's Story* (New York, 1969); *The O'Hara Generation* (New York, 1969); *The Ewings* (New York, 1972); *The Time Element and Other Stories* (New York, 1972); *A Cub Tells His Story* (Iowa City, Iowa, 1974); *Good Samaritan and Other Stories* (New York, 1974); *"An Artist Is His Own Fault,"* ed. by Matthew J. Bruccoli (Carbondale, Ill., 1977); *The Second Ewings* (Bloomfield Hills, Mich., 1977); *Two by O'Hara* (New York and London, 1979); *Collected Stories of John O'Hara,* ed. by Frank MacShane (New York, 1984).

REFERENCES: Charles Bassett, "John O'Hara: Irishman and American," *John O'Hara Journal* 1 (Summer 1979): 1–81; Matthew J. Bruccoli, *The O'Hara Concern: A Biography of John O'Hara* (New York, 1975); Finis Farr, *O'Hara: A Biography* (Boston, 1972); Sheldon Grebstein, *John O'Hara* (New York, 1966); Frank MacShane, *The Life of John O'Hara* (New York, 1980); Charles Walcutt, *John O'Hara* (Minneapolis, 1969).

Ojampa, Brian (4 August 1949–   ). Brian Ojampa is columnist, general assignment reporter, and feature writer for the *Mankato* [Minnesota] *Free Press.*

Originally from Austin, Minnesota, Ojampa received a degree in sociology from Winona State University and later a journalism degree from Mankato State University. His column appears once a week, and he is also the paper's writing coach.

O'Neill, Brian Robert (22 March 1956–   ). Brian O'Neill has been a general columnist since 1983 and is currently with the *Pittsburgh Post-Gazette.*

O'Neill was born in Flushing, New York, and received the B.A. in English and newspaper journalism from Syracuse University in 1978.

After a year as city hall reporter for Virginia's *Danville Register* (1978–1979), O'Neill joined the *Roanoke Times and World News,* first as a New River Valley bureau reporter, covering business and government (1980–1981), then as a feature writer (1982–1983), and finally as a columnist (1983–1988). He joined the *Pittsburgh Press* as a columnist in 1988 and took the same position with the *Pittsburgh Post-Gazette* in 1993.

O'Reilly, Jane (5 April 1936–   ). Jane O'Reilly wrote a weekly column syndicated by the Newspaper Enterprise Association from 1976 to 1978.

O'Reilly was born in St. Louis, Missouri. She received the B.A. from Radcliffe College in 1958 and began working as a free-lance writer. From 1968 to 1975 she was a contributing editor for *New York* magazine, after which she began her column. She contributed to such magazines as *Ms., Atlantic,* and *New Republic* and has authored one book on feminism and coauthored another.

BOOKS: *The Girl I Left Behind* (New York, 1980); with Barbara Ferraro and Patricia Hussey, *No Turning Back: Two Nuns' Battle with the Vatican over Women's Right to Choose* (New York, 1990).

Overstreet, Sarah (?–   ). Sarah Overstreet has been a weekly viewpoint columnist for Newspaper Enterprise Association since 1987.

Overstreet, born in Springfield, Missouri, attended Southwest Missouri State University. She free-lanced for the local paper while a student, then after graduation, worked as an English and art teacher. She got into journalism in 1979 at the *Springfield Leader and Press,* for which she was a reporter and columnist until 1987. She started the Southwest Missouri Speakers Bureau, is public access manager for TeleCable in Springfield, and hosts a cable show called "Springfield Scene." Prior to her TeleCable job, she was a reporter for KSPR-TV news. Overstreet's column is devoted to social and political issues.

P ——————————————————

Packard, Vance Oakley (22 May 1914–   ). Known primarily for his books of popular investigative sociology, Vance Packard was also a columnist for about a year with the *Boston Record* (1937–1938).

Packard was born in Granville Summit, Pennsylvania. He received the B.S. in 1936 from Pennsylvania State College and the M.A. in 1937 from Columbia University.

In 1936 Packard worked as a reporter for the *Centre Daily Times* in State College, Pennsylvania. After a year as a *Record* columnist, he worked as a feature writer and editor for the Associated Press Feature Service in New York City (1938–1942) and as a writer/editor for *American* magazine (1942–1956). He was a staff writer for *Collier's* in 1956. Packard also taught journalistic writing at Columbia University from 1941 to 1944. After the success of his 1957 book *The Hidden Persuaders,* a look at the use of motivational research in advertising, Packard retired from full-time newspaper and magazine work to concentrate on his future as a book author. He did, however, continue to make occasional contributions to such magazines as *Atlantic, Saturday Review, Saturday Evening Post,* and *McCall's.*

BOOKS: With Clifford R. Adams, *How to Pick a Mate, the Guide to a Happy Marriage* (New York, 1946); *Animal IQ: The Human Side of Animals* (New York, 1950); *The Hidden Persuaders* (New York, 1957); *The Status Seekers* (New York, 1959); *The Waste Makers* (New York, 1960); *The Pyramid Climbers* (New York, 1962); *The Naked Society* (New York, 1964); *The Sexual Wilderness* (New York, 1968); *A Nation of Strangers* (New York, 1972); *The People Shapers* (Boston, 1977); *Our Endangered Children: Growing Up in a Changing World* (Boston, 1983); *The Ultra Rich: How Much Is Too Much?* (Boston, 1989).

REFERENCES: Daniel Horowitz, *Vance Packard and American Social Criticism* (Chapel Hill, N.C., 1994).

Page, Clarence Eugene (2 June 1947–). Clarence Page is a columnist for the *Chicago Tribune* and a political commentator and news analyst for Chicago's station WGN-TV.

Page was born in Dayton, Ohio, and received the B.S. in journalism from Ohio University in 1969.

He was a reporter and later city editor for the *Chicago Tribune* (1969–1980) and has been director of community affairs for Chicago station WBBM-TV since 1980. Since 1984 he has been a *Tribune* columnist and member of the paper's editorial board. In 1972 he was part of a *Tribune* task force that won a Pulitzer Prize for a series on vote fraud, and he won his own Pulitzer for commentary in 1989. Page is a member of the Chicago Association of Black Journalists and the Chicago Academy of Television Arts and Sciences.

Palmer, L. F. (?–). Lu Palmer was a syndicated *Chicago Tribune* black-affairs columnist whose column appeared in more than one hundred papers. He chose to specialize in this topic because of his conviction that race was and would continue to be the nation's number-one story.

Palmer was born in Newport News, Virginia, and was a sociology graduate of Virginia Union University. He went on to receive a master's in journalism at Syracuse University and began work on a Ph.D. at the University of Iowa but dropped out of that program to become a *Chicago Defender* reporter.

During the 1950s, Palmer worked as a hospital public information officer in Chicago and was news bureau director for Fisk University in Nashville, Tennessee. He then returned to newspaper work, this time as a rewrite man on the *Chicago American,* from which he eventually moved to the *Chicago Daily News.* He also did a radio news analysis program, "Lu's Notebook," in Chicago.

REFERENCES: M. L. Stein, *Blacks in Communications* (New York, 1972): 48–51.

Palomo, Juan R. (7 July 1946–). Juan Palomo, who includes on his résumé that he once won the "Most Infuriating Columnist" award in Houston, Texas, has been an op-ed columnist and editorial writer for the *Houston Post* since September 1991.

Palomo grew up in Crystal City, Texas. He received the A.A. from Southwest Texas Junior College in 1967, the B.S. in art education from Southwest Texas State University in 1970, and the M.A. in journalism and public affairs from American University in 1980.

From 1970 to 1972 he taught art at San Marcos High School, then in January 1972 became a reporter for *La Otra Voz* in San Marcos. He worked as reporter/editor for the *Hays County Citizen* in the same city (1972–1976) and for a four-month period in 1976 was assistant press director for the Carter-Mondale campaign in Austin. He was assistant to the publisher of Central Texas Newspapers from 1977 to 1978, then press aide and speech writer for Warren Harding's campaign for Texas state treasurer. After graduate school in Washington, D.C., he became a general assignment reporter for the *Houston Post* in October 1979. From June 1981 to July 1982 he was a *Post* political reporter; for the remainder of 1982, a reporter for the national desk of *USA Today*. He returned to the *Post* in February 1983 as general assignment reporter and was that paper's Caribbean and Central America correspondent in 1984 and 1985, then Washington bureau reporter (1985–1990). From October 1990 to August 1991 Palomo was a *Post* metro columnist. He was fired on 30 August over disagreements with management concerning his revealing that he is gay but was rehired shortly thereafter. His column has appeared on the op-ed page since September 1991. He taught journalism as an adjunct instructor at the University of Houston in 1992, has won numerous writing awards, and served as national director of the National Lesbian and Gay Journalists Association from 1991 to 1993. His general interest column often emphasizes politics, gay/lesbian issues, and items of interest to the Hispanic community. Palomo has also written for such periodicals as *Texas Observer, Quill, Vista* magazine, and *Outlook*.

REFERENCES: Tony Case, "Fired, Rehired," *Editor and Publisher* (14 September 1991): 14, 35.

Parrillo, Rosemary (7 September 1951–). Rosemary Parrillo has been a general-interest metro columnist for the *Courier-Post* in Cherry Hill, New Jersey, since 1987. Before that time, she spent a decade on the paper's metro desk as night editor, regional editor, and projects editor.

Parrillo's column ranges from the serious to the whimsical—from interviews with the governor of her state and accounts of alcoholics fighting to stay on the wagon to her own efforts in weight loss or an interview with the world's smallest woman. More often than not, her column is humorous, whatever the subject. One hundred of her columns were published in book form in 1993.

BOOKS: *Welcome to Exit 4: Enter at Own Risk* (Sicklerville, N.J., 1993).

Parris, John A. (23 Nov. 1914–). *Asheville* [North Carolina] *Citizen-Times* columnist John Parris is known for his weekly column and for the books he has written about the North Carolina mountains.

Parris was born in the mountain town of Sylva, North Carolina. He began his newspaper career at age thirteen as a reporter for the *Jackson County Journal* in Sylva and as Sylva correspondent for the *Asheville Citizen-Times*. He joined the United Press in Raleigh, North Carolina, in 1934, and later moved to New York City as a feature writer. He returned to his native state as a roving correspondent for the *Winston-Salem Journal-Sentinel*, then a year later was rehired by United Press as a cable editor. In 1941 he was posted to London to cover the diplomatic beat, and in 1944 he covered the invasion of North Africa.

Next Parris switched to the Associated Press as a London-based diplomatic correspondent and in 1946 relocated to New York to cover the United Nations.

He left wire service work in 1947 and returned to the North Carolina mountains. After writing *The Cherokee Story* (1950), he became public relations director for the Cherokee Historical Association. In February 1955 he became a columnist for the Asheville paper; his column, "Roaming the Mountains," specializes in mountain legends, people, stories, and traditions.

BOOKS: With Ned Russell, *Springboard to Berlin* (New York, 1943); *The Cherokee Story* (Asheville, N.C., 1950); *Roaming the Mountains with John A. Parris* (Asheville, N.C., 1955); *My Mountains, My People* (Asheville, N.C., 1957); *Mountain Bred* (Asheville, N.C., 1967); *These Storied Mountains* (Asheville, N.C., 1972).

Parsons, Louella Oettinger (6 Aug. 1893–9 Dec. 1972). Hollywood gossip columnist Louella Parsons began her first movie column in 1914 at the *Chicago Record-Herald.* From 1922 to 1965 she wrote her column for the Hearst newspapers.

She was born Louella Oettinger in Freeport, Illinois. During high school, in or around 1909, she was drama editor and assistant city editor of the *Dixon Morning Star* in Dixon, Illinois. She sold a movie script, *Chains,* to the Essanay Company in 1912. Her script became a one-reel film starring Francis X. Bushman, and she was hired by Essanay as a story editor. In 1914 she moved to Chicago, became a reporter on the *Tribune,* and later that year began writing a movie column for the *Chicago Record-Herald.* When publisher William Randolph Hearst bought that paper in 1918, he let Parsons go but soon rehired her after discovering that she had written complimentary remarks about his mistress, Marion Davies. Later in 1918, Parsons moved to New York City and became film critic for the *Morning Telegraph* in addition to writing her column, which was syndicated to the Hearst papers. Like the other early Hollywood columnists, she reported romances and divorces of the stars, wrote up (and gave) glittery parties, tried to give her readers inside information on the film industry, and feuded with rival columnists, especially Hedda Hopper. Her column appeared in more than four hundred papers at its zenith.

In 1926 she relocated to Hollywood, where she continued writing her column until 1965. She extended her reach by radio, starting in 1928. Her most successful radio program was "Hollywood Hotel," which premiered in 1934 and ran until 1938. She also reviewed movies for *Cosmopolitan,* wrote for *Modern Screen* and *Photoplay,* and authored four books.

BOOKS: *How to Write for the "Movies"* (Chicago, 1915); *Jean Harlow's Life Story* (New York, 1937); *The Gay Illiterate* (Garden City, N.Y., 1944); *Tell It to Louella* (New York, 1963).

REFERENCES: George Eells, *Hedda and Louella* (New York, 1972).

Parton, Sara Payson Willis (9 July 1811–10 Oct. 1872). Sara Parton was one of the earliest U.S. columnists, writing as "Fanny Fern" for the *New York Ledger* from 1855 until just prior to her death in 1872. She is also remembered as an early feminist and as the first reviewer to extol the poetry of Walt Whitman.

Parton was born in Portland, Maine, and as a child moved to Boston with her family. Her father founded a religious paper, the *Boston Recorder,* in 1816, and her older brother, Nathaniel Parker Willis, became a recognized poet and was coeditor of the *New York Mirror* and editor of the *American Monthly Magazine.* Sara Willis attended Catherine Beecher's Young Ladies' Seminary in Hartford, Connecticut, and wrote essays for another of her father's periodicals, *Youth's Companion.* After two unsuccessful marriages, she began in 1851 to write free-lance as ''Fanny Fern'' for such magazines as the *True Flag,* the *Mother's Assistant,* and the *Olive Branch* (as ''Olivia Branch'' in this one). Her work was collected and republished in three highly successful books, and in or around 1855, she moved to New York City, where Robert Bonner, publisher of the *New York Ledger,* paid her $100 per weekly column. She wrote for the *Ledger* for the next twenty years and was also a frequent contributor to other newspapers.

She married a third time, this time to a fellow writer. Sara Parton is remembered as an advocate of women's rights, an able satirist of mankind's many foibles, and a writer whose stories for children and sentimental treatment of home life were in keeping with the times in which she lived.

BOOKS: *Fern Leaves from Fanny's Portfolio* (Auburn, N.Y., first series, 1853; second series, 1854); *Little Ferns for Fanny's Little Friends* (Auburn, N.Y., 1854); *Ruth Hall: A Domestic Tale of the Present Time* (New York, 1855); *Rose Clark* (New York, 1856); *The Play-Day Book: New Stories for Little Folks* (New York, 1856); *Fresh Leaves* (New York, 1857); *A New Story Book for Children* (New York, 1864); *Folly As It Flies* (New York, 1868); *Ginger-Snaps* (New York, 1870); *Caper-Sauce: A Volume of Chit-Chat About Men, Women, and Things* (New York, 1872); *Fanny Fern: A Memorial Volume,* ed. by James Parton (New York, 1873).

REFERENCES: Florence B. Adams, *Fanny Fern* (West Trenton, N.J., 1966); Fanny Fern, *The Life and Beauties of Fanny Fern* (Philadelphia, 1855); Elizabeth B. Schlesinger, ''Fanny Fern: Our Grandmothers' Mentor,'' *New York Historical Society Quarterly* (October 1954).

Patinkin, Mark (12 January 1953–). Mark Patinkin has written a column for the *Providence* [Rhode Island] *Journal-Bulletin* since 1979. He is syndicated nationally by the Scripps-Howard News Service.

Patinkin was born in Chicago and earned the B.A. from Middlebury College in 1974.

He has been with the Providence paper since 1979; his column appears four times a week and couples humor and human interest. He also hosts a Sunday morning interview show on Channel 10 TV in Providence. Patinkin's work has taken him on extended trips abroad to Africa, Eastern Europe, and the Middle East. These travels produced not only columns, but two books.

BOOKS: *An African Journey* (Providence, R.I., 1985); with Ira C. Magaziner, *The Silent War: Inside the Global Business Battles of America's Future* (New York, 1989).

Patterson, Eugene Corbett (15 Oct. 1923–   ). Gene Patterson wrote a daily column in the *Atlanta Constitution* from June 1960 until 1968, the years in which he was also editor of the *Journal and Constitution.* Later, as chief executive officer of the *St. Petersburg* [Florida] *Times,* he wrote a Sunday column for that paper (1978–1988).

Patterson was born in Valdosta, Georgia. As a boy he worked part-time for the *Adel News* and worked on his high school paper. He attended North Georgia College from 1940 to 1942, editing the school newspaper, then transferred to the University of Georgia, where he received the A.B. in journalism in 1943. He served in World War II as a tank platoon leader in Gen. George Patton's Third Army, after which he became an army pilot.

He returned to civilian life in 1947 and began reporting, first for the Temple (Texas) *Daily Telegram,* then for the *Macon* [Georgia] *Telegraph.* He next was hired by the United Press in Atlanta and in 1948 became manager for South Carolina. From 1949 to 1953 he was night bureau manager in New York City, then was stationed in London for three years.

In 1956 Patterson was made executive editor of the *Atlanta Journal and Constitution* under Ralph McGill. After McGill's retirement in 1960, Patterson moved up to editor in chief and replaced his former boss as seven-days-a-week columnist and editorial writer. He won the Pulitzer Prize for editorial writing in 1967, then in 1968 became managing editor of the *Washington Post* after disagreements with *Constitution* executives. His three years with the *Post* were difficult because of tension between him and head editor Ben Bradlee. During Patterson's time with the *Post,* the paper was involved in the Pentagon Papers affair.

In 1971 Patterson resigned from the *Post* and taught political science at Duke University, and in 1972 he was picked to succeed Nelson Poynter as editor of the *St. Petersburg* [Florida] *Times.* He also was editor of Poynter's other periodical, the *Congressional Quarterly.* When Poynter died in 1978, Patterson replaced him as CEO of the St. Petersburg Times Company. He also wrote a Sunday column for the *Times.* He was known as a proponent of increasing the hiring of minorities and was president of the American Society of Newspaper Editors in 1977–1978. He retired from the *Times* in 1988.

REFERENCES: Tom Kelly, *The Imperial Post: The Meyers, the Grahams and the Paper That Rules Washington* (New York, 1983); Chalmers M. Roberts, *In the Shadow of Power: The Story of the Washington Post* (Cabin John, Md., 1989); Nicholas von Hoffman, "The Night They Wore Old Gene Down," *ASNE Bulletin* (August 1977): 23.

Paul, Maury Henry Biddle (14 April 1890–17 July 1942). Maury Paul was society editor and columnist for the *New York Evening Mail* (1918–1923) and the *New York Journal-American* (1919–1942). He was better known by his byline, Cholly Knickerbocker, and appears to have been the most read and highest paid society columnist of the early 1900s.

Paul was reportedly born in Philadelphia, though his origins are anything but clear. He attended the University of Pennsylvania but did not graduate. Prior to finding his proper niche in life, he worked in a typefounder's office and as a salesman for Philadelphia's posh jewelry store Bailey, Banks & Biddle. His entry into journalism was in 1913 as society editor for the *Philadelphia Times.* When owner Frank Munsey shut this paper down in 1914, Paul moved to another Munsey paper, the *New York Press,* as a society reporter. When the *Press* was merged with the *New York Morning Sun,* Paul left journalism for a brief career as a Wall Street bond salesman, later writing society news part-time for the *New York Evening Post.* He eventually added a third job writing for the *New York Evening Mail,* signing his work in the *Mail* with a woman's name, Dolly Madison. At other times he wrote as Polly Stuyvesant (in the *New York Morning Telegraph*) and as Billy Benedick (in the *New York Evening Journal*). In 1919, he joined Hearst's *New York Journal-American,* writing as Cholly Knickerbocker; it was 1922, however, before he began writing exclusively for Hearst, apparently thanks to Hearst's longtime mistress, Marion Davies, who enjoyed Paul's work.

As Cholly Knickerbocker, Paul chronicled the moneyed activities of the Old Guard, and the goings-on of New York's lesser socialites, for whom Paul coined the term "café society." The columnist used innumerable features, or recurring sections of his column, such as "Ask Cholly," for what purported to be questions sent in by readers: "Many Happy Returns," for wedding anniversary material on the rich and famous; "First Families," a genealogy feature run complete with the family's coat of arms; and "Tragedies of Society" on unhappy events in the lives of society figures.

Working in the era of "society with an upper-case *S,*" Paul, with his outrageous expressions and chit-chat style, was a considerable financial success, as evidenced by his Rolls Royce, his Manhattan penthouse, and his Connecticut country estate.

REFERENCES: Eve Brown, *Champagne Cholly: The Life and Times of Maury Paul* (New York, 1947); Margaret Case Harriman, "Dolly and Polly, Billy and Cholly," *New Yorker* (16 October 1937): 23–27; (23 October 1937): 22–27.

Payne, Ethel L. (14 Aug. 1911–28 May 1991). Ethel Payne's journalistic reputation derives mainly from her reporting of the civil rights movement for the *Chicago Defender,* but late in life, from 1982 to 1985, she self-syndicated a column to a number of black newspapers around the nation.

Payne was born in Chicago. She had youthful hopes of becoming a lawyer yet was financially able to attend college only briefly. She was a clerk at the Chicago Public Library, then in 1948 became a hostess for an Army Special Services club in Japan. Excerpts from her diary were published by *Chicago Defender* reporter Alex Wilson, and her accounts of illegal discrimination against black soldiers caused the *Defender's* circulation to rise. Payne was offered a feature writing job by the *Defender's* editor, Louis E. Martin, in 1951. She accepted but soon gravitated to hard news coverage—prior to the Supreme Court's landmark decision in *Brown* v. *Board of Education* in 1954. She irritated President Dwight Eisenhower by asking pointed questions at press conferences and was called on the carpet by White House Press Secretary James Hagerty. Columnist Drew Pearson rose to her defense and accused Hagerty of harassing Payne.

Payne went on to cover the Montgomery, Alabama, bus boycott and the violent civil rights clashes in Little Rock, Arkansas. She also interviewed and profiled the Reverend Martin Luther King, Jr. When President Lyndon Johnson signed the Civil Rights Act of 1964 and the Voting Rights Act of 1965, Payne was the only black woman journalist invited to the signings.

She went to Vietnam in 1966 to write about the experiences of black American troops there and in 1969 covered the civil war in Nigeria. In the 1970s, she traveled with Secretary of State Henry Kissinger on a six-nation African tour. She also became the first black woman to work as a commentator on a national network, CBS (1972–1982). She appeared first on "Spectrum," then on "Matters of Opinion." She was named associate editor of the *Chicago Defender* and in that position was placed in charge of local news coverage until in 1978 she ended her twenty-seven-year association with the paper and launched her column at age seventy. One of her last campaigns was joining the effort to gain the release of Nelson Mandela. She was sometimes called the "first lady of the black press."

REFERENCES: Rodger Streitmatter, *Raising Her Voice: African-American Women Journalists Who Changed History* (Lexington, Ky., 1994): 118–128.

Payton, Brenda (24 Aug. 1952–   ). Brenda Payton writes a general-interest column for California's *Oakland Tribune.*

Payton was born in Omaha, Nebraska. She earned the B.A. in 1973 at Pomona College and the M.A. in 1975 at the Boston University School of Public Communication. She began her career at the *New Bedford Standard Times* in 1975, then moved to the *Boston Phoenix* later that same year. In 1977 she moved again, this time to the *San Francisco Examiner,* and in 1980, she joined the *Oakland Tribune.*

Her column emphasizes social issues and local politics and frequently employs humor. She also was associate producer and director of a 1992 PBS documentary about lending discrimination, "Your Loan Is Denied."

Pearson, Andrew Russell (13 Dec. 1879–1 Sept. 1969). Drew Pearson, controversialist and Washington socialite, combined the techniques of the gossip columnist with those of the political pundit in his widely syndicated column "Washington Merry-Go-Round."

Pearson was born in Evanston, Illinois, and, like his professor father, became a Quaker. He attended Phillips Exeter Academy and in 1919 was a Phi Beta Kappa graduate of Swarthmore College, where he was editor of the school paper, the *Phoenix,* and was founder of the Intercollegiate Press Association. He worked with his father in Chautauqua, first as a helper, then as a lecturer. He spent two years working for the British Red Cross in the Balkans and for the American Friends Service Committee in Serbia, Albania, and Montenegro. Pearson returned home in 1921 and spent a year teaching industrial geography at the University of Pennsylvania, after which he traveled around the world, supporting himself by writing for newspapers and news syndicates. In 1924 he taught briefly for Columbia University, then returned to Asia for more travel.

In 1926 Pearson became foreign editor of the *United States Daily,* continuing to travel abroad. Three years later he began covering the State Department for the *Baltimore Sun* and soon became head of that paper's Washington bureau. Pearson met *Christian Science Monitor* reporter Robert S. Allen, who suggested the two write a muckraking book together; the result, in 1931, was *Washington Merry-Go-Round,* which was published anonymously, sold well, and caused quite a stir. The two published a sequel, *More Merry-Go-Round,* in 1932, after which the coauthors' identities were discovered. Allen was promptly fired by the *Monitor,* went to work for Hearst, and was also fired from that job. Later in the year, Pearson was sacked by the *Sun.* The two unemployed writers decided to launch a daily column, handled by United Feature Syndicate; it began to appear in December 1932 in a scant six papers. Pearson hired his brother, Leon, as an assistant; Allen hired a legman named Tom McNamara; and the sassy new column began printing inside information on Washington politics, often gathered by tipsters who were disgruntled informants or ambitious underlings impatient to have a shot at the boss's job. Allen had the almost stereotypical manner of the hardboiled newshound; Pearson, aristocratic of manner and habit, more closely resembled the diplomat he had once hoped to become.

Allen left Pearson to write the column solo in 1942 and became an Army Intelligence officer. By this time the column was appearing in roughly 350 papers and the two columnists were doing their own radio show, which had begun in 1935, plus a comic strip, "Hap Hopper." Eventually, the "Merry-Go-Round" was in more than six-hundred papers, second only to Walter Winchell's record eight-hundred.

Pearson's unusual column got him sued for libel roughly 120 times, making him the most-sued American columnist on record. Although he was a New Deal supporter, Pearson was called a liar by President Franklin Roosevelt. He was physically attacked by Sen. Joe McCarthy and was called an "S.O.B." by President Harry Truman. His insider revelations, which often were intensely personal, gave him a tremendous readership and considerable influence in the nation's capital, but his tendency to dramatize, vilify, and make frequent predictions cost him respect among his fellow journalists. About a decade prior to his death, Pearson hired Jack Anderson as an assistant; later he shared the column's byline with him. Anderson took over the column after Pearson's death.

BOOKS: With Robert S. Allen, *Washington Merry-Go-Round* (New York, 1931); with Robert S. Allen, *More Merry-Go-Round* (New York, 1932); *The American Diplomatic Game* (London, 1935); with Robert S. Allen, *The Nine Old Men* (Garden City, N.Y., 1936); with Jack Anderson, *U.S.A.—Second Class Power?* (New York, 1958); with Jack Anderson, *The Case Against Congress: A Compelling Indictment of Corruption on Capital Hill* (New York, 1968); *The Senator* (Garden City, N.Y., 1968); *The President* (Garden City, N.Y., 1970); *Diaries, 1949–1959,* ed. by Tyler Abell (New York, 1974).

REFERENCES: Jack Alexander, "Pugnacious Pearson," in *More Post Biographies,* ed. by John E. Drewry (Athens, Ga., 1947): 218–238; Morris A. Bealle, *All-American Louse: A Candid Biography of Drew A. Pearson* (Frenchtown, N.J., 1965); Charles Fisher, *The Columnists* (New York, 1944): 210–247; Herman Klurfeld, *Behind the Lines: The World of Drew Pearson* (Englewood Cliffs, N.J., 1968); Oliver Pilat, *Drew Pearson: An Unauthorized Biography* (New York, 1973).

Pegler, Francis Westbrook (2 Aug. 1894–24 June 1969). Angry, ornery journalist Westbrook Pegler began his column at the *New York World-Telegram* in 1933 and continued as a columnist until 1962.

Pegler was born in Minneapolis, Minnesota, the son of an English-born journalist. Part of his youth was spent in Chicago, where he attended the Horace Greeley School and Lane Technical High School. He also attended Loyola Academy for two years before dropping out in 1912 to take a job as a telephone reporter in Chicago for the International News Agency. After only two weeks he got another job with United Press in Des Moines, Iowa, and went from there to St. Louis, Missouri, and after that to Texas as a United Press (UP) reporter and bureau manager. In 1916 he was a UP correspondent in London, and during 1917–1918 he was a war correspondent in Europe. After irritating generals and admirals with his insistent questions, he joined the navy (1918–1919). After the war he spent 1919–1925 as a sportswriter and editor for the United Press. He began to featurize his sports stories and in 1925 was hired as a sportswriter by the *Chicago Tribune* and syndicated by the Tribune News Syndicate.

In 1933 he moved to the *New York World-Telegram* and began writing a general column, "Fair Enough," which was distributed by United Feature Syndicate. He won the Pulitzer Prize for reporting in 1941 for his stories on labor union racketeering. After four years, he switched to King Features Syndicate, changing his column title to "As Pegler Sees It." Pegler was an exciting, forceful writer but too often oversimplified and was prone to vilify those he didn't like, who included most political and labor union leaders, by assigning them derogatory nicknames. He developed an endless hatred for Franklin Roosevelt, who became, in Pegler's column, "the momma's boy." Other Americans he "Peglerized" over the years included Eleanor Roosevelt, Huey Long, Upton Sinclair, Frank Sinatra, and John F. Kennedy, whom Pegler labeled a "Boston gang politician." As Alistair Cooke once put it, the path to Pegler's prose led through his bile duct. Pegler held grudges, and his writing became ever more acrimonious, though as author Charles Fisher has noted, his circulation tended to rise with his blood pressure.

In 1954 Pegler lost a libel suit that had been brought against him by reporter Quentin Reynolds in 1949 for comments in "As Pegler Sees It" that made Reynolds out to be a war profiteer and a cowardly "absentee war correspondent" during the London blitz. Damages of $175,000 were paid by Hearst's King Features Syndicate thanks to a provision in Pegler's syndicate contract, but his standing with the public never recovered. He was canceled by his syndicate in August 1962 after he attacked the Hearst organization itself. During 1962 and 1963 Pegler wrote a column for the John Birch Society's magazine *American Opinion* but proved too vituperative for even that periodical. At the time of his death, an invasion of privacy suit Pegler had filed against the "Ed Sullivan Show" and CBS-TV was pending.

BOOKS: *T'aint Right* (Garden City, N.Y., 1936); *The Dissenting Opinions of Mister Westbrook Pegler* (New York, 1938); *George Spelvin, American, and Fireside Chats* (New York, 1942); *Lady I* (New York, 1942).

REFERENCES: Alistair Cooke, "An Outrageous Man," in Karl E. Meyer, *Pundits, Poets, and Wits* (New York, 1990): 227–230; Finis Farr, *Fair Enough: The Life of Westbrook Pegler* (New York, 1975); Charles Fisher, *The Columnists* (New York, 1944); Oliver Ransay Pilat, *Pegler, Angry Man of the Press* (Westport, Conn., 1963).

Peirce, Neal R. (5 January 1932–   ). Neil Peirce began a weekly column on local and state issues and relations with the federal government that began in 1975. He is syndicated by the Washington Post Writers Group.

Peirce was born in Philadelphia. He made Phi Beta Kappa and earned the A.B. at Princeton University in 1954, spent 1954–1957 in counterintelligence for the U.S. Army, then did graduate study in international relations at Harvard University in 1957 and 1958. After that he was legislative assistant to Rep. Silvio O. Conte of Massachusetts (1958–1959).

From 1960 to 1969 he was political editor of the *Congressional Quarterly*, after which he helped found and served as a contributing editor to the *National Journal* (1969), a government-watching periodical for which a yearly subscription cost $300. The *Journal* was sponsored by the Government Reporting Corporation in Washington.

Peirce was an election consultant to NBC News in 1964 and 1966, and to CBS News in 1962 and from 1967 to 1974. He was a Fellow of the Woodrow Wilson International Center for Scholars from 1971 to 1974. In 1975 he began his column, at first self-syndicating it to about sixty-five regular subscribers plus other papers that used the column occasionally. He has written for *Christian Science Monitor* and the *New York Times* and has done a series of books on various blocks of states, beginning with what he termed the "megastates": New York, Massachusetts, Pennsylvania, New Jersey, Ohio, Illinois, Michigan, Florida, Texas, and California.

BOOKS: *The People's President: The Electoral College in American History and the Direct-Vote Alternative* (New York, 1968); *The Megastates of America* (New York, 1972); *The Pacific States of America* (New York, 1972); *The Mountain States of America* (New York, 1972); *The Great Plains States of America* (New York, 1973); *The Border South States* (New York, 1975); *The Deep South States of America* (New York, 1974); *The New England States* (New York, 1976); *The Mid-Atlantic States of America* (New York, 1977); *The Great Lake States* (New York, 1980); *The Book of America: Inside 50 States Today* (New York, 1983); *Over New England* (San Francisco, 1990); *Citistates: How Urban America Can Prosper in a Competitive World* (Washington, D.C., 1993).

REFERENCES: "The Other End of the Telescope," *Time* (9 May 1977): 49.

Petacque, Arthur Martin (20 July 1924–   ). Pulitzer Prize–winning investigative reporter Art Petacque wrote a column for the *Chicago Sun-Times* starting in 1974.

Petacque was born in Chicago and studied from 1940 to 1942 at the University of Illinois. He was a *Chicago Sun* reporter from 1942 to 1947 and with the *Sun-Times* from 1947. He became an investigative reporter in 1957 and in 1974 won a Pulitzer Prize for his work and became a columnist.

One of his investigative efforts helped solve the murder of the daughter of Sen. Charles Percy. Another was instrumental in the stock fraud conviction of William Rentschler, one of President Richard Nixon's campaign managers. Petacque was also crime editor for *World Book Encyclopedia* from 1970 to 1975.

Peters, Michael Ray (6 March 1944–   ). Columnist Mike Peters has written for the *Greeley Tribune* since 1972. He does three columns a week: a humor column that appears under the unlikely column title "The Gnarly Trombone"; a consumer column, "Action Line"; and a history column, "This Week."

Peters was born in Colorado Springs, Colorado, and received the B.A. from Colorado State College in Greeley in 1968. From 1969 through 1971 he taught high school in Flagler, Colorado.

Peters joined the *Greeley Tribune* in 1972 as a columnist and general assignment reporter. The strange title of his weekly humor column is taken from an 1871 news story in which a reporter back East confused the handwritten name for the Greeley paper and printed it as "Gnarly Trombone."

BOOKS: *Quick—Call a Cop* (Greeley, Colo., 1977); *76 Gnarly Trombones* (Greeley, Colo., 1987).

Pfaff, William Wendle, III (29 December 1928–   ). William Pfaff writes a political column handled by the Los Angeles Times Syndicate.

Pfaff was born in Council Bluffs, Iowa. He received the B.A. from the University of Notre Dame in 1949.

He worked as associate editor of *Commonweal* from 1949 to 1955, with time out for Infantry and Special Forces service in the U.S. Army, 1951–1952. From 1955 to 1957 he was a writer for ABC News and from 1957 to 1961 was with the Free Europe Committee, Inc., in New York City. Pfaff was with the Hudson Institute, Inc., from 1961 to 1978 and worked in Paris for Hudson Research Europe Ltd. in 1971–1978. His column is done out of Paris. He has also written columns for the *International Herald Tribune* and was a political commentator for the *New Yorker* starting in 1972.

BOOKS: With Edmund Stillman, *The New Politics* (New York, 1961); with Edmond Stillman, *The Politics of Hysteria: The Sources of Twentieth-Century Conflict* (New York, 1964); with Edmund Stillman, *Power and Impotence: The Failure of America's Foreign Policy* (London, 1966); *Condemned to Freedom* (New York, 1971); *The Wrath of Nations: Civilization and the Furies of Nationalism* (New York, 1993).

Phillips, Harry Irving (26 Nov. 1887–?). H. I. Phillips wrote humor columns for the *New York Globe* and the *New York Sun* during the 1920s and 1930s.

Phillips was born in New Haven, Connecticut, and was educated in that city's public schools. Before making his start in journalism, he held a succession of other jobs: driver of a horse for an undertaker, hotel bellhop, stock clerk in a Woolworth store, candy salesman in an opera house, and grocery deliveryman.

He first reported for the *New Haven Register* (1906–1908). Phillips hoped to be a cartoonist but at age twenty-three found himself the paper's managing editor instead. After six years with the *Register,* he relocated to New York City. He was fired after a short stay on the *New York Tribune,* then got a copyediting job on the *Globe.* Soon he began an editorial page column in which he satirized items in the news; the column was soon syndicated. He moved to the *New York Sun,* where his column was titled "Sun Dial." Here he poked fun at Roosevelt's New Deal. When World War II began, he originated two regular characters: lovable dogface Private Purkey and All-Out Arlene of the Women's Army Corps. He was syndicated by Associated Newspapers and also wrote comic material for radio and Broadway musicals. Several books made up of material from his columns were published, as well.

BOOKS: *The Globe Trotter* (Garden City, N.Y., 1923); *The Foolish Question Book* (New York, 1927); *Calvin Coolidge, 1872–1933* (New York, 1933); *On White or Rye, Including Some of the Deeper Speculations of Elmer Twitchell* (New York, 1941); *The Private Papers of Private Purkey* (New York, 1941); *Private Purkey in Love and War* (New York, 1942); *All-Out Arlene, a Story of the Girls Behind the Boys* (Garden City, N.Y., 1943).

Phillips, John Sanburn (2 July 1861–28 Feb. 1949). John Phillips, best remembered as cofounder of *McClure's* magazine and later as part-owner of *American Magazine,* wrote a column for the *Goshen Independent-Republican* during his retirement years.

Phillips was born in Council Bluffs, Iowa, and grew up in Galesburg, Illinois. He received the A.B. from Knox College in 1882. One of his college friends, with whom he worked on student publications, was S. S. McClure. When McClure took over a bicycling magazine, *Wheelman,* in 1882, Phillips went along as his assistant. After a year he left McClure to study literature at Harvard, where he earned the A.B., magna cum laude, in 1885. He attended the University of Leipzig in Germany for further study, then rejoined McClure in a syndicate the latter had founded to handle the work of fiction writers who wanted to reach the newspaper audience.

In 1893 Phillips and McClure started *McClure's,* a highly successful magazine that became known for its muckraking stories just after the turn of the century. The two founders parted ways in 1906, after which Phillips and former *Mc-Clure's* writers Ray Stannard Baker, Ida Tarbell, and Lincoln Steffens bought the *American Magazine.* They sold the magazine in 1911 because of financial strains, and Phillips went on to edit the *Red Cross Magazine* from 1917 to 1920. Retiring in 1920, he began writing a column for the Goshen paper. Some of his columns were about literature; others were of a more general nature.

REFERENCES: Peter Lyon, *Success Story: The Life and Times of S. S. McClure* (DeLand, Fla., 1967); Harold S. Wilson, *McClure's Magazine and the Muckrakers* (Princeton, N.J., 1970).

Phillips, Kevin Price (30 Nov. 1940–   ). Kevin Phillips, who is credited with coining the term "the Sun Belt," has written columns for King Features Syndicate and for *TV Guide.*

Phillips was born in New York City. He holds the A.B. from Colgate University (1961) and the LL.B. from Harvard University (1964). During 1959–1960 he attended the University of Edinburgh in Scotland.

He began his career as administrative assistant to Congressman Paul Fino in 1964–1968, then served as an assistant to John Mitchell, Richard Nixon's campaign manager, in 1968–1969. When Mitchell became U.S. attorney general, Phillips was hired as an assistant (1969–1970). Phillips's book *The Emerging Republican Majority* (1969) made him a highly regarded political analyst before his thirtieth birthday. After leaving the attorney general's office in 1970, Phillips edited and published two periodicals: *American Political Report* and *Business and Public Affairs Fortnightly.* He wrote a political column for King Features Syndicate (1970–1983) and became a contributing columnist for the *Los Angeles Times* in 1984. He has been a commentator for CBS since 1978 and for National Public Radio since 1984 and has published several books, most of which focus on our increasingly polarized society.

BOOKS: *The Emerging Republican Majority* (New Rochelle, N.Y., 1969); *Mediacracy: American Parties and Politics in the Communications Age* (Garden City, N.Y., 1975); *Post-Conservative America: People, Politics, and Ideology in a Time of Crisis* (New York, 1982); *Staying on Top: The Business Case for a National Industrial Strategy* (New York, 1984); *The Politics of Rich and Poor: Wealth and the American Electorate in the Reagan Aftermath* (New York, 1990); *Boiling Point: Republicans, Democrats, and the Decline of Middle-Class Prosperity* (New York, 1993).

Phillips, Pauline Esther Friedman (4 July 1918–   ). In her guise as Abigail Van Buren, Pauline Phillips writes "Dear Abby," one of the most widely syndicated columns ever published.

Born Pauline Esther Friedman in Sioux City, Iowa, she is the twin of Eppie Lederer, who writes a similar column as "Ann Landers." She majored in journalism and minored in psychology at Morningside College in Sioux City from 1936 to 1939. She and her twin collaborated on a campus gossip column called "PEEP," but both dropped out of school in favor of marriage and volunteer work. At age thirty-seven, Phillips began giving her sister a hand with replying to letters drawn by the "Ann Landers" advice column that Lederer had begun writing in Chicago in 1955. Enjoying the work, she decided upon a similar column of her own. Within three months, in January 1956, she was writing the "Dear Abby" column for the *San Francisco Chronicle*. Her pen name, "Abigail Van Buren," was a combination of a biblical character, Abigail, who advised King David, and the classy sounding last name of President Martin Van Buren.

The McNaught Syndicate picked up the column (1956–1974), then the Chicago Tribune Syndicate (1974–1980), and finally, the Universal Press Syndicate (since 1980). The column was an immediate success; Universal now claims that the column reaches eighty million readers a day and that "Dear Abby" receives around ten thousand letters weekly. Whereas earlier advice columnists were prone to wring every conceivable ounce of pathos out of people's troubles, "Abby" is able to combine serious advice with witty one-liners. Considering her frequent suggestions that those who write in seek counseling, it is little wonder that the American College of Psychiatrists has made her an honorary life member.

The column appears seven times weekly. People's letters—at least those that come with a stamped, self-addressed envelope—are answered with the help of a staff of seven. At times, the more seriously troubled letter writer will receive a phone call from "Abby." The column can generate tremendous direct response, as in January 1990, when a column that mentioned Ralph Nader's *Consumer Guide to Toll-Free Hotlines* generated eighty-four thousand requests for a copy. Phillips has used her considerable influence to help numerous causes, such as Planned Parenthood, Goodwill Industries, and the Salvation Army. She has received a long list of honors and has published six books.

BOOKS: *Dear Abby* (Englewood Cliffs, N.J., 1958); *Dear Teen-Ager* (New York, 1959); *Dear Abby on Marriage* (New York, 1962); *The Best of Dear Abby* (Kansas City, Mo., 1981); *Dear Abby on Planning Your Wedding* (Kansas City, Mo., 1988); *Where Were You When President Kennedy Was Shot? Memories and Tributes to a Slain President, as Told to Dear Abby* (Kansas City, Mo., 1993).

REFERENCES: David Astor, "No Slowing Down for Abigail Van Buren," *Editor and Publisher* (16 August 1986): 36–37; Richard Weiner, *Syndicated Columnists,* 3rd Ed. (New York, 1979): 103–113.

Pinkerton, Robert John (28 July 1932–   ). Bob Pinkerton, owner and publisher of the *Western Nebraska Observer* in Kimball, Nebraska, has for many years written a general column titled "On the Bobsled" for his paper.

Pinkerton was born in Madison, Nebraska, and grew up in Kimball. He earned the B.S. in journalism from the University of Nebraska in 1954. After college he began working for the paper he now owns, then spent the end of 1954 through 1956 in the U.S. Air Force as chief of advertising and publicity for the 3504th Recruiting Group in San Antonio, Texas. He then returned to the *Observer* in December 1956 as news reporter and then editor. He purchased the *Observer* on 1 December 1962.

Plagenz, George Richard (11 Dec. 1923–   ). George Plagenz writes the column "Saints and Sinners," which is syndicated by the Newspaper Enterprise Association (NEA).

Plagenz was born in Lakewood, Ohio. He holds the B.A. cum laude from Western Reserve University (1945) and the S.T.B. from Harvard University (1949). He also studied for the ministry and was ordained in the Unitarian church in 1951.

His work life has combined media work and ministry. He began as a sportswriter for the *Cleveland Press* (1943–1946) and after his ordination, was assistant minister of King's Chapel in Boston (1951–1954). He was in news broadcasting on Boston station WEEI radio (1955–1963) and a writer for the *Boston Sunday Advertiser* (1963–1970). From 1970 to 1982 he was religion editor for the *Cleveland Press* and began a syndicated column for Scripps-Howard Newspapers in 1974. He switched to NEA in 1980.

Pogrebin, Letty Cottin (9 June 1939–   ). Letty Pogrebin (pronounced PO-greb-in) has written columns for the *New York Times, Newsday, Ms.,* and the *Ladies' Home Journal.*

Pogrebin was born Letty Cottin in New York City. She received the A.B. cum laude in English and American literature from Brandeis University in 1959.

She worked from 1957 to 1959 as a part-time assistant and secretary for Simon & Schuster, then from 1959 to 1960 as an editorial assistant for Coward-McCann. She was as an advertising copywriter for the New York firm of Sussman & Sugar in 1960 and began work for a publisher, Bernard Geiss Associates, later that same year. From 1960 to 1979 she was vice president of that firm. From 1971 to 1981, Pogrebin wrote the column "The Working Woman" for *Ladies' Home Journal.* She was one of the founders of *Ms.* magazine and was its editor from 1971 to 1987. From 1987 to 1989, she was a *Ms.* columnist and editor at large and has been a contributing editor since 1990. She conducted the "Hers" column in the *New York Times* in 1983 and from 1988 to 1991, and wrote a column for *Newsday* in 1985. Her columns' focus has been on women's and family issues. She has written several books and has contributed to such magazines as *TV Guide, Nation, Cosmopolitan,* and *Good Housekeeping.*

BOOKS: *How to Make It in a Man's World* (Garden City, N.Y., 1970); *Getting Yours: How to Make the System Work for the Working Woman* (New York, 1975); *Growing Up Free: Raising Your Child in the 80's* (New York, 1980); ed., *Stories for Free Children* (New York, 1982); *Family Politics: Love and Power on an Intimate Frontier* (New York, 1983); *Among Friends* (New York, 1987); *Deborah, Golda, and Me: Being Female and Jewish in America* (New York, 1991).

Poore, Benjamin Perley (2 Nov. 1820–29 May 1887). Benjamin Perley Poore is remembered as one of the earliest Washington correspondents to achieve a national reputation and, because of his "Perley" letters that appeared regularly for thirty years in the *Boston Journal,* deserves recognition as one of America's prototype columnists.

Poore was born near Newburyport, Massachusetts, at his family's farm, Indian Hill. Part of his youth was spent in New York City, where he attended the public schools. In 1831, his father, a successful merchant, took him to Europe, where he met such greats as the Marquis de Lafayette and Sir Walter Scott. Poore was enrolled at Dummer Academy in Massachusetts but ran away to learn printing at a Worcester print shop. He became editor of the *Southern Whig* in Athens, Georgia, in 1839, after his father bought the paper for him. A paper run by a "Yankee" did not fare well in pre–Civil War Athens, however, and after a scandal, the so-called Mulatto Ball Affair, and a subsequent trial (in which Poore was cleared), the paper was sold in August of 1841.

Next Poore served as attaché to the U.S. legation in Brussels (1841–1844). He traveled extensively and wrote letters signed simply as "Perley" that appeared in the *Boston Atlas* and the *Hartford Courant.* He returned to the United States and worked briefly during 1847–1848 as Washington correspondent for the *Atlas,* then moved to Boston as editor of the *Boston Daily Bee* in December 1848. He founded an ill-fated Sunday paper, *Perley's Sunday Picnic,* in January 1849. When it failed, he again worked as Washington correspondent for the *Boston Atlas.* In December of 1849 he again relocated to Boston and started another paper of his own, the *Sunday Sentinel* (also known as the *American Sentinel*), which he sold in 1851.

Poore began writing books: a biography of Napoleon and a few novels, which appeared in serial form in *Gleason's Pictorial Drawing-Room Companion.* He also wrote for a variety of other magazines. He became the *Boston Journal's* Washington correspondent, and in 1854 his column "Waifs from Washington" began appearing in that paper. Its content was that of modern-day general columns, and it appeared, always signed "Perley," for twenty-nine years. Poore ended his column in 1883 after salary disagreements with the *Journal's* management.

The prolific Poore also wrote for several other newspapers scattered about the nation and for such magazines as *Atlantic* and *Harper's Weekly.* His final years were spent as congressional correspondent for the *Boston Budget,* the *Omaha Republican,* and the *Albany Evening Journal.* He was chosen as the first president of Washington's Gridiron Club in 1885, two years before his death.

BOOKS: *The Rise and Fall of Louis Philippe, Ex-King of the French* (Boston, 1848); *Life of Gen. Zachary Taylor, the Whig Candidate for the Presidency* (Boston, 1848); *The Early Life and First Campaigns of Napoleon Bonaparte* (Boston, 1851); *The Marmaluke: Or The Sign of the Mystic Tie: A Tale of the Camp and Court of Bonaparte* (Boston, 1852); *The Russian Guardsman: A Tale of the Seas and Shores of the East* (New York, 1852); *Historical Material for the Biography of W.T.G. Morton, M.D., Discoverer of Etherization* (Washington, D.C., 1856); *The Scout: Or Sharpshooters of the Revolution* (Boston, 1860); *The West Point Cadet: Or The Turns of Fortune's Wheel* (Boston, 1863); *Trial of Andrew Jackson, President of the United States* (Washington, D.C., 1868); *The Life and Public Services of John Sherman* (Cincinnati, 1880); *The Life and Public Services of Ambrose E. Burnside, Soldier,—Citizen,—Statesman* (Providence, R.I., 1882); with O. H. Tiffany, *Life of U.S. Grant* (Philadelphia and New York, 1885); *Perley's Reminiscences of Sixty Years in the National Metropolis,* 2 vols. (Philadelphia, 1886).

REFERENCES: Josephine P. Driver, "Ben: Perley Poore of Indian Hill," *Essex Institute Historical Collections* 89 (January 1953): 1–18; Joseph P. McKerns, *Benjamin Perley Poore of the Boston Journal: His Life and Times as a Washington Correspondent, 1850– 1887,* Ph.D. Dissertation, University of Minnesota, 1979; John E. Talmadge, "Ben: Perley Poore's Stay in Athens," *Georgia Historical Quarterly* 41 (September 1957): 247– 254.

Posner, Jack (25 May 1916–   ). Jack Posner self-syndicates two columns out of Deerfield Beach, Florida: "Capitol Comedy," featuring political satire, and "Dear Daffy," a spoof of personal advice features. Earlier in his career, he wrote the column "Potomac Fever," which was handled by the Register/Tribune Syndicate of Des Moines, Iowa.

Posner was born in New York City and received the B.A. from New York University. He worked as advertising manager for Consolidated Retail Stores for two years and as a principal in the Posner-Zabin ad agency for sixteen years. His Register/Tribune Syndicate column ran for five years, and he spent six years as a Retail Reporting Bureau editor. He has contributed material to Jay Leno and various sitcom television shows and has authored one book.

BOOKS: *Say Something Funny, Instantly* (Great Neck, N.Y., 1967).

Post, Emily Price (3 Oct. 1873–25 Sept. 1960). One of the household name arbiters of taste in the first half of the 1900s was Emily Post, who wrote a column distributed by the Bell Syndicate from 1932 until her death.

She was born into wealth and social standing as Emily Price in Baltimore, Maryland. The family moved to New York when she was still a child. She was educated at Miss Graham's and other private schools, had a German governess and was taken abroad for extensive travel, which acquainted her with the manners of European aristocracy. Her New York debut was in 1891. Her 1892 marriage to banker Edwin Post failed after he had lost most of his fortune in the financial panic of 1903, and she began to write for two magazines: *Ainslee's* and *Everybody's*. She also wrote novels of manners, set in Europe; her work often contrasted the social conventions of America with those of the Old World.

Post's great success began when Richard Duffy of Funk and Wagnall's suggested that she write an etiquette book. The result, *Etiquette: The Blue Book of Social Usage,* appeared in 1922 and, with its subsequent editions, made her wealthy and famous. She began appearing on radio in 1929 and in 1932 replied to her readers' and listeners' inquiries by launching a newspaper column with the Bell Syndicate. The column, carried in more than two-hundred papers, contained her replies to some of the 250,000 letters she received each year. She also continued to write books, most of the later ones on proper behavior, home decorating, and the like.

BOOKS: *The Flight of the Moth* (New York, 1904); *Purple and Fine Linen* (New York, 1905); *Woven in Tapestry* (New York, 1908); *The Title Market* (New York, 1909); *By Motor Car to the Golden Gate* (New York, 1916); *Parade: A Novel of New York Society* (New York, 1925); *Etiquette: The Blue Book of Social Usage* (New York, 1922); *How to Behave—Though a Debutante* (Garden City, N.Y., 1928); *The Personality of a House: The Blue Book of Home Design and Decoration* (New York, 1930); *The Secret of Keeping Friends* (Boston, 1938); *101 Common Mistakes in Etiquette—and How to Avoid Them* (New Haven, Conn., 1939); *Children Are People, and Ideal Parents Are Comrades* (New York, 1940); *The Emily Post Cookbook,* ed. by Edwin M. Post, Jr. (New York, 1951); *Your Reference Book of Silver Etiquette* (Newark, N.J., 1952).

Prather, Paul David (29 March 1956–   ). Columnist/religion writer Paul Prather has written for the *Lexington* [Kentucky] *Herald-Leader* since 1988.

Prather was born in Somerset, Kentucky, and before getting into journalism held a wide variety of jobs, which he describes as "a janitor, a newspaper carrier, a clothing salesman, a farm laborer, a substitute school teacher, a university instructor, a jack-leg preacher, an insurance peddler—and several other things." His educational attainments include three degrees from the University of Kentucky: the B.A. (1982) and M.A. (1984) in English and the M.A. in communications (1992).

From 1988 to 1990 Prather was a business writer for the *Herald-Leader,* since 1990, a religion writer. His column has appeared since late 1990, and on a regular weekly schedule since mid-1991. His general column is frequently directed at social issues, religion, and ethics and has been reprinted in other publications, such as *Catholic Digest* and the *Chicago Tribune*. Prather has taught journalism and English part-time for the University of Kentucky since 1982 and has been pastor of a small independent rural church, Grace Church, in Montgomery County, Kentucky, also since 1982.

Preston, Keith (29 Sept. 1884–7 July 1927). Known for his humor verse, Keith Preston wrote two columns for the *Chicago Daily News:* the humorous

"Hit or Miss" on the paper's editorial page and "The Periscope," a book column.

Preston was born in Chicago and studied the classics at the University of Chicago, where he earned the Ph.B. in 1905. From 1906 to 1910 he taught Latin at the University of Indiana and also received a master's degree there in 1907. He returned for graduate study and in 1914 received the Ph.D. from the University of Chicago. He then taught Latin and Greek at Princeton University (1912–1913) and at Northwestern University (1913–1923).

Preston began his book column for the *Daily News* in 1918, and in 1926 he became the paper's literary editor. His humor column, usually done in verse, was launched in 1922. He was a member of Phi Beta Kappa and published four books.

BOOKS: *Types of Pan* (Boston, 1919); *Splinters* (New York, 1921); ed., *Column Poets* (Chicago, 1924); *Pot Shots from Pegasus* (New York, 1929).

Price, Deb (27 Feb. 1958–   ). Deb Price appears to have been the first U.S. columnist working for a mainstream paper to write a column exclusively devoted to gay and lesbian issues. She launched the column at the *Detroit News,* where she is also Washington news editor, on 8 May 1992. Gannett, which owns the *News,* offered the weekly column to the other papers in its chain.

Price was born in Lubbock, Texas. She holds both the B.A. (1981) and M.A. from Stanford University.

Price had been a journalist for eleven years prior to starting this column, which has drawn both praise and angry diatribes from readers. In 1982 she was a reporter for the *Northern Virginia Sun.* From 1982 to 1984 she reported for the States News Service, then from 1984 to 1989 was an editor at the *Washington Post.* From 1989 to 1993 she was the *Detroit News*'s deputy bureau chief in Washington.

Prince, Richard E. (26 July 1947–   ). Richard Prince has served the Rochester (New York) *Democrat and Chronicle* since 1988 as columnist and since February 1993 as op-ed page editor.

Prince was born in New York City and received the B.S. in journalism in 1968 from New York University.

In 1967 and 1968 he was a reporter for the *Star-Ledger* in Newark, New Jersey. He was with the *Washington Post* from 1968 until 1977, first as city hall reporter (1968–1972), then as education writer (1972–1975), and finally as general assignment reporter, Metro (1975–1977). In 1977–1979 he worked as a free-lance writer-photographer in Washington, and in 1979 he joined the *Democrat and Herald* as assistant metro editor. Prince was assistant news editor from 1981 to 1985, when he was named to the paper's editorial board. He was editor of letters to the editor (1986–1988) and has written editorials since 1985. His column has been transmitted by the Gannett News Service since 1988. It is an issues-oriented editorial page column, often offering African-American perspective. Prince is a member of the New York State Association of Black Journalists, the National Association of Black Journalists, the Trotter Group, and the National Society of Newspaper Columnists.

Pyle, Ernest Taylor (3 Aug. 1900–18 April 1945). Ernie Pyle was America's best loved columnist during World War II and prior to that time wrote an unusual column of travel commentary rather in the manner of a print medium Charles Kuralt.

Pyle was born on a farm near Dana, Indiana. He finished high school in 1918, enlisted in the navy and served a few months before the end of World War I, then majored in economics with a second concentration in journalism at Indiana University. He edited the school paper, the *Student,* and the campus humor periodical, *Smokeup,* but left school before the end of his senior year to work as a reporter for the *LaPorte* [Indiana] *Herald.* After only three months, he took a new reporting job for the *Washington* [D.C.] *Daily News.* He married, and he and his wife, who became known to America as "the girl who rides beside me," bought a car and drove around the nation for ten weeks in 1926, writing about the people and places they found. Later in 1926 he got a job on the copy desk of the *New York Evening World* and the next year moved to the *New York Evening Post* in the same capacity. The end of 1927 found him back at the *Washington Daily News* as telegraph editor. Here he wrote a column about aviation, and in 1929 he became the paper's full-time aviation writer/editor. In his column Pyle specialized in the human aspect of flying. He left this assignment in 1932 to become the *Daily News*'s managing editor. Recuperating from influenza, Pyle took his wife traveling once again and wrote a series of columns about their experiences. These columns filled the space normally occupied by columnist Heywood Broun during Broun's vacation. The success of Pyle's work was such that in 1935 the paper created a unique roving reporter position for him: traveling the nation by car and writing six columns a week about what he found. The column was syndicated by Scripps-Howard in 1939. Like the work of CBS's roving commentator Charles Kuralt, Pyle's writing combined sharp observation of detail, humor, a sense of melancholy, and more than a touch of the poetic.

Pyle's enduring fame, however, is derived from his coverage of World War II. In late 1940 he sailed to England, where he covered the London blitz. His stories concentrated on the war's effects on the English people.

Pyle returned to America in 1941 to continue his travel commentaries for Scripps-Howard, but the bombing of Pearl Harbor caused him to return to Europe, where he became a combat columnist. He went with the troops to North Africa, Sicily, and Italy, writing mainly about the war as experienced by the foot soldier. He landed with the Allied Forces on D-Day and was present at the liberation of Paris. Pyle won the Pulitzer Prize in 1944 for his war correspondence, briefly returned to the United States, then in January 1945 sailed to the

Pacific theater of war. His last published column was written on April 15, 1945. Pyle was killed by three bullets from a Japanese sniper on the island of Ie Shima. At the time of his death, Pyle was his nation's favorite columnist. His column appeared in more than four hundred dailies and around three hundred weeklies.

BOOKS: *Ernie Pyle in England* (New York, 1941); *Here Is Your War* (New York, 1943); *Brave Men* (New York, 1944); *Last Chapter* (New York, 1946); *Home Country* (New York, 1947); *Ernie's War,* ed. by David Nichols (New York, 1986).

REFERENCES: Charles Fisher, *The Columnists* (New York, 1944): 296–317; Lee G. Miller, *An Ernie Pyle Album: Indiana to Ie Shima* (New York, 1946); Miller, *The Story of Ernie Pyle* (New York, 1950); Frederick C. Painton, "The Hoosier Letter-Writer," in *More Post Biographies,* ed. by John E. Drewry (Athens, Ga., 1947): 274–288.

Q _____

Quindlen, Anna (1951–). From 1990 to September 1994, Anna Qunidlen of the *New York Times* wrote the op-ed column "Public & Private," a sort of synthesis of her two earlier *Times* columns.

She was brought up in a New Jersey suburb of Philadelphia. She wrote for her school paper in high school and after graduation did part-time writing for the *New Brunswick Home News*. At age nineteen, while a student at Barnard College, she took a summer job with the *New York Post*. She returned for full-time work as a *Post* reporter after her graduation in 1974 and with the help of her former *Post* city editor, Warren Hoge, and a class-action suit that had charged the *New York Times* with hiring too few women, she became in February 1977 a general assignment reporter for the *Times*. Next she had the city hall beat until 1981, when she was assigned to the "About New York" column, which had been started in 1939 by Meyer Berger; had run, with more than a decade's interruption, until his death in 1959; then resumed in 1979 and handled by a variety of writers. Here she could write about the city's movers and shakers, its homeless, its runaways, the hard-working people who prevent it from collapsing, and the like.

From 1983 to 1985 she had a taste of *Times* management as the paper's deputy metropolitan editor. She left the paper in June 1985 when her first child was born, planning to combine motherhood and novel writing. Her plans changed when the *Times* asked her to handle the "Hers" column for a few weeks on a free-lance basis. She so enjoyed the assignment that she arranged with editor Abe Rosenthal to return as a full-time columnist, this time writing an intensely personal weekly column titled "Life in the 30s." Her new column established her as a prominent voice of the "baby boomer" generation.

Quindlen took a leave of absence in 1988 for the birth of her second child, then in 1990 launched her weekly column, "Public & Private," a general mix of social issues, politics, and anything else that interests her. She follows Anne O'Hare McCormick and Flora Lewis as the third woman to have a column on the *Times's* op-ed page. In mid-September 1994, she announced that she was giving up the column to concentrate on novels. She had won the Pulitzer Prize for commentary in 1992 for her columns supporting abortion rights, defending Anita Hill, and opposing the Persian Gulf War and was syndicated by the New York Times News Service. She has written for such magazines as *Ladies' Home Journal, Ms.,* and *McCall's* and has written five books.

BOOKS: *Living Out Loud* (New York, 1988); *Object Lessons* (New York, 1991); *The Tree That Came to Stay* (New York, 1992); *Thinking Out Loud: On the Personal, the Political, the Public, and the Private* (New York, 1993); *One True Thing* (New York, 1994).

REFERENCES: Chris Lamb, "A 'Public and Private' Talk with a Columnist," *Editor and Publisher,* (30 November 1991): 32–34; Sherry Ricchiardi and Virginia Young, *Women on Deadline* (Ames, Iowa, 1991): 117–134.

R

Ragan, Samuel Talmadge (31 Dec. 1915–   ). Sam Ragan, North Carolina's poet laureate since 1982, currently editor and publisher of the *Pilot* in Southern Pines, North Carolina, wrote the Sunday column "Southern Accents" for the *News and Observer* in Raleigh for many years, beginning in 1948.

Ragan was born in Raleigh and received the B.A. from Atlantic Christian College in 1936. His first job was on the weekly *Hemp Plain Dealer* in the late 1930s. He worked for dailies in Concord, Goldsboro, and Wilmington, North Carolina, as well as San Antonio, Texas, before joining the *News and Observer* as city editor. After serving in the army, he returned to the *News and Observer* as managing editor (1948–1957), then was executive editor from 1956 to 1969. He was also executive editor of the evening paper, the *Raleigh Times,* starting in 1957. In 1968 he moved to Southern Pines and took over publishing the *Pilot.* He has taught as a lecturer at North Carolina State University, Sandhills College, and St. Andrews College. He was chairman of the North Carolina Arts Council from 1967 to 1972, has published books of verse as well as prose, and has written for magazines including the *Reader's Digest, Saturday Evening Post,* and the *Progressive.*

BOOKS: *The Tree in the Far Pasture* (Winston-Salem, N.C., 1964); ed., *The New Day* (Zebulon, N.C., 1964); with Elizabeth Ives, *Back to Beginnings: Adlai Stevenson and North Carolina* (Charlotte, N.C., 1969); *To the Water's Edge* (Durham, N.C., 1971); *Journey into Morning* (Laurinburg, N.C., 1981); with Thad Stem, Jr., *In the Beginning* (Tryon, N.C., 1984); *Poems of Sam Ragan* (New Rochelle, N.Y., 1986); ed., *Weymouth: An Anthology of Poetry* (Laurinburg, N.C., 1987); *Collected Poems of Sam Ragan, Poet Laureate of North Carolina* (Laurinburg, N.C., 1990).

Rascoe, Burton (22 Oct. 1892–19 March 1957). Highly published Burton Rascoe wrote a column entitled ''The Daybook of a New Yorker'' that was syndicated to a reported four hundred papers from 1924 to 1928.

Rascoe was born in Fulton, Kentucky. He attended the University of Chicago from 1911 to 1913 after working at the Shawnee (Oklahoma), *Herald* from 1908 to 1911.

From 1912 to 1920 he was literary and dramatic editor of the *Chicago Tribune,* and during 1920–1921, manager of the Newspaper Enterprise Association's Chicago bureau. He was literary editor of *McCall's* magazine (1921–1922), literary editor of the *New York Tribune* (1922–1924), and editor of Johnson Features, Inc. (1924–1927). Rascoe edited the *Bookman* during 1927–1928 and was also associated with *Arts and Decorations Magazine* and *Vanity Fair* during this same general period.

He was associate editor of *Plain Talk* (1929–1930), the *New York Sun's* literary critic (1930–1932), and literary critic for *Esquire* (1932–1938) and *Newsweek* (1938–1939). From 1939 to 1941 he was a critic for *American Mercury* and from 1934 to 1937, editorial adviser to Doubleday, Doran & Company. He was also the drama critic and an editorial writer for the *New York World-Tribune* from 1942 to 1946. In addition to his newspaper and magazine writing, Rascoe published numerous books.

BOOKS: Translator of Abbé Prevost, *Manon Lescaut* (New York, 1919); with Vincent O'Sullivan and F. C. Henderson, *H. L. Mencken* (New York, 1920); translator of Thaeophile Gautier, *Mademoiselle de Maupin* (New York, 1920); *Theodore Dreiser* (New York, 1925); translator of Emile Zola, *Nana* (New York, 1925); *A Bookman's Daybook,* ed. by C. Hartley Grattan (New York, 1929); ed., *Floyd Gibbons, Knight of the Air* (New York, 1930); *Titans of Literature: From Homer to the Present* (New York, 1932); *Prometheans, Ancient and Modern* (New York, 1933); *Smart Set History* (New York, 1934); ed. with Groff Conklin, *The Smart Set Anthology* (New York, 1934); *Before I Forget* (Garden City, N.Y., 1937); *The Joys of Reading: Life's Greatest Pleasure* (San Francisco, 1937); ed., *An American Reader* (New York, 1938); *Belle Starr: ''The Bandit Queen''* (New York, 1941); *We Were Interrupted* (Garden City, 1947); *The Case of Leo Frank* (Girard, Kan., 1947).

Raspberry, William James (12 Oct. 1935–   ). One of the most widely read of all America's black columnists, 1994 Pulitzer Prize winner William Raspberry has worked as a columnist for the *Washington Post* since 1966. His work is syndicated by the Washington Post Writers Group.

Raspberry was born in Okolona, Mississippi. He earned the B.S. in history from Indiana Central College in 1958. From 1956 to 1960 he was a reporter/editor for the *Indianapolis Recorder,* and from 1960 to 1962 he served in the U.S. Army, after which he joined the Los Angeles Times–Washington Post News Service as a teletype operator. Soon he was hired by the *Washington Post* as a reporter/editor. He began writing the paper's urban affairs column, ''Potomac Watch,'' in 1966. It is widely syndicated and deals more often than not with the various causes of conflict in our cities or with education. Raspberry has written for numerous magazines and has frequently appeared on radio and television programs. He had been a commentator for WRC-TV since 1973 and a contributing editor for ABC-TV's evening news. He also taught journalism at Howard University from 1971 to 1973. Unlike many other columnists, Raspberry believes in using direct quotations in his columns. He also believes that affirmative action programs should be based on financial need rather than on race.

BOOKS: *Looking Backward at Us* (Jackson, Miss., 1991).

REFERENCES: David Astor, ''William Raspberry Talks About His Work,'' *Editor and Publisher* (2 February 1991): 36–38.

Reed, Rex Taylor (2 Oct. 1940–   ). Rex Reed is known for his magazine writing, for his film column in the *New York Daily News,* and for his arts-oriented Sunday column syndicated starting in 1971 by the Chicago Tribune–New York News Syndicate.

Reed was born in Fort Worth, Texas, and grew up in several small towns in Texas, Mississippi, and Louisiana. He received the B.A. in journalism in 1960 at Louisiana State University after having served as editor of the campus literary magazine and columnist/reviewer/editorial writer for the school newspaper, the *Daily Reveille.* Reed had a variety of odd jobs—singer, cook, actor, salesman—before 1965, when he had his first success as a writer. He sold interview stories on the comedian Buster Keaton and the actor Jean-Paul Belmondo to the *New York Times* and *New York* magazine. The recognition these articles gave him enabled him to become film critic for two magazines: *Cosmopolitan* and *Status.* He later did similar work for *Women's Wear Daily, Holiday* magazine, *Vogue, Gentleman's Quarterly,* and the *New York Post,* plus his columns. His *Esquire* profile of Ava Gardner is something of a New Journalism classic. Reed has authored eight books, many of which have been constructed around celebrity interviews.

BOOKS: *Do You Sleep in the Nude?* (New York, 1968); *Conversations in the Raw: Dialogues, Monologues, and Selected Short Subjects* (New York, 1969); *Big Screen, Little Screen* (New York, 1971); *People Are Crazy Here* (New York, 1974); *Valentines and Vitriol* (New York, 1977); *Travolta to Keaton* (New York, 1979); *Personal Effects* (New York, 1986); *Rex Reed's Guide to Movies on TV and Video* (New York, 1992).

Reese, Charley (19 Jan. 1937–   ). Charley Reese writes a conservative thrice-weekly general column syndicated by King Features.

Reese was born in Washington, Georgia, and grew up there, in East Texas and in Northwest Florida. Before he was twenty, he had been a printer, cub reporter, and caption writer for Planet News Pictures, Ltd. (in London, England). He served two years in the army, and in 1955 he became a reporter at the

Pensacola [Florida] *News.* After more than a decade of newspaper reporting, Reese worked from 1969 to 1971 as a political campaign staffer in a variety of races. He was hired as assistant metro editor of the *Orlando Sentinel* in 1971 and later became assistant to the publisher and an editorial board member.

Reese's column is generally conservative. He has referred to the General Agreement on Tariffs and Trade (GATT) as "the latest assault on U.S. independence" and is an advocate of a strong U.S. military. He also does lighter columns, such as one about an unusual character named Po Piedmont, the "Taoist sage" of Northeast Georgia. Reese has authored two books.

BOOKS: *Great Gods of the Potomac* (Orlando, Fla., 1978); *Common Sense for the 80s* (Orlando, Fla., 1981).

Reeves, Richard (28 November 1936–   ). Richard Reeves writes a twice-weekly political column for Universal Press Syndicate and has also written regularly for the *New York Times* and the *New Yorker.*

Reeves was reared in Jersey City. He is a 1960 engineering graduate of Stevens Institute of Technology (in Hoboken) and once worked as an engineer while also editing a weekly paper. He became an investigative reporter for the *Newark Evening News* and from there went to the *New York Times,* where he became chief political reporter. He resigned the *Times* job in 1971 in favor of writing for *Harper's* and *New York,* hosting a television talk show, doing a syndicated radio program, and working as a consultant with the Ford Foundation. The *Harper's* job lasted only a year, and Reeves gave up his TV show in 1974. In 1975 the first of his eight books appeared, a none-too-flattering portrait of President Gerald Ford.

Reeves has hosted a number of award-winning television documentaries, and his column has appeared in as many as 150 newspapers.

BOOKS: *A Ford, not a Lincoln* (New York, 1975); *Old Faces of 1976* (New York, 1976); *Convention* (New York, 1977); *Jet Lag: The Running Commentary of a Bicoastal Reporter* (Kansas City, Kan., 1981); *American Journey: Traveling with Tocqueville in Search of Democracy in America* (New York, 1982); *Passage to Peshawar: Pakistan, Between the Hindu Kush and the Arabian Sea* (New York, 1984); *The Reagan Detour* (New York, 1985); *President Kennedy: Profile of Power* (New York, 1993).

REFERENCES: "Thumping the Pols," *Time* (10 November 1975): 46.

Reid, Ogden Rogers (24 June 1925–   ). Ogden Reid wrote a column for a brief period beginning in 1950 for his family's paper, the *New York Herald Tribune.* From 1955 to 1959, he was that paper's editor.

Reid, son of Ogden Mills Reid and grandson of *Tribune* owner Whitelaw Reid, was born in New York City. He attended Deerfield Academy from 1940 to 1943 and earned the A.B. from Yale in 1949.

In 1940 the young Reid was a part-time photographer, then mail clerk for his family's paper. Prior to enrolling at Yale, he enlisted in the army and served in the Pacific theater as a paratrooper and as public relations officer for the Eleventh Airborne Division.

Returning to the *Herald Tribune* in 1949, Reid worked as columnist and reporter. His principal accomplishments during this period of his life were two series of coauthored stories: "How Strong Is America? The Score on National Defense," written with Robert S. Bird, and "The Threat of Red Sabotage," written with Fendall Yerxa. Reid's primary interest was the threat of communism; his column's title was "The Red Underground."

In 1953 he became president of the paper's Paris edition, and in 1954 he was appointed vice president of the parent company and was put on the board of directors. In the following year he moved up to president and publisher of the *Herald Tribune*. The Reids sold the paper to John Hay Whitney in 1958, and from 1959 to 1961 Ogden Reid served as U.S. ambassador to Israel. He represented New York in Congress for two terms and from 1961 to 1962 was chairman of the New York State Commission for Human Rights.

Reston, James Barrett (3 Nov. 1909–). James "Scotty" Reston of the *New York Times* was one of the most influential political columnists of the twentieth century.

Reston was born in Clydebank, Scotland, and grew up in Alexandria in Dunbartonshire. He attended the Vale of Leven Academy before moving with his parents to Dayton, Ohio, in 1920. After graduation from high school, where he was a championship golfer, Reston worked for a year as editor of *Doings,* the house organ of General Motors' Delco division. He studied journalism at the University of Illinois and received the B.S. in 1932.

Next Reston was for two years a sportswriter for the *Springfield* [Ohio] *Daily News,* a sports publicist for Ohio State University, and in press relations for the Cincinnati Reds. In 1934 he began a three-year hitch with the Associated Press (AP) Feature Service, writing a column, "A New Yorker at Large," plus feature stories. From 1937 to 1939 he covered sports for the AP in London, after which he was hired by the *New York Times* and assigned to their London bureau to report on Nazi bombing of that city. In 1941 he relocated to Washington to cover the State Department and also took leave to help set up the U.S. Office of War Information in London. In 1943 he returned to New York, then moved again to Washington, D.C., as a *Times* diplomatic correspondent. Here he covered the Dunbarton Oaks Conference, where his work earned him the 1945 Pulitzer Prize for national reporting. Reston won the Pulitzer a second time, in 1957, for his series on American political drift.

In 1953 Reston was offered the editorship of the *Washington Post.* Instead, he replaced Arthur Krock as *Times* bureau chief in Washington. In addition to running the bureau, he was a prolific writer, doing a weekly D.C. gossip column, essays, and book reviews. He began writing a three-times-a-week editorial page column titled "Washington" in March 1960, and in 1964, he resigned as bureau head to devote his energies to his column. In 1968 he was made executive editor of the *Times,* and from 1969 to 1974 he was vice president in charge of news. After stepping down as an executive, he continued writing his "Washington" column until 1989.

Reston bought a weekly paper, the *Vineyard Gazette,* in 1968. His writing awards have been many, and he has received roughly twenty honorary degrees from colleges and universities.

BOOKS: *Prelude to Victory* (New York, 1942); ed. with Marquis Childs, *Walter Lippmann and His Times* (New York, 1959); *Sketches in the Sand* (New York, 1967); *Artillery of the Press: Its Influence on American Foreign Policy* (New York, 1967).

REFERENCES: Karl E. Meyer, "James Reston," in *Pundits, Poets, and Wits: An Omnibus of American Newspaper Columnists* (New York, 1990); Gay Talese, *The Kingdom and the Power* (New York, 1969).

Riesel, Victor (1917–   ). Widely syndicated Victor Riesel wrote columns that concentrated on the concerns of American workers from 1937 through the 1960s. His career was impeded when, in 1956, he was blinded by acid thrown into his face by a labor goon.

Riesel was born in New York City, the son of a garment industry worker who was a militant unionist. The younger Riesel attended City College of New York.

After a variety of jobs in a hat factory, in a saw mill, and in various mines and other mills, Riesel began writing on labor affairs for foreign newspapers. He began a labor column in 1937 and was eventually syndicated to a reported 356 papers. He was managing editor of *New Leader* and wrote for the *New York Post* starting in 1941. His column, "Inside Labor," appeared from 1942 to 1950. He also wrote a column for the *New York Daily Mirror* from 1948 to 1963.

In 1956 his column was attacking the International Union of Operating Engineers and its leader, William De Koning. One of his columns brought an anonymous telephone call warning him to cease his attacks on labor racketeering. Shortly thereafter, Riesel appeared on WMCA in New York and took to the air with his charges. As he left the building after the broadcast, a vial of sulfuric acid was flung into his face by an assailant. He was blinded by the acid. The Post-Hall Syndicate offered a reward for information leading to the capture of his attacker, but the man's identity was never established. Riesel had also been known for his militant anticommunism. At one point he campaigned to stop the flow of Russian goods into the United States, and for a period, American dock workers refused to unload Soviet cargo ships.

Rivers, Joan (8 June 1933–   ). Comedian Joan Rivers wrote a column from 1973 to 1976 that was distributed by Publishers-Hall.

Rivers was born in New York City and received the B.A. at Barnard College in 1958. Before entering show business in 1960, she was fashion coordinator for the Bond clothing stores. Rivers made her television debut on the "Tonight

Show'' in 1965 and in the 1980s was one of that show's guest hosts. Her own short-lived talk show, ''The Late Show Starring Joan Rivers,'' appeared during 1986–1987, and since that time, she has appeared on ''Hollywood Squares.'' Safe to say Rivers's New Yorkish brand of comedy came across better on television or on stage than in a newspaper column. She has written an autobiography, *Enter Talking* (1986), and a follow-up, *Still Talking* (1991), plus two other books.

BOOKS: *Having a Baby Can Be a Scream* (Los Angeles, 1974); *The Life and Hard Times of Heidi Abromowitz* (New York, 1984); with Richard Meryman, *Enter Talking* (New York, 1986); *Still Talking* (New York, 1991).

Robarchek, Douglas Robert (23 July 1943–). Doug Robarchek has been the *Charlotte* [North Carolina] *Observer*'s humor columnist since 1986. His column title is ''Outfront.''

Robarchek was born in McCook, Nebraska. He is a not-so-old journalist of the old school who skipped college and went directly to work.

Robarchek began as a reporter for the *Grand Island* [Nebraska] *Independent* (1961–1963), then moved to a similar job with the Columbus (Nebraska) *Telegram* (1964–1965). Thereafter he was sports editor for the Fremont (Nebraska) *Tribune* (1965–1966); was associate editor of the *High Plains Journal* in Dodge City, Kansas (1966); worked the copy desk of the Port Arthur (Texas) *News* (1967); was city editor of the Coffeyville (Kansas) *Journal* (1967); then moved to New England to work as first reporter, then managing editor of the Attleboro (Massachusetts) *Sun* (1968–1970). Next the well-traveled Robarchek moved to California to become city editor of the Fontana *Herald-News* (1972–1974), returned east to edit the Lewistown (Pennsylvania) *Sentinel* (1972–1974), then south to be news editor of the Tallahassee (Florida) *Democrat* (1974–1978). In 1980 he took a job on the *Charlotte Observer*'s copy desk before becoming a columnist in 1986.

Robb, Inez Callaway (1901–4 Apr. 1979). Inez Robb wrote three columns but was best known for the column that was widely syndicated by Scripps-Howard and the United Feature Syndicate from 1953 to 1969.

Robb was born Inez Callaway in Middletown, California, and grew up on her grandparents' fifteen thousand-acre ranch near Caldwell, Idaho. As a high school reporter she won a scholarship to study journalism at the University of Idaho, where she earned the A.B. in 1924.

She worked as a general assignment reporter for the *Tulsa* [Oklahoma] *Daily World* for roughly two years, then went to the *New York Daily News* as a Sunday section editor. In 1928 she became the paper's society editor and from 1928 to 1938 wrote a light-hearted society column as ''Nancy Randolph.'' She joined Hearst's International News Service (INS) in 1938 and began her column ''Assignment America,'' written from about forty countries. She was on Pan American's first transatlantic round-trip flight (in 1939) and wrote from England and Ireland during World War II.

After war ended, she became a sort of latter-day Nellie Bly by being the first woman to fly around the world in six days, a stunt done to celebrate the resumption of tourism. As a Hearst columnist she traveled the world, interviewing Juan Peron in Argentina in 1947, covering the wedding of England's Princess (now Queen) Elizabeth in that same year, and beating out most of the press for a seat at Elizabeth's 1953 coronation.

In November 1953 Robb left INS to launch a column of general commentary handled by Scripps-Howard and United Feature. She is remembered, among other things, for her disdain for the women's fashion industry, arguably one of the world's silliest businesses. She retired in 1969.

BOOKS: *Don't Just Stand There* (New York, 1962).

Roberts, Osborne Sinclaire, Jr. (8 March 1949–   ). Ozzie Roberts has been with the *San Diego Tribune/San Diego Union-Tribune* since 1974 and writes the human interest column "Making It."

Osborne was born in Manhattan. He received the B.A. in 1972 from Syracuse University, where he majored in English. He interned at *Life* during the summer of 1968, was with *Psychology Today* during 1972–1973, and worked for *Ebony* in 1973–1974. He then joined the *Tribune* in San Diego.

Roberts, Paul Craig (3 April 1939–   ). Educator, consultant, columnist Paul Craig Roberts has done three columns: in the *Wall Street Journal,* 1978–1980; in *Business Week,* starting in 1983; and in a column syndicated nationally by Scripps-Howard News Service since 1989.

Roberts was born in Atlanta, Georgia. His B.S. is from the Georgia Institute of Technology (1961), his Ph.D. from the University of Virginia (1967). He has also studied at the University of California, Berkeley (1962–1963); Merton College, Oxford (1964–1965); and Goethe Institute in Germany (1964).

His work life began as an economics professor at Virginia Tech (1965–1969). During 1969–1971 he taught economics at the University of New Mexico; he has been a Fellow of the Hoover Institution on War, Revolution and Peace since 1971. He has also taught at Tulane University, Georgetown University, and George Mason University. Roberts has also worked as an economics adviser for Representative Jack Kemp and Senator Orrin Hatch. In addition to his column writing, he has been a contributing editor of *Harper*'s and has written for various political/finance/economic journals, including *Soviet Studies* and *Slavic Review.*

BOOKS: *Alienation and the Soviet Economy: Toward a General Theory of Marxian Alienation, Organizational Principles, and the Soviet Economy* (Albuquerque, N. Mex., 1971); with Matthew A. Stephenson, *Marx's Theory of Exchange, Alienation, and Crisis* (Stanford, Calif., 1973); *The Supply-Side Revolution: An Insider's Account of Policymaking in Washington* (Cambridge, Mass., 1984).

Robinson, Edwin Meade (1878–Sept. 1946). Novelist, poet, and literary critic Ted Robinson wrote columns in the papers of Cleveland, Ohio, from before 1910 until his death in 1946.

Robinson wrote for the *Cleveland Leader* from 1905 to 1910, in the column "Just by the Way." In 1910, he switched to the *Cleveland Plain Dealer,* where he wrote "Philosopher of Folly," which, like Franklin Pierce Adams's more famous "The Conning Tower," used contributions from other writers. Robinson himself had been a "Conning Tower" contributor. He went on to become the *Plain Dealer*'s associate editor and literary editor. Robinson was a lecturer in language and philology at Cleveland College in the 1930s and served as president of the American Press Humorists. He published five books.

BOOKS: *Mere Melodies* (Philadelphia, 1918); *Piping and Panning* (New York, 1920); *Enter Jerry* (New York, 1921); *Poems on An Archaic Pattern* (Cleveland, 1946); *Ted Robinson's New Testament Jazzes* (Cleveland, 1963).

Robinson, Elsinore Justina (30 April 1883–Sept. 1956). Elsie Robinson wrote two columns for King Features Syndicate: "Listen, World" for the adult reader and "Listen World to Young America" for children.

Robinson was born in Benicia, California, and attended the public schools of that city. She spent ten years in an unhappy marriage in Vermont, then took her ailing son and left for the West, where she worked as a hard-rock miner in a mining camp. Giving up mining, she moved to San Francisco and eventually found work at nearby Oakland writing children's stories for the *Tribune.* Her stories were an immediate success, and, writing as Aunt Elsie, she soon was in charge of an eight-page children's tabloid section on Sundays. The George Matthew Adams Service began syndicating her children's feature after two years, and around the same time she launched her column for adults.

William Randolph Hearst's right-hand man Arthur Brisbane signed her as a Hearst writer, and she continued writing "Listen World" out of New York until 1929, when she returned to California. Her only book was her autobiography. Her column was heavy on human interest. Robinson was bedridden after an accident in 1940.

BOOKS: *I Wanted Out* (New York, 1934).

Roche, John Pearson (7 May 1923–). Political science professor John Roche has written two columns: "A Word Edgewise," syndicated by King Features, and "News Watch," in *TV Guide.*

Roche was born in Brooklyn, New York. He holds the A.B. from Hofstra College (1943), the A.M. from Cornell University (1947), and the Ph.D. (1949), also from Cornell. He served with the Army Air Forces from 1943 to 1946. He has taught political science and history at Haverford College (1949–1956), Brandeis University (1956–1961), and Tufts University (since 1973). At Brandeis he was dean of arts and sciences (1958–1961) and at Tufts, academic dean of the

School of Law and Diplomacy (1973–1985). He has been active with various federal and United Nations commissions. He has published a number of books on politics and has been a frequent contributor of articles to scholarly journals and journals of commentary. His newspaper column appeared weekly, the *TV Guide* column, monthly.

BOOKS: With Murray S. Stedman, Jr., *The Dynamics of Democratic Government* (New York, 1954); *Courts and Rights: The American Judiciary in Action* (New York, 1961); ed. with Leonard W. Levy, *Readings in American Government,* 4 vols. (New York, 1962–1963); ed. with Leonard W. Levy, *The American Political Process* (New York, 1963); *The Quest for the Dream: The Development of Civil Rights and Human Relations in Modern America* (New York, 1963); *Shadow and Substance: Essays on the Theory and Structure of Politics* (New York, 1964); *Parties and Pressure Groups* (New York, 1964); with Leonard W. Levy, *The Judiciary* (New York, 1964); with Eugene J. Mechan and Murray S. Stedman, Jr., *The Dynamics of Modern Government* (New York, 1966); ed., *Origins of American Political Thought: Selected Readings* (New York, 1967); ed. with Stanley B. Bernstein, *John Marshall: Major Opinions and Other Writings* (Indianapolis, 1967); ed., *American Political Thought: From Jefferson to Progressivism* (New York, 1967); *Sentenced to Life* (New York, 1974); with Leonard W. Levy, *The Congress* (New York, 1984).

Rock, Howard (11 Aug. 1911–20 April 1976). Howard Rock, founding editor of the *Tundra Times* in Alaska, wrote a column titled "Arctic Survival" for that paper until his death in 1976.

Rock, whose Inupiat name was Siqvoan Weyahok, was born in Point Hope, a native village said to be the oldest continually inhabited site on the North American continent. His given name "Howard" was after a missionary who worked in this region of Alaska, and "Rock" is the translation of the Inupiat word *Weyahok.* Rock began his formal education at a mission school at Point Hope and later, in 1926, attended the White Mountain Vocational School in a more southerly part of the state. At the latter school Rock edited the yearbook, the *Nasevik.* In the early 1930s he spent three years studying art at the University of Washington in Seattle, after which he supported himself as an artist. He was drafted in 1942 and served as an Army Air Corps radio operator in North Africa, returning to Seattle after the war.

Rock returned to Alaska in 1961, and the inhabitants of Point Hope asked him to write to the Department of the Interior to protest proposed nuclear experiments known as Project Chariot. From this start, plans were made to start a native weekly paper, which originally was to be called *Inupiat Okatut,* which means "The Eskimos Speak." Working with a white reporter for the *Fairbanks Daily News-Miner,* Thomas Snapp, Rock became founding editor of the paper, which appeared in October 1962 and was given a more inclusive name, the *Tundra Times,* so as not to exclude the other native peoples, such as the Aleuts and Tlingits. The paper's reason for existence was to serve as a voice for the concerns of all Native American Alaskans. Rock and his paper were important in organizing these peoples politically to push for legislation vital to their interests. His column also presented a picture of their lives.

REFERENCES: Patrick Daley and Beverly James, "An Authentic Voice in the Technocratic Wilderness: Alaskan Natives and the Tundra Times," *Journal of Communication* 36 (Summer 1986): 10–30; Shirley E. Fogarino, *The Tundra Times: Alaska Native Advocate, 1962–1976,* Master's Thesis, University of Maryland, 1981; Lael Morgan, *Art and Eskimo Power* (Fairbanks, 1988).

Rodericks, Daniel J. (8 March 1954–   ). Dan Rodericks has written a column for the *Baltimore Sun* since 1979.

Rodericks was born in Brockton, Massachusetts, and earned the B.A. at the University of Bridgeport in 1976. From 1973 to 1975 he reported for the *Patriot Ledger* in Quincy, Massachusetts, and for the remainder of 1975 he was wire editor for the *Middletown Times Record* in New York state.

Rodericks joined the *Evening Sun* in Baltimore in 1976 as a reporter. He has been a reporter/commentator for WBAL-TV in Baltimore since 1980 and has hosted a radio talk show since 1989. He has authored one book.

BOOKS: *Mencken Doesn't Live Here Anymore: Tales of Baltimore in the 1980s* (Baltimore, 1989).

Rodriguez, Roberto (7 June 1954–   ). A former columnist for *La Opinion,* a Spanish-language daily in Los Angeles, and for *Black Issues in Higher Education,* Roberto Rodriguez also teams with his wife, Patrisia Gonzales, in writing "Latino Spectrum," an op-ed column syndicated by Chronicle Features.

Rodriguez was born in Aguascalentes, Mexico, and moved with his family to the United States at age five. He was reared in East Los Angeles and holds a 1976 history degree from the University of California, Los Angeles.

He began his career as a reporter/photographer for the magazine *Lowrider.* On an early assignment, he was beaten by sheriff's deputies in Los Angeles County after he had photographed the beating they gave a Latino street preacher. Rodriguez brought suit and eventually won a judgment of a reported $150,000. From 1985 to 1989 he wrote for the Hispanic Link News Service. Rodriguez began writing for *La Opinion,* America's largest Spanish-language daily, in 1987. One of his specialties has been writing about racial issues in general, with emphasis on relations between Latinos and African Americans.

"Latino Spectrum" began in syndication in March 1994. It covers issues of particular interest to what is rapidly becoming the nation's largest ethnic minority. The column's second purpose is to provide illumination for non-Latino readers.

REFERENCES: "Writing Team Covers a Latino Spectrum," *Editor and Publisher* (19 February 1994): 47.

Roeper, Richard (17 Oct. 1959–   ). Richard Roeper is lead columnist for the *Chicago Sun-Times* and has been with that paper for many years, since age twenty-four.

Roeper is a Chicago native and is a graduate of Illinois State University. He began at the *Sun-Times* as a cityside reporter and features writer and has written his general column since 1986. He has also written for *Playboy, Spy,* and *TV Guide* and has appeared on such television talk shows as the "Oprah Winfrey Show" and "Chicago Tonight."

Roessner, Barbara T. (?–). Barbara Roessner is a free-lance columnist for the *Hartford Courant* in Connecticut.

Roessner is a 1975 graduate of Wesleyan University, where she majored in Greek and Latin. From 1980 to 1985 she was the *Courant*'s chief political writer but gave up full-time work with the paper to raise a family. Her columns are distributed by the Los Angeles Times–Washington Post News Service, and she has also contributed to the *International Herald Tribune, Northeast Magazine,* and *Connecticut Magazine.*

Rogers, Joseph Lewis (28 June 1953–). Joe Rogers has written the "et cetera" column for the *Tennessean* in Nashville, Tennessee, since 1990.

Rogers was born in Moss Point, Mississippi, and received the B.A. in journalism from the University of Mississippi in 1974. He was a copy editor for the *Daily Herald* in Gulfport, Mississippi, in 1974–1975, then worked as a reporter/copy editor for the *Mississippi Press* in Pascagoula (1975–1978). From 1978 to 1984 he was a reporter and columnist for the *Jackson Daily News* in Jackson, Mississippi, moving to his present paper in 1990 as general columnist, feature writer, and reporter.

Rogers, Warren Joseph, Jr. (6 May 1922–). Warren Rogers wrote the syndicated Washington column "Countdown" from 1971 to 1973 and a much earlier column, "A. Labas," for the *New Orleans Item* (1945–1947).

Rogers was born in New Orleans. He attended both Tulane University (1940–1941) and Louisiana State University (1951) and served in the Marine Corps from 1941 to 1945. His initial contact with journalism was as a copyboy, then a cub reporter, with the *New Orleans Tribune.* He was a copyreader and columnist for the *Item* in that city from 1945 to 1947. In 1947 he went with the Associated Press, as a reporter in Baton Rouge until 1951 and in Washington, D.C., until 1959. From 1959 to 1963 he was a military affairs correspondent for the *New York Herald Tribune,* and from 1963 to 1966 he was chief Washington correspondent for Hearst Newspapers.

Look magazine employed Rogers as its Washington editor (1966–1969) and as its Washington bureau chief (1969–1970). He then worked in Washington as military and foreign affairs specialist for the *Los Angeles Times* (1970–1971), after which he wrote his "Countdown" column for the Chicago Tribune–New York News Syndicate (1971–1973).

Rogers was vice president of public affairs for the National Forest Products Association (1973–1976), editor in chief of Plus Publications (1977–1979), editor of the newsletter *White House Weekly* (1981–1989), editor of *This Week in the White House* (1989–1990). He was with the *Georgetown Courier* in 1991–1992. He has authored or coauthored six books.

BOOKS: *The Floating Revolution* (New York, 1962); with Roger Donlon, *Outpost of Freedom* (New York, 1965); *An Honorable Profession: A Tribute to Robert F. Kennedy* (New York, 1966); *Sea Shepherd* (New York, 1982); *Hickory Hill: Bob Kennedy at Home* (New York, 1985); *When I Think of Bobby: A Personal Memoir of the Kennedy Years* (New York, 1993).

Rogers, William Penn Adair (4 Nov. 1879–15 Aug. 1935). One of the best loved of all American humorists, Will Rogers wrote both daily and weekly newspaper columns that enjoyed wide syndication from 1922 until his tragic death in 1935.

Rogers was born on the Claremore, Oklahoma, ranch of his well-to-do parents. Whether he graduated from high school is unclear, but he attended Scarritt College in Neosho, Missouri, in 1895–1896, and in the following academic year, Kemper Military Academy in Booneville, Missouri, from which he ran away. He worked on the family ranch, then after winning trick roping competitions, traveled to South America and from there to South Africa, where he appeared as "The Cherokee Kid" in Texas Jack's Wild West Show. Next he performed his trick roping, trick riding act in Australia and New Zealand with Wirth Brothers Circus.

Rogers, whose father and mother were both part Cherokee, progressed from the circus to burlesque to, in 1904 Chicago, vaudeville. In 1905 he incorporated stand-up comedy routines, some of which were based on news items, into his roping act, and by 1916 he was a headliner in the Ziegfield Follies. His first acting job in a silent film was in 1918, and his first two humor books appeared in 1919. He wrote humorous magazine articles, became a regular on the lecture circuit, and in 1922 began writing a column for the McNaught Newspaper Syndicate. His slang-filled, down-home style writing, which appeared in both a daily and a weekly column, appeared in around three hundred papers until his death. He also did well-paid radio commentaries that began in 1926, donating much of the proceeds to charity. His first talking picture was in 1929, and overall, he was in some seventy films.

Rogers was perhaps the most omnipresent entertainer of the early twentieth century—he was in every medium, including Broadway. He was an aw-shucks, self-effacing humorist, the culmination of the cracker-barrel school. He leveled his gentle satire at the powerful, especially Congress; crusaded for the needy; and seemed to embody the sentiments of the everyday American. Like his contemporary Kin Hubbard, he was known for his aphorisms: "I love a dog. He does nothing for political reasons." "Nobody wants to be called the common people, especially the common people."

It is sadly ironic that Rogers had promoted flying in his columns and broadcasts. In 1927 he became the first U.S. civilian to fly coast to coast, and in

August of 1935, he and famed aviator Wiley Post were killed at Point Barrow, Alaska, when their Lockheed Orion-Explorer crashed into a river.

BOOKS: *Rogers-isms, The Cowboy Philosopher on the Peace Conference* (New York, 1919); *Rogers-isms, The Cowboy Philosopher on Prohibition* (New York, 1919); *The Illiterate Digest* (New York, 1924); *Letters of a Self-Made Diplomat to His President* (New York, 1926); *There's Not a Bathing Suit in Russia* (New York, 1927); *Ether and Me: Or Just Relax* (New York, 1929); *Twelve Radio Talks Delivered by Will Rogers During the Spring of 1930* (New York, 1930); *Will Rogers Wit and Wisdom,* comp. by Jack Lait (New York, 1936); *The Autobiography of Will Rogers,* ed. by Donald Day (Boston, 1949); *How We Elect Our Presidents,* ed. by Donald Day (Boston, 1952); *Sanity Is Where You Find It,* ed. by Donald Day (Boston, 1955); *The Writings of Will Rogers,* 13 vols., ed. by Joseph A. Stout, Jr., and James M. Smallwood (Stillwater, Okla., 1973–1980).

REFERENCES: Paul E. Alworth, *Will Rogers* (New York, 1974); Homer Croy, *Our Will Rogers* (New York, 1953); Donald Day, *Will Rogers* (New York, 1962); Betty Rogers, *Will Rogers: The Story of His Life As Told by His Wife* (Garden City, N.Y., 1943).

Rooney, Andrew Aitken (14 Jan. 1919–   ). Humorist Andy Rooney is best known for his curmudgeonly appearances on the CBS program "60 Minutes," but he also has written a column syndicated to newspapers by the Tribune Company since 1979.

Rooney was born in Albany, New York. He attended Colgate University in 1942, working for the campus literary-humor magazine and during the summer as a copyboy for an Albany paper. He was drafted into the army and sent to England as an artilleryman, later to be transferred to work with *Stars and Stripes.* He teamed with fellow military journalist Oram C. "Bud" Hutton and wrote three books, the second of which was the story of *Stars and Stripes* itself. MGM bought movie rights to the story and summoned the two ex-sergeants to Hollywood to work on the screenplay, after which they returned to Europe as free-lance writers, turning out articles for *Life, Look, Esquire,* and other magazines.

Rooney decided that the life of a free-lancer held little financial promise and from 1949 to 1955 wrote for the popular entertainer Arthur Godfrey. He next worked as a gag writer for comics Sam Levinson, Herb Shriner, and Victor Borge. In 1959 he began his long association with CBS, starting as a writer for "The Garry Moore Show." In 1962 he and CBS newsman Harry Reasoner collaborated on a series of TV news features done with genial satire. Rooney became unhappy with the network's treatment of his more serious ideas and left it in 1970 for two years as a writer for public television. He returned to CBS in 1972, and in 1978 he was featured as a summer substitute for "60 Minutes'" Point-Counterpoint segment, which featured journalists James J. Kilpatrick and Shana Alexander. Rooney's droll examination of seemingly mundane topics was so popular that he has been a "60 Minutes" regular since that time. He extended his reach as a "popular philosopher" through his column, which since 1979 has been syndicated to as many as 250 newspapers. In February 1990, Rooney was accused of making racist and antigay comments and was temporarily suspended by CBS. He denied having made the remarks attributed to him and was reinstated after three months. His column was never suspended.

BOOKS: With Oram C. Hutton, *Air Gunner* (New York, 1944); with Oram Hutton, *The Story of the Stars and Stripes* (New York, 1946); with Oram Hutton, *Conqueror's Peace: A Report to the American Stockholders* (Garden City, N.Y., 1947); *The Fortunes of War, Four Great Battles of World War II* (Boston, 1962); *A Few Minutes with Andy Rooney* (New York, 1981); *And More by Andy Rooney* (New York, 1982); *Pieces of My Mind* (New York, 1984); *Word for Word* (New York, 1986); *The Most of Andy Rooney* (New York, 1986); *Not That You Asked—* (Norwalk, Conn., 1989); *Sweet and Sour* (New York, 1992).

Roosevelt, Anna Eleanor (11 Oct. 1884–7 Nov. 1962). Eleanor Roosevelt, wife of President Franklin Roosevelt, wrote a column titled "My Day" for United Feature Syndicate from 1936 until her death in 1962.

Anna Roosevelt, niece of President Theodore Roosevelt, was born in New York City. She was educated at home until being enrolled in Allenwood, an English school for girls, where she studied for three years. She and Franklin Roosevelt, her fifth cousin, were married in 1905 while he was a law student.

During her husband's long political career, including her dozen years as First Lady (1933–1945), she became the most visible and involved president's wife ever. She campaigned, traveled to promote U.S. interests, spoke in favor of the various social programs of the New Deal, addressed the nation in fifteen minute radio broadcasts, and in 1936 began a widely syndicated newspaper column, "My Day," which at first was diarylike, but which later dealt with more substantial public issues. The original home base for her column was the *New York World-Telegram,* but after her husband's death, she moved to the *New York Post.*

Her first print media experience was as editor of *Babies, Just Babies,* a magazine created for her by the flamboyant publisher Bernarr Macfadden as a fairly transparent way to curry favor with FDR in hopes of securing an ambassadorship or some other prestigious political appointment. Macfadden was disappointed, and Mrs. Roosevelt edited this unusual magazine for only a short while—June 1932–March 1933. Later in 1933 she began doing a page for another magazine, *Woman's Home Companion.* These jobs, combined with her column and her several books, gave her so much public exposure that she became the subject of "Eleanor jokes" in much the same way that in more recent years, Hillary Rodham Clinton has been the object of many jibes. Overall, however, Eleanor Roosevelt was much loved and admired.

BOOKS: Ed., *Hunting Big Game in the Eighties: The Letters of Elliot Roosevelt, Sportsman* (New York, 1932); *It's Up to the Women* (New York, 1933); *This Is My Story* (New York, 1937); *The Lady of the White House* (London, 1938); with Frances Cooke Macgregor, *This Is America* (New York, 1942); *This I Remember* (New York, 1949); with Helen Farris, *Partners: The United Nations and Youth* (Garden City, N.Y., 1950); *India and the Awakening East* (New York, 1953); with William De Witt, *UN: Today and Tomorrow* (New York, 1953); *It Seems to Me* (New York, 1954); with Lorena A. Hickok, *Ladies of Courage* (New York, 1954): *On My Own* (New York, 1958); *You Learn by Living* (New York, 1960); with Helen Ferris, *Your Teens and Mine* (Garden City, N.Y., 1961); *The Autobiography of Eleanor Roosevelt* (New York, 1961); *The Wisdom of Eleanor Roosevelt: Eleanor Roosevelt Writes About Her World* (New York, 1962); *Book of Common Sense Etiquette* (New York, 1962); *Tomorrow Is Now* (New York, 1963); *Eleanor Roosevelt's Christmas Book* (New York, 1963).

REFERENCES: Ruby A. Black, *Eleanor Roosevelt, A Biography* (New York, 1940); Rochelle Chadakoff, ed., *Eleanor Roosevelt's My Day, 1936–1945* (New York, 1989); David Emblidge, ed., *Eleanor Roosevelt's My Day* (New York, 1994); Joseph Lash, *Eleanor: The Years Alone* (New York, 1972).

Roosevelt, Edith Kermit (19 Dec. 1926–   ). Edith Roosevelt was writer of the syndicated weekly column "Between the Lines." Her specialties were health and fitness.

Roosevelt was born in New York City and received the B.A. in 1948 from Barnard College. She was a United Press International (UPI) reporter in California and Washington, D.C., from 1950 to 1955; wrote for the communication consulting firm of McConn Erickson from 1956 to 1957; and was a feature writer and editor with the Spadea Syndicate from 1957 to 1959. From 1959–1963 she was a reporter for the *Newark* [New Jersey] *Star Ledger,* and beginning in 1963 she worked as Washington correspondent for a variety of newspapers, including the *Manchester Union Leader, Vermont Sunday News,* and *Connecticut Sunday Herald.* Increasingly concentrating on health issues, she became Washington correspondent for *Nutrition and Health Review* in 1980. Her column was launched in 1963, and she also wrote for such magazines as *Barron's, Your Health, Popular Medicine,* and *Karate International.*

Rose, Billy (6 Sept. 1899–10 Feb. 1966). New York showman Billy Rose wrote a column, "Pitching Horseshoes," which was nationally syndicated from 1946 to 1953.

Rose was born William Samuel Rosenberg in New York City. He had his name changed legally to Billy Rose. His formal education was limited to Public School 44 in the Bronx.

Rose first achieved fame as an expert at Gregg shorthand. Gregg himself used Rose to demonstrate the effectiveness and speed of his system. Rose's ability to take dictation from several sources at once attracted the attention of the financier Bernard Baruch, who employed the gifted teenager to take all his confidential dictation. At age twenty, Rose gave up shorthand to become a songwriter. His first published song was "Barney Google;" possibly his best was "Without a Song." Next he went into the nightclub business, then moved to Hollywood for a brief and generally unsuccessful stint as a movie writer. His first wife was the stage great Fanny Brice.

A Rose original was the combined restaurant/nightclub/theater. Among his best remembered shows were the circus spectacular *Jumbo;* the *Aquacade,* a leggy water show put on at the New York World's Fair in 1939–1940; and *Carmen Jones.*

BOOKS: *Wine, Women and Words* (New York, 1948).

Rosenfeld, Stephen Samuel (26 July 1932–   ). Stephen Rosenfeld is a columnist at the *Washington Post,* where he has worked since 1959.

He was born in Pittsfield, Massachusetts, and earned his B.A. from Harvard University in 1953, his M.A. from Columbia University in 1959.

Rosenfeld worked as a reporter for the *Berkshire Eagle* in Pittsfield from 1955 to 1957. In 1959 he began as a reporter for the *Washington Post,* then was a foreign correspondent, columnist, and department editor on the *Post* editorial page. He has written two books.

BOOKS: With Barbara Rosenfeld, *Return from Red Square* (Washington, D.C., 1967); *The Time of Their Dying* (New York, 1977).

Rosenthal, Abraham Michael (2 May 1922–   ). A. M. Rosenthal, executive editor of the *New York Times* from 1977 to 1986, began his conservative political column "On My Mind" in 1986.

Rosenthal was born in Sault Ste. Marie, Ontario. He earned the B.S. from City College in New York in 1944 and became a U.S. citizen in 1951.

A one-newspaper man, Rosenthal began working for the *Times* in 1944, was the paper's UN correspondent from 1946 to 1954, and spent most of the next decade as a foreign correspondent: in India (1954–1958), Poland (1958–1959), Switzerland (1960–1961), and Japan (1961–1963).

He worked from 1963 to 1967 as the *Times*'s metropolitan editor, during 1967–1968 as assistant managing editor, and in 1967–1968 as associate managing editor. He was managing editor from 1969 to 1977 and executive editor thereafter. Rosenthal won a Pulitzer Prize in 1960 for his stories out of Poland. He has taken part in editing several books and has often written for the *New York Times Magazine, Foreign Affairs,* and other periodicals. His column is handled by the New York Times News Service. In 1990 he made headlines by accusing fellow conservative columnist Patrick Buchanan of anti-Semitism over comments Buchanan had made about ties between Israel and that nation's Jewish supporters in the United States.

BOOKS: Edited with Arthur Gelb, *The Pope's Journey to the United States* (New York, 1965); edited with Arthur Gelb, *The Night the Lights Went Out* (New York, 1965); with Arthur Gelb, *One More Victim* (New York, 1967); edited with Arthur Gelb, Michael J. Leahy, and Nora Kerr, *The Sophisticated Traveler: Beloved Cities, Europe* (New York, 1984); edited with Arthur Gelb, Michael J. Leahy, and Nora Kerr, *Winter: Love It or Leave It* (London, 1984); edited with Arthur Gelb and Marvin Siegel, *The New York Times World of New York: An Uncommon Guide to the City of Fantasies* (New York, 1985); edited with Arthur Gelb, Michael J. Leahy, and Nora Kerr, *Great Tours and*

Detours (London, 1985); ed. with Arthur Gelb, Michael J. Leahy, and Nora Kerr, *The Sophisticated Traveler: Enchanting Places and How to Find Them* (New York, 1986); ed. with Arthur Gelb and Marvin Siegel, *New York Times Great Lives of the Twentieth Century* (New York, 1988).

Rowan, Carl Thomas (11 Aug. 1925–). One of America's most prominent and experienced journalists, Carl Rowan has been writing a nationally syndicated column since 1965.

Rowan was born in Ravenscroft, Tennessee, but grew up mainly in another Tennessee town, McMinnville. He attended an ill-equipped all-black school in McMinnville, graduating in 1942 as class president and valedictorian. He attended Tennessee Agricultural and Industrial State College in Nashville during 1942–1943, then joined the navy for wartime service. In 1944 he became one of the first fifteen blacks to become commissioned navy officers and served as a communications officer on two ships in the Atlantic. After the war, Rowan attended Oberlin College, where he received the A.B. in mathematics in 1947. He earned the M.A. in journalism from the University of Minnesota in 1948, writing during that year for two black papers, the *Minneapolis Spokesman* and the *St. Paul Recorder* as well as doing public opinion survey work for the *Baltimore Afro-American.*

He was hired by the *Minneapolis Tribune* in November 1948. He worked for two years as a copyreader, then from 1950 to 1961 as the paper's first black reporter. In 1951 he took on a major assignment, traveling six thousand miles around the South to gauge race relations. His series of stories "How Far from Slavery?" won much acclaim and were turned into a book, *South of Freedom* (1952). Rowan spent much of 1954 in Asia lecturing for the U.S. State Department and filing stories on what he saw there. Again, a book resulted: *The Pitiful and the Proud* (1956).

In 1960 the *Tribune* sent Rowan to Washington to cover the Nixon-Kennedy presidential race. On New Year's Day 1961, President-Elect Kennedy asked Rowan, whose stories he had found balanced and fair, to take charge of the State Department's press relations as deputy assistant secretary of state for public affairs. Rowan was party to the 1962 swap of U-2 pilot Francis Gary Powers for the Russian spy Rudolph Abel and in general was subject to the usual pressures of a journalist suddenly thrust into public relations work.

In 1963 Kennedy appointed Rowan ambassador to Finland, the fifth African American to become an ambassador. After nine months in this role, President Lyndon Johnson made Rowan head of the United States Information Agency to replace the retiring Edward R. Murrow. As such, Rowan was the highest-ranking black in the federal government and the first black on the National Security Council. After a disagreement with Johnson in July 1965, Rowan resigned and began writing a thrice-weekly column for the *Chicago Daily News* and the Field Enterprises Syndicate. He also became a roving editor for *Reader's Digest,* writing about four stories yearly for that magazine. Finally, he signed on for three radio commentary broadcasts a week for the Westinghouse Broadcasting Company. Without the help of his staff of seven, these commitments would probably have been unworkable.

Despite his many, many columns urging fair treatment for black Americans, he has been, on occasion, called an Uncle Tom by more militant blacks. He frequently exhorts young African-Americans to aim high and get the best possible education. Rowan is not at all a one-issue columnist, commenting on other social problems, national politics, and international affairs. Like many another primarily political columnist, he has found that his nonpolitical, personal columns are often the ones that provoke the most mail. His column is presently syndicated by King Features and was earlier handled by North America Syndicate.

A political independent and moderate, he was on Nixon's celebrated enemies list, found Jimmy Carter an inept president, and was displeased by Reaganomics and some of its holdovers during the Bush years. He has sparred with George Will and James J. Kilpatrick on television's "Agronsky & Co." and has made frequent appearances on "Meet the Press." Rowan has won a long list of awards and roughly forty honorary degrees.

BOOKS: *South of Freedom* (New York, 1952); *The Pitiful and the Proud* (New York, 1956); *Go South to Sorrow* (New York, 1957); with Jackie Robinson, *Wait till Next Year: The Life Story of Jackie Robinson* (New York, 1960); *Just Between Us Blacks* (New York, 1974); *Breaking Barriers: A Memoir* (Boston, 1991); *Dream Makers, Dream Breakers: The World of Justice Thurgood Marshall* (Boston, 1993).

REFERENCES: Neil A. Grauer, *Wits and Sages* (Baltimore and London, 1984): 195–212.

Rowell, Chester Harvey (1 Nov. 1867–12 April 1948). An influential California newspaper editor and columnist, Chester Rowell was born in Bloomington, Illinois.

He received the Ph.B. in modern languages from the University of Michigan in 1888, completing the degree in three years. After one more year studying philosophy, he took a position his father had arranged for him as clerk for the U.S. House of Representatives' Committee on Elections. Next he spent two years in Germany at universities in Halle and Berlin, studying political economics and philosophy, after which he taught for four years at schools in four states: Kansas, Wisconsin, California, and Illinois.

In 1898 Rowell became editor of a newspaper founded and owned by his uncle, also Chester Rowell. As editor of the *Fresno Republican,* he became politically active in California, campaigning against the power of the big rail interests and for passage of the state's workmen's compensation laws in 1911 and 1913. He favored California's Alien Land Act of 1913, which disallowed ownership of farm land by aliens. In 1914, Rowell ran unsuccessfully for the U.S. Senate. In 1920, the *Republican* was sold, and Rowell spent the next decade lecturing and writing a syndicated newspaper column. In 1932 he became editor (1932–1935) of the *San Francisco Chronicle,* for which he also wrote a column from 1935 to 1947. He was opposed to the New Deal and increasingly wrote on world politics.

REFERENCES: Miles C. Everett, *Chester Harvey Rowell, Pragmatic Humanist and California Progressive,* Ph.D. Dissertation, University of California, Berkeley, 1966; George E. Mowry, *The California Progressives* (Berkeley and Los Angeles, 1951); Spencer C. Olin, Jr., *California's Prodigal Sons: Hiram Johnson and the Progressives, 1911–1917* (Berkeley, Calif., 1968).

Rowen, Hobart (31 July 1918–   ). Longtime syndicated columnist Hobart Rowen comments mainly on politics and the economy.

Rowen was born in Burlington, Vermont, and earned the B.S. in 1938 from City College of New York. He began his career as a reporter and Washington correspondent for the *Journal of Commerce* (1938–1942) and from 1942 to 1944 worked with the War Production Board in Washington. From 1944 to 1965 he was a Washington correspondent for *Newsweek* and also served as that magazine's business trends editor (1957–65). Rowen wrote a column that was syndicated by the North American Newspaper Alliance from 1960 to 1963. He then became financial editor and assistant managing editor of the *Washington Post* (1966–1975) and later its economics editor (1975–1991). His *Post* column was launched in 1975; it is syndicated via the Washington Post Writers Group. He has also contributed to such magazines as *New Republic* and *Harper's.*

BOOKS: *The Free Enterprisers—Kennedy, Johnson and the Business Establishment* (New York, 1964).

Rowland, Helen (1876–?). Witty Helen Rowland is remembered for her daily columns that offered satirical treatment of one of the oldest stories of all: the battle of the sexes.

Rowland was born in Washington, D.C., and was educated in the public schools of Washington, D.C., in a private school in Louisville, Kentucky, and at Emerson College. While still a teenager, she sold material to the *Washington Post.*

Later Rowland wrote interview stories for the *Post,* humor verse for the old *Life* magazine, and short stories for various other magazines. Eventually she left Washington for New York City and a job at the *Sunday Press,* where she did feature stories, fashion coverage, humor verse, and other material. A year later, the *Press* gave her a column, which she later self-syndicated. Her column was picked up by the McClure Syndicate, which called it "Widow Wordalogues." Later columns appeared under the title "The Sayings of Mrs. Solomon," and around this time she moved from the *Press* to the *Evening World.* She also changed syndicates, going with the Wheeler Syndicate after eleven years with McClure. Her columns for Wheeler appeared under the column title "Meditations of a Married Woman." Finally, in 1924 she left Wheeler to join King Features Syndicate, and at this time her daily column became the "Marry-Go-Round." Her various columns were collected into eight books.

BOOKS: *The Digressions of Polly* (New York, 1905); *Reflections of a Bachelor Girl* (New York, 1909); *The Sayings of Mrs. Solomon: Being the Confessions of the Seven Hundredth Wife as Revealed to Helen Rowland* (New York, 1913); *The Rubaaiyaat of a Bachelor* (London, 1915); *A Guide to Men: Being Encore Reflections of a Bachelor Girl* (New York, 1922); *If* (New York, 1927); *This Married Life* (New York, 1927); comp. with Franklin P. Adams, Deems Taylor, and Percival Wilde, *The Week End Companion* (Cleveland and New York, 1941).

REFERENCES: Ishbel Ross, *Ladies of the Press* (New York, 1974): 379–381.

Royko, Mike (19 Sept. 1932–   ). In Chicago, a city known for its great columnists, Mike Royko has been the head billy goat for years. He was a columnist for the *Daily News* from 1959 to 1978, the *Sun-Times* from 1978 to 1984, and the *Tribune* since 1984.

He was born—where else?—in Chicago, in a tough Polish neighborhood on the city's northwest side. His parents were Ukrainian immigrants who ran a saloon. At age twelve he worked as a pinboy in a bowling alley, at fifteen as a bartender. He left high school at age sixteen, worked as a department store stock clerk and a theater usher, then returned to complete high school. After spending 1951–1952 at Wright Junior College, Royko joined the air force and went to Korea as a radio operator. Transferred to Chicago to become a military policeman, he lied and instead became editor of a base newspaper. He claimed to have worked at the *Chicago Daily News.*

When he left the service in 1956, Royko became a reporter for Lerner newspapers, a group of weeklies in Chicago's suburbs. He soon left Lerner for the City News Bureau, there to work the police beat, then to cover city hall. He was night city editor and assistant day editor before joining the *Daily News* in 1959 as a beat reporter. He was given a county government column that appeared weekly, an assignment that in September 1963 was followed by a general thrice-weekly column. By 1964 he was the top local columnist, appearing five times a week.

Royko was now in his element, attacking Mayor Richard Daley and other Chicago politicos, writing about the city's Runyonesque low-lifes, recounting the stories of ordinary Chicagoans of all sorts. Here and at his subsequent papers, he used his column to speak against discrimination, and later, to rail against political correctness. He was against the war in Vietnam, disgusted with beatniks and hippies, distrustful of feminists, one of Jane Fonda's least ardent fans, and the columnist who called California's Jerry Brown "Governor Moonbeam."

In 1978 the *Daily News* folded, and Royko switched to the *Sun-Times,* continuing to mix irony and exaggeration with a sort of macho indignation that made some readers laugh with delight and others fume. Most delightful of his creations are Slats Grobnik, a skinny Huck Finn of inner-city Chicago, who in one column called the police on his own "fodder" when he thought he had caught the old fellow stealing his Easter basket, and Slats's friend, Skinny Archie, who was, in Royko's words, "so dumb he couldn't find his teeth with his tongue.'' While Royko was with the *Sun-Times,* his column was syndicated by the Independent Press to around two hundred other papers.

Royko left the *Sun-Times* in 1984, the day after the paper had been bought by Australian press magnate Rupert Murdock. Royko went with the *Tribune* and has been there since. His column is now syndicated by Tribune Media Services to 550 papers. Royko is at the top of the heap among the columnists of his city, yet he, unlike so many other successful columnists today, keeps clear of television appearances and the lecture circuit and has decided to concentrate on the column rather than writing books, with the exception of collections of his columns. The main exception to this decision, *Boss,* an unsympathetic account of Mayor Daley, appeared in 1971.

Although mellowed somewhat, Royko still manages to raise hackles. Some of the papers that use his column refused in late 1993 to run a column that reprinted suggestive limericks about the John Bobbitt case. In typical fashion, the seriocomically gruff columnist called them prudes. Probably slobs and jerks, too.

BOOKS: *Up Against It* (Chicago, 1967); *I May Be Wrong, but I Doubt It* (Chicago, 1968); *Boss: Richard J. Daley of Chicago* (New York, 1971); *Slats Grobnik and Some Other Friends* (New York, 1973); *Sez Who? Sez Me* (New York, 1982); *Like I Was Sayin'* (New York, 1984); *Dr. Kookie, You're Right* (New York, 1989).

REFERENCES: William Brashler, "The Man Who Owns Chicago," *Esquire* (8 May 1979): 44–55; Neil A. Grauer, *Wits and Sages* (Baltimore and London, 1984): 215–236; Howard Kurtz, "Lunchbox Laureate," *Washington Post* (28 September 1993): C1, C9.

Royster, Vermont Connecticut (30 April 1914–   ). Two-time Pulitzer Prize winner Vermont Royster was editor of the *Wall Street Journal* from 1958 to 1971 and wrote a weekly column for that paper from 1971 throughout most of the 1980s.

Royster was born in Raleigh, North Carolina, and spent part of his youth in nearby Chapel Hill. After two years of study at the Webb School in Bell Buckle, Tennessee, he went to the University of North Carolina, where he majored in classical languages, worked for the *Daily Tar Heel,* and graduated Phi Beta Kappa in 1935.

Moving to New York City after graduation, Royster and two Chapel Hill classmates founded the unsuccessful Metropolitan News Service, which focused on North Carolinians living in New York. He then took a job as a messenger/reporter for the New York News Association, but his job was eliminated after a few weeks. In February 1936 he found work with the Dow Jones News Service, and a month later he was sent to Washington, D.C., to cover the Department of Agriculture for the *Wall Street Journal*'s bureau there. His assignments broadened, and he also wrote for Dow Jones's weekly magazine *Barron's.* He was assigned to cover the Supreme Court, then served with the Navy Reserves and returned to the *Journal* in 1945. He became Washington bureau chief in 1946, then moved to New York and wrote editorials, with the title of associate editor. In 1951 he became senior associate editor and won his first Pulitzer, for editorial writing. He was chairman of the National Conference of Editorial Writers in 1957 and became editor of the *Journal* in 1958. Until his retirement in 1971, Royster wrote extensively on national and international politics.

After retirement, he began his weekly column, "Review and Outlook," for which he won his second Pulitzer in 1984. He also began teaching journalism at his alma mater in 1971 and began appearing on CBS's "Spectrum."

BOOKS: *Journey Through the Soviet Union* (New York, 1962); *A Pride of Prejudices* (New York, 1967); *My Own, My Country's Time: A Journalist's Journey* (Chapel Hill, N.C., 1983); *The Essential Royster: A Vermont Royster Reader* (Chapel Hill, N.C., 1985).

REFERENCES: Lloyd Wendt, *The Wall Street Journal: The Story of Dow Jones and the Nation's Business Newspaper* (Chicago, 1982).

Runyon, Alfred Damon (4 Oct. 1884–10 Dec. 1946). Damon Runyon, chronicler of New York City's underworld and Broadway scene, did several columns for the *New York American*. One, "The Brighter Side," was carried by hundreds of newspapers.

He was born in Manhattan, Kansas. His family name was actually Runyan; after a printer misspelled it with an *o,* he decided that he preferred it that way. Some years later, one of his editors, Harry Cashman of the *New York American,* told him his byline was too long, and "Alfred" was dropped for good. In 1887, the Runyan family moved to Pueblo, Colorado, where Damon eventually worked as a reporter on the *Pueblo Evening Press.* He enlisted in the army in 1889 and was sent to the Philippines, where he wrote for the military paper the *Manila Freedom* and the magazine *Soldier's Letter.* He returned to the Pueblo paper in 1899 and spent part of the early 1900s as an itinerant semihobo reporter for small town papers before being hired in 1905 as a sportswriter for the *Denver Post.* He was fired the next year but was hired by the *Rocky Mountain News,* also in Denver, to cover local politics. By 1908 he was placing stories and poetry in *Collier's, McClure's,* and other magazines, and here was born his use of "Runyonese"—the slang and argot of society's underside.

In 1910 he got a job writing about sports for the *New York American.* He gave sports stories a humorous spin, and in 1914, he began the column "Th' Mornin's Mornin'," which was more or less given over to humor. The versatile Runyon also wrote western stories and covered major trials for the *American.* In 1928 the title of his column was changed to "I Think So," and in the following year he changed it again to "Between You and Me," once again concentrating more on sports, especially boxing and horse racing. His popular tales of Broadway appeared in *Cosmopolitan, Saturday Evening Post,* and *Collier's* from 1929 to 1940. Runyon spent his nights among entertainment, sports, and underworld figures and police, drinking a reported forty to fifty cups of coffee daily. In the mid-1930s, he wrote a sports column titled "Both Barrels" for the *American.* In 1937 he put aside sports to begin a new column, "As I

See It,'' which was syndicated to other Hearst papers, and later in this same year, he retitled the column ''The Brighter Side.'' It was widely syndicated. He also wrote a column for the *New York Daily Mirror* toward the end of the 1930s. He became one of America's highest paid columnists, bought his own string of race horses, and began wintering in Florida. After his death, some of his Broadway tales were adapted for the acclaimed musical *Guys and Dolls* (1950). Runyon's ashes were scattered from a plane over Manhattan by his old friend Capt. Eddie Rickenbacker.

BOOKS: *The Tents of Trouble* (New York, 1911); *Rhymes of the Firing Line* (New York, 1912); *Guys and Dolls* (New York, 1932); *Blue Plate Special* (New York, 1934); *Money from Home* (New York, 1935); *More than Somewhat* (London, 1937); *Take It Easy* (New York, 1938); *Furthermore: A Companion Book of Stories to "More than Somewhat"* (London, 1938); *The Best of Damon Runyon* (New York, 1938); *My Old Man* (New York, 1939); *My Wife Ethel* (London, 1939); *The Damon Runyon Omnibus* (New York, 1939); *A Slight Case of Murder* (New York, 1940); *Runyon a la Carte* (Philadelphia, 1944); *The Three Wise Guys and Other Stories* (New York, 1946); *In Our Town* (New York, 1946); *Short Takes, Reader's Choice of the Best Columns of America's Favorite Newspaperman* (New York and London, 1946); *Poems for Men* (New York, 1947); *Trials and Other Tribulations* (Philadelphia, 1948); *Runyon First and Last* (Philadelphia, 1949); *More Guys and Dolls* (Garden City, N.Y., 1951); *Runyon from First to Last* (London, 1954).

REFERENCES: Tom Clark, *The World of Damon Runyon* (New York, 1978); Patricia Ward D'Itri, *Damon Runyon* (Boston, 1982); Edwin P. Hoyt, *A Gentleman of Broadway: The Story of Damon Runyon* (Boston, 1964); Damon Runyon, Jr., *Father's Footsteps* (New York, 1954); Jean Wagner, *Runyonese: The Mind and Craft of Damon Runyon* (Paris, 1965); Edward H. Weiner, *The Damon Runyon Story* (New York, 1948).

Rusher, William Allen (19 July 1923–   ). Conservative William Rusher was a columnist with the Universal Press Syndicate from 1973 to 1982 and has written ''The Conservative Advocate'' for the Newspaper Enterprise Association since that time.

Rusher was born in Chicago. He received the A.B. from Princeton in 1943, the J.D. from Harvard in 1948. He was admitted to the New York bar in 1949 and worked with the New York firm of Shearman & Sterling & Wright from 1948 to 1956. Rusher was special counsel for the finance committee of the New York Senate in 1955 and was associate counsel of the internal security subcommittee of the U.S. Senate in 1956–1957. In 1957 he joined William F. Buckley as publisher and vice president of the *National Review,* which had been founded two years earlier. He served in this capacity until 1988. His conservative column has appeared since 1973, enjoying wide syndication. In recent years, Rusher has been known for his remarks charging a predominant liberal bias in the U.S. news media.

BOOKS: *Special Counsel* (New Rochelle, N.Y., 1968); with Arlie Schardt and Mark O. Hatfield, *Amnesty?* (Croton-on-Hudson, N.Y., 1973); *The Making of the New Majority Party* (New York, 1975); *How to Win Arguments* (Garden City, N.Y., 1981); *The Rise of the Right* (New York, 1984); *The Coming Battle for the Media: Curbing the Power of the Media Elite* (New York, 1988).

Russell, Mark (23 Aug. 1932–   ). Known mainly as a comedian who specializes in political satire, Mark Russell has also written a humor column syndicated by the Los Angeles Times Syndicate since 1975.

He was born Mark Ruslander in Buffalo, New York, and later legally changed his name to Russell. He attended the University of Miami and George Washington University in 1952, then enlisted in the Marines (1953–1956). While stationed at Quantico, Virginia, Russell began playing piano in area night spots. He held similar jobs in Washington, D.C., after leaving the service. Here he discovered that original songs that satirized politicians were extremely popular with his audiences. His first steady job of this sort was at the cocktail lounge of the Carroll Arms. In 1961 he moved to more upscale surroundings at Washington's Shoreham Hotel, where he was the featured performer until 1981. Since 1975 he has done a number of "Mark Russell Comedy Specials" on PBS, cohosted NBC's "Real People" from 1979 to 1984, and contributed to ABC-TV's "Good Morning, America." He also entertains on the college and banquet circuits and gives his merry one-liners a still wider audience via his syndicated column.

BOOKS: *Presenting Mark Russell* (New York, 1980).

Ryskind, Morrie (20 Oct. 1895–24 Aug. 1985). The versatile Morrie Ryskind came to be a successful syndicated columnist by a most unusual route. He began writing a political column in 1960 after a career as a lyricist, playwright, screenwriter, and poet. "The Morrie Ryskind Column" ran until Ryskind's retirement in 1978.

Ryskind was born in New York City. While a high school student, he contributed to "The Conning Tower," the popular column of Franklin P. Adams. He studied journalism at Columbia University and worked part-time as an assistant to George S. Kaufman, drama editor of the *New York Times*. After brief experience free-lancing poems and song lyrics, he assisted Kaufman in writing *The Cocoanuts*, a musical starring the Marx Brothers, and in 1928 the two collaborated on a second Marx Brothers project, *Animal Crackers*.

Ryskind did screenwriting and wrote for Broadway plays and musicals in the 1930s. One of his musicals, the satirical *Of Thee I Sing* (1931), was the first musical play to win a Pulitzer Prize for drama. The prize was shared by collaborators Ryskind, Kaufman, and the Gershwins, Ira and George. A few years later, Ryskind worked with Gregory La Cava on the 1936 comedy hit *My Man Godfrey*. His last projects as a screenwriter/playwright were in 1946.

In the late 1940s, Ryskind became caught up in the anticommunist fervor of the times, testifying in 1947 against other Hollywood film industry figures before the House Un-American Activities Committee. He was a supporter of Senator Joseph McCarthy. Ryskind was instrumental in founding the *National Review* in 1955, and in 1960 he began writing a political column that was handled by the Los Angeles Times Syndicate. More than a decade later he left the syndicate over a disagreement about one of his columns and took his column to the *Los Angeles Herald Examiner,* where he remained until his retirement in 1978.

BOOKS: *Unaccustomed As I Am* (New York, 1921); with C. F. Stevens and James Englander, *The Home Movie Scenario Book* (New York, 1927); *The Diary of an Ex-President* (New York, 1932).

REFERENCES: Charlotte Chandler, *Hello, I Must Be Going: Groucho and His Friends* (Garden City, N.Y., 1978); Richard Corliss, *Talking Pictures* (Woodstock, N.Y., 1974); Scott Meredith, *George S. Kaufman and His Friends* (Garden City, N.Y., 1974); Howard Teichmann, *George S. Kaufman: An Intimate Portrait* (New York, 1972).

S

Safire, William L. (17 Dec. 1929–   ). Readable and widely syndicated conservative columnist William Safire writes two columns for the *New York Times:* his political column titled "Essay" and another devoted to words and writing titled "On Language," which appears in the *New York Times Magazine.* His work is syndicated by the New York Times News Service.

Born William Safir in New York City, he attended Syracuse University in 1948–1949 but had to drop out because of finances. He took a job as a legman for columnist Tex McCrary, whose "New York Close-Up" column appeared in the *New York Herald Tribune.* He next entered broadcasting and worked in Europe and the Middle East for WNBC and WNBT-TV. After spending 1952–1954 in the U.S. Army, Safire became producer of Tex McCrary's show for radio and television, "Tex and Jinx," named for McCrary and his wife, Jinx Falkenburg. In 1955 he became a vice president of Tex McCrary, Inc., a public relations firm that had major clients.

In January 1961, Safire founded Safire Public Relations, Inc., his own firm, and was active in Republican campaign work. He began writing speeches for Richard Nixon in 1965 and assisted Patrick Buchanan in writing for a syndicated column under Nixon's byline. In 1969, Safire became a special assistant to President Nixon and served as the president's wordsmith. He worked for Vice President Spiro Agnew in 1970 and was the author of many of Agnew's heavy-handed alliterative phrases that made conservatives glow with pleasure while liberals and moderates gagged.

Safire has written for numerous magazines, including *Redbook, Playboy,* and the *Harvard Business Review,* and he has authored around twenty-five books.

BOOKS: *The Relations Explosion, a Diagram of the Coming Boom and Shakeout in Corporate Relations* (New York, 1963); *Plunging into Politics* (New York, 1964); *The New*

Language of Politics (New York, 1968); *Before the Fall: An Inside View of the Pre-Watergate White House* (Garden City, N.Y., 1975); *Full Disclosure* (Garden City, N.Y., 1977); *Safire's Political Dictionary* (New York, 1978); *On Language* (New York, 1980); *Safire's Washington* (New York, 1980); *What's the Good Word?* (New York, 1982); compiled and edited with Leonard Safir, *Good Advice* (New York, 1982); *I Stand Corrected: More on Language* (New York, 1984); *Take My Word for It* (New York, 1986); *Freedom* (Garden City, N.Y., 1987); *You Could Look It Up* (New York, 1988); *Words of Wisdom: More Good Advice* (New York, 1989); *Fumblerules: Guide to Grammar and Good Usage* (New York, 1990); *Language Maven Strikes Again* (Garden City, N.Y., 1990); *Coming to Terms* (Garden City, N.Y., 1991); *The First Dissident: The Book of Job in Today's Politics* (New York, 1992); with Leonard Safir, *Good Advice on Writing* (New York, 1992); *Lend Me Your Ears: Great Speeches in History* (New York, 1992); *Quoth the Maven* (New York, 1993); *Safire's New Political Dictionary* (New York, 1993); *In Love with Norma Loquendi* (New York, 1994).

Sandburg, Carl August (6 Jan. 1878–22 July 1967). America's great poet of democracy and the common man and Abraham Lincoln's biographer, Carl Sandburg was also a newspaper columnist.

Sandburg was born in Galesburg, Illinois, the son of Swedish immigrant parents. At age thirteen he dropped out of school, worked at a variety of menial jobs, and rode the rails as a hobo until in 1898 he volunteered for service in the Spanish-American War. After a brief period in Puerto Rico, he attended Lombard College in his hometown. He had an opportunity to attend the U.S. Military Academy (West Point) but failed two entrance exams: math and grammar. He remained at Lombard College until the spring of 1902, serving as editor of the *Lombard Record* but leaving without completing a degree. His literary career began there thanks to Professor Philip Green Wright, whose Asgard Press published the young writer's first four books between 1904 and 1910. Uneasy about his Swedish roots, the fledgling author signed these as Charles A. Sandburg.

Sandburg worked in Wisconsin as an organizer for the Social Democratic party from 1907 to 1912, and in 1910 he was secretary to Emil Seidel, Milwaukee's socialist major. In 1911 Sandburg became a reporter for the *Social Democratic Herald* in Milwaukee, and in the following year he took a job on the *Chicago Evening World,* also a socialist paper. When the *World* closed, Sandburg worked for E. W. Scripps's adless newspaper the *Day Book,* which was closed in 1917. He wrote for the National Labor Defense League and was an editorial writer for a brief time on the *Chicago Evening American,* a Hearst property. Later in 1917 he took a job as a labor reporter and editorial writer for the *Chicago Daily News.* He reviewed movies for a decade for that paper and was finally given his own column, which was initially titled "Chips from Carl Sandburg." The title was soon changed to "From the Notebook of Carl Sandburg." His columns on racial tensions and rioting in 1919 were collected into a book, *The Chicago Race Riots* (1919). He worked with the *Daily News* until 1932.

Concurrently, Sandburg published articles and free-verse poetry. His poetry was "discovered" after editor Harriet Monroe published six of his works in the March 1914 issue of *Poetry*. He also worked on his multivolume biography of Lincoln during these years, publishing the first two volumes in 1926. In 1928 he moved to Harbert, Michigan, and continued his literary career. In 1939 he completed his Lincoln volumes, for which he won the Pulitzer Prize for history in 1940. From 1941 to 1945 he wrote a weekly political column for the Chicago Times Syndicate and made radio appearances on behalf of the Office of War Information. Some of this material was collected into the book *Home Front Memo* (1943). In 1945 he moved to his final home, Connemara Farm in Flat Rock, North Carolina, where he and his family shared their house with their goats. In 1951 he won the Pulitzer Prize for poetry for his *Complete Poems* (1950). Sandburg is a perfect example of the literary figure whose belles lettres owe their sinew to long journalistic experience.

BOOKS: *In Reckless Ecstasy* (Galesburg, Ill., 1904); *Incidentals* (Galesburg, Ill., 1907); *The Plaint of a Rose* (Galesburg, Ill., 1908); *Joseffy* (Galesburg, Ill., 1910); *Chicago Poems* (New York, 1916); *Cornhuskers* (New York, 1918); *The Chicago Race Riots, July, 1919* (New York, 1919); *Smoke and Steel* (New York, 1920); *Slabs of the Sunburnt West* (New York, 1922); *Rootabaga Stories* (New York, 1922); *Rootabaga Pigeons* (New York, 1923); *Abraham Lincoln: The Prairie Years,* 2 vols. (New York, 1926); *Selected Poems* ed. by Rebecca West (London, 1926); *Carl Sandburg,* ed. by Hughes Mearns (New York, 1926); ed., *The American Songbag* (New York, 1927); *Good Morning, America* (New York, 1928); *Abe Lincoln Grows Up* (New York, 1928); *Steichen, The Photographer* (New York, 1929); *Potato Face* (New York, 1930); *Early Moon* (New York, 1930); with Paul Angle, *Mary Lincoln: Wife and Widow* (New York, 1932); *The People, Yes* (New York, 1936); *Abraham Lincoln: The War Years,* 4 volumes (New York, 1939); *Storm over the Land* (New York, 1943); *Home Front Memo* (New York, 1943); with Frederick Hill Meserve, *The Photographs of Abraham Lincoln* (New York, 1944); *Remembrance Rock* (New York, 1948); *Lincoln Collector: The Story of Oliver R. Barrett's Great Collection* (New York, 1949); *Complete Poems* (New York, 1950); *Always the Young Strangers* (New York, 1953); *A Lincoln Preface* (New York, 1953); *The Sandburg Range* (New York, 1957); *Harvest Poems, 1910–1960* (New York, 1960); *Wind Song* (New York, 1960); *Honey and Salt* (New York, 1963); *The Wedding Procession of the Rag Doll and the Broom Handle and Who Was in It* (New York, 1967); *Breathing Tokens,* ed. by Margaret Sandburg (New York, 1978); *Ever the Winds of Chance,* ed. by Margaret Sandburg and George Hendrick (Urbana-Champaign, Ill., 1983).

REFERENCES: North Callahan, *Carl Sandburg: Lincoln of Our Literature* (New York, 1970); Norman Corwin, *The World of Carl Sandburg: A Stage Presentation* (New York, 1960); Richard Crowder, *Carl Sandburg* (New York, 1964); Karl Detzer, *Carl Sandburg: A Study in Personality and Background* (New York, 1941); Hazel Durnell, *The America of Carl Sandburg* (Seattle, 1965); Harry Golden, *Carl Sandburg* (Chicago, 1961); Joseph Haas and Gene Lovitz, *Carl Sandburg: A Pictorial Biography* (New York, 1967); Paula Steichen, *My Connemara* (New York, 1969).

Saunders, Debra J. (8 Dec. 1954–   ). Irreverent political columnist Debra Saunders began her syndicated column based at the *San Francisco Chronicle* in July 1992.

Saunders was born in Massachusetts and is a 1980 graduate (in Latin and Greek) of the University of Massachusetts. Her first political job was with the Republican political consulting firm of Todd Domke Associates in Boston. She later moved to Sacramento, California, with another consulting firm, Russo Watts & Rollins.

In 1987 Saunders began writing speeches and newsletter copy for the Republican leader of the California legislature as well as free-lancing in column format. She became a full-time columnist/editorial writer for the *Los Angeles Daily News* in 1987, remaining there until going with the *Chronicle* in 1992.

Scandale, Frank (28 May 1957–   ). Frank Scandale has written a column for the *Denver* [Colorado] *Post* since September 1990.

Scandale was born in Brooklyn, New York. He received the B.A. in communications from Glassboro State College in 1979.

Scandale was a reporter/columnist for the *Daily Journal* of Elizabeth, New Jersey, from 1980 to 1985, then free-lanced for various travel trade periodicals from late 1985 to 1987. In February 1987 he was employed by Reuters News Service, and he returned to the *Daily Journal* as city editor and columnist from February 1989 to September 1990.

His column's specialty is humor written from the male point of view.

Schanberg, Sydney Hillel (17 Jan. 1934–   ). Sydney Schanberg was a *New York Times* columnist from 1981 to 1985 and became a columnist for *Newsweek* in 1986.

Schanberg was born in Clinton, Massachusetts. He received the B.A. from Harvard University in 1955, then served in the U.S. Army from 1956 to 1958.

Hired in 1959 by the *New York Times,* Schanberg began reporting in 1960. He was the paper's Albany bureau chief from 1967 to 1969; bureau chief in New Delhi, India, 1969–1973; and Southeast Asia correspondent working out of Singapore, 1973–1975. In 1975 he won the Pulitzer Prize for his stories about the fall of Phnom Pehn. He was metropolitan editor of the *Times* from 1977 to 1980 and for the next five years wrote a column that concentrated on New York politics. In 1986 he began writing a column for *Newsweek.*

BOOKS: *The Killing Fields* (Sydney, Australia, 1984); *The Death and Life of Dith Pran* (New York, 1985).

Schiff, Dorothy (11 March 1903–30 Aug. 1989). Owner-publisher of the *New York Post* Dorothy Schiff wrote a column for her paper from 1951 to 1958.

Schiff was born into a wealthy family in New York City. The Schiff fortune had come from investment banking. She attended the Brearley School in the city, then failed Bryn Mawr College in 1923 after her freshman year. She lived the life of a wealthy socialite during the 1920s, dabbling in charitable activities on the side. Her closest brush with journalism at this time of her life was as an occasional guest at the Algonquin Round Table.

Schiff's media holdings began with the purchase of radio stations in Brooklyn, Los Angeles, and San Francisco. Then in June 1939 she bought a controlling interest in the venerable *New York Post*. At first she allowed her second husband, George Backer, the titles of publisher and president, making herself vice president and treasurer. Backer had to step down for health reasons, and Schiff became publisher in name as well as in fact. She and Backer divorced, and in 1943, her third husband, newsman Theodore Thackery, took over as editor and publisher. By 1949 he was out, as both husband and head of the paper.

To popularize the *Post,* Mrs. Schiff made it a tabloid in 1949. She had earlier added a San Francisco edition and a Paris edition, neither of which had proved successful. She also added a comics section, more concentrated attention to glamour and gossip, her own foreign bureau and syndication service, and columnists, mostly of the liberal stamp. By the late 1940s the *Post* had become the most column-friendly of all American newspapers, publishing nearly fifty at one time. In September 1951, Mrs. Schiff began her own column, at first titled ''Publisher's Notebook'' but later changed to the more friendly sounding ''Dear Reader.'' She wrote the copy longhand for her thrice-weekly column and found the work satisfying but more time-consuming than she had expected. She discontinued the column in 1958, citing the strain on her time as publisher.

In the 1960s the *Post* suffered the effects of a 114-day strike called over Schiff's attempts to automate. In December 1976 she sold the paper to press magnate Rupert Murdock for about $31 million.

REFERENCES: Jeffrey Potter, *Men, Money and Magic: The Story of Dorothy Schiff* (New York, 1976).

Schlafly, Phyllis Stewart (15 Aug. 1924–   ). In 1976, conservative advocate Phyllis Schlafly began a political column syndicated by the Copley News Service.

She was born Phyllis Stewart in St. Louis, Missouri. She attended Maryville College of the Sacred Heart for two years, then transferred to Washington University (in St. Louis), where she graduated Phi Beta Kappa in 1944. She received her M.A. in political science from Radcliffe in 1945. During her undergraduate years, she worked nights at an arms factory. After earning her master's degree, she was a congressional researcher, and from 1946 to 1949 she was a researcher/librarian for a St. Louis bank. She became a politically active Republican and did commentary on a local radio station in the early 1950s. In 1952 she made the first of several unsuccessful bids for public office, running for Congress from Illinois. She was a researcher for Sen. Joseph McCarthy in the 1950s and with her husband founded the anticommunist Cardinal Mindszenty Foundation. In 1962 she returned to radio with her own show, ''America Wake Up.'' Her first book, *A Choice not an Echo,* was written in the early 1960s to support Barry Goldwater's bid for the presidency; the book sold a reported three million copies. In 1964 she was elected vice president of the National Federation of

Republican Women, and in 1967 she started a newsletter, the *Phyllis Schlafly Report*. With this forum, she attacked the Equal Rights Amendment as a threat to women's interests. Shortly thereafter, in 1973, she became a commentator on the CBS program "Spectrum" and on Chicago radio station WBBM's "Matters of Opinion." She received her J.D. from Washington University in 1978. From 1980 to 1983 she was a CNN television commentator.

BOOKS: *A Choice not an Echo* (Alton, Ill., 1964); with Chester Ward, *The Gravediggers* (Alton, Ill., 1964); with Chester Ward, *Strike from Space* (New York, 1966); *Safe—not Sorry* (Alton, Ill., 1967); with Chester Ward, *Kissinger on the Couch* (New Rochelle, N.Y., 1974); *The Power of the Positive Woman* (New Rochelle, N.Y., 1977); *The Power of the Christian Woman* (Cincinnati, 1981); ed., *Child Abuse in the Classroom* (Alton, Ill., 1984); ed., *Who Will Rock the Cradle? The Battle for Control of Child Care in America* (Dallas, 1989).

Schneider, John Benjamin (14 March 1949–   ). John Schneider has been a daily general/personal columnist for the *Lansing* [Michigan] *State Journal* since 1988.

He was born in Detroit, Michigan, and holds the B.A. from Wayne State University. Schneider was a reporter/columnist/news editor for the *Sidney* [Ohio] *Daily News* from 1973 to 1977. He joined the staff of the *Lansing State Journal* in 1977, first as reporter, then as weekly columnist. He has published two collections of his columns.

BOOKS: *Kin* (Lansing, Mich., 1981); *Kin, Too* (Lansing, Mich., 1983).

Schorr, Daniel Louis (31 Aug. 1916–   ). Mainly known for his controversial twenty-three-year career with CBS television, Daniel Schorr began writing a column for the *Des Moines* [Iowa] *Register* and the Register/Tribune Syndicate in 1978.

Schorr was born in New York City and in 1939 received the B.S. in sociology from City College. During his high school years, he edited his school newspaper and yearbook and worked as a stringer for the *Bronx Home News* and the *Jewish Daily Bulletin*. In college he also wrote for the school paper, the *Campus;* wrote for several papers; and worked for the Jewish Telegraphic Agency.

Upon graduation from college, Schorr took a job with the Jewish Telegraphic Agency as its assistant editor (1939–1941). For two years he was New York news editor for ANETA, the Netherlands news agency. Drafted into the army in 1943, he worked in public relations and military intelligence and after his 1945 discharge, returned to ANETA, which posted him to the Hague. In 1948 he left this job to free-lance out of Europe for the *New York Times, London Daily Mail, Christian Science Monitor, Time,* and *Newsweek.*

Schorr was hired by Edward R. Murrow as a CBS correspondent in 1953, working first in Washington, D.C., then in 1955 in Moscow, where he set up a CBS bureau. He was a roving European correspondent for CBS in 1958–1960, then headed the bureau for Germany and Central Europe from 1960 to 1966. In

1966 he became head of the Washington bureau of the network. His hard-hitting investigative work on Watergate earned him three Emmys, but his probing of the CIA's activities in the mid-1970s got him into a controversy that eventually led to his September 1976 resignation from the network. In February of that year, Schorr gave a copy of the House Intelligence Committee's report on its investigation of CIA activities, which the House had voted to suppress, to the *Village Voice.* CBS's accommodating executives had not wanted to make the material public, so Schorr acted on his own to see that it was published. Press reaction to what he had done was negative, and he soon resigned.

Schorr spent one term (spring 1977) teaching journalism at the University of California at Berkeley, then began writing his political column for the Register-Tribune Syndicate. In 1980 he also became a Washington correspondent for CNN. He has written two books.

BOOKS: *Don't Get Sick in America* (Nashville, Tenn., 1970); *Clearing the Air* (Boston, 1977).

Schram, Martin Jay (15 Sept. 1942–   ). Martin Schram is currently a liberal political columnist syndicated by the Newspaper Enterprise Association and was formerly writer of the column ''1600 Pennsylvania Avenue'' for the *Washington Post.*

Schram was born in Chicago. He received the B.A. from the University of Florida in 1964.

He began his career as a reporter for the *Miami News* (1963–1965), then spent more than a decade with *Newsday,* as a reporter (1965–1967), Washington correspondent (1967–1969), and White House correspondent (1969–1973). He was a reporter for the *Washington Post* from 1979 to 1981 and a *Post* national affairs writer thereafter. His column on the presidency ran from 1972 to 1979. His later syndicated column was handled by United Feature Syndicate until he switched to the Newspaper Enterprise Association in 1991. Schram is also a commentator for Cable News Network.

BOOKS: *Running for President* (New York, 1976); *The Great American Video Game: Presidential Politics in the Television Age* (New York, 1987); ed. with Will Marshall, *Mandate for Change* (New York, 1993).

Schuyler, George Samuel (25 Feb. 1895–31 Aug. 1977). Black columnist and reporter George Schuyler is remembered for his conservative columns for the *Pittsburgh Courier* (1924–1966), Spadeau Columns (1953–1962), and North American Newspaper Alliance (1965–1977). He is sometimes dubbed ''the black H. L. Mencken.''

Schuyler was born in Providence, Rhode Island, and grew up in Syracuse, New York. He was largely self-educated, having dropped out of high school in 1912 to enlist in the army. While stationed in Hawaii, he produced a post newspaper and began writing occasionally for the *Honolulu Commercial Advertiser.*

After leaving the service, he held a variety of jobs: civil service clerk, factory worker, dishwasher, handyman, and construction worker. In 1921 he became a member of the American Socialist party, and in 1923 he began working for the magazine of the Friends of Negro Freedom, the *Messenger*. His monthly feature "Shafts and Darts: A Page of Calumny and Satire" brought humor to this otherwise serious magazine.

In 1924 he began writing a column "Views and Reviews" for the successful black weekly the *Pittsburgh Courier*. He quickly turned away from socialism and became an ardent anticommunist. Schuyler was also the *Courier*'s head editorial writer for thirty-eight years. Part of his reputation also rests on the many special series he did as a reporter. The first of these was on the continuing slave trade in Liberia. He traveled to Africa in late 1930 for the *New York Evening Post*, which published his findings in February 1931. Other later series by Schuyler included comparisons of civil rights in various state capitals to conditions in Washington, D.C.; housing and general living conditions in Harlem; race relations in Latin America; the better side of race relations in the American South; and living conditions for blacks in various parts of the world.

A frequent theme in Schuyler's columns was what he regarded as a Communist conspiracy to enlist the sympathy of U.S. blacks. His conservative views often brought him into conflict with established black leaders, such as William Jones of the *Baltimore Afro-American*, W.E.B. DuBois, Adam Clayton Powell (against whom Schuyler ran unsuccessfully for Congress in 1964), and the Reverend Martin Luther King, Jr. Schuyler was frequently called an Uncle Tom and a traitor to the black cause.

In 1937 he became business manager of the National Association for the Advancement of Colored People's (NAACP's) magazine *Crisis*, and in 1942, associate editor of the *Courier*. In 1949 he began a weekly radio program, "The Negro World," on WLIB in New York City, and in 1950 he was chosen as a U.S. delegate to the Congress of Cultural Freedom held in Berlin. In 1953 he launched his "For the Record" column for Spadeau Columns; using this forum, he irritated most black leaders by contending that African colonies were not yet ready for independence. In 1961 he began writing for *American Opinion*, an organ of the John Birch Society, and in 1964 he became a regular contributor to the *Manchester Union Leader*, in which he lambasted Martin Luther King, Jr. He was syndicated by the North American Newspaper Alliance in 1965 and attacked those who participated in the Watts riots. He became an editor and movie critic for another John Birch periodical, *Review of the News*, in 1967 and was in that same year made the *Manchester Union Leader*'s literary editor. To the end of his career, he remained a man who went against the conventional grain.

BOOKS: *Racial Intermarriage in the United States* (Girard, Kan., 1929); *Black No More* (New York, 1931); *Slaves Today: A Story of Liberia* (New York, 1931); *Black and Conservative: The Autobiography of George S. Schuyler* (New Rochelle, N.Y., 1966).

REFERENCES: George Goodman, Fr., "George S. Schuyler, Black Author," *New York Times* (8 September 1977): 40; Michael W. Peplow, *George S. Schuyler* (Boston, 1980).

Schwartz, Gary Richard (21 Oct. 1944–   ). Gary Schwartz self-syndicates his humor column "Life in the Slow Lane" from his home in Mukilteo, Washington.

Schwartz was born in Hollywood, California, and received the B.S. in journalism from California State University, Northridge, in 1971.

He was a sportswriter for the Santa Monica *Evening Outlook* in 1970 and was publications manager of the California Credit Union League from 1971 to 1974. During 1975 he worked as a public relations specialist for Toyota Motors, U.S.A., and traveled in Europe during 1976. His next position was as manager of employee communications for Hyrdil Company (1977–1983), after which he was a PR consultant for Clive Hoffman Associates from 1985 to 1990. Schwartz launched his humor column in 1987.

REFERENCES: "Weekly Humor Feature Is Offered," *Editor and Publisher* (4 April 1992): 54.

Scripps, Ellen Browning (18 Oct. 1836–3 Aug. 1932). One of the few columnists who became wealthy enough also to be a philanthropist, Ellen Scripps wrote the column "Matters and Things," also known as "Miss Ellen's Miscellany."

Scripps was born in London, the sister of James and George Scripps and the half-sister of Edward Willis Scripps. Her family moved to the United States in 1844, and she received the A.B. at Knox College in Galesburg, Illinois, in 1859. After working as a schoolteacher, she joined her brothers in Detroit, on their paper the *Evening News*. Here she worked as a proofreader until her father fell ill and she returned home to care for him until his death in 1873. She then rejoined her brothers at the *Detroit News,* where she bought into the paper, read proofs, became literary editor, and began her own column.

In the succeeding years, she participated with E. W. Scripps, eighteen years her junior, in building what is ususally described as the first modern newspaper chain, the Scripps-McRae League, which later became Scripps-Howard Newspapers. Her column, "Matters and Things," was the seed from which grew the Scripps' feature service, the Newspaper Enterprise Association, feeding feature material to more than one thousand newspapers.

Ellen Scripps was part owner of E.W.'s Miramar Ranch, but she preferred to retire to a house she built in La Jolla, California, and in her remaining years, used her considerable fortune to fund various philanthropic projects. With E.W., she funded what became the Scripps Institution for Oceanography and the Scripps Memorial Hospital in La Jolla. With her sister, Eliza, she founded the Bishop School for Girls in that same city, and her largest project was funding Scripps College in Claremont, California, which was a school for women. Ellen Scripps never married.

REFERENCES: N. D. Cochran, *E. W. Scripps* (New York, 1933); A. McRae, *Forty Years in Newspaperdom* (New York, 1924); J. E. Scripps, *A General History of the Scripps Family* (Detroit, 1903).

Seaman, Elizabeth Cochrane (5 May 1867–27 Jan. 1922). Famed for her 1890 trip around the world as "Nellie Bly" while working as a stunt reporter for the *New York World,* Elizabeth Cochrane had her own Sunday column in that paper for roughly one year (1894–1895).

She was born Elizabeth Cochran on a farm near the community of Cochran's Mills, Pennsylvania, which was named for her father. She added the final *e* to her family name after becoming a journalist. Her family moved to Apollo, Pennsylvania, and her formal education was limited to one year (1880–1881) at a boarding school in Indiana, Pennsylvania.

After the death of her father, she and her mother moved to Pittsburgh, where in 1885 she secured a job as the first woman reporter with the *Pittsburgh Dispatch.* Elizabeth Cochrane was an investigative journalist roughly fifteen years before this approach to news became fashionable. She also did interview features with interesting people, such as Andrew Carnegie and James Whitcomb Riley. Her biggest assignment for the *Dispatch* was a series on life in Mexico after the execution of Emperor Maximilian. She and her mother traveled there in the winter of 1886–1887, and these stories eventually were turned into a book: *Six Months in Mexico* (1888).

In 1887 she relocated to New York City, where she was hired as a *New York World* reporter by Joseph Pulitzer. Her first story called for her to pose as a mentally disturbed Cuban immigrant and to be committed to the mental facilities at Blackwell Island. Her story dramatized the ill treatment of mental patients and generated publicity for the *World.* She produced other exclusives by posing as a sweatshop worker, a chorus girl, and a thief, and in addition, did a series on the living wives of ex-presidents (Mmes. Tyler, Polk, and Grant) and wrote about the suffragettes. The assignment that made her known to virtually all literate Americans, however, was a stunt story: her trip around the world in an attempt to beat Jules Verne's time in his tale *Around the World in Eighty Days.* She went as "Nellie Bly," a name borrowed from a popular song by Stephen Foster, though she altered the spelling from Foster's "Nelly." She began the trip, alone and carrying only one small suitcase, on 14 November 1889 and returned to New York on 25 January 1890, for a successful time of seventy-two days, six hours, ten minutes, and eleven seconds, according to the *World.*

After a forty-week lecture tour of the nation, she returned to reporting for the *World* and was given her own column. Her time as a columnist was cut short, however, by her sudden marriage to a wealthy Brooklyn manufacturer, Robert L. Seaman, forty years her senior. She left journalism for the life of a society woman, but in 1904, Seaman died. Her attempts to run his companies were unsuccessful, and by 1914, most of her money gone, she left for Europe. Because of World War I, she was unable to return home until 1919, after which she began writing for the *New York Evening Journal,* which she continued until her death in 1922, a forgotten figure after having been undoubtedly the most famous woman reporter in history.

BOOKS: *Ten Days in a Mad-House, or, Nellie Bly's Experience on Blackwell's Island* (New York, 1887); *Six Months in Mexico* (New York, 1888); *Nellie Bly's Book: Around the World in Seventy-Two Days* (New York, 1890).

REFERENCES: Madelon Golden Schlipp and Sharon M. Murphy, *Great Women of the Press* (Carbondale and Edwardsville, Ill., 1983): 133–147.

Seib, Charles Bach (22 Aug. 1919–). Charles Seib, ombudsman for the *Washington Post,* began a column in that paper in 1977.

Seib was born in Kingston, New York. He earned the B.A. from Lehigh University in 1941.

He was a reporter for the Allentown (Pennsylvania) *Chronicle* from 1942 to 1944, an Associated Press (AP) reporter in 1944–1945, and on the desk of the *Philadelphia Record* in 1945–1946. From 1946 to 1952 he was a reporter for International News Service and was assistant Washington bureau chief for Gannett News Service, 1952–1954. Seib spent the next twenty years at the *Washington Star,* from 1968 to 1974 as managing editor. In 1974 he became associate editor and ombudsman of the *Washington Post* and started his column, ''The News Business.''

BOOKS: *The Woods: One Man's Escape to Nature* (Garden City, N.Y., 1971).

Seldes, Gilbert Vivian (3 Jan. 1893–29 Sept. 1970). Journalist, author, essayist, educator, and popular culture maven Gilbert Seldes was a *New York Journal* columnist from 1930 to 1937.

Seldes was born in Alliance, New Jersey, which was a utopian colony his parents had founded. He received the A.B. from Harvard University in 1914, graduating Phi Beta Kappa.

After graduation, Seldes worked as a reporter for the *Pittsburgh Sun* and was music critic for the *Philadelphia Evening Ledger* from 1914 to 1916. From 1916 to 1918 he was a free-lance war correspondent in England, after which he was a Washington correspondent for *L'Echo de Paris* (1918). He was associate editor of *Collier's* in 1919 and associate managing editor of the *Dial* from 1920 to 1923. He then relocated to Paris and wrote his opus *The Seven Lively Arts,* in which he championed twentieth-century popular culture. Upon his return to New York, he was drama critic for *Dial* as well as for the *New York Evening Graphic.* After writing his column in the *Journal* from 1930 to 1937, he became director of programming for CBS (1937–1945). In 1950 he joined the faculty of the Annenberg School of Communications at the University of Pennsylvania and served as communications dean from 1959 to 1963. He also worked as a radio commentator and was a prolific author of books. In his later writings, he became less sanguine about the influence of mass culture and its media purveyors, which had grown more monopolistic and ever more prone to trivialize.

BOOKS: *The United States and the War* (London, 1917); *The Seven Lively Arts* (New York, 1024); *The Stammering Century* (New York, 1928); *An Hour with the Movies and the Talkies* (Philadelphia, 1929); *The Wings of the Eagle* (Boston, 1929); *The Future of Drinking* (Boston, 1930); *Aristophanes' Lysistrata, a New Version* (New York, 1930); *Against Revolution* (New York, 1932); *The Years of the Locust, 1929–1932* (Boston, 1933); *Movies for the Millions* (London, 1937); *The Movies Come from America* (New York, 1937); *Your Money and Your Life, a Manual for "the Middle Classes"* (New York, 1938); *Proclaim Liberty!* (New York, 1942); *The Great Audience* (New York, 1950); *Preview of Entertainment, Through June 1952* (New York, 1951); *Writing for Television* (Garden City, N.Y., 1952); *The Popular Arts* (New York, 1956); *The New Mass Media: Challenge to a Free Society* (Washington, D.C., 1957).

REFERENCES: Norman Jacobs, ed., *Culture for the Millions?* (Boston, 1964).

Senn, Dorothy Sartin (6 Oct. 1931–   ). Dorothy Senn has written a weekly general-interest column for the *Oak Ridger* in Tennessee since 1976.

Senn was born in Ardmore, Oklahoma. She received the B.A. in journalism from the University of Oklahoma in 1953. While in college, she reported for the campus paper, the *Oklahoma Daily,* and was women's editor in 1953.

After graduation, Senn edited the *Maryville Enterprise* and the *Maryville Free Press* (Maryville, Tennessee) during 1954–1955. From 1969 to 1972 she was a reporter and feature writer for the *Oak Ridger,* also serving as editor for special editions. From 1972 to 1976 she edited the entertainment tabloid *Intermission,* then began her column, which often deals with people in the arts. Senn also writes on travel topics and sometimes takes a humorous approach. She doubles as a feature writer. Her column, which usually includes her own photos, appears on Fridays.

Sevareid, Arnold Eric (26 Nov. 1912–9 July 1992). Best known for his stern but savvy commentaries on the CBS Evening News with Walter Cronkite, Eric Sevareid began his journalistic career as a newspaperman and from 1960 to 1966 wrote a weekly column distributed to more than one hundred papers by the Robert Hall Syndicate.

Sevareid was born in Velva, North Dakota, the son of Norwegian immigrants. The family later moved to Minneapolis, where Eric Sevareid graduated from high school in 1930, having served as editor of his school paper. His first column-writing experience occurred at age seventeen, when he and a friend paddled a canoe more than two thousand miles from Minneapolis to Hudson Bay. Sevareid wrote a series of ten columns detailing the trip for the *Minneapolis Star.* He did further assignments for that paper while a student at the University of Minnesota, from which he graduated with a B.A. in political science in 1935. He also reported for the college paper, the *Minnesota Daily.*

Sevareid was a reporter for the *Minneapolis Journal* during 1936–1937, then did graduate study at the London School of Economics and Political Science later in 1937, and at the Alliance Française in 1938. In Paris, he worked as a reporter for the Paris edition of the *New York Herald Tribune* and was its city editor in 1939. He also worked as night editor for United Press.

At this juncture, the twenty-six-year-old Sevareid made the switch to broadcasting, signing on with CBS on 21 August 1939, the day Hitler signed a peace pact with Stalin. He worked as a war correspondent in England and France during 1939–1940, was in Washington during 1940–1943, and again was a war correspondent—in China during 1943 and in Italy in 1944. After the war, he held a variety of CBS assignments and from 1964 to 1977 was commentator on the Cronkite news show. Chief among his later assignments was his work as interviewer/host of "Conversations with Eric Sevareid" from 1975 to 1977. His career earned him a long list of awards and honors.

Sevareid's column first appeared in the *Wisconsin State Journal* in June 1960. During 1960–1961, most of his columns were written from abroad; thereafter, they were done out of New York City and Washington, D.C. By 1962 he was writing about civil rights and about environmental conservation issues. When he became Cronkite's regular commentator in 1966, he had to give up writing his column. His final column appeared in March of that year. He also published nine books, including an autobiography, *Not So Wild a Dream* (1946).

BOOKS: *Canoeing with the Cree* (New York, 1935); *Not So Wild a Dream* (New York, 1946); *In One Ear* (New York, 1952); *Small Sounds in the Night: A Collection of Capsule Summaries on the American Scene* (New York, 1956); *Candidates 1960: Behind the Headlines in the Presidential Race* (New York, 1959); *This Is Eric Sevareid* (New York, 1964); with Robert A. Smith, *Washington: Magnificent Capital* (Garden City, N.Y., 1965); with Malcolm Boyd, *You Can't Kill the Dream* (Richmond, Va., 1968); with John Case, *Enterprise: Doing Business in America* (New York, 1983).

REFERENCES: Elsie Marie Patterson, *Eric Sevareid: The Making and the Art of a Television News Analyst,* 2 vols., Ph.D. Dissertation, University of Wisconsin—Madison, 1976.

Shamy, Ed (17 Aug. 1958–). Ed Shamy (rhymes with "whammy") was a *Roanoke* [Virginia] *Times and World News* columnist who professed to hate editors above all living creatures. He is now an editor.

Shamy, a Pennsylvanian by birth, graduated in 1980 from Columbia University with a major in political science. He served three years in Paraguay as a Peace Corps volunteer, then in 1983 became a reporter for *Today's Sunbeam* in Salem, New Jersey. He moved to the *Gloucester County Times* in Woodbury, New Jersey, then reported for the *Express* in Easton, Pennsylvania, where he wrote his first column.

In March 1989, Shamy joined the Roanoke paper as a full-time columnist. By this time, he had formed unprintable opinions about editors, considered most reporters lazy and overly dependent on official news releases, and held public relations people and drug dealers in roughly equal esteem. He also thought that people in the South were too placid in their reactions to their newspapers, unlike northerners, who, he said, love to hate their newspapers.

Consequently, he assumed the wise-cracking, smart-talking persona of the "professional Yankee" in his column—sometimes snide, sometimes arrogant or curmudgeonly. Another Shamy crotchet was hating to have his column jumped to an inside page. To prevent this, he wrote short, claiming to be the "shortest" columnist in the nation. Shamy began by writing four columns a week for the Roanoke paper, then volunteered to do five—for no additional pay. In December 1993 he was named editor of the Westminister (Maryland) *Carroll County Times,* a smaller paper owned by Landmark Communications, the Roanoke paper's parent group.

Shannon, William Vincent (24 Aug. 1927–1988). William Shannon wrote a political column for the *New York Post* from 1957 to 1964.

Shannon was born in Worcester, Massachusetts, and received the A.B. cum laude in 1948 at Harvard, where he was also a member of Phi Beta Kappa.

From 1949 to 1951 he worked as a free-lancer in Washington, D.C., and from 1951 to 1957 he was Washington correspondent for the *New York Post.* He was a member of the editorial board of the *New York Times* from 1964 to 1977, after which he served as U.S. ambasador to Ireland (1977–1981). Finally, he wrote for the *Boston Globe* from 1982 to 1988.

BOOKS: *The American Irish* (New York, 1963); *The Heir Apparent: Robert Kennedy and the Struggle for Power* (New York, 1967); *They Could Not Trust the King: Nixon, Watergate and the American People* (New York, 1974); *A Quiet Broker? A Way Out of the Irish Conflict* (New York, 1985).

Shaw, Henry Wheeler (21 April 1818–14 Oct. 1885). Humorist Henry Shaw, who made himself famous as "Josh Billings," was one of America's earliest humor columnists. His column was carried by the *New York Weekly* from 1867 until his death in 1885—and after.

Shaw was born in Lanesboro, Massachusetts. He spent a year (1833–1834) at Hamilton College but was expelled for taking the clapper out of the college's chapel bell. Shaw was one of those individuals who take considerable time to find their niche in life. He spent roughly twenty years unsuccessfully seeking his fortune, moving back and forth between the East and West. At various times he worked as a farmer, a steamboat owner on the Ohio River, an auctioneer, and a real estate salesman. In midlife he began writing for the New Ashford (Massachusetts) *Eagle* and for the papers in Poughkeepsie, New York. He used comic pseudonyms, such as Efrem Billings and Si Sledlength, and made use of the comic misspellings and dreadful syntax of the crackerbarrel school. He turned the corner of fame and fortune in 1864 with his "Essa on the Muel, bi Josh Billings," which attracted the attention of established humorist Charles Farrar Browne (Artemus Ward), who helped Shaw find a publisher for his first humor book, *Josh Billings, Hiz Sayings* (1865). The book's success led to his

New York Weekly column, which appeared as "The Josh Billings Papers" and sometimes as "Josh Billings' Spice Box" or "Josh Billings' Philosophy." It was such a popular feature that when Shaw died in 1885, the paper made no mention of his death and simply began to rerun the column, rather in the manner of the sponsor of Lydia Pinkham.

Shaw met with considerable success, making $100 per talk on the lecture circuit and selling humor books. His biggest money-maker was his spoof of the *Farmer's Almanac,* which he called *Josh Billings' Farmer's Allminax* and which he published each year from 1869 to 1879. His humor was mainly nonpolitical. He became a friend of fellow humorists Samuel Clemens (Mark Twain) and David Ross Locke (Petroleum Vesuvius Nasby).

BOOKS: *Josh Billings, Hiz Sayings* (New York, 1865); *Josh Billings on Ice, and Other Things* (New York, 1868); *Twelve Ancestrals Sighns in the Billings' Zodiac Gallery* (New York, 1873); *Everybody's Friend, or Josh Billings' Encyclopedia and Proverbial Philosophy of Wit and Humor* (Hartford, Conn., 1874); *Josh Billings' Wit and Humor* (London, 1874); ed., *Josh Billings' Spice Box* (New York, 1874); *The Complete Comical Writings of Josh Billings* (New York, 1876); *Josh Billings' Trump Kards: Blue Grass Philosophy* (New York, 1977); *Old Probability: Perhaps Rain—Perhaps Not* (New York, 1879); *Josh Billings' Cook Book and Picktorial Proverbs* (New York, 1880); *Josh Billings Struggling with Things* (New York, 1881); *Wit and Wisdom of Josh Billings* (Winston-Salem, N.C., 1913); *Selections from the Writings of Josh Billings* (Athens, Ga., 1940); *Uncle Sam's Uncle Josh* (Boston, 1953).

REFERENCES: David B. Kesterson, *Josh Billings* (New York, 1973).

Shields, Mark (?–). Liberal Mark Shields, probably best known as one of the five-member "Capitol Gang" for CNN, also writes a weekly commentary column distributed by Creators Syndicate.

Shields was reared in Weymouth, Massachusetts. He is a 1959 graduate of the University of Notre Dame, where he majored in philosophy and minored in history. He served in the Marine Corps, then in 1964 moved to Washington, D.C., as a legislative assistant to former Sen. William Proxmire of Wisconsin. Shields then worked on a number of political campaigns, including Robert Kennedy, Edmund Muskie, and Morris Udall's runs for the presidency and Sargent Shriver's bid for the vice presidency.

Shields was hired by the editorial department of the *Washington Post* in 1979 and launched his column there in 1980. He also became active in television and radio in the early 1980s. In 1984 he appeared daily on the ABC radio show "Look at Today," and from 1987 to 1993, he and David Gergen did the "MacNeil/Lehrer News Hour"'s political analysis. He has published one book.

BOOKS: *On the Campaign Trail: Wise and Witty Dispatches from the Front Lines of the 1984 Presidential Race* (Chapel Hill, N.C., 1985).

Shumaker, James H. (7 Oct. 1923–). Jim Shumaker, a journalism professor at the University of North Carolina at Chapel Hill, has written an op-ed column for the *Charlotte* [North Carolina] *Observer* since 1973.

Shumaker was born in Winston-Salem, North Carolina. He now teaches for the school at which he received his own journalism degree, in 1972. He had studied journalism at Chapel Hill from 1945 to 1948 but had left without completing the degree, then did graduate study at Columbia University in 1949.

From 1946 to 1948 Shumaker was a city hall reporter for the *Durham* [North Carolina] *Herald,* after which he wrote for the Associated Press (AP) in Columbia, South Carolina, and Charlotte, North Carolina. From 1950 to 1953 he was also night editor for AP. He returned to Durham and the *Herald* from 1953 to 1958, first as state editor, then as managing editor.

Shumaker was with the *Chapel Hill Weekly* and its successor, the *Chapel Hill Newspaper,* from 1958 to 1967 and from 1968 to 1972 was editor and general manager of Florida's *Boca Raton News.* He then returned to Chapel Hill as editor and publisher from 1968 to 1972. Since 1973 he has taught journalism at Chapel Hill, with a one-year leave as editorial page editor of the *Wilmington* [North Carolina] *Star News.*

Shumaker's column in the *Charlotte Observer* appears on Sundays and offers a mixture of the general, the personal, humor, and discussion of current events. He has done one book, a collection of his columns. He also enjoys the distinction of being the man after whom the editor/crow was modeled in the popular comic strip "Shoe," drawn by Jeff MacNelly.

BOOKS: *SHU* (Chapel Hill, 1989).

Sibley, Celestine (23 May 1917–). Celestine Sibley is the best known woman in Georgia journalism and has been a columnist and reporter for the *Atlanta Constitution* since 1941.

Sibley was born in Holly, Florida, and grew up in Mobile County, Alabama. She attended Spring Hill College and the University of Florida. While still in high school, she worked as a reporter for the *Mobile* [Alabama] *Press-Register.* She covered the Georgia House of Representatives for the *Constitution* for more than twenty years. Her columns, published over such a span of years, provide a rich record of how her adopted city and state have changed, and of how they have stayed the same. Sibley has also had considerable civic involvement in Atlanta and has been an active publisher of books, largely novels and memoirs.

BOOKS: *The Malignant Heart* (Garden City, N.Y., 1958); *Peachtree Street, U.S.A.,* (Garden City, N.Y., 1963); *A Place Called Sweet Apple* (Garden City, N.Y., 1967); *Dear Store: An Affectionate Portrait of Rich's* (Garden City, N.Y., 1967); *Especially at Christmas* (Garden City, N.Y., 1969); *The Sweet Apple Gardening Book* (Garden City, N.Y., 1972); *Day by Day with Celestine Sibley* (Garden City, N.Y., 1975); *Small Blessings* (Garden City, N.Y., 1977); *Jincey* (New York, 1978); *Children, My Children* (New York, 1981); *Young 'Uns: A Celebration* (New York, 1982); *For All Seasons* (Atlanta, 1984); *Christmas in Georgia* (Atlanta, 1985); *Mothers Are Always Special* (Atlanta, 1985); *Turned Funny: A Memoir* (New York, 1988); *Tokens of Myself* (Atlanta, 1990); *Ah, Sweet Mystery* (New York, 1991); *Straight as an Arrow* (New York, 1992); *Dire Happenings at Scratch Ankle* (New York, 1993).

Sifford, Charles Darrell (19 Sept. 1931–1992). Darrell Sifford wrote a *Philadelphia Inquirer* column that dated from 1976 and a four-times-a-week column syndicated by Knight-Ridder News Service from 1972.

Sifford was born in Moberly, Missouri, and received the B.J. from the University of Missouri in 1953.

He was a reporter on the *Columbia Missourian* while a student (1952–1953). After graduation he served in the U.S. Army Corps of Engineers from 1953–1955, then became sports editor of the *Jefferson City* [Missouri] *News-Tribune* for 1955–1956. He became this paper's city editor (1956–1961) and its managing editor (1961–1962) before joining the *Louisville* [Kentucky] *Courier-Journal* as night city editor (1962–1966). Sifford was executive editor of the *Charlotte News* in North Carolina from 1966 to 1976, joining the *Philadelphia Inquirer* as a columnist in 1976. He died at age sixty while snorkeling in the Caribbean.

BOOKS: *A Love of the Land* (Philadelphia, 1980); *Father and Son* (Philadelphia, 1982); *The Only Child: Being One, Loving One, Understanding One, Raising One* (New York, 1989); *What Do You Think? The 100 Best Columns of Darrell Sifford* (Philadelphia, 1992).

Simon, Roger Mitchell (29 March 1948–). Now distributed by the Los Angeles Times Syndicate, Roger Simon has been a columnist since 1970.

He was born in Chicago and received the B.A. in 1970 from the University of Illinois. Simon wrote a column for the campus paper and worked as a reporter for the Danville (Illinois) *Commercial-News* while he was a student. After graduation, he took a job with the City News Bureau of Chicago, quickly becoming a columnist for the *Waukegan* [Illinois] *News-Sun* (1970–1972). He joined the *Chicago Sun-Times* in 1972 as a reporter and began a column for that paper in 1974. His next move was to the *Baltimore Sun*, for which he began writing a column in 1984. The column was handled by Creators Syndicate. From 1986 to 1991 he also did a column for *Regardie's* magazine. His *Sun* column is syndicated nationally, four times a week, by the Los Angeles Times Syndicate. The column defies categorization, as it varies from satirical to somber, from political to domestic. Simon travels considerably in search of good human interest copy. He has also done television commentary and has free-lanced for *TV Guide* and other magazines.

BOOKS: *Simon Says: The Best of Roger Simon* (Chicago, 1985); *Road Show: In America, Anyone Can Become President: It's One of the Risks We Take* (New York, 1990).

REFERENCES: David Astor, ''A Generalist in an Age of Specialization,'' *Editor and Publisher* (14 June 1986): 52–54.

Sims, Lydel (1917–3 June 1995). Lydel Sims was a feature columnist for the *Commercial Appeal* in Memphis, Tennessee. While in retirement, he continued to write a weekly column, ''Watch Your Language,'' for the *Commercial Ap-*

peal. He was reared in Louisiana and graduated from Northwest Louisiana State College. He was an active free-lancer to a variety of magazines and an author of books for juveniles.

BOOKS: *The Burning Thirst: A Story of John Wesley* (New York, 1958); George Grider as told to Lydel Sims, *War Fish* (New York, 1959); *Thaddeus Lowe: Uncle Sam's First Airman* (New York, 1964); *Assignment Memphis* (Oxford, Miss., 1982).

Sinberg, Stan (25 Feb. 1952–   ). Humor columnist Stan Sinberg was born in New York City and received the B.A. from Queens College in New York in 1976.

Sinberg broke in as a columnist for *Westsider* (1985–1987) and from 1988 to 1991 free-lanced for such papers as *Newsday,* the *Baltimore Sun,* the *Washington Post,* the *Los Angeles Times,* and the *Wall Street Journal.* Since 1991 he has written for the *Marin Independent Journal* in California.

Sinor, John (24 Dec. 1930–   ). John Sinor (pronounced SIGH-ner) writes a daily column for the *San Diego Evening Tribune* as well as a weekly column titled the "John Sinor Column" that is syndicated to several hundred newspapers.

Sinor was born in Elk City, Oklahoma. He attended Modesto Junior College (1953–1959) and San Jose State University. He served in the U.S. Air Force.

Sinor has free-lanced since the late 1940s and has written several books. His weekly column is syndicated by the Copley News Service.

BOOKS: *Eleven Albatrosses in My Bluebird Tree* (San Diego, 1976); *Finsterhall of San Pasqual* (San Diego, 1976); *Ghosts of Cabrillo Lighthouse* (San Diego, 1977); *Finsterhall Goes over the Wall* (San Diego, 1978); *Some Ladies in My Life* (San Diego, 1979); *The Best of San Diego* (La Jolla, Calif., 1982).

Smith, Hazel Brannon (5 Feb. 1914–   ). Weekly newspaper editor and publisher Hazel Smith wrote a front-page column, "Through Hazel Eyes," that dates from 1936 and that was continued for most of her fifty-year career.

She was born Hazel Brannon in Alabama City, Alabama. After graduation from high school, she worked as a reporter and ad salesperson for the weekly *Etowah Observer* near Gadsden, Alabama. She went on to study journalism at the University of Alabama, where she was managing editor of the campus paper. Brannon graduated with the B.A. in 1935 and in August 1936 bought a weekly paper of her own: the *Durant News,* which was in Holmes County, Mississippi. She titled her column "Through Hazel Eyes"—hers were actually blue—and used it to voice the usual southern view at that time regarding race: that each race had and should keep its place in society. She bought a second paper in 1943, the *Lexington* [Mississippi] *Advertiser,* and here she first ran afoul of local authority by chiding law enforcement officials about their winking at bootlegging and gambling violators. She also was strongly anticommunist and a supporter of Sen. Joseph McCarthy.

Brannon began to move toward the side of the angels in 1954 when she took the local sheriff to task for brutality toward blacks. The sheriff sued her for libel, and a jury found her guilty. Although she was cleared on appeal, her opposition was formidable. In 1958, her Lexington enemies founded the *Holmes County Herald* in an attempt to drive her out of business. Advertisers boycotted her paper and a cross was burned on the lawn of her columned home, Hazelwood. As her financial troubles mounted, a group of moderate southern editors formed a committee to raise money for her. Among her supporters were Nelson Poynter of the *St. Petersburg* [Florida] *Times,* Mark Etheridge of the *Louisville Courier-Journal,* Ralph McGill of the *Atlanta Constitution,* and J. N. Heiskell of the *Arkansas Gazette.* Although she never became a true integrationist, she nevertheless continued to advocate equal rights under the law for all citizens, regardless of race, and in 1964 she became the first woman to win a Pulitzer Prize for editorial writing.

Hazel Brannon Smith had in the mid-1950s bought two more Mississippi weeklies: the *Banner County Outlook* in Flora (1955) and the *Northside Reporter* in Jackson (1956). The latter paper was firebombed in 1964. She borrowed heavily and mortgaged her home to keep publishing but in the 1970s had to close the Banner County paper and sell the *Northside Reporter.* Eventually she found herself a pariah to whites and to blacks, an ally they no longer needed. She filed for bankruptcy in autumn 1985, closing both her remaining papers. Her house was taken by a bank, and after a long, courageous career of voicing what she thought right, she was taken in by her sister in Gadsden, Alabama.

REFERENCES: Hodding Carter, Jr., "Woman Editor's War on Bigots," in *First Person Rural* (Garden City, N.Y., 1963): 217–225; T. George Harris, "The 11-Year Siege of Mississippi's Lady Editor," *Look* 29 (16 November 1965): 121–128; Mark Newman, "Hazel Brannon Smith and Holmes County, Mississippi, 1936–1964: The Making of a Pulitzer Prize Winner," *Journal of Mississippi History* 54 (February 1992): 59–87.

Smith, Jack Clifford (27 Aug. 1916–   ). A giant among U.S. local columnists is Jack Smith of the *Los Angeles Times,* where his column has appeared since 1958.

Smith was born in Long Beach, California, and got his first taste of journalism as editor of the student paper for Belmont High School in Los Angeles. He attended Bakersfield College in 1937–1938 while working for the *Bakersfield Californian.*

Smith was a copy editor for the *Honolulu Advertiser* from 1940 until 1942, then returned to the mainland to become a reporter for the *Sacramento Union* (1943) and the Hollywood *Citizen News* (1946). He was also a reporter for the *Los Angeles Daily News* (1946–1949) and the *Los Angeles Herald-Express* (1950–1953) before joining the *Los Angeles Times* in 1953 as reporter and rewrite man. He became a columnist in 1958 and until recently wrote five a week. Now in semiretirement, he writes one column per week.

BOOKS: *Three Coins in the Birdbath* (Garden City, N.Y., 1965); *Smith on Wry* (Garden City, N.Y., 1970); *God and Mr. Gomez* (New York, 1974); *The Big Orange* (Pasadena, Calif., 1976); *Spend All Your Kisses, Mr. Smith* (New York, 1978); *Jack Smith's L.A.* (New York, 1980); *How to Win a Pullet Surprise: The Pleasures and Pitfalls of Our Language* (New York, 1982); *Cats, Dogs and Other Strangers at My Door* (New York, 1984); *Alive in La La Land* (New York, 1989); with Robert Cameron, *Above Los Angeles* (San Francisco, 1990); with Frank Blair, *Let's Be Frank About It* (Garden City, N.Y., 1979).

REFERENCES: *New York Times* (22 Jan. 1979), p. C19.

Smith, John L. (2 May 1960–   ). John L. Smith's column has appeared four days a week in the *Las Vegas Review-Journal* since 1988.

Smith was born in Henderson, Nevada. His 1982 B.A. in journalism is from Western Washington University.

Smith has worked in Las Vegas for his entire career, and, like many other general columnists before him, he began as a sportswriter and editor. His first job was as sports columnist/sports editor of the *Las Vegas Sun* (1982–1985). In 1985 he went with the *Review-Journal* as a sports columnist and in 1988 became a general/news columnist. He writes, he says, about "aging boxers, two-bit mobsters, bookmakers, loansharks and waitresses at Denny's—preferably a combination of two or more." He considers Las Vegas the best city in America for a columnist to work. He has three books scheduled for publication in 1995: one on the mob in his city, one on Las Vegas itself, and a collection of his columns.

Smith, Mary Elizabeth (2 Jan. 1923–   ). Versatile columnist Liz Smith's career has spanned four media: newspapers, magazines, radio, and television. She is currently a gossip columnist with the Los Angeles Times Syndicate.

Smith was born in Ft. Worth, Texas. She received the B.J. from the University of Texas at Austin in 1948.

She began her career as an associate radio producer for CBS in New York (1952–1954), then moved to NBC as associate producer of "Wide, Wide World" (1954–1956). She was a freelance writer for several years starting in 1956 and from 1957 to 1962 wrote the "Cholly Knickerbocker" column (originated in 1919 by Maury Paul). Next she became the film critic for *Cosmopolitan* magazine (1964–1966) and a writer for *Sports Illustrated* (1966–1967). In 1970 she began writing the "Instant Gotham" column for the *Palm Beach Social Pictorial* and the "Liz Smith" column syndicated to various newspapers from 1976 to 1991 by Tribune Media Services. Her work has also appeared in such magazines as *Esquire, Vogue, Redbook,* and *Good Housekeeping,* and she has been a television commentator since 1978—for WNBC-TV in New York (1978–1991) and with Fox since 1991.

BOOKS: *The Mother Book* (Garden City, N.Y., 1978).

Snow, Aubert Calvin (16 July 1924–). A. C. Snow's column has been a fixture in Raleigh, North Carolina, journalism since 1950.

Snow was born in Surry County in western North Carolina. He served in the Air Force in World War II, then attended Mars Hill Junior College and went on for an A.B in journalism in 1950 from the University of North Carolina (UNC) at Chapel Hill. In May 1993 he was inducted into UNC's North Carolina Journalism Hall of Fame.

After seven years with the Burlington (North Carolina) *Times-News* (1950–1957), Snow joined the now-defunct *Raleigh Times,* first as a government reporter, then as city editor, news editor, associate editor, and in 1974, editor, the position he held until the paper was closed in 1989. His column appeared from 1958 in the *Times,* then in the city's remaining paper, the *News and Observer.* Snow's gentle humor appeared under the column title "Sno' Foolin' " for thirty-seven years, and since the Paper's redesign in 1992, simply as "A. C. Snow." He retired from full-time work in 1990, but his column still appears.

BOOKS: *Dust of Snow* (Raleigh, N.C., 1980); *Snow Flurries* (Raleigh, N.C., 1985); *Comfort Me with Apples* (Raleigh, N.C., 1989).

Sobran, Joseph (1946–). Joseph Sobran writes a thrice-weekly column for Universal Press Syndicate. He has been nationally syndicated for ten years.

Sobran (pronounced SO-bran) was born in Ypsilanti, Michigan, and is a graduate of Eastern Michigan University. He worked as an English department teaching fellow during and after his years in college. After college, he became a member of the staff of *National Review.* He has contributed regularly to the *Rothbard-Rockwell Report* and the *Wanderer,* and he has also written for *Harper's* and the *American Spectator.* The conservative Sobran describes himself as "the kind of guy who still gets mad at Jane Fonda." As a columnist he is known as a witty, thoughtful moralist. He has authored two books, one on social ethics, the other on individualism and the right of privacy.

BOOKS: *Single Issues* (New York, 1983); *The Conservative Manifesto: The Philosophy, the Passion, the Promise* (New York, 1984).

REFERENCES: C. H. Simonds, "Joseph Sobran," *National Review* (25 June 1982): 764–765.

Sokolsky, George Ephraim (5 Sept. 1893–12 Dec. 1962). George Sokolsky, a columnist for the *New York Herald Tribune* and King Features, is remembered as an enthusiastic advocate of capitalism and the American way of life.

Sokolsky was born in Utica, New York, but grew up mainly in New York City. He graduated from Columbia University in 1917 with a degree in journalism. Excited by the possibilities of the Russian revolution, he went to Russia in 1917 and edited the Petrograd *Daily News,* an English-language paper. The realities of communism did not live up to Sokolsky's expectations, and he was ordered out of the country. He went by train to Peking, where he worked as assistant editor of the *North China Star.* In 1919 he became a reporter for the *Shanghai Gazette,* and from 1921 to 1924 he was president of the *Journal of Commerce* in that city. He spent the next decade writing for various metropolitan dailies, including the London *Daily Express,* the New York *Evening Post,* and the Philadelphia *Public Ledger.*

Sokolsky returned to the United States in 1932 and became a broadcaster for the National Association of Manufacturers and a *New York Herald Tribune* columnist (1935–1940). From 1944 he wrote a column for Hearst's syndicate King Features. He also wrote books as well as articles for magazines such as *Liberty* and *Atlantic Monthly.*

BOOKS: Ed., *China, a Sourcebook of Information* (Shanghai, 1920); *The Tinder Box of Asia* (Garden City, N.Y., 1933); *Labor's Fight for Power* (Garden City, N.Y., 1934); *We Jews* (New York, 1935); *The Labor Crisis in the United States* (New York, 1938); *The American Way of Life* (New York, 1939).

REFERENCES: W. H. Cordell, ed., *Molders of American Thought* (New York, 1933–1934): 376–390.

Soren, Tabitha L. (19 Aug. 1967–). One of the youngest U.S. newspaper columnists at this writing is Tabitha Soren, best known as an MTV announcer/anchor/reporter, who in October 1993 launched her column "Something to Think About" for the New York Times Syndicate.

Soren was born in San Antonio, Texas, into a military family. Part of her youth was spent in Germany and the Philippines. She received the B.A. cum laude in journalism in 1989 at New York University and worked as a student intern at CNN in New York City and at WABC-TV, also in New York.

Her first job after graduation was at New York's WNBC-TV. She next worked as a state capital reporter, acting news director, talk-show host, and news anchor for Burlington, Vermont's WVNY-TV before being hired in 1991 as a reporter and anchor for Music Television. The New York Times Syndicate was attracted to her column by her high name recognition as a means of reaching the eighteen-to thirty-four-year-old age group, and as a way for older readers to find out what is on the minds of this same age group. The biweekly column deals with politics in a broad sense and with any other topic of interest to younger readers. Although the column was intended to run on opinion pages, some papers use it in their entertainment, youth, or feature section. Some of the papers in addition to the *Times* that carry the column are the *Denver Post, Las Vegas Review-Journal,* and *Seattle Post-Intelligencer.* Soren is also a correspondent for NBC's "Today" show.

REFERENCES: David Astor, "Unplugged Tabitha Soren Tries Column," *Editor and Publisher* (20 November 1993): 42–44.

Sowell, Thomas (30 June 1930–). One of America's leading black conservative intellectuals, economist Thomas Sowell writes a column distributed by Creators Syndicate.

Sowell was born in Gastonia, North Carolina. From 1951 to 1953 he served in the Marine Corps. He earned the A.B., magna cum laude, at Harvard University in 1958; the A.M. at Columbia University in 1959; and the Ph.D. in economics at the University of Chicago in 1968. He began his career as an economist for the U.S. Department of Labor (1961–1962), then moved through a succession of teaching/research positions at a number of universities and colleges: Rutgers, Douglass College, Howard University, Cornell, Brandeis, University of California—Los Angeles, and Stanford. In 1980 he joined the Hoover Institution at Stanford University.

Sowell has been an outspoken conservative. He has attacked affirmative action, quotas, forced busing, government assistance programs aimed at minorities, and even desegregated schools and the minimum wage. Sowell argues that basing government policy on the premise of minorities as victims does more harm than good and argues instead for free market policies. His columns, books, and other writings picture "political correctness" on U.S. campuses as largely self-serving and destructive. He has been a prolific author of books.

BOOKS: *Economics: Analysis and Issues* (Glenview, Ill., 1971); *Black Education: Myths and Tragedies* (New York, 1972); *Say's Law: An Historical Analysis* (Princeton, N.J., 1972); *Classical Economics Reconsidered* (Princeton, N.J., 1974); *Affirmative Action: Was It Necessary in Academia?* (Washington, D.C., 1975); *Race and Economics* (New York, 1975); *Patterns of Black Excellence* (Washington, D.C., 1977); ed., *American Ethnic Groups* (Washington, D.C., 1978); ed., *Essays on Data on American Ethnic Groups* (Washington, D.C., 1978); *Markets and Minorities* (New York, 1981); *Pink and Brown People, and Other Controversial Essays* (Stanford, Calif., 1981); *Knowledge and Decision* (New York, 1982); *Ethnic America: A History* (New York, 1983); *The Economics and Politics of Race* (New York, 1983); *Marxism: Philosophy and Economics* (New York, 1985); *Civil Rights: Rhetoric or Reality?* (Stanford, Calif., 1986); *Education: Assumptions vs. History* (Stanford, Calif., 1986); *Compassion vs. Guilt, and Other Essays* (New York, 1987); *A Conflict of Visions: Ideological Origins of Political Struggles* (New York, 1987); *Choosing a College: A Guide for Parents and Students* (New York, 1989); *Preferential Policies: An International Perspective* (New York, 1990); *Race and Culture: A World View* (University Park, Pa., 1992); *Inside American Education: The Decline, the Deception, the Dogmas* (New York, 1993); *Is Reality Optional? And Other Essays* (Stanford, Calif., 1993).

Spear, Joseph (?–). Joseph Spear's twice-weekly commentary on national and international politics, written from a populist viewpoint, is syndicated by the Newspaper Enterprise Association to around six hundred papers. The column was launched in 1989.

Spear is a graduate of Western Maryland College and holds a master's degree in communication from American University. He has been an army officer and taught high school chemistry and biology prior to earning his master's degree. Spear became a member of investigative columnist Jack Anderson's staff in 1969, was Anderson's editor and chief of staff from 1979 to 1989, and shared Anderson's byline for several years.

Spear has also contributed to such magazines as *Washingtonian* and *Saturday Evening Post*, and he has authored one book.

BOOKS: *Presidents and the Press: The Nixon Legacy* (Cambridge, Mass., 1984).

Spencer, James Littleton (22 Sept. 1951–). General columnist Jim Spencer writes for the *Daily Press* of Newport News, Virginia.

Spencer was born in Newport News and received the B.A. in urban affairs from the College of William and Mary in 1973 and the B.S. in mass communications from Virginia Commonwealth University in 1975.

Spencer began his career as a writer/editor for the *Virginia Gazette* in Williamsburg (1975–1977). He then spent a decade as a feature writer, first at the *Virginian-Pilot* in Norfolk (1977–1983), then at the *Chicago Tribune* (1983–1987). His column in the *Daily Press* dates from 1988.

Sperling, Jr., Godfrey (25 Sept. 1915–). Known for his many years with the *Christian Science Monitor*, Godfrey Sperling has been a Washington columnist since 1984.

He was born in Long Beach, California, and received the B.S. from the University of Illinois in 1937, the LL.B from the University of Oklahoma in 1940. While practicing law in Urbana, Illinois, he began reporting for the Champaign-Urbana *News-Gazette* (1940–1941), and from 1941 to 1946 he served in the U.S. Army Air Forces.

Sperling joined the *Monitor* in 1946, was its Midwest bureau chief from 1957 to 1962, and served as New York bureau chief from 1962 to 1965. He was assistant chief of its Washington bureau from 1965 to 1973 and chief from 1973 to 1983, after which he began his column.

Stahl, Nancy (1937–). Nancy Stahl wrote "Jelly Side Down," a column of gentle humor that focused on family life.

Stahl was born in Chicago, attended DePaul University, and was an art major at the University of Massachusetts, finishing in 1959. From 1959 to 1960 she was an editorial assistant with *Iowa Farm Science* in Ames, Iowa. Her humor column began at the *Calgary Herald* in Calgary, Alberta, in 1969, and was syndicated to various U.S. papers during the 1970s by the Universal Press Syndicate.

BOOKS: *Jelly Side Down* (Greenwich, Conn., 1972); *If It's Raining This Must Be the Weekend* (Kansas City, 1979).

Stanton, Frank Lebby (22 Feb. 1857–7 Jan. 1927). Frank L. Stanton was, in a sense, the Lewis Grizzard of turn-of-the-century Georgia: in other words, he was that state's best known humorist and journalist. His "Just from Georgia" column ran in the *Atlanta Constitution* from 1890 to 1927.

Stanton was born in Charleston, South Carolina, and in 1862 moved with his family to Savannah, Georgia. He was mainly self-educated and at age twelve went to work as a copyboy for the *Savannah Morning News*. He moved to the back shop of this paper as a printer's devil and began writing humorous verse, which attracted the attention of *Morning News* reporter Joel Chandler Harris. Apparently, Stanton spent almost a decade as an itinerant printer before joining the weekly *Smithville* [Georgia] *News* as a reporter/columnist. He bought into this paper in 1887, became its editor, and continued to write his column as "Mr. Smith of Smithville." His work was occasionally reprinted in the *Atlanta Constitution*. In 1888 he moved to Rome, Georgia, to become night editor of the *Rome Daily Tribune* under John Temple Graves, and in 1889 Joel Chandler Harris helped him secure a job as reporter/feature writer with the *Constitution* in Atlanta. Stanton's long-lived column began less than a year later and was a miscellany of prose, epigrams, material reprinted from other sources, and light verse. Mostly his fame came from his optimistic, sentimental, nostalgic dialect verse, some of which was adapted by others as popular songs. While his paper espoused the New South, Stanton celebrated the Old South. He was selected as Georgia's first poet laureate in February 1925, two years before his death.

BOOKS: *Songs of a Day and Songs of the Soil* (New York, 1892); *Songs of the Soil* (New York, 1894); *Comes One with a Song* (Indianapolis, 1898); *Songs from Dixie Land* (Indianapolis, 1900); *Up from Georgia* (New York, 1902); *Little Folks down South* (New York, 1904); *Just from Georgia,* comp. By Marcelle Stanton Megahee (Atlanta, 1927).

REFERENCES: Walter Chambers, "He Sings of Simple Things," *American Magazine* 19 (February 1925): 118–126; Mel R. Colquitt, "Frank L. Stanton," *Magazine of Poetry* (October 1892): 369–372; Bertha Sheppard Hart, *Introduction to Georgia Writers* (Macon, Ga., 1929): 129–131; Lucian L. Knight, *Reminiscences of Famous Georgians,* vol. 1 (Atlanta, 1907).

Steele, Judy McConnell (?–   ). Judy McConnell Steele combined the jobs of columnist and reporter for the *Idaho Statesman* in Boise; she held these dual positions from 1978 to 1994.

Steele grew up in Denver, Colorado. She was a Peace Corps volunteer, translator, and teacher prior to entering journalism. She seems equally at home writing humor and human interest copy.

Stein, Ruthe (7 Nov. 1945–   ). Ruthe Stein writes the syndicated column "The Company We Keep," which deals with a broad range of human relationships. She is based at the *San Francisco Chronicle,* and her work is distributed by Chronicle Features.

Stein is a native of Chicago and received both the B.A (1966) and M.S. (1967) from the Medill School of Journalism at Northwestern University.

In 1968 Stein became associate editor of *Jet* magazine, for which she reported on issues of interest to the African-American community; she was both the only woman and the only white on the staff. In 1970 she became a feature writer for the *San Francisco Chronicle,* where she broke the story that identified First

Lady Nancy Reagan's astrologer. In 1987 she began writing a column, "First Person Singular," that dealt with the single life and ran in thirty papers. This column ended in June 1993 when Stein launched her present column. She has written for various magazines, including *Cosmopolitan, US, Ebony,* and *San Francisco,* and since 1987 has made frequent radio and television appearances on stations in her city plus "Sonya Live" on CNN, "All Things Considered" on National Public Radio, the British Broadcasting Corporation, and the Canadian Broadcasting Corporation, mainly to comment on issues that affect singles. She has also worked as a feature writing instructor and special programs coordinator for the University of California at Berkeley since 1974.

BOOKS: *The Art of Single Living: A Guide to Going It Alone in the 90s* (New York, 1990).

Stephenson, Malvina (?–   ). Syndicated columnist Malvina Stephenson was handled by Knight Newspapers Wire Service from 1969 and by the Chicago Tribune Syndicate from 1970.

Stephenson was born in Paris, Texas. She received the A.B. in history from Southeast State College and the M.S. in journalism (1936) from the University of Oklahoma.

She was a reporter and feature writer for the *Tulsa World.* She was a columnist with the Stephenson News Bureau starting in 1963 and was a radio reporter for ABC in Washington, D.C. From 1951 to 1963, she was an editorial and research assistant for Sen. Robert S. Kerr, then began her column "Washington Offbeat" for Knight Newspapers in 1969. She continued to combine newspaper and radio work, beginning in 1972 as a commentator on Washington's all-news station WTOP.

Stinson, Roddy (17 Sept. 1940–   ). Roddy Stinson has been a daily columnist for the *San Antonio* [Texas] *Express-News* since 1974.

He was born in Mt. Vernon, Texas, and holds two degrees from the University of Texas at Austin: a bachelor's in journalism in 1963 and a master's in journalism in 1969.

Stinson began his career as editor of the *Baptist Men's Journal,* a periodical of the Southern Baptist Convention, from 1964 to 1970. Next he was editor of *San Antonio,* the Chamber of Commerce magazine for that city, 1970–1974. He wrote a column for this magazine, which led to his being hired as a daily newspaper columnist for the *Express-News.*

BOOKS: *My Church Helps Me Learn* (Nashville, Tenn., 1967).

Stokes, Thomas Lunsford, Jr. (1 Nov. 1898–14 April 1958). Thomas Stokes was a political columnist for United Feature Syndicate from 1944 until 1958.

Stokes was born in Atlanta, Georgia, and was a Phi Beta Kappa graduate of the University of Georgia in 1920. While a student, he wrote for the *Atlanta*

Constitution, the *Atlanta Georgian,* and the student paper the *Red and Black,* and was editor of the campus literary magazine.

Stokes's first job out of college was as a reporter for the *Savannah Press* (1920). In 1921 he reported for two other Georgia papers, the *Macon News* and the *Athens Herald.* Before the end of 1921 he took a job with the United Press (UP) doing rewrite and shortly was sent to Washington to report on Congress, then the White House. His bureau chief and mentor was Raymond Clapper. Stokes remained with UP until 1933, when he became Washington correspondent for the *New York World-Telegram,* and from 1936 to 1944 he was a Washington correspondent for Scripps-Howard Newspaper Alliance. He won a Pulitzer Prize in 1939 for his reporting on corrupt politicization of the Works Progress Administration in Kentucky.

Stokes began writing his liberal column for United Feature in 1944 and was widely respected for his objectivity and fairness. His column ran in roughly one hundred newspapers. He was elected president of Washington's Gridiron Club in 1950 and was also active in the National Press Club. He wrote two books, one his autobiography and the other about the Savannah River.

BOOKS: *Chip off My Shoulder* (Princeton, N.J., 1940); *The Savannah* (New York, 1951).

REFERENCES: Delbert Clark, *Washington Dateline* (New York, 1941); Cabell Phillips, ed., *Dateline: Washington* (New York, 1968).

Stone, Charles Sumner, Jr. (21 July 1924–   ). Chuck Stone, now a member of the journalism faculty at the University of North Carolina (UNC) at Chapel Hill, was a columnist for the *Philadelphia Daily News* and Universal Press Syndicate starting in 1973.

Stone was born in St. Louis, Missouri. He received the A.B. from Wesleyan University in 1948 and the M.A. from the University of Chicago in 1950. From 1943 to 1945 he served in the Army Air Forces.

Stone worked as a field representative for World Politics and American Foreign Policy from 1952 to 1956, and from 1956 to 1957 as a representative for Cooperative for American Relief Everywhere (CARE). He was an editorial consultant for *New York Age* from 1957 to 1958 and edited that newspaper from 1958 to 1960.

In 1960 he became editor and White House correspondent for the *Washington Afro-American,* and in 1963 he became editor of a third black newspaper, the *Chicago Daily Defender.* He was fired from the *Defender* in 1964 because of his criticism of Chicago Mayor Richard Daley and in 1965 became an assistant to New York congressman Adam Clayton Powell. This job evaporated in 1967 when Powell lost his post as a result of charges of misuse of public funds, and Stone worked during 1968 as a research aide to Congressman Robert Nix.

In 1969 Stone served as a visiting professor of government at Trinity College in Hartford, Connecticut, and doubled as a "Today" show commentator on NBC-TV. From 1970 to 1972 he was minority affairs director for the Educational Testing Service in Princeton, New Jersey, and in 1972 he began writing his column in Philadelphia.

Stone's column soon gave him the image of Philadelphia journalism's champion of the common man. He was outspoken in his criticism not only of Philadelphia's two-gun police-chief-turned-mayor Frank Rizzo and a later mayor, Wilson Goode, but of the city's only black congressman, William H. Gray III, as well. His willingness to take on the establishment and his criticism of racism in law enforcement resulted in his becoming mediator for two prison disturbances, one in 1972 and the other in 1981. Also, several criminal fugitives turned themselves in to Stone rather than directly to Philadelphia police.

Stone has been on the UNC journalism faculty since 1991 and continues to write his column, now syndicated by the Newspaper Enterprise Association. He also continues to ruffle feathers, as he did recently when he took the position that South Carolina should be able to fly the Confederate flag if its citizens choose to do so.

Stone has been a contributing editor of *Black Scholar* and has authored three books, including one novel.

BOOKS: *Tell It Like It Is* (New York, 1967); *Black Political Power in America* (Indianapolis, 1968); *King Strut* (Indianapolis, 1970).

Stone, Isador Feinstein (24 Dec. 1907–19 June 1989). Best known as editor/publisher of *I. F. Stone's Weekly* and later *I. F. Stone's Bi-Weekly,* journalist I. F. Stone was a New York City newspaper columnist from 1942 to 1952.

He was born Isador Feinstein in Philadelphia. He legally adopted his pen name in 1938. His family moved to Haddonfield, New Jersey, while he was in his teens. He and a friend briefly published their own newspaper, the *Progressive,* during high school. After this experience, he worked part-time for the *Haddonfield Press,* then attended the University of Pennsylvania, majoring in philosophy and working part-time for the *Courier Post* in Camden, New Jersey, and the *Philadelphia Inquirer.* He left college without a degree and went to work for the *Courier Post* as a reporter/editor (1927–1933). He was a copy editor for the *Philadelphia Inquirer* (1925–1927), then spent six years as an editorial writer, first for the *Philadelphia Record* (1933), then for the *New York Post* (1933–1939). Stone was associate editor of the liberal monthly the *Nation* from 1938 to 1940 and its Washington editor from 1940 to 1946. His decade as a New York City columnist and editorial writer began in 1942; he wrote for *PM,* the *New York Star,* the *New York Post,* and the *New York Daily Compass.* He was one of the first columnists to question the United States's role in the Korean conflict.

Stone's non-conformist views had made him unpopular, even with the press, and when the *Compass* closed in 1952, he found himself without job offers and decided to start his own periodical. In *I. F. Stone's Weekly,* he lambasted the enormities and evasions of big government, criticized the tactics of Sen. Joseph

McCarthy, supported racial integration, and questioned America's involvement in Vietnam. After developing heart trouble, he changed his periodical in 1967 to a biweekly, also changing its title to *I. F. Stone's Bi-Weekly,* and continued his duties until 1971.

Stone was a contributing editor to the *New York Review of Books* from 1971 until his death in 1989. He also developed an intense interest in ancient Greece and learned to read Greek literature in the original. His book *The Trial of Socrates* (1988) was a surprise best-seller. In his final years he was hailed as a hero by liberals and became something of a cult figure.

BOOKS: *The Court Disposes* (New York, 1937); *Business as Usual* (New York, 1941); *This Is Israel* (New York, 1948); *The Hidden History of the Korean War* (New York, 1952); *The Truman Era* (New York, 1953); *The Haunted Fifties* (New York, 1963); *In a Time of Torment* (New York, 1967); *Polemics and Prophecies* (New York, 1970); *The Killings at Kent State; How Murder Went Unpunished* (New York, 1971); *The Best of I. F. Stone's Weekly: Pages from a Radical Newspaper* (New York, 1973); *The I. F. Stone's Weekly Reader,* ed. by Neil Middleton (New York, 1973); *Underground to Palestine* (New York, 1978); *The Trial of Socrates* (Boston, 1988); *A Nonconformist History of Our Times* (Boston, 1988).

REFERENCES: Thomas G. Paterson, ed., *Cold War Critics* (Chicago, 1971); Andrew Patner, *I. F. Stone: A Portrait* (New York, 1988).

Stroup, Sheila T. (28 Nov. 1943–). Sheila Stroup has been a columnist for the *Times-Picayune* in New Orleans since April 1988. Her thrice-weekly general interest column has appeared on the metro page since September 1990.

Stroup was born in Aurora, Illinois. She received the B.A. in English education from the University of Illinois in 1965, the M.S. in creative writing from Southeastern Louisiana University in 1982.

Prior to becoming a journalist, she was a teacher, at both the high school and college levels, and a computer consultant. She was hired by the *Times-Picayune* in 1988 as a community news writer and weekly columnist. Stroup has also published short stories in such magazines as *Yankee, Woman's World,* and *First.* She became president of the National Society of Newspaper Columnists in 1994.

Strout, Richard Lee (14 March 1898–19 Aug. 1990). Richard Strout was from 1943 to 1983 writer of the liberal political column "TRB from Washington" that appeared in *New Republic* magazine and was syndicated to roughly sixty newspapers.

Strout was born in Cohoes, New York, but grew up in Brooklyn. After two years at Dartmouth he entered the U.S. Army, then entered Harvard, where he earned the A.B. in 1919 and the M.A. in economics and political science in 1923. He wrote for the *Harvard Crimson* and the *Harvard Advocate.*

After his undergraduate days, Strout went to England and a reporting job on the Sheffield *Independent.* Two years later he returned to the United States and a short-lived job as a reporter for the *Boston Post.* He joined the *Christian*

Science Monitor staff as reporter/copy editor and concurrently worked on his master's degree. In 1925, his graduate degree in hand, he transferred to the *Monitor's* Washington bureau, where he remained for roughly sixty years as a Washington correspondent. He wrote free-lance for *Reader's Digest* and the *New Yorker,* as well. In 1943 he took over the "TRB" column in *New Republic* magazine, a column first written in January 1925 by Frank Kent of the *Baltimore Sun,* then by *Newsweek* writer Kenneth Crawford. The column's initials are said to stand for a backward version of Brooklyn Rapid Transit, an unlikely explanation, since in 1925 there was no such thing. In this widely distributed column, Strout covered every presidential administration from Harding to Carter. The liberal columnist was often highly critical of conservative congressmen, as well as the more conservative presidents. Increasingly, he saw the American political system as flawed and barely able to function. He wrote the column until April 1983.

BOOKS: ed., *Maud* (New York, 1939); with E. B. White as Lee Strout White, *Farewell to the Model T* (New York, 1936); *TRB: Views and Perspectives on the Presidency* (New York, 1979).

Strunsky, Simeon (23 July 1879–5 Feb. 1948). Known for his combination of erudition and gentle wit, Simeon Strunsky wrote the column "The Patient Observer" for the *New York Evening Post* starting in 1906 and two columns for the *New York Times:* "Topics of the Times" (1933–1947) and "About Books—More or Less" (1924–1929).

Strunsky was born in Vitebsk, Russia, and immigrated with his parents to New York City when he was seven. He received the A.B. from Columbia College in 1900.

From 1900 to 1906 he was a department editor for the *New International Encyclopedia* under editor Frank Moore Colby. During these years, Strunsky also free-lanced for magazines and newspapers. In 1906 he was hired by the *New York Evening Post* as a columnist and editorial writer. As an editorial writer, he supported U.S. involvement in World War I, and he was also a supporter of unfettered capitalism and of the League of Nations. He was named head editorial writer in 1920.

He moved to the *New York Times* in 1924, also as a columnist and editorial writer, and worked there until his death at age sixty-eight. As conductor of the miscellaneous column "Topics of the Times," he succeeded Frederick Carig Mortimer, who had written the column since 1896. Strunsky also published a number of books, many of which were of a whimsical, satirical nature.

BOOKS: *Through the Outlooking Glass* (New York, 1912); *Post-Impressions: An Irresponsible Chronicle* (New York, 1914); *Belshazzar Court: Or Village Life in New York City* (New York, 1914); *Smith on Preparedness* (New York, 1916); *Professor Latimer's Progress: A Novel of Contemporaneous Adventure* (New York, 1918); *Little Journeys Towards Paris, 1914–1918* (New York, 1918); *Sinbad and His Friends* (New York, 1921); *King Akhnaton, a Chronicle of Ancient Egypt* (New York, 1928); *The Living*

Tradition: Change and America (New York, 1930); *The Rediscovery of Jones: Studies in the Obvious* (Boston, 1931); *No Mean City* (New York, 1944); *Two Came to Town* (New York, 1947); *Simeon Strunsky's America; "Topics of the Times,"* 1933–1947 (New York, 1956).

REFERENCES: Herbert Mitgang, ed., *American at Random* (New York, 1970); Harold Phelps Stokes, ed., *Simeon Strunsky's America* (New York, 1956).

Sullivan, Edward Vincent (28 Sept. 1902–13 Oct. 1974). Ed Sullivan's re-markable career combined writing columns with hosting radio and television variety shows. His most lasting fame comes from the "Ed Sullivan Show," which appeared Sunday nights on CBS from 1955 to 1971.

Sullivan was born in Manhattan but grew up in Port Chester, New York. His formal education was limited to high school in that city.

Sullivan's first job was with the Port Chester *Daily Item,* for which he covered police news, the courts, and sports. In 1919 he was hired as a reporter by the ill-fated *Hartford Post,* which folded a few days after Sullivan was hired. He then covered sports for the *New York Evening Mail* from 1920 until that paper was bought out by the *New York Sun* in 1924. He worked briefly for the *New York World,* then in 1925 went with the *New York Morning Telegraph.* Two years later he joined the staff of Bernarr Macfadden's racy *New York Evening Graphic,* which at that time employed Walter Winchell as writer of the "Broad-way Hearsay" column. Winchell left to join the *New York Daily Mirror* in 1929, whereupon Sullivan took his place at the *Graphic* until that paper's closing in 1932. Sullivan's column then began a long run in the *New York Daily News* as "Little Old New York," appearing until his death in 1974.

Sullivan's career in broadcasting began in 1932 with his hosting the CBS radio show "Broadway's Greatest Thrills," on which he introduced such per-formers as Jack Benny, Jimmy Durante, George M. Cohan, and Irving Berlin. Sullivan also had a vaudeville troupe that toured the country during the 1930s, and during World War II, he was known for hosting benefits and fund-raisers. In 1942 he began a second CBS radio show, "Ed Sullivan Entertains," and in 1948 he made his television debut as host of the variety show "Toast of the Town," which in 1955 was retitled the "Ed Sullivan Show." On it, he intro-duced the nation to Elvis Presley, the Beatles, Rudolph Nureyev, and countless other entertainers.

BOOKS: *Mister Lee: The Story of the Shuberts* (New York, n.d.); *Christmas with Ed Sullivan* (New York, 1959).

REFERENCES: Jerry G. Bowles, *A Thousand Sundays: The Story of the Ed Sullivan Show* (New York, 1980).

Sullivan, Frank (22 Sept. 1892–19 Feb. 1976). From 1924 to 1931 Frank Sullivan was a humor columnist for the *New York World.*

Sullivan was born in Saratoga Springs, New York. He reported part-time for the *Saratogian* while in high school, then in 1914 graduated with the A.B. from

Cornell University and returned to the *Saratogian,* where he worked until he was drafted into the army in 1917. Upon his discharge, Sullivan moved to New York City and wrote for first the *Herald,* then the *Sun,* and finally, in 1922, the *World.* Here he began as a reporter/feature writer. He briefly did a news column, but his editor, Herbert Bayard Swope, saw his unusual talent for the comic and made him a humor columnist in 1924.

As a humorist, Sullivan was known for his gentle touch and for the collection of fictitious characters he created: Aunt Sally Gallup, Martha Hepplethwaite, the Forgotten Bach (a member of the Bach family who was tone deaf), and Mr. Arbuthnot the cliché expert. Sullivan wrote his column until the *World* closed down in 1931, but he had also been writing humor articles for the *New Yorker* since 1926 and continued to do so through the 1950s. He was also one of the celebrated Algonquin Round Table wits. A lifelong bachelor, Sullivan returned to his childhood home in Saratoga Springs in the 1960s and lived there until his death in 1976. He also contributed to *Harper's, Atlantic Monthly, Good Housekeeping,* and other magazines and published a dozen humor books.

BOOKS: *The Life and Times of Martha Hepplethwaite* (New York, 1926); *The Adventures of an Oaf* (New York, 1927); *Innocent Bystanding* (New York, 1928); *Broccoli and Old Lace* (New York, 1931); *In One Ear* (New York, 1933); *A Pearl in Every Oyster* (Boston, 1938); *Sullivan at Bay* (London, 1939); ed., *The Sergeant Says* (New York, 1943); *A Rock in Every Snowball* (Boston, 1946); *The Night the Old Nostalgia Burned Down* (Boston, 1953); *Sullivan Bites News: Perverse News Items* (Boston, 1954); *A Moose in the Hoose* (New York, 1959); *Frank Sullivan Through the Looking Glass* (Garden City, N.Y., 1970).

REFERENCES: Margaret Case Harriman, *The Vicious Circle: The Story of the Algonquin Round Table* (New York, 1951); John K. Hutchens, "The Happy Essence of Frank Sullivan," *Saturday Review* 53 (12 September 1970): 88–89.

Sullivan, Mark (10 Sept. 1874–13 Aug. 1952). Mark Sullivan is probably best remembered for his muckraking articles in *Ladies' Home Journal* and *McClure's* just after 1900, but he also wrote a political column for the *New York Herald-Tribune* and thirty-four other papers from 1923 until his death.

Sullivan was born in Avondale, Pennsylvania. As a schoolboy he worked for the *Daily News* in the nearby town of West Chester. He attended West Chester Teachers College, graduating in 1892. At this time he bought half interest in the *Phoenixville* [Pennsylvania] *Republican* and used his income from this paper to pay for his studies at Harvard, where he received the A.B. in 1900 and, after brief employment with the *Philadelphia North American,* the LL.B. from Harvard in 1903. While attending Harvard, he worked part-time for the *Boston Transcript.*

Sullivan's big break came in 1904 with an investigative story on the patent medicine industry for *Ladies' Home Journal.* Among other things, he revealed that Lydia Pinkham, to whom American women thought they were writing for medical advice (and from whom they received written replies), had actually been dead for about twenty years. He did muckraking for *McClure*'s in 1905 and from 1906 to 1917 worked for *Collier*'s, first as its political editor, then as its editor in chief from 1914 to 1917. During most of this time he wrote a column, "Comment on Congress," for *Collier*'s. After stepping down as editor, he continued writing for the magazine. Then in 1919 he was hired as Washington correspondent for the *New York Evening Post*, and in 1923 he joined the *New York Tribune*, which became the *Herald-Tribune*, and launched his column. In this same year he began *Our Times*, a six-volume popular history of U.S. life in the first twenty-five years of the century.

BOOKS: *Wake Up America* (New York, 1918); *The Great Adventure at Washington* (London, 1922); *Our Times: The United States, 1900–1925*, 6 vols. (New York, 1926–1935); *The War Begins* (New York, 1932); *The Education of an American* (New York, 1938).

REFERENCES: Edward LaRue Weldon, *Mark Sullivan's Progressive Journalism, 1874–1925: An Ironic Persuasion*, Ph.D. Dissertation, Emory University, 1970.

Sullivan, Richard (12 August 1964–   ). Richard Sullivan, columnist and feature writer for the *Indianapolis News*, is distributed by Universal Press Syndicate. His column, "The 20s," is devoted to the concerns of post–baby boom readers and itself dates from fall 1990.

Sullivan grew up in Huntington, West Virginia, and is a 1986 graduate of Marshall University, with majors in journalism and English. He first worked as a reporter for the *Charleston* [West Virginia] *Gazette* and from there relocated to the *Indianapolis News* as an editorial writer. As such, Sullivan was one of the nation's youngest editorial writers, holding this position for three and a half years prior to beginning his column. He points out that the irony of his unusual professional progression is that as a very young editorial writer, he was paid to "write old." Now as a columnist, he is paid to "write young."

REFERENCES: David Astor, "A Rise in Features for Young Adults," *Editor and Publisher* (17 October 1992): 38–39.

Sulzberger, Cyrus Leo, II (27 Oct. 1912–   ). C. L. Sulzberger wrote the column "Foreign Affairs" for the *New York Times* from 1954 to 1978.

Sulzberger was born in New York City, the nephew of Arthur Hays Sulzberger, publisher of the *New York Times*, and received the B.S. magna cum laude and Phi Beta Kappa from Harvard University in 1934.

From 1934 to 1935 he was a reporter and rewrite man for the *Pittsburgh Press*, and from 1935 to 1938 he was a Washington, D.C.–based reporter for United Press (UP). Sulzberger then began a long career as a foreign correspondent: with the *London Evening Stardard* (1938–1939); for UP, the North American Newspaper Alliance, and CBS (1939–1940); then with the *New York Times* beginning in 1940. He covered the war in Europe for the *Times*, interviewed world leaders, and traveled on every continent. His beat from 1940 to 1944 was Russia, the Balkans, and the Middle East, and he was the *Times*'s head of all foreign service from 1944 to 1954. Sulzberger was also a prolific author, most of whose books concerned politics.

BOOKS: *Sit Down with John L. Lewis* (New York, 1938); *The Big Thaw: A Personal Exploration of the "New" Russia and the Orbit Countries* (New York, 1956); *What's Wrong with U.S. Foreign Policy* (New York, 1959); *My Brother Death* (New York, 1961); *The Test: DeGaulle and Algeria* (New York, 1962); *Unfinished Revolution: America and the Third World* (New York, 1965); *The American Heritage Picture History of World War II* (New York, 1966); *A Long Row of Candles* (New York, 1969); *The Last of the Giants* (New York, 1970); *The Tooth Merchant: A Novel* (New York, 1973); *Unconquered Souls: The Resistentialists* (Woodstock, N.Y., 1973); *An Age of Mediocrity* (New York, 1973); *The Coldest War: Russia's Game in China* (New York, 1974); *Postscript with a Chinese Accent* (New York, 1974); *Go Gentle into the Night* (Englewood Cliffs, N.J., 1976); *The Fall of Eagles* (New York, 1977); *The Tallest Liar* (New York, 1977); *Seven Continents and Forty Years* (New York, 1977); *Marina* (New York, 1978); *How I Committed Suicide: A Reverie* (New Haven, Conn., 1982); *Such a Peace: The Roots and Ashes of Yalta* (New York, 1982); *The World and Richard Nixon* (New York, 1987); *Fathers and Children* (New York, 1987); *Paradise Regained: Memoir of a Rebel* (New York, 1989).

T

Tammeus, William David (18 Jan. 1945–). Bill Tammeus (pronounced Tam-may-us) has written columns for the *Kansas City Star* since 1977. His daily column appears under the title "Starbeams"; his every-other-Sunday column is untitled. His work has been distributed by the New York Times News Service since 1989.

Tammeus was born in Woodstock, Illinois; attended two years of high school in Mussoorie and Allahabad, India; and in 1967 received the B.A. in journalism at the University of Missouri. He did graduate work in English at the University of Rochester in 1967–1969.

His career began at the Rochester (New York) *Times-Union,* where he was a reporter from 1967 to 1970. He joined the *Kansas City Star* as a reporter in 1970 and became a columnist and editorial board member in 1977. Tammeus was a stringer for *Time* (1966–1967) and *Newsweek* (1967–1970) and has written free-lance for the *Washington Post, New York Times, Newsday,* the *Milwaukee Journal, Rolling Stone, Reader's Digest, Missouri Life,* and *Theology Today.* In 1993 he was editor at large for the *Presbyterian Outlook* and since 1987 has been a commentator on Kansas City's station KCPT-TV. He has served as vice president (1990–1992) and president (1992–1994) of the National Society of Newspaper Columnists and was a member of the staff that won the 1982 Pulitzer Prize for local reporting for their story on the Hyatt Hotel disaster. Three days a week his column is mainly given to humor, mostly political satire. Other columns are of a more serious nature, often political.

REFERENCES: David Astor, "A New President Is Elected by NSNC," *Editor and Publisher* (23 May 1992): 30.

Taylor, Bert Leston (13 Nov. 1866–19 March 1921). Bert Leston Taylor is remembered as writer of the humorous *Chicago Tribune* column "A Line o' Type or Two" in the early 1900s.

Taylor was born in Goshen, Massachusetts. He attended City College of New York during 1881–1882, then worked as a reporter and sometimes as a printer for the *Montpelier* [Vermont] *Argus and Patriot,* the *Manchester* [New Hampshire] *Union,* the *Boston Traveler,* and the *New York Herald.* He was an editorial writer for the Duluth (Minnesota), *News-Tribune* in 1896, and from 1899 to 1901 he wrote a column titled "A Little About Everything" for the *Chicago Journal.* The *Chicago Tribune* doubled his pay in January 1901, and Taylor launched his column "A Line o' Type or Two."

He returned to New York in 1903 and did a new column, "The Way of the World," for the *New York Telegraph.* He then joined the humor periodical *Puck* as a subeditor in 1904. Offered a far better salary, Taylor returned to Chicago and the *Tribune,* where he resumed writing "A Line o' Type or Two," keeping it going until 1921, the year of his death. He became known as B.L.T., as he signed each column in this manner.

B.L.T. had the ability to be funny in both prose and verse and is sometimes referred to as a "colyumnist," a spoof of the unlearned printshop accent and an indication of a writer whose column also aired the work of readers and fellow professional writers. He frequently received around one hundred letters or submissions a day from hopefuls who wanted to "make the Line." He was fascinated by words and their use and misuse and was politically independent of the *Tribune*'s own positions. After Taylor's death, the "Line" column was continued by a succession of other writers until June 1969.

BOOKS: With A. T. Thoits, *Under Three Flags* (Chicago, 1896); *Line-O-Type Lyrics* (Evanston, Ind., 1902); *The Well in the Wood* (Indianapolis, 1904); with W. C. Gibson, *The Log of the Water Wagon: Or The Cruise of the Good Ship "Lithia"* (Boston, 1905); with John Kendrick Bangs and Arthur Hamilton Folwell, *Monsieur d'En Brochette* (New York, 1905); with W. C. Gibson, *Extra Dry: Being Further Adventures of the Water Wagon* (New York, 1906); *The Charlatans* (Indianapolis, 1906); *A Line-O'-Verse or Two* (Chicago, 1911); *The Pipesmoke Carry* (Chicago, 1912); *Motley Measures* (Chicago, 1913); *A Penny Whistle: Together with the Babette Ballads* (New York, 1921); *The So-Called Human Race* (New York, 1922); *A Line o' Gowf or Two* (New York, 1923); *The East Window, and The Car Window* (New York, 1924); with Walter Henry Lewis, *Captain Kidd, Coin Collector* (N.p., n.d.); with Walter Henry Lewis, *The Explorers* (N.p., n.d.).

REFERENCES: Franklin P. Adams, "Bert Leston Taylor," *American Magazine* 77 (April 1914): 68; "Bert L. Taylor, 'Colyumnist' of The Chicago Tribune," *Everybody's* (April 1916): 478–479; "The Lost 'Colyumnist,' " *Literary Digest* (9 April 1921): 27; Harriet Monroe, "The Death of B.L.T.," *Poetry* 18 (May 1921): 97–98.

Taylor, Henry Junior (2 Sept. 1902–24 Feb. 1984). Henry J. Taylor made his fortune in the pulp and paper business but was also a war correspondent and from 1961 to 1981, a social and economic issues columnist for the Scripps-Howard papers.

Taylor was born in Chicago. He attended the University of Virginia. After a successful business career, Taylor came to newspapering in 1945 as a war correspondent for the Scripps-Howard Syndicate. He was U.S. ambassador to Switzerland from 1957 to 1961 and was a delegate to the Geneva Disarmament and Nuclear Control Conference from 1958 to 1960. His column for Scripps-Howard began in 1961. He also contributed to many magazines, including *Saturday Evening Post, Life, Reader's Digest,* and *Saturday Review of Literature.*

BOOKS: *Why Hitler's Economy Fooled the World* (Boston, 1941); *Time Runs Out* (Garden City, N.Y., 1942); *Men in Motion* (Garden City, N.Y., 1943); *The Big Man* (New York, 1964); *Men and Moments* (New York, 1966).

Teepen, Thomas Henry (19 Jan. 1935–   ). Tom Teepen has been national correspondent for Cox Newspapers since January 1992. His editorial page column for Cox's twelve papers appears twice a week and is also distributed nationally by the New York Times News Service.

Teepen was born in Nashville, Tennessee, and as a child also lived in Mobile, Alabama, and Cincinnati, Ohio. In 1957 he received the B.S. in journalism from Ohio University. He has since studied African history and African affairs at Stanford University as a Professional Journalism Fellow.

From 1957 to 1958 Teepen was a reporter for the Urbana (Ohio) *Daily Citizen.* He was assistant editor of the *Kettering-Oakwood Times* in Dayton, Ohio, in 1958 and 1959, and from 1959 to 1968 a reporter and editorial writer for the *Dayton Daily News.* He became editorial page editor of the *Atlanta Constitution* in 1982, remaining in that position until 1992. He has traveled on assignment to China, Africa, the Middle East, and the former Soviet Union and has appeared on the "MacNeil Lehrer News Hour," CNN, ABC's "Good Morning, America," and Canadian television's "The Editors."

terHorst, Jerald Franklin (11 July 1922–   ). J. F. terHorst was a columnist with the *Detroit News* and the Universal Press Syndicate from 1974 to 1981.

He was born in Grand Rapids, Michigan, and received the A.B. from the University of Michigan in 1947 after serving three years in the Marines.

From 1946 to 1951 terHorst was a reporter for the *Grand Rapids Press,* then was recalled by the Marines for duty in Korea. He was a political writer for the *Detroit News* from 1953 to 1957, that paper's Washington correspondent from 1958 to 1960, and head of its D.C. bureau from 1961 to 1974.

Regarded as a calm, respected moderate, terHorst was appointed President Gerald Ford's press secretary in 1974 and also took over directing the White House Office of Communication. An important part of his assignment was to reestablish good press relations in the wake of his predecessor, Ron Ziegler. After only thirty days in office, however, terHorst resigned as a matter of conscience after Ford pardoned former president Richard Nixon for his role in the

Watergate affair. Rejoining the *Detroit News,* terHorst began writing his column, and in 1981, he took a new position as director of public affairs for Ford Motor Company in Washington. From 1958 to 1974, he wrote for the North American Newspaper Alliance. He wrote regularly for *Reporter* and also contributed to a variety of magazines.

BOOKS: With Ralph Albertazzie, *The Flying White House: The Story of Air Force One* (New York, 1979); with Jody Powell and George Reedy, *Gerald Ford and the Future of the Presidency* (Lanham, Md., 1983).

Thimmesch, Nicholas Palen (13 Nov. 1927–11 July 1985). Nick Thimmesch was a syndicated Washington columnist from 1969 to 1985.

Thimmesch was born in Dubuque, Iowa. He received the B.A. from the University of Iowa in 1950. He was a Davenport (Iowa) *Times* reporter from 1950 to 1952 and a reporter for the *Des Moines Register* from 1952 to 1955. In 1955 he joined *Time* magazine as a correspondent and became chief of *Time*'s New York bureau before taking the same job at *Newsday* in 1967.

Thimmesch wrote his column, which was handled by the Los Angeles Times Syndicate, from 1969 to 1985. From 1981 to 1985, he was also journalist in residence at the American Institute for Public Policy Research. He has been a commentator on Mutual Radio and on both radio and television for CBS. He has done commentary for CNN and has often appeared on "Face the Naiton" and on "Meet the Press." From 1976 to 1978 he was a contributing editor of *New York* magazine.

BOOKS: With William O. Johnson, *Robert Kennedy at 40* (New York, 1965); with William O. Johnson as William Nicholas, *The Bobby Kennedy Nobody Knows* (Greenwich, Conn., 1967); *The Condition of Republicanism* (New York, 1968).

Thomas, Cal (2 December 1942–). Conservative Cal Thomas writes a twice-weekly column distributed by the Los Angeles Times Syndicate (LATS) and is a rising star among columnists who address politics, values, and ethics.

Thomas is a native of Washington, D.C., and is a graduate of American University. Prior to becoming a columnist, he had a twenty-one-year career as a broadcast journalist, including more than seven years with NBC News in Washington. He also was a reporter/anchor for KPRC-TV in Houston, Texas, and during his military service, was with Armed Forces Radio and Television in New York City. During his broadcast career, he covered a variety of beats, including the White House, civil rights, the space program, Watergate, and medicine.

After the 1983 publication of the fourth of his nine books, *Book Burning,* a denunciation of censorship, Thomas began submitting guest columns to such major papers as the *New York Times* and the *Washington Post.* He then approached several syndicates and was accepted by the Los Angeles Times Syndicate in April 1984. He presently appears in roughly 350 newspapers and does commentaries aired on more than one hundred radio stations. In May 1994 he became the host on CNBC's Tuesday night talk show and is known for his ability to take a staunchly conservative approach to issues in such a way as not to alienate liberals. Fellow columnist George Will points out that Thomas frequently concerns himself with the nonmaterial and calls him "a moral environmentalist."

LATS publicity materials quote Senator Edward Kennedy as saying, "Cal Thomas usually says the far right thing instead of the right thing, but I like reading him anyway." Thomas lives in northern Virginia.

BOOKS: With Ralph Webster, *Target-Group Evangelism* (Nashville, Tenn., 1975); *A Freedom Dream* (Waco, Tex., 1977); *Public Persons and Private Lives: Intimate Interviews* (Waco, Tex., 1979); *Book Burning* (Westchester, Ill., 1983); *Occupied Territory* (Brentwood, Tenn., 1987); *The Death of Ethics in America* (Waco, Tex., 1988); *Uncommon Sense* (Brentwood, Tenn., 1990); *Gays in the Military: The Moral and Strategic Crisis* (Franklin, Tenn., 1993); *The Things That Matter Most* (New York, 1994).

REFERENCES: Chris Lamb, "Conservative Has a Growing Readership," *Editor and Publisher* (27 February 1993); pp. 32–33.

Thomas, Keith L. (8 Feb. 1959–   ). Keith Thomas has written a column for the *Tallahassee Democrat* since March 1993.

Thomas was born in Tallahassee. He received the B.S. in journalism, magna cum laude, in 1981 from Florida A & M University and the M.S., also magna cum laude, from the Medill School of Journalism at Northwestern University in 1982.

From 1982 to 1985 Thomas was a staff writer for the *Miami Herald*. He worked as a feature writer for the *Atlanta Journal-Constitution* from late 1985 to 1993 and in March 1993 became columnist, contributing editor, and senior writer for the *Tallahassee Democrat*. He has taught as an adjunct professor for Florida A & M's school of journalism. Thomas, who is African American, often uses his column to demonstrate that problems involving human relationships are not at all simple or capable of being reduced to stock answers.

Thompson, Dorothy (9 July 1893–30 Jan. 1961). Intrepid foreign correspondent and probably the first American woman to serve as a bureau chief abroad, the exciting, outspoken Dorothy Thompson was a political columnist for the *New York Herald Tribune* (1936–1941) and for the Bell Syndicate (1941–1958).

Thompson was born in Lancaster, New York, and lived in Gowanda, New York, and other upstate New York towns where her father, a Methodist minister, worked. As an adolescent she was sent to Chicago to live with an aunt, and here she attended the Lewis Institute, receiving her A.A. degree in 1912. She graduated from Syracuse University with a B.A. in 1914 and became a spokesperson for women's suffrage while in school there.

Once out of school, she worked in Buffalo, New York, for the New York State Suffrage Association; took a short-lived job at a religious publishing firm;

and then was publicity director for an antipoverty social program. When she had saved enough money for passage to Europe, she sailed there in June 1920 aboard the S.S. *Finland*. Thompson was a publicist for the Red Cross and at the same time free-lanced for the International News Service, the *New York Evening Post*, and the *Christian Science Monitor*, quickly gaining the reputation of a gutsy reporter with a nose for news. She found a mentor in Marcel Fodor of the *Manchester Guardian* and wrote with him for that distinguished paper. In 1925 the *New York Evening Post* made her head of its Berlin bureau, and there she met the famous American novelist Sinclair Lewis. The two were married (her second marriage) in London in May 1928, after which she resigned her position, returned to the United States, and combined free-lancing and home life for two years.

The couple returned to Europe in 1930. On assignment for *Saturday Evening Post*, Thompson interviewed Adolph Hitler. Calling him a "little man," she predicted that he was too ineffectual ever to take power in Germany—not one of her more successful predictions. Her mistake was compounded when she expanded this episode into a book, *I Saw Hitler!* (1932). She continued writing for the *Saturday Evening Post*, had a brief affair with an Austrian baroness, and in 1936 began writing a thrice-weekly column, "On the Record," for the *New York Herald Tribune*. Her monthly nonpolitical column for the *Ladies' Home Journal* began in 1937, covering such topics as children, pets, and gardening. By this time it was said that, aside from Eleanor Roosevelt, she was the most influential of American women.

Thompson used her newspaper column, which was syndicated to roughly 170 papers, to campaign for U.S. entry into the war in Europe. She took on American hero Charles Lindbergh for his isolationist stand, upset the *Herald Tribune* by supporting Franklin Roosevelt for president in 1940, and left the paper to write for the *New York Post* and the Bell Syndicate. As a wartime sideline, she did a weekly shortwave broadcast to Europe, in German, that began, "Listen, Hans. . . ." After the war, her main interest became the Middle East, specifically the conflict between the Zionists and the Palestinians. Her pro-Palestinian columns drew charges of anti-Semitism, and in March 1947 the *Post* severed ties with her. She suffered a considerable loss of prestige and finally ended her Bell Syndicate column in August 1958. Thompson was also a fairly active author, writing just under twenty books from the 1920s to the 1950s.

BOOKS: *The New Russia* (New York, 1928); *I Saw Hitler!* (New York, 1932); *Concerning Vermont* (Brattleboro, Vt., 1937); *Once on Christmas* (London and New York, 1938); *Dorothy Thompson's Political Guide: A Study of American Liberalism and Its Relationship to Modern Totalitarian States* (New York, 1938); *Refugees: Anarchy or Organization?* (New York, 1938); *Let the Record Speak* (Boston, 1939); *Christian Ethics and Western Civilization* (New York, 1940); *A Call to Action* (New York, 1941); *Our Lives, Fortunes, and Sacred Honor* (San Francisco, 1941); *Listen, Hans* (Boston, 1942); *To Whom Does the Earth Belong?* (London, 1944); *I Speak Again as a Christian* (New York, 1945); *Let the Promise Be Fulfilled: A Christian View of Palestine* (New York,

1946); *The Developments of Our Times* (De Land, Fla., 1948); *The Truth About Communism* (Washington, D.C., 1948); *The Crisis of the West* (Toronto, 1955); *The Courage to Be Happy* (Boston, 1957).

REFERENCES: Barbara Belford, *Brilliant Bylines* (New York, 1986): 220–230; Paul Boyer, "Dorothy Thompson, Journalist," in *Notable American Women: The Modern Period,* ed. by Barbara Sickerman and Carol Hurd Green (Cambridge, Mass., 1980): 683–686; Charles Fisher, *The Columnists* (New York, 1944): 16–51; Ishbel Ross, *Ladies of the Press* (New York and London, 1936): 360–366; Marion K. Sanders, *Dorothy Thompson: A Legend in Her Time* (Boston, 1973); Madelon Golden Schlipp and Sharon M. Murphy, *Great Women of the Press* (Carbondale, Ill., 1983): 168–178; Vincent Sheean, *Dorothy and Red* (Boston, 1963).

Thurber, James Grover (8 Dec. 1894–2 Nov. 1961). James Thurber's lasting fame is derived from his years as a humorist employed by the *New Yorker* magazine. Only recently have scholars begun to document his column "Credos and Curios," written early in his career for the *Columbus* [Ohio] *Evening Dispatch* in 1923. His later column in the New York paper *PM* (early 1940s) appears to remain unstudied.

Thurber was born in Columbus, Ohio. He attended Ohio State University from 1913 to 1918, working for the school paper, the *Ohio State Lantern,* and the literary/humor magazine, the *Sundial,* but departing sans degree. Unable to join the military because of an eye injury, he became a code clerk at the U.S. Embassy in Paris (1918–1920). Returning to his hometown, he became a reporter for the *Columbus Dispatch,* where he worked until 1924, when he left the paper, hoping to free-lance for magazines. When given a column in 1923, Thurber adopted the style of Franklin Adams, writer of the famous Chicago column "The Conning Tower." Included in Thurber's "Credos and Curios" were satire, verse, fiction, and epigramatic paragraphs. One section of the column was subtitled the "Dad Dialogs," in which a rather plain midwestern dad gives his views on current life-styles. A second section was "The Adventures of Blue Ploermell," a parody of Sherlock Holmes featuring a bumbling detective who puts one in mind of Inspector Clouseau. A later addition was "The Book-End," a miscellaneous section made up of essays and anecdotes. Thurber's half-page Sunday column was cancelled in July 1923 as a cost-cutting measure, upon which he departed to try his luck at free-lancing. Luck was not with him, and in September 1925 he took a job as a rewrite man for the Paris edition of the *Chicago Tribune.* He became coeditor of this paper's Riviera edition in December 1925. In June 1926 he arrived in New York City, again finding his work rejected until in February 1927 writer E. B. White introduced him to *New Yorker* editor Harold Ross, who gave him an editing job. Here he found his niche as a humorist, working with the magazine until his death in 1961 and also publishing many successful humor books.

BOOKS: *Is Sex Necessary? Or Why You Feel the Way You Do* (New York, 1929); *The Owl in the Attic and Other Perplexities* (New York, 1931); *The Seal in the Bedroom and Other Predicaments* (New York, 1932); *My Life and Hard Times* (New York, 1933); *The Middle-Aged Man on the Flying Trapeze* (New York, 1935); *Let Your Mind Alone! And More or Less Inspirational Pieces* (New York, 1937); *Cream of Thurber* (London, 1939); *The Last Flower* (New York, 1939); *Fables for Our Time and Famous Poems Illustrated* (New York, 1940); with Elliott Nugent, *The Male Animal* (New York, 1940); *My World—and Welcome to It* (New York, 1942); *Thurber's Men, Women and Dogs* (New York, 1943); *Many Moons* (New York, 1943); *The Great Quillow* (New York, 1944); *The Thurber Carnival* (New York, 1945); *The White Deer* (New York, 1945); *The Beast in Me and Other Animals* (New York, 1948); *The 13 Clocks* (New York, 1950); *The Thurber Album* (New York, 1952); *Thurber Country* (New York, 1953); *A Thurber Garland* (London, 1955); *Thurber's Dogs* (New York, 1955); *Further Fables for Our Time* (New York, 1956); *The Wonderful O* (New York, 1958); *Alarms and Diversions* (London, 1957); *The Years with Ross* (Boston and Toronto, 1959); *Lanterns and Lances* (New York, 1961); *Credos and Curios* (London, 1962); *A Thurber Carnival* (New York, 1962); *Vintage Thurber,* 2 vols. (London, 1963); *Thurber and Company* (New York, 1966).

REFERENCES: Burton Bernstein, *Thurber* (New York, 1975); Stephen A. Black, *James Thurber: His Masquerades* (The Hague, 1970); Edwin T. Bowden, *James Thurber: A Bibliography* (Columbus, Ohio, 1968); Thomas Jackson Carter, *"Credos and Curios": James Thurber's Practice and Spadework on the Columbus Dispatch,* Ph.D. Dissertation, University of Tennessee, 1993; Alistair Cooke, "James Thurber: In Conversation with Alistair Cooke," *Atlantic* 198 (August 1956): 36–40; Charles S. Holmes, *The Clocks of Columbus: The Literary Career of James Thurber* (New York, 1972).

Tiede, Tom Robert (24 Feb. 1937–   ). Tom Tiede retired in the summer of 1992 as a columnist to become owner-publisher of the weekly *Richmond Hill–Bryan County News* just outside Savannah, Georgia. His column had been syndicated by the Newspaper Enterprise Association (NEA) since 1965 and appeared in as many as seven hundred papers at its peak.

Tiede (pronounced like the initials *T.D.*) was born in Huron, South Dakota. He received the B.A. in journalism from Washington State University in 1959, after which he served in the U.S. Army.

He was sports editor of the *Kalispell Daily Interlake* in Kalispell, Montana, in 1961–1962, then worked as a sports columnist for the *Daytona* [Florida] *News-Journal* from 1962 to 1964. Tiede was editor of *Outdoor Empire* in Sacramento, California, during 1964–1965, after which he began reporting and writing his column for NEA. He covered the war in Vietnam and traveled in more than fifty countries for NEA. His favorite assignments, he once reported in *Editor and Publisher,* involved driving the full length of the Pan-American Highway from Alaska to Panama in 1981 and retracing the journeys of St. Paul in 1983. His last years as a columnist were devoted to covering current events as seen through the eyes of ordinary Americans. Tiede also authored half a dozen books.

BOOKS: *Your Men at War* (Cleveland, 1966); *Coward* (New York, 1968); *Calley, Soldier or Killer?* (New York, 1971); *Welcome to Washington, Mr. Witherspoon* (New York,

1979); with Jack Findleton, *The Great Whale Rescue: An American Folk Epic* (New York, 1986); *American Tapestry: Eyewitness Accounts of the Twentieth Century* (New York, 1988).

Tims, Jane Neblett (24 Sept. 1946–). Jane Tims has been a general columnist for the *Vindicator* in Youngstown, Ohio, since 1987.

Tims was born in Tampa, Florida. She received the B.A. in economics from Randolph Macon Woman's College in 1968.

Her first experience as a columnist was at the *Boardman Leader,* a weekly in Niles, Ohio (1985–1986). At this time she held the unusual distinction of being a columnist who was also president of her local chapter of the Junior League (in Youngstown). She joined the *Vindicator* in 1987.

Toledano, Ralph de (17 Aug. 1916–). Ralph de Toledano has dual claims to fame: one, as a nationally syndicated political columnist since 1960, the other, as an authority on jazz music.

He was born in the International Zone of Tangier, Morocco, the son of a foreign correspondent mother and a businessman/journalist father. His family returned to New York City when he was five. He attended the Fieldston School in Riverdale, New York, where he edited the school magazine *Inklings* and helped launch a weekly paper titled *Crosstown.* In 1934 he enrolled at Columbia College, majoring in literature and philosophy. He wrote for the *Columbia Daily Spectator,* was managing editor of the campus humor magazine the *Columbia Jester,* and was associate editor of the *Columbia Review.* He received the B.A. in 1938.

During 1938–1939 de Toledano was an editor for Lex Publications in New York, then in 1940 became associate editor of the anticommunist weekly the *New Leader.* He also was a music critic for *American Mercury.* He served in the U.S. Army from 1943 to 1946, after which he returned to New York as editor of the *Standard,* a periodical of the American Ethical Union. Later in 1946 he helped found and became managing editor of *Plain Talk,* an anticommunist monthly, and in 1947 he became publicity director for the International Ladies' Garment Workers' Union. He was hired by *Newsweek* in 1948, became associate editor in 1949, and served as national reports editor from 1950 to 1960. His final four years with *Newsweek* were spent in Washington, where he covered then–Vice President Richard Nixon and traveled with him to Russia and Poland.

By this time, de Toledano, who had begun his career as a radical, had become a staunch conservative, and close to Nixon, as his two biographies of Nixon will show. De Toledano began writing a syndicated column, "In Washington," for King Features in 1960; was also a broadcast commentator for Taft Broadcasting; and edited *Washington World,* a conservative tabloid news weekly, from 1961 to 1962.

In 1971 he switched to the National News-Research Syndicate, in 1974 to

Copley News Service, and in 1989 to Heritage Features Syndicate. His close association with Nixon ended in 1970 as a result of comments made to the president by W. R. Haldeman, on whom de Toledano places much of the blame for Watergate.

De Toledano has written extensively for magazines and opinion journals, including *Commonweal, National Review, American Scholar, American Mercury, Reader's Digest,* and *Coronet.* He has published in *Poetry* and became a contributing editor of *National Review* in 1960. In 1938 he was cofounder of the periodical *Jazz Information,* which he coedited with Eugene Williams from 1938 to 1939. He has been a prolific author in a variety of genres.

BOOKS: *Frontiers of Jazz* (New York, 1947); *Spies, Dupes, and Diplomats* (New York, 1952); *Day of Reckoning* (New York, 1955); *Nixon* (New York, 1956); *Lament for a Generation* (New York, 1960); with Victor Lasky, *Seeds of Treason* (Chicago, 1962); *The Greatest Plot in History* (New York, 1963); *The Winning Side: The Case for Goldwater Republicans* (New York, 1963); *R.F.K.: The Man Who Would Be President* (New York, 1967); *America, I Love You* (Washington, D.C., 1968); *One Man Alone: Richard Nixon* (New York, 1969); *Claude Kirk: Man and Myth* (New York, 1970); *Little Cesar* (Washington, D.C., 1971); *J. Edgar Hoover: The Man in His Time* (New York, 1973); with Edward W. O'Brien, *Seeing Is Believing* (Taipei, Taiwan, 1974); *The Municipal Doomsday Machine* (Ottawa, Ill., 1975); *Hit and Run: The Rise—and Fall?—of Ralph Nader* (New Rochelle, N.Y., 1975); *Let Our Cities Burn* (New Rochelle, N.Y., 1975); *Poems, You and I* (Gretna, La., 1978); *Devil Take Him* (New York, 1979).

Trillin, Calvin (5 Dec. 1935–). A prolific writer known for his wit, Calvin Trillin has written a column for King Features Syndicate since 1986 and from 1978 to 1985 wrote his column of intelligent, understated humor, "Uncivil Liberties," for the *Nation.*

Trillin was born in Kansas City, Missouri. He received the A.B. from Yale University in 1957.

Trillin began his career as a reporter for *Time* (1960–1963), then in 1963 became a staff writer for the *New Yorker,* where he has remained. Wanting access to a wider audience, he decided to syndicate "Uncivil Liberties" in 1986 via the Cowles Syndicate. The feature had appeared in *Nation* on an every-third-week basis; as a newspaper column, it was shortened and has appeared weekly. The column is now distributed by King Features and gives readers an iconoclastic, somewhat acerbic look at matters both political and social. Collections of the column have been published in three of Trillin's books: *Uncivil Liberties* (1982), *With All Disrespect* (1985), and *If You Can't Say Something Nice* (1987). Trillin has written for many other periodicals, including *Esquire, Harper's,* and *Atlantic,* and has authored nearly twenty books.

BOOKS: *An Education in Georgia: The Integration of Charlayne Hunter and Hamilton Holmes* (New York, 1964); *Barnett Frummer Is an Unbloomed Flower* (New York, 1969); *U.S. Journal* (New York, 1970); *American Fried: Adventures of a Happy Eater* (Garden City, N.Y., 1974); *Runestruck* (Boston, 1977); *Alice, Let's Eat: Further Adven-*

tures of a Happy Eater (New York, 1978); *Floater* (New Haven, Conn., 1980); *Uncivil Liberties* (New Haven, Conn., 1982); *Third Helpings* (New Haven, Conn., 1983); *Killings* (New York, 1984); *With All Disrespect: More Uncivil Liberties* (New York, 1985); *If You Can't Say Anything Nice* (New York, 1987); *Enough's Enough (And Other Rules of Life)* (New York, 1990); *American Stories* (New York, 1991); *Remembering Denny* (New York, 1993); *The Tummy Trilogy* (New York, 1994); *Deadline Poet* (New York, 1994).

Trohan, Walter Joseph (4 July 1903–   ). Walter Trohan was a columnist with the *Chicago Tribune* from 1968 to 1978.

Trohan was born in Mt. Carmel, Pennsylvania. He was awarded the B.A. from the University of Notre Dame in 1926.

In 1922 he was a reporter for the *Daily Calumet,* and after finishing college, he took a job with the City News Bureau of Chicago (1927–1929). Later in 1929 he joined the *Tribune* as a reporter (through 1934), then as a Washington correspondent (1934–1948), and as D.C. bureau chief from 1949 to 1969. His final years with the *Tribune* were spent as a columnist. Trohan was president of the White House Press Correspondents in 1939 and president of the Gridiron Club in 1967. He was named to the Sigma Delta Chi Hall of Fame in 1976 and was a member of the Baker Street Irregulars. Between 1951 and 1969 he also did commentary for WGN, a *Tribune* property, and for the Mutual Broadcasting System.

BOOKS: Ed., *Jim Farley's Story: The Roosevelt Years* (New York, 1948); *Political Animals: Memoirs of a Sentimental Cynic* (Garden City, N.Y., 1975).

Tucker, Cynthia Anne (13 March 1955–   ). Cynthia Tucker's weekly column "As I See It" is syndicated by Chronicle Features. She is also the *Atlanta Constitution*'s editorial page editor.

Tucker was born in Monroeville, Alabama. She received the B.A. from Auburn University in 1976. Tucker began her career as a reporter for the *Atlanta Journal* (1976–1980). From 1983 to 1986 she was an editorial writer and columnist for the *Philadelphia Inquirer,* then returned in 1986 to Atlanta as associate editorial page editor of the *Constitution.* She was promoted to editorial page editor in 1992 and has also made frequent appearances on the "MacNeil Lehrer News Hour." She writes two columns a week for her section, one of which is distributed by Chronicle Features. Her subject matter is sometimes political, sometimes about other issues, and at last report, the column was appearing in more than twenty-five papers. As a black woman columnist, Tucker does not limit herself to traditional subjects dealing with blacks and women, but writes on a wide variety of topics. She was a Nieman Fellow at Harvard during 1988–1989.

Tully, Andrew Frederick, Jr. (24 Oct. 1914–27 Sept. 1993). Andrew Tully was a longtime Washington columnist and a successful book author whose specialties were espionage and law enforcement.

Tully was born in Southbridge, Massachusetts, and was educated in that city's public schools. He was a reporter for the *Southbridge News* (1933–1936) and for the *Worcester* [Massachusetts] *Gazette* (1936–1939), after which he became the nation's youngest newspaper owner when he bought the *Southbridge Press,* a weekly, in 1939.

From 1943 to 1945 he was a war correspondent for the *Boston Traveler,* covering the war in Europe. Tully was one of the journalists who entered Berlin with Soviet troops when that city was taken from the Nazis in 1945. After the war, he was a reporter for the *New York World Telegram* from 1945 to 1947; he then began his many years as a Washington columnist, working for the Scripps-Howard Newspaper Alliance (1948–1961). In 1961 he became a Bell–McClure Syndicate columnist, and in 1969 he switched to the McNaught Syndicate. His column appeared in at least 150 newspapers while he was with McNaught.

In 1962, Tully also had the distinction of being the only author ever to have simultaneous books on the *New York Times*'s best-seller lists in both fiction and nonfiction. Those books were his novel *Capitol Hill* and his exposé *CIA: The Inside Story.*

BOOKS: *Era of Elegance* (New York, 1947); *Treasury Agent: The Inside Story* (New York, 1958); *A Race of Rebels* (New York, 1960); *When They Burned the White House* (New York, 1961); *Capitol Hill* (New York, 1962); *CIA: The Inside Story* (Greenwich, Conn., 1962); *Supreme Court* (New York, 1963); *Berlin: Story of a Battle* (New York, 1963); with Milton Britten, *Where Did Your Money Go? The Foreign Aid Story* (New York, 1964); *The FBI's Most Famous Cases* (New York, 1965); *The Time of the Hawk* (New York, 1967); *White Tie and Dagger* (New York, 1967); *The Super Spies: More Secret, More Powerful than the CIA* (New York, 1969); *The Secret War Against Dope* (New York, 1973); *The Brahmin Arrangement* (New York, 1974); *Inside the FBI* (New York, 1980).

Tyler, Gus (18 Oct. 1911–   ). Known mainly for his work with the International Ladies' Garment Workers' Union, Gus Tyler has also been a thrice-weekly syndicated columnist with United Feature Syndicate since 1974.

Tyler was born Gus Tilove in Brooklyn, New York. He earned the B.A. from New York University in 1933.

From 1922 to 1934 he was assistant labor editor for the *Jewish Daily Forward* in New York, and from 1936 to 1938, editor of *Socialist Call,* also in New York. He was education director of Local 91 of the Ladies' Garment Workers' Union from 1939 to 1947 with time out for service in the U.S. Army Air Force (1942–1945) and after that, director of the union's politics department. He became assistant president of the union in 1963.

Tyler was a much-sought-after speaker and a prolific writer of magazine articles for *New Republic, Saturday Review, New Leader,* and other periodicals. He wrote or edited six books.

BOOKS: Ed., *Organized Crime in America* (Ann Arbor, Mich., 1962); *The Labor Revolution: Trade Unions in a New America* (New York, 1967); *The Political Imperative:*

The Corporate Character of Unions (New York, 1968); *Labor in the Metropolis* (Columbus, Ohio, 1972); ed., *Mexican-Americans Tomorrow: Educational and Economic Perspectives* (Albuquerque, N.Mex., 1975); *Scarcity: A Critique of the American Economy* (New York, 1976).

Tyrrell, R. Emmett, Jr. (14 Dec. 1943–   ). Bob Tyrrell is known primarily as founder (1967) and editor of the conservative cultural/political monthly journal the *American Spectator* but also writes a weekly column, "Public Nuisances," distributed to newspapers by Creators Syndicate. Known for his hard-hitting, sarcastic wit, Tyrrell saw the circulation of his magazine advance from 30,000 to 300,000 during the Clinton administration.

Tyrrell was born in Chicago and reared in affluent circumstances in Oak Park, Illinois. He received his A.B. in government in 1965 and his M.A. in American history in 1967 at Indiana University. While doing his graduate work, he founded a campus magazine called the *Alternative* to combat a liberal student government. In 1970, he went national with the magazine and in 1977 changed its title to the *American Spectator*.

Tyrrell is known for his adoration of President Ronald Reagan and for his equally great disdain for President Bill Clinton, whom Tyrrell calls "the eternal man-child." A much talked about article in the *Spectator* called First Lady Hillary Clinton the "Winnie Mandela of American politics," and others have espoused a conspiracy theory regarding the death of Clinton aide Vince Foster.

Tyrrell has authored or edited four books and has contributed to the *Wall Street Journal, Harper's, National Review,* the *Washingtonian,* and other periodicals. He also makes frequent appearances on television on such programs as ABC's "Good Morning America" and "The MacNeil/Lehrer Report," and PBS's "Firing Line."

BOOKS: Ed., *The Future That Doesn't Work: Social Democracy's Failure in Britain* (Garden City, N.Y., 1977); *Public Nuisances* (New York, 1979); *The Liberal Crack-Up* (New York, 1984); *The Conservative Crack-Up* (New York, 1992).

REFERENCES: Jennet Conant, "The Hazing of the President," *Esquire* (June 1944): 87–92.

U

Utley, Clifton Maxwell (31 May 1904–19 Jan. 1978). Primarily remembered as a radio and television commentator, Clifton Utley also wrote a syndicated column for the *Chicago Sun-Times* in the 1950s.

Utley was born in Chicago and received the Ph.B. from the University of Chicago in 1926, majoring in English. He remained there for postgraduate study, fulfilling all requirements for a Ph.D. in political science except the dissertation. He also studied abroad at the University of Munich and the University of Algiers and spoke German, French, Spanish, and Russian.

From 1931 to 1941 he directed the Chicago Council on Foreign Relations. He was also a commentator for Chicago radio stations WGN, WBBM, and WMAQ and in addition did commentary for the BBC from 1945 to 1953. His column, which focused on foreign affairs, appeared in the 1950s. Utley was an early television commentator and anchor in Chicago with WMAQ-TV, starting in 1949. One of his three sons is Garrick Utley of NBC News.

V

Vanderbilt, Amy (22 July 1908–27 Dec. 1974). Amy Vanderbilt, known for her pronouncements on etiquette, wrote a syndicated column titled "Amy Vanderbilt's Etiquette" from 1954 until her death in 1974.

Vanderbilt, a descendant of the wealthy Commodore Cornelius Vanderbilt, was born in New York City. While in high school, she worked part-time for the *Staten Island Advance* as a feature and society writer. She took courses in home economics at the Institute Heubi in Lausanne, Switzerland; returned to study at Packer Collegiate Institute in Brooklyn; and studied journalism at New York University from 1926 to 1928.

In 1933 she became business manager of the *American Spectator,* a literary magazine, and began a one-year-long column for International News Service. She was home service director of Tower Magazines in 1934 and from 1935 to 1939 worked in advertising. From 1939 to 1945 Vanderbilt was with a New York public relations firm, Publicity Associates, Inc., as president from 1940. When one of her clients, Doubleday, asked her to write an etiquette book, she found her true calling. The book appeared in 1952 and was republished in several updated versions.

Vanderbilt began writing her column in 1954 and in that same year also began to host a television program titled "It's Good Taste," which ran until 1960. From 1960 to 1962 she hosted a similar radio show, "The Right Thing to Do." She was a regular contributor to *McCall'*s and *Ladies' Home Journal* and also wrote for the *New Yorker, Collier's, Better Homes and Gardens,* and other periodicals. Her newspaper column was carried by United Feature from 1954 to 1968 and by the Los Angeles Times Syndicate from 1968 to 1974.

BOOKS: *Amy Vanderbilt's Complete Book of Etiquette* (Garden City, N.Y., 1952); *Amy Vanderbilt's Everyday Etiquette* (Garden City, N.Y., 1956); *Amy Vanderbilt's Complete Cookbook* (New York, 1961).

Van Horne, Harriet (17 May 1920–   ). Harriet Van Horne was hired in 1942 to write a radio column for the *New York World-Telegram.* Since then, her column, which began appearing in the *New York Post* in 1967, has been syndicated by the New York Times Syndicate and the Los Angeles Times Syndicate. Her work has transcended the narrowness of the usual radio or TV review column.

Van Horne was born in Syracuse, New York, and spent part of her youth in Rochester. She majored in government and history at the University of Rochester; edited the campus paper, the *Tower Times;* wrote for the campus literary magazine; and wrote part-time for the *Rochester Democrat and Chronicle.* After receiving the B.A. in 1940, she worked for *Greenwich* [Connecticut] *Time* as reporter/feature writer/society editor/weekly general columnist.

The glamorous Van Horne began writing a radio column for the *World-Telegram* in September 1942. In it she did reviews of programs, wrote about industry trends, interviewed celebrities, and spoke out against bad taste and trivialization. In 1947 she added television to her agenda, and in this same year, she was given her own television interview show. She later moved her column to the *New York Post.*

BOOKS: *Never Go Anywhere Without a Pencil* (New York, 1972).

Vanocur, Sander (8 Jan. 1928–   ). Sander Vanocur, known mainly for his television work with NBC and public broadcasting, began his career as a newspaper reporter and wrote a television column for the *Washington Post* from 1975 to 1977.

He was born Sander Vinocur (with an *i*) in Cleveland, Ohio. He was a 1950 graduate of Northwestern University, studied at the London School of Economics (1950–1951), and served in the U.S. Army in Austria and Germany (1952–1954). Upon his release from the service, he secured a job as a reporter for the *Manchester Guardian* in England (1954–1955). He branched out as a weekly commentator for the North American Service of the BBC, did some writing for the *Observer* in London, and was a CBS London stringer. Vanocur covered Winston Churchill's retirement and the Princess Margaret–Peter Townsend romance.

He returned to America and covered the Queens police beat for the *New York Times* in 1955–1957, then became an NBC News Washington correspondent. Transferred to Chicago, he covered Soviet Premier Nikita Khrushchev's U.S. tour and reported on the early stages of school desegregation in Little Rock, Arkansas. He was one of the newsmen who asked the candidates questions after the Kennedy-Nixon debates in 1960. He left NBC in 1971 after being passed over as evening news anchor and worked in public broadcasting from 1971 to 1977. He then spent two years writing his *Post* column and has been with ABC since 1977.

BOOKS: Ed. with Pierre Salinger, *A Tribute to John F. Kennedy* (New York, 1964).

Vaughan, William Edward (8 Oct. 1915–26 Feb. 1977). Bill Vaughan was associate editor (1965–1977) of the *Kansas City Star* and from 1945 until his death, wrote the column ''Starbeams'' as well as two other columns for national syndication.

Vaughan was born in St. Louis, Missouri, and received the B.A. in journalism in 1936 from St. Louis University. From 1936 to 1939 he was a reporter for the Springfield (Missouri) *Leader and Press*. He joined the *Star* in 1939 and remained with the paper for the rest of his life, with the exception of his military service with the U.S. Army Air Forces (1943–1945).

In addition to ''Starbeams,'' Vaughan wrote the column ''Senator Soaper Says,'' syndicated by North American Newspaper Alliance, and ''Vaughan at Large'' for the Bell-McClure Syndicate. His columns were collected in four books.

BOOKS: *Bird Thou Never Wert* (New York, 1962); *Sorry I Stirred It* (New York, 1964); *Half the Battle* (New York, 1967); *The Best of Bill Vaughan,* ed. by Kirk W. Vaughan and Robert W. Butler (Independence, Mo., 1979).

REFERENCES: Karl E. Meyer, *Pundits, Poets, and Wits* (New York, 1990): 394–399.

Viets, Elaine Frances (5 Feb. 1950–). Elaine Viets (pronounced Veets) has been a life-style humor columnist for the *St. Louis Post-Dispatch* since 1979.

Viets was born in St. Louis, attended the University of Missouri at St. Louis from 1968 to 1970, and received a bachelor's degree in journalism from the University of Missouri at Columbia in 1972.

She was employed by the *Post-Dispatch* as a fashion writer in May 1972 and two years later became youth page editor, then feature writer. Her column runs four days a week and has been carried by the Scripps-Howard wire. She has twice won an Emmy for her local television shows and has had a syndicated national radio show since 1992. She is a member of the Authors Guild of New York.

BOOKS: *Urban Affairs* (St. Louis, 1988); *The Viets Guide to Sex, Travel and Anything That Will Sell This Book* (St. Louis, 1989); *Images of St. Louis* (Columbia, Mo., 1989); *Censored Viets: Stories You Couldn't Read in the Newspaper* (audio book) (St. Louis, 1991).

Viorst, Milton (18 Feb. 1930–). Respected political journalist and author Milton Viorst wrote a syndicated column out of the *Washington Evening Star* from 1971 to 1975.

Viorst was born in Paterson, New Jersey. He received the B.A. summa cum laude from Rutgers University in 1951; was a Fulbright Scholar at the University of Lyon, France, in 1952; served in the U.S. Air Force from 1952–1954; received the M.A. from Harvard University in 1955; and earned the M.S. from Columbia University in 1956.

From 1955 to 1956 he was a reporter for the *Bergen Record* in Bergen, New

Jersey. He progressed to other reporting jobs with the *Newark* [New Jersey] *Star Ledger* (1956–1957) and the *Washington Post* (1957–1961). From 1961 to 1964 he was Washington correspondent for the *New York Post,* and from 1971 to 1975 he wrote his political column at the *Star.* He has been a staff writer for the *New Yorker* since 1987. Viorst was board chairman of the Fund for Investigative Journalism from 1968 to 1978 and has written a number of well received books dealing with politics and political figures. He has also been published in such magazines as *Nation, Esquire,* and *Harper's.*

BOOKS: *Liberalism: A Guide to Its Past, Present, and Future in American Politics* (New York, 1963); *Hostile Allies* (New York, 1965); *The Great Documents of Western Civilization* (Philadelphia, 1965); *Fall from Grace: The Republican Party and the Puritan Ethic* (New York, 1968); with Clinton P. Anderson, *Outsider in the Senate* (New York, 1970); with Judith Viorst, *The Washington D.C., Underground Gourmet* (New York, 1970); *Hustlers and Heroes: An American Political Panorama* (New York, 1971); *Fire in the Streets: America in the 1960s* (New York, 1979); ed., *Making a Difference: The Peace Corps at Twenty-Five* (New York, 1986); *Sands of Sorrow: Israel's Journey from Independence* (New York, 1987); *Sandcastles: The Arabs in Search of the Modern World* (New York, 1994).

Voina, Vladimir (?–   ). In 1991, Vladimir Voina became the first Soviet journalist to be nationally syndicated in the United States, and in 1989 he was the first Soviet journalist to become a Nieman Fellow at Harvard University. He has also been senior editor of *USA Magazine* in Moscow since 1971 and is presently journalist in residence at the Foundation for American Communications.

Voina was the son of a prominent Soviet diplomat who figured in the formation of the United Nations in 1945. Voina, however, never joined the Communist party and hence was denied status as a Soviet foreign correspondent. His work experience in the former Soviet Union includes writing for such periodicals as *Pravda, Izvestia, Ogonyok, Moscow News,* and *New Times.*

Voina's column, which began with Creators Syndicate in September 1991, combines writing about his home country with discussing American affairs from his unusual perspective. He has written for such U.S. papers as the *Boston Globe, Los Angeles Times, Atlanta Journal and Constitution,* and *Village Voice,* and he has appeared on CNN and other U.S. television outlets.

REFERENCES: "CS Distributing a Soviet Journalist," *Editor and Publisher* (28 September 1991): 28.

von Hoffman, Nicholas (16 Oct. 1929–   ). Incisive writer Nicholas von Hoffman did the column "Poster" for the *Washington Post* (1966–1976).

He was born in New York City and was educated at Fordham Prep School, graduating in 1948. His work life began in 1954 at Chicago's Industrial Area Foundation, where he was associate director under Saul Alinsky. In 1963 he was hired as a labor reporter for the *Chicago Daily News,* and in 1966 he was hired away by Ben Bradlee of the *Washington Post* as a reporter and columnist. He covered the civil rights and antiwar movements and Watergate, and his provocative column, which often spoke for the younger segment of the U.S. population, was syndicated by King Features. He doubled as a commentator on the ''60 Minutes'' segment ''Point-Counterpoint,'' as well.

In 1976 von Hoffman left the *Post* and moved to London to work with the venerable magazine *Spectator*. His work has also appeared in such periodicals as *New Republic, Esquire, Progressive,* and *Harper's Bazaar,* and he has authored eleven books.

BOOKS: *Mississippi Notebook* (New York, 1964); *The Multiversity: A Personal Report on What Happens to Today's Students at American Universities* (New York, 1966); *We Are the People Our Parents Warned Us Against* (Greenwich, Conn., 1968); *Two, Three, Many More* (Chicago, 1969); *Left at the Post* (Chicago, 1970); with Garry Trudeau, *The Fireside Watergate* (New York, 1973); *Make-Believe Presidents* (New York, 1978); *Organized Crimes* (New York, 1984); *Citizen Cohn* (Toronto, 1988); *Capitalist Fools: Tales of American Business, from Carnegie to Forbes to the Milken Gang* (New York, 1992).

REFERENCES: Karl E. Meyer, *Pundits, Poets, and Wits* (New York, 1990): 363–366.

W

Wagman, Robert John (11 Nov. 1942–). Robert Wagman has written "The Wagman File," a twice-weekly political, investigative Washington column, for the Newspaper Enterprise Association (NEA) since 1980.

Wagman was born in Chicago. He received the B.A. in 1965, the M.A. in 1968, and the J.D. in 1971, all from St. Louis University. His varied career began with Dun & Bradstreet, where he was a reporter from 1963 to 1966. Next he spent 1966–1969 with CBS's News Election Unit and from 1969 to 1973 worked for his alma mater as assistant to the law school dean and director of both the Student Medical/Legal Institute and the law school's continuing education program.

Wagman then returned to CBS as a producer in the network's Midwest bureau (1973–1975), a member of its evening news investigative team in New York City (1975–1976), and as part of the "60 Minutes" team (1976–1977). In 1977 he became D.C. bureau head and chief political correspondent for the North American Newspaper Alliance, and in 1980 he launched his NEA column.

BOOKS: With Sheldon D. Engelmayer, *Hubert Humphrey: The Man and His Dream* (New York, 1978); with Sheldon D. Engelmayer, *The Taxpayer's Guide to Effective Tax Revolt* (New York, 1978); with Sheldon D. Engelmayer, *Tax Revolt 1980: A How-To Guide* (Westport, Conn., 1980); with Sheldon D. Engelmayer, *Hostage* (Ottawa, Ill., 1981); with Sheldon D. Engelmayer, *Lord's Justice* (Garden City, N.Y., 1985); *Instant Millionaires: Cashing in on America's Lotteries* (Kensington, Md., 1986); with Charles Ashman, *The Nazi Hunters* (New York, 1988); *The First Amendment Book* (New York, 1991); *The Supreme Court: A Citizen's Guide* (New York, 1993).

Waldmeir, Peter Nielsen (16 Jan. 1931–). Pete Waldmeir has written a general feature column for the *Detroit News* since 1972 and from 1963 to 1972 did a sports column for the same paper.

Waldmeir was born in Detroit, attended Wayne State University, and during 1951–1953 served in the U.S. Marine Corps. He has been with the *Detroit News* since 1949, when he began as a copyboy. He worked as a reporter for 1950–1951, then as a sportswriter from 1951 until 1972, when his sports column began. He was also associate sports editor from 1971 to 1973. His present column appears on a Monday-Wednesday-Friday schedule and on Sunday.

Walker, Danton MacIntyre (26 July 1899–8 Aug. 1960). Danton Walker was a freewheeling Broadway columnist for thirty-seven years, most of that time with the *New York Daily News.*

Walker was born in Marietta, Georgia, and gave up schooling at age twelve to work as a Western Union messenger. When the United States entered World War I, Walker was too underweight to enlist but managed to get to Europe in a civilian capacity. He worked there with the Relief Administration (the Hoover Food Mission) for three years after hostilities ceased.

Returning to the United States, he moved to New York City and worked as a bit actor from 1922 to 1927. He was theater critic Alexander Woollcott's private secretary during 1928–1929 and from 1930 to 1932 worked in the same capacity for Harold Ross, editor of the *New Yorker.* In 1933 he was hired as assistant financial editor of the *New York Daily News* but was quickly reassigned as assistant drama editor. He was a *News* music critic from 1934 to 1936, the paper's radio columnist during 1936–1937, nightclub editor beginning in 1937, and Ed Sullivan's replacement as the *Daily News*'s Broadway columnist, also starting in 1937.

BOOKS: *Danton's Inferno: The Story of a Columnist and How He Grew* (New York, 1955); *Spooks Deluxe: Some Excursions into the Supernatural* (New York, 1956); *Guide to New York Nitelife* (New York, 1958); *I Believe in Ghosts: True Stories of Some Haunted Celebrities and Their Celebrated Haunts* (New York, 1969).

REFERENCES: Charles Fisher, *The Columnists* (New York, 1944): 270–273.

Walters, Robert Mark (24 Aug. 1938–). Robert Walters began writing a column syndicated by the Newspaper Enterprise Association in 1977. During some of his time as a columnist, he was paired with fellow journalist Martha Angle.

Walters was born in New York City. He received the B.S. in 1960 at Lehigh University. He was a United Press International (UPI) reporter in Harrisburg, Pennsylvania, in 1962 and UPI bureau chief in Cincinnati, Ohio, in 1963. Starting in 1964, he spent a decade as a *Washington Star* reporter. Then, from 1974 to 1976, he doubled as a contributing editor of *National Journal Reports* and associate editor of *Parade,* the Sunday newspaper feature magazine.

Ward, Kent H. (4 May 1932–). Though retired since 1991, Kent Ward still contributes a weekly humor column to the Bangor (Maine) *Daily News,* the paper where he spent a thirty-year career.

Ward was born in Limestone, Maine, and attended Becker Junior College in Worcester, Massachusetts, where in 1951 he received the A.S. in journalism. After two years in the U.S. Army, he began work with the weekly *Limestone Leader* in 1954, becoming its editor and remaining there for eight years. In 1962 he became Rockland bureau chief for the *Bangor Daily News* and in the years that followed was a general assignment reporter, statehouse reporter, state editor, Maine editor (city and state desks combined), and from 1982 until his retirement, associate managing editor.

REFERENCES: Jim Brunelle, *Over to Home and from Away* (Portland, Me., 1980).

Waters, Linton "Earl" (1 Feb. 1935–   ). Earl Waters has been a columnist for the *Chattanooga Times* since 1984.

Waters was born in Waycross, Georgia. He attended Berry College (1953–1955) as well as the Army School of Photolithography (1955).

Waters has worked for three newspapers: the Alma (Georgia) *Times* (1958), the Waycross (Georgia) *Journal-Herald* (1958–1966), and the *Chattanooga Times* (since 1966). He switched from reporting to the *Times*'s copy desk in 1980. Waters has also free-lanced since the 1970s. His fiction has appeared in the *Georgia Review,* his nonfiction in the *Atlanta Journal-Constitution Magazine.* He describes his general column, "Life in the Slow Lane," as a mixture of humor, the personal, and nostalgia. His generation, he writes, "has one foot in the plowed field and the other on the moon," which "makes for interesting prose possibilities."

BOOKS: *Life in the Slow Lane: Don't Play Possum with a Pulpwood Truck* (Rossville, Ga., 1988).

Watson, Muriel Susan (19 May 1943–   ). Columnist Susan Watson has been on the staff of the *Detroit Free Press* since 1968.

She was born in Detroit and received the B.A. with honors from the University of Michigan in 1965. While doing postgraduate work at Howard University, she worked as a speech writer for Senator Philip A. Hart (1967). She was a general assignment reporter for the *Detroit Free Press* from 1968 to 1972, then spent two years as administrative assistant to the president of New Detroit Inc. She rejoined the *Free Press* in 1974. Her columns often offer the perspective of the black woman.

BOOKS: Ed. with Scott McGehee, *Blacks in Detroit* (Detroit, Mich., 1980); *Susan Watson* (Detroit, Mich., 1990).

Wattenberg, Ben J. (26 Aug. 1933–   ). A man who began his career as a political speech writer and aide, Ben Wattenberg has been a syndicated columnist since 1981, first with United Feature and currently with the Newspaper Enterprise Association (NEA).

Wattenberg was born in New York City. He was a Phi Beta Kappa graduate of Hobart College in 1955 and served in the Air Force from 1956 to 1958.

He was a speech writer for President Lyndon Johnson (1966–1968) and an aide and adviser to two senators, Hubert Humphrey (1970) and Henry "Scoop" Jackson (1972). From 1968 to 1979 he was also a business consultant in Washington. Wattenberg was on the faculty of Mary Washington College in 1973 and 1974 and was active in various institutes and associations during the 1970s. In 1981 he became host of "Ben Wattenberg at Large" on PBS and began a political column for United Feature. He continues his column with NEA and his work in public broadcasting and has been an active author.

BOOKS: *The Story of Harbors* (New York, 1960); with Ralph Lee Smith, *New Nations of Africa* (New York, 1963); *Busy Waterways, the Story of America's Inland Water Transportation* (New York, 1964); with Richard M. Scammon, *This U.S.A.* (Garden City, N.Y., 1966); with Richard M. Scammon, *The Real Majority* (New York, 1970); *The Real America* (Garden City, N.Y., 1974); *In Search of the Real America: A Challenge to the Chaos of Failure and Guilt* (New York, 1974); with Ervin S. Duggan, *Against All Enemies* (Garden City, N.Y., 1977); *The Good News Is the Bad News Is Wrong* (New York, 1984); *The Birth Dearth* (New York, 1987); *The First Universal Nation* (New York, 1991).

Weber, Tom (20 October 1952–   ). Tom Weber is a once-weekly columnist for the *Bangor Daily News* in Maine.

Weber was born in Brooklyn, New York, and is a 1974 graduate of the University of Maine. He began his career in 1979 as a correspondent for the *Portland* [Maine] *Press Herald* and joined the *Bangor Daily News* in 1982. He began as a sportswriter/editor then moved to the city beat and from there to the features desk, where he began contributing occasional columns and magazine pieces.

Wechsler, James Arthur (31 Oct. 1915–11 Sept. 1983). James Wechsler was a longtime columnist for the *New York Post*.

Wechsler was born in New York City. He received a B.A. from Columbia University in 1935. He was editor of *Student Advocate* (1936–1937), assistant editor of *Nation* (1938–1939), and labor editor of *PM* (1940–1941). In 1942 he went to work for the *New York Post* as Washington bureau chief. He was that paper's Washington correspondent from 1946 to 1949, then its executive editor from 1949 until 1961. From 1961 to 1980 he edited the *Post*'s editorial page. His column ran from 1949 until shortly before his death in 1983.

BOOKS: *Revolt on the Campus* (New York, 1935); with Joseph P. Lash, *War Our Heritage* (New York, 1936); with Harold Lavine, *War Propaganda and the United States* (New Haven, Conn., 1940); *Labor Baron, a Portrait of John L. Lewis* (New York, 1944); *The Age of Suspicion* (New York, 1953); *Reflections of an Angry Middle-Aged Editor* (New York, 1960); with Nancy F. Wechsler and Holly W. Karpf, *In a Darkness* (New York,

1972); *Kentucky's Pritchard: Brightest of Roosevelt's Young Aides* (Louisville, Ky., 1979).

Wells-Barnett, Ida Baker (16 July 1862–25 March 1931). A forceful spokesperson for racial justice and a newspaper owner, Ida Wells-Barnett wrote two columns, one for *New York Age* during 1892 and 1893, the other in the *Chicago Inter Ocean* during 1894.

She was born Ida Wells, a slave, in Holly Springs, Mississippi, and educated at a Freedmen's Aid School from 1866 to 1878.

Wells taught school in Holly Springs beginning in 1878. In 1880 she moved to Memphis, Tennessee, and taught for another nine years; she also became editor of the *Evening Star,* a Memphis, Tennessee, paper. She then was editor of a black weekly Baptist paper, *Living Way.* In 1887 Wells won a lawsuit against the Chesapeake, Ohio and Southwestern Railroad because she had been forced to move to a car designated for blacks despite her first-class ticket. Black editors around the nation asked her for articles on the experience, and in 1889 she became a part owner and editor of a larger Memphis paper, the *Memphis Free Speech.* With this forum, she spoke out forcefully against lynching and other forms of racial harassment. As a result of her editorials, the *Free Speech*'s offices and equipment were destroyed by a mob. She was also fired from her teaching job in 1891.

Wells moved to New York City and bought into the *New York Age,* in which her columns continued to press for racial justice. In addition to columns, she also wrote or cowrote pamphlets. In 1893 she relocated to Chicago and wrote for the *Chicago Conservator.* Also, on a lecture tour of England, she wrote a new column, "Ida B. Wells Abroad," for the *Chicago Inter Ocean.*

In 1895 Wells married the owner of the *Conservator* and became that paper's editor. She continued crusading against discrimination and also became an advocate of women's suffrage.

BOOKS: *The Reason Why the Colored American Is not in the World's Columbian Exposition* (Chicago, 1893); *On Lynchings* (New York, 1969); *Crusade for Justice: The Autobiography of Ida B. Wells,* ed. by Alfreda M. Duster (Chicago, 1970); *Selected Works of Ida B. Wells-Barnett,* compiled by Trudier Harris (New York, 1991); *The Memphis Diary,* ed. by Miriam DeCosta-Willis (Boston, 1995).

REFERENCES: T. Thomas Fortune, "Ida B. Wells, A.M.," *Women of Distinction,* ed. by Lawsen A. Scruggs (Raleigh, N.C., 1893); Mary B. Hutton, *The Rhetoric of Ida B. Wells: The Genesis of the Anti-Lynch Movement,* Ph.D. Dissertation, University of Indiana, 1975; Mildred Thompson, *Ida B. Wells-Barnett: An Exploratory Study of an American Black Woman, 1893–1930,* Ph.D. Dissertation, George Washington University, 1979.

West, Dick Sheppard (26 Dec. 1920–   ). Dick West's humor column "The Lighter Side" appeared in 1960.

West was born in Merkel, Texas, and received the B.A. from Trinity University in San Antonio in 1942. He was a reporter for the *Corpus Christi* [Texas]

Caller-Times in 1942, served in the U.S. Army in 1942–1945, then returned to the *Caller-Times* in 1946. In 1947 he joined United Press International. He became a correspondent in its Washington bureau in 1952.

BOOKS: *The Backside of Washington* (Garden City, N.Y., 1961).

White, Sallie Joy (1847–25 March 1909). Sallie Joy White wrote a society column for the *Boston Herald* under the pen name Penelope Penfeather starting in 1875.

Born Sallie Joy Sargent in Brattleboro, Vermont, she was a 1865 graduate of the Glenwood Seminary in Brattleboro. She was the niece of Nathan Sargent, who wrote as "Oliver Oldschool" and was an early Washington correspondent. From 1865 to 1868 she worked for Loring's Circulating Library and taught home economics in Charlestown, Massachusetts. Inspired by Lucy Stone, then a *New York Tribune* reporter, she found a job in 1869 writing for the *Boston Post,* the first woman reporter in that city. In 1874 she married and switched to the *Boston Advertiser*. The following year she again changed employers and launched her column for the *Boston Herald*. It ran for ten years.

White was a founder of the New England Woman's Press Association (1885) and was its first president (1885–1891). She also was instrumental in founding the General Federation of Women's Clubs. White lectured, wrote for magazines, and published at least two books on home economics topics.

BOOKS: *Housekeepers and Home-Makers* (Boston, 1888); *Cookery in the Public Schools* (Boston, 1890).

REFERENCES: Myra B. Lord, *History of the New England Woman's Press Association* (Newton, Mass., 1932).

Whitehead, Donald F. (8 April 1908–12 Jan. 1981). Pulitzer Prize–winning reporter Don Whitehead wrote a column for the *Knoxville* [Tennessee] *News-Sentinel* from 1957 to 1981.

Whitehead was born in Inman, Virginia. He studied journalism at the University of Kentucky from 1926 to 1928, working for the campus newspaper. He was city editor of the *Harlan* [Kentucky] *Daily Enterprise* from 1929 to 1933 and a reporter for the *Knoxville* [Tennessee] *Journal* from 1934 to 1935.

From 1935 to 1942, Whitehead was an Associated Press (AP) reporter and feature writer in New York City; from 1942 to 1945, an AP war correspondent. He landed with U.S. troops in Sicily, in Italy at Salerno and Anzio, and in Normandy on D-Day. After the war, he served as AP bureau chief in Hawaii (1945–1948), then as a Washington correspondent for AP (1948–1956). His first Pulitzer was awarded in 1951 for his coverage of the Korean War, his second in 1953 for his stories on President Eisenhower's secret trip to Korea. During 1956–1957, he headed the D.C. bureau of the *New York Herald Tribune,* and in 1959 he joined the Knoxville paper as a columnist.

BOOKS: *The FBI Story* (New York, 1956); *Journey into Crime* (New York, 1960); *Border Guard: The Story of the United States Customs Service* (New York, 1963).

Whitfield, Arthur Davis (25 April 1927–   ). Archie Whitfield was a general/humor columnist for the *Savannah* [Georgia] *Morning News* from 1966 until his retirement in June 1991.

Whitfield was born in Savannah. He attended the Citadel and Armstrong Junior College.

Whitfield began as a cub reporter for the *Morning News* in February 1950. In the succeeding years he worked all beats, as assistant city editor, city editor, Sunday editor, chief copy editor, and news editor. He describes the nature of his column as "humor, depending upon the reader."

Wicker, Thomas Grey (18 June 1926–   ). Now retired, Tom Wicker wrote a general political column for the *New York Times* from 1966 to 1991.

Wicker was born in Hamlet, North Carolina. He earned the A.B. in journalism at the University of North Carolina at Chapel Hill in 1948.

From 1948 to 1949 Wicker was director of the Chamber of Commerce in Southern Pines, North Carolina, and for a short time in 1949 he was editor of the *Sandhill Citizen* in Aberdeen, North Carolina. He was managing editor of the *Robesonian* in Lumberton, North Carolina (1949–1950), public information director of the North Carolina Board of Public Welfare (1950–1951), and a copy editor of the *Winston-Salem Journal* (1951–1952). After two years of service in the U.S. Navy, Wicker returned to become the *Journal*'s sports editor (1954–1955), its Sunday features editor (1955–1956), its first Washington correspondent (1957, assigned to cover Sen. Sam Ervin), and an editorial writer and city hall reporter (1958–1959). Part of 1957–1958 was spent at Harvard as a Nieman Fellow.

In 1959–1960 Wicker was associate editor of the Nashville *Tenneseean,* after which he joined the *New York Times* as a member of its Washington bureau. He remained there until 1971, and from 1964 to 1968 was bureau chief. He was associate editor of the *Times* from 1968 to 1985. Wicker's column ran in the *Times* for twenty-five years, ending when he retired in 1991. Wicker, who had originally intended to be a novelist, wrote several novels as well as a number of nonfiction books.

BOOKS: As Paul Connolly, *Get Out of Town* (New York, 1951); as Paul Connolly, *Tears Are for Angels* (New York, 1952); *The Kingpin* (New York, 1953); as Paul Connolly, *So Fair, So Evil* (New York, 1955); *The Devil Must* (New York, 1957); *The Judgment* (New York, 1961); *Kennedy Without Tears, the Man Beneath the Myth* (New York, 1964); *JFK and LBJ: The Influence of Personality upon Politics* (New York, 1968); *Facing the Lions* (New York, 1973); *A Time to Die* (New York, 1975); *On Press* (New York, 1978); *Unto This Hour* (New York, 1984); *One of Us: Richard Nixon and the American Dream* (New York, 1991); *Donovan's Wife* (New York, 1992).

Wickham, DeWayne (22 July 1946–   ). DeWayne Wickham is a general columnist for *USA Today* and the Gannett News Service.

Wickham was born in Baltimore, Maryland, and holds the B.S. in journalism from the University of Maryland (1974) and the M.P.A. from the University of Baltimore (1982).

Wickham worked in 1973 as a copyediting intern for the *Richmond* (Virginia) *Times-Dispatch* and since that time has been a reporter for the *Sun* and the *Evening Sun* in Baltimore, as well as a Capitol Hill correspondent for *U.S. News and World Report.* He has also been a contributing editor for *Black Enterprise* magazine. Wickham is a founding member and former president (1987–1989) of the National Association of Black Journalists. He is a panelist on the Black Entertainment Television news analysis program "Lead Story."

BOOKS: *Fire at Will* (Washington, D.C., 1989).

Widener, Alice (1905–24 Jan. 1985). Alice Widener's conservative national and international affairs column was syndicated to roughly one hundred newspapers. She was also a magazine writer and founder.

Widener was born in New York City. She wrote for *Atlantic Monthly, Life,* and other magazines and in 1954 founded her own magazine, *U.S.A.* It was published in New York City and continued publication until 1984, just before her death. Widener also wrote or edited five books between 1955 and 1979.

BOOKS: *Behind the U.N. Front* (New York, 1955); *Student Subversion: The Origin of America's Leftist Agitators* (New York, 1968); *The Detonators: Their Break with America* (New York, 1969); *Teachers of Destruction: Their Plans for a Socialist Revolution: An Eyewitness Account* (Washington, D.C., 1970); translator and ed., *Gustave Le Bon, the Man and His Works* (Indianapolis, Ind., 1979).

Wieghart, James Gerard (16 Aug. 1933–   ). James Wieghart's Washington column "Capitol Stuff" was syndicated by the Knight News Service. Wiegart was also executive editor of the *New York News,* beginning in 1981.

Wieghart was born in Chicago. After service in the U.S. Army (1951–1954), he attended Central Michigan University in 1954, then transferred to the University of Wisconsin, where he received the B.A. cum laude in 1958.

Wieghart was a reporter with the *Milwaukee Journal* (1958–1962) and the *Milwaukee Sentinel* (1962–1965). He was Senator William Proxmire's press secretary in 1965, then returned to the *Sentinel* as head of its Washington bureau (1966–1969). He was a Washington correspondent for the *New York News* (1969–1975) and its D.C. bureau chief (1975–1981), after which he was promoted to executive editor.

Wiemer, Robert A. (11 June 1931–   ). Bob Wiemer has written a weekly general column for *Newsday* since 1972.

Wiemer was born in Manhattan and grew up in Queens. He served in the U.S. Marine Corps from 1948 to 1952, then attended Hofstra University, where he earned the B.A. in 1957. Fresh from college, he signed on with *Newsday* as a switchboard operator/city room gofer in September 1957. Later in the same year he began reporting and from then until 1960 worked as beat reporter, general assignment reporter, and copy editor. His next two years were spent as the paper's United Nations correspondent. For the two subsequent years he was night city editor, and in 1965 he became a full-time editorial writer—a conservative among liberals.

Wiggins, James Russell (4 Dec. 1903–   ). The *Ellsworth* [Maine] *American*'s James Russell Wiggins in December 1993 celebrated his ninetieth birthday and his seventy-year newspaper career, which included writing a column for the *American.*

Wiggins was born in Luverne, Minnesota, and received his formal education in that city's public schools, later being awarded honorary degrees from eight colleges and universities.

His first job was as reporter for the *Rock County Star* in Luverne (1922–1925), after which at age twenty-two he became one of the nation's youngest publishers when he bought the *Luverne Star,* which he edited and published until 1930. From 1930 to 1933 he wrote editorials for the *Dispatch-Pioneer Press* in St. Paul, Minnesota, then joined the *New York Times,* first as Washington correspondent (1933–1938), second as managing editor (1938–1945, with time out for service in the U.S. Army Air Forces as an air combat intelligence officer), and finally as assistant to the publisher (1946–1947).

Wiggins moved to the *Washington Post* as managing editor (1947–1955) and in 1953 was also made a vice president. He was the *Post*'s executive editor from 1955 to 1960 and editor and executive vice president from 1960 to 1968. He was U.S. ambassador to the United Nations during 1968–1969, then bought the *Ellsworth American,* which he owned from 1969 to 1991. After selling the paper in 1991, he remained as its editor and columnist. Wiggins was president of the American Antiquarian Society from 1969 to 1977.

BOOKS: *Freedom or Secrecy?* (New York, 1956); with Archibald Cox and Mark DeWolfe Howe, *Civil Rights, the Constitution, and the Courts* (Cambridge, Mass., 1967).

REFERENCES: Dorothy Giobbe, "Sage Advice from a Newspaper Veteran," *Editor and Publisher* (29 January 1994): 16–17.

Wiggins, Ron (3 March 1942–   ). Ron Wiggins began as a *Palm Beach Post* columnist in 1974.

Wiggins was born in Jacksonville, Florida, and received the B.J. from the University of Florida in 1966.

Wiggins was with the *St. Petersburg* [Florida] *Evening Independent* from 1970 to 1974, then joined the Palm Beach paper, where he has remained since. His column is of the general interest/humor variety.

BOOKS: *The First Book of Last Times* (West Palm Beach, Fla., 1988).

Wile, Frederic William (30 Nov. 1873–7 April 1941). Frederic Wile was a foreign correspondent, columnist, and pioneer radio commentator. His column "Washington Observations" appeared in the *Washington Star* in 1923.

Wile was born in La Porte, Indiana. He was a student at the University of Notre Dame but had to drop out for financial reasons.

From 1898 to 1900 he was a reporter for the *Chicago Record*, and during the Boer War he was a correspondent for the *Record* and the *Chicago Daily News* in London (1900–1901). Later in 1901 he worked as the *Record*'s Berlin correspondent. He remained there and in 1906 left the Chicago paper to become Berlin correspondent for the *London Daily Mail*. Two years later he began to cover Berlin for the *New York Times* as well. When war came, Wile was arrested as a spy and expelled from Germany. He later sued for false arrest and in 1929 won $6,400. He wrote the column "Germany Day by Day" for the *London Daily Mail* during the war years, summarizing the news that appeared in German papers.

Wile was in the intelligence service of the American Expeditionary Forces when the United States entered the war. He returned home after the war and in 1920 became head of the *Philadelphia Public Ledger*'s D.C. bureau. In 1923 he switched to the *Washington Star* and launched his column "Washington Observations," an early political column. In 1923 his weekly radio show "The Political Situation in Washington Tonight," began on NBC; in 1929 he switched networks to CBS. He also authored a number of books.

BOOKS: *Men Around the Kaiser: The Makers of Modern Germany* (London, 1913); *The German-American Plot* (London, 1915); *The Assault: Germany Before the Outbreak and England in War-Time* (Indianapolis, Ind., 1916); *Newscuttings of the War* (N.p., 1916); *"Who's Who" in Hunland* (London, 1916); *Explaining the Britishers* (London, 1918); *Emile Berliner, Maker of the Microphone* (Indianapolis, Ind., 1926); ed., *A Century of Industrial Progress* (Garden City, N.Y., 1928); *News Is Where You Find It: Forty Years of Reporting at Home and Abroad* (Indianapolis, Ind., 1939).

Wilkins, Roy (30 Aug. 1901–8 Sept. 1981). Civil rights leader Roy Wilkins, executive director of the National Association for the Advancement of Colored People (NAACP) from 1965 to 1977, began his career as a journalist and wrote two columns: one in New York City's *Amsterdam News* and the other for national syndication by the Register and Tribune Syndicate (1969–1980).

Wilkins was born in St. Louis, Missouri. He received the A.B. in journalism and sociology in 1923 from the University of Minnesota. He was night editor of the *Minnesota Daily*, his campus paper, and also worked for a black weekly, the *St. Paul* [Minnesota] *Appeal*. Upon graduation, Wilkins became managing editor of another black paper, the *Kansas City* [Missouri] *Call*, holding that position until 1931, when he joined the NAACP as assistant executive secretary, the job he held until 1949. He also succeeded W.E.B. DuBois as editor of the organization's magazine, the *Crisis*, from 1939 to 1949. He was acting executive secretary (1949–1950), head of internal affairs (1950–1955), and executive secretary (1955–1964) before taking over as executive director. On his retirement in 1977, Wilkins was replaced by Benjamin Hicks.

Throughout his career with the NAACP and in reaction to his columns, Wilkins was frequently criticized as an accommodationist by those within the civil rights movement more inclined to be militant, yet he is remembered by most Americans as a calm, dignified voice of reason that consistently condemned violence and separatism.

BOOKS: *The Reminiscences of Roy Wilkins* (New York, 1962); *The Roy Wilkins Column: Selections from Mr. Wilkins' Nationally Syndicated Columns Published During 1972 and 1973* (New York, 1973); *Talking It Over with Roy Wilkins,* comp. by Helen Solomon and Aminda Wilkins (Norwalk, Conn., 1977); *Standing Fast: The Autobiography of Roy Wilkins* (New York, 1982).

Will, George Frederick (4 May 1941–   ). Well-read conservative columnist George Will has written a syndicated column from the *Washington Post* since 1973 and since 1975 has also done a biweekly column for *Newsweek* magazine.

Will was born in Champaign, Illinois, the son of a philosophy professor. He took his B.A. (1962) at Trinity College, Hartford, Connecticut, where he edited the school newspaper. He attended Magdalen College, Oxford, during 1962–1964, studying philosophy, politics, and economics and earning a second bachelor's and a master's degree. His Ph.D. is in political science from Princeton (1967). He taught political philosophy at Michigan State University (1967–1968) and at the University of Toronto (1968–1969) and left teaching to become an aide to a conservative Republican senator, Gordon Allott of Colorado (1970–1972). During this time he began writing occasional articles for *National Review,* and in January 1973 he was named the *Review*'s Washington editor. He remained with the *Review* until 1975.

With the encouragement of Meg Greenfield, Will submitted guest columns for the op-ed page of the *Washington Post.* His column became a *Post* regular and was syndicated by the Washington Post Writers Group starting in September 1973, going out three times a week, now twice weekly, to roughly four hundred papers. In 1976 he began a separate column for the back page of *Newsweek,* alternating weeks with his friend Meg Greenfield.

Having established himself as a major conservative presence in print journalism, Will furthered his reach as a panelist on the "Agronsky and Company" show (1979–1984); by appearances on "This Week with David Brinkley" starting in 1981, and as a "World News Tonight" commentator for ABC-TV starting in 1984.

His well-researched probing of America's often short-sighted Never-Never Land economic policies and politics of denial won him the Pulitzer Prize for commentary in 1977. His writing style manages to be both academic and stylish. He examines fundamental issues rather than mere events, such as the youth culture of the 1980s and 1990s, or the tendency of liberals to regard tolerance as the only meaningful principle. His newspaper columns average around 750 words, and, unlike most columnists who came up through the reporting ranks, he writes them longhand on a legal pad with a Mont Blanc pen. He has been a staunch defender of the military budget, pro–nuclear power, antiabortion, and anti–affirmative action. He has been criticized by fellow journalists for on occasion becoming part of the political process rather than simply observing and writing about it, for example, in his assistance to Ronald Reagan in preparing for a debate with Jimmy Carter.

Although writing books has been less of a priority for Will than for some of his fellow columnists of a similarly intellectual stripe, such as Garry Wills, he has written seven. Six are about politics, the seventh about his favorite sport, baseball.

BOOKS: *The Pursuit of Happiness, and Other Sobering Thoughts* (New York, 1978); *The Pursuit of Virtue and Other Tory Notions* (New York, 1982); *Statecraft as Soulcraft: What Government Does* (New York, 1983); *The Morning After: American Successes and Excesses, 1981–1986* (New York, 1986); *The New Season: A Spectator's Guide to the 1988 Election* (New York, 1987); *Men at Work: The Craft of Baseball* (New York, 1990); *Restoration: Congress, Term Limits, and the Recovery of Deliberative Democracy* (New York, 1992); *Suddenly: The American Idea Abroad and at Home* (New York, 1990).

REFERENCES: David S. Broder, *The Changing of the Guard* (Harmondsworth, England, 1980); David Burner and Thomas R. West, *Column Right: Conservative Journalists in the Service of Nationalism* (New York and London, 1988); Neil A. Grauer, *Wits and Sages* (Baltimore and London, 1984): 239–261.

Williams, Walter Edward (31 March 1936–   ). Conservative black columnist Walter Williams is presently with Creators Syndicate and has also written columns for the *Philadelphia Tribune* and Heritage Features.

Williams was born in Philadelphia. He received the B.A. from California State University in 1965 and the M.A. (1967) and Ph.D. (1972) from UCLA. His first job was teaching economics at California State University (1967–1971). He was a research associate with the Urban Institute (1971–1973), then taught economics at Temple University, beginning in 1973.

Williams's columns espouse individual accountability, picture affirmative action and quotas as morally bankrupt, and argue that social programs intended to help blacks and other poor Americans actually do more harm than good. His present column, "A Minority View," handled by Creators Syndicate and appearing in roughly one hundred papers, infuriates some readers, but he is a most unusual columnist in that he has a fan club. Williams has also written for various economics journals and authored or coauthored five books.

BOOKS: With Frank L. Cleaver, *Precalculus Algebra and Trigonometry* (New York, 1971); with James H. Reed, *Fundamentals of Business Mathematics* (Dubuque, Iowa, 1977); with Betty Jane Narver, *Government by Agency* (New York, 1980); *The State Against Blacks* (New York, 1982); *America, a Minority Viewpoint* (Stanford, Calif., 1982).

REFERENCES: Chris Lamb, "Columnist Doesn't Follow Liberal Agenda," *Editor and Publisher* (1 September 1990): p. 30.

Wills, Garry (22 May 1934–). Intellectual journalist, educator, book author Garry Wills has written a column, "Outrider," since 1970 for Universal Press Syndicate.

Wills was born in Atlanta, Georgia, and spent part of his formative years in Michigan and Wisconsin. He attended various public schools and was a 1957 graduate of St. Louis University, where he majored in philosophy with plans to become a Jesuit brother. He decided against joining the order and went for the M.S. in philosophy at Xavier University, finishing in 1958. In the following year, he earned another M.A. at Yale University, from which he also received the Ph.D. in the classics in 1961. While working on his dissertation, he wrote editorials for the *Richmond* [Virginia] *News Leader,* and during 1961–1962 he was a fellow at the Center for Hellenic Studies in Washington, D.C. After publishing his first book, *Chesterton: Man and Mask,* in 1961, Wills began writing a column for a religious paper, the *National Catholic Reporter,* which was also distributed to other Roman Catholic periodicals.

As an academic, Wills began his career at Johns Hopkins University, where he was an assistant professor from 1962 to 1967. Denied tenure because of the kinds of writing he had chosen to do, he found he could improve his income by working as a contributing editor for *Esquire,* which asked four articles a year from him. Some of his *Esquire* assignments, such as a story on President John Kennedy's assassin Jack Ruby and his coverage of the 1968 Democratic National Convention, were expanded into books. He was an adjunct professor at Johns Hopkins from 1968 to 1980, and from 1980 to 1988 was the Henry R. Luce Professor of American Culture and Public Policy at Northwestern University, where he has been an adjunct professor since that time. He also worked for a time with William F. Buckley, Jr., and the *National Review,* though he and Buckley found themselves at cross-purposes.

Wills's syndicated column is hard to characterize, as the columnist himself is regarded by some as a liberal and by others as a conservative. Whatever its leaning, it is most certainly an individual voice and well grounded in history as it examines contemporary issues.

BOOKS: *Chesterton: Man and Mask* (New York, 1961); *Politics and Catholic Freedom* (Chicago, 1964); *Roman Culture: Weapons and the Man* (New York, 1966); *The Second Civil War: Arming for Armageddon* (New York, 1968); with Ovid Damaris, *Jack Ruby* (New York, 1968); *Nixon Agonistes: The Crisis of the Self-Made Man* (New York, 1969); *Bare Ruined Choirs: Doubt, Prophecy, and Radical Religion* (New York, 1972); ed., *Values Americans Live By* (New York, 1973); *Inventing America: Jefferson's Declaration of Independence* (New York, 1978); *Confessions of a Conservative* (Garden City, N.Y., 1979); *At Button's* (Kansas City, Mo., 1979); *Explaining America: The Federalist* (Garden City, N.Y., 1981); *The Kennedy Imprisonment: A Meditation on Power* (Boston, 1982); *Lead Time: A Journalist's Education* (Garden City, N.Y., 1983); *Cincinnatus:*

George Washington and the Enlightenment (Garden City, N.Y., 1984); *Reagan's America: Innocents at Home* (Garden City, N.Y., 1987); *Under God: Religion and American Politics* (New York, 1990); *Lincoln at Gettysburg: The Words That Remade America* (New York, 1992); *Certain Trumpets: The Call of Leaders* (New York, 1994).

Wilson, Earl (3 May 1907–16 Jan. 1987). From 1942 to 1983, Earl Wilson commented on Broadway and show business in general in his widely syndicated column "It Happened Last Night."

Wilson was born in Rockford, Ohio. He attended Heidelberg College, then transfered to Ohio State University, and received the B.S. degree in 1931. To earn money for college, he worked as a sportswriter for the Piqua (Ohio) *Daily Call.* In 1931 he became an International News Service reporter and also reported for the *Akron Beacon Journal* before becoming a copy editor for the *Washington Post.* In 1935 he took a job as a rewrite man for the *New York Post.* He soon became the paper's amusement editor, and in 1942 he began his famous six-day-a-week column. The Field Newspaper Syndicate picked it up, syndicating it to more than two hundred papers. Wilson and his wife, known to his readers as "the B.W.," for "beautiful wife," would spend most nights on the town, gathering material, then Wilson would do his writing in the wee hours, sending his copy to the *Post* via taxi.

Though his usual material was celebrity tittle-tattle, he also had more significant stories. He credited himself with scooping the nation's hard news reporters on the Salk polio vaccine story. He also helped Woody Allen get a start in show business. Wilson often appeared on television talk shows, free-lanced to magazines, and wrote a number of books.

BOOKS: With Clyde Beatty, *Jungle Performers* (New York, 1941); *I Am Gazing into My 8-Ball* (Garden City, N.Y., 1945); *Pikes Peak or Bust* (Garden City, N.Y., 1946); *Let 'Em Eat Cheesecake* (Garden City, N.Y., 1949); *Look Who's Abroad Now* (Garden City, N.Y., 1953); *The NBC Book of Stars* (New York, 1957); *Das Ist New York* (Munich, Germany, 1966); *Earl Wilson's New York* (New York, 1964); *The Show Business Nobody Knows* (Chicago, 1971); *Show Business Laid Bare* (New York, 1974); *Hot Times: True Tales of Hollywood and Broadway* (Chicago, 1984).

Wilson, John Steuart (6 Jan. 1913–). Known mainly as an authority on jazz music, John S. Wilson was a columnist for *PM* from 1942 to 1949.

Wilson was born in Elizabeth, New Jersey. His A.B was from Wesleyan University in Middletown, Connecticut, in 1935; his M.A. in journalism from Columbia University in 1942.

From 1935 to 1941 he worked in promotion for the Vick Chemical Company in New York City. After his master's program, he became entertainment editor, then sports editor and columnist for the New York paper *PM.* His interests turned more and more to music, and from 1948 to 1950 he was New York editor for the magazine *Down Beat.* He was jazz critic for the *New York Times* and for *High Fidelity* magazine beginning in 1952. Wilson also worked as a producer and commentator for "The World of Jazz" on radio station WQXR in New York (1954–1970) and for the Voice of America starting in 1971. He wrote three books on the history of jazz.

BOOKS: *The Collector's Jazz: Traditional and Swing* (Philadelphia, 1958); *The Collector's Jazz: Modern* (Philadelphia, 1959); *Jazz: The Transition Years, 1940–1960* (New York, 1966).

Wilson, Keith, Jr. (3 March 1928–). Lawyer/columnist Keith Wilson, Jr., has been a general columnist for the *Examiner* in Independence, Missouri, since 1969.

Wilson was born in Independence. He received the B.A. in 1949 and the J.D. in 1951, both from the University of Kansas.

From 1960 to 1963 Wilson was city attorney for Kansas City, Missouri. He was city manager of Independence from 1980 to 1986, after which he was president and CEO of the University of Health Sciences in Kansas City from 1986 to 1989. Wilson reports owning the largest collection of paintings by Adolph Hitler in the Western Hemisphere.

Wilson, Lyle Campbell (2 Aug. 1899–23 May 1967). Longtime United Press (UP) journalist and executive Lyle Wilson also wrote a Washington column for the UP.

Wilson was born in Topeka, Kansas. He attended the University of Oklahoma (1917–1918), served a year (1918) in the U.S. Army, received the B.J. from the University of Missouri in 1922, and studied at the University of London (1923–1924).

He began his career as a *Daily Oklahoman* reporter in Oklahoma City (1920–1921), then went to work for the UP in London. He was New York City cable editor (1924–1927), then a reporter for the D.C. bureau (1927–1932). He was D.C. bureau manager from 1933 to 1942 and was UP general manager from 1943 to 1964. He ended his career as United Press International (UPI) vice president and columnist.

Wilson, Richard Lawson (3 Sept. 1905–18 Jan. 1981). Pulitzer Prize winner Richard Wilson worked for the *Des Moines Register and Tribune* for roughly fifty years and wrote a syndicated column.

Wilson was born in Galesburg, Illinois. He studied at Iowa State College (1922–1925) and the University of Iowa (1925–1926) and received the LL.D. from Drake University in 1956.

He was a reporter on the *Des Moines Register* in 1926, moving to the *St. Louis Globe-Democrat* in 1928. He returned to the *Register* later in 1928 as a political reporter and was city editor from 1930 to 1933. He was Washington correspondent for the *Register and Tribune* starting in 1933 and served as head of Cowles Publications' Washington bureau from 1938 to 1970. His Pulitzer was for distinguished reporting in 1954. Wilson also wrote for *Look* and for other magazines.

Winchell, Walter (7 April 1897–20 Feb. 1972). Walter Winchell, originator of the gossip column, was one of the most widely syndicated columnists of them all.

Winchell, who changed the spelling of his family name from Winchel, was born in the Harlem section of New York City, the son of Russian Jewish immigrants. He left school after failing the sixth grade for the third time and joined a vaudeville troupe. He was a song and dance man until 1916, when he joined the navy. Discharged in 1920, he returned to the stage and shortly thereafter got his first writing experience by doing a typed gossip sheet for his fellow vaudevillians. With this start, he began contributing to *Variety* and other established show business periodicals. In 1922 he became a reporter, columnist, and advertising manager for the *Vaudeville News* in New York City. The two columns he wrote for this periodical were titled "Merciless Truth" and "Broadway Hearsay."

Winchell was hired in 1925 by the *New York Evening Graphic*. He had a variety of jobs at this tabloid: ad manager, drama critic and editor, amusement editor, and Broadway columnist. He gathered material at the Stork Club and was a regular at the Algonquin Round Table. His column was successful and was soon in syndication.

After disagreements with the *Graphic*'s managing editor, Emil Gauvreau, Winchell moved his column to William Randolph Hearst's *New York Mirror* in June 1929 and in this same year began his fifteen-minute Sunday night radio show on CBS, where his fast-paced "news" was presented with flair and drama with a background of phony Morse code dots and dashes. Years later the brash columnist/commentator made the move to television, hosting the "Walter Winchell Show" in 1956 and the "Walter Winchell File" in 1957. His distinctive voice lives on in reruns of "The Untouchables," for which Winchell did the voiceover from 1959 to 1963.

At its peak, Winchell's column appeared in nearly one thousand papers, including newspapers in all fifty states and numerous other nations. As time moved on, he became increasingly combative and more frequently moved away from entertainment and into politics. He wrote much about organized crime, flatly declared Bruno Hauptmann guilty before trial in the Lindbergh kidnapping case, and was an early hater of Adolph Hitler and the Nazis, who, in Winchell's slang were referred to as the "Ratzis." Part of Winchell's popularity came from his inventiveness in the use of words. In 1933, H. L. Mencken named Winchell as one of the ten most productive inventors of slang in America. "Makin' whoopee," "blessed event," and "bundle from Heaven" are three examples that remain in use today, though others, such as "debutramp" and "merged and middle-aisled" (for married), seem to have faded from use.

Winchell began feuding with rival columnists Leonard Lyons and Ed Sullivan, as well as with *New York Post* publisher Dorothy Schiff. Winchell pictured the *Post* as having communist leanings and in 1952 lost a libel suit filed by that paper. Also, Winchell sided with Sen. Joseph McCarthy, and when McCarthy was discredited in 1954, Winchell's own popularity plummeted. The *New York Mirror* folded in 1963, and Winchell moved to the *New York Journal-American*. He was dropped by King Features in 1968 and was picked up by the McNaught Syndicate, though his number of papers was now down to perhaps 150. The old scrapper retired in February 1968. His autobiography appeared in 1975.

BOOKS: *Winchell Exclusive—Things That Happened to Me—and Me to Them* (Englewood Cliffs, N.J., 1975).

REFERENCES: Charles Fisher, *The Columnists* (New York, 1944): 87–135; Herman Klurfeld, *Winchell: His Life and Times* (New York, 1976); St. Clair McKelway, *Gossip* (New York, 1940); Lyle Stuart, *The Secret Life of Walter Winchell* (New York, 1953); Edward H. Weiner, *Let's Go to Press* (New York, 1955).

Winter, Ruth Grosman (29 May 1930–   ). Ruth Winter has done a variety of columns handled by three syndicates and is a prolific author, specializing in books on medical topics.

Born Ruth Grosman in Newark, New Jersey, she received the B.A. from Upsala College in 1951. From that year until 1955 she was a general assignment reporter for the *Newark Star Ledger*. During 1951–1956 she was a reporter for the *Houston Press* in Texas, then returned to the Newark paper as its science editor (1956–1969). She was a columnist for the North American Newspaper Alliance, then went with the Los Angeles Times Syndicate (1974–1978). Since 1981 she has been handled by the Register and Tribune Syndicate.

Winter has written more than one column at a time. Titles of some of her columns are "Currently with Ruth Winter," "Celebrities at Midlife," "Beat the Clock," "Medical Breakthroughs," and "Vitamins." She has been a frequent contributor of articles to such periodicals as *Science Digest, Woman's Day, Ladies' Home Journal, Town and Country,* and *Reader's Digest,* and she has published more than twenty books, some of the more recent coauthored with her husband, Arthur Winter, a neurosurgeon.

BOOKS: *Poisons in Your Food* (New York, 1969); *How to Reduce Your Medical Bills* (New York, 1970); *Beware of the Food You Eat* (New York, 1971); *Vitamin E: The Miracle Worker* (New York, 1972); *So You Have Sinus Trouble* (New York, 1973); *So You Have a Pain in the Neck* (New York, 1974); *A Consumer's Dictionary of Cosmetic Ingredients* (New York, 1974); *Don't Panic: What to Do and What Not to Do in All Kinds of Family Emergencies* (New York, 1975); *Triumph over Tension: 100 Ways to Relax* (New York, 1976); *The Smell Book: Scents, Sex, and Society* (Philadelphia, 1976); *The Fragile Bond: Marriage Now* (New York, 1976); *Scent Talk Among Animals* (Philadelphia, 1977); *Cancer-Causing Agents: A Preventive Guide* (New York, 1979); *Feet First* (San Francisco, 1980); *The Great Self-Improvement Sourcebook* (New York, 1980); *The Scientific Case Against Smoking* (New York, 1980); *The People's Handbook of Allergies and Allergens* (Chicago, 1984); with Mindy Cohen and Louis Abramson, *Thin*

Kids (New York, 1985); with Toni Marotta and Lolly Wurtzel *One Month Lighter* (New York, 1985); with Arthur Winter, *Build Your Brain Power* (New York, 1986); with Arthur Winter, *Eat Right, Be Bright* (New York, 1988); with Arthur Winter, *Consumer's Guide to Free Medical Information by Phone and Mail* (Englewood Cliffs, N.J., 1993); with Bonnie Eaker-Weil, *Adultery, the Forgivable Sin* (Secaucus, N.J., 1993).

Witcover, Jules (16 July 1927–). Jules Witcover wrote a Washington column for Newhouse News Service from 1968 to 1970 and since 1977 has cowritten another syndicated political column with Jack W. Germond.

Witcover was born in Union City, New Jersey. He served in the U.S. Navy from 1945 to 1946, then earned the A.B. (1949) and the M.S.J. (1951) from Columbia University. He worked as a reporter in Hackensack, New Jersey (1949–1950); Providence, Rhode Island (1951–1953); and Newark, New Jersey (1953). From 1954 to 1962 he was Washington correspondent for the *Syracuse* [New York] *Herald-Journal,* and from 1962 to 1968, chief political writer for Newhouse News Service. After two years as a Newhouse columnist, he became a Washington correspondent for the *Los Angeles Times* (1970–1972). Witcover joined the *Washington Post* in 1973 and later went with the *Baltimore Sun,* home base of the national political column he now writes with Jack Germond. Witcover has also been an active commentator on politics in his books.

BOOKS: *85 Days: The Last Campaign of Robert Kennedy* (New York, 1969); *The Resurrection of Richard Nixon* (New York, 1970); *White Knight: The Rise of Spiro Agnew* (New York, 1972); with Richard M. Cohen, *A Heartbeat Away: The Investigation and Resignation of Vice President Spiro T. Agnew* (Toronto, 1974); *Marathon: The Pursuit of the Presidency, 1972–1976* (New York, 1977); *The Main Chance* (New York, 1979); with Jack W. Germond, *Blue Smoke and Mirrors: How Reagan Won and Why Carter Lost the Election of 1980* (New York, 1981); with Jack W. Germond, *Wake Us When It's Over: Presidential Politics of 1984* (New York, 1985); *Sabotage at Black Tom: Imperial Germany's Secret War in America, 1914–1917* (Chapel Hill, N.C., 1989); with Jack W. Germond, *Whose Broad Stripes and Bright Stars? The Trivial Pursuit of the Presidency, 1988* (New York, 1989); *Crapshoot: Rolling the Dice on the Vice Presidency: From Adams and Jefferson to Truman and Quayle* (New York, 1992); with Jack W. Germond, *Mad as Hell: Revolt at the Ballot Box, 1992* (New York, 1993).

Wong, William (7 July 1941–). One of American's few Asian-American political columnists, William Wong has written a thrice-weekly column of political and social commentary for the *Oakland* [California] *Tribune* since 1988.

Wong was born in Oakland, California. He received the B.A. at the University of California, Berkeley, in 1962 and the M.S. from Columbia University in 1970.

From 1962 to 1964 Wong worked for three San Francisco Bay Area papers: the *San Francisco Chronicle,* the *San Leandro Morning News,* and the *San Francisco News Call Bulletin.* He was a Peace Corps volunteer in the Philippines from 1964 to 1968, then studied for his master's degree. Wong was a reporter for the *Wall Street Journal,* based in Cleveland, Ohio, from 1970 to 1972 and in San Francisco from 1972 to 1979, the year he joined the *Oakland Tribune* as its business editor. In 1981 he became assistant managing editor and from 1984 to 1986 was the paper's ombudsman. After two more years as assistant managing editor (1986–1988), Wong became a columnist and editorial writer for the *Tribune*. Wong's column varies in subject matter among local, national, and international issues and also addresses the interests and concerns of the Asian-American community.

Wood, Charles Osgood, III (8 Jan. 1933–   ). This CBS news correspondent, who uses the professional name Charles Osgood, also writes a humorous column syndicated by Tribune Media Services.

Wood was born in New York City and earned the B.S. at Fordham University in 1954. He worked at Washington station WGMS prior to World War II, played in the army band during the war, then returned to the station, working there until 1963. From 1963 to 1964 he was general manager of station WHCT in Hartford, Connecticut, then spent 1964–1967 as a reporter for ABC Radio News. He was anchorman for radio station WCBS from 1967 to 1972, when he also began working for CBS's television news operation.

Both his columns and his broadcast commentaries are known for their light verse, which often satirizes people or things in the news. He has authored four whimsical books.

BOOKS: *Nothing Could Be Finer Than a Crisis That Is Minor in the Morning* (New York, 1979); *There's Nothing That I Wouldn't Do If You Would Be My POSSLQ* [persons of the opposite sex sharing living quarters] (New York, 1981); *Osgood on Speaking: How to Think on Your Feet Without Falling on Your Face* (New York, 1988); *The Osgood Files* (New York, 1991).

Woodson, Carter Godwin (19 Dec. 1875–3 April 1950). Sometimes referred to as the "father of black history," author, editor, and educator Carter Woodson also wrote a column that was syndicated to various black U.S. weeklies in the 1930s.

Woodson was born in New Canton, Virginia. He was self-taught as a youngster but entered high school in 1895 at age twenty after he had moved to Huntington, West Virginia. He went on to earn the Litt.B. from Berea College in Kentucky (1903), then briefly worked as a high school principal before accepting a job teaching English in the Philippines. He trained Filipino teachers in Manila from December 1903 until he returned to the United States in February 1907. Woodson then enrolled at the University of Chicago; he received the B.A. in 1907 and the M.A. in 1908. He enjoyed a travel/study year in Europe, studying history at the Sorbonne, then returned and entered Harvard, where he earned the Ph.D. in 1912. His studies had revealed to him the absence of written history of black Americans, and he set out to correct the situation.

Woodson was a founder of the Association for the Study of Negro Life and History, set up in Chicago in 1915. He founded and edited the association's quarterly periodical, the *Journal of Negro History,* which dates from 1916, and in 1937 founded and edited the *Negro History Bulletin,* which was directed at schoolteachers and their pupils.

In his role as an educator, Woodson was dean of the School of Liberal Arts at Howard University from 1919 to 1920 and dean of West Virginia State College (1920–1922). While in the latter position, he established Associated Publishers, a book publishing firm that would publish black history. In 1922 Woodson retired from teaching and spent the remainder of his life as a chronicler of black history. The lifelong bachelor wrote thirteen books, edited five more, collected rare manuscripts, and gathered material for a major work to be titled the *Encyclopedia Africana,* a project that was never brought to fruition because of lack of funds.

BOOKS: *The Education of the Negro Prior to 1861* (New York and London, 1915); *A Century of Negro Migration* (Washington, D.C., 1918); *The History of the Negro Church* (Washington, D.C., 1921); *Early Negro Education in West Virginia* (Institute, W.Va., 1921); *The Negro in Our History* (Washington, D.C., 1922); ed., *Free Negro Owners of Slaves in the United States in 1830* (Washington, D.C., 1924); ed., *Free Negro Heads of Families in the United States in 1830* (Washington, D.C., 1925); ed., *Negro Orators and Their Orations* (Washington, D.C., 1925); ed., *The Mind of the Negro as Reflected in Letters Written During the Crisis, 1800–1860* (Washington, D.C., 1926); *African Myths, Together with Proverbs* (Washington, D.C., 1928); with John H. Harmon and Arnett C. Lindsay, *The Negro as a Businessman* (Washington, D.C., 1929); with Lorenzo J. Greene, *The Negro Wage Earner* (Washington, D.C., 1930); *The Rural Negro* (Washington, D.C., 1930); *The Mis-Education of the Negro* (Washington, D.C., 1933); *The Negro Professional Man and the Community* (Washington, D.C., 1934); *The African Background Outlined* (Washington, D.C., 1936); *African Heroes and Heroines* (Washington, D.C., 1939); ed., *The Works of Francis J. Grinke,* 4 vols. (Washington, D.C., 1942).

REFERENCES: Frank J. Klingberg, "Carter G. Woodson, Historian, and His Contribution to American Historiography," *Journal of Negro History* 41 (January 1956): 66–68; Rayford W. Logan, "Carter Godwin Woodson," *Journal of Negro History* 35 (1950): 344–348; Charles H. Wesley, "Carter G. Woodson as a Scholar," *Journal of Negro History* 36 (January 1951): 12–24.

Worden, Helen (12 July 1896–?). Feature writer and society editor Helen Worden wrote columns for the Scripps-Howard Syndicate (1935–1944) and the *New York Herald Tribune* (1947–1949) and picked up the Dorothy Dix column after Dix's death (1960–1964).

Worden was born in Denver, Colorado, but grew up in the East. Her father, a lawyer, at one time edited the first American paper in Mexico City, *Two Republics.* From 1906 to 1915 Worden studied with private tutors. She was at the University of Colorado from 1915 to 1919, then studied portrait painting in New York and at the Academie Julien in Paris (1925–1926). Her original intention was to be an artist, but she became involved in journalism when she had some of her drawings published in a Denver (Colorado) weekly, the *Community-Herald*, on the condition that she write copy to accompany them.

In 1926 she began a six-year stint as a feature writer for the *New York World*. She drew sketches to illustrate her "Sally Lunn" cooking feature, drew a feature titled "Fashions of the Theatre," and wrote "Belle Brummel," a style column that outlasted the other other two. Later she started the *World*'s society page and was its editor from 1927 to 1931. During this time she also specialized in hard-to-get interviews, most noteworthy of which were one with Col. Charles Lindbergh after the birth of his child and a second with the wealthy Mrs. Charles M. Schwab. Perhaps her most unusual story involved the eccentric carbon magnate C. Harold Smith, who, prior to the Great Depression, proposed to give $10 million away to the winner of a contest run by Worden for the proposal that would best aid humanity. The winner was a Columbia University psychology professor who wanted to found an institute to study mental illness, but the Depression and Smith's death prevented the completion of the plan.

Worden began a new column, "Miss Manhattan," for Scripps-Howard in 1935. She continued the column until 1944, when she became a writer for *Reader's Digest* and *Liberty* magazine. She wrote for these magazines until 1947, then spent two years as a *New York Herald Tribune* columnist. From 1951 to 1956 she was an associate editor of *Collier's* magazine, then took over the Dorothy Dix column from 1960 to 1964. Worden was a highly prolific writer of magazine articles and published several books about New York City.

BOOKS: *The Real New York* (Indianapolis, 1933); *Round Manhattan's Rim* (Indianapolis, 1934); *Society Circus: From Ring to Ring with a Large Cast* (New York, 1936); *Here Is New York* (New York, 1939); *Discover New York with Helen Worden* (New York, 1943).

REFERENCES: Ishbel Ross, *Ladies of the Press* (New York, 1974): 387–392.

Woster, Kevin (1951–   ). Kevin Woster was until 1993 a weekly columnist and the capital reporter for the *Rapid City* [South Dakota] *Journal*.

Woster is a native of central South Dakota and has been a journalist for at least eighteen years. He has worked for several weeklies and dailies in South Dakota. In addition to his column and his government reporting, he also wrote feature articles on people and projects in the Pierre area, plus outdoors and environmental stories.

Wright, James Claud, Jr. (22 Dec. 1922–   ). Former congressman and House majority leader Jim Wright's column in the *Fort Worth Star-Telegram* is now syndicated by the New York Times News Service.

Wright was born in Fort Worth, Texas. A debater and Golden Gloves boxer in high school, Wright studied at Weatherford College in Weatherford, Texas, then majored in politics and economics at the University of Texas. He served in the Army Air Forces (1941–1945) as a B-24 pilot, flying combat missions against Japanese targets. After the war he started an advertising business and in 1946 was elected to the Texas legislature. His liberal views made him a one-term member of that body. He served two terms as mayor of Weatherford, then was president of the League of Texas Municipalities. He was elected to the U.S. House of Representatives in 1955 and was returned to office many times there-after, becoming majority leader in 1976.

Before launching his column, Wright was a frequent contributor of articles to such magazines as *Saturday Evening Post, Coronet,* and *Harper's.*

BOOKS: *You and Your Congressman* (New York, 1965); *The Coming Water Famine* (New York, 1966); *Of Swords and Plowshares: A Collection of the Best Short Writings of Congressman Jim Wright* (Fort Worth, Tex., 1967).

Wundram, Bill (?–   ). Bill Wundram, columnist for the *Quad City Times* in Davenport, Iowa, says he has been writing "since the lava dried." He may very well be the only U.S. local columnist today whose column appears seven days a week.

Wundram has held a variety of newspaper jobs: reporter, photographer, city editor, associate editor. As a columnist, he sees himself mainly as a storyteller. His column runs long and is crafted with the skill of experience.

BOOKS: *The Best of Bill Wundram: Favorite Columns from the Quad City Times* (Eldridge, Iowa, 1990).

Y ⸻

Yardley, Jonathan (27 Oct. 1939–   ). Jonathan Yardley is book critic and columnist for the *Washington Post*. His columns, however, often diverge from book reviewing and appear to cover anything he wishes to discuss.

Yardley was born in Pittsburgh, Pennsylvania. He was a 1961 A.B. graduate of the University of North Carolina at Chapel Hill, where he was editor of the *Daily Tarheel*. After graduation, he became James Reston's first intern at the *New York Times*. From 1962 to 1964 Yardley was employed by the *Times* to write unsigned capsule news stories for the section called This Week in Review.

For the next decade he worked in North Carolina at the *Greensboro Daily News*, initially as one of that paper's three editorial writers, then as book page editor and finally book columnist. He did graduate study at Harvard during the 1968–1969 school year, then returned to the Greensboro paper. From 1970 to 1974 he made regular contributions to the book review sections of the *New Republic*, the *New York Times Book Review*, and *Washington Post Book World*. In 1974, he was hired as book editor of the *Miami Herald* and began a weekly book column syndicated by Knight Newspapers. Five years later he went with the *Washington Star* as book editor, winning the 1981 Pulitzer Prize for criticism shortly before the paper folded. Since that time he has been book editor and columnist at the *Washington Post*.

Yardley has also contributed to *Sewanee Review* and *Partisan Review* and has been a contributing editor of *Sports Illustrated*. He has authored four books.

BOOKS: *Ring: A Biography of Ring Lardner* (New York, 1977); *Our Kind of People: The Story of an American Family* (New York, 1989); *Out of Step: Notes from a Purple Decade* (New York, 1991); *States of Mind: A Personal Journey Through the Mid-Atlantic* (New York, 1993).

REFERENCES: Sam Staggs, "Jonathan Yardley," *Publishers Weekly* (17 March 1989): 75–76.

Yerkes, Susan Gamble (5 Sept. 1951–   ). Susan Yerkes (pronounced YER-keys) has written a column for the *San Antonio Express-News* since 1993 and from 1984 to 1993 wrote a six-day-a-week metro column for the *San Antonio Light.*

Yerkes was born in Evanston, Illinois. She graduated magna cum laude and Phi Beta Kappa in 1974 from the University of Texas and received the M.A. in mass communications from Wichita State University in 1976.

From 1974 to 1981 she worked in broadcasting, as reporter and anchor for both radio and television at KAKE-Radio and TV, the ABC affiliates in Wichita, Kansas. From 1981 to 1984 she was a biweekly travel columnist for the *Wichita Eagle-Beacon* and free-lance writer based abroad, writing for the Knight-Ridder papers and also publishing in the *International Herald Tribune, Christian Science Monitor, Chicago Sun-Times, San Francisco Chronicle, Toronto Star, Illustrated London News, Pan Am Clipper,* and other newspapers and magazines.

Yerkes combined public relations and free-lance writing out of San Antonio, Texas, from 1984 to 1986. She was coowner of Y & S Communicators, a PR firm, and wrote for various airline in-flight magazines, Chamber of Commerce magazines, and corporate magazines, such as the John Deere Company *Furrow.* She began her column at the *Light* in 1984 and has also taught PR, broadcasting, and media ethics at Incarnate Word College. Since 1988 she has also contributed to the outstanding regional magazine *Texas Monthly.* Yerkes does a talk show on KTKR AM, as well.

Yoakum, Robert (8 March 1922–   ). Robert Yoakum wrote the syndicated humor column "Another Look," which he started in 1972. He is also remembered as Art Buchwald's partner in another column, "Mostly About People," which the two wrote for the Paris edition of the *New York Herald Tribune.* Yoakum left that project, thinking there was little future in it.

Yoakum was born in Phoenix, Arizona. He studied at Northwestern University (1940–1942) and the University of Chicago (1945–1947). He served in the U.S. Air Force in Europe (1942–1945). He free-lanced in Europe during 1947–1948 and was a Reuters News Service correspondent in Paris (1948–1949). Yoakum was city editor of the *Paris Herald* from 1949 to 1956, the period when he and Buchwald wrote their column. From 1952 to 1956 he was deputy secretary of the World Veterans Federation in Paris, then free-lanced out of Greenwich and Lakeville, Connecticut, from 1956 to 1972. He began writing "Another Look" in 1972, first placing it in the *London Sunday Times.*

Yoder, Edwin Milton, Jr. (18 July 1934–   ). Now a journalism professor, Edwin Yoder began his syndicated column for The Washington Post Writers Group in 1982.

Yoder was born in Greensboro, North Carolina. He earned his B.A. from the University of North Carolina at Chapel Hill in 1956 and was a Rhodes Scholar, earning the M.A. at Oxford University in 1958.

He worked as an editorial writer for the *Charlotte* [N.C.] *Observer* from 1958 to 1961 and in the same capacity for the *Greensboro* [N.C.] *Daily News* from 1961 to 1964. He spent 1964–1965 teaching history at the University of North Carolina at Greensboro, then was associate editor of the *Daily News* from 1965 to 1975.

Yoder was editorial page editor for the *Washington Star* (1975–1981), then began writing his column from the *Washington Post* in 1982. His interest in history is apparent in his column, which appears twice weekly and varies from a focus on the American South to examination of international issues. He has written two books.

BOOKS: *The Night of the Old South Ball, and Other Essays and Fables* (Oxford, Miss., 1984); *The Unmaking of a Whig and Other Essays in Self-Definition* (Washington, D.C., 1990).

Young, Catherine A. (10 Feb. 1963–   ). Cathy Young has written a column of social/political/cultural commentary for the *Detroit News* since October 1993.

Young was born in Moscow, Russia. She emigrated to the United States in July 1980 and was naturalized in October 1987. Young received the A.A. in 1984 at Brookdale Community College and the B.A. in English in 1988, and membership in Phi Beta Kappa, at Rutgers University.

From 1990 to 1993 she was the Soviet/Russian Presswatch columnist for the *American Spectator* and since 1991 has been a contributing editor of *Reason*. She became a *Detroit News* columnist in October 1993, has been a frequent contributor of reviews and articles to other major newspapers, and has made numerous appearances on radio and television talk shows. She is the author of a book about her Moscow youth.

BOOKS: *Growing Up in Moscow: Memories of a Soviet Girlhood* (New York, 1989).

Young, Elizabeth (?–   ). Writing as "Mary Haworth," Elizabeth Young was a columnist for the *Washington Post* from 1934 to 1944 and was syndicated by the *Post* and by King Features.

Young was born in Riverside, Ohio, and studied at Wilmington College in Ohio (1924–1926). She worked in the office of the *Wilmington Daily News-Journal* during 1923–1924, then was a reporter (1924–1926) for that paper. From 1926 to 1928 she was editor of a Columbus, Ohio, weekly, the *Community News*. Young spent 1928–1930 selling ads for the *Ohio State Journal* and the *Lima Daily News*, then joined the *Washington Post* as a feature writer in 1933. In 1934 she became assistant woman's editor and started her column.

Z

Zeiger, Larry (19 Nov. 1933–). Known by his professional name Larry King, this media personality is the host of the political interview television show "Larry King Live" and a columnist for *USA Today*. Many years earlier, he also wrote a weekly column for the *Miami News*.

Zeiger was born in Brooklyn, New York. He broke into broadcasting the hard way—by sweeping floors at a radio station in Miami. From this humble start he became a popular Miami performer/commentator, in both radio and television. He wrote for the entertainment section of the *Miami Herald* for seven years and did his *Miami News* column before going to Washington, D.C., to do a late-night talk show for Mutual Radio and to host "Let's Talk" on station WLA-TV. He has now achieved a national audience with both his current TV interview show and his column. He has written an autobiography and several other books.

BOOKS: With Peter Occhiogrosso, *Tell It to the King* (Thorndike, Me., 1988); *Mr. King, You're Having a Heart Attack* (New York, 1989); *Tell Me More* (New York, 1990); *When You're from Brooklyn, Everything Else Is Tokyo* (Boston, 1992); *On the Line* (New York, 1993).

Zezima, Jerry (11 Jan. 1954–). Jerry Zezima has written a humor column for the *Stamford* [Connecticut] *Advocate* since 1985.

Zezima (pronounced ZEZ-im-a) was born in Stamford. He received the B.A. in political science from St. Michael's College in Winooski, Vermont, in 1975. He has been with the *Advocate* since 1976, successively working as copyboy, police reporter, sportswriter, and assistant metro editor until 1985, when he became a columnist. He is distributed by the Los Angeles Times–Washington Post News Service. In typical Zezima style, he notes, "As a chilling example of just how low journalistic standards have sunk in this country, my column has won several national, regional and state awards.''

Asked whether he had any books to his credit, he replied, ''Over the years, I have completed literally hundreds of books. Unfortunately, none of them were written or edited by me.''

Selected Bibliography

Adams, Franklin P. *Column Book of F.P.A.* Garden City, N.Y.: Doubleday, Doran, 1928.
———. *The Melancholy Lute: Selected Songs of Thirty Years.* New York: Viking, 1936.
Ade, George. *The Permanent Ade: The Living Writings of George Ade.* Edited by Fred C. Kelly. Indianapolis: Bobbs-Merrill, 1947.
Alexander, Holmes. *Never Lose a War: Memoirs and Observations of a National Columnist.* Greenwich, Conn.: Devin-Adair, 1984.
Allen, Robert S., and Drew Pearson. *Washington Merry-Go-Round.* New York: Liveright, 1931.
Alsop, Joseph and Stewart Alsop. "Our Own Inside Story." *Saturday Evening Post* (November 8–15, 1958).
———. *The Reporter's Trade.* New York: Reynal & Company, 1958.
Alworth, E. Paul. *Will Rogers.* Boston: Twayne, 1974.
Anderson, Douglas A. "The Muckraking Books of Pearson, Allen, and Anderson." *American Journalism* 2 (1985): 5–21.
Anderson, Jack, with James Boyd. *Confessions of a Muckraker.* New York: Random House, 1979.
Anderson, J.W. "Op-Ed." In Laura Longley Babb, ed., *The Editorial Page.* Boston: Houghton Mifflin, 1977, pp. 135–145.
Anthony, Edward. *O Rare Don Marquis: A Biography.* Garden City, N.Y.: Doubleday, 1962.
Ashley, Sally. *F.P.A.* New York: Beaufort Books, 1986.
Baer, Arthur "Buggs." *The Family Album.* New York: A. C. Boni, 1925.
Baker, Russell. *All Things Considered.* Philadelphia: Lippincott, 1965.
———. *An American in Washington.* New York: Knopf, 1961.
Beasley, Maurine H. *Eleanor Roosevelt and the Media.* Urbana: University of Illinois Press, 1987.
Beebe, Lucius. *The Lucius Beebe Reader.* Edited by Charles Clegg and Duncan Emrich. Garden City, N.Y.: Doubleday, 1967.

Belford, Barbara. *Brilliant Bylines*. New York: Columbia University Press, 1986.
Berger, Meyer. *The Eight Million: Journal of a New York Correspondent*. New York: Simon and Schuster, 1942.
———. *Meyer Berger's New York*. New York: Random House, 1960.
Berkove, Lawrence I., ed. *Skepticism and Dissent: 1898–1901,* by Ambrose Bierce. Ann Arbor, Mich.: UMI Research Press, 1986.
Bernstein, Burton. *Thurber*. New York: Dodd, Mead, 1975.
Bishop, James A. *The Mark Hellinger Story*. New York: Appleton-Century-Crofts, 1952.
———. *A Bishop's Confession*. Boston: Little, Brown, 1981.
Blair, Walter, and Hamlin Hill. *America's Humor*. New York: Oxford University Press, 1978.
Bode, Carl. *Highly Irregular: The Newspaper Columns of Carl Bode*. Carbondale: Southern Illinois University Press, 1974.
———. *Mencken*. Carbondale: Southern Illinois University Press, 1969.
Braden, Maria. *She Said What? Interviews with Women Newspaper Columnists*. Lexington: University Press of Kentucky, 1993.
Bradlee, Benjamin C. "Comments on the Columnists." In Laura Longley Babb, ed., *Of the Press, by the Press, for the Press, and Others, Too*. Boston: Houghton Mifflin, 1976, pp. 173–174.
Breslin, Jimmy. *Damon Runyon*. New York: Ticknor & Fields, 1991.
———. *The World According to Breslin*. Edited by James G. Bellows and Richard C. Wald. New York: Viking, 1967.
Briggs, Emily P. E. *The Olivia Letters*. New York: Neale, 1906.
Broder, David. *Behind the Front Page*. New York: Simon & Schuster, 1987.
Broun, Heywood. *Collected Edition of Heywood Broun*. Edited by Heywood Hale Broun. New York: Harcourt, Brace, 1941.
———. *Sitting on the World*. New York: Putnam, 1924.
Broun, Heywood Hale. *Whose Little Boy Are You? A Memoir of the Broun Family*. New York: St. Martin's Press, 1983.
Brown, Eve. *Champagne Cholly: The Life and Times of Maury Paul*. New York: E.P. Dutton, 1947.
Bruccoli, Matthew J. *The O'Hara Concern: A Biography of John O'Hara*. New York: Random House, 1975.
Buchwald, Ann, and Art Buchwald. *Seems Like Yesterday*. New York: Putnam, 1980.
Caen, Herb. *Only in San Francisco*. Garden City, N.Y.: Doubleday, 1960.
Carter, Boake. *I Talk as I Like*. New York: Dodge, 1937.
Carter, Thomas Jackson. *"Credos and Curios": James Thurber's Practice and Spadework on the Columbus Dispatch*. Ph.D. Dissertation, University of Tennessee, 1993.
Chapman, Elisabeth Cobb. *My Wayward Parent: A Book About Irvin S. Cobb*. Indianapolis: Bobbs-Merrill, 1945.
Cheshire, Maxine, and John Greenya. *Maxine Cheshire, Reporter*. Boston: Houghton Mifflin, 1978.
Childs, Marquis. *I Write from Washington*. New York: Harper, 1942.
———. *Witness to Power*. New York: McGraw-Hill, 1975.
———, and James Reston, eds. *Walter Lippmann and His Times*. New York: Harcourt Brace Jovanovich, 1959.

Clapper, Raymond. *Watching the World.* Edited by Olive Ewing Clapper. New York: Whittlesey House, 1944.

Cobb, Irvin S. *Exit Laughing.* Indianapolis: Bobbs-Merrill, 1941.

———. *Stickfuls: Compositions of a Newspaper Minion.* New York: George H. Doran, 1923.

Cohen, Richard. "The Syndicated Columnist." *Gannett Center Journal* 3 (Spring 1989): 9–16.

Conrow, Robert. *Field Days: The Life, Times and Reputation of Eugene Field.* New York: Scribner, 1974.

Considine, Bob. *It's All News to Me: A Reporter's Deposition.* New York: Meredith, 1967.

Cousins, Paul M. *Joel Chandler Harris: A Biography.* Baton Rouge: Louisiana State University Press, 1968.

Croy, Homer. *Our Will Rogers.* Boston: Little, Brown, 1953.

Dam, Hari N. *The Intellectual Odyssey of Walter Lippmann.* New York: Gordon Press, 1973.

Davis, Hallam Walker. *The Column.* New York: Alfred A. Knopf, 1926.

DeMott, Benjamin. "The Pursuit of Charm." *Nation* (March 27, 1982): 353.

DeMuth, James. *Small Town Chicago: The Comic Perspective of Finley Peter Dunne, George Ade, and Ring Lardner.* Port Washington, N.Y.: Kennikat, 1980.

Driscoll, C. B. *Life of O. O. McIntyre.* New York: Greystone, 1938.

DuBois, W.E.B. *The Autobiography of W.E.B. DuBois.* ed. by Herbert Aptheker. New York: International Publishers, 1968.

Dunne, Finley Peter. *Mr. Dooley and the Chicago Irish: An Anthology.* Edited by Charles Fanning. New York: Arno, 1976.

———. *Mr. Dooley at His Best.* Edited by Elmer Ellis. New York: Scribners, 1938.

———. *The World of Mr. Dooley.* Edited by Louis Fuller. New York: Collier, 1962.

Eban, Abba. *Abba Eban: An Autobiography.* New York: Random House, 1977.

Eells, George. *Hedda and Louella.* New York: G. P. Putnam's Sons, 1972.

Elder, Donald. *Ring Lardner: A Biography.* Garden City, N.Y.: Doubleday, 1956.

Ellis, Elmer. *Mr. Dooley's America: A Life of Finley Peter Dunne.* New York: C. Scribner's, 1938.

Emblidge, David, ed. *Eleanor Roosevelt's My Day.* New York: Pharos, 1994.

Everett, Miles C. *Chester Harvey Rowell, Pragmatic Humanist and California Progressive.* Ph.D. Dissertation, University of California, Berkeley, 1966.

Fanning, Charles. *Finley Peter Dunne and Mr. Dooley: The Chicago Years.* Lexington: University of Kentucky Press, 1978.

Farr, Finis. *Fair Enough: The Life of Westbrook Pegler.* New Rochelle, N.Y.: Arlington House, 1975.

Fetherling, Doug. *The Five Lives of Ben Hecht.* Toronto: Lester & Orpen, 1977.

Field, Eugene. *The Writings in Prose and Verse of Eugene Field.* 12 vols. New York: Scribners, 1898–1901.

Fisher, Charles. *The Columnists.* New York: Howell, Soskin, 1944.

Fountain, Charles. *Another Man's Poison: The Life and Writings of Columnist George Frazier.* Chester, Conn.: Globe Pequot, 1984.

Gaines, James R. *Wit's End: Days and Nights of the Algonquin Round Table.* New York: Harcourt Brace Jovanovich, 1977.

Geyer, Georgie Anne. *Buying the Night Flight.* New York: Delacorte, 1983.

Gilbreth, Frank Bunker. *Ashley Cooper's Doing the Charleston.* Charleston, S.C.: Post & Courier, 1993.

Gilmer, Elizabeth Meriwether. *Dorothy Dix—Her Book.* New York: Funk & Wagnalls, 1926.

Golden, Harry. *Carl Sandburg.* Cleveland: World, 1961.

———. *The Right Time: An Autobiography.* New York: Putnam, 1969.

Goodman, Ellen. *At Large.* New York: Summit Books, 1981.

Gould, John. *The Shag Bag.* Boston: Little, Brown, 1972.

Graham, Sheilah. *Confessions of a Hollywood Columnist.* New York: William Morrow, 1969.

Grauer, Neil A. *Wits and Sages.* Baltimore: Johns Hopkins University Press, 1984.

Greene, Bob. *Johnny Deadline, Reporter: The Best of Bob Greene.* Chicago: Nelson-Hall, 1976.

Grossvogel, David I. *Dear Ann Landers.* Chicago: Contemporary Books, 1987.

Hamill, Pete. *Irrational Ravings.* New York: Putnam, 1971.

Hansen, Harry. *Midwest Portraits: A Book of Memories and Friendships.* New York: Harcourt, Brace, 1923.

Hapgood, Hutchins. *A Victorian in the Modern World.* New York: Harcourt, Brace, 1939.

Harris, Michael David. *Always on Sunday, Ed Sullivan: An Inside View.* New York: Meredith, 1968.

Harsch, Joseph Close. *At the Hinge of History: A Reporter's Story.* Athens: University of Georgia Press, 1993.

Hearst, William Randolph. *William Randolph Hearst: A Portrait in His Own Words.* New York: Simon & Schuster, 1952.

Hecht, Ben. *A Child of the Century.* New York: Simon and Schuster, 1954.

———. *Gaily, Gaily.* Garden City, N.Y.: Doubleday, 1963.

———. *1001 Afternoons in Chicago.* Chicago: Covici-McGee, 1922.

Hinkle, Olin E., and John M. Henry. *How to Write Columns.* Ames: Iowa State College Press, 1952. Reprinted, Westport, Conn.: Greenwood Press, 1969.

Hopper, Hedda, and James Brough. *The Whole Truth and Nothing But.* New York: Pyramid, 1963.

Horowitz, Daniel. *Vance Packard and American Social Criticism.* Chapel Hill: University of North Carolina Press, 1994.

Hoyt, Edwin P. *A Gentleman of Broadway* [Damon Runyon]. Boston: Little, Brown, 1964.

Hudson, Edmund. *An American Woman's Life and Work: A Memorial of Mary Clemmer.* Boston: Ticknor, 1886.

Hulteng, John L. *The Opinion Function.* New York: Harper & Row, 1973, pp. 127–133.

Ickes, Harold Le Claire. *The Autobiography of a Curmudgeon.* New York: Reynal & Hitchcock, 1943.

Judis, John B. *William F. Buckley, Jr.: Patron Saint of the Conservatives.* New York: Simon & Schuster, 1988.

Kelly, Fred C. *George Ade, Warmhearted Satirist.* Indianapolis: Bobbs-Merrill, 1947.

———. *The Life and Times of Kin Hubbard, Creator of Abe Martin.* New York: Dutton, 1952.

Kempton, Murray. *America Comes of Middle Age: Columns, 1950–1962.* New York: Viking, 1972.

Kesterton, David B. *Josh Billings.* New York: Twayne, 1973.

Ketchem, Richard M. *Will Rogers: His Life and Times*. New York: American Heritage, 1973.

Kilgallen, Dorothy. *Girl Around the World*. Philadelphia: David McKay, 1936.

Klobuchar, Jim. "The Local Columnist." *Gannett Center Journal* 3 (Spring 1989): 34–38.

Klurfeld, Herman. *Winchell, His Life and Times*. New York: Praeger, 1976.

Kramer, Dale. *Heywood Broun*. New York: A. A. Wyn, 1949.

Krock, Arthur. *Memoirs: Sixty Years on the Firing Line*. New York: Funk and Wagnalls, 1968.

———. *Myself When Young: Growing Up in the 1890's*. Boston: Little, Brown, 1973.

Kuhn, Irene Corbally. *Assigned to Adventure*. New York: Grosset & Dunlap, 1938.

Kunst, Arthur E. *Lafcadio Hearn*. New York: Twayne, 1969.

Kupcinet, Irv. *Kup: A Man, an Era, a City*. Chicago: Bonus Books, 1988.

Kurth, Peter. *American Cassandra: The Life of Dorothy Thompson*. Boston: Little, Brown, 1990.

Lash, Joseph. *Eleanor: The Years Alone*. New York: Norton, 1972.

Lawrence, David. *Diary of a Washington Correspondent*. New York: H. C. Kinsey, 1942.

Lee, Lynn. *Don Marquis*. Boston: Twayne, 1974.

Leonard, John. *Private Lives in the Imperial City*. New York: Knopf, 1979.

Lerner, Max. *Actions and Passions: Notes on the Multiple Revolution of Our Time*. New York: Simon and Schuster, 1949.

Lewin, Leonard C., ed. *A Treasury of American Political Humor*. New York: Dial Press, 1964.

Lewis, John L., et al. *Heywood Broun As He Seemed to Us*. New York: Random House, 1940.

Lippmann, Walter. *The Essential Lippmann: A Political Philosophy for Liberal Democracy*. Edited by Clinton Rossiter and James Lare. New York: Random House, 1963.

———. *Interpretations, 1933–1935*. Edited by Allan Nevins. New York: Macmillan, 1936.

Luskin, John. *Lippmann, Liberty and the Press*. Alabama: University of Alabama Press, 1972.

Marquis, Don. *The Best of Don Marquis*. Garden City, N.Y.: Doubleday, 1946.

Martin, Harold H. *Ralph McGill, Reporter*. Boston: Little, Brown, 1973.

Marzolf, Marion. *Up from the Footnote: A History of Women Journalists*. New York: Hastings House, 1977.

Maxwell, Elsa. *R.S.V.P.: Elsa Maxwell's Own Story*. Boston: Little, Brown, 1954.

May, Antoinette. *Witness to War: A Biography of Marguerite Higgins*. New York: Beaufort Books, 1983.

McGill, Ralph. *The Fleas Come with the Dog*. Nashville, Tenn.: Abingdon, 1954.

McHugh, Robert, ed. *The Bathtub Hoax and Other Blasts and Bravos from the Chicago Tribune*. New York: Knopf, 1958.

McIntyre, Oscar Odd. *The Big Town: New York Day-by-Day*. New York: Dodd, Mead, 1935.

McKelway, St. Clair. *Gossip: Life and Times of Walter Winchell*. New York: Viking, 1940.

McKerns, Joseph P. *Benjamin Perley Poore of the Boston Journal*. Ph.D. Dissertation, University of Minnesota, 1979.

Meltzer, Milton. *Langston Hughes: A Biography.* New York: Crowell, 1968.

Mencken, Henry L. *A Carnival of Buncombe.* Edited by Malcolm Moos. Baltimore: Johns Hopkins Press, 1956.

Meyer, Ernest L. *Making Light of the Times.* Madison, Wis.: Capital Times Publishing, 1928.

Meyer, Karl E. *Pundits, Poets, and Wits: An Omnibus of American Newspaper Columnists.* New York: Oxford University Press, 1990.

Miller, Lee G. *The Story of Ernie Pyle.* New York: Viking, 1950.

Molloy, Paul. *All I Said Was . . .* Garden City, N.Y.: Doubleday, 1966.

Morehouse, Ward. *Just the Other Day: From Yellow Pines to Broadway.* New York: McGraw-Hill, 1953.

Mowrer, Lilian Thompson. *Journalist's Wife.* New York: W. Morrow, 1937.

Nelson, Roy Paul. *Articles and Features.* Boston: Houghton Mifflin, 1978, pp. 47–53.

Newhouse, Nancy, ed. *Hers, Through Women's Eyes.* New York: Villard Books, 1985.

Nye, Frank Wilson. *Bill Nye: His Own Life Story.* New York and London: Century, 1926.

Oakley, Helen. *Three Hours for Lunch, The Life and Times of Christopher Morley.* New York: Watermill, 1976.

O'Connor, Richard. *Ambrose Bierce, A Biography.* Boston: Little, Brown, 1967.

———. *Heywood Broun: A Biography.* New York: G. P. Putnam's Sons, 1975.

O'Daniel, Therman, ed. *Langston Hughes: Black Genius.* New York: Morrow, 1971.

Parsons, Louella O. *The Gay Illiterate.* Garden City, N.Y.: Doubleday, Doran, 1944.

———. *Tell It to Louella.* New York: Putnam, 1961.

Patner, Andrew. *I. F. Stone: A Portrait.* New York: Pantheon, 1988.

Patrick, Walton R. *Ring Lardner.* New York: Twayne, 1963.

Patterson, Elsie Marie. *Eric Sevareid: The Making and the Art of a Television News Analyst.* 2 vols. Ph.D. Dissertation, University of Wisconsin—Madison, 1976.

Pearson, Drew. *Drew Pearson Diaries, 1949–1959.* Edited by Tyler Abell. New York: Holt, Rinehart and Winston, 1974.

Pegler, Westbrook. *The Dissenting Opinions of Mr. Westbrook Pegler.* New York: C. Scribner's Sons, 1938.

———. *T'Aint Right.* Garden City, N.Y.: Doubleday, 1936.

Peplow, Michael W. *George S. Schuyler.* Boston: Twayne, 1980.

Pilat, Oliver. *Drew Pearson: An Unauthorized Biography.* New York: Harper's Magazine Press, 1973.

———. *Pegler, Angry Man of the Press.* Boston: Beacon, 1963.

Post, Edwin. *Truly Emily Post.* New York: Funk & Wagnalls, 1961.

Potter, Jeffrey. *Men, Money and Magic: The Story of Dorothy Schiff.* New York: Coward, McCann, 1976.

Pottker, Jan and Bob Speziale. *Dear Ann, Dear Abby.* New York: Dodd, Mead, 1987.

Preston, Keith., ed. *Column Poets.* Chicago: P. Covici, 1924.

Pyle, Ernie. *Home Country.* New York: William Sloane, 1947.

Quindlen, Anna. *Living Out Loud.* New York: Random House, 1988.

Rascoe, Burton. *We Were Interrupted.* Garden City, N.Y.: Doubleday, 1947.

Raspberry, William. *Looking Backward at Us.* Jackson: University Press of Mississippi, 1991.

Reston, James. *Sketches in the Sand.* New York: Knopf, 1967.

Riley, Sam G. *The Best of the Rest: Non-Syndicated Newspaper Columnists Select Their Best Work.* Westport, Conn.: Greenwood Press, 1993.

Rivers, William L. *The Opinionmakers.* Boston: Beacon Press, 1965.

————, and Alison R. Work. *Writing for the Media.* Mountain View, Calif.: Mayfield, 1988, pp. 146–152.

Robb, Inez Callaway. *Don't Just Stand There.* New York: D. McKay, 1962.

Robinson, Elsinore Justina. *I Wanted Out.* New York: Farrar & Rinehart, 1934.

Rogers, Will. *The Autobiography of Will Rogers.* Edited by Donald Day. Boston: Houghton Mifflin, 1949.

Roosevelt, Eleanor. *This I Remember.* New York: Harper, 1949.

Root, Robert L., Jr. *Working at Writing: Columnists and Critics Composing.* Carbondale: Southern Illinois University Press, 1991.

Rose, Billy. *Wine, Women and Words.* New York: Simon & Schuster, 1948.

Ross, Ishbel. *Ladies of the Press.* New York: Harper & Brothers, 1936, pp. 379–399.

Rowland, Helen. *Reflections of a Bachelor Girl.* New York: Dodge, 1909.

Royko, Mike. *Like I Was Sayin'. . .* New York: Dutton, 1984.

Royster, Vermont. *My Own, My Country's Time: A Journalist's Journey.* Chapel Hill, N.C.: Algonquin, 1983.

Runyon, Damon. *Runyon from First to Last.* London: Constable, 1954.

————. *Runyon on Broadway.* London: Constable, 1954.

————. *Short Takes.* New York: McGraw-Hill, 1946.

Rystrom, Kenneth. *The Why, Who and How of the Editorial Page.* New York: Random House, 1983, pp. 271–280.

Safire, William. *Safire's Washington.* New York: Times Books, 1980.

Sanders, Marion. *Dorothy Thompson: A Legend in Her Time.* Boston: Houghton Mifflin, 1973.

Saturday Evening Post: More Post Biographies: Articles of Enduring Interest About Famous Journalists and Journals and Other Subjects Journalistic. Edited by John E. Drewry. Athens: University of Georgia Press, 1947.

Schaaf, Barbara C. *Mr. Dooley's Chicago.* Garden City, N.J.: Anchor, 1977.

Schapsmeier, Edward L., and Frederick H. Schapsmeier. *Walter Lippmann, Philosopher-Journalist.* Washington, D.C.: Public Affairs Press, 1969.

Schlipp, Madelon Gordon, and Sharon Murphy. *Great Women of the Press.* Carbondale: Southern Illinois University Press, 1983.

Schuyler, George S. *Black and Conservative: The Autobiography of George S. Schuyler.* New Rochelle, N.Y.: Arlington House, 1966.

Seib, Charles B. "Columnists and Conflicts." *Of the Press, by the Press, for the Press, and Others, Too.* In Laura Longley Babb, ed. Boston: Houghton Mifflin, 1976, pp. 177–179.

Seitz, Don C. *Artemus Ward: A Biography and Bibliography.* New York: Harper, 1919.

Seldes, George. *Tell the Truth and Run.* New York: Greenberg, 1953.

Seldes, Gilbert. *The Seven Lively Arts.* New York: Harper & Brothers, 1924.

Shaw, David. "The Death of Punditry." *Gannett Center Journal* 3 (Spring 1989): 1–8.

Sheean, Vincent. Dorothy and Red [on Dorothy Thompson]. Boston: Houghton Mifflin, 1963.

Shepard, Bernard A. *C. K. McClatchy and the Sacramento Bee.* Ph.D. Dissertation, Syracuse University, 1960.

Shepherd, Jean, ed. *The America of George Ade, 1866–1944.* New York: Putnam, 1960.

Sibley, Celestine. *Turned Funny: A Memoir.* New York: Harper & Row, 1988.

Steel, Ronald. *Walter Lippmann and the American Century.* Boston: Atlantic–Little, Brown, 1980.

Stokes, Thomas L. *Chip Off My Shoulder.* Princeton, N.J.: Princeton University Press, 1940.

Streitmatter, Roger. *Raising Her Voice: African-American Women Journalists Who Changed History.* Lexington: University Press of Kentucky, 1994.

Strickland, Michael, ed. *The Best of Ralph McGill.* Atlanta, Ga.: Cherokee, 1980.

Stuart, Lyle. *Secret Life of Walter Winchell.* New York: Boars Head Books, 1953.

Sullivan, Mark. *The Education of an American.* New York: Doubleday, Doran, 1938.

Sulzberger, C. L. *An Age of Mediocrity: Memoirs and Diaries, 1963–1972.* New York: Macmillan, 1973.

———. *A Long Row of Candles: Memoirs and Diaries, 1934–1954.* New York: Macmillan, 1969.

Taylor, Bert Leston. *A Line-o'-Verse or Two.* Chicago: Reilly and Britton, 1911.

Thompson, Dorothy. *Let the Record Speak.* Boston: Houghton Mifflin, 1939.

Thompson, Slason. *Life of Eugene Field, The Poet of Childhood.* New York: D. Appleton, 1927.

Trohan, Walter Joseph. *Political Animals: Memoirs of a Sentimental Cynic.* Garden City, N.Y.: Doubleday, 1975.

Van Doren, Carl. *Many Minds.* New York: Knopf, 1924.

Van Horne, Harriet. *Never Go Anywhere Without a Pencil.* New York: Putnam, 1972.

Von Hoffman, Nicholas. "Behold the Columnist." *Quill* (October 1975): 18–21.

———. *Left at the Post.* Chicago: Quadrangle, 1970.

Waldrop, A. Gayle. *Editor and Editorial Writer.* Dubuque, Iowa: Wm. C. Brown, 1967, pp. 354–370.

Weiner, ed. *The Damon Runyon Story.* New York: Longmans, Green, 1948.

———. *Let's Go to Press: A Biography of Walter Winchell.* New York: Putnam, 1955.

Weldon, Edward LaRue. *Mark Sullivan's Progressive Journalism, 1874–1925.* Ph.D. Dissertation, Emory University, 1970.

Wells-Barnett, Ida B. *Crusade for Justice: The Autobiography of Ida B. Wells.* Edited by Alfreda M. Duster. Chicago: University of Chicago Press, 1970.

Wile, Frederic William. *News Is Where You Find It: Forty Years of Reporting at Home and Abroad.* Indianapolis: Bobbs Merrill, 1939.

Wilkie, Franc B. *"Walks about Chicago," and Army and Miscellaneous Sketches.* Chicago: Church, Goodman and Donnelley, 1869.

Wilkins, Roy. *Standing Fast: The Autobiography of Roy Wilkins.* New York: Viking, 1982.

Will, George F. "The Syndicated Column." In *The Editorial Page.* Edited by Laura Longley Babb. Boston: Houghton Mifflin, 1977, pp. 147–150.

Wills, Gary. *Lead Time: A Journalist's Education.* Garden City, N.Y.: Doubleday, 1983.

Winchell, Walter. *Winchell Exclusive: Things That Happened to Me—and Me to Them.* Englewood Cliffs, N.J.: Prentice-Hall, 1975.

Yardley, Jonothan. *Ring: A Biography of Ring Lardner.* New York: Random House, 1977.

Yoder, Edwin Milton, Jr. *The Unmaking of a Whig and Other Essays in Self-Definition.* Washington, D.C.: Georgetown University Press, 1990.

Young, Catherine A. *Growing Up in Moscow: Memories of a Soviet Girlhood.* New York: Ticknor & Fields, 1989.

Zeiger, Larry. *On the Line.* New York: Harcourt Brace, 1993.

Index

Pages in **bold** represent main entries.

Capital Reporter (Jackson, Miss.), 216
Capital Times (Madison, Wis.), 7, 215, 216
"Capitol Comedy" column, 253
"Capitol Gang, The," 300
"Capitol Journal" TV show, 56
"Capitol Parade" column, 8, 159
"Capitol Punishment" column, 45
"Capitol Stuff" column, 89, 346
Caplan, Deborah, 114
Cardinal Mindszenty Foundation, 290
CARE (Cooperative for American Relief Everywhere), 312
Carey, Ernestine, 100
Carlinsky, Dan, **54–55**
Carnegie, Andrew, 295
Carolina Israelite, The, 103
Carr, Rosemary, 168
Carroll County Comet (Flora, Ind.), 177
Carroll County Times (Westminster, Md.), 299
Carter, Boake, **55**
Carter, Harold Thomas Henry, 55
Carter, Jimmy, 56, 148, 237, 278, 315, 350
Carter, William Hodding, III, **55–56**
Cartoonews International, 80
Casey, Maura, **56**
Cashman, Harry, 282
Castro, Fidel, 52
Catholic Digest, 49, 254
Catholic Messenger, The, 176
Catholic Standard and Times, 70
Catholic Universe Bulletin, 205
Catholic Voice, 49
"Cathy" comic strip, 116
Cato Institute, 20
CBS (Columbia Broadcasting System), 55, 81, 84, 97, 105, 112, 124, 153, 157, 158, 169, 210, 219, 243, 246, 249, 256, 273, 282, 291, 292, 296, 297, 298, 305, 316, 323, 339, 348, 354, 357
"CBS Evening News" TV show, 297
"CBS Morning News" TV show, 90
"CBS Sunday Morning" TV show, 169
Cedar County News, 49
Cedar Rapids Gazette, 73, 74

"Celebrities at Midlife" column, 355
Central Texas Newspapers, 237
Centre Daily Times (State College, Pa.), 236
Century magazine, 78, 126, 174
"Chaff" column, 115
"Chains" movie script, 239
Chamberlain, John Rensselaer, **56–57**
Champaign-Urbana Courier (Ill.), 230
Chapel Hill Weekly, 301
Chaplin, Charlie, 115
Charen, Mona, **57**
Charleston Gazette (W.Va.), 15, 318
Charleston News & Courier (S.C.), 100, 173, 200
Charlotte News (N.C.), 169, 302
Charlotte Observer (N.C.), 32, 96, 103, 266, 300, 301, 363
Chattanooga News (Tenn.), 162
Chattanooga Times (Tenn.), 22, 154, 341
Chavez, Cesar, 52
Chennault, Claire, 9
"Cherokee Kid," 272
Cheshire, Maxine, **57**
Cheyenne Sun (Wyo.), 231
Chicago Academy of Television Arts and Sciences, 237
Chicago American, 39, 171, 237
Chicago Association of Black Journalists, 237
Chicago Chronicle, 145
Chicago Conservator, 343
Chicago Daily Defender, 148, 312
Chicago Daily News, 13, 22, 26–27, 49, 77, 99, 110, 124, 131, 163, 188, 215, 218, 222, 223, 237, 254, 255, 277, 280, 287, 337, 348
Chicago Daily Times, 123, 169
Chicago Defender, 140, 141, 237, 242, 243
Chicago Evening American, 287
Chicago Evening Post, 13, 78, 120
Chicago Evening World, 287
Chicago Examiner, 171
Chicago Herald, 78
Chicago Herald-Examiner, 123
Chicago Inter Ocean, 171, 343
Chicago Journal, 3, 78, 128, 321

About the Author

SAM G. RILEY is Professor of Communication Studies at Virginia Polytechnic Institute and State University. His previous books include *The Best of the Rest: Non-Syndicated Newspaper Columnists Select Their Best Work* (1993), *Consumer Magazines of the British Isles* (1993), *Corporate Magazines of the United States* (1992), *Regional Interest Magazines of the United States* (1990), *Index to City and Regional Magazines* (1989), *Magazines of the American South* (1986), and *Index to Southern Periodicals* (1986), all published by Greenwood Press.

ISBN 0-313-29192-6

EAN

9 780313 291920

HARDCOVER BAR CODE